Textiles in America
1650–1870

Dry goods merchant Elijah Boardman (1760–1823), New Milford, Connecticut.
Portrait by Ralph Earl, dated 1789. Oil on canvas; H. 83″; W. 51″.
(Collection of Mrs. Cornelius Boardman Tyler:
Photo, Metropolitan Museum of Art.)

£34.00

Textiles in America
1650–1870

A DICTIONARY BASED ON ORIGINAL DOCUMENTS,
PRINTS AND PAINTINGS,
COMMERCIAL RECORDS, AMERICAN MERCHANTS' PAPERS,
SHOPKEEPERS' ADVERTISEMENTS, AND
PATTERN BOOKS WITH ORIGINAL SWATCHES OF CLOTH

Florence M. Montgomery

W · W · NORTON & COMPANY   NEW YORK

A WINTERTHUR/BARRA BOOK

Published simultaneously in Canada by George J. McLeod Limited, Toronto.

The text of this book is composed in Bembo, with display type set in Centaur.
Composition by Vail Ballou Press Inc.
Manufacturing by Dai Nippon Printing Company Ltd., Tokyo, Japan.
Book design by Jacques Chazaud.

First Edition

Library of Congress Cataloging in Publication Data

Montgomery, Florence M.
   Textiles in America, 1650-1870.

   (A Winterthur book)
   Bibliography: p.
   1. Textile fabrics—United States—History.
   2. Textile fabrics—United States—Dictionaries.
   I. Title.
   TS1767 .M66 1984   677'.02864'0973   83-25339

ISBN 0-393-01703-6

W. W. Norton & Company, Inc., 500 Fifth Avenue, New York, N.Y. 10110
W. W. Norton & Company Ltd., 37 Great Russell Street, London WC1B 3NU

Contents

*"Ah, remember? Organdie, taffeta, dimity, lawn, batiste, chiffon,
China silk, voile, muslin, damask, percale, cambric, tulle."*

Drawing by Alan Dunn; © 1973 The New Yorker Magazine, Inc.

Acknowledgments

To several keepers at the Victoria and Albert Museum, I am greatly indebted for their interest in this book and for their generosity in sharing their research with me. Natalie Rothstein first told me of the Moccasi manuscript and the Hilton manuscript. She also gave me many references to documents in the Public Record Office which she has systematically studied for her own work on Spitalfields silk weavers and exports of English cloth to the American colonies. On numerous visits to the museum, she and other members of the Textile Department have generously allowed me to study important records such as the Kelly books, the Warner Archive, and the Barbara Johnson scrapbook. Peter Thornton's splendid book *Baroque and Rococo Silks* and, more recently, his keen interest in upholstery as keeper of furniture and woodwork rekindled my enthusiasm for textiles and furnishings. He and Simon Jervis provided the photographs and information concerning the late eighteenth-century Science Museum manuscript. Peter Floud first brought the important Berch collection to my attention.

Over the years, John Cornforth and I have engaged in a dialogue about textile furnishings, and his many articles in *Country Life* have brought English furnishing practices much closer to me than was possible on the few trips I made to England.

ACKNOWLEDGMENTS

I am grateful to Elisabet Hidemark of the Nordiska Museet for granting me permission to reproduce selected pages from the Berch collection.

For many years, I have had a friendly exchange of information with Mildred Lanier, former curator of textiles at Colonial Williamsburg. She shared her research on textiles imported to Virginia from Great Britain and advertised for sale by Virginia merchants. Her work on Marseilles quilting is embodied in the dictionary entry for marcella. Over the years something of value was gleaned on each visit to the textile collections at Colonial Williamsburg.

The textiles and swatch books at the Cooper-Hewitt Museum were made available to me first by Alice Baldwin Beer and Calvin Hathaway and more recently by curator Milton Sonday. Edith Standen and Jean Mailey of the Textile Study Room at the Metropolitan Museum of Art and Larry Salmon, former curator of textiles at the Museum of Fine Arts, Boston, have always been helpful to me. Miss Standen brought the typescript of London Newspaper References to my attention. I have had many fruitful discussions about textiles and furnishings with Jane C. Nylander at Old Sturbridge Village and Richard C. Nylander and Abbott Lowell Cummings at the Society for the Preservation of New England Antiquities. Brock Jobe's discovery of the Fitch and Grant upholsterers' accounts was generously shared.

Cora Ginsburg is a friend to all lovers of textiles and embroideries. She spent hours showing me examples from her fine collection. Katherine A. Kelloch and Margaret Fitzpatrick have given me important references which added further documentation for identifying textiles. Mrs. Samuel Schwartz provided me with photographs from her copy of *Die Tapezierkunst in Allen Stielen.* Betty Vijard, formerly of the Castle Museum, sent photographs of Norwich worsteds. Catherine W. Lynn, author of *Wallpaper in America,* and I have exchanged notes in these comparable fields. W. Scott Braznell brought to my attention many periodicals and trade publications on furnishing fashions.

Many other colleagues contributed to my knowledge of textiles: Katharine B. Brett, Dorothy K. Burnham, and Harold B. Burnham, Royal Ontario Museum; Linda Baumgarten, curator of textiles, Colonial Williamsburg; Christa Mayer-Thurman, curator of textiles, Art Institute of Chicago; and Irene Emery, curator emeritus, Textile Museum, Washington, D.C.

During the years I was at the Winterthur Museum, we were able to acquire the important Maurepas Papers and the worsted swatch books discovered by Ruth Cox Page while she was a fellow in the Winterthur Program in Early American Culture. Many members of the Winterthur staff were helpful, especially Helen R. Belknap, Benno M. Forman, Charles F. Hummel, and Frank H. Sommer.

In New Haven I have been privileged to use the great libraries at Yale University including Sterling Memorial Library, the Beineke Rare Book and Manuscript Library, and the Center for British Art.

I am much indebted to Ian M. G. Quimby, editor of Winterthur Publications, who put this book all together with the assistance of Catherine E. Hutchins, Patricia R. Lisk, and Catherine H. Maxwell.

Not only did Charles F. Montgomery encourage me to persevere with the manuscript, but he read it and made excellent suggestions; I like to think he would have been proud of it. Tangible evidence of his belief in the project is his color photography of swatches from the Alexander, Berch, Holker, Kelly, Moccasi, and Richelieu papers, the Warner Archive, and the Yorkshire pattern book.

Robert L. McNeil, Jr., through the Barra Foundation, made it possible to include a greater number of color plates than we had thought possible. By presenting so many well-preserved antique textiles in color, the reader can sense not only their beauty but their true character as well.

To Emita Ferriday Stockwell I am grateful for friendship in accompanying me on research trips which did not interest her and for companionship which is the best antidote for tedious work.

Introduction

Textiles played an important part in the lives of American colonists. Estate inventories indicate that bedding and bed curtains were among the most highly valued possessions, exceeded in value only by land, buildings, and, in rare instances, wrought silver. In monetary terms textiles were by far the largest commodity imported into the colonies. Many of the textiles mentioned in early newspapers, inventories, and manuscripts are no longer known. This study, begun while the author was a member of the curatorial staff of the Henry Francis du Pont Winterthur Museum, grew out of the need for accurate information on the kinds of textiles used in early American homes. To furnish period rooms authentically, it is necessary to know what kinds of textiles were available and how to distinguish one from another.

Answers were sought to questions about clothing materials for men, women, children, and infants; household linen for tabling, toweling, ticking, and other bedding; and suitable textiles for bed and window curtains, upholstery, slipcovers, table and chest covers, and floor coverings. The names of high-priced fashionable clothing materials had to be distinguished from common, coarse goods worn by laborers in various agricultural and craft occupations; and, among woolen goods, heavy fishermen's clothing and Indian blankets from fine-quality worsteds for bed furniture or a gentleman's coat. Which linen and cotton textiles were for the house and which were used for grain bags, sieves, sails, or horse coverings?

There are many pitfalls in the identification and study of textile terms. Technological changes from traditional hand methods to mechanization of fiber preparation, spinning, weaving, and finishing have been enormous. Over the centuries many textiles ceased to be manufactured as they were superseded by new types. Sometimes the old names persisted but were applied to cloth of quite different character.

Commerce was closely linked with fashion and powerfully influenced textile production throughout the seventeenth, eighteenth, and nineteenth centuries. Exotic embroideries, painted cottons, and silks brought from the Orient by the East India Companies in the early 1600s had become the rage sixty years later. Their popularity led to imitation by English and European manufacturers. Such fabrics as alacha, cherryderry, dunjars, and seersucker were among those copied. More importantly, European textile printing with woodblocks (in itself a technological advance over painting by hand) arose from a desire to meet the demand for brilliantly colored, washable cottons from India. The generic term *calico* included a wide variety of "plain, printed, stained, dyed, chintz, muslins, and the like."[1]

Magnificent garments worn by Siamese ambassadors on a state visit to the court of Louis XIV in 1684 are said by French economist Jacques Savary des Bruslons to have inspired French imitations, called *siamoises*.[2] First woven of cotton brightened with colorful silk stripes, they later were made of linen and cotton. These inexpensive textiles, in turn, rivaled English-made goods. In an attempt to capture the trade with the Levant, *drap londre, londrin,* and several other worsted cloths woven in Languedoc, were made in imitation of English cloths exported by the Turkey Company from the port of London to the Levant.

From about 1650 French silk weaving was centered at Lyons where the finest artists and *ornemanistes* designed rich brocades for those Europeans who could afford the luxury of silk. These highly prized textiles were shipped to England clandestinely to avoid high duties or total import prohibition. English-woven silks patterned after French models were marketed as French.

In England silk weaving was carried on largely at Spitalfields in the east end of London where Huguenot weavers settled when they fled France after the revocation of the Edict of Nantes in 1685. Over eight hundred Spitalfields watercolor patterns are owned by the Victoria and Albert Museum. Together with the archive from Warner's, one of the largest English silk-weaving firms, the two collections form an unusually complete record of fashionable dress silks from the eighteenth and nineteenth centuries.

The popularity of certain textiles caused their names to become generic, such as holland for good-quality bleached linen long woven in that country. Textile names were often derived from towns first made famous by their manufacture. Cambric and shalloon originated in Cambrai and Chalons in France, while osnaburg is clearly a product of the German city of Osnabrück.

Problems of language and changing terminology caused confusion among merchants. During the American Revolution, when the merchants of Providence, Rhode Island, sought to establish trade with France, they found that

> All the Dictionaries in the World could not translate the names of the goods ordered. Order a French Merchant to ship a piece of *Mousseline de Livre* but no Manufacturer in Europe would be able to furnish him, and he would write in answer that it was not to be found, unless some American were to tell him that a piece of Goods called *ourgandi* answers to Book Muslin, except in the folding it.[3]

From medieval times the English economy depended upon the woolen trade. As late as 1694, Sir Josiah Child cited the statement of Sir Edward Coke (1552–1634), that "nine parts in Ten of our Exported Commodities doth come from the Sheep's Back, and from hence alone is the Spring of our Riches."[4] In early times English wool was exported in the fleece or in unfinished and undyed cloths, but from the sixteenth century the government encouraged the production and export of finished goods because of the great profit to be derived from them. The staple English cloth manufacture was the broadcloth made of "short-stapled carded wool, in both warp and weft, and fulled so that the woven mass of fibres was thoroughly felted, to give an enduring, strong, weather resistant fabric."[5] Considerable variety was afforded among these Old Draperies with differences in breadth, weight, and finish, to say nothing of pattern and color. Some cloths took their names from the towns or areas wherein they were then woven, such as Bath beaver, Bocking bay, Bristol, dorsetteen, pennystone, and stroud.

During the sixteenth century skilled weavers from Flanders and Holland were enticed to settle in England for the purpose of improving textile manufactures. A new class of fabrics called the New Draperies was the result of this infusion of foreign technical skills. The New Draperies consisted of worsted yarn warp (spun from combed, long-staple wool) mixed with a woolen weft (spun from carded, short-staple wool). In general they were lighter in weight than the Old Draperies and were suitable for wear on warm days or in hot climates. They needed little or no fulling or elaborate finishing. Barracan, bay, bombazine, calimanco, grogram, mockado, perpetuana, rash, say, serge, shalloon, and stammet are some of the names given to them.[6] The names, weights, and values of twenty-nine New Draperies are listed and described in a manuscript dated 1592 which is reproduced in John James, *History of the Worsted Manufacture in England*.[7]

By the close of the reign of James I (d. 1625) other types of worsted cloth had been invented which are described in "Allegations on behalf of the worsted weavers of Norwich," a manuscript preserved in the British Museum. Alleging that there was little difference between the New Draperies and the Old Draperies, it argued that

> a buffyn, a catalowne, and the pearl of beauty, are all one cloth; a peropus and paragon all one; a saye and piramides, all one; the same cloths bearing other names in times past. The paragon, peropus, and philiselles may be affirmed to be double chambletts; the difference being only, the one was double in the warp, and the other in the weft. Buffyn, cattalowne, and pearl of beauty, &c., may be affirmed single chamblett, differing only in the breadth. The say and piramides may also be affirmed to be that ancient cloth, mentioned in the said statute [7 Edward IV], called a bed; the difference only consisting in the breadth and fineness.
>
> To make of this worsted a stamin, was but to make it narrower and thinner in the stay; to make the bed a say, which

served for apparel, was to make the same much narrower and finer; this cloth hath continued its name and fashion till this day; but, now lately, by putting the same into colours, and twisting one third of one colour with another colour, being made narrow, it is now called piramides.

From worsted are derived, in another line, other cloths. A worsted was wrought with four treadles; to make thereof a bustian, is to weave with three of the same treadles; to make the same double chamblet, is to use the two right foot treadles; to make it single, is to use the two left foot treadles; to make this a philisello, a peropus, a paragon, or a buffyn, is but to alter the breadth, and to make them double, treble, or single in the striken [weft, or shoot]; and to make this buffyn a cata-lowne, it is to twist a thread of one colour with a thread of another, and strike it with another colour; to make the same a pearl of beauty, is to make it striped, by colours in the warp, and tufted in the striken.[8]

In addition to these worsted and part-worsted textiles, Dutch and Walloon weavers fleeing Spanish rule in the Netherlands brought to the Norwich area the art of mixing linen and silk with combing wools. Some of the names applied to these goods are alapeen, anterne, bombazine, darnex, drugget, frizadoe, grogram, hair camlet, and poplin.[9]

The West Country was famous not alone for broadcloths but for a variety of other goods, some probably woven in broad widths and others in narrow. "Some new sorts of Drapery invented, as Du Roys, druggets and durantes" also included everlasting, perpetuana, and sempiternum, all suggesting the quality of durability.[10] Druggets, related to sagathys, shalloons, and silesias, were striped, corded, or patterned in mosaic or with flowers. Serge, usually of twill weave and often combining combed and carded yarns, was produced in great quantities. Samples dating from 1716 in "rich, bright colours—pink, cream, tawny, light and golden brown, yellows, whites, and blacks" are preserved in the collection of the Archief Brants in Amsterdam.[11]

Weavers in the north of England, especially in the area of Yorkshire known as the West Riding, made a specialty of coarse broadcloths and narrow kerseys in solid colors, used for uniforms all over Europe, and in mixed colors for the clothing of servants and common people. Before the end of the sixteenth century Yorkshire weavers undertook the production of worsteds. Their manufacture, for the most part limited to the middle and lower grades, included bay; calimanco, glazed and in brilliant colors; shalloon, thin, twilled, glazed, lining material; camlet, thick, rough, rain-resistant material suitable for cloaks; and tammy in glazed varieties for curtain linings and flour and meal sieves.

Norwich, "the chief seat of the chief manufacture of the realm," produced finer qualities of worsteds including calimanco, camlet, and damask, suitable for dress and furnishing materials. The most flourishing period of their manufacture occurred during the mid-eighteenth century when the export market included all of Europe, China, the Levant, the West Indies, Spanish America, and the North American colonies.

Names for the various kinds of Norwich stuffs—including those made entirely of worsted yarns, wool and worsted, and silk and worsted mixed—are particularly difficult to identify. Novelty titles abound, and when the sale of a material languished it was given a new name in the hope of captivating buyers. Speaking of Norwich manufacturers in 1662, Thomas Fuller said "Expect not I should reckon up their several names, because daily increasing, and many of them are binominous, as which, when they begin to tire in sale, are quickened with a new name."[12]

Camlet was woven in striped, shaded, spotted, sprigged, changeable, and brocaded patterns. Camleteen, narrower and thinner than camlet, was also produced in great variety. Worsted damask, sometimes called bed satin, was woven in single colors or in two contrasting shades. Black Norwich crape was adopted for official court mourning, but it was also woven in bright colors. Within a large category called calimanco were included striped, flowered, and checked patterns. Others bore such names as dresden, espolinados, and martinique (names penned in the pattern books), probably invented to appeal to certain markets. Some names suggested small allover patterns: cheverett, diamantine, esterett, floretta, and harlequin. A group of fabrics featuring white lace bands woven on colored grounds with polychrome brocaded flowers was called variously batavia, blondine, grandine, taboratt, or brilliant, mecklenburgh, and russaline. Camlet became china, or cheney when waved or moiréd, grograms and grogrinetts, harateens and moreens.

Woolen materials in everyday use for linings, interlinings, undercloths, and outer garments were woven in several grades and in many European countries. These included bay, flannel, and serge. Related to serge was ratteen, which was well fulled and napped with teasels on one or both sides of the cloth. Say, a light, inexpensive, twilled wool is defined as a kind of serge. Half thicks and longcloth, some with weft cording, were also twill woven. Other heavy materials, whose appearance we can only imagine, are bearskin, beaver, fearnaught, forest cloth, shag, swanskin, naps, spotted ermin, and thunder and lightning.

From the beginning of the seventeenth century, Lancashire, especially the area around Manchester, became the center for cotton and linen / cotton weaving in England. The main production between 1670 and 1700 consisted of barmillian, jean, pillow, stripes, and tufts. By the mid-eighteenth century the general categories of dimity, fustian, and muslin included such textiles as "herringbones, pillows for pockets and outside wear, strong cotton ribs and barragon, broadraced linen thicksets and tufts, dyed, with white diapers, striped dimities, and lining jeans."[13] From shortly after the middle of the century these textiles were imitated in manufactories near Rouen in France.

Fortunately, early trade practices bequeathed to us a surprising number of documents which made this book possible. Scattered about the world are books of cloth swatches containing contemporary names, dimensions, colors, prices, and the names of their manufacturers. Some were prepared by British agents acting for American merchants or those of other countries; other accumulations, such as the Berch Papers, were compiled by economists or historians; and still other collections resulted from the efforts of government officials to promote textile manufactures within their own countries. These swatch books, merchants' records, and business papers are described in greater detail in the bibliography.

A wealth of textile samples, especially of dress goods, is found in trade publications and mill pattern books. Interesting for their designs, they are often not identified or dated. Collections are found in the Merrimack Valley Textile Museum, North Andover, Massachusetts; the Goldie Paley Design Center at the Philadelphia College of Textiles and Science; the Rhode Island School of Design and the Rhode Island Historical Society, Providence; and at the Metropolitan Museum of Art and the Cooper-Hewitt Museum, New York.

Scrapbooks form another vast source for textile swatches. For instance, a huge scrapbook of French textiles shown at the 1855 Paris Exhibition and grouped by manufacturer is owned by the Design Library, New York, which also owns an equally large French book of paisley calico patterns printed in red, brown, black, and orange, popular from the 1840s through the 1870s in both Europe and America.

[1] Thomas Sheraton, *The Cabinet-Maker, Upholsterer and General Artist's Encyclopedia* (London, 1804–7), p. 235.

[2] Jacques Savary des Bruslons, *Dictionnaire Universel de Commerce,* 4 vols. (Geneva, 1750), 3:864.

[3] James B. Hedges, *The Browns of Providence Plantation* (Cambridge, Mass.: Harvard University Press, 1952), p. 253.

[4] Josiah Child, *The Interest of England Considered in an Essay on Wool* (London: Walter Kettilby, 1694), p. 3.

[5] D. C. Coleman, "An Innovation and Its Diffusion: The 'New Draperies,' " *Economic History Review,* 2d ser., 22 (1969): 419.

[6] Coleman, "Innovation and Its Diffusion," p. 418.

[7] John James, *History of the Worsted Manufacture in England* (1857; reprint ed., London: Frank Cass, 1968), pp. 125–27. Lansdowne Ms. No. 71, Art. 51.

[8] James, *Worsted Manufacture in England,* pp. 143–44.

[9] For a complete list, see Eric Kerridge, "Wool Growing and Wool Textiles in Medieval and Early Modern Times," in *The Wool Textile Industry in Great Britain,* ed. J. Geraint Jenkins (London: Routledge & Kegan Paul, 1972), pp. 19–33.

[10] Sir John Elwill to David Leeuw, merchant of Amsterdam, as quoted in Charles Henry Wilson, *Anglo-Dutch Commerce and Finance in the Eighteenth Century,* ed. M. M. Postan (Cambridge: At the University Press, 1941), p. 37.

[11] Wilson, *Anglo-Dutch Commerce and Finance,* p. 38.

[12] Thomas Fuller, *Worthies of England* (1662; reprint ed., London: George Allen & Unwin, 1952), p. 419.

[13] John Aikin, *A Description of the Country from Thirty to Forty Miles Around Manchester* (London, 1795), p. 158.

Textiles in America
1650–1870

Furnishing Practices in England and America

In times past the quality and richness of textiles in clothes indicated the social station of the person wearing them. The same principle applied to houses where fine curtains differentiated the houses of the rich from those of the middling sort. Cloth arranged in ornamental folds was called drapery, and artful displays of drapery—whether on the human form, in an architectural setting, or in a portrait—provided the requisite touch of luxury and elegance.

In the eighteenth century, men—at least gentlemen—concerned themselves far more with the appearance of their houses than most men do today. They took pains to express their taste both in designing their houses and in furnishing them. For exterior as well as for interior decoration, the American colonist turned to English architectural books which showed elevations, plans, and interior details. Imported copies were generally available, and the first American edition of Abraham Swan's popular *British Architect* was printed in Philadelphia in 1775.[1]

Thomas Chippendale (1718–79) addressed his great book of furniture designs (1754) to men. He called it the *Gentleman and Cabinet-Maker's Director,* stating that it was "calculated to assist the one [gentleman] in the choice, and the other [cabinetmaker] in the execution of the Designs."[2] This book and others, such as those of Thomas Sheraton (1751–1806) and George Hepplewhite (d. 1786), were owned in America and served as guides for furniture styles and for upholstery and bed hangings.[3]

There is no doubt that English upholstery and furnishing practices were followed in America. Being for the most part Englishmen, the colonists had a natural preference for English fashions which they saw in the rich furniture, curtains, and bed hangings brought to the colonies by royal governors and imported by wealthy merchants. At least in the larger cities, curtains could be ordered from London according to specifications. Furthermore, English upholstery and furnishing materials were imported in great quantities. Not only were fabrics available, but so could all the trimmings be imported—borders, fringes, tapes, tassels, pulleys, lines, and hooks.

Upholsterers, "lately from London," as they described themselves in newspaper advertisements, and entirely familiar with English practices, were eager to provide furnishings "in the newest fashion" and "the most approved manner now in vogue." Pattern books such as Chippendale's *Director* provided clues to the "newest and genteelest fashions practised in London."

Another pictorial guide to English practice was the print, long lists of which were advertised in American newspapers. Satirical and political prints of the day were passed around the drawing room or were viewed through a perspective glass as evening entertainment. Beds, windows, and upholstered and slipcovered furniture shown in these prints at least popularized English furnishing practices, if indeed they did not provide models for the colonists.[4] Many immigrant upholsterers brought practical knowledge and firsthand experience when they came from London to urban centers in America. They also imported vast quantities of English textiles which were used almost exclusively.

French influence in the decorative arts strengthened in the last decade of the eighteenth century and in the first decades of the nineteenth century. In America this influence came in a variety of ways.

Thomas Jefferson, our most famous Francophile, served as the American minister to France from 1785 to 1789. While living in Paris he furnished his *hôtel* with French furniture and other French decorative arts. When he accepted George Washington's appointment as secretary of state in 1790, eighty-six packing cases of household goods were shipped from Paris to Philadelphia.[5] Jefferson was particularly captivated by neoclassicism in the arts, and his French furnishings reflected the most up-to-date expression in the decorative arts. Other prominent Americans, such as James Monroe and John Quincy Adams, also served in Paris and helped to popularize French styles on their return.

The most elegant collection of high-style European art and decorative arts to be found in America during the second decade of the nineteenth century was that of Joseph Bonaparte, exiled brother of Napoleon Bonaparte and former king of Naples and Spain. Point Breeze, his home near Bordentown, New Jersey, from 1816 to 1839, was richly furnished.[6] Socially astute Americans of the time flocked to Point Breeze to be awed by the former king and his magnificent collection.

French influence in American decorative arts probably owes more, however, to the influx of French refugees following the French Revolution and the black uprisings in Haiti. During the 1790s most American cities along the East Coast had a French colony and many of these people were craftsmen and shopkeepers. Charles-Honoré Lannuier is, perhaps the best-known cabinetmaker among the French émigrés, and Simon Chaudron the most celebrated silversmith.[7]

Still another transmitter of styles were the fashion magazines of the day. In addition to illustrating stylish clothes, they also included prints illustrating the latest designs in furniture, window curtains, and bed hangings. Rudolph Ackermann's *Repository of Arts, Literature, Commerce, Manufactures, Fashions, and Politics* (1809–28) was published in London but distributed widely in the English-speaking world. Some of Ackermann's plates were freely borrowed from Pierre de La Mésangère's *Meubles et objets de goût,* published in Paris irregularly from 1802 to 1835.[8] La Mésangère, in turn, copied the designs of such prominent French architects and designers as Charles Percier (1764–1838) and Pierre F. L. Fontaine (1762–1853). The sophisticated English traveler and dilettante Thomas Hope (ca. 1770–1831) was well acquainted with French styles. He published his own book of designs in 1807 called *Household Furniture and Interior Decorations,*[9] a widely circulated book that was advertised in New York in 1819. By this time fashions traveled quickly, and the stylistic differences between countries became less distinct as the century progressed.

As the age of neoclassicism passed, after one final burst of creativity in the Greek revival style, it was replaced by the spirit of eclecticism which encouraged the simultaneous revival of various historical styles. Spokesmen for the new age included John Claudius Loudon (1783–1843) whose *Encyclopedia of Cottage, Farm, and Villa Architecture and Furniture,* first published in London in 1833, became one of the most influential books on interior design of the nineteenth century. The American author Andrew Jackson Downing (1815–52) depended heavily on Loudon's work for his own *Architecture of Country Houses* published in New York in 1850. Both books include general descriptions of the revival styles and illustrations of appropriate furnishings. The revival styles were thought to evoke moods appropriate to functions of rooms. Downing pointed to the advantages of using the Gothic style for domestic settings. "A great beauty of this style, when properly treated, is the home-like expression which it is capable of, in the hands of a person of taste. This arises, mainly, from the chaste and quiet colours of the dark wood-work, the grave, though rich hue of the carpets, walls, etc., and the essentially fire-side character which the apartments receive from this type of treatment." By way of contrast, "The prevailing character of the Grecian and Italian styles partakes of the gay spirit of the drawing-room and social life; that of the Gothic, of the quiet, domestic feeling of the library and the family circle."[10]

Downing also spoke approvingly of "modern French furniture," in what he and others at the time called the Louis XIV style. (We know this style today as Louis XV.) He said it "stands much higher in general estimation in this country than any other. Its union of lightness, elegance, and grace renders it especially the favorite of ladies. For country-houses we would confine its use, chiefly, to the drawing-room or boudoir, using the more simple and massive classical forms for the library, dining-room and other apartments." Downing then quotes Thomas Webster's description of this style from *An Encyclopaedia of Domestic Economy:* "The style of Louis XIV [Louis XV] is known by its abundance of light, ornamental scrollwork, and foliage.

Its elegance of form . . . together with its admission of every species of enrichment, as carving, gilding, painting, inlaying, with coverings of the richest silks, velvets, and the choicest stuffs, admirably adapt it for the modern drawing-room. Certainly no kind of furniture equals it in general splendour of appearance." In a note Downing explains that a large collection of furniture in "the most tasteful designs of Louis Quatorze, Renaissance, Gothic, etc." may be found "at the warehouse of Mr. A. Roux, Broadway."[11]

By Victorian times both rooms and furnishings had achieved a high degree of specialization. There was a proliferation of furniture forms as well as a tendency to confine activities to certain designated rooms. That this had not always been true is evident from surviving illustrations showing the way furniture was arranged in rooms prior to the nineteenth century. Almost invariably furniture is depicted against the walls of the room. This is evident in the interior scenes engraved by the French artist Abraham Bosse (1602–76), by the French designer Daniel Marot (ca. 1663–1752), or by the English artist Edmund Marmion (seventeenth century).[12] (See Bed Hangings, Figs. 1, 2). Chairs are ranked against the walls except for those drawn into the room for the assembled company. Pier tables with looking glasses hung on the wall above them were fixed features of the room. That this formality continued throughout the eighteenth century can be seen in the elevation drawings of the four walls of an English drawing room of about 1760 (Fig. 1). In characteristic eighteenth-century fashion, the arrangements on each wall are, for the most part, symmetrical. Room plans published by George Hepplewhite and Thomas Sheraton, in 1789 and 1793 respectively, adhere to the same formula in spite of the radical changes in the furniture itself as a result of the introduction of the neoclassical style (Figs. 2, 3). Group portraits in the eighteenth century often show the family gathered around a tea table, but it is certain that once the tea ceremony was completed the chairs and tables were returned to their places against the wall. Rooms specifically intended for dining are not found in house plans before the second quarter of the eighteenth century. More frequently, food was brought to the master and mistress and their family and friends in whichever room was suitable for the occasion.

By about 1825 the drawings of Gillow and Company, a London furniture firm, and the plates from George Smith's *The Cabinet-*

The Upper end of a Drawing Room

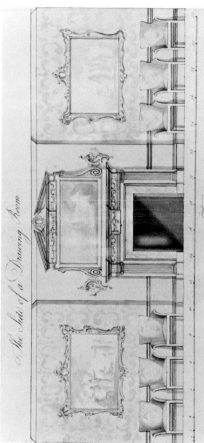

The Side of a Drawing Room

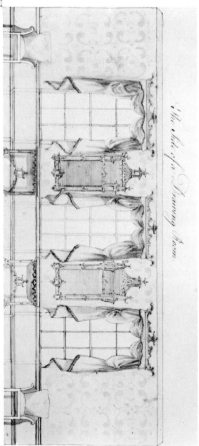

The Side of a Drawing Room

FIG. 1A–D. *Four walls of a drawing room. Wash drawings by William Gomm, London upholsterer, ca. 1760. (Joseph Downs Manuscript and Microfilm Collection, Winterthur Museum Library, purchase from funds given by Agnes Downs.)*

The Entrance of a drawing Room

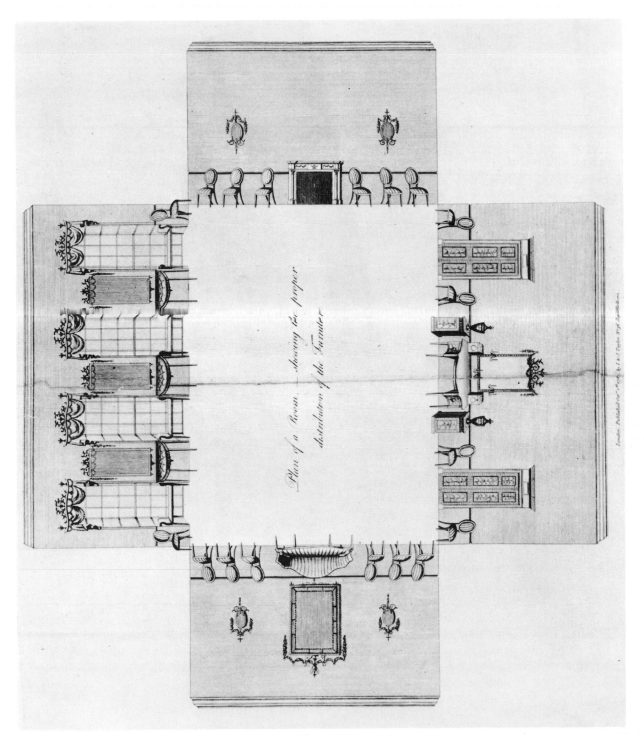

FIG. 2. *"Plan of a Room showing the proper distribution of the Furniture."* From George Hepplewhite, The Cabinet-Maker and Upholsterer's Guide (London, 1789), pl. 124. (Winterthur Museum Library.) The furniture, which includes four benches in the window embrasures, is placed against the walls. Note the use of striped upholstery material to complement the neoclassical furniture. It is a question whether the curtains would have fallen to the floor if released or whether they were made to simulate draw-up curtains.

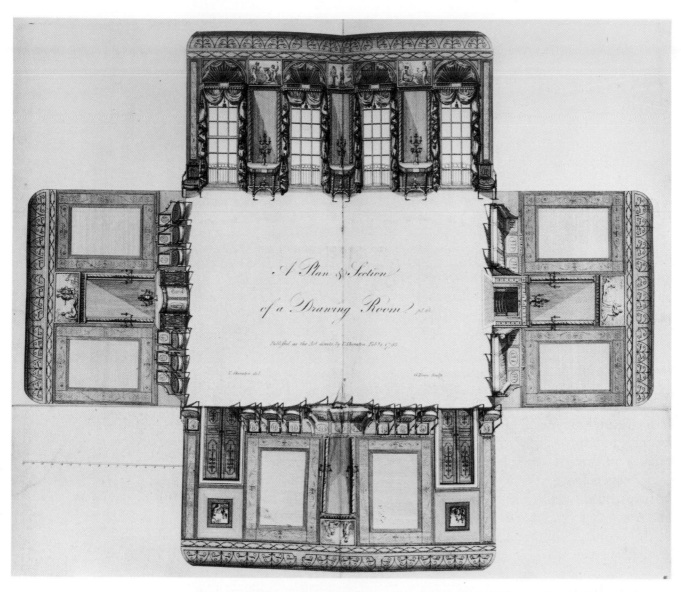

FIG. 3. *"A Plan and Section of a Drawing Room." From Thomas Sheraton,* The Cabinet-Maker and Upholsterer's Drawing-Book (*London, 1793*), *pl. 61.* (*Winterthur Museum Library.*) *Chairs, sofas, pier tables, and a commode are arranged around the walls with an open center space. Of the upholstery, Sheraton says that the sofas "are bordered off in three compartments, and covered with figured silk or satin. The ovals may be printed separately, and sewed on. These sofas may have cushions to fill their backs, together with bolsters at each end"* (*p. 444*).

Maker and Upholsterer's Guide (1826) show couches, comfortable chairs with footstools, and tables placed out in the room (Figs. 4, 5). Indeed, the center table in the parlor soon became the focus of activity for the Victorian family (Pl. 1). In the second half of the century, in America as in England, furniture was routinely grouped for conversation, reading, eating, or even enjoying the view from a window.

In 1878 Harriet P. Spofford described the drawing room as, historically, "the result of the first separation of the lady's chamber from the great hall . . . and [it] is therefore essentially one of the feminine apartments."[13] Twenty years later Edith Wharton and Ogden Codman, Jr., agreed while noting that the drawing room "is still considered sacred to gilding and discomfort." It "must have its gilt chairs covered with brocade, its *vitrines* full of modern Saxe, its guipure curtains and velvet carpet." "Circulation must not be impeded" and "chairs should be so light and easily moved that groups may be formed and broken up at will."[14]

In the present century, prior to World War II, two divergent trends in furnishing are seen. The eclectic styles continued with broader scope to include the Spanish style (especially in large New York apartments) and the Tudor revival or Elizabethan style favored for large estates on Long Island. Fireplace walls or entire rooms were brought over, especially from England, with appropriate tapestries, lighting fixtures, and furniture. What could not be found was reproduced. More modest was the colonial revival style with white woodwork and walls presumably suitable for antiques or reproductions in early American styles.

As opposed to this continued eclecticism, the modern movement was beginning to make itself felt. Frank Lloyd Wright began his career following a long line of nineteenth-century English reform artists which included Augustus Welby Pugin, who stressed qualities of propriety, repose, and unity in architecture; Owen Jones, the ornamentist; and Christopher Dresser whose stylizations of natural floral forms were influential. Wright inherited the honest, straightforward qualities of the arts and crafts movement established by William Morris but grew to greater sophistication and subtlety. A giant among designers and architects, he looked to total organic schemes including architecture, furniture, lighting fixtures, and fabrics.

Visual sources are inadequate to inform us completely concern-

FIG. 4. *Drawing by Gillow and Company, 176 Oxford Street, London, about 1825. (Victoria and Albert Museum Print Room.) A variety of furniture is now placed out in the room, including sofas with library tables and tub chairs, a round upholstered confidant, and a piano and stool (sketched in plan). Five suggestions for window curtains, three of which have scrolled cornices and two with pleated and fringed valances, are shown. The curtains hang to the floor, and two have sheer glass curtains beneath. A concept to be developed more fully later when a conservatory or garden room adjoined the house is suggested by the addition of trees placed in front of the windows in tubs (sketched in plan).*

FIG. 5. *"Octangular Tent Room."* From George Smith, The Cabinet-Maker and Upholsterer's Guide *(London, 1826), pl. 145. (Winterthur Museum Library.) In the romantic mood of the Regency period when the beauties of nature were admired on every hand, architects sought to bring the out-of-doors into homes. Of great importance was the Prince Regent's fantastic complex of domed buildings at Brighton that has been likened to a giant tent. This idea is adapted here to a room with a draped ceiling and continuous window pelmet with floor-length draperies. Brilliant color contrasts were favored, and here the tent ceiling is painted in red and green stripes. A center table is the focal point, and an armchair and footstool are drawn into the room.*

Eastman Johnson, The Hatch Family, *New York City, 1871. Oil on canvas; H. 48″, W. 73⅜″. (Metropolitan Museum of Art, gift of Frederic H. Hatch.) The Hatch family is shown in the library of their Park Avenue home. Grouped around the center table illuminated by a large gas fixture are three generations at work and play. The splendid red curtains with deep fringed lambrequins are suspended beneath a Renaissance revival continuous cornice matching the mantelpiece, bookcases, and table.*

ing the use of rooms in the larger houses of the sixteenth, seventeenth, and eighteenth centuries, and to some degree even the nineteenth century. Several recent studies have described in detail the function of rooms in English great houses and demonstrated how the furnishings conformed to the social demands of the time. Of particular interest are Mark Girouard's *Life in the English Country House* and Peter Thornton's *Seventeenth-Century Interior Decoration in England, France, and Holland.*[15] These studies refer to the processional sequence from public reception areas to semiprivate and finally to private rooms, such as the bed chamber, closet, or *cabinet,* reserved for the owner's intimate friends and his most splendid possessions. Studies of this kind are needed for early American houses as well.

In American furnishing plans of some of the older restorations have recently been the object of intense scrutiny. Studies with a view to more accurate historical interpretation have been undertaken at Pennsbury Manor, the reconstructed home of William Penn, and at Colonial Williamsburg where the furnishing plans of all the restored structures are under continuing review. A timely book on the subject is William Seale's *Recreating the Historic House Interior,* published in 1979.[16] Seale castigates the period room as being the artificial product of the decorator. He proposes instead the "historical interior" based on solid research and well-defined educational objectives. It is clear that furnishing old houses is a far more complex matter than it was once thought to be. Generalizations about household furnishings remain difficult whether discussing the twentieth century or the seventeenth century. It does appear that the survival of the concept of state or formal rooms, as opposed to the comfortable and informal rooms for family use, continued. The nineteenth century distinguished between the parlor and the sitting room, while the twentieth century clearly understands the difference between the living room and the family room. As always, the distinctions increase with position and wealth.

[1] Abraham Swan, *The British Architect; or, The Builder's Treasury of Stair-Cases,* was first published in London in 1745. Later London editions were published in 1748, 1750, and 1758. A second American edition was published in Boston in 1794.

[2] Thomas Chippendale, *The Gentleman and Cabinet-Maker's Director* (1762, 3d ed.; reprint ed., New York: Dover Publications, 1966), preface.

[3] Thomas Sheraton, *The Cabinet-Maker and Upholsterer's Drawing-Book* (1791–93; selections in reprint ed., New York: Dover Publications, 1972); George Hepplewhite, *The Cabinet-Maker and Upholsterer's Guide . . . from Drawings by A. Hepplewhite and Co., Cabinet-Makers* (1974, 3d ed.; reprint ed., New York: Dover Publications, 1969).

[4] Florence M. Montgomery, "Room Furnishings as Seen in British Prints from the Lewis Walpole Library," pt. 1, "Bed Hangings," pt. 2, "Window Curtains, Upholstery, and Slip Covers," *Antiques* 104, no. 6 (December 1973): 1068–75; 105, no. 3 (March 1974): 522–31.

[5] For contents of shipment, see Thomas Jefferson, *The Papers of Thomas Jefferson,* ed. Julian P. Boyd et al., 19 vols. to date (Princeton: Princeton University Press, 1950–), 18:33–39.

[6] Clarence E. Macartney and Gordon Dorrance, *The Bonapartes in America* (Philadelphia: Dorrance, 1939).

[7] Lorraine Waxman, "French Influence on American Decorative Arts of the Early Nineteenth Century: The Work of Charles-Honoré Lannuier" (M.A. thesis, University of Delaware, 1958); and *Philadelphia: Three Centuries of American Art (1676–1976)* (Philadelphia: Philadelphia Museum of Art, 1976), pp. 226–27.

[8] Samuel J. Dornsife, "Design Sources for Nineteenth-Century Window Hangings," in *Winterthur Portfolio 10,* ed. Ian M. G. Quimby (Charlottesville: University Press of Virginia, 1975), pp. 66–69.

[9] Thomas Hope, *Household Furniture and Interior Decoration* (1807; reprint ed., New York: Dover Publications, 1971).

[10] Andrew Jackson Downing, *The Architecture of Country Houses* (1850; portions on furniture and furnishings from this work and Loudon excerpted and reprinted in *Furniture for the Victorian Home* [Watkins Glen, N.Y.: American Life Foundation, 1978], pp. 23, 24).

[11] *Furniture for the Victorian Home,* p. 62.

[12] For the Bosse engravings, see Peter Thornton, *Seventeenth-Century Interior Decoration in England, France, and Holland* (New Haven and London: Yale University Press, 1978), pls. 1, 2, 4.

[13] Harriet P. Spofford, *Art Decoration Applied to Furniture* (New York: Harper, 1878), p. 215.

[14] Edith Wharton and Ogden Codman, Jr., *The Decoration of Houses* (1897; reprint ed., New York: W. W. Norton, 1978), pp. 124–25.

[15] Mark Girouard, *Life in the English Country House: A Social and Architectural History* (New Haven and London: Yale University Press, 1978); and Peter Thornton, *Seventeenth-Century Interior Decoration in England, France, and Holland* (New Haven and London: Yale University Press, 1978).

[16] William Seale, *Recreating the Historic House Interior* (Nashville: American Association for State and Local History, 1979).

Bed Hangings

Symbol of station and wealth, the bed was the most important object in the house. The quality of its hangings made it so. Louis XIV's bed of state at Versailles, sumptuously furnished with silk hangings and a carved and upholstered cornice topped with ostrich plumes, was set apart behind a balustrade, important in courtly hierarchy. The monarch received his courtiers at his levée seated on the edge of his bed fully clothed and wearing a plumed hat. In England royal and noble accounts show large expenditures for bed furnishings, and surviving beds, lavishly hung, attest to the richness and importance of the bed.

The engravings of Abraham Bosse and Daniel Marot show the lavish hangings found on certain seventeenth-century beds. Bosse, working from about 1629 to 1645, recorded intimate details of French court life and was explicit in his representations of dress, furniture, and hangings. An English print of a lady's bedroom is reminiscent of Bosse's work (Fig. 1). Marot, a Huguenot, served as designer to Louis XIV before fleeing France in 1685 with many other French Protestants. He became designer to William of Orange and accompanied him to London at the time of his marriage to Queen Mary. Marot's work brought fashions in room furnishings to the importance of an international style based on French modes (Fig. 2).

FIG. 1. *A lady's bedroom, engraving by Edmund Marmion, ca. 1640. (By permission of the Master and Fellows, Magdalene College, Cambridge.) The toilet table draped to the floor matches the straight, deeply fringed valances and curtains that completely surround the bed. Portraits in elaborately carved frames hang high on the walls above pictorial tapestries. High-backed chairs stand against the walls. This engraving and others of a group usually referred to under the title "The Five Senses" are pasted in a volume of miscellaneous prints by Samuel Pepys entitled "London and Westminster vol. II," pp. 410–11.*

English upholsterers may have dreamed of rich commissions like the room seen in figure 2, but probably few such rooms were created. Most were simpler. Chimney pieces and some interior paneling at Hampton Court in the manner of Marot's engravings show the simplification which occurred in the transfer from printed design to actual construction. That such simplification was not unexpected is borne out by Thomas Sheraton's remarks a hundred years later concerning his design entitled "An English State Bed":

Upon the whole, though a bed of this kind is not likely to be

Fig. 2. *Royal bedroom as shown in an engraving by Daniel Marot. From* Werken van D. Marot, opperboumeester van Zyne Maiesteit Willem den Derden Konig van Groot Britanje (*Amsterdam, [1707?], p. 76. (Winterthur Museum Library.) Following French custom, as established at the court of Louis XIV, the area around the bed of state is set apart by carpeting, and high-backed chairs are ranked around the wall.*

executed according to this design, except under the munificence of a royal order, yet I am not without hopes that useful ideas may be gathered from it, and applied to beds of a more general kind.[1]

English designers continued to produce designs for beds throughout the eighteenth century and into the nineteenth century. While designs such as those of Thomas Chippendale and George Smith for state beds may represent merely an ideal rather than a practical solution, their other designs, along with those of other designers, provided a vocabulary of elements from which customer, upholsterer, and cabinetmaker could assemble a bed of impressive character (Figs. 3–9). "Beds," observed George Hepplewhite, "are an article of much importance, as well on account of the great expense attending them, as the variety of shapes, and the high degree of elegance which may be shewn in them."[2]

A complete set of bed "furniture" for a four-post bed consisted of valances, headcloth, bedspread, and four curtains made wide enough to enclose the bed and long enough to reach nearly to the floor. Measurements for head and foot curtains, headcloth, tester, bedspread, matching chair cushions, and "two small Carpetts" were sent out to India from London by East India Company merchants for bed hangings. An order of 1682 reads:

> 100 Suits of painted Curtains and Vallances, ready made up of Several Sorts and Prices, strong, but none too dear, nor any overmean in regard you know our Poorest people in England lye without any Curtains or Vallances and our richest in Damask, etc. The Vallances to be 1 foot deep and 6½ yards compass. Curtains to be from 8 to 9 foot deep, and two lesser Curtains each 1½ yards wide, the two larger Curtains to be 3½ yards wide. The Tester and Headpiece proportionable. A Counterpane of the same work to be 3½ yards wide and 4 yards long, half of them to be quilted and the other half not quilted. Each bed to have to it 2 small Carpetts, 1½ yards wide and 2 yards long. Each bed to have 12 Cushions for Chairs of the same work.[3]

No seventeenth-century American high-post bedstead is known to survive, and few hangings or bedcovers are attributable to that early period. There are, however, some clues concerning their appearance. That some lavishly dressed beds existed in seventeenth-century America can be deduced from the warning issued to the Philadelphia Yearly Meeting of Women Friends in 1698 "that no superfluous furniture be in your houses, as great fringes about your valances, and double valances, and double curtains, and many such like needless things; wich the Truth maketh manifest to the humble minded."[4] A few bedsteads with low, turned posts are known, and there are references to boxed beds in the Dutch tradition.[5]

FIG. 3. *Design for a state bed. From Thomas Chippendale,* The Gentleman and Cabinet–Maker's Director (*3d ed.; London, 1762*), *pl. 47. (Winterthur Museum Library.)*

FIG. 4. *Design for a bed. From Thomas Chippendale,* The Gentleman and Cabinet-Maker's Director (*3d ed.; London, 1762*), *pl. 40. (Winterthur Museum Library.) Side and foot curtains are not shown presumably to allow the carving to be seen.*

FIG. 5. *Design for "a Gothick Bed, with a flat Tester." From Thomas Chippendale,* The Gentleman and Cabinet-Maker's Director *(3d ed.; London, 1762), pl. 44. (Winterthur Museum Library.)*

FIG. 6. *Design for a state bed. From George Smith,* A Collection of Designs for Household Furniture and Interior Decoration *(London, 1808), pl. 28. (Winterthur Museum Library.) Smith proposes curtains "made of Genoa velvet, satin or superfine cloth, a suitable border being worked round them on an embroidery of gold; the ground also of the tester must be of the same material and colour as the curtains. . . . This species of Bed does not admit of drapery. . . . This style is applicable only in a real Gothic mansion; if otherwise used, it would be highly improper and out of taste."*

FIG. 7. *Design for a dome bed. From George Smith,* A Collection of Designs for Household Furniture and Interior Decoration *(London, 1808), pl. 24. (Winterthur Museum Library.) Smith suggests that the furniture for this bed "may be of calico or silk, the exterior green, and the linings yellow."*

FIG. 8. *Design for a French bed. From George Smith,* A Collection of Designs for Household Furniture and Interior Decoration *(London, 1808), pl. 29. (Winterthur Museum Library.) Smith advises that "the tester with the dome is attached to the wall, and supports the curtains, which draw round the bedstead, which is in the form of a sofa. The furniture may be of rich materials as before described, such beds being calculated for elegant apartments."*

In seventeenth-century English paintings and prints, four-post beds are shown with valances made straight and ornamented with fringe, sometimes elaborately netted (Fig. 10). From Boston Samuel Sewall wrote to London in 1719 for what seems to be a bed of this kind.

> To be Bought. Curtains and Vallens for a bed, with Counterpane, Head-Cloth and Tester, of good yellow waterd worsted camlet, with Trimming, well made, and Bases, if it be the fashion. Send also of the same Camlet and Trimming, as may be enough to make Cushions for the Chamber Chairs.[6]

FIG. 9. *Design for a field bed. From George Smith,* A Collection of Designs for Household Furniture and Interior Decoration (*London, 1808), pl. 21. (Winterthur Museum Library.) Smith suggests furniture of "plain or printed calicoes; the border cut out in black Manchester velvet and sewed on."*

FIG. 10. *Alcove and bed designed for Charles II at Greenwich Palace. Engraving after a drawing dated 1665 by John Webb (1611–72). From John Vardy,* Some Designs of Mr. Inigo Jones and Mr. William Kent *(London, 1744), pl. 4. (Winterthur Museum Library.) The bed, completely enclosed with curtains, is ornamented with fringed valances, borders, and plume finials.*

Colonial newspaper advertisements suggest the general appearance of beds including the kinds of textiles, their colors, and sometimes the manner of draping. Thus we read of "one work'd [embroidered] Cloth Bed, lin'd with Silk, . . . one Green Camblet Bed and bedstead,"[7] "a genteel four post Bedstead and Cornices, with fine blue and white copper-plate Furniture . . . trimmed with fringe, made to draw in double drapery, with lines, tassels and brass pins. Two Window Curtains and Six Chair Cases of the same pattern,"[8] or "a painted four post bedstead, with calico furniture fringed, and made to draw in drapery, with cornices" (Figs. 11a, b; 12a, b; 13a, b).[9]

FIG. 11A,B. *Blue and white checked linen curtain from Stenton, the Germantown home of James Logan. (Stenton Mansion, The National Society of Colonial Dames of America in the State of Pennsylvania. Photo, Winterthur Museum.) The curtain is shown here drawn up in "double drapery." It measures 9 feet 6 inches in length and 3 feet 6 inches in width. The checks are 2¼ by 2 inches. Presumably these curtains were made for Logan sometime between the completion of Stenton (1731) and his death (1751). B, Back of the Stenton curtain showing two parallel curving lines of narrow tape with brass rings stitched to them at intervals through which cords were run to raise the curtain. A single set of rings and tape would make a single swag. To our eyes the effect may be bunchy, but it was a practical way to manage large curtains.*

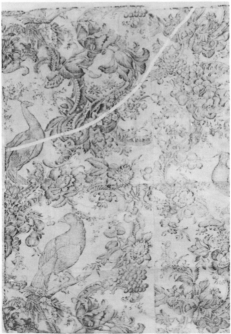

FIG. 12A,B. *Window or bed curtain of English copperplate-printed cloth edged with fringe. The peacock and rococo scroll pattern was probably printed about 1765 to 1775. B, Back of curtain showing tape and rings through which cord was run to raise the curtain. (Litchfield [Conn.] Historical Society.)*

FIG. 13A,B. *Detail of headcloth printed from copperplates in a chinoiserie pattern show-*
ing tape applied in scallops at the top. The valances, which no longer survive, were proba-
bly made with matching scalloped edges. B, *Detail of headcloth showing a pair of bound*
holes through which the headboard fit into slots in the bed posts. Tapes stitched to the side
edges at intervals were tied around the posts. Despite the advantages claimed for washable
printed textiles, in this instance it would have been necessary to dismantle the bed to remove
the headcloth for laundering. (Stenton Mansion, The National Society of Colonial Dames
of America in the State of Pennsylvania.)

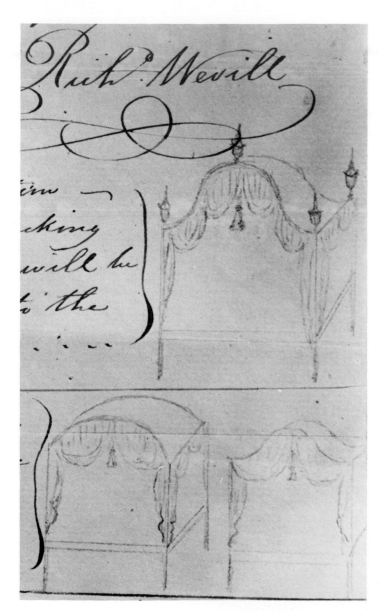

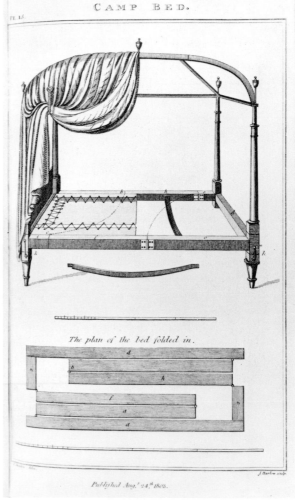

CAMP BED.

The plan of the bed folded in.

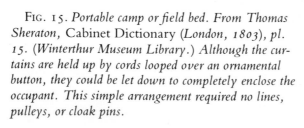

Published Aug.ᵗ 24.ᵗʰ 1803.

FIG. 14. *Drawings of canopy and field beds by Richard Wevill, Philadelphia upholsterer, dated July 17, 1802. (Ridgely Collection, Public Archives Commission, Division of Historic and Cultural Affairs, Dover, Delaware.) The sketches were made at the request of Mrs. Williamina Cadwalader on behalf of Mrs. Ann Ridgely of Dover, Delaware. Mrs. Cadwalader notes in her letter accompanying Wevill's estimates that the prices are for bedsteads without curtains and that she "can purchase white Muslin very low which will look neat at present and hereafter serve to line better."*

FIG. 15. *Portable camp or field bed. From Thomas Sheraton,* Cabinet Dictionary *(London, 1803), pl. 15. (Winterthur Museum Library.) Although the curtains are held up by cords looped over an ornamental button, they could be let down to completely enclose the occupant. This simple arrangement required no lines, pulleys, or cloak pins.*

Canopy, dome, field, and four-post beds were advertised by urban colonial upholsterers (Fig. 14), and all except the dome bed have survived in considerable numbers. Camp or field beds, according to Sheraton, could "be folded in the most compact manner."[10] Even though designed to be portable, these beds were often fitted with curtains (Figs. 15, 16). The nomenclature for bed types was loosely applied, invention and fantasy being most important to designers and upholsterers. Between 1737 and 1760 Samuel Grant of Boston filled commissions for raised beds (possibly a low-post bed with a canopy suspended from the ceiling); woodwork beds; joined and field beds; coach (couch) beds; and satie (settee) beds. A listing for a "couch frame, squab and pillow" suggests a daybed.

FIG. 16. *Doll's bed, American, early nineteenth century. (Winterthur Museum.) The arched tester bed is shown with fringed curtains held back by buttons and cords in the manner of Sheraton's drawing (Fig. 15). The bed does not fold.*

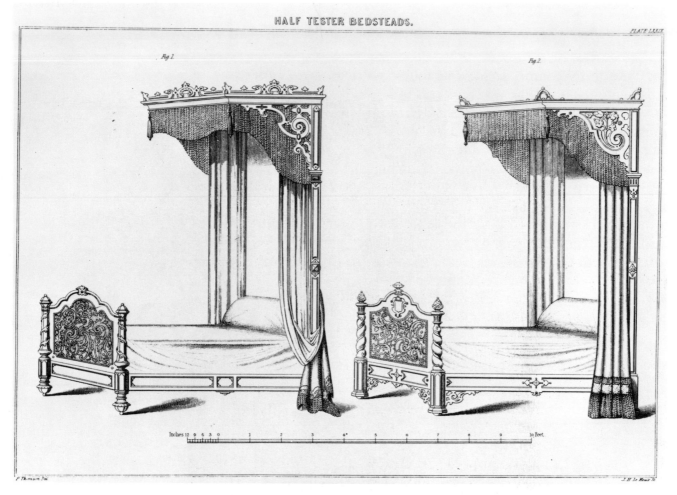

FIG. 17. *Half-tester bedsteads. From* The Cabinet-Maker's Assistant *(London: Blackie & Son, 1853), pl. 79. (Photo, Winterthur.) Such designs are characteristic of the mid-nineteenth century. These beds were "in frequent use" and "very suitable for moderately-sized apartments." The long fringe is suspended beneath the carved wooden testers with long head curtains fringed to match.*

Eighteenth-century bed curtains might be hung from a continuous iron rod fastened to the wall above the head of the bed and suspended from hooks in the ceiling above the foot.[11] Half-tester beds, like more recent Murphy beds, could be turned up during the day and concealed beneath a headcloth and long curtains. The tester and side curtains of such half-headed beds were sometimes suspended from a hook in the ceiling,[12] or long curtains were hung from a narrow wooden tester frame braced to two high posts. Mid-nineteenth-century half-tester beds are illustrated in figure 17.

Cloak pins, or mirror knobs as they are described in brass founders' catalogues, were used for holding curtains in place. On the bed shown in figure 18 cloak pins attached to a head post secured the cords. The author has seen pairs of transfer-printed cloak pins attached to the foot posts of an American Chippendale bed.

FIG. 18. *Four-post bed fitted with curtains which could be let down by releasing cords running on pulleys and fastened to a pair of brass cloak pins at the head post. From Thomas Malton,* A Compleat Treatise on Perspective *(2d ed.; London, 1778), pl. 34. (Winterthur Museum Library.)*

FIG. 19. *Canopy bed from the engraved trade card of Richard Kip, Jr., New York upholsterer, dated 1771. (New York Public Library, Astor, Lenox, and Tilden Foundations.)*

FIG. 20. *Four shaped bed valances. (Winterthur Museum.) The top example of red wool ornamented and bound with shirred scrolls of buff colored silk tape and cords may date from the second quarter of the eighteenth century. The valance beneath is block printed in blue with huge flowers and curling leaves, and together with its shape featuring broad "ears," it can be dated about 1740. Darker unfaded areas indicate that a printed strip of cloth was once gathered and applied in scrolls about an inch from the bottom edge of the valance paralleling its contour. The unfaded blue resist-dyed valance with modified curves dates from mid-century, and the bottom valance, edged with fine white fringe, from after the Revolution. The English copperplate print of Franklin and Washington, the latter ruthlessly cut at the waist, probably in the interest of economic use of the material, was printed about 1785.*

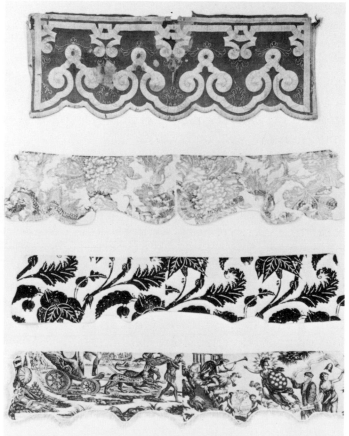

It is difficult to determine whether eighteenth-century American upholsterers actually created the elaborate drapery sometimes shown on their trade cards. The elegant 1771 advertisement of Richard Kip shows alternate designs for bed pillars and short drapery in the Chinese Chippendale taste (Fig. 19). By the 1770s carvers excelled at their craft, and owners wished their fine work to show; it is possible that Kip's curtains fell to the floor when released.

In 1725 Thomas Fitch, a Boston upholsterer, asked a London merchant to commission an upholsterer to make up valances, and to cover a set of cornices and a headboard which Fitch would then complete in Boston. On another occasion he requested "a few pretty patterns of Vallances and headcloths."[13] Surviving bed valances in American collections provide further information about the appearance of eighteenth-century beds (Fig. 20). A few valances exist made of watered worsted with rounded "ears" and with applied ornamental tapes and cords, following the curvilinear patterns depicted by artists like William Hogarth (Fig. 21), William De La Cour, and other designers working in the first half of the century. Other valances, particularly those made from copperplate-printed textiles, follow the more elaborate and frivolous rococo style (Fig. 22). By the end of the century straight valances were again in vogue, and the broad foot curtains enclosing the bed were no longer obligatory. Many washable curtains were finished without linings. The use of interior valances and extra swags of drapery probably depended upon the fancy of the upholsterer or his client's taste.

Two carved and scrolled American wooden bed cornices survive (Figs. 23, 24). One fragment, covered in red and white copperplate-printed cotton, and another with blue and white resist-dyed cotton, testify to the custom of upholstering carved wooden parts— simplified versions of princely English beds. In 1770 Thomas Affleck, famous Philadelphia cabinetmaker, billed his wealthy client John Cadwalader for a "Sett of Cutt open Cornices" and "2 Window ditto."[14] In 1759 George Washington ordered a "Tester Bedstead" from London with "a Neat cut Cornish" to be covered with "Chintz Blew Plate Cotton furniture" to match in color a sample of wallpaper sent with the order. A coverlet, four chair seats, festoon curtains, and "2 Neat cut window Cornishes" to be covered to match would, according to Washington, make the room "uniformly handsome and genteel."[15]

FIG. 22. *A continuous unlined valance hangs beneath a late eighteenth-century painted wooden cornice on this mahogany bedstead. The valance descended in the family of Eleazer Arnold of Lincoln, Rhode Island. (Society for the Preservation of New England Antiquities. Photo, Richard Cheek.) The valance is pleated in the center of each side and gathered at the corners to hang in points edged with netting and delicate fly fringe. The English copperplate pattern, printed in blue, comes from the Bromley Hall printworks where it was called "Farmyard" and dates from 1770 to 1780.*

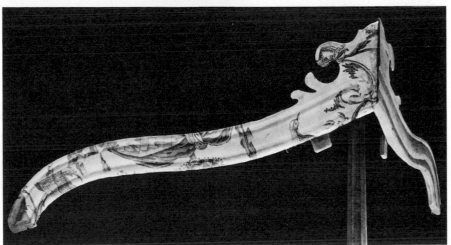

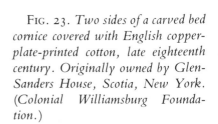

FIG. 23. *Two sides of a carved bed cornice covered with English copperplate-printed cotton, late eighteenth century. Originally owned by Glen-Sanders House, Scotia, New York. (Colonial Williamsburg Foundation.)*

OPPOSITE

FIG. 21. *"After," engraving by William Hogarth, ca. 1736. (Colonial Williamsburg Foundation.) Details of the bed with inner and outer shaped valances, headcloth, curtain, and rod are shown. Scrolled braid ornaments the headcloth, and the valances with pronounced "ears" were either embroidered or had applied tapes and cords.*

FIG. 24. *Bed with carved and pierced cornice covered in blue and white resist-dyed cotton. (Metropolitan Museum of Art, purchase from Joseph Pulitzer Bequest.) The bed was made for Abigail Porter who married Col. Thomas Belden of Wethersfield, Connecticut, in 1753. At that date, the foot posts were probably also covered with long curtains enclosing the bed when drawn together.*

Of all the materials available, worsteds—cheney, harateen, moreen, and camlet—were the most widely used before the American Revolution. These were made from long woolen fibers which were combed rather than carded before spinning. By this process the fibers were laid parallel to one another, and, when lightly twisted together, they formed hard, silky, shiny yarns like those used for crewelwork. After weaving, the cloth was finished by pressing or stamping to give watered, waved, or flowered patterns.

Boston tastes in textiles, possibly for bed hangings, are suggested by a 1723 order for camlet from Fitch to a London agent.

> I generally deal in double Camblets which by my Friends I get seasonally bespoke of the makers and so have the fresh and good Colours. . . . Invest the money in good double Camlets of fresh lively fashionable colours, a pretty many of copperish cast, some lighter than others, but none of a sad dull Colour, severall blews though they may cost a little more, others of the colours of the enclosed patterns and more lively.[16]

In 1725 Fitch wrote to a London upholsterer asking that his best draftsman draw patterns for bed hangings in the newest fashion which he would make of "very good broad scarlet in grain double worsted camlet." At the same time he asked for "good fashionable silk lace binding and breed [braid] very fresh, lively and sutable" leaving the choice to the Londoner's fancy.[17]

Silk mixed with worsted for curtains in the best bedroom or parlor (Fig. 25) is occasionally mentioned in advertisements. Richard Kip lists "rich yellow silk and worsted damask," and "a sofa, twelve chairs, and three window curtains of sky-blue silk and worsted damask stuffs garnished and fringed."[18] In 1739 John Banister of Rhode Island lists "2 ps Crimson Silk and Worsted Bed Damask 80 yds."[19] In 1765 Benjamin Franklin's son William ordered "Three curtains of Yellow Silk and Worsted Damask. . . . to be hung festoon fashion" with yellow fringe for binding.[20] These would match chairs covered in yellow damask.

Unlike patterns for silk dress fabrics, with new designs produced as often as once or twice a year and woven in small yardages, silks for furnishing were more conservative. Various stylized leafy patterns, some featuring large pomegranates, first woven in Italy in the late seventeenth century, were produced at Spitalfields into the 1770s. Silk hangings remained in fashion for the few who could afford them. Certainly they were costly and far less durable than worsteds. In 1773 John Apthorp, a wealthy Bostonian, had "a very rich Silk Damask Bed, with Window Curtains, Chairs, and an easy Chair, all in the newest Taste" together with "a large Sopha and ten Chairs covered with the best crimson Silk-Damask, and four large Window Curtains of the same" as well as "a small Sopha and five Chairs of the same Damask, in the Chinese Taste." In 1771, John Cadwalader of Philadelphia ordered from London mercers for his front parlor deep blue silk damask which John Webster, a London-trained upholsterer, made into window curtains lined with blue sarcenet, a thinner silk. The same blue damask covered three sofas and twenty chair seats in the room. Yellow silk damask, also from London, was used in the back parlor.[21]

FIG. 25. *Curtain and fringed valance made of gold colored silk and worsted damask. Originally owned by the Burnham family of Newburyport, Massachusetts, ca. 1765. (Winterthur Museum.)*

After the middle of the eighteenth century, cotton materials were listed with increasing frequency among upholsterers' goods. Advertisements noted, for example, "elegant printed Cottons for Bed Furniture [and] a Variety of printed Cottons and Linnens . . . just imported."[22] A 1779 Philadelphia advertisement of H. Taylor mentioned "a few pieces of the most elegant chintz, both for fineness and richness of pattern, that has been imported into this country."[23] More specific was his 1775 offer for sale of "a genteel four post Bed, with very fine flowered cotton furniture, fringes, and ornamented with a cornice."[24] These referred to block-printed, polychrome materials printed in vertical repeating patterns suitable for window curtains, bed hangings, and matching slipcovers.

In 1794 George Hepplewhite was quite specific in his recommendations for fabrics for beds:

> They may be executed of almost every stuff which the loom produces. White dimity, plain or corded, is peculiarly applicable for the furniture, which, with a fringe with a gymp head, produces an effect of elegance and neatness truly agreeable.
>
> The Manchester stuffs have been wrought into Bed-furniture with good success. Printed cottons and linens are also very suitable; the elegance and variety of patterns of which, afforded as much scope for taste, elegance, and simplicity, as the most capricious fancy can wish. . . . In state-rooms where a high degree of elegance and grandeur are wanted, beds are frequently made of silk or satin, figured or plain, also of velvet, with gold fringe, &c.[25]

In *The Cabinet-Maker and Upholsterer's Guide* (1826), George Smith, who styled himself "Upholsterer and Furniture Draughtsman to His Majesty," offered beds dressed to suit his furniture in the Chinese, Gothic, rustic, Egyptian, Etruscan, Greek, and Roman styles, among others. French beds with a long side against the wall are shown with drapery suspended from a rod extending out from the wall above and thrown loosely over rods at each end of the couch (Fig. 26). According to Thomas Webster, the most elegant French beds were made of mahogany "and have canopies and draperies of a more fanciful kind" while "the cottage French pole-bed is of very simple construction" and "consists merely of a piece of drapery thrown over a

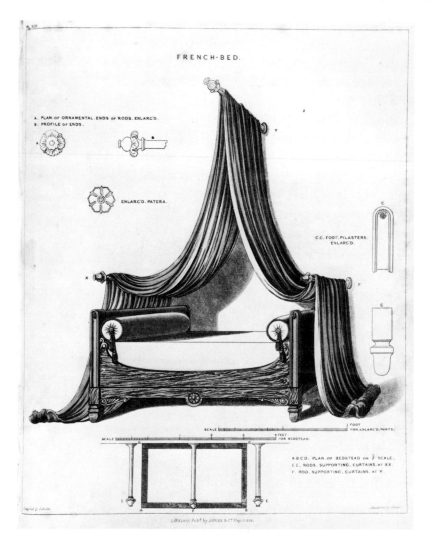

FIG. 26. *A "French-Bed" with short rods placed above the bed and at each end, as shown on the plan, to accommodate the drapery. From* George Smith, The Cabinet-Maker and Upholsterer's Guide (*London, 1826*), *pl. 13.* (*Winterthur Museum Library.*)

OPPOSITE

FIG. 27. *Bed hangings. From* The Workwoman's Guide (*London and Birmingham, 1838*), *pl. 22.* (*Winterthur Museum Library.*) *Included are templates for cutting swags and points (7–10); the manner of gathering material to a center rosette for the ceiling of a bed (17); half-tester (19, 20) and French pole beds (21, 22); and illustrations for folding beds, cots, sacking bottoms, and a hanging bed (26–30).*

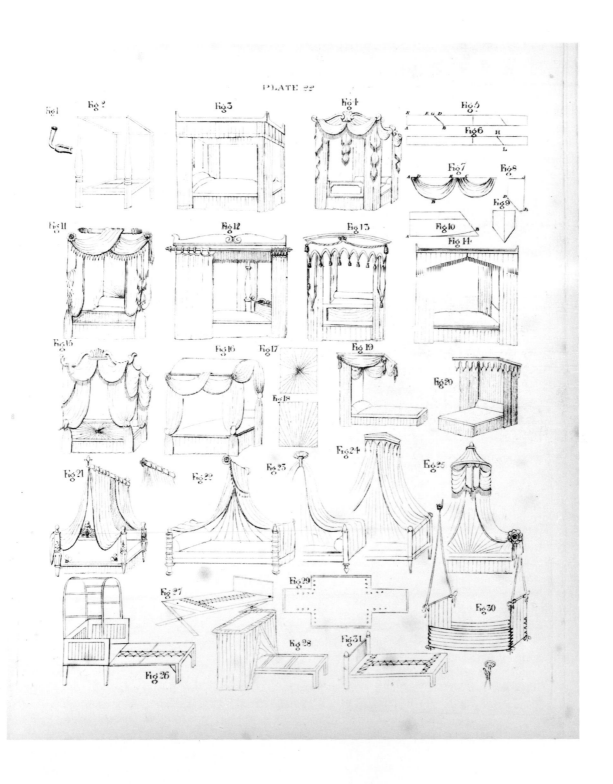

PLATE 22

FIG. 28. *Cuts from Thomas Webster,* An Encyclopaedia of Domestic Economy *(New York: Harper, 1845). (Winterthur Museum Library.) Figure 399 shows the bracket for suspending a curtain over the middle of a bed to drape over each end of the high head and foot boards as seen in figure 400.*

pole which is generally fixed to the wall at the place where the bed is to stand" (Figs. 27–29).[26]

Continuing the earlier precept, as illustrated in figure 30, John Claudius Loudon wrote in 1833, "The curtains of all beds ought to correspond with those of the windows of the rooms in which they are placed." Pictures of bed hangings taken from all the best-known English pattern books may be found in the *Pictorial Dictionary of British Nineteenth-Century Furniture Design.* In America Andrew Jackson

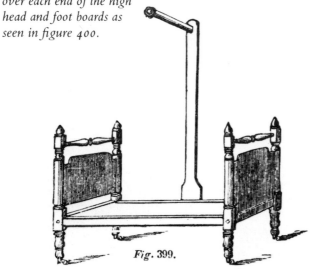

Fig. 399.

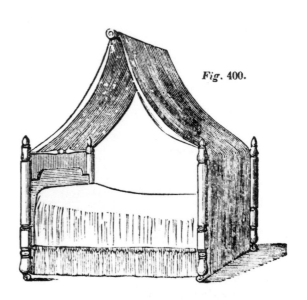

Fig. 400.

FIG. 29. *Bedspread fitted to accommodate a pillow. Cotton cloth block printed in the drab style of yellow and dark brown, England, 1800–1805. The bedspread descended in the Lewis family of Gorham, Maine. (Society for the Preservation of New England Antiquities.) French bedspreads with ends fashioned to fit over round, stiff bolsters have long been known, but the custom was unknown in America until the discovery of this spread. This detail shows the original welting and inserted oval of cloth.*

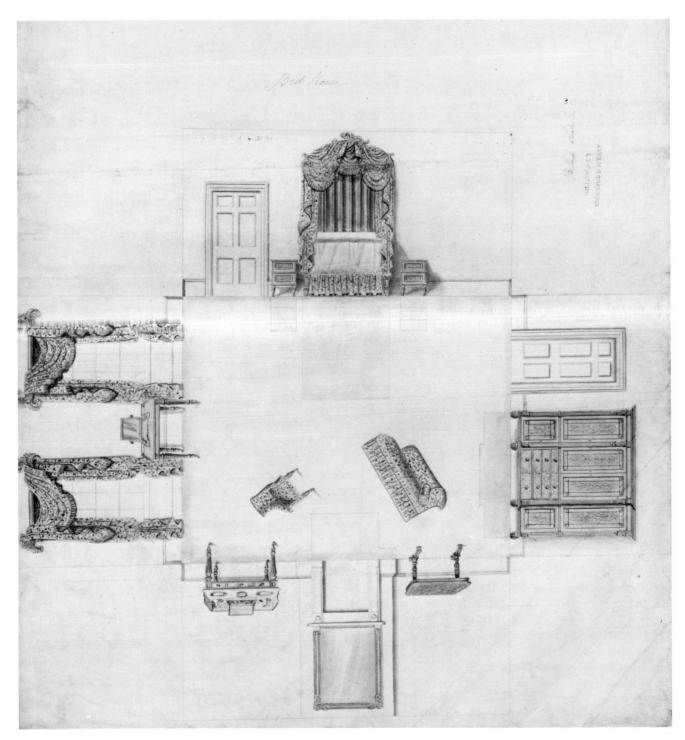

FIG. 30. *Drawing for a bedroom by Gillow and Company, 176 Oxford Street, London, ca. 1825. (Victoria and Albert Museum.) The window curtains and bed are heavily draped in flowered chintz with a slipcovered couch and tub chair to match.*

Downing commented in 1850 that "the high four-post bedstead, with curtains, still common in England, is almost entirely laid aside in the United States for the French bedstead, low, and without curtains" (Fig. 31).[27] Loudon's suggestions for materials to be used are practical:

> The usual material for the hangings of cottage beds, especially for tent beds, is dimity, which has the advantage of being easily washed, and may thus be always contrived to have a clean appearance. Printed cottons, Manchester stripes, and chintzes are also very suitable, particularly the latter, for French beds; but moreens and other woollen stuffs should never be used in cottages, as they have not only too heavy an appearance for a small room, but are liable to harbour dust and vermin.[28]

FIG. 31. *"A very good specimen of a modern bedstead with canopy and drapery complete, in the English taste [left], . . . and another in the French taste [right]." From A. J. Downing,* The Architecture of Country Houses *(New York: D. Appleton, 1850), p. 431, figs. 233, 234. (Winterthur Museum Library.)*

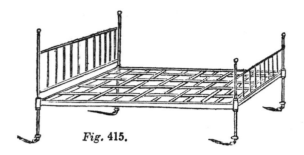

Fig. 415.

FIG. 32. *An iron bedstead. From Thomas Webster,* An Encyclopaedia of Domestic Economy (*New York: Harper, 1845*), *fig. 415.* (*Winterthur Museum Library.*)

FIG. 33. *A cast-iron bed "high-post Gothic" style. From Hutchinson and Wickersham,* A New Phase in the Iron Manufacture . . . Descriptive Catalogue of the Manufacturers of the New York Wire Railing Company (*New York, 1857*), *p. 62, fig. 9.* (*Atheneum of Philadelphia.*)

In 1845 Thomas Webster recommended iron bedsteads for their durability and found that they had "become very general, and are much more easily kept clean than those of wood" (Figs. 32, 33). He added that "some are made with standards for curtains, in the manner of French bedsteads."[29] Twenty years later Charles Eastlake's iron bed scarcely seems a simplification of the preceding styles to our eyes (Fig. 34). The medieval flavor is carried out in the spears serving as rods for the heavily fringed valances. Quite in contrast is the washable, tufted bedspread with sheets and pillows uncovered.

In some homes ornamental swags or valances were attached to the wall above the head of the bed; totally without function, they were the last remnants of bed hangings until the revival of colonial and other earlier styles when the pendulum swung back to curtained four-posters (Fig. 35). By the late nineteenth century hygiene and cleanliness were of great concern. People were persuaded that open windows and night air were healthy, and the sleeping porch adjacent to a bedroom was thought beneficial by many. In 1883 Laura Holloway declared, "We have discarded in great degree the old-fashioned feather bed, and also the curtains of the past generation."[30]

FIG. 34. *"Iron Bedstead, with Canopy."* From Charles Locke Eastlake, Hints on Household Taste (*London, 1868*), pl. 31. (*Winterthur Museum Library.*) *The canopy is hung on rods suspended from the exposed ceiling beam and fastened to the wall behind "as in old days." For London where "white curtains rapidly soil," Eastlake suggested "cretonne, chintz, or damask" to reach within two or three inches of the floor and "simply tied back when not in use" (p. 189). He further added: "The canopy may be either disposed in plaits or decorated with fringe, but where plaits are used the fringe should be omitted, as it is apt to get tangled and pull the plaits out of shape. Box-plaits are the best to use, and should never be less than four or five inches in width, at intervals of about eight or ten. They should be pressed down as flat as possible, and when necessary, may be kept in shape by a stitch on either side" (p. 190).*

FIG. 35. *A bedstead in the " 'Renaissance' style . . . [with] draperies . . . of raw silk, drab and blue, and canopy . . . of light blue silk tufted." Made by Herts and Company, New York. From Walter Smith,* Industrial Art, Masterpieces of the Centennial Exhibition, *vol. 2 (Philadelphia: Gebbie & Barrie, 1876), 2:26. (Winterthur Museum Library.)*

[1] Thomas Sheraton, *The Cabinet-Maker and Upholsterer's Drawing-Book* (London, 1802), appendix, p. 40.

[2] George Hepplewhite, *The Cabinet-Maker and Upholsterer's Guide* (2d ed.; London, 1789), p. 17.

[3] John Irwin and P. R. Schwartz, *Studies in Indo-European Textile History* (Ahmedabad, India: Calico Museum of Textiles, 1966), p. 35.

[4] Frederick B. Tolles, *Meetinghouse and Counting House: The Quaker Merchants of Colonial Philadelphia* (Chapel Hill: University of North Carolina Press, 1948), p. 128.

[5] According to Norman B. Rice of the Albany Institute, such beds were listed in seventeenth-century inventories. The Museum of Fine Arts, Boston, recently acquired a seventeenth-century turned-post bed that was exhibited in the 1982 exhibition "New England Begins."

[6] Samuel Sewall, *The Letter-Book of Samuel Sewall,* in *Collections of the Massachusetts Historical Society,* 6th ser., vols. 1 and 2 (Boston: Published by the society, 1886, 1888), p. 105.

[7] Advertisment of Benjamin Church, *Boston Gazette,* December 20, 1748, as quoted in George Francis Dow, *The Arts and Crafts in New England, 1704–1775* (Topsfield, Mass.: Wayside Press, 1927), p. 112.

[8] Advertisement of H. Taylor, upholsterer, *Pennsylvania Journal,* February 23, 1782, as quoted in Alfred Coxe Prime, *The Arts and Crafts in Philadelphia, Maryland, and South Carolina, 1721–1785* (Topsfield, Mass.: Wayside Press for the Walpole Society, 1929), p. 214.

[9] Advertisement of H. Taylor, *Pennsylvania Journal,* January 19, 1780, as quoted in Prime, *Arts and Crafts,* p. 213.

[10] Thomas Sheraton, *The Cabinet Dictionary* (London: W. Smith, 1803), p. 123.

[11] Abbott Lowell Cummings, *Bed Hangings: A Treatise on Fabrics and Styles in the Curtaining of Beds, 1650–1850* (Boston: Society for the Preservation of New England Antiquities, 1961), fig. 21.

[12] Florence M. Montgomery, "Room Furnishings as Seen in British Prints from the Lewis Walpole Library," pt. 1, "Bed Hangings," *Antiques* 104, no. 6 (December 1973): 1068–75. Cummings, *Bed Hangings,* fig. 22, note the hook in the ceiling.

[13] Brock Jobe, "The Boston Furniture Industry, 1720-1740," in *Boston Furniture of the Eighteenth Century,* ed. Walter Muir Whitehill (Charlottesville: University Press of Virginia for the Colonial Society, 1974), p. 30; and Fitch to John East, December 13, 1726, letter book of Thomas Fitch, 1723–33, Massachusetts Historical Society.

[14] Nicholas B. Wainwright, *Colonial Grandeur in Philadelphia: The House and Furniture of General John Cadwalader* (Philadelphia: Historical Society of Pennsylvania, 1964), p. 44.

[15] Helen Maggs Fede, *Washington Furniture at Mount Vernon* (Mount Vernon, Va.: Mount Vernon Ladies' Association of the Union, 1966), p. 18.

[16] Fitch to Robert Harrison, January 22, 1723, Fitch letter book, 1723–33.

[17] Jobe, "Boston Furniture Industry," p. 28; Fitch to John East, April 6, 1725, Fitch letter book, 1723–33.

[18] Richard Kip, Jr., *New York Packet and the American Advertiser,* December 13, 1784, in Rita Susswein Gottesman, *The Arts and Crafts in New York, 1777–1799* (New York: New-York Historical Society, 1954), p. 147.

[19] John Banister, account of Thomas Hall, invoice no. 6, 1739, John Banister letter books, 1739–50, M-191, Joseph Downs Manuscript and Microfilm Collection, Winterthur Museum Library.

[20] Charles Henry Hart, ed., "Letters from William Franklin to William Strahan," *Pennsylvania Magazine of History and Biography* 35, no. 4 (1911): 440–41.

[21] *Boston News-Letter,* May 13, 1773, as quoted in Dow, *Arts and Crafts in New England,* p. 126; Wainwright, *Colonial Grandeur,* pp. 51–52.

[22] Advertisement of Nathaniel Rogers, *Boston Gazette,* August 8, 1763, as quoted in Dow, *Arts and Crafts in New England,* p. 171.

[23] Advertisement of H. Taylor, upholsterer, *Pennsylvania Packet,* December 23, 1779, as quoted in Prime, *Arts and Crafts,* p. 213.

[24] Advertisement of H. Taylor, upholsterer, *Pennsylvania Journal,* May 31, 1775, as quoted in Prime, *Arts and Crafts,* p. 212.

[25] Hepplewhite, *Cabinet-Maker and Upholsterer's Guide,* p. 17.

[26] Thomas Webster, *An Encyclopaedia of Domestic Economy* (New York: Harper, 1845), p. 292.

[27] John Claudius Loudon, *An Encyclopedia of Cottage, Farm, and Villa Architecture and Furniture* (London, 1833). Excerpts reprinted in *Furniture for the Victorian Home* (Watkins Glen, N.Y.: American Life Foundation, 1978), p. 183; *Pictorial Dictionary of British Nineteenth-Century Furniture Design,* intro. by Edward T. Joy (Woodbridge, Suffolk: Baron Publishing for the Antique Collectors' Club, 1977), pp. 1–28. Andrew Jackson Downing, *The Architecture of Country Houses* (New York, 1850). Excerpts reprinted in *Furniture for the Victorian Home,* p. 61.

[28] *Furniture for the Victorian Home,* p. 123.

[29] Webster, *Encyclopaedia of Domestic Economy,* p. 296.

[30] Laura C. Holloway, *The Hearthstone; or, Life at Home* (Philadelphia and Chicago, 1883), p. 158.

Jeremiah Platt, merchant, New York City; oil on canvas by John Mare, 1767.
(Metropolitan Museum of Art: Photo, Antiques.)

Window Curtains

Studies of early American estate inventories lead to the conclusion that window curtains were less common than we once thought.[1] When they do appear in inventories, they are usually found in the best parlor or, almost as often, in the best bedroom. Nevertheless, it is clear that some handsome and elaborate window curtains were in use in America by the late colonial period. In his portrait of Jeremiah Platt of New York, painted in 1767, John Mare surrounded his sitter with a red damask curtain edged with fringe and complete with tassel (Pl. 1). Ordinarily, such an elaborate curtain would be considered an artist's studio prop or a background borrowed from an engraving to enhance the status of the sitter. In this case, however, Platt's inventory lists three red window curtains with red cords and tassels. Thus, while statistically such showy displays of expensive textiles were not common, neither were they unusual among the well-to-do segment of American society. Window curtains have a particularly low rate of survival because of the deleterious effects of ultraviolet radiation in daylight which causes them to fade and rot. We are dependent for information on their appearance, therefore, on paintings and prints of interiors and books and magazines that instructed people in the current fashions of the day.

In seventeenth-century western Europe the most common form of window curtain apparently consisted of a single piece of cloth

FIG. I. *Drawing of the narrow end of a proposed reception chamber by Paul Decker for his* Fürstlicher Baumeister *published in Augsburg, 1711–16. From P. Dohme, Paul Decker's* Fürstlicher Baumeister *in Siebenundfünfzig Tafeln (Berlin: Ernst Wasmuth, 1885), pl. 38. (Winterthur Museum Library.) The curtains shown at left are gathered up at each side by cords; that at the right is shown released.*

hanging from the top of the window frame. It was opened by drawing it to one side or the other of the window. In 1673 the French journal *Mercure Galant* refers to the division of the single curtain into two vertical parts as a novelty. The curtains "are now split down the middle instead of being drawn to one side; they are drawn apart to the two sides; this method has been introduced because it is more convenient and also because the curtains look handsomer like this."[2] One such curtain is shown in a drawing by Paul Decker (1677–1713), a German designer who showed the strong influence of French artists (Fig. 1). Throughout much of the eighteenth century, in simple homes, both in England and in America, straight hanging curtains in two parts were the dominant form of window curtain. They covered the window completely, they were cut to the size of the window, and they fell only to the sill. In their simplest form they consisted of two strips of material held back during the day by cords or tiebacks (Fig. 2). Sometimes a valance concealed the top, and sometimes the two parts of the curtain were simply stitched together at the top to give the effect of a valance.

A second important curtain type in the eighteenth century was one that pulled up in much the same manner as a venetian blind. It may, in fact, have been called a venetian curtain. This type consisted

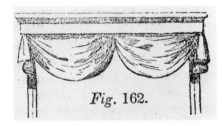

Fig. 162.

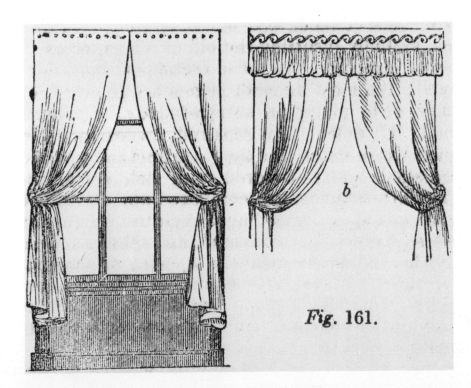

Fig. 161.

FIG. 2A,B,C. *Window curtains as illustrated in Thomas Webster,* Encyclopaedia of Domestic Economy *(New York: Harper, 1845), p. 250. (Winterthur Museum Library.)* A, *Two panels tacked to the top of the window frame.* B, *The same curtains with the addition of a fringed valance.* C, *Festoon curtains.*

of one piece of material drawn up from the sill by means of cords run through rings attached to the back of the curtain. When it was raised the fabric bunched at the top (Fig. 3). Sometimes, depending on the fabric employed, swags or festoons were formed by the fabric between the cords, and this may account for their being described as festoon curtains also. Both venetian and festoon curtains are mentioned in eighteenth-century accounts, and it is difficult to distinguish between them.[3] The pull-up curtain is illustrated by Daniel Marot (ca. 1663–1752) in several versions in the first decade of the eighteenth century (Fig. 4), and it continued in use throughout much of the century (Figs. 5,6).

In 1803 Sheraton described "festoon window curtains" as "those which draw up by pullies, and hang down in a swag. These curtains are still in use in bed rooms, notwithstanding the general introduction of the French rod curtains in most genteel houses."[4] As late as 1845 Thomas Webster, addressing a less genteel and hence less fashionable audience, described them in detail:

> Another simple mode is to have the curtain in one piece to draw up by means of lines and pulleys. . . . To effect this, a pulley is fixed at each end of a flat piece of wood as long as the window is wide; and another pulley is let into the wood, so as to divide the lath into two equal parts. The curtain is nailed to this wood, and pieces of tape are then sewed down the curtains at the two sides, and also just under the middle pulley, and there a number of rings are fixed. Through these rings are passed three cords, which go over the pulleys, and are then fastened together; by means of these cords the curtains can be raised or lowered at pleasure. The boards, with the pulleys, may be concealed by a lath covered with a border, and having a small valance; these are called by upholsterers *festoon* curtains, and were very general before the French manner was introduced of making them slide on a rod.[5]

For large window openings double festoons, or double drapery, with two sets of cords, were made. Embellishments of fringe, cords, tassels, and tapes were prevalent. Valances concealing the mechanics of pulleys and lines were shaped and ornamented in accord with bed valances in the room.

FIG. 3. Morning, *an English interior scene drawn and engraved by I. S. Miller and dated 1766. (Metropolitan Museum of Art, gift of Vincent D. Andrus.) The window curtain is raised behind a stiff upholstered valance edged and scrolled with tape. Cords for drawing the curtain are fastened around cloak pins at the right of the window frame. This print served as a model for the curtains created for the assembly room from Gadsby's Tavern, Alexandria, Virginia, after the installation of the room in the American Wing of the Metropolitan Museum of Art.*

FIG. 4. *Four designs for window curtains by Daniel Marot, architect to William of Orange. From Werken van D. Marot . . . (Amsterdam, [1707?]), p. 81. (Winterthur Museum Library.) All four examples are of the pull-up type. The second one includes the cord and tassel for raising and lowering it. The third curtain is drawn up under a stiff upholstered valance.*

FIG. 5. *John Phillips of Exeter, N.H.; oil by Joseph Steward, ca. 1793. (Dartmouth College Collection.) Through the open door a raised window is dressed with a fringed curtain which probably fell to the sill when released. A fringed and ruffled valance conceals the pulleys and cords ending in tassels by which it was drawn.*

FIG. 6. *An illustration from* The Suspicious Husband, *a play by Benjamin Hoadly published July 6, 1776. (Lewis Walpole Library: Photo, Yale University Library.) The engraving shows a variation on the pull-up window curtain of the eighteenth century. It appears to have been made in one piece and, presumably, it would have covered the window to the floor when released. Here, it is shown drawn up beneath a stiff scalloped valance. The sides are allowed to droop in points suggesting a V-shaped arrangement of tapes and rings on the back.*

French rod curtains, a fourth type, were a major innovation of the late eighteenth century. The mechanism, roughly equivalent to the modern traverse rod, made it possible to open curtains without their being raised from the floor. The awkward puffs and bunches of raised-up curtains were thereby eliminated. As Sheraton said in 1803, "At present the most approved way of managing window curtains is to make them draw from the centre to each side of the window," as shown in figure 7.[6] The novelty of the French rod is suggested by his comments on plate 51 of *The Cabinet-maker and Upholsterer's Drawing-Book:*

> These curtains are drawn on French rods. When the cords are drawn the curtains meet in the center at the same time, but are in no way raised from the floor. When the same cord is drawn the reverse way, each curtain flies open, and comes to their [sic] place on each side. . . . The cord passes on a side pulley fixed on the right-hand.[7] [Fig. 8.]

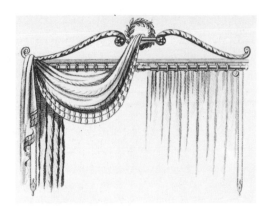

FIG. 7. *Detail of a French rod from Thomas Shera-ton,* The Cabinet Dictionary *(London, 1803), pl. 46. (Winterthur Museum Library.) The rod actually con-sisted of two rods spaced so that one panel of the curtain overlapped the other slightly when the curtains were closed.*

FIG. 8. *"Cornices, Curtains & Drapery for Drawing Room Windows." From Thomas Sheraton,* The Cab-inet-Maker and Upholsterer's Drawing Book *(London, 1793), pl. 51. (Winterthur Museum Library.)*

Rare surviving upholsterers' bills, newspaper advertisements of sales and auctions, and inventory listings all indicate that during the eighteenth century furnishing materials within a room matched. This was especially true of window and bed curtains but frequently included upholstery as well. As stated in the section on bed curtains, worsteds were the most widely used materials in the first half of the century. They were known by the common name of camlets, but when they were given a watered, waved, or flowered finish, they were called by names like harateen, moreen, and cheney. A combination of silk warp and worsted weft was next most expensive, superseded by all-silk damasks, satins, and velvets for the well-to-do.

FIG. 9. *Window curtains from Rudolph Ackermann,* The Repository of Arts, Literature, Commerce, Manufactures, Fashions, and Politics *4, no. 22 (October 1810): 246. (Yale Center for British Art.) Borrowing from a plate in La Mésangère's* Meubles et objets de goût, *the author says that the valance on the left is made of "lemon-coloured silk" with embroidered muslin curtains; that on the right is made of "fine spotted muslin hung over a gilt dart." Alternate fabrics suggested by Ackermann were silk, muslin, or chintz.*

WINDOW CURTAINS.

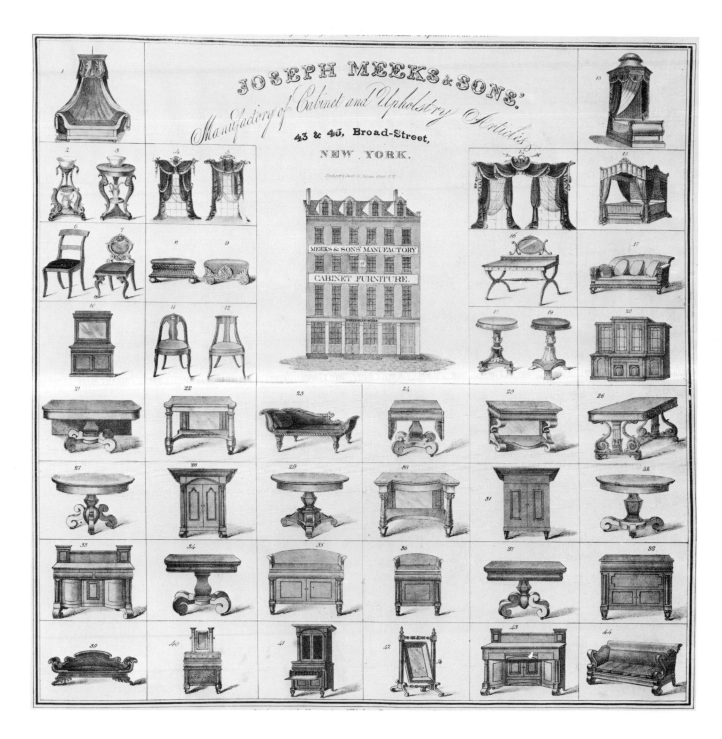

FIG. 10. *Detail from trade card of Joseph Meeks and Sons, 43 and 45 Broad Street, New York, dated 1833. (Metropolitan Museum of Art, gift of Mrs. R. W. Hyde.) Meeks copied patterns for bed and window curtains from design books such as Ackermann's* Repository *and La Mésangère's* Meubles et objets de goût. *Window curtains cost from $200 to $300.*

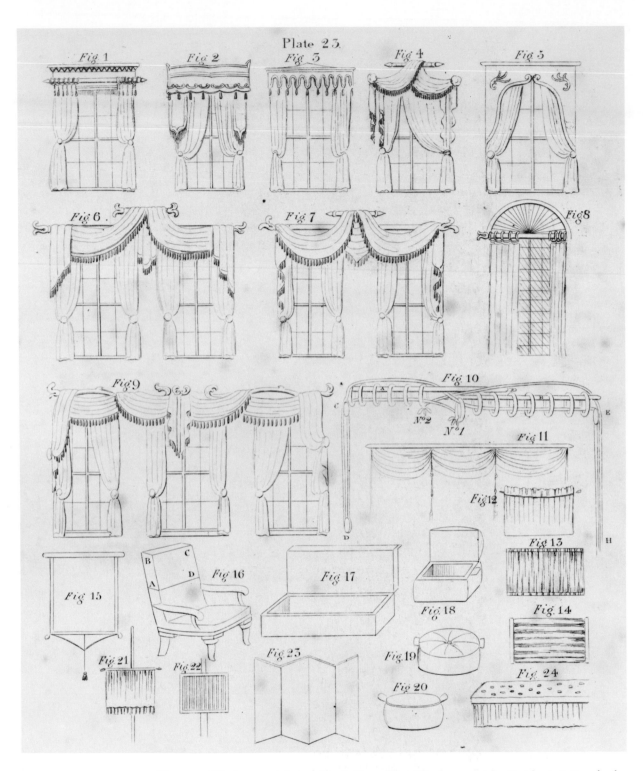

FIG. 11. *Window curtains and rods from* The Workwoman's Guide (*1838; 2d ed., London and Birmingham, 1840*), *pl. 23. (Winterthur Museum Library.) Figures 6, 7, and 9 are continuous cornices. Figure 5 is a solid lambrequin. Figure 10 shows the mechanism of pulleys, cords, and rings for a French curtain, and figure 11 is a draw-up curtain with tapes and rings stitched at the back.*

In the second half of the century, cotton materials such as furniture checks, cotton velvets (Manchester stuffs), and dimity, either plain or corded, came into use. For more colorful and elegant rooms, a wide variety of printed textiles, both block and copperplate patterns, were favored.

With the coming of the nineteenth century, designers like Sheraton, Hepplewhite, and George Smith gave recommendations for furnishing fabrics and for the cut of curtains. Rudolph Ackermann described materials available in fashionable London linendrapers' shops in his monthly *Repository* (1809–28). The periodical contains many hand-colored engravings of designs for window curtains as well as fashionable furniture (Fig. 9) which were widely copied by others (Fig. 10).

Among the seemingly endless possibilities suggested for window treatments, the tops of the windows were singled out for decoration (Fig. 11). In 1808 George Smith wrote of "continued drapery," or long valances suspended from an ornamental pole (Fig. 12). He also

FIG. 12. *"Continued Drapery is suitable to Venetian, Bow, or large Windows; the materials may be of plain-coloured or printed calicoes; the Curtains to draw on rods after the French manner, and the Draperies suspended from an ornamental Cornice, which may be executed in gold and bronze; the fringe in silk and cotton."* From George Smith, A Collection of Designs for Household Furniture and Interior Decoration (*London, 1808*), *pl. 10.* (*Winterthur Museum Library.*)

wrote about swags made to look as if they were slung over a pole (Fig. 13) when in fact these pieces were carefully precut and stitched before being attached to the rod or cornice (Fig. 14). Smith stated:

> We often see silk and calico tormented into every other form than agreeable, natural Drapery. The mystery and difficulty of *cutting-out* would vanish, did the artist but apply his mind with resolution to conquer his established prejudices: to the work-man very little knowledge is requisite beyond cutting-out what is usually called a festoon, the arrangement, whether for continued Drapery or for a single window, forming the principal difficulty; one festoon, well and properly cut out, will answer for the whole.[8]

FIG. 13. *Designs for window curtains. From James Barron,* Modern and Elegant Designs of Cabinet and Upholstery Furniture (*London: W. M. Thiselton, 1814*), *pl. 9.* (*Winterthur Museum Library.*) *The curtains are suspended from a gilt pole continued across two windows. A pink valance lined with green surmounts the center hanging pelmet of green, while the two colors are reversed in the long curtains. The inner curtains are white mull.*

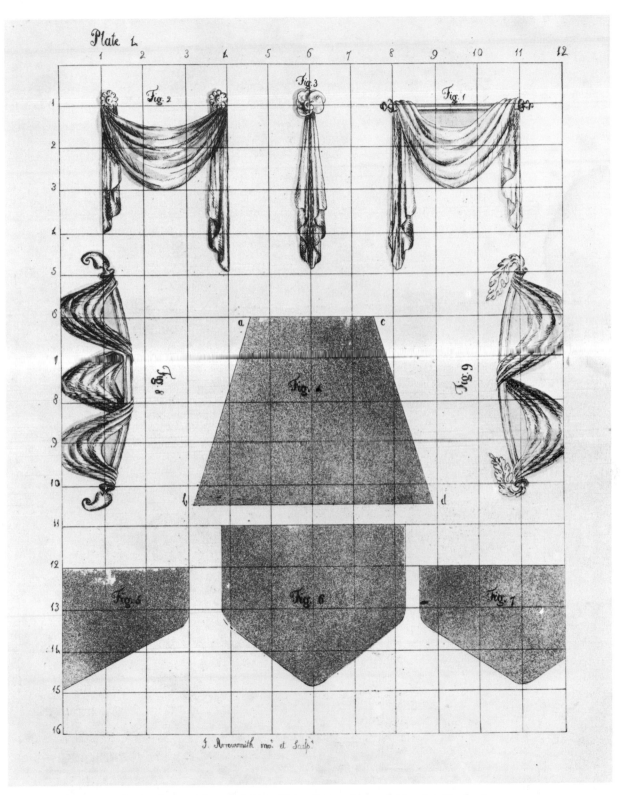

FIG. 14. *Patterns for cutting window draperies. From James Arrowsmith,* An Analysis of Drapery *(London, 1819), pl. 4. (Winterthur Museum Library.)*

63

Valance or cornice boxes were useful to conceal the mechanism for opening and closing the curtains as well as being ornamental. Some valance boxes were veneered and inlaid with fine woods; others were painted to achieve the same effect (Fig. 15). One elaborate valance printed on glazed cotton was intended to give the illusion of expensive silk moiré with elaborate tassels, fringe, and cord (Fig. 16). Gilded poles holding swags of drapery were often adorned with three-dimensional gilded gesso terminals (see Figs. 11, 12). By 1815 Rudolph Ackermann was publishing illustrations showing colored drapery hung from poles with large exposed rings. Also new at this time were the sheer white cotton glass curtains draped beneath to soften the light. (See also Fig. 4 in "Furnishing Practices.")

Plain materials are used in these illustrations, probably because drawloom-woven patterned silks were prohibitively expensive.[9] The lavish use of borders, fringes, tassels, and sometimes embroidered or painted medallions compensated for the lack of pattern and created a handsome effect (Fig. 17). Brilliant color contrasts of bright blue and pink, red and yellow, or green and rose were advocated by designers.

FIG. 15. *Family group by an unknown artist; oil, 1810–15. (Collection of Bertram K. and Nina Fletcher Little.) The curtains here were probably made of separate pieces of cloth cut and shaped in a precise swag, with flat fringed tails falling down the sides over longer draperies looped over curtain knobs.*

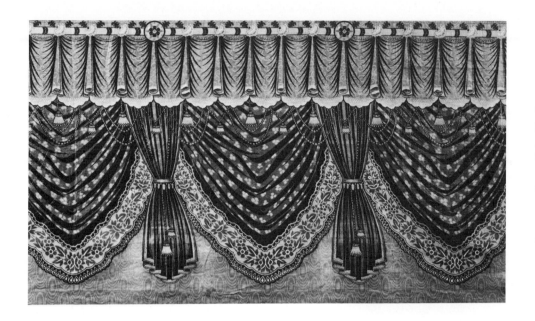

FIG. 16. *Simulated valance of cotton cloth roller printed in brown, blue, and yellow, England, midnineteenth century. (Winterthur Museum.) The chintz is intended for use as window or bed valances. It is printed on a moiré ground resembling silk.*

FIG. 17. *Patterns for fringes made of wooden spools covered with silk thread. From James Barron,* Modern and Elegant Designs of Cabinet and Upholstery Furniture *(London: W. M. Thiselton, 1814), unnumbered plate. (Winterthur Museum Library.) The fringes measure about four inches including the heading. Only rarely can fringes be precisely dated, in this case to 1814.*

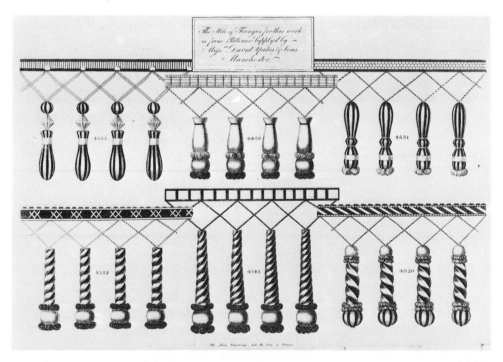

Ackermann sometimes included in issues of the *Repository* swatches of fabric. In 1810 he labeled a swatch of glazed cotton printed with a damask pattern "ruby damask." He said it was "calculated for curtains, sofas beds, &c. The linings which form the most pleasing contrast to this elegant article are Sicilian or celestial blue, spring or pea-green. For dining rooms, deep borders, of plain or fancy cut velvet, have a rich and appropriate effect. For drawing-rooms, the draperies should be the colour of the lining, tastefully blended and fringed to correspond."[10] Other nineteenth-century authors favored furnishing rooms according to their function. In 1826, George Smith specified textiles suitable for various types of rooms:

> For Eating Rooms and Libraries, a material of more substance is requisite than for Rooms of a lighter cast; and for such purposes superfine cloth, or cassimere, will ever be the best; the colours as fancy or taste may direct; yet scarlet and crimson will ever hold the preference . . . calico when used should be of one colour, in shades of moroon or scarlet.
>
> In elegant Drawing Rooms, plain coloured satin or figured damask assumes the first rank, as well for use as for richness; lustring and tabarays the next; the latter, however, makes but indifferent drapery. Calico, the next in choice, and of so great variety of patterns, should, where good drapery is required, be glazed mellow. . . .
>
> The arrangement of Drapery for the different descriptions of apartments will ever be subject to the control of fancy; Dining Rooms and Libraries being simple and plain in their decorations, require less variety in the drapery for their curtains.[11]

In 1845 Thomas Webster also offered valuable suggestings about the kinds of materials appropriate for various rooms:

> The materials for window curtains must necessarily vary with the apartments where they are to be used. . . . In forming graceful drapery, the material is of great importance. It is impossible to form them well of stiffened materials, such as highly-glazed calicoes, which will not, of themselves, fall into graceful folds, and must consequently have a stiff appearance.

Fig. 165.

Fig. 166 is another design for a cornice and a piped valance.

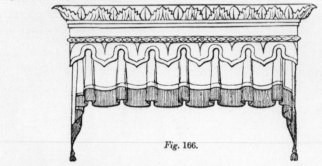

Fig. 166.

Fig. 167 is a cornice and valance in the style called of Louis XIV., now much in fashion. The cornice is wholly gilded, and the valance may be of rich silk and fringe.

Fig. 167.

FIG. 18. *Window cornices and valances from Thomas Webster,* Encyclopaedia of Domestic Economy *(1845), figs. 165, 166, 167. (Winterthur Museum Library.) Figure 167 is described by Webster as "Window curtain with cornice and valance"; he says of this curtain that it is "in the style very prevalent in the present day," adding that "there is a double set of curtains; one . . . for evening, and another of figured muslin for day."*

FIG. 19. *Group silhouette of an American family by Auguste Edouart (1789–1861), dated 1842. (Winterthur Museum.) About the window curtains, which are particularly complex, Harold Peterson commented in* Americans at Home: *"There seem to be three different fabrics involved in the treatment that combines the two windows and the pier mirror between them as a single unit. First are the outer drapes that hang in big swags and festoons. These drapes are fringed, and there is a gold(?) rope with tassel for accent. Beneath these drapes are others of an apparently lighter material, long on the outer edges and short on the inner edges where they are held by flower-shaped tiebacks. Finally there are lace glass curtains held back on the inner edges by stamped ormolu tiebacks."*

FIG. 20. *Elevation of a Greek revival house, probably by Joseph C. Howard, Boston. Wash drawing, ca. 1845. (Society for the Preservation of New England Antiquities, Luther Briggs, Jr. Collection.) Although intended as a precise architectural drawing, it also shows ample curtains pulled to one side downstairs and crossed in pairs upstairs. Ball fringe and netting finish all the curtains.*

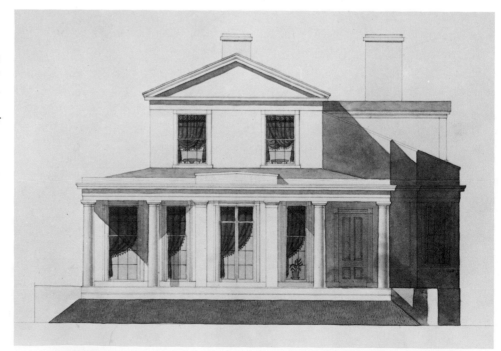

Pliability of the material is essential; and, for this purpose, silk and fine cloth are considered the best substances. In drawing-rooms, plain coloured satin, or figured damasks, bear the first rank for richness. Lutestring and tabarets next, though they do not make so good drapery. Salisbury flannel, fine cloth, or cassimer, are sometimes used. For eating-rooms and libraries, a material of more substance is requisite than for drawing-rooms; in these, moreen is most usually employed. When chintses are used, they should not be much glazed.[12] [Fig. 18.]

Light colors prevailed during the English Regency period (from about 1810 to 1830) and presumably in the United States as well, but toward the middle of the century they were replaced by somber, dark colors, especially the deep crimson and bottle green found in heavier fabrics like worsted damasks, velvet or plush, and brocatelle (made of a combination of silk and a filler fiber) (Figs. 19, 20). About the second decade of the nineteenth century, moreen, other worsteds, and silk and worsted materials returned to fashion, although in different patterns and colors from those of the previous century. Cotton damasks and velvets and quantities of printed chintzes, many in imitation of expensive silk damasks, were imported by American upholsterers. After the first quarter of the century, with the gradual adoption of the jacquard weaving apparatus which drastically reduced production costs, more elaborate patterns were introduced. A wealth of revival styles and exuberant, lush floral patterns were executed in both woven and printed designs. With accelerated production and continuous experimentation within the industry, many new materials were developed that were made from a combination of fibers that frequently included cotton.

Mid-nineteenth-century curtains, upholstery, carpeting, and wallpaper in the parlor of the Farnsworth Homestead, Rockland, Maine, illustrate the types of materials available to well-to-do clients with easy access to an urban center (Figs. 21, 22a,b,c). William A. Farnsworth was a Rockland merchant who made several trips each year to Boston. He built his home about 1850 and presumably purchased the furniture at that time. It is difficult to explain why furniture in a matched set should be upholstered in three different materials, all of which appear to be original and which together with the curtains, wallpaper, and carpet produce a decidedly busy effect.

FIG. 21. *Window curtains in the parlor of the Farnsworth Homestead, Rockland, Maine, ca. 1850. They are fashioned of red, white, and black silk and wool in a design of roses and leaves alternating with stripes of more formal ornament suggestive of metalwork. (William A. Farnsworth Library and Art Museum.)*

FIG. 22A,B,C. *Rococo revival parlor suite in the parlor of the Farnsworth Homestead, Rockland, Maine, ca. 1850. The armchair (A), one of a pair, is upholstered in peach colored brocatelle. It bears the label of Blake, Ware & Co. of Boston "manufacturers and importers of furniture and upholstery." The side chair (B) is covered in red satin with green and white figures. The sofa (C) is covered with a blue and gold floral damask. (William A. Farnsworth Library and Art Museum.)*

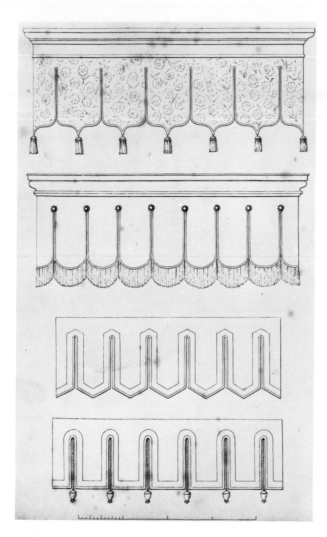

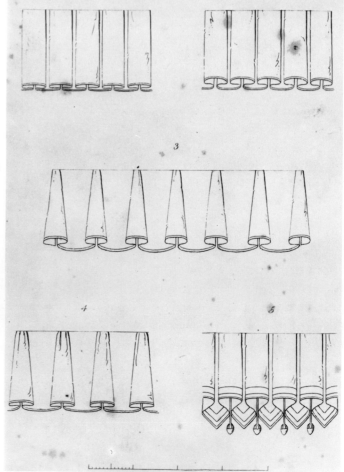

FIGS. 23 AND 24. *"Piped" and "geometric" valances for either window or bed hangings. From* The Upholsterers' Accelerator; Being Rules for Cutting and Forming Draperies, Valances, etc. . . . *(London: At the Architectural and Scientific Library, Bloomsbury, [ca. 1840]), pls. 31 and 36. (Winterthur Museum Library.)*

Unlike the eighteenth century when fashion decreed that furnishing materials match throughout a room, Webster suggested that "the colours of window curtains should harmonize with the rest of the room, as well as with the richness of the materials. When we say harmonize, we do not mean they should correspond, or be the same, but that there should not be any violent contrasts, and that the colours should agree with each other."[13] He wrote of the current taste for "plain or piped valances" which "harbour less dust, from the folds being perpendicular," of "massive brass rods and large rings," and "rich gilt cornices over the valances" in what we now know as the rococo revival style. *The Upholsterers' Accelerator,* published in London about 1840, gives directions for measuring and tacking "piped" valances and "geometrical" valances then in vogue (Figs. 23, 24). Flat geometrical valances for beds or windows had the "advantage in not allowing the dust to accumulate," while piped, or pleated, valances required "more care in their formation than is commonly supposed," "the pipes should appear to hang with ease," "be well proportioned, and not seem to drag the other parts."[14]

According to J.C. Loudon different colors and materials should be chosen for mahogany than for oak furniture:

> If the furniture be chiefly mahogany, the material of the curtains should be moreen or cloth; and the colour should be of the same tone, and strong or dark; say some shade of red, brown, or scarlet. If on the other hand, the furniture be chiefly of oak, or of different-coloured foreign woods . . . light-coloured cloth, or moreen, or some description of chintzes or cottons, will be more suitable.[15] [Fig. 25.]

Lambrequins seem to have evolved from flat valances hung over long curtains such as those seen in figure 26. At a three-part window where six long curtains would have been voluminous and unmanageable, the center window had only a flat lambrequin (p. 76). Lambrequins were unquestionably cheaper and easier to make. A continuous stiff lambrequin with long curtains beneath is shown in No. 5 of the *Workwoman's Guide,* first published in 1838 (see Fig. 11). A mid-nineteenth century example is seen in the bright red-orange worsted piece in figure 27. Another example of the same period is shown in figure 28. Catharine Beecher and Harriet Beecher Stowe offered lambrequins

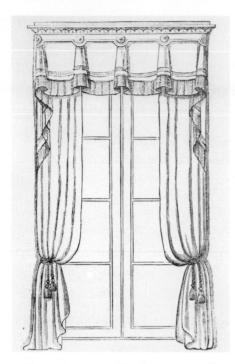
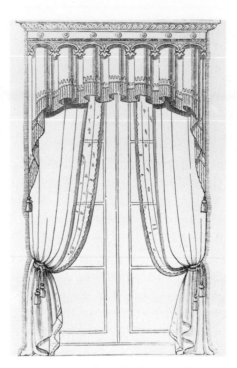

FIG. 25A,B,C,D. *Window curtains for a drawing room. From John Claudius Loudon,* An Encyclopaedia of Cottage, Farm and Villa Architecture and Furniture (*London: Longman et al., 1833), figs. 1976–79. (Winterthur Museum Library.) Loudon described* (A) *as "a window curtain with a gilt cornice and handsome drapery, the hangings being either of damask or chintz, with bullion fringe . . . with silk drops";* (B) *"muslin hangings are shown beneath the damask ones";* (C) *features "a richly carved and gilt cornice"; in* (D) *the valance is attached to "gilt brass rings, which move along a wooden pole sheathed in gilt brass. A silk drop is attached to each ring, and from each ring the fringe turns a swag. . . . The curtains draw behind the valance on a rod."*

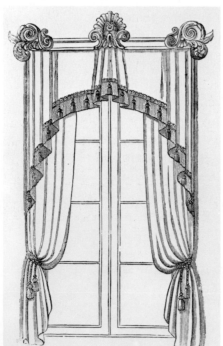
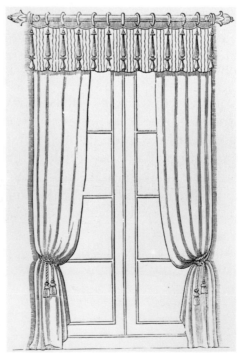

FIG. 26. *Unidentified artist,* View from the House of Henry Thomas Briscoe. *Baltimore, ca. 1841. Pen and ink, crayon, and wash on paper. (Metropolitan Museum of Art, gift of Lydia Bond Powel.) A shaped valance and gathered tails trimmed with borders and fringe hang in front of thin glass curtains, Venetian blinds, and indoor shutters. The cords, tassels, and hardware are all explicitly represented, leaving no doubts except for the materials and colors.*

Parlor window of Camden, a house near Port Royal, Virginia, built 1856 to 1859 for William Carter Pratt. (Photo, Walter Smalling, Jr.) The three-part window is finished with a continuous gilded brass cornice from which the blue and gold rococo revival curtains are suspended. Purchased for the house in 1859, they are rare survivals complete with tassels suspended from the central lambrequin edged with braid. Lattice-patterned upholstery material matched in color.

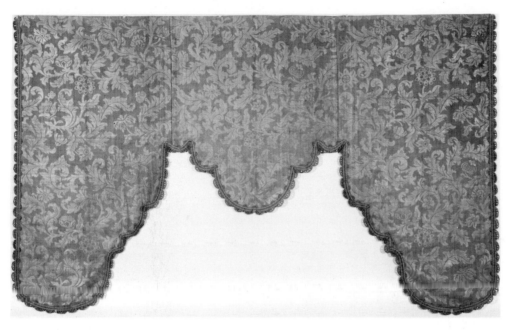

FIG. 27. *Lambrequin, American, mid-nineteenth century. Fashioned of bright orange, stamped or embossed worsted (moreen) of English manufacture. (Winterthur Museum.)*

FIG. 28. *Ornamental fringe for a window manufactured by R. Burgh of London. From* The Industry of All Nations 1851. The Art Journal Illustrated Catalogue *(London: George Virtue, 1851), p. 141. (Photo, Winterthur.)*

 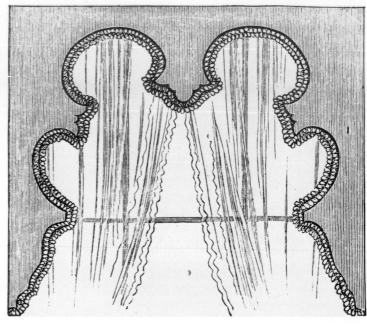

FIGS. 29 AND 30. *Patterns for lambrequins. From Catharine E. Beecher and Harriet Beecher Stowe,* The American Woman's Home *(New York: J. B. Ford; Boston: H. A. Brown, 1869), pp. 88–89. (Winterthur Museum Library.) The authors gave practical and inexpensive ideas for furnishing. Windows were to have "lambrequins . . . a kind of pendent curtain-top" trimmed with "fringe or gimp of the same color." White muslin curtains beneath could be ornamented with "hems an inch in width" in which "a strip of gingham or chambray" of the same color as the chintz was inserted. An English furniture print was recommended for the lambrequins and a cushioned lounge and an easy chair were to be covered in the same material.*

as practical and inexpensive solutions to the problem of window curtains (Figs. 29, 30). Their popularity for modest homes seems to have been at its height in the 1870s to judge from illustrations in *Hearth and Home* intended as suggestions for "home-tied house-keepers in the country" (Fig. 31).

By the mid-nineteenth century, fashionable window curtains reflected all manner of eclectic styles (Figs. 32–36). The styles include Adamesque, neo-Grec and Gothic, modern English and "Elizabethian," modern German, Flemish, French, and Italian, the latter divided into Cinque Cento, Florentine, Renaissance, and Pompeian (Fig. 37). Designs "for Chintzes" include the Louis XIII and Louis XVI styles. Pictures taken from all the best-known English pattern books are found in the *Pictorial Dictionary of British Nineteenth-Century Furniture Design.*[16]

FIG. 31A,B,C. *"Lambrequin with Curtain." From Hearth and Home 18, no. 3 (May 6, 1871): 349. (Lehigh University: Photos, Winterthur.)* (A) *"For winter use, heavy materials are appropriate; but for summer, this style looks well only in lace or thin muslin, or in striped chintz of delicate colors. The lambrequin alone, made of white piqué or marseilles, with long narrow side-pieces of the same, hanging full from the corners so as to conceal the window-frame—the whole trimmed with white bullion fringe—is effective for bedchambers"*; (B) *hung beneath a cornice of black walnut inlaid with oak was a lambrequin "of blue satin damask, the trimming blue gimp, and the garniture a heavy silk cord"*; (C) *the wooden cornice strip was covered with colored cambric over which lace was gathered in a ruffle. The same cambric was used to line the lace lambrequin.*

FIG. 33. The Four Seasons of Life: Old Age, *colored lithograph by Currier and Ives, 1868. (Mabel Brady Garvan Collection, Yale University Art Gallery.) The curtains in this cozy room (with furniture of several previous periods) are hung from an elaborately carved cornice. Heavy, dark patterned draperies with lace glass curtains beneath are held back with cords looped over knobs.*

OPPOSITE
FIG. 32. A Window, House on the Hudson River *by Worthington Whittredge; oil, 1863. (New-York Historical Society.) Sunlight and summer breezes flow into this spacious window alcove with thin patterned curtains suspended from an arched cornice and tied back with ribbons.*

FIG. 35. *The music room in the Morse-Libby Mansion (Victoria Mansion), Portland, Maine, 1858–60. The gold damask curtains have blue fringes and tassels. The wall panels are painted in imitation of fabric. (The Morse-Libby Mansion; photo, Richard Cheek.)*

OPPOSITE
FIG. 34. *The Turkish room in the Morse-Libby Mansion (Victoria Mansion), Portland, Maine, 1858–60. The red and gold room has its original window curtains in the Turkish taste in a star-and-crescent patterned material over gold net. (The Morse-Libby Mansion; photo, Richard Cheek.)*

From my room window
May 1869
W W Harding
fecit

65 Columbia St
Brooklyn Heights

FIG. 37. *The full range of nineteenth-century eclectic styles are presented in R. Charles,* 300 Designs for Window-Draperies, Fringes and Mantle-Board Decorations *(London: R. Charles, 1874), p. 16. (Metropolitan Museum of Art Library.) These two cornices with stiff valances are in the "Elizabethian" or "Modern English" mode.*

OPPOSITE
FIG. 36. New York Harbor from Brooklyn Heights *by William M. Harding; pen and watercolor, 1869. (M. & M. Karolik Collection, Museum of Fine Arts, Boston.) Shadows from the arched window mullions are seen through the thin striped material of the lambrequin edged with ball fringe. The curtain fits over the wide moldings and folded shutters.*

Following severe criticism from many sources of the excesses of ornament and overelaboration of design characteristic of all exhibits at the 1851 Crystal Palace Exhibition, a reform movement gradually got under way. One of the most influential reformers of taste was Charles L. Eastlake whose *Hints on Household Taste* was published in London in 1868 and in New York in 1872. He said that "decorative art is degraded when it passes into a direct imitation of natural objects," and he expressed his admiration for Indian shawls and oriental textiles for their abstract ornament. On the subject of window curtains and fixtures, he deplored the flimsy hollow poles ending in "gigantic fuchsias, or other flowers, made of brass, gilt bronze, and even china, sprawling downwards in a design of execrable taste." He suggested for a portiere a simple curtain, diagonally striped, hanging from rings (Fig. 38). For curtain materials he recommended a German fabric of silk, wool, and cotton, "often worked in diaper patterns of excellent design," or a heavy ribbed material from France "decorated with broad bands or stripes of colour running transversely to its length, and resembling the pattern of a Roman scarf" (Fig. 39). Algerian cloth, chiefly of cotton, "was designed with horizontal stripes of colour on an unbleached white ground"; it was inexpensive and washable. Eastlake also favored William Morris's cretonnes, damasks of plain colors, "either green or crimson, enriched with stripes worked in various patterns with gold-colored silk."[17]

A similar plea for recognition of the nature of materials and the suitability of pattern to its function is expressed in *Art Education, Scholastic and Industrial* (1873) by Walter Smith, state director of art education for Massachusetts. Of machine-made lace, he wrote:

> The most *general* use to which lace is put is that of curtains, and in this the best and worst taste is displayed. . . . Many designs for lace curtains are composed of huge and barbarous scrolls, squandered irregularly over the surface as if by accident, half hidden by the drapery in which the curtain hangs; immense and vulgar bouquets of flowers, in which not only the unsymmetrical natural flower is closely copied but attempts at shading are made.

FIG. 38. *Portiere with rod and bracket for hanging. From Charles L. Eastlake,* Hints on Household Taste *(London: Longmans, Green, 1868). (Winterthur Museum Library.)*

FIG. 39. *"Embroidered Curtains." From Charles L. Eastlake,* Hints on Household Taste *(London: Longmans, Green, 1868). (Winterthur Museum Library.) The curtain at the right is decorated in "appliqué work with a representation of Aesop's fable, 'the Fox and the Stork.'" Both patterns have the horizontal bands so dear to Eastlake and other reformers.*

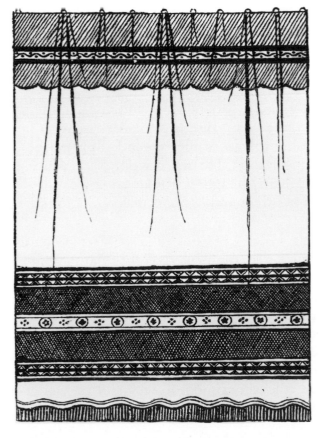

Smith further stated that:

> the best designs for curtains are those which consist largely of
> an enriched border, founded on some light and graceful natural
> foliage forms, in which the outline is characteristic; the body
> of the curtain being slightly powdered over with some detail
> of the plant used, such as a conventional treatment of the flower
> or bud of the subject which forms the border.[18]

Articles by Clarence Cook first serialized in *Scribner's Monthly*
were published in 1878 as *The House Beautiful*. Following Eastlake's
dictates, he urged homemakers to "Give up the cornices and the lambrequins . . . give up fringes and borders, and straps by which to hold
the curtains back, and you can then throw the whole weight of your
purse upon the main stuff of your curtains and the bands they are to
be crossed with." Of the new style he wrote: "The decoration of the
curtain by bands across the stuff, not by vertical stripes, has every-
thing to recommend it—oriental usage (almost always a sure guide in
decoration), and the fact that it is always to be reckoned on to produce
its pictorial effect, since the bands cannot be hid, no matter how many
folds the curtain makes."

Reflecting his predilection for oriental art and the Aesthetic
Movement, he urged women to give up Berlin woolwork or what he
called "little love-and-friendship tokens of the cap-and-slipper tribe"
and turn to Japanese art for inspiration. He urged women to embroider "coverings for furniture [and] hangings for doors and walls."
Describing embroidered motifs frequently found on crazy quilts he
wrote:

> Now, on a pale sapphire silk, she made a flight of apple-blos-
> som petals drift before the wind, at one side the branch that
> bore them, with its tips of leaves; or across one corner of a
> square of amber satin a geometric spider had woven her silver
> web, darting from tip to tip of the white rose-tree; or cat-o'-
> nine-tails against a blue-green water, with a rose-red mallow,
> or the neck and head of a duck sailing through her kingdom;
> or autumn leaves, sad colored, raining down against a welter-
> ing sky of gray; or hips and haws, or black elderberries, or—
> anything.[19]

In the last quarter of the century one may add to the excesses of upholstery and curtaining the addition of portieres (Fig. 40). They are pictured in collections of photographs of interiors, such as William Seale's *Tasteful Interlude*. Almon C. Varney wrote of portieres in *Our Homes and Their Adornments:* "They should not repeat the curtains of the room, but represent a separate idea, though in harmony with the room. They are frequently made double to correspond with rooms of different colors." Smyrna blankets and prayer carpets were used at doorways, but especially designed for the purpose is the curtain with the head of an American Indian painted on it (Fig. 41), reminding us of Rookwood pottery with dusky noble savages dating from the same time.[20]

An 1883 trade journal acknowledged the rage for portieres as "legitimate and justified in every respect." Not only did they "cut off draughts much more effectually than doors," they also acted as "a strong preventive of bickerings, backbitings and family jars" because sound penetrated them readily. Aside from tapestry and "rich embroidered velvet" for the wealthy, "nearly all double-faced goods are used for portieres, and at the present moment cashmeres, silk turcomans, double-faced jute and linen velours, chenille and plush are the prevailing materials for this purpose."[21]

Early in the present century Gustav Stickley carried the ideals of honesty and simplicity in the crafts even further. Quoting the English author Edward Carpenter's *England's Ideal* he writes: "As a rule all curtains, hangings, cloths and covers, which are not absolutely necessary, would be dispensed with. They all create dust and stiffness, and all entail trouble and recurring expense, and they all tempt the housekeeper to keep out the air and sunlight." Stickley experienced difficulty in finding fabrics of the right texture and character for his furniture:

> Silks, plushes and tapestries, in fact delicate and perishable fabrics of all kinds, were utterly out of keeping with Craftsman furniture. What we needed were fabrics that possessed sturdiness and durability; that were made of materials that possessed a certain rugged and straightforward character of fiber, weave and texture,—such a character as would bring them into the same class as the sturdy oak and wrought iron and copper of the other furnishings.

FIG. 40. *Door and wall decoration in the latest English taste, designed by G. Remon, Paris. From* Die Tapezierkunst in Allen Stielen *(Berlin: Verlag von Ernst Wasmuth, 1895), pl. 17. (Photo, courtesy Mrs. Samuel Schwartz.) The chair upholstery matches the green and cream drapery and valance. A predilection for sunflowers and floral sprigs among designers in the aesthetic taste is seen in the frieze, door panels, chair backs, and walls.*

FIG. 41. *Interior of a wigwam suitable for garden houses, verandahs, and country houses, designed by Gariboldi. From* Die Tapezierkunst in Allen Stielen *(Berlin: Verlag von Ernst Wasmuth, 1895), pl. 10. (Photo, courtesy Mrs. Samuel Schwartz.) A romantic interest in the American Indian and the wilderness was widespread at the turn of the century.*

His preference was for fabrics "of a robust sort of beauty" such as "flax left in the natural color or given some one of the nature hues," "certain roughly-woven dull-finished silks," and "nets and crepes of the same general character." Stylized natural elements, such as pinecones, poppies, and dragonflies, as well as neat geometric borders, were suggested for embroidery on curtains.[22]

How-to books in conservative good taste continued to appear in the early years of this century. Lucy Abbot Throop of New York attempted to harmonize period styles with modern houses with "huge panes of glass and simple framework" which require "curtains of a high standard of beauty and practicality—simple, appropriate, and serving the ends they were intended for." The author writes that "the average window needs two sets of curtains and a shade. . . . Thin curtains in combination with side curtains of some thicker material are most often used." Her illustration of a formal drawing room is reminiscent of Daniel Marot (see Fig. 4), but she also suggests curtains of "arras cloth with an applique design of linen couched on it" "to go with the Mission or Craftsman furniture." Her advice was: "When curtains stand out and astound one, they are wrong. It is not upholstery one is trying to display, but to make a perfect background for one's furniture, one's pictures and one's friends."[23]

Far more subtle and sophisticated, although for a much smaller audience, were the furnishing plans of Frank Lloyd Wright. Insistent not only on color harmonies which included the plaster walls, paint colors, the floors, the upholstery, decorative wall hangings, and rugs, he also was concerned with pattern and texture. To carry out the organic unity of his houses, he used the floor plan of the house as a decorative device which was woven into the carpet. In one instance, window draperies were made of soft ecru silk and wool casement cloth and embroidered to match the rugs. Leaving nothing to chance that might disturb the total harmony within his house, he even designed dresses for the owner.

Style changes in late nineteenth-century decorative arts are exciting to study, and more is being published about them each year. However, during the period of the American renaissance and well into this century rooms were designed in Newport, in Long Island houses, and in large New York apartment buildings in conservative period styles. More study is needed on the interior designers commissioned by wealthy clients and the textiles produced for them (Fig. 42).

FIG. 42. *One of a set of gold-embroidered damask curtains made by Jules Allard et Fils of Paris. (Preservation Society of Newport County.) The curtains were made for Chetwode, the home of W. Storrs Wells built in Newport, Rhode Island, in 1900 from designs of Horace Trumbauer. They hung in the house during the season of 1902 and were then stored until 1980 when they were exhibited at the Rhode Island School of Design.*

Fashions for window curtains changed greatly over the centuries with new mechanisms and hardware invented for managing them. Their essential purposes to lend privacy or to shield the occupants from the weather remained constant, but taste dictated the fabrics and styles to be used. Their elegance depended on the size of the owner's purse and the ability of his upholsterer or decorator.

[1] Susan Prendergast Schoelwer, "Form, Function, and Meaning in the Use of Fabric Furnishings: A Philadelphia Case Study, 1700–1775," *Winterthur Portfolio* 14, no. 1 (Spring 1979): 25–40.

[2] As quoted in Margaret Jourdain, "Window Curtains of the Eighteenth Century," *Country Life* 99, no. 2569 (April 12, 1946): 668–69. See also Peter Thornton, *Seventeenth-Century Interior Decoration in England, France, and Holland* (New Haven and London: Yale University Press, 1978), p. 135ff.

[3] John Fowler and John Cornforth, *English Decoration in the Eighteenth Century* (Princeton, N.J.: Pyne Press, 1974), pp. 100–122.

[4] Thomas Sheraton, *The Cabinet Dictionary* (London, 1803; reprint ed., New York: Praeger Publishers, 1970), pp. 208–9.

[5] Thomas Webster, *An Encyclopaedia of Domestic Economy* (New York: Harper, 1845), p. 250. Similar descriptions are offered in John Claudius Loudon, *An Encyclopedia of Cottage, Farm and Villa Architecture and Furniture* (London, 1833), and in *The Workwoman's Guide* 2d ed.; London, 1840).

[6] Thomas Sheraton, *Cabinet Dictionary,* p. 185.

[7] Thomas Sheraton, *The Cabinet-maker and Upholsterer's Drawing-Book* (London, 1793; reprint ed., New York: Dover Publications, 1972), p. 408 (original pagination), p. 106 (Dover ed.).

[8] George Smith, *A Collection of Designs for Household Furniture and Interior Decoration* (London, 1808; reprint ed., New York: Praeger Publishers, 1970), "Preliminary Remarks," pp. xi–xiii.

[9] At that time the silk-weaving industry of Spitalfields was in a depressed state.

[10] Rudolph Ackermann, *The Repository of Arts, Literature, Commerce, Manufactures, Fashions, and Politics* 3, no. 13 (January 1810): 57.

[11] Smith, *Household Furniture,* p. xii.

[12] Webster, *Encyclopaedia,* p. 251.

[13] Webster, *Encyclopaedia,* p. 251.

[14] *The Upholsterers' Accelerator; Being Rules for Cutting and Forming Draperies, Valances, etc. . . . ,* by an upholsterer of forty-five years' experience (London: At the Architectural and Scientific Library, Bloomsbury, [ca. 1840]), p. 33. The Winterthur Museum Library's copy bears neither author's name nor date. However, Barbara Morris attributes this work to Thomas King and gives 1833 as the probable

date of publication ("Textiles," in *The Early Victorian Period, 1830–1860,* The Connoisseur Period Guides, ed. Ralph Edwards and L. G. G. Ramsay [New York: Reynal, 1958], pp. 118–19).

[15] John Claudius Loudon, *An Encyclopedia of Cottage, Farm and Villa Architecture and Furniture* (London, 1833). Excerpts reprinted in *Furniture for the Victorian Home* (Watkins Glen, N.Y.: American Life Foundation, 1978), p. 178.

[16] For designs for chintzes, see Richard Charles, *Three Hundred Designs for Window-Draperies, Fringes, and Mantle-Board Decorations* (London: R. Charles, 1874); *Pictorial Dictionary of British Nineteenth-Century Furniture Design,* intro. Edward T. Joy (Woodbridge, Suffolk: Baron Publishing for the Antique Collectors' Club, 1977), pp. 565–72.

[17] Charles Locke Eastlake, *Hints on Household Taste* (1868; reprint of 4th British ed., 1878, New York: Dover Publications, 1969), pp. 64, 68, 100.

[18] Walter Smith, *Art Education, Scholastic and Industrial* (Boston: J. R. Osgood, 1873), p. 200.

[19] Clarence Cook, *The House Beautiful: Essays on Beds and Tables, Stools and Candlesticks* (New York: Scribner, Armstrong, 1878), pp. 136, 138, 141.

[20] William Seale, *The Tasteful Interlude: American Interiors Through the Camera's Eye, 1860–1917* (New York: Praeger Publishers, 1975); Almon C. Varney, *Our Homes and Their Adornments* (Detroit: J. C. Cheton, 1883), p. 259.

[21] *Carpet and Trade Review* 14, no. 7 (April 1, 1883): 43.

[22] Gustav Stickley, *Craftsman Homes* (1909; reprint ed., New York: Dover Publications, 1979), pp. 4, 165, 166.

[23] Lucy Abbot Throop, *Furnishing the Home of Good Taste* (New York: McBride, Nast, 1912), pp. 181–83, 186.

Walnut-framed easy chair upholstered with polychrome wool embroidery worked in Irish stitch. (Metropolitan Museum of Art, gift of Mrs. J. Insley Blair.) The top rail, beneath the upholstery, is inscribed "Gardner, Junr. | Newport May | 1758 | W." Fragments of green calimanco, probably the original upholstery, were found when the chair was repaired. The present covering was probably put on by Gardner in 1758. One Caleb Gardner advertised as an upholsterer in the Providence Gazette in 1783. The walnut frame was probably made about 1725. The chair has a history of ownership in the Keech family of Newport and Providence, Rhode Island.

Upholstery

Completely upholstered easy chairs were fashioned to accompany state beds upholstered and curtained in damask or velvet. As early as 1610 or 1620 no wood was left uncovered on an easy chair with X-shaped legs and sloping arm rests at Knole, Sevenoaks. A daybed, perhaps made for the same apartment, is upholstered to the floor in crimson velvet sectioned off with galloon, to hold the stuffing in place, and ornamented with rows of long fringe and large gilt nails (Fig. 1). Equipped with adjustable wings, it has comfortable matching cushions. The seat, back posts, and back panel of a turned walnut chair of about the same date are covered with dark blue wool embroidered in silk.[1] Materials used for padding and stuffing were generally hair, straw, chaff, or wool. Feathers, probably because of their high cost, were reserved for cushions and feather beds. The insides of bedticks were gummed or sized to prevent the down from coming through the cloth. Feathers in the cushion of an easy chair in the Victoria and Albert Museum are encased in soft chamois beneath the finished upholstery material.

Leather was far more practical for upholstery than textiles, although it required special skills. Indeed the upholsterer may have learned from the saddle maker how to quilt padding materials firmly in place and from trunk makers how to use ornamental brass tacks.

XXVIII.

FIG. I. "Ancient Sofa" in the Long Gallery, Knole, Sevenoaks, ca. 1620. From Charles L. Eastlake, Hints on Household Taste (London: Longmans, Green, 1868), p. 144. (Winterthur Museum Library.) The "moveable sides, like the back, are stuffed with feathers, while the seat itself is provided with two ample cushions of the same material [red velvet]." This sofa and several other pieces of seventeenth-century upholstered furniture were singled out by Eastlake as examples of "thoroughly good design" and compatible with the taste of his time. Of a similar armchair, also at Knole, he says that "the side rails which support the back are studded, over the velvet, with large round copper-gilt nails punched with a geometrical pattern" (p. 79).

FIG. 2. Low-back chairs upholstered in leather were popular in England and the American colonies during the seventeenth century. Boston, 1665–95. (Winterthur Museum.)

Low-back leather chairs, otherwise known as "Cromwellian" chairs, were especially common in Britain and the American colonies during the seventeenth century (Fig. 2). Their backs and seats were often upholstered in "Russia leather," which was frequently imported for upholstery. A popular alternative to leather was Turkey work. It was generally used on side chairs except in bedchambers where upholstery matched the important bed hangings. On chairs given hard use in eating, meeting, and parade rooms, it formed an especially satisfactory covering, being both durable and colorful (Fig. 3). Both types of upholstery were displaced in the William and Mary period when caning was much used.

FIG. 3. *Couch or settee owned by the Appleton family of Salem, Massachusetts, from the late seventeenth century until it was purchased by the Reverend William Bentley in 1819. The frame is American maple and the original upholstery is English Turkey work. (Essex Institute.)*

Woolen needlework on canvas has survived as the covering on a few colonial easy chairs where it is used to cover the inside of the chairs while the outer back and side surfaces, which showed less, are covered with practical watered worsted. Flame patterns worked in Irish stitch are listed in English inventories from the sixteenth century to the eighteenth century and were made here as well. Around 1750, other needlework patterns worked in tent stitch on canvas imitated formal foliate furnishing damasks or patterned velvets. Others, which follow the freer style of crewelwork on plain linen, or fustian, have a heavy border of needlework, often a rolling hillside with animals and birds to provide a strong front edge where wear first occurs (Fig. 4, p. 96).

Haircloth was a widely used upholstery fabric from at least the mid-eighteenth century. Durable and not subject to moth, it could be woven in patterns which shone like silk damask (Figs. 5, 6). Black was the predominant color, but green, plum, shades of red, and light

FIG. 4. *Chair seat, one of a set of four said to have been made in the eighteenth century by a Mrs. Southmayd in Middletown, Connecticut. Crewel embroidery in rose, green, blue, and brown. (Metropolitan Museum of Art, gift of Mrs. J. Insley Blair.)*

FIG. 5. *Chair seat patterned with a leafy central medallion and floral trails; gold silk paired warps with pattern warp of blue-green silk; white horsehair wefts; French or English. (Lewis Collection, National Museum of American History, Smithsonian Institution.) On one of a set of twelve mahogany side chairs made for George Washington by John Aitken of Philadelphia near the end of the eighteenth century. More delicate than the heavy foliate medallions typical of the early nineteenth century Empire style, this pattern is probably contemporary with the chairs.*

FIG. 6. *Patterned, black haircloth panel removed from a couch. England or France, nineteenth century. (Old Sturbridge Village. Photo, Henry E. Peach.)*

blue are known. Surviving examples date from the late eighteenth and early nineteenth centuries and are woven in patterns suited to furniture of that time. Wool plush with similar woven medallion patterns was also fashionable (Fig. 7).

Leafy medallions, characteristic of Napoleonic ornament, were woven of worsted on a cotton warp in red with white or gold. Matching strips for the skirts of chairs and sofas were designed *en suite* (Figs. 8, 9).

John Cadwalader, a wealthy Philadelphian, ordered deep blue silk damask from London mercers in 1771 for his front parlor which John Webster, a London-trained upholsterer, made into window curtains lined with blue sarcenet, a thinner silk. The same blue damask covered three sofas and twenty chair seats in the room. Yellow silk damask, also from London, was used in the back parlor.[2]

FIG. 7. *Mahogany sofa, New York, ca. 1820. (Metropolitan Museum of Art, bequest of May Blackstone Huntington.) The upholstery is crimson wool velvet stamped with a foliate pattern on a field of small flowers that repeats the carved motifs of the frame. The same patterns were also woven in brilliant yellow and emerald green. The upholstery is held in place with cast brass strips. (The upholstery on the sofa has been changed.)*

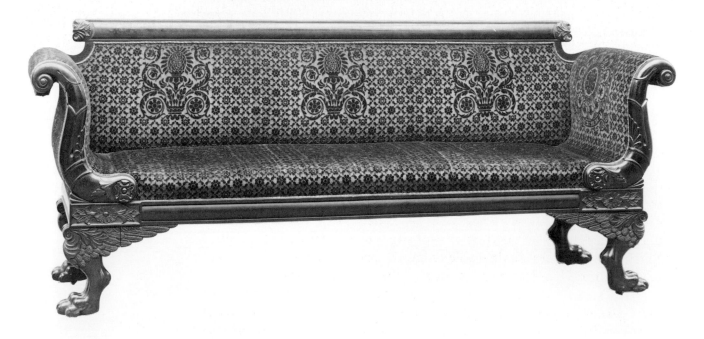

FIG. 8. *Patterned upholstery. (Winterthur Museum.) Red worsted on white cotton warp with green and black Empire medallions for a back, seat, and apron strip. Panels could be stitched together for a longer couch or settee.*

Worsted materials, known in the eighteenth century by such names as embossed camlet, cheney, harateen, moreen, and grogrinett were widely used not only for bed curtains but also for upholstery. From merchants' pattern books we know that these textiles were dyed in many bright colors such as red, indigo blue, dark green, and a strong yellow or gold. Vulnerable to moth, few early pieces have survived; occasionally a fragment is found when a chair is stripped.

A plate in Diderot's encyclopedia (1751–65) illustrating the craft of the *tapissier* depicts an armchair ready to be covered with muslin (Fig. 10). Hints as to the appearance of eighteenth- and nineteenth-

FIG. 9. *Designs for three sofas colored (top to bottom) pink, blue, and yellow, showing pendant fringe, bolsters, and flat cushions of contrasting colors. The plain materials are embellished with wreaths, flat leaves, and borders. From James Barron,* Modern and Elegant Designs of Cabinet and Upholstery Furniture *(London: W. M. Thiselton, [1814]), unnumbered plate. (Winterthur Museum Library.)*

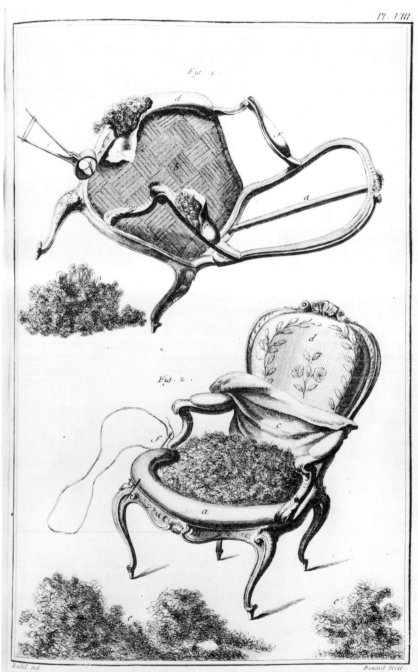

Pl. VIII.

Fig. 1.

Fig. 2.

Radel Del   Benard Fecit

Tapissier, 1ere et 2me préparation de la façon de faire les Fauteuils.

FIG. 10. *"Le Tapissier." From Denis Diderot and Jean d'Alembert,* Encyclopédie, ou dictionnaire raisonné des sciences, des arts et des métiers. . . . Recueil de planches, *11 vols. (Paris: Briasson et al., 1762–72), 8: pl. 8. (Winterthur Museum Library.) Illustrated are eighteenth-century upholstering techniques. The upper illustration shows the webbing and the firm rolls of horsehair being applied to the front edge of an armchair. Below, the seat cavity is filled with hair, and the muslin is ready to be tacked in place.*

FIG. 11. Mahogany framed easy chair, New England, ca. 1750. (Winterthur Museum.) Original stuffing of marsh grass or hay and linen covering. The wings, arms, and vertical arm supports were firmly stuffed.

FIG. 12. Armchair with label of Adam Hains, Philadelphia, 1825. Mahogany and ash frame upholstered in red striped velvet. (Privately owned: Photo, New England Gallery, Andover, Mass.) The back is upholstered in the French style, raised or squared to follow the contour of the curved and arched back.

century upholstery can be found in original pieces. In America firm rolls of padding filled with tough grass or hay were found on a chair which has lost its outermost covering (Fig. 11). Easy chairs, some fitted with commodes, were generally used in bedrooms and are seen in portraits of elderly people to whom they were allocated for their comfort. The inner surfaces of such chairs, including the back, the cheeks of the high wings, the arms, and the seat were comfortably padded, while the outer surfaces were left unpadded. An example of "French stuffing," crisp in outline and smart in appearance, is seen on the raised, squared back of an armchair made by Adam Hains of Philadelphia (Fig. 12).[3]

The original upholstery on a few easy chairs and lolling chairs is tufted. Seven or eight tufts in a back, depending upon the contour of the chair, kept the padding from slipping down.[4] Occasionally one finds a tuft of fringed silk, like a soft tassel, which conceals the stitch of coarse linen thread beneath and prevents it from ripping the cloth. The arms of sofas, lolling chairs, and easy chairs were gently rounded for comfort (Fig. 13). The neat trim lines of upholstered furniture continued well into the nineteenth century. Cabinetmakers' pattern books show side chairs with flat seats which do not obscure the cyma-curve molding at the base of the splat.

By the mid-1840s coiled wire springs were generally used in comfortable seating furniture. These were held in place by deeply recessed buttons. Many settees, poufs or hassocks, conversation chairs or confidants, and sofas were upholstered in this manner (Figs. 14, 15, 16).

In original eighteenth-century upholstery, narrow worsted ribbon or tape matching the upholstery color was placed beneath the tacks not only to hold the covering and any loose threads in place but also to prevent the tacks from tearing the material beneath.

Brass tacks adorned the chair, just as a necklace of gold beads enhanced a dress. Randle Holme in his *Academy of Armory* used the term *garnishing* when he described the process of finishing upholstered furniture with brass nails. Especially ornamental is the double row of tacks placed tight against each other around the base of the lolling chair in the portrait of an American girl by John Singleton Copley (Fig. 17). Other decorative nailing patterns are found in Ince and Mayhew (Figs. 18, 19). In the Federal period, two methods of tacking

FIG. 13. *John Singleton Copley,* Mrs. Thomas Boylston. *Boston, 1766. Oil on canvas.* (*Harvard University Portrait Collection.*) *The arms of this lolling chair are comfortably but firmly rounded. A dent in the back can be seen where the layers of padding were stitched together to hold them firmly in place. A similar chair, perhaps a studio property, is shown in Copley's* Young Lady with a Bird and Dog (*Fig. 17*).

FIG. 14. *A lady's boudoir. From Ella Rodman Church,* How to Furnish a House *(New York: D. Appleton, 1883), p. 94. (Winterthur Museum Library.) With deep-buttoned chairs and sofa, heavily curtained bed alcove, wall-to-wall carpeting, and upholstered fireplace, this view might as well bear the caption "The Upholsterer's Dream."*

FIG. 15. *Sofa, United States, ca. 1870. Walnut and chestnut with burl walnut veneer. (St. Louis Art Museum, gift of Mrs. Milton Greenfield in memory of Blanche Sterne and Maude Sterne Bauman.) While not original to the piece, the blue wool damask with vaguely Gothic and Renaissance motifs is old and entirely suitable to the sofa. Furniture in the Brooklyn Museum collection of the same date is covered in this material.*

FIG. 16. *Platform rocking chair, United States, ca. 1880. Walnut frame with original gold and cream silk upholstery. (Newark Museum, gift of Mr. and Mrs. Irving J. Soloway.) This armchair with deep buttoning, gathered edges, and fancy gimp and fringe can be said to epitomize the late nineteenth-century ideal in comfortable seating furniture.*

OPPOSITE
FIG. 17. *John Singleton Copley,* Young Lady with a Bird and Dog *(also known as* Mary Warner). *New England, 1767. Oil on canvas. (Toledo Museum of Art, gift of Florence Scott Libbey.)*

Plate IX.

Parlour Chairs.

M:Ince inv.t et delin. Darly sculp.

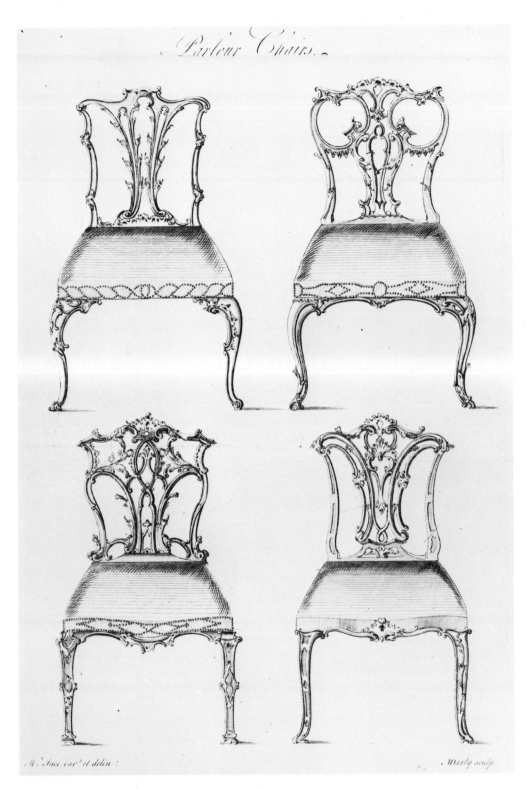

W. Ince invt et delint.   Darly sculp.

FIGS. 18,19. *Designs for English Chippendale side chairs. From William Ince and Thomas Mayhew,* The Universal System of Household Furniture *(London, 1762), pls. 9 and 10. (Winterthur Museum Library.) Shown is a variety of patterns for ornamental brass tacking to hold the upholstery in place.*

FIG. 20. *Ralph Earl,* Chief Justice and Mrs. Oliver Ellsworth. *Connecticut, 1792. Oil on canvas. (Wadsworth Atheneum.) The judge's side chair appears to be covered in pink haircloth held in place with brass tacks and trimmed around the skirt with fringe. Haircloth was most frequently dyed black, but other lighter colors, particularly green, were produced.*

were followed: either a double row, at top and bottom of a chair rail, or festoons above a single row at the bottom of the seat frame (Fig. 20). Later Federal and Empire furniture is occasionally seen with a metal strip replacing tacks or a welt. Soft metals like pewter or lead were easy to work around the contours of the stuffing. One set of chairs had a beaded brass strip through which a round-headed tack was nailed about every tenth bead, a laborsaving, and yet ornamental method. Large brass tacks were again used in the late nineteenth century, a practice harking back to the seventeenth century and advocated by Eastlake (Fig. 21).

FIG. 21. *Side chair, United States, ca. 1880. Ebonized hardwood with metal insets and original velvet upholstery. (National Museum of American History, Smithsonian Institution, gift of Mrs. Eustis Emmet.) This chair is trimmed with galloon, fringe, and copper gilt nails in the manner of English furniture of about 1620 at Knole as described by Charles Eastlake in* Hints on Household Taste *(1869).*

In lieu of tacks or strips, welting, and increasingly, matched or contrasting cords or fancy tapes were manufactured to conceal the utilitarian nails. Welting was used in the eighteenth century, as now, to define the crisp lines of a wing chair or a sofa (Figs. 22, 23).

FIG. 23. *Easy chair, New England, 1740–50. Walnut frame with original red harateen upholstery. (Brooklyn Museum, Henry C. Batterman Fund and others.)*

OPPOSITE
FIG. 22. *John Singleton Copley,* Unknown subject *(traditionally known as* Mrs. Henry Thrale). *England or America, 1771. Oil on canvas. (Hyde Collection, Somerville, N.J.) Welting is used around the arm, seat, and cushions of this Chippendale sofa upholstered in what appears to be silk damask.*

FIG. 24. *Chaise longue from Rudolph Ackermann,* The Repository of Arts, Literature, Commerce, Manufactures, Fashions and Politics *1, no. 1 (January 1809): 54. (Winterthur Museum Library.) In addition to the carving the couch is handsomely trimmed with a Greek border along the skirt, fringed shawls suspended from the ends, and both a round bolster and a flat cushion.*

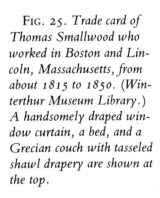

FIG. 25. *Trade card of Thomas Smallwood who worked in Boston and Lincoln, Massachusetts, from about 1815 to 1850. (Winterthur Museum Library.) A handsomely draped window curtain, a bed, and a Grecian couch with tasseled shawl drapery are shown at the top.*

A fashion especially favored by Thomas Sheraton was the addition of drapery over the upholstery at the back of a couch or duchesse or beneath the arch of a lady's writing cabinet or a dressing table. In the Regency period, this practice was extended to the use of extra drapery suspended from the arms, or long netted fringe hanging below chair rails (Figs. 24, 25). Perhaps the informality of room arrangements, whereby furniture was seen from several sides, accounts for these additional pieces of drapery, or it may have been the upholsterer's fancy. Vulnerable to wear and tear these textile ornaments rarely survived, and the fashion is seldom followed when furniture is reupholstered today.

Framed needlework panels made for firescreens were supplanted by draped and fringed hangings often of banner or shield shape (Fig. 26). The storage bag or compartment of sewing tables was frequently elaborately pleated and draped.

FIG. 26. *Designs for pole screens with suspended cloth banners, two handsome upholstered stools, and Gothic chairs. From James Barron,* Modern and Elegant Designs of Cabinet and Upholstery Furniture (*London: W. M. Thiselton, [1814]), pl. 33. (Winterthur Museum Library.*)

FIG. 27. *Interior of a boudoir displayed by Carrington, de Zouché and Company of Philadelphia at the International Exhibition in 1876. From Walter Smith,* Industrial Art, *Masterpieces of the Centennial International Exhibition, vol. 2 (Philadelphia: Gebbie & Barrie, 1876), p. 121. (Winterthur Museum Library.)*

The skill of the upholsterer reached its apogee at the time of the Centennial in this country to judge by the "boudoir" of Carrington, de Zouché and Co. from Philadelphia (Fig. 27). The catalogue describes "this abode of luxury" in detail:

> The ceiling and sides of this apartment are panelled with tufted cretonne of rich, warm colors, relieved by a stile of drab-colored damask with mouldings of ebony and gilt. . . . The upholstering of the chairs, pillow lounge and ottoman is in a cretonne matching the panels, and the same material is used around the large mirror at the end of the apartment and on the shelf at its foot. Puffing and box-plaits are used to make curved and broken lines and to give additional effectiveness to the arrangement. The room in its suggestions of repose, comfort and refinement is the beau-ideal of a boudoir.[5]

Writing in England as early as 1873, reform designer Christopher Dresser insisted that a "wood frame should appear in every work of furniture" and found that "sofas are now made as if they were feather beds." About upholstery materials, he commented on haircloth as being durable but "inartistic in its effect." For library chairs he suggested either plain or embossed Utrecht velvet, leather for dining room chairs, and silk and satin damasks, rep, and plain cloth for drawing rooms. Chintz he "was not fond of" for chair covers.[6]

Reform in room arrangement was soon advocated in this country as well, for Clarence Cook wrote in 1877 that "every piece of furniture in the room must have a good and clear reason for being there" and that "it will be found good for the health, and conducive to the freshness and simplicity of a small apartment to get rid of upholstery and stuffing in our furniture as far as possible. The wooden chairs, and chairs seated with rushes or cane of the old time, were as comfortable as the stuffed and elastic seats we are so fond of."[7]

Clean lines and visible wooden frames are evident in the set of parlor furniture made for the Rockefellers about 1880 (Fig. 28). Plainness is offset by embroidered seats and backs and an abundance of swags and tassels required to make this furniture acceptable in the eyes of its original owners.

In this country reform principles of "fitness, proportion and harmony" were developed by Frank Lloyd Wright with his built-in furniture comprising an organic unity with his houses.

FIG. 28A,B. *Side chair and arm-chair, United States, ca. 1880. (Brooklyn Museum, gifts of John D. Rockefeller, Jr., and John D. Rockefeller III.) Blue velvet upholstery embroidered in creams, blues, and reds.*

Slipcovers or Cases

In the eighteenth century, handsome furnishing materials were protected by cases or slipcovers as they are today (Figs. 29, 30). Thomas Chippendale included cases at the same time that he offered a selection of upholstery materials to a patron.[8] For green silk damask, he suggested green serge cases. On occasion he also advised crimson or yellow serge. A certain nicety of judgment or protocol was demanded on the part of the chief steward to determine which guests warranted

Fig. 29. Israel Israel, *by an unknown artist, Delaware or Pennsylvania, ca. 1775. Oil on canvas. (Abby Aldrich Rockefeller Folk Art Collection, Colonial Williamsburg.) With characteristic exaggeration the folk artist painted the slipcovered seat of a Chippendale side chair. The fringe with a scalloped heading edges the deep ruffled skirt.*

FIG. 30. *An eighteenth-century slipcover, or case, on a mahogany side chair, Philadelphia, 1760–70. (Winterthur Museum.) The deep ruffled skirt is tied to the chair legs with narrow tapes. The linen-cotton material was printed from copper plates with pastoral scenes by Robert Jones, Old Ford, in 1761.*

the removal of these coverings. The reverse was also practiced; from the late seventeenth century some furniture was finished in muslin over which was placed a richer covering of damask or velvet made as a slip case. A set of Queen Anne chairs in the Victoria and Albert Museum finished only in coarse linen is provided with slipcovers of handsome red and green patterned velvet neatly fitted to the seats and backs. They are held in place by tabs of buckram with eyelets made to slip over nails beneath the seat frame. For ordinary use the fine coverings were removed. Similar loose covers of red Genoa velvet on gilt chairs by William Kent are found at Houghton Hall in Norfolk, England. Cords threaded through holes in the front rail hold the covers in place.

Later in the eighteenth century, with less formality of living, costly materials were increasingly supplanted by lighter, less permanent textiles (Fig. 31). Washable slipcovers became popular, in spite of the fact that after washing they seldom fit so nicely because of the

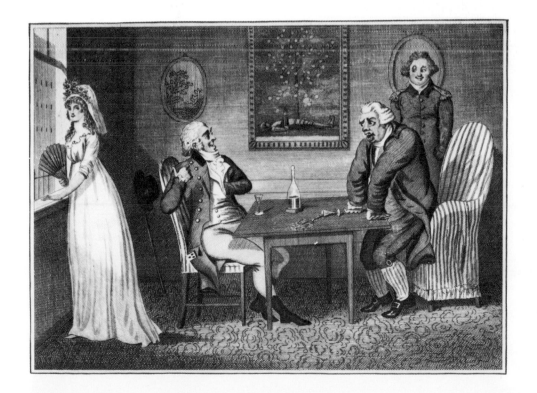

FIG. 31. *Illustration for a poem entitled "Speculation; or, A New Way of Saving A Thousand Pounds"* (London: Laurie & Wittle, 1798). *(Lewis Walpole Library.) Both chairs are covered with striped slipcovers.*

difficulty of ironing them smoothly. Furniture check became one of the most popular materials for cases (Fig. 32). Red, green, and especially blue and white checks gave a neat, clean appearance when used for an entire room—bed hangings, window curtains, and slipcovers. In lesser houses cases sometimes served to conceal shabby, worn materials beneath. In America, especially in the South, it was long customary to use lighter, washable materials for slipcovers during the summer months.

FIG. 32. *John Hamilton Mortimer,* Sergeant-at-Arms Bonfoy, His Son, and John Clementson, Sr. *England, ca. 1770. (Paul Mellon Collection, Yale Center for British Art.) The two back stools and a lolling chair are furnished with checked slipcovers with deep skirts. The slipcover on the lolling chair is tied beneath the arm supports with cords.*

The *Workwoman's Guide* of 1838 describes the proper method for making slipcovers:

When chairs and sofas are fitted up with damask, merino, stuff, horse hair, or other material that does not wash, they are generally covered with Holland, chintz, or glazed calico, which protects them from dust and dirt, and are easily removed, when required for company. Holland covers are the most durable, but look cold; chintz, unless very strong, should be lined with thin glazed calico. The cover should be made exactly to fit the chair or sofa, with or without piping at the edge, and with loops sewed on three of the sides underneath, and a pair of strings through the three loops, and making it tie. Ottomans generally have the covers to fit along beneath the edging of wood, in which case, they must be pinned to the stuffing with very strong pins, which from their length are called sofa pins.[9]

[1]Ralph Edwards, *The Shorter Dictionary of English Furniture* (London: Country Life, 1964), pp. 121, 264, 121.

[2]Nicholas B. Wainwright, *Colonial Grandeur in Philadelphia: The House and Furniture of General John Cadwalader* (Philadelphia: Historical Society of Pennsylvania, 1964), pp. 51–52.

[3]For other examples of Hains's work upholstered in this manner, see Kathleen Catalano and Richard C. Nylander, "New Attributions to Adam Hains, Philadelphia Furniture Maker," *Antiques* 117, no. 5 (May 1980): 1112–16.

[4]John Fowler and John Cornforth, *English Decoration in the Eighteenth Century* (Princeton, N.J.: Pyne Press, 1974), p. 156.

[5]Walter Smith, *Industrial Art,* Masterpieces of the Centennial International Exhibition, vol. 2 (Philadelphia: Gebbie & Barrie, 1876), p. 121.

[6]Christopher Dresser, *Principles of Decorative Design* (1873; reprint ed., New York: St. Martin's Press, 1973), pp. 70, 72.

[7]Clarence Cook, *The House Beautiful: Essays on Beds and Tables, Stools and Candlesticks* (New York: Scribner, Armstrong, 1877), p. 58.

[8]Geoffrey Beard, ed., "The Harewood Chippendale Account, 1772–77," *Furniture History* 4 (1968): 70–80.

[9]*The Workwoman's Guide* (1838; 2d ed., London: Simpkin, Marshall; Birmingham: Thomas Evans, 1840).

Textiles for the
Period Room in America

At the opening of the American Wing of the Metropolitan Museum of Art in 1924, Robert W. de Forest, museum president, pointed out that to exhibit American art "in our large Museum galleries," with beaux arts architectural details and lofty, skylighted ceilings, resulted in a loss of "its distinctive charm of simplicity and that it could be adequately shown only in the modest rooms for which it was made." Until the 1970s, period rooms have been the accepted background for the display of American decorative arts. According to R. T. Haines Halsey, trustee of the Metropolitan Museum and chairman of the committee on American decorative art, and Charles O. Cornelius, curator, "in furnishing and equipping the rooms [of the American Wing] a great effort has been made to insure historical accuracy" based on "an exhaustive study of the inventories and newspaper advertisements of the early days."[1]

In early installations, however, it mattered little to some collectors whether window openings and doors were cut where they had not been, whether rooms were enlarged or thrown together, or whether woodwork from several houses was combined. At that time, fielded paneling, feather-edge sheathing, and boldly molded fireplace surrounds and doorways were considered the ideal background for antique furniture; mellow old wood, soft lighting, and dark, rich textiles created an ambience in accord with the veneration in which antique furniture was held.

Like the paneling, it seemed more important that textiles used in these rooms be antique than that they be of a kind originally used with the furniture. Study of the suitability of textiles for furnishing period rooms was begun by curators in the American decorative arts field rather than by textile curators who concerned themselves primarily with the acquisition and cataloguing of the finest and most sumptuous examples of the textile arts since ancient times.

The *American Wing Handbook,* in seven editions, beginning in 1924, has been a primary source for students of all the American arts including furnishing. In 1931, an entire book, *Early American Textiles* by Frances Little, was published as part of a series on early American crafts. Although sparsely illustrated and now out of date, it remains a valuable pioneer work. Like the many volumes by such indefatigable antiquarians as Alice Morse Earle and Esther Singleton, it is without footnotes, but present-day studies often corroborate the discoveries of these early writers. *The Homes of Our Ancestors* by R. T. H. Halsey and Elizabeth Tower included textile research through 1936, and the research of Hazel E. Cummin undertaken in the late 1930s for the restoration of Stratford Hall in Virginia was published in *Antiques.* Miss Cummin's findings stimulated the interest of dealers, among them Mrs. Lawrence Ullman who invited her to address a group of antiquarian friends at the Ullman home in Tarrytown, New York.[2]

Homer Eaton Keyes, editor of *Antiques,* stated in 1931 that "the problem of correctly furnishing a renovated old-time mansion or a new dwelling in an early period style involves many difficulties, whose solution depends primarily upon documentary research and the just interpretation of its results."[3] Among those who were "singularly successful" at research and interpretation was Marie G. Kimball, whose husband Fiske Kimball was a restoration architect and director of the Pennsylvania Museum, now the Philadelphia Museum of Art. Mrs. Kimball's articles on the furnishings of John Penn's town and country houses and two on Jefferson's White House furnishings and "Jefferson's Curtains at Monticello," which she coauthored with her husband, were published in *Antiques*.[4]

Joseph Downs, who began his career under Fiske Kimball as curator of the Pennsylvania Museum, was to become America's foremost authority on textile usage at the American Wing. As early as the 1930s and 1940s and at the Henry Francis du Pont Winterthur Museum in the 1950s, Downs touched on textiles in his articles for the bulletins of both the Pennsylvania Museum and the Metropolitan Museum of Art, in his several revisions of the *American Wing Handbook,* and in his master work, a catalogue of the Winterthur Museum's collection of Queen Anne and Chippendale furniture. His broad knowledge of European decorative arts included prints as sources for window curtain treatments, and two articles on draperies were published in *Fine Arts*. Joseph Downs took great pains in supervising the repairs made by museum craftsmen and independent upholsterers engaged in making curtains and bed hangings. What they learned from him is now standard practice.[5]

A similar study of bed hangings, upholstery, and slipcovers as found in English satirical and political prints in the Lewis Walpole Library, Farmington, Connecticut, resulted in two articles by this writer published in *Antiques*.[6]

In recent years graduate students have undertaken serious research on textiles. For her 1963 doctoral dissertation, the first in this field, Anna Brightman wrote on fabrics and styles of colonial window hangings in Boston and Salem. Out of this study, she developed two articles on window curtains.[7]

For theses in the Winterthur Program in Early American Culture, Ruth Y. Cox Page studied textiles used in Philadelphia, Barbara Gilbert Carson wrote on dated examples of American crewelwork embroidery, and Linda Baumgarten Berlekamp surveyed the textile trade in Boston from 1650 to 1700, portions of which appear in *Arts of the Anglo-American Community in the Seventeenth Century*. Most recently Susan Prendergast Schoelwer studied 324 inventories for her thesis on fabric furnishings used in eighteenth-century Philadelphia houses and condensed some of her findings into an article for *Winterthur Portfolio: A Journal of American Material Culture*.[8] Another comprehensive study of crewelwork was done for the Museum of Fine Arts, Boston, by Ann Pollard Rowe.[9]

An interest in the craft of weaving and the preparation of fibers was developed at the Farmers' Museum, Cooperstown, New York, where Virginia Parslow Partridge held demonstrations for visitors and taught in the summer seminars conducted by the American Association for State and Local History. A remarkable collection of household textiles and needlework owned by several generations of the Copp family in Stonington, Connecticut, was presented to the United States National Museum in the 1890s, but not until 1971, with Grace Rogers Cooper's publication and exhibition, including craft demonstrations, was it studied comprehensively.[10] At Colonial Williamsburg, Mildred Lanier, a weaver before she became curator, studied textiles used in the southern colonies. Over the years important lectures on textiles have been delivered at Williamsburg's annual antiques forums, when the splendid collections and textile storage facilities are opened to forum participants.

Dealers have searched out textiles from early American homes where they long had been stored in attic trunks. Their discoveries made it possible to link actual fabric with period terminology culled from advertisements, merchants' accounts, upholsterers' bills, house inventories, and early dictionaries. Beginning in the 1930s, collectors vied for textiles in the booths of the semiannual White Plains Antique Show, as well as in the shops of Mary Allis, Alice B. Beer, Lillian B. Cogan, Mr. and Mrs. Fred Fuessenich, Rockwell and Avis Gardiner, Ginsburg and Levy, Josephine Howell, J. A. Lloyd Hyde, Mary Johnson, Elinor Merrell, Charlotte and Edgar Sittig, Thurston and Doris Thacher, and Winsor White. Among the collectors who seldom missed an antiques show were Mrs. De Witt C. Howe (later Mrs. Austin Palmer) and Henry Francis du Pont, the latter often accompanied by Mrs. Harry Horton Benkard from whom he frequently sought advice on questions of furnishing. Hobe Erwin, like many other designers and manufacturers, availed himself of the Cooper-Union Museum's great collections of textiles and wallpapers for design sources. More recently the fabric houses of Schumacher, Scalamandré, and Brunschwig et Fils, among others, have reproduced or adapted old textiles to modern production methods.

In the 1930s and 1940s, silks and satins, preserved in considerable quantities in Europe, especially in the hot, dry climates of Spain and Italy, were most readily available to collectors through dealers.

Customarily, wealthy urban churches on feast days hung silk damask in colors designated by the church calendar. For this reason church vestries held rich stores of handsome brocaded silks in the form of vestments and altar hangings. Indeed, a late seventeenth-century Italian green silk damask with a chalice in its pattern was made up into curtains for one American period room. Quantities of eighteenth-century ladies' dresses and gentlemen's vests and coats also provided fabrics for upholstery.

Early eighteenth-century woven wall hangings from the northern French provincial towns of Elbeuf and Rouen somehow found their way to America in this century. They were brocaded in patterns reminiscent of coarse flamestitch needlework and were used in Europe instead of costly pictorial tapestries. In America their original function as inexpensive wall coverings was misunderstood, and they were cut up for upholstery, daybed cushions, and table and floor carpets.[11]

In other instances, American homespun coverlets in overshot and summer-and-winter weaves were made to serve as upholstery for country easy chairs, and patchwork quilts were cut apart for bed valances. Until English examples were identified, French *toiles* for the most part were used for furnishing, overlooking our enormous and nearly exclusive trade with England during the eighteenth century. Woolen and especially worsted fabrics were almost entirely unknown. Moths have taken their toll, and, indeed, we did not always understand what moreen and harateen looked like when we met the terms in household inventories.

Several textile conferences grew out of the common interests of collectors, dealers, and curators. In 1957 Constance R. Williams of Litchfield, Connecticut, in search of information about a recently acquired example of blue resist, brought it to Alice Beer, at that time curator at the Cooper-Union Museum. At Mrs. Williams's suggestion, a seminar was organized at the Cooper-Union around the puzzling subject of indigo blue-resist textiles, a type which turned up repeatedly in the New York area and was unknown in European collections. At about this time, the Winterthur staff began to hear of research in English printed textiles being carried on by Peter Floud and Barbara Morris at the Victoria and Albert Museum. In 1958 a seminar was held at Winterthur, at which Floud was the principal speaker. This writer's book, *Printed Textiles: English and American Cottons and Linens, 1700–1850,* based on the Winterthur Museum collection, was an outgrowth of those beginnings. *Bed Hangings: A Treatise on Fabrics and Styles in the Curtaining of Beds, 1650–1850,* compiled by Abbott Lowell Cummings, grew out of a meeting held in 1960 at the Society for the Preservation of New England Antiquities in Boston. In this valuable book, bed hangings are considered from the point of view of both pictorial and documentary sources, the former discussed by Nina Fletcher Little, a collector long interested in the scholarly documentation of period furnishings. In 1975 the Irene Emery Roundtable on Museum Textiles held annually at the Textile Museum in Washington, D.C., considered imported and domestic textiles in eighteenth-century America. Textiles have frequently been topics of discussion at the Pennsbury Manor Americana forums. In 1977 the English-based Furniture History Society devoted a workshop to upholstery of all ages, and the 1979 annual workshop of the Decorative Arts Chapter of the Society of Architectural Historians, with responsibilities shared by Old Sturbridge Village and the Museum of Fine Arts, Boston, focused on the same topic.[12]

Over the years *Antiques* published notices and pictures of boldly patterned bed rugs made of homespun and home-dyed wools. Finally in 1972 the Wadsworth Atheneum held a large exhibition of these materials and published a catalogue.[13] Research has been conducted on coverlet weaving in Canada and in various areas of the United States. Quilts, many now seen as related to Op-Art in their intricate eye-catching patterns, have been the subject of several exhibitions and books. The Metropolitan Museum of Art's centennial exhibition "19th-Century America" and restorations like Lyndhurst, Olana, and the Mark Twain house have focused on the later nineteenth century, an era now popular for research topics among students. Installations at the Yale University Art Gallery and the Philadelphia Museum of Art now cover all periods of American arts up to the present, and the collections of the Metropolitan Museum of Art have recently been brought forward to about 1930.

Each year research provided more and more information about the kinds of textiles used in American homes, while fewer and fewer old textiles remained for installation. For a century or more, frugal housewives had altered old sets of bed curtains beyond recognition, and window curtains were discarded after sun, rain, and dirt had taken their toll. Few pieces of furniture with original upholstery survived in usable condition; most were stripped of every fragment of their first upholstery in preparation for new coverings. Often successive layers of upholstery dating from the eighteenth century were discarded and the evidence lost.

The textiles in the Winterthur Museum long have been one of its great glories and the pride of its founder. Until shortly before his death, Mr. du Pont personally selected old materials, decided the room in which each was to be used, and supervised the manner in which they were to be made up. He designed suitable storage facilities for bedspreads, window curtains, and bed hangings—installations which have become models for other institutions.

Over the years as Mr. du Pont furnished the rooms at Winterthur he also supervised repairs made to textiles at Ernest Lo Nano's workrooms in New York. No records were kept of the treatment they received. Sometimes pieces were dry cleaned or washed (in what we do not know). Sometimes new braid was applied and even entire sections of the original background material of a crewelwork bedspread were replaced. Of course this would no longer be acceptable practice among textile conservators.

Textile conservation has progressed a long way since that time. Among the pioneers in the field was Junius Bird at the Museum of Natural History, New York, with its rich collections of Peruvian textiles. Louisa Bellinger at the Textile Museum, Washington, devised many techniques in use today. There also Col. James Rice, a trained chemist, became interested in the subject in his retirement years and published ten articles in the *Textile Museum Journal* in the 1960s. An international conference held in Delft in 1964 pointed up the grave concerns of curators all over Europe for their precious textiles, including those of churches, monasteries, and tombs. The Abegg-Stiftung in Bern, Switzerland, became the ideal laboratory and served as a model for several other installations.

The Textile Museum trained several able young people who are now well known in the field, notably Nabuko Kajitani at the Metropolitan Museum of Art, Milton Sonday at Cooper-Hewitt, and Margaret Fikioris at Winterthur.

In recent years textile conservation has been greatly fostered by the establishment of two laboratories where museums which lack their own facilities can send their work, and these laboratories will also accept pieces owned privately. These are the Textile Conservation Workshop in South Salem, New York, opened in June 1978, and the Textile Conservation Center of the Merrimack Valley Textile Museum, North Andover, Massachusetts. Within the profession conservators generally are interested in sharing their techniques and methods with one another, although there is not always agreement from nation to nation.

Eighteenth-century furnishing practices in both England and America emphasize the problems faced by the curator endeavoring to furnish a room with old textiles. By midcentury, and earlier in England, rooms were furnished *en suite* using the same fabric for bed and window hangings and for upholstery. If more durable material was required, then it would at least be of the same color. With printed textiles, slipcovers matched the drapery materials. From upholsterers' bills we note that over fifty yards of material were required for a set of bed curtains to enclose the bed. For period rooms, it is no longer possible to find sufficient yardage of one pattern to follow this practice. Furthermore, few local preservation societies could afford antique textiles even if they were available.

Ideally one might wish that here in America we had a team of experts well acquainted with period styles of window curtains and bed hangings, correct textile patterns, and methods of upholstery. John Cornforth, editor at *Country Life,* put forth such an idea for the English National Trust houses in two articles he published about the refurnishing of Ham House in Surrey.[14] His team would include craftsmen skilled in the mixing of paint, and, as in earlier centuries, others who could do marbleizing and graining. With textiles it would be helpful if modern spinning could simulate the irregularities found in the yarn of old textiles and if workmen could be trained once again to make the fringes, tassels, and tapes that add so much to the dressing of a bed or window. Today it is often necessary to use synthetic fibers because silk, wool, and even cotton are too expensive. Modern fabrics are made of mechanically spun fibers which, lacking the unevenness of hand-spun yarn, catch the light differently thereby changing the color effect. Patterns cannot be reproduced with absolute accuracy on modern wide looms. Synthetic dyes are also what one might call too perfect. Too many reproduction fabrics are based on faded or soiled examples which are distortions of the original fresh, bright colors.

For all the reasons cited above it seems necessary to come to reproduction fabrics. In the Governor's Palace at Colonial Williamsburg, reopened in 1981, the beds and windows are furnished with reproductions. Considering the hordes of people who visit the Palace annually, this is surely the only route to have followed. For reproduction fabrics we are fortunate to have Jane Nylander's 1983 book published by the National Trust for Historic Preservation listing fabrics available on the market today.[15]

With the revival of interest in needlework and the availability of good worsted yarns, crewelwork bed curtains and needlework seats now can be accurately copied to replace the original pieces which, in turn, can be preserved under safer conditions.

Unfortunately there are few museums that have in-house facilities for making curtains. Historically this was the province of upholsterers and is today the business of decorators. But much additional research is necessary to sort out correct patterns for various types of period furniture. In particular, the revival styles are not yet well understood. For larger scale revival furniture, bolder patterns were in order which could be readily produced in jacquard-woven versions. Many patterns produced today for use on eighteenth-century antique furniture were probably first woven in the nineteenth century and not in the seventeenth or eighteenth centuries as suggested in showrooms. Nineteenth-century patterns, although perhaps adapted from late seventeenth-century Italian damasks, have fat, fleshy leaves with tightly curled tips, and large-scale motifs are coupled with tiny, fussy details. Large flat areas and a lack of clear definition in the drawing are noted. Eighteenth-century damasks and brocades by well-known French designers such as Jean Pillement, François Boucher, and Philippe de Lasalle were revived in blown-up scale with coarsened details. Subtle discrepancies in scale also appear in neoclassical revival patterns. Geometric motifs such as paterae, ovals, and brackets derived from formal architectural ornament are in different scale from the curling acanthus leafage surrounding them. Pendant jewels and pearls are found together with birds, cherubs, and classical figures—now sentimentalized. Work in the archives of French and English textile firms will be necessary to assign firm dates of first manufacture to such patterns. Eighteenth-century dress patterns in stripes with polychrome floral trails or sprigs were copied for use on delicate rococo revival parlor or boudoir furniture, especially gilded pieces. Similarly, small-scale geometric velvets, once used for gentlemen's clothing, were revived for upholstery. The altered color palette of these revival fabrics, with their strange, less naturalistic hues, is probably due to the use of new synthetic dyes. Characteristic of many revival textiles are striped, or *strié*, backgrounds designed to make them look antique. Much more work is needed to sort out these fabrics from those of earlier centuries.

Antique textiles are too precious to be used up. Pieces in good condition are needed as documents, and these should be carefully stored and handled or displayed infrequently. Under optimum conditions textiles may last a long time, but sunlight, their worst enemy, rots and fades them as does fluorescent light. Changes in moisture affect textiles, and without humidity control their life expectancy is short. Dirt and chemicals in polluted air cause discoloration. Over the years abrasion, inevitable with good housekeeping, frays the edges of curtains and the corners of seating furniture. If the life of a textile is short, frequent reupholstering is necessary. This is not only expensive; it riddles seat rails of chairs and sofas with tack holes.

Perhaps the final blow is the hard, cold fact that in rooms without climate controls textiles will last only ten or fifteen years before they look shabby and we must start over again.

[1]For Robert W. de Forest, see "Address by the President," *Addresses on the Occasion of the Opening of the American Wing* (New York: Metropolitan Museum of Art, 1925), p. 5; for R. T. H. Halsey and C. O. Cornelius, see "The American Wing," *Metropolitan Museum of Art Bulletin* 29, no. 11 (November 1924): 251.

[2]*American Wing Handbook*, (7 eds., New York: Metropolitan Museum of Art, 1924–42). The seventh edition (1942) by Joseph Downs supersedes all other editions and is an invaluable guide. Frances Little, *Early American Textiles* (New York: Century Co., 1931), R. T. H. Halsey and Elizabeth Tower, *The Homes of Our Ancestors* (Garden City, N.J.: Doubleday, Page & Co., 1925); Hazel E. Cummin, "Calamanco," *Antiques* 39, no. 4 (April 1941): 182–83; "Camlet," 42, no. 6 (December 1942): 309–12; "Colonial Dimities, Checked and Diapered," 38, no. 3 (September 1940): 111–12; "Moreen—A Forgotten Fabric," 38, no. 6 (December 1940): 286–87; "Tammies and Durants," 40, no. 3 (September 1941): 153–54; "What was Dimity in 1790?" 38, no. 1 (July 1940): 23–25. In addition to this series, three short notes

on Miss Cummin's research also appeared in *Antiques:* "A Dimity in 1737," 39, no. 5 (May 1941): 255–56; "Early Seersucker," 38, no. 5 (November 1940): 231–32; and "A Note on Nankin, Colonial Calico," 41, no. 3 (March 1942): 197.

[3]Homer Eaton Keyes, editorial note, *Antiques* 19, no. 5 (May 1931): 375.

[4]Marie G. Kimball, "The Furnishings of Governor Penn's Town House," *Antiques* 19, no. 5 (May 1931): 375–78; "The Furnishings of Lansdowne, Governor Penn's Country Estate," 19, no. 6 (June 1931): 450–55; "Thomas Jefferson's French Furniture," 15, no. 2 (February 1929): 123; "The Original Furnishings of the White House," 15, no. 6 (June 1929): 481–85, and 16, no. 1 (July 1929): 33–37. Fiske Kimball and Marie Kimball, "Jefferson's Curtains at Monticello," *Antiques* 52, no. 4 (October 1947): 266–68.

[5]Joseph Downs, *American Furniture: Queen Anne and Chippendale Periods in the Henry Francis du Pont Winterthur Museum* (1952; reprint ed., New York: Bonanza, 1978); "Authentic Draperies Reconstructed from Old Pictures," *Fine Arts* 18 (January 1932): 17–21; "Neo-Classic Draperies from Original Designs," *Fine Arts* 18 (February 1932): 29–32.

[6]Florence M. Montgomery, "Room Furnishings as seen in British Prints from the Lewis Walpole Library, Part 1: Bed Hangings," *Antiques* 104, no. 6 (December 1973): 1068–75; "Part 2: Window Curtains, Upholstery, and Slip Covers," 105, no. 3 (March 1974): 522–31.

[7]Anna Brightman, "Fabrics and Styles of Colonial Window Hangings as Revealed through Boston and Salem, Massachusetts, Records, 1700–1760" (Ph.D. diss., Florida State University, 1963); "Window Curtains in Colonial Boston and Salem," *Antiques* 86, no. 2 (August 1964): 184–87; *Window Treatments for Historic Houses, 1700–1850,* Preservation Leaflet Series, no. 14 (Washington, D.C.: National Trust for Historic Preservation, 1968).

[8]Ruth Yvonne Cox, "Textiles Used in Philadelphia, 1760–75" (M.A. thesis, University of Delaware, 1960); Barbara L. Gilbert, "American Crewelwork, 1700–1850" (M.A. thesis, University of Delaware, 1965); Linda Baumgarten Berlekamp, "The Textile Trade in Boston, 1650–1700" (M.A. thesis, University of Delaware, 1976); and "The Textile Trade in Boston, 1650–1700," in *Arts of the Anglo-American Community in the Seventeenth Century,* ed. Ian M. G. Quimby (Charlottesville: University Press of Virginia, 1974), pp. 221–73; Susan Margaret Prendergast, "Fabric Furnishings Used in Philadelphia Homes, 1700–1775" (M.A. thesis, University of Delaware, 1978); Susan Prendergast Schoelwer, "Form, Function, and Meaning in the Use of Fabric Furnishings: A Philadelphia Case Study, 1700–1775," *Winterthur Portfolio* 14, no. 1 (Spring 1979): 25–40.

[9]Ann Pollard Rowe, "Crewel Embroidered Bed Hangings in Old and New England," *Bulletin of the Museum of Fine Arts, Boston* 71, nos. 365 and 366 (1973): 102–66.

[10]Grace Rogers Cooper, *The Copp Family Textiles,* Smithsonian Studies in History and Technology, no. 7 (Washington, D.C.: Smithsonian Institution Press, 1971).

[11]See also Florence M. Montgomery, "A Pattern-Woven 'Flamestitch' Fabric," *Antiques* 80, no. 5 (November 1961): 453–55.

[12]Florence M. Montgomery, *Printed Textiles: English and American Cottons and Linens, 1700–1850* (New York: Viking Press, 1970); Abbott Lowell Cummings, comp., *Bed Hangings: A Treatise on Fabrics and Styles in the Curtaining of Beds, 1650–1850* (Boston: Society for the Preservation of New England Antiquities, 1961); Patricia L. Fiske, ed., *Imported and Domestic Textiles in Eighteenth-Century America,* Proceedings of the 1975 Irene Emery Roundtable on Museum Textiles (Washington, D.C.: Textile Museum, 1975).

[13]*Bed Ruggs, 1722–1833,* exhibition catalogue, intro. William L. Warren, catalogue by J. Herbert Callister (Hartford, Conn.: Wadsworth Atheneum, 1972).

[14]John Cornforth, "Ham House Reinterpreted" *Country Life* 169 (Jan. 29, Feb. 5, 1981): 250–53, 322–25.

[15]Jane C. Nylander, *Fabrics for Historic Buildings* (3rd ed.; Washington, D.C.: Preservation Press for the National Trust for Historic Preservation, 1983).

PL. D-1. *Swatches of calmuc. From the Aix-la-Chapelle pattern book, 1807. (Musée des Arts Décoratifs.)*

PL. D-2. *Two pieces of heavy coating. From the Aix-la-Chapelle pattern book, 1807. (Musée des Arts Décoratifs.)*

PL. D-3. *Swatches of duvetyn. From the Aix-la-Chapelle pattern book, 1807. (Musée des Arts Décoratifs.)*

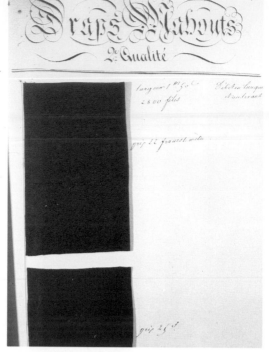

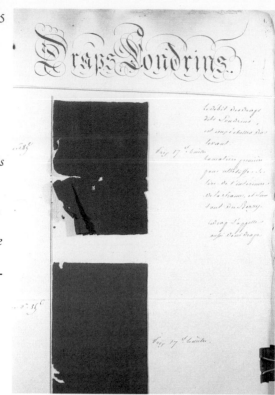

PL. D-4. *Swatches of mahouts, one of the woolen cloths featured in French trade with the Levant. The red swatches are second quality. Many textiles in the Levant trade were patterned on English broadcloths. From the Aix-la-Chapelle pattern book, 1807. (Musée des Arts Décoratifs.)*

PL. D-5. *Swatches of Londrins, one of the woolen cloths featured in French trade with the Levant. In the hope of capturing the market from the British they were given an imitative name. From the Aix-la-Chapelle pattern book, 1807. (Musée des Arts Décoratifs.)*

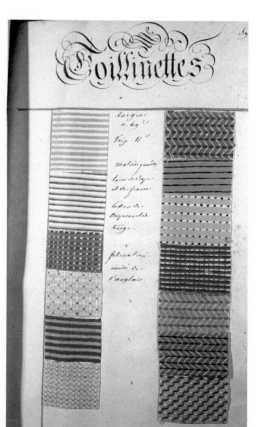

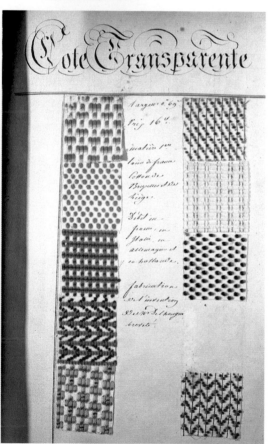

PL. D-6. Toillinettes, *waistcoat materials in cotton and wool with some silk. From the Aix-la-Chapelle pattern book, 1807. (Musée des Arts Décoratifs.)*

PL. D-7. *Vestings called* Côte Transparente *made of cotton and wool. From the Aix-la-Chapelle pattern book, 1807. (Musée des Arts Décoratifs.)*

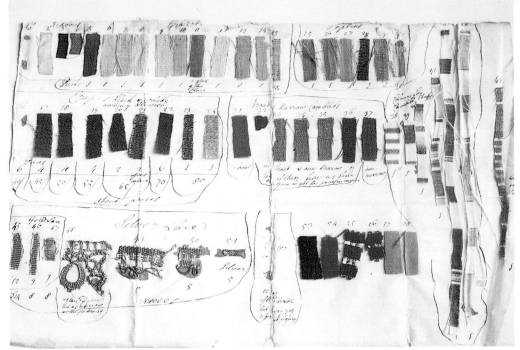

PL. D-9. *Patterns of eighteenth-century ribbons, grazets, poplins, crapes, broad and narrow camlets, camlet stuffs, gold and silver lace, and various unidentified textiles. From the Alexander Papers. (New-York Historical Society.)*

PL. D-8. *Part of an order from James Alexander to London, June 1738. Scraps of calimanco, camlet, russel, lustring, and hairbine are pasted to the page. From the Alexander Papers. (New-York Historical Society.)*

PL. D-10. *Patterns of garterings sent to Mary Alexander in 1736. From the Alexander Papers. (New-York Historical Society.)*

PL. D-11. *Cuttings of tobines: white linen with blue cotton warp stripes. The wider stripes on the top swatch are purple. Preserved with the copy of a letter, dated 1746, from James and Mary Alexander, merchants of New York, to William Hunt in England. (New-York Historical Society.)*

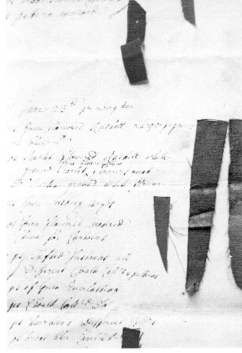

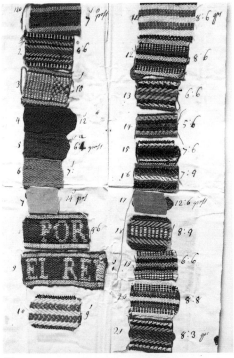

Pl. D-12. *Detail of Berlin work sampler. Inscribed 1866 M W. (Helen Louise Allen Textile Collection, University of Wisconsin.)*

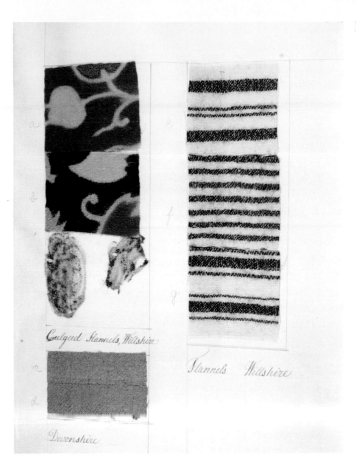

Culgeed Flannels, Wiltshire

Flannels Wiltshire

Devonshire

PL. D-13A, 13B. *Culgeed, or discharge-printed, flannel made in Wiltshire. From the Lindegreen pattern book, ca. 1750. (Berch Papers, Nordiska Museet.)*

PL. D-14. Doreas aga-bannas, *fine white cotton cloth embroidered in silk.* (*Berch Papers, ca. 1750. Nordiska Museet.*)

PL. D-15. *Silk and worsted figured grograms. From a paperbound pattern book of English worsteds with English titles.* (*Berch Papers, ca. 1750, Nordiska Museet.*)

PL. D-16. *Swatches of superfine grogrinetts, fine worsteds with a watered finish. From the Lindegreen pattern book, ca. 1750.* (*Berch Papers, Nordiska Museet.*)

PL. D-17. *Embossed serge and Kidderminster stuffs. From the Lindegreen pattern book, ca. 1750.* (*Berch Papers, Nordiska Museet.*)

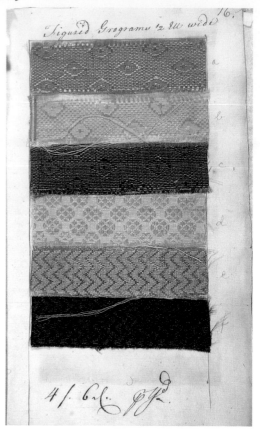

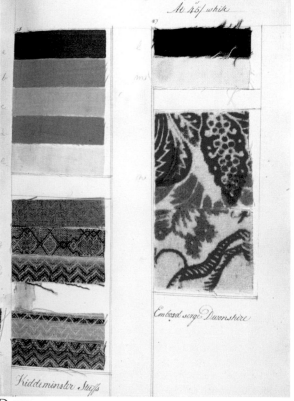

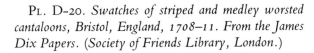

PL. D-18. *Four warp-patterned glazed worsted tobines. From a pattern book with English titles, ca. 1750. (Berch Papers, Nordiska Museet.)*

PL. D-19. *Swatches of wool velvets from Spital-fields. From the Lindegreen pattern book, ca. 1750. (Berch Papers, Nordiska Museet.)*

PL. D-20. *Swatches of striped and medley worsted cantaloons, Bristol, England, 1708–11. From the James Dix Papers. (Society of Friends Library, London.)*

PL. D-21. *Striped duffel, a trucking cloth of English manufacture, was found at Burr's Hill, Warren, Rhode Island, a seventeenth-century burial site of Wampanoag Indians. (Haffenreffer Museum of Anthropology.)*

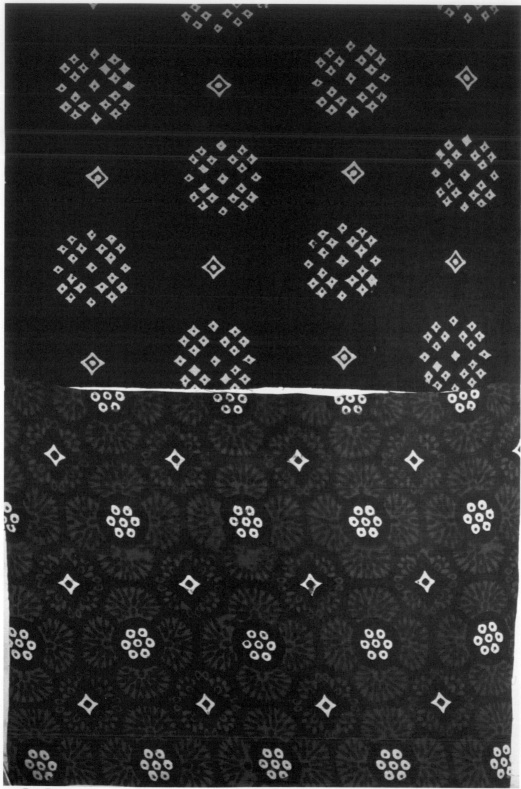

PL. D-22. *Samples of resist-printed handkerchiefs made in the Manchester area in imitation of Indian goods. From the Holker manuscript, ca. 1750. (Musée des Arts Décoratifs.)*

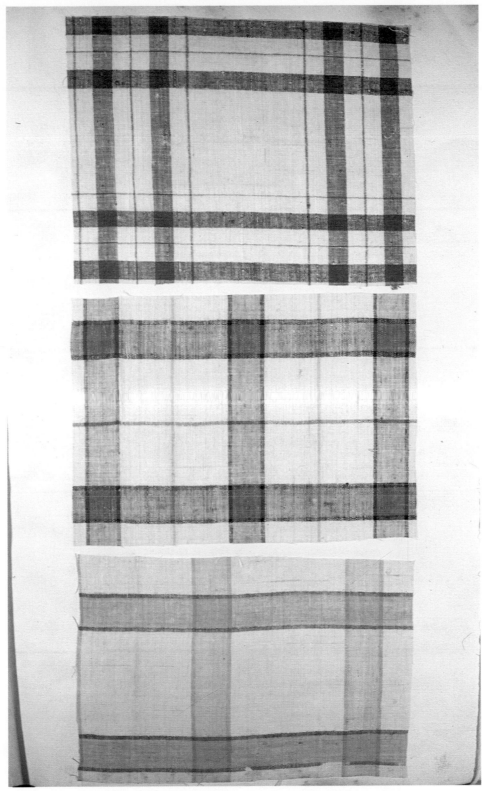

PL. D-23. *Furniture checks "made and sold in Manchester for curtains and chair coverings." From the Holker manuscript, ca. 1750. (Musée des Arts Décoratifs.)*

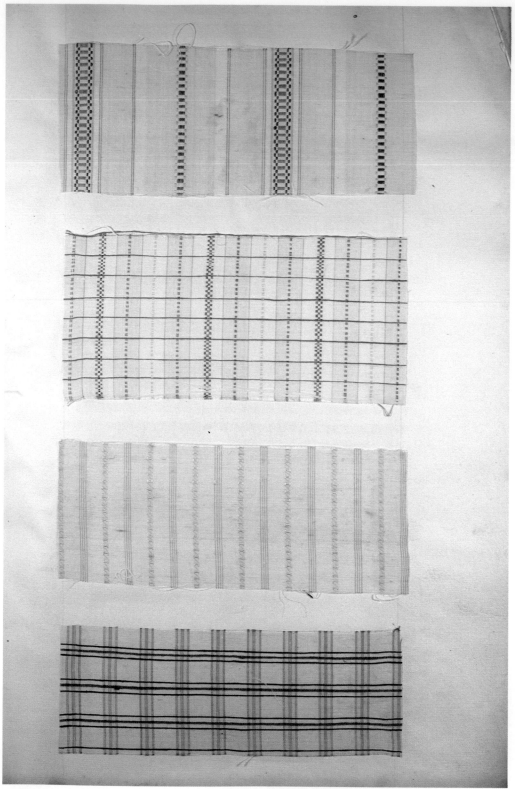

Pl. D-24A, 24B. *Cherryderrys of silk warp and cotton weft.*
From the Holker manuscript, ca. 1750. (Musée des Arts Décoratifs.)

D-24B

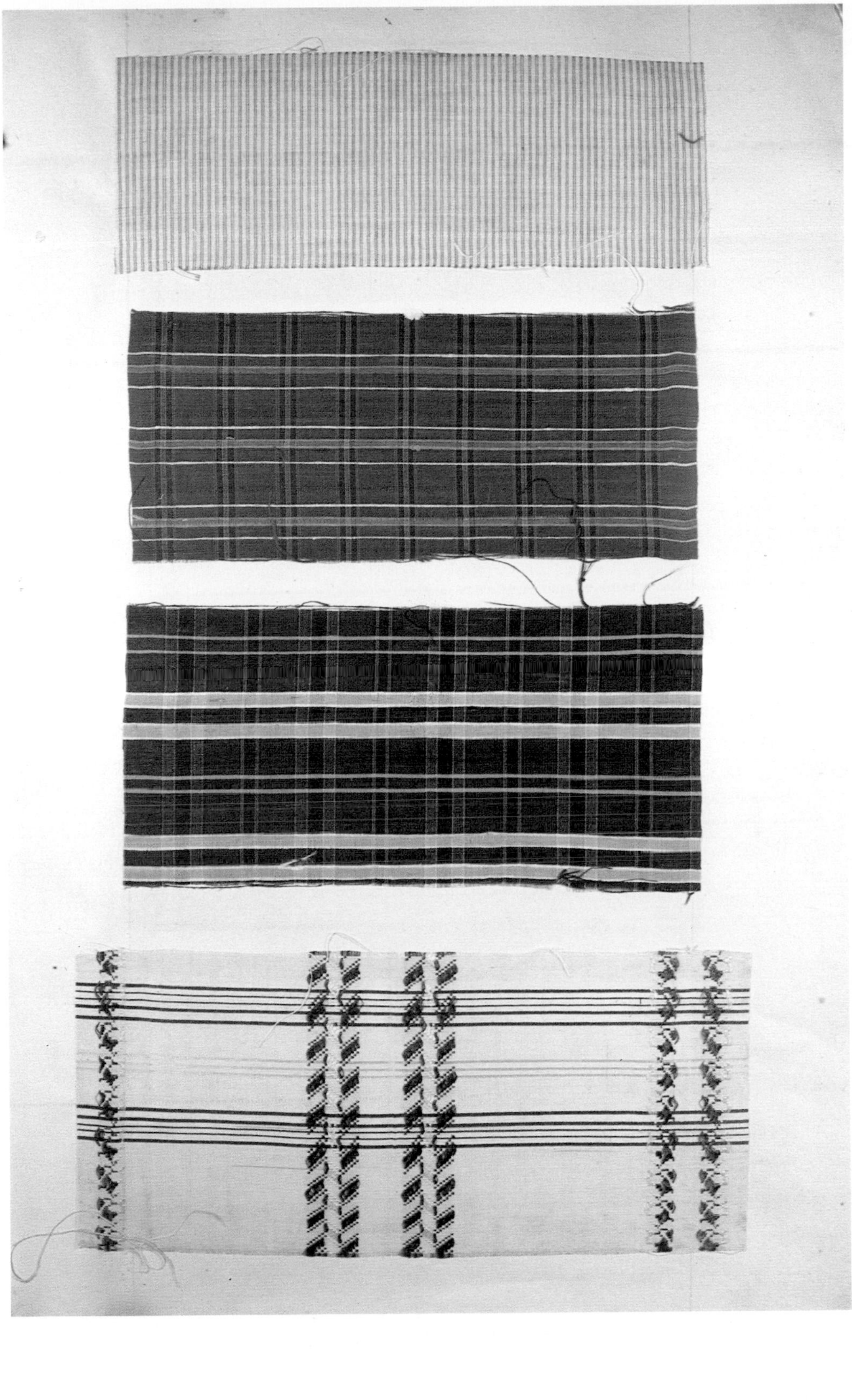

PL. D-25. *Cotton diaper flowered, woven of linen warp and cotton weft.*
From the Holker manuscript, ca. 1750. (Musée des Arts Décoratifs.)

PL. D-26. *Piece from a silk foulard handkerchief in twill weave.*
From the Holker manuscript, ca. 1750. (Musée des Arts Décoratifs.)

D-27A

D-27B

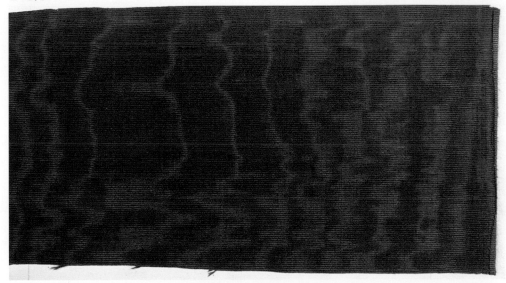

Pl. D-27A, 27B, 27C, 27D. *Swatches of harateen. The two pieces in green and red were given a watered finish; the two pieces in yellow and green were stamped with a wavy pattern by means of a hot copper cylinder. From the Holker manuscript, ca. 1750. (Musée des Arts Décoratifs.)*

D-27C

D-27D

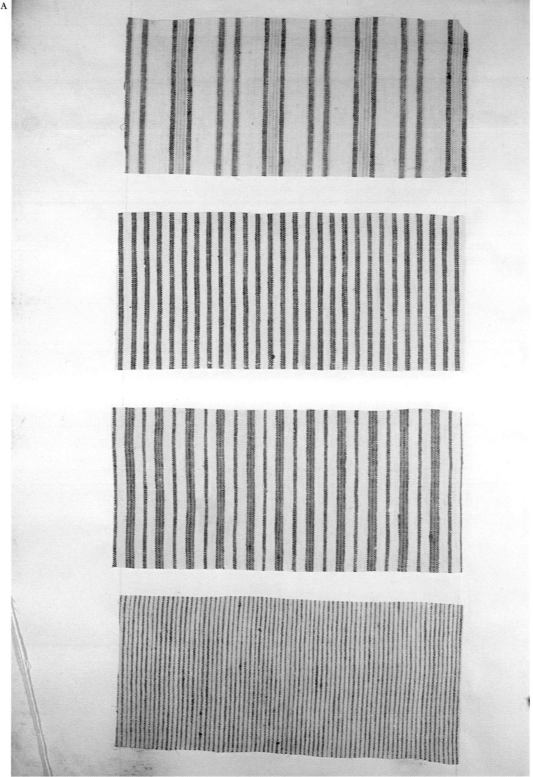

PL. D-28A, 28B. *Striped hollands, linen warps with additional colored cotton warps to form the stripes. From the Holker manuscript, ca. 1750. (Musée des Arts Décoratifs.)*

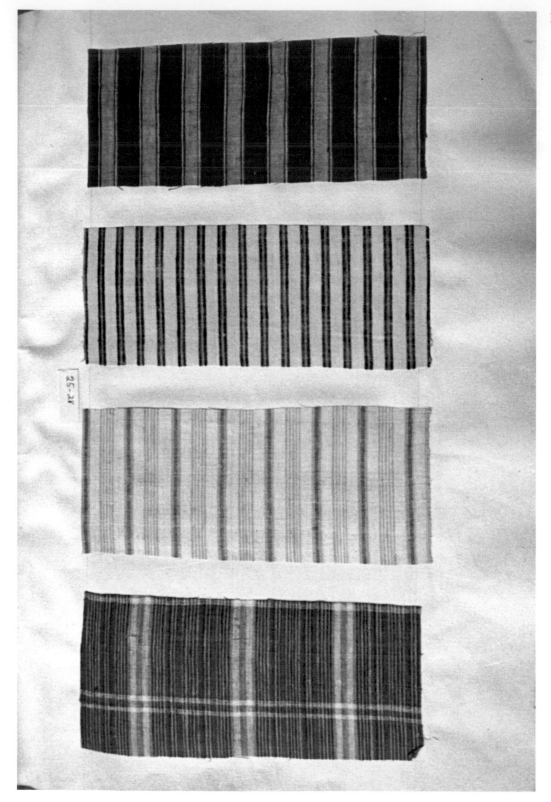

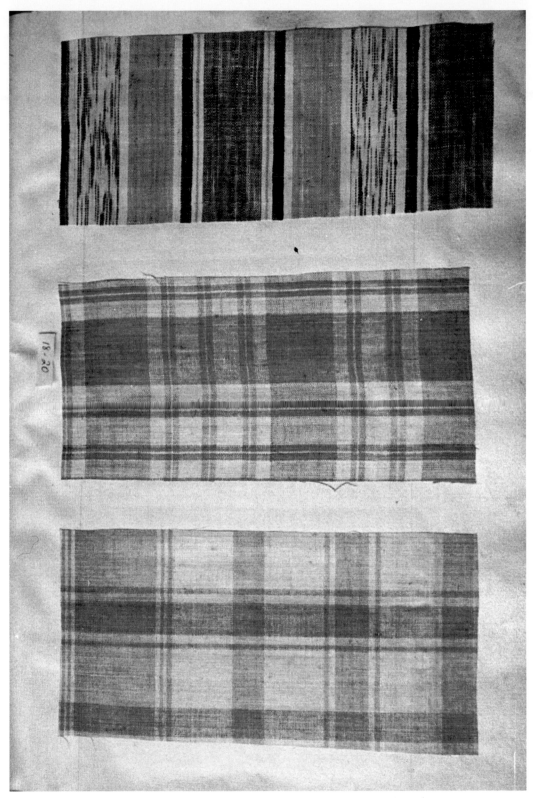

PL. D-29. *Swatches of linen hooping. From the Holker manuscript, ca. 1750. (Musée des Arts Décoratifs.)*

PL. D-30. *Silk and worsted dress fabrics called Irish stuffs.*
From the Holker manuscript, ca. 1750. (Musée des Arts Décoratifs.)

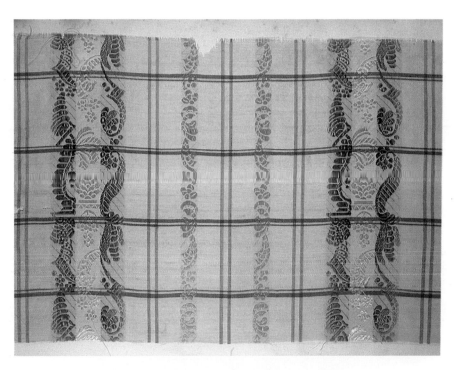

PL. D-31. *Messinet with stripes of yellow and brown silk.*
From the Holker manuscript, ca. 1750. (Musée des Arts Décoratifs.)

Pl. D-32. *Worsted "Scotch Pload".*
From the Holker manuscript, ca. 1750. (Musée des Arts Décoratifs.)

PL. D-33. *Samples of twill-woven worsted shalloon.*
From the Holker manuscript, ca. 1750. (Musée des Arts Décoratifs.)

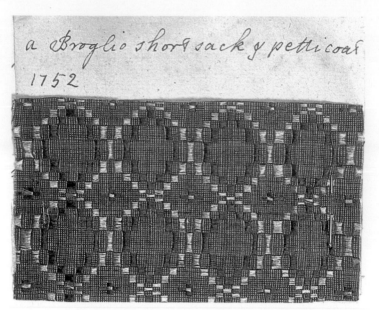

PL. D-34. *A swatch of broglio dated 1752. From the Johnson album. (Victoria and Albert Museum.)*

PL. D-35. *A swatch of fine taffeta with warp-faced floral sprigs shown with matching corded trimming. "A Laylock figur'd Ducape Negligee" was worn at the Stamford races, June 1767. From the Johnson album. (Victoria and Albert Museum.)*

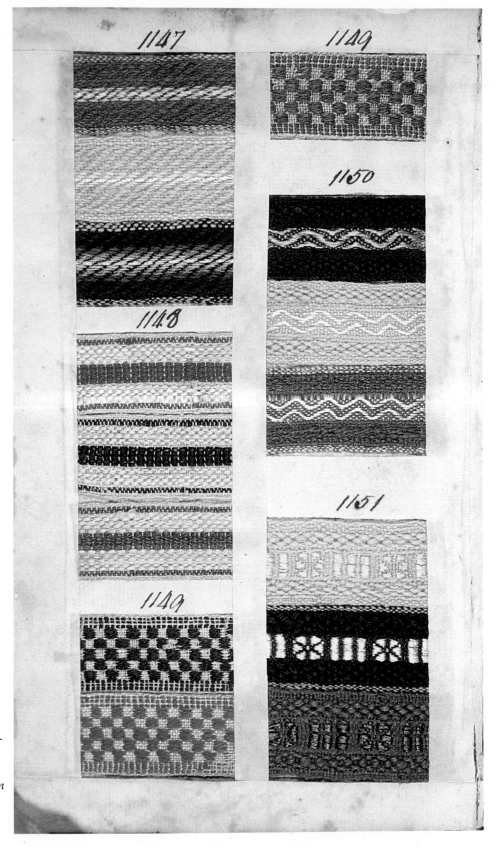

PL. D-36A, 36B. *The Hydes of Manchester offered "Garters, Quality Bindings, & tapes of all Sorts. Coat Bindings, Shoe Bindings, & Laces of all Sorts. Bed Lace, Livery lace, & Coach Lace." From a pattern book of Robert and Nathan Hyde of Manchester, 1771. (Privately owned.)*

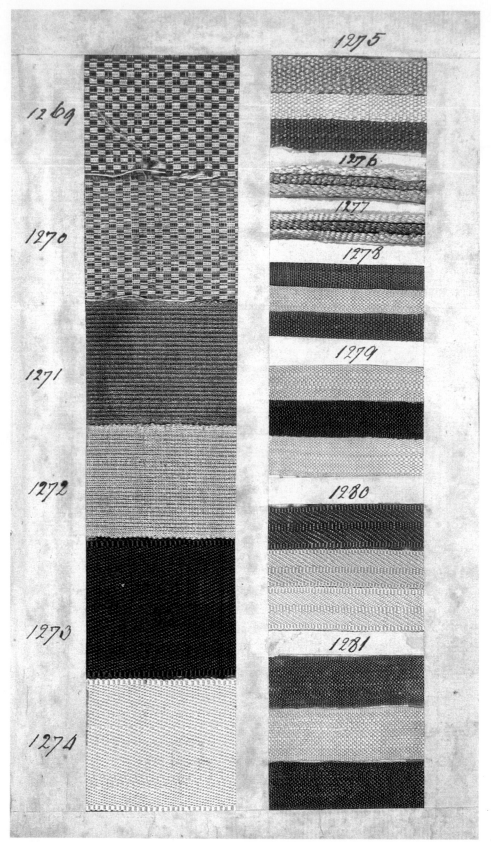

PL. D-37. *Block-printed cotton velvets. From a Manchester pattern book of 1783. (Winterthur Museum Library.)*

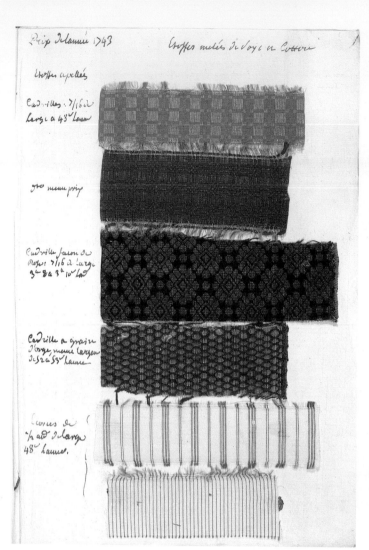

D-38

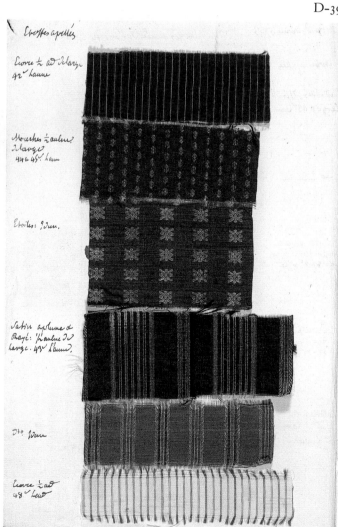

D-39

PL. D-38. *Swatches of silk and cotton checked patterns, a barleycorn, and two écorces (at bottom). From the Maurepas Papers, 1743. (Winterthur Museum Library.)*

PL. D-39. *Swatches of silk and cotton textiles with spots, stars, and feather-edge stripes. The top and bottom samples are écorce. From the Maurepas Papers, 1743. (Winterthur Museum Library.)*

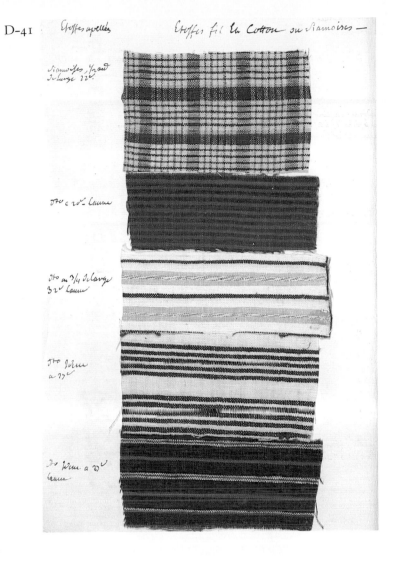

PL. D-41. *Swatches of linen and cotton siamoises made in Rouen. From the Maurepas Papers, 1743. (Winterthur Museum Library.)*

D-40

PL. D-40. *Swatches of silk and cotton textiles. The top sample is écorce; the others are draw-loom woven floral patterns. From the Maurepas Papers, 1743. (Winterthur Museum Library.)*

PL. D-43. *Swatches of linen and cotton siamoises made in Rouen. From the Maurepas Papers, 1743. (Winterthur Museum Library.)*

D-42

D-43

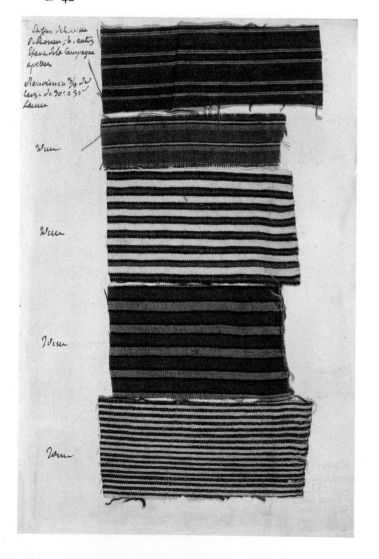

PL. D-42. *Swatches of linen and cotton siamoises made in Rouen. From the Maurepas Papers, 1743. (Winterthur Museum Library.)*

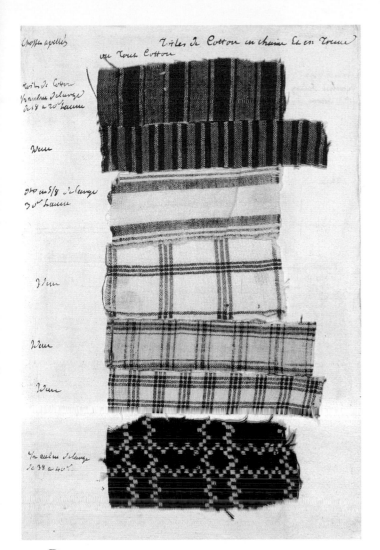

D-44

PL. D-44. *Swatches of all-cotton textiles made in Rouen. From the Maurepas Papers, 1743. (Winterthur Museum Library.)*

PL. D-44. *Swatches of all-cotton textiles made in Rouen. From the Maurepas Papers, 1743. (Winterthur Museum Library.)*

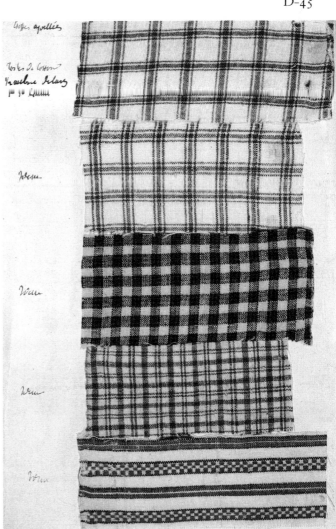

D-45

PL. D-45. *Swatches of all-cotton textiles made in Rouen. From the Maurepas Papers, 1743. (Winterthur Museum Library.)*

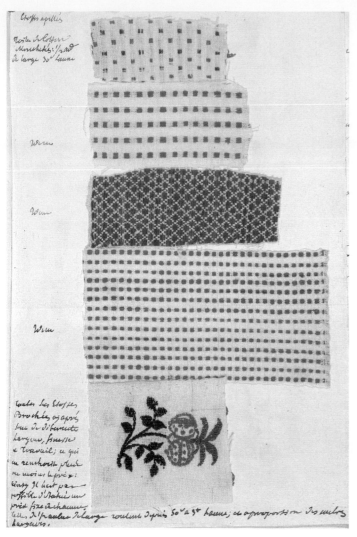

D-46

D-47

D-48

D-49

PL. D-49. *Swatches of English woolens of types used by the Spanish in Europe and in America. Included are four bays, sempiternum, scarlet cloth, and three serges used for lining garments. From the Maurepas Papers, 1743. (Winterthur Museum Library.)*

PL. D-48. *Swatches of linen and cotton textiles. The cloth, probably known as barrage, is brocaded in wool and was made in Rouen. From the Maurepas Papers, 1743. (Winterthur Museum Library.)*

PL. D-50. *Striped, checked, and broacaded Cha-moisa (siamoise?) made of cotton and colored silks. From the Moccasi manuscript, ca. 1760. (Bibliothèque Forney.)*

PL. D-51. *Cotton velvets manufactured in Rouen, ca. 1760. From the Moccasi manuscript. (Bibliothèque Forney.)*

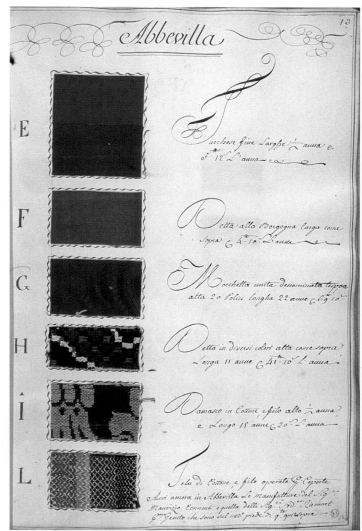

PL. D-52. *Manufactures of Abbeville: (E, F) Turchese; (G, H) moquette or trippe; (I) linen/cotton damask; and (L) linen/cotton diamond pattern. From the Moccasi manuscript, ca. 1760. (Bibliothèque Forney.)*

PL. D-54. *London woolen and worsted manufactures include (Y) amens, (Z) broglios, (A–C) camlets, (DD) duroys, (HH) serge, (II) calamancos, (LL) tammys, and (MM) everlastings. From the Moccasi manuscript, ca. 1750. (Bibliothèque Forney.)*

D-53

D-54

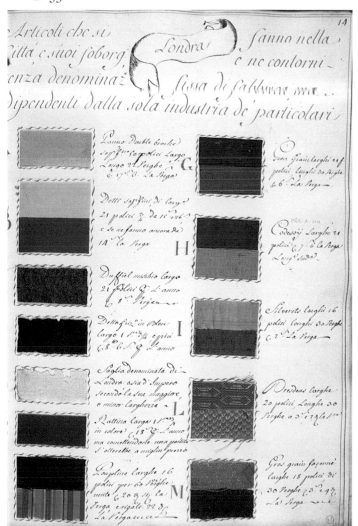

PL. D-53. *(A) Velvets, (B) duffel, (C) frized duffel, (D) serge, (E) ratteen, (F) poplins, (G) grosgrains, (H) codesoys, (I) silverets, (L) dresdens, and (M) patterned grosgrains made in London and environs, ca. 1760. From the Moccasi manuscript. (Bibliothèque Forney.)*

PL. D-56. *Manufactures of Norwich: (A) tapiza-doe, (B) brocade, (C) damask, (D) satin. From the Moccasi manuscript, ca. 1760. (Bibliothèque Forney.)*

D-55

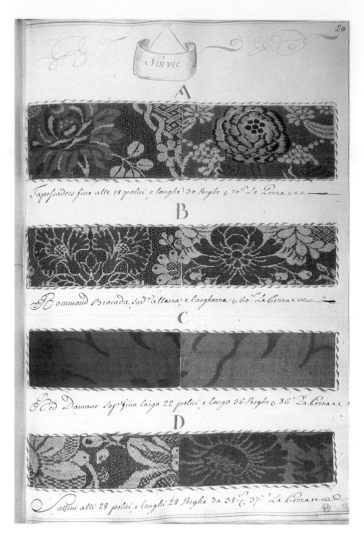

D-56

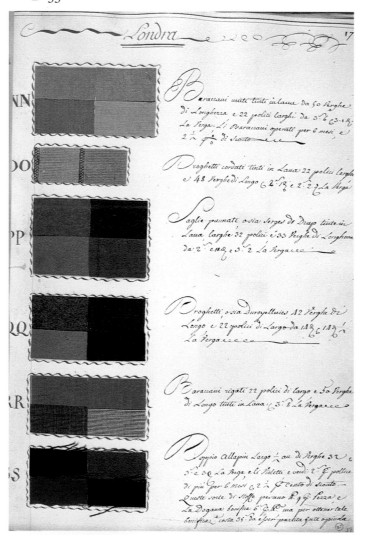

PL. D-55. *(N) Woolen barracans, (O) corded drug-gets, (P) serges, (Q) druggets or duroys, (R) striped bar-racans, and (S) double alapeens made in London, ca. 1760. From the Moccasi manuscript. (Bibliothèque For-ney.)*

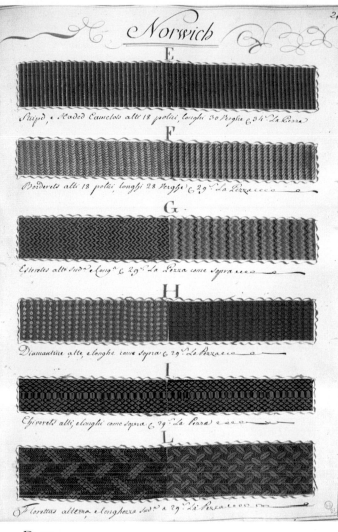

PL. D-57. *Norwich worsteds: (E) camlets, (F) bor-derets, (G) "esteretes," starrets, (H) diamantines, (I) cheveretts, and (L) florettas. From the Moccasi manu-script, ca. 1760. (Bibliothèque Forney.)*

PL. D-58. *Swatches of glazed Norwich worsteds: (M) taboratt, (N) Brussels, (O) belle-isles, (P) martiniques, (Q) blondine. From the Moccasi manuscript, ca. 1760. (Bibliothèque Forney.)*

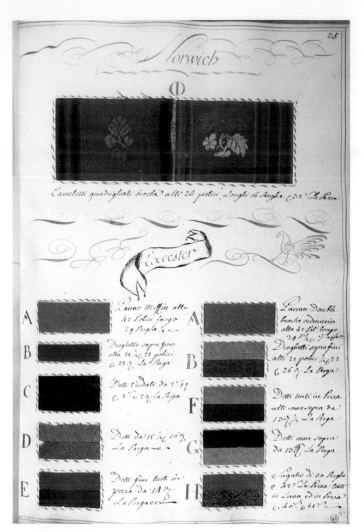

D-59

Pl. D-59. *Two swatches of Norwich worsted camlets and sixteen swatches of woolens woven at Exeter: (A) velvets, (B–G) druggets, and (H) sagathy. From the Moccasi manuscript, ca. 1760. (Bibliothèque Forney.)*

D-60

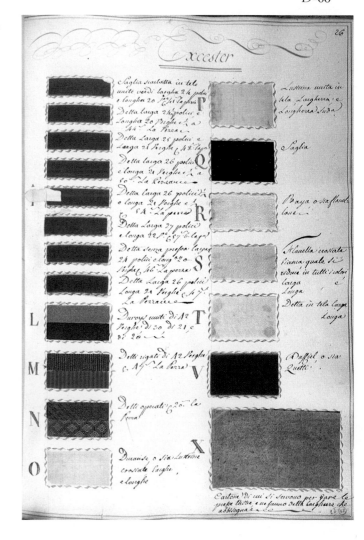

Pl. D-60. *Woolen fabrics made near Exeter include (I) eight kinds of red serge: (L) plain, (M) ribbed, and (N) figured duroys; (O) durance; (P) lustrene; (Q) serge; (R) bays, (S, T) flannels, (V) duffel, and (X) an example of the slick pasteboard used for giving woolens a fine luster in pressing. From the Moccasi manuscript, ca. 1750. (Bibliothèque Forney.)*

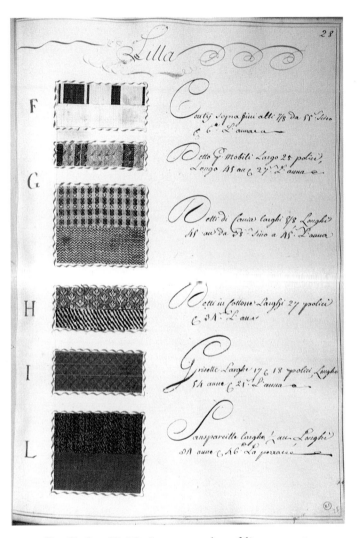

PL. D-61. (F–H) *Seven swatches of linen or cotton* coutys, *some intended for furniture;* (I) grisette, *small diamond-patterned worsted;* (L) *two samples of sans-*pareille *worsteds. From the Moccasi manuscript. (Bibliothèque Forney.)*

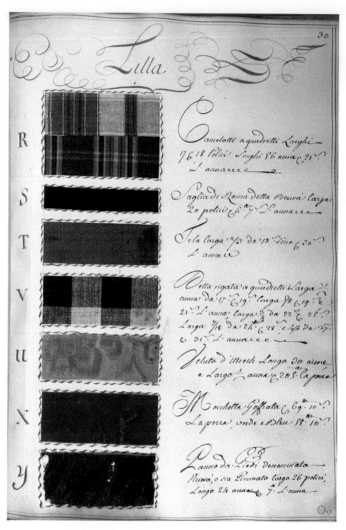

PL. D-62. *Manufactures of Lille: (R) checked camlets, (S) serge, (T) linen, (U) Utrecht velvet, (V) striped or checked linen, (X) stamped mockado, and (Y) velvet. From the Moccasi manuscript. (Bibliothèque Forney.)*

D-63

PL. D-63. Battavias à Dentelles, *floral and lace patterns, striped glazed worsteds. From a Norwich pattern book, ca. 1785. (Winterthur Museum Library.)*

PL. D-65. Callamandres Rayés à Flammes Fins. *From a Norwich pattern book, ca. 1785. (Winterthur Museum Library.)*

D-65

D-64

PL. D-64. Callamandres à la Reine Fins. *From a Norwich pattern book, ca. 1785. (Winterthur Museum Library.)*

PL. D-66. Camlettines Rayés et à Quadrille Super-fins glacés. *From a Norwich pattern book, ca. 1785. (Winterthur Museum Library.)*

D-66

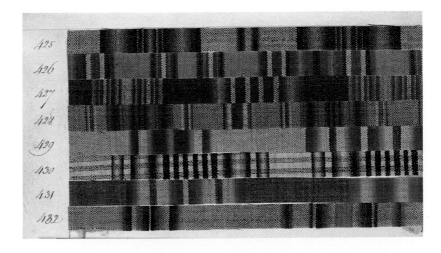

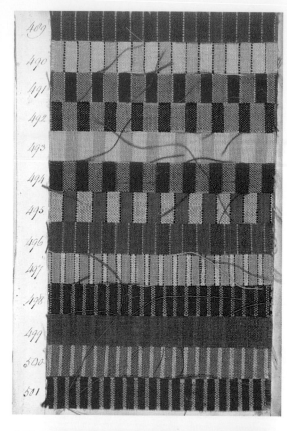

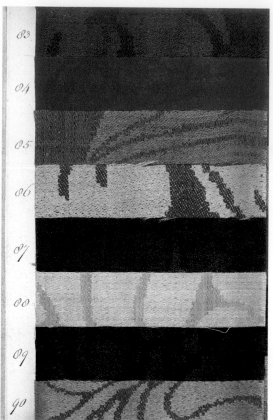

PL. D-67. Camlettines Rayés sans Lustre. *From a Norwich pattern book, ca. 1785. (Winterthur Museum Library.)*

PL. D-68. Sattins de lit très Fins, *or bed damasks made of worsted and highly glazed and pressed. From a Norwich pattern book, ca. 1785. (Winterthur Museum Library.)*

PL. D-69. Duroys Fins. *Diaper-patterned glazed worsteds. From a Norwich pattern book, ca. 1785. (Winterthur Museum Library.)*

PL. D-70. Fleurets Fins. *From a Norwich pattern book, ca. 1785. (Winterthur Museum Library.)*

D-71

D-72

PL. D-71. Grandines à
Fleurs Brocheés fins. *From
a Norwich pattern book, ca.
1785. (Winterthur Museum
Library.)*

PL. D-72. Mecklenburgs
Fins. *From a Norwich pattern
book, ca. 1785. (Winterthur
Museum Library.)*

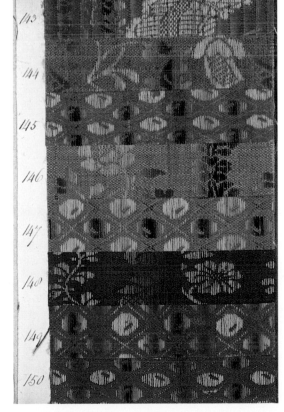

PL. D-73. *Swatches of worsted* Satins de lit Fins. *From
a Norwich pattern book, ca.
1785. (Winterthur Museum
Library.)*

PL. D-74. Tabourets
Nuancés Fins, *or taboratts.
From a Norwich pattern book,
ca. 1785. (Winterthur
Museum Library.)*

D-73

D-74

D-75

PL. D-75. Tabourets à deux Couleurs Fins. *From a Norwich pattern book, ca. 1785. (Winterthur Museum Library.)*

PL. D-76. Tabourets Rayés et Nuancés. *From a Norwich pattern book, ca. 1785. (Winterthur Museum Library.)*

D-76

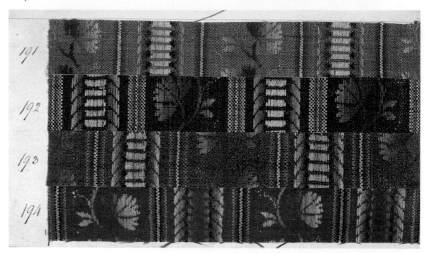

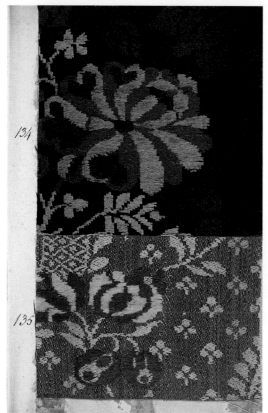

PL. D-77. Tapizados Fins. *From a Norwich pattern book, ca. 1785. (Winterthur Museum Library.)*

PL. D-78. "Fine Batavias." *Woven 16 inches wide in 28-yard lengths. From a Norwich pattern book, ca. 1794. (Winterthur Museum Library.)*

D-77   D-78

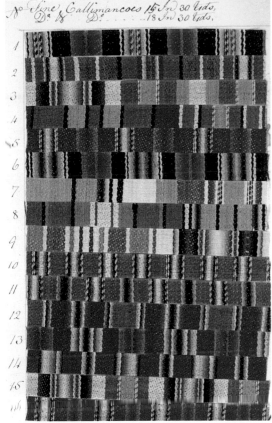

PL. D-79. *"Fine Calli-mancoes."* Woven 15 inches and 18 inches wide in 30-yard lengths. from a Norwich pattern book, ca. 1794. (Winterthur Museum Library.)

PL. D-80. *"Fine Broc[ade]d Callimancoes."* Woven 18 inches wide in 31-yard lengths. From a Norwich pattern book, ca. 1794. (Winterthur Museum Library.)

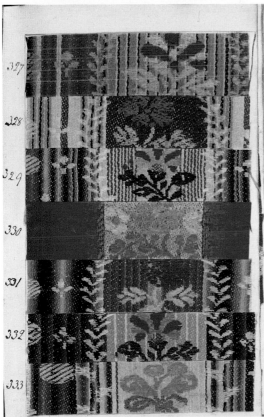

PL. D-81. *"Fine Calli-mancoes."* Woven 15 or 18 inches wide in 30-yard lengths. From a Norwich pattern book, ca. 1794. (Winterthur Museum Library.)

PL. D-82. *"Fine single cambletts."* Woven 26 inches wide and 30 yards long. From a Norwich pattern book, ca. 1794. (Winterthur Museum Library.)

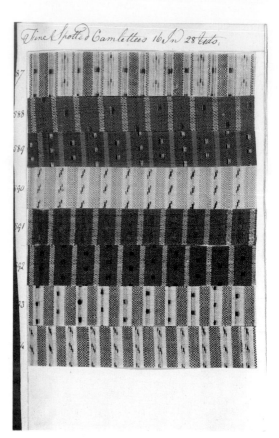

PL. D-83. *"Fine cheque Camlettes." Coarse worsteds woven 16 inches wide in 28-yard lengths. From a Norwich pattern book, ca. 1794. (Winterthur Museum Library.)*

PL. D-84. *"Fine Spotted Camlettees." Woven 16 inches wide in 28-yard lengths. From a Norwich pattern book, ca. 1794. (Winterthur Museum Library.)*

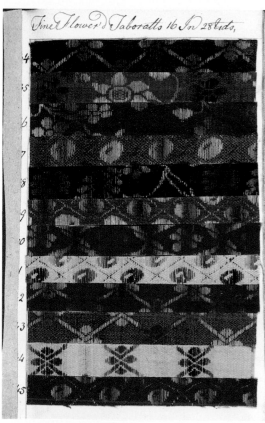

PL. D-85. *"Fine Flower'd Taboratts" woven 16 inches wide and 28 yards long. From a Norwich pattern book, ca. 1794. (Winterthur Museum Library.)*

PL. D-86. *"Fine Tappizadoes." From a Norwich pattern book, ca. 1794. (Winterthur Museum Library.)*

No. I. January, 1809.

The Repository

Of Arts, Literature, Commerce, Manufactures, Fashions, and Politics.

MANUFACTURERS, Factors, and Wholesale Dealers in Fancy Goods, that come within the scope of this Plan, are requested to send Patterns of such new Articles, as they come out; and if the requisites of Novelty, Fashion, and Elegance, are united, the quantity necessary for this Magazine will be ordered.

R. Ackermann, 101, Strand, London.

PL. D-87. *Rudolph Ackermann's selections included (1) plush made of mohair "for gentlemen's wear," (2) silk velvet, (3) brocade, or tissue, and (4) flowered satin for evening wear. From Repository 1, no. 1 (January 1809): facing 58. (Winterthur Museum Library.)*

PL. D-88. (1) *Fawn-colored luster for evening or half dress;* (2) *seaweed print on cotton;* (3) *merino;* (4) *cassimere of wool. From Repository 6, no. 35 (November 1811): facing 305. (Winterthur Museum Library.)*

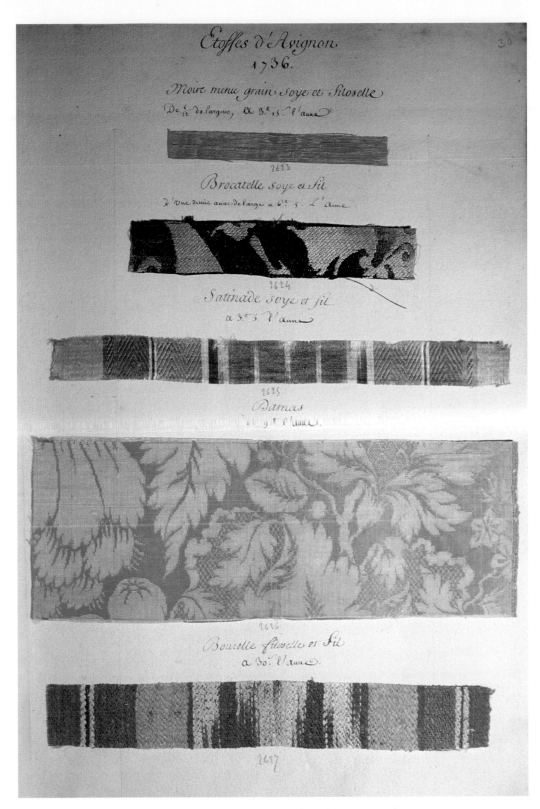

Pl. D-89. *Moiré, brocatelle, silk and linen striped satin, damask, and bourette on a page dated 1736. From the Richelieu Papers. (Bibliothèque Nationale.)*

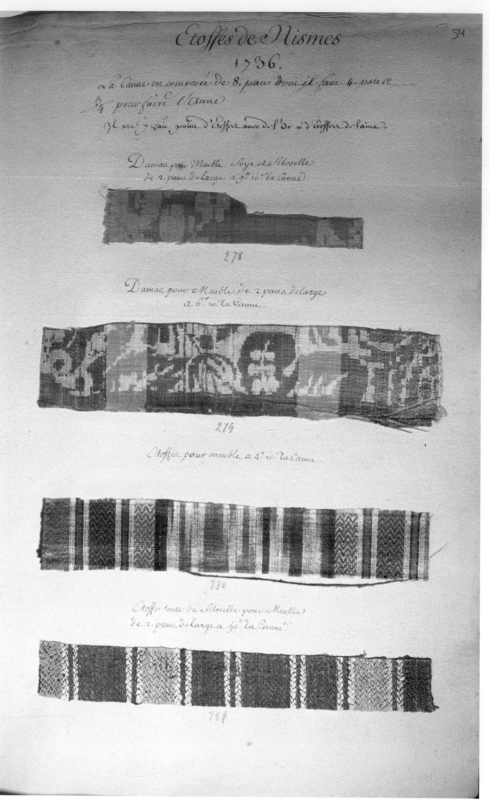

PL. D-90. *Low-grade furnishing silks made at Nîmes, 1736. Included are two damasks (part filoselle); a chiné, or shaded, stripe; and a stripe made entirely of filoselle. From the Richelieu Papers. (Bibliothèque Nationale.)*

PL. D-91. *Linen and cotton textiles woven in damask*
patterns in imitation of Indian goods, Rouen, 1737.
From the Richelieu Papers. (Bibliothèque Nationale.)

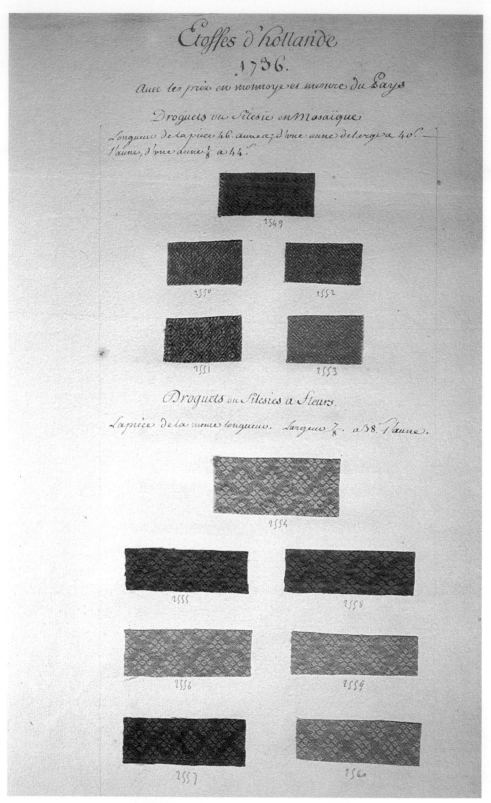

PL. D-92. *Woolen druggets or silesies from Holland, 1736.*
From the Richelieu Papers. (Bibliothèque Nationale.)

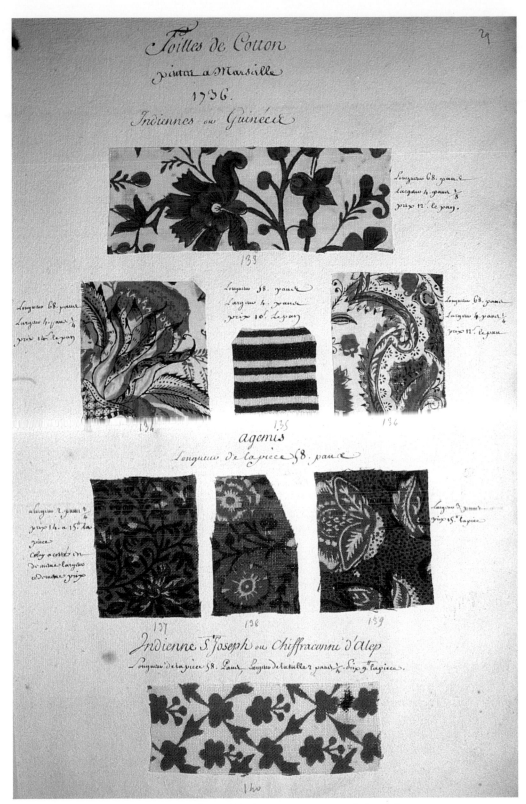

PL. D-93. *Printed Indian cottons exported through the port of Marseilles in the Guinea trade. From the Richelieu Papers. (Bibliothèque Nationale.)*

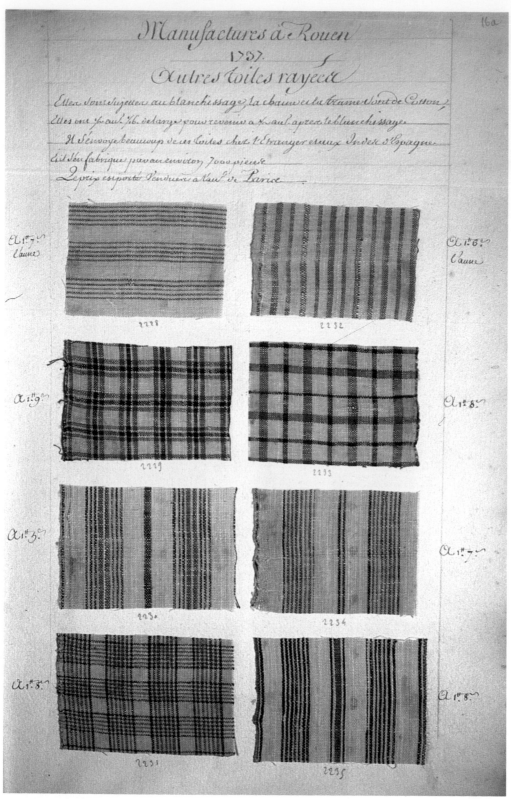

PL. D-94. *Striped and checked cotton textiles woven at Rouen, 1737.*
From the Richelieu Papers. (Bibliothèque Nationale.)

PL. D-95. *Cloth of linen warp and woolen weft, possibly darnex.*
This material was found at Chastleton, Gloucestershire, where
a 1633 inventory lists "dornix hangings." The flower slips
are brocaded in gold wool on the dark green ground.
(Victoria and Albert Museum.)

PL. D-96. *Florentines. From a French pattern book, ca. 1760.*
(Warner Archive, Victoria and Albert Museum.)

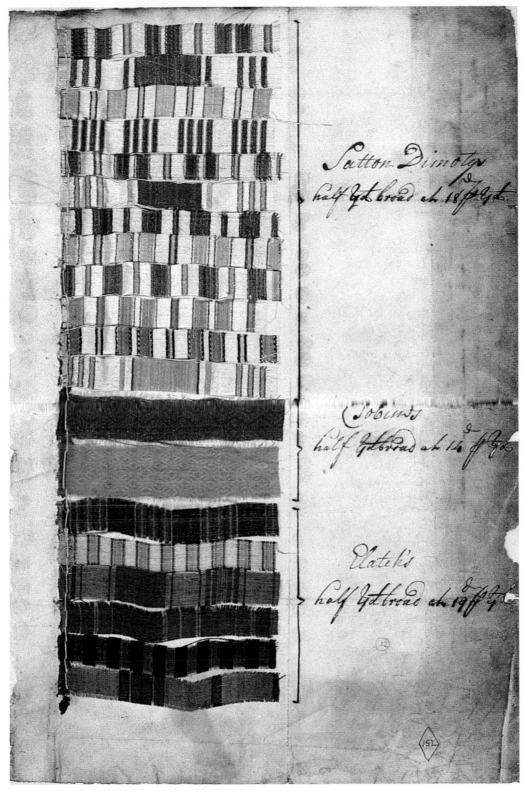

PL. D-97. *Linen and silk "Satton Dimotys," "Tobines,"*
and "Elatch's" made in imitation of imported Indian goods, ca. 1720.
From the Weavers' Company manuscript. (Public Record Office.)

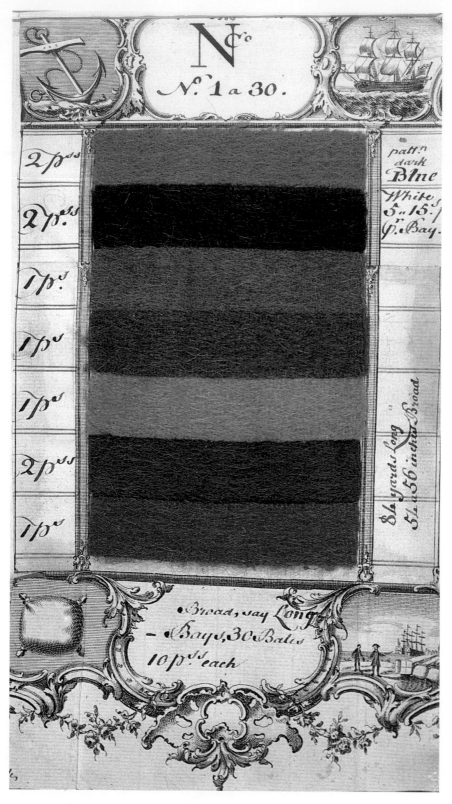

PL. D-98. *Swatches of "Long bays" pasted to an engraved*
pattern sheet. From the Yorkshire pattern book, ca. 1770.
(Collection of Mrs. George R. Stansfeld.)

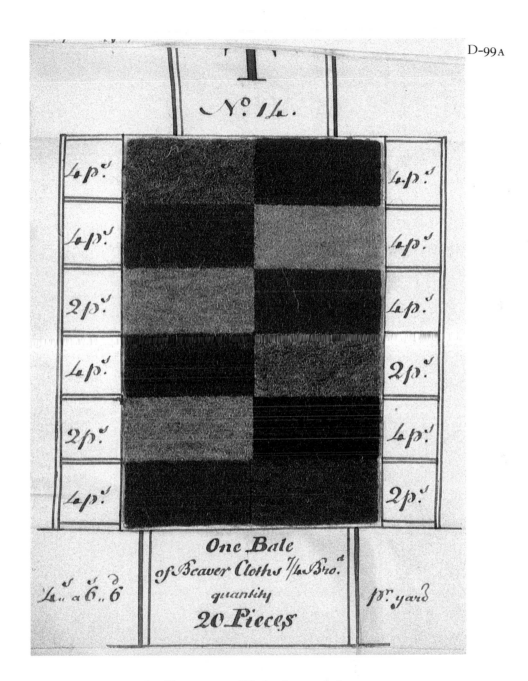

PL. D-99A, 99B. *Woolen beaver cloth.*
From the Yorkshire pattern book, ca. 1770.
(Collection of Mrs. George R. Stansfeld.)

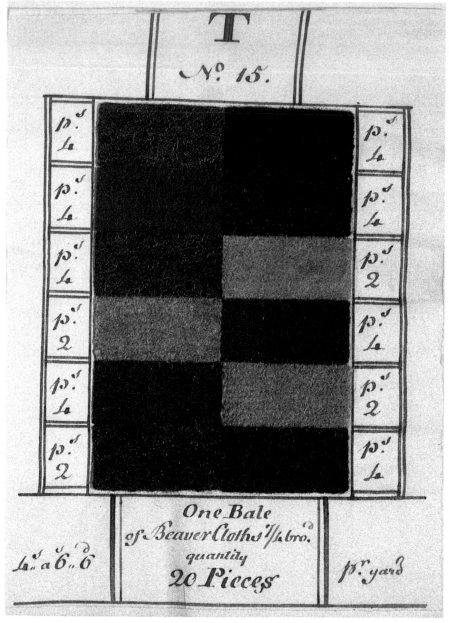

T

№ 15.

One Bale
of Beaver Cloths ⅞ bro.
quantity
20 Pieces

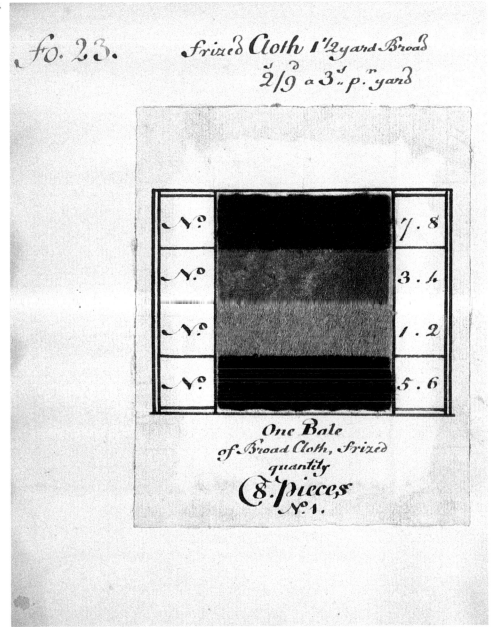

PL. D-100A, B. *Swatches of woolen frieze.*
From the Yorkshire pattern book, ca. 1770.
(Collection of Mrs. George R. Stansfeld.)

Beaver Cloth, for great Coats, 7/4 yard Broad

3..9.. a 4..p. yard

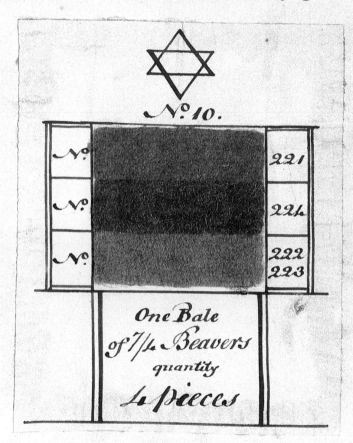

Nº 10.

One Bale
of 7/4 Beavers
quantity
4 pieces

fo. 58.

fo. 33 N.º 1 a 12

Everlastings, com. quality, but good sort
20 inches 30 yds a 39ˢ finished

fo. 34 N.º 1 a 6 Bird eyes
Large Figure 29ˢ small 27ˢ pˢ pᵈ
22 inches 30 yds

D-101A

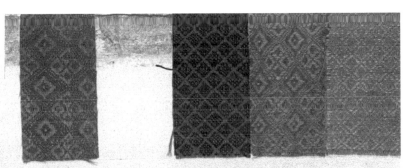

fo. 34 N.º 1 a 5 Fine Worsted Shags
16 inches Broad 30 a 40 yds Long — com. colors 2./2ᵈ pᵉ yᵈ finished

D-101B

fo. 14.   Broad Kersey, super Fine, 1½y.? Bro.?
the mo.t perfect Cloth made in this Kingdom. 27.s p.r yard

Spinning, Wool, and
substance, super excellent.

300

Honley Plains
27 yds Long 27 in: Broad

Italian Goods, that is, chiefly
sent to Italy

50   p.ces

50   p.ces

10 Bales
quant.y in each Bale
50 p.ces

fo. 32. N.o 301 a 316
Broad Cloths
sup.r Fine

18.s p. yard full ⅓ ½ Broad

PL. D-102 A, B. Broadcloths and kerseys.
From the Yorkshire pattern book, ca. 1770.
(Collection of Mrs. George R. Stansfeld.)

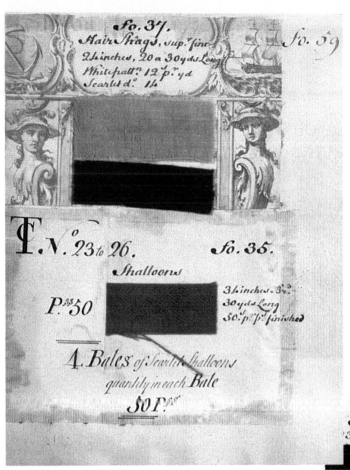

D-103A

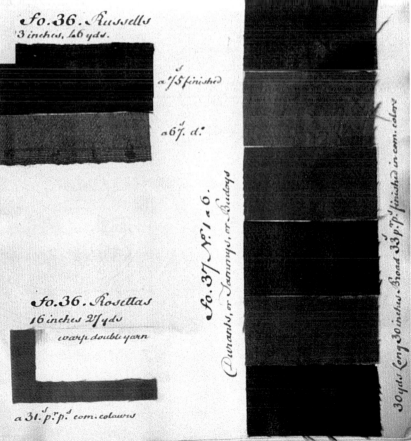

D-103 B

PL. D-103 A, B. *Worsted textiles including hair shags, shalloons, russels, rosettas, and "durants, or tammys, or budoys." From the Yorkshire pattern book, ca. 1770. (Collection of Mrs. George R. Stansfeld.)*

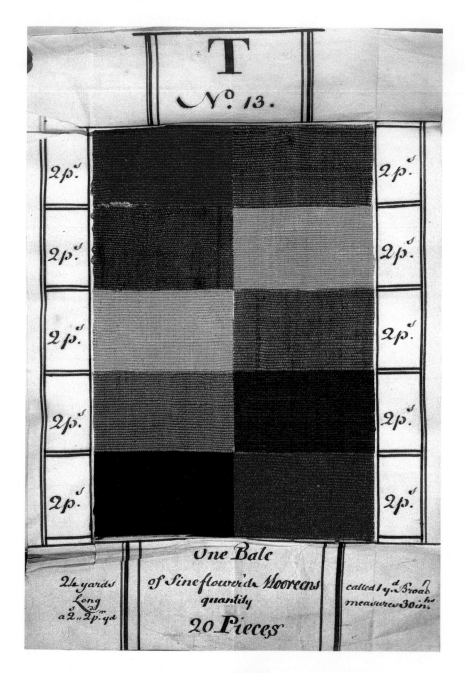

PL. D-104. *Swatches of moreen. From the Yorkshire pattern book, 1770. (Collection of Mrs. George R. Stansfeld.)*

Introduction to the Dictionary

The pictorial documentation for this book is based largely on manuscript sources which contain actual textile swatches pasted to their pages. The manuscripts, scattered about Europe and this country, contain contemporary names, dimensions, colors, prices, and manufacturers. Some were prepared by British agents acting for American merchants. Other accumulations, such as the Berch Papers (ca. 1750), were compiled by economists or historians. And still others were prepared by government officials interested in promoting textile manufacture within their own countries. These swatch books, merchants' records, and business papers are described, and the institution and place of ownership for each is given in the bibliography under a key word, for example, Beekman, Holker, Richelieu.

In the dictionary entries, a definition is given first, then chronological instances of the textile's use in England and/or America along with the manuscript in which named textile swatches were found. Many of the entries are illustrated with black and white photographs or in color. The color plates are arranged alphabetically by the name of the particular manuscript collection.

To find a word in the dictionary, the reader is urged to be orthographically imaginative, because not every vagary of spelling is cross-referenced. The reader is further urged to wander from word to word, for, in the interest of saving space, passages listing several textiles are sometimes quoted under only one of the words. For instance, a 1767 letter to James Beekman of New York documenting the importation of barley corns, hungarians, and prunellas is cited only under *barley corn*.

In order to unclutter dictionary entries from hundreds of footnotes, the author chose to use the bibliography as a reference tool. Therefore, within entries, sources are given by author and page; the complete references are found in the bibliography. When an entry refers to a dictionary or an encyclopedia with words arranged alphabetically, page numbers are omitted. Should a page number for a source seem incorrect, the book may be a different edition than the one cited in the bibliography; for example, there are dozens of editions of Daniel Defoe's *Tour*.

The cutoff date of about 1870 for descriptions in dictionary entries is somewhat arbitrary. Modern dictionaries give definitions for fabrics after this time. Entries to be found in *Webster's New International Dictionary,* second edition unabridged, are for the most part not duplicated.

Period dress was not an area of particular study for the author. The definitions of clothing materials were included in order to help differentiate them from furnishing materials. No special emphasis has been laid on needlework stitches except for a few employed for chair coverings and bed furnishings.

Fiber analysis of swatches posed problems because while traveling about doing research the author found it impractical to carry a microscope, and sometimes even the use of a linen counter for magnification proved to be too time-consuming. Thus, some fiber analyses in the dictionary may not be precise. Similarly, if a complete description of a fabric's structure is lacking, the reader should remember that in the manuscripts studied swatches are glued to the page, making it impossible to see the reverse. Many others, especially wools, are heavily napped. With small swatches and no selvedges, it is difficult to distinguish the warp from the weft and therefore to describe the weave.

A

ADATAIS
(adathaies, addaties)

"A muslin or cotton cloth, very fine and clear" imported from India (Postlethwayt). Used for furnishing (Havard).

ALACHA
(allegae, allejae, alligeer, elatch)

"Originally a striped cloth of mixed cotton-and-silk, commonly red-and-white or blue-and-white, sometimes flowered and embellished with gold and silver thread. Gujarat *Alachas* usually contained a higher proportion of cotton than Bengal cloth of the same name which sometimes led to their being classified as calicoes." Bengal alachas were "much in demand in Europe for petticoats." Alachas made on the Coromandel coast "were similarly striped . . . but made entirely of cotton." "Checkered *allejaes* are also mentioned. They do not appear in Coromandel trade before 1670, whence they were shipped to Europe as handkerchiefs" (Irwin and Schwartz).

In 1680 "Callicoes, Romalls Alligeers and other cours painted Callicoes [were] fitt for childrens coates and Necloths" (Baumgarten, p. 235). In London, silk, tick, and "taffachela allejaes" were listed in "An Extract from the Dutch Printed Cargoes of the Several Sorts of Goods . . . Imported from the East-Indies between the Years 1686 and 1696" (Kress S1994). About 1700 "Elatches 185, at 18s" were listed in "A Particular of the Silks . . . which came from the East India, . . . and were sold . . . at the East-India House" (Kress S2180).

Alachas were among the East India goods considered a threat to English cloth manufactures, and their importation was prohibited. By about 1720 English imitations were being woven, and swatches of six dark striped linen and silk alachas are in the Public Record Office (see Pl. D-97).

A Boston inventory of 1695 lists "3 handkerchiefs of allejars" (SCPR, 13:659). By 1711 other colors were used, e.g., "one Alejah Petticoat Stript with Green, Gold and White" (*Daily Courant* [London], December 29, 1711).

Alachas were related to charconnaes and were more substantial in texture than the generally flimsy doreas (*Hobson-Jobson*).

ALAMODE

A thin silk identified in a 1695 London broadside: "Silks were made in England, Time out of mind, fit for Hoods and Scarves, tho not then known by the Name of Alamodes and Lustrings" (Kress, S1866). "A thin, light, glossy, black silk, not quilled [corded] or crossed [twilled]" (Postlethwayt). *Taffetas noir de Lyon, appellés taffetas à la mode* (Savary des Bruslons).

From Boston, Samuel Sewall wrote for narrow and broad alamodes in 1690, and in 1693 he asked for "a pattern of good strong colour'd Silk for a Jacket, a pc of Alamode" (Letter book, 1: 116, 137). John Banister ordered alamode in 1739 from a pattern card or book: "1 Ps rich ½ yd black Allamode No. 14, 60 ½ Ells, 2 /" (Banister Papers). Although it was generally dyed black for mourning, James Beekman ordered "Sky-colored figured" alamode in 1766 (Beekman Papers, 2:769).

ALAPEEN
(allopeen)

A mixed cloth of wool and silk primarily used for men's clothing but also sold by upholsterers. In 1739 John Banister of Newport ordered "Cloth col[ore]d, blew, pink, scarlet and rose allopeens." In the following year James Alexander of New York ordered similar colors and, in 1760, changeable varieties in black / white, brown / white, brown / orange, and blue / orange.

"88 yds. Allepeen" were listed among the "Goods in the shop" of Thomas Baxter, "Upholder" of Boston in 1751 (Cummings, *Bed Hangings*), and in 1760 Blanch White of Philadelphia advertised alapeens for sale at his "Upholstery and Ironmongery warehouse, the Crown and Cushion" (Prime, *1721–85*, p. 219).

James Beekman's London agent explained its resemblance to poplin: "You order 2 pieces of Single Allopeens 30 yards long each at 105 / Maze[rine] Blue, and yellow Silk warp, which we suppose to be a mistake, as theres nothing of that sort of Goods made so high, have sent you 2 pieces of the nearest to an Allopeen of any thing thats made. and what we call here Irish Poplings" (Beekman Papers, 2: 534).

Four swatches of *Doppio allapin* (see Pl. D-55) and two of *Alopino simplici* made in London are included in the Moccasi manuscript of about 1760. Of silk and wool in plain weave, the colors are red, black, and two shades of green and white.

ALBERT CLOTH
(or cord, crape, diagonal, twill)

Names of coating, dress, and lining materials probably first woven or marketed in 1840, the year of Queen Victoria's marriage to Albert, prince of Saxe-Coburg-Gotha.

See also Coburg.

ALGERIAN
(algerienne)

A woolen furnishing fabric made in Algiers and imitated in France in the 1880s. Algerian stripe is a cloth manufactured in "alternate stripes of rough knotted cotton web, and one of a delicate gauze-like character, composed of silk. It is employed for the making of women's burnouses, in imitation of those worn by the Arabs. It used to be produced in scarlet and cream-white, as well as in the latter only" (Caulfeild and Saward). Used especially for portieres, curtains, and wall hangings and for covering divans and sofas (Havard). Those of wool with fancy colored weft stripes were used for tents, curtains, and awnings (Harmuth).

Clarence Cook wrote in 1878 that "The stuffs called Algeriennes, made of silk and cotton, in gay but well-harmonized stripes, are serviceable, and look well to the last; there are serges, too, but probably the prettiest coverings for cushions are the stamped plushes which are now made in England, with patterns and colors that leave nothing to be desired" (p. 67).

ALLIBANNEE
(alibany)

Of mixed silk and cotton, probably striped; imported from India beginning in the seventeenth century (Irwin and Schwartz).

ALPACA

A type of llama native to Peru. Its fleece "in its natural state is either black, brown, or white," and is "superior to the sheep in length and softness" (James, Appendix, p. 25; p. 452). "There is also a transparency, a glittering brightness upon the surface giving it the glossiness of silk, which is enhanced on its passing through the dye-vat" (James, p. 453). Combined with silk or cotton for the warp of cloth, alpaca yarn was manufactured into "an endless variety of goods suited both for male and female dress" (James, p. 457). The cloth was fashionable from about 1840. Four swatches of alpaca are in the *Journal of Design* for 1840 (6:107).

AMAMEE

Cotton cloth, plain weave, made from smooth fine yarns in Bengal. Three qualities including finer bissuti and coarser tissuti were made, and bleached, dyed, and printed varieties were known. They were used for shirts, bedcovers, and curtains (*Textile Mercury Dictionary*).

AMBERTEE
(amberty)

A kind of calico woven in several widths in the Patna area of India and exported to London, especially in the first quarter of the seventeenth century (Irwin and Schwartz).

AMENS

"A figured stuff made with double warp" (James, p. 363). "A species of fine worsted lasting, with warp cords and fancy patterns" (Harmuth). Its name was probably derived from the town of Amiens, France, where it was once made. See figure D-1.

In 1746 John Banister of Newport ordered scarlet, black, and cloth colored amens. The Moccasi manuscript of about 1760 contains two swatches of corded London amens in black and crimson and two of flowered amens in blue and crimson (see Pl. D-54). Other eighteenth-century swatches of flowered and figured amens, also called everlastings, are found in the Yorkshire pattern book (see Pl. D-101). One swatch of black German amens is a figured worsted to be used for the upholstery of chairs and sofas (*Journal für Fabrik* [August 1793], p. 117). (See also Fig. D-48.)

AMERICAN CLOTH

A plain weave cotton fabric produced in the latter part of the nineteenth century in many qualities and treated with colored mixtures of linseed oil and other materials to make it waterproof (*Textile Mercury Dictionary*). It was much used for cheap furniture covering and was often termed imitation leather. An enameled oilcloth much employed in needlework for traveling and toilet "necessaries," and "housewives"; "it possesses much elasticity, and is sold in black, sky-blue, white, and green, silver and gold" (Caulfeild and Saward).

A substitute for leather on "Cromwell" chairs (Eastlake, p. 81).

ANABASSE

Originally a blue and white striped loincloth made in India. It formed part of the cargo of African traders from all nations (Wadsworth and Mann, p. 126). "Commonly striped with blue and white equal stripes, about an inch broad" (Postlethwayt). In the early eighteenth century, it was imitated in the West, especially in Lancashire, and was described as a coarse blanketing probably made of woolen warp and cotton weft.

Fifty small and fifty large anabasse blankets valued at 24 and 28 stivers each are listed in the 1671 account and invoice of the ship *de Witte Kloodt* (van Laer, *van Rensselaer Bowier Manuscripts*, p. 796).

ANACOSTE
(Sp. anascote)

Twilled and with a short nap (Savary des Bruslons). "A woollen diaper stuff . . . generally sent white or black into Spain" (Postlethwayt).

Hondschoote says, first manufactured in a Flemish town of that name, were a light worsted cloth imitated in other areas of Europe where the

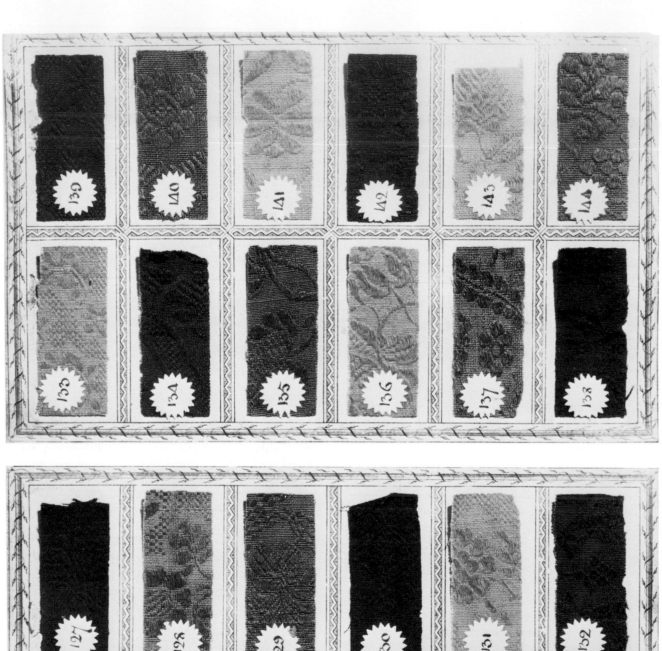
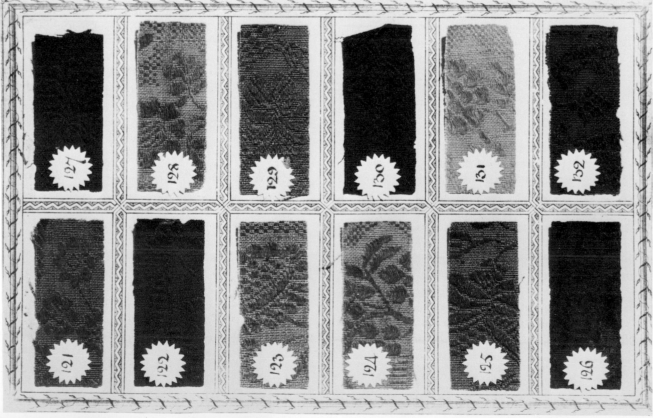

name was altered to hounscots and anascotes (Coleman, p. 426).

Anacostes are listed in one of the Maurepas Papers, circa 1743: "English wools which have the best sale in Spain and in the West Indies are . . . bays, sempiternums, scarlets, anacostes, white and black for religious orders, and wool serges for lining robes" (Lamontagne, p. 120).

"Fine all-worsted English dress goods, woven in a 2-and-2 twill with a weft face, as the number of picks is much higher than the number of ends. It is woven in gray and dyed in the piece" (Harmuth).

See also Perpetuana.

ANGLETERRE

Nine swatches of *Angleterre chang[ean]t rayé et en drillé pour robe et pour habit d'homme* in a French pattern book in the Warner Archive present striped, checked, and changeable silks in plain weave (Fig. D-2). The term may have been intended to suggest silks patterned in the English taste. No other reference has been found.

ANGOLA

At the end of the eighteenth century, every fashionable lady aspired to own a cashmere shawl. Soon manufacturers in Norwich, Edinburgh, and Lyons attempted imitations, not in the laborious twill tapestry hand technique of India but on the drawloom and, later, the jacquard loom. Experiments with various wool fibers were conducted, among them angora goat fur. *Angola,* a word probably derived from *angora,* is the name of one of these fashionable fabrics.

In 1810 Ackermann showed a swatch of "an Imitative Angola Shawl Dress of blended green and amber" (Fig. D-3) with a "shawl" sprig brocaded on fine woolen cloth of twill weave.

FIG. D-1. *Flowered and figured worsted amens. From an eighteenth-century folding pattern card. (Public Record Office.)*

An entry in the Great Exhibition of 1851, "a new and perfectly original fabric, made with weft spun from the down or fur of the Angola rabbit" was "exceedingly soft, and much resembles Cashmere" (James, Appendix, p. 22). "The warp is a fine spun silk coloured, and the weft Angora or Syrian white wool, which was thus thrown on the surface. . . . By adopting a cotton warp the same article is now made in England, . . . and it is found that the cotton warp as a mixture suits the goats' hair best" (Beck).

ANGOLA SHIRTING

Khaki shirting made of a mixture of wool and cotton in twill weave.

ANTELOON

Probably a woolen clothing material. Samuel Rowland Fisher ordered "10 drab Antilloons 33 / 6" and blue "antilloons" with pruncllas during his journeys to England in 1768 and again in 1784. Samuel Boardman's Wethersfield, Connecticut, account book of 1772 contains entries for light blue and "dark Colour anteloon" ordered by number from pattern cards.

ANTERNE
(anterine, antherine)

"A stuff of wool and silk mixed, or of mohair and cotton" (Beck). In 1695, they were a recent manufacture which "look as handsome as Indian silks, and serve as well in Linings for our Cloaths" (Cary, p. 57). The loss of "a light green coloured Coat and Wastcoat lined with Antherin of the same colour, with Mohair Buttons" was advertised in the December 30, 1699, London *Post-Boy*.

A long Boston inventory of expensive silks and haberdashery includes "56 yds. of Antherine" (SCPR, 13:670). "Antroine" was imported into Virginia in 1708 / 9 at 12 shillings a yard (Virginia Records).

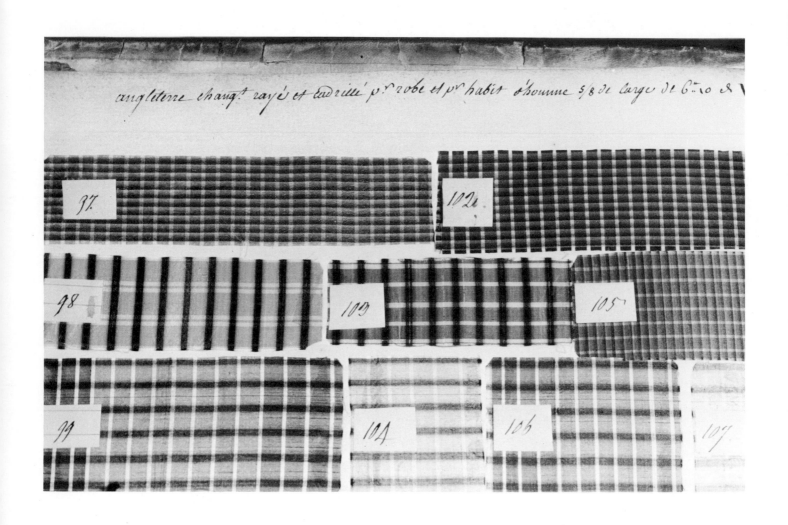

FIG. D-2. *Striped and checked silk angleterres. From a French pattern book, ca. 1760.*
(Warner Archive, Victoria and Albert Museum.)

FIG. D-3. *Among fabrics fashionable for the winter season in 1810 were (1) "royal embossed satin," (2) "imperial orange bombazeen," (3) "imitative angola shawl" pattern, and (4) "India rib [marcella] permanent green print." From Repository 3, no. 14 (February 1810): facing p. 130. (Winterthur Museum Library.)*

Anterne is listed among "Goods made of long wool, silk, mohair and cotton mixed" and "divers sorts of different stuffs both figured, clouded, spotted, plain and striped, too tedious to name" in *Observations on Wool* (1738).

ARDASSE
(Fr. ablaque)

Raw silk fiber of Persia. "Very beautiful, and hardly inferior in fineness to the Sourbastis. It is but little used, however, in the manufactures of silk stuffs at Lyons and Tours, because it will not bear hot water in the winding" (Postlethwayt). In Europe it was manufactured into embroidery silk.

Thomas Fitch ordered "Ardas and Sarsnet handkerchiefs," East India goods, from his agent in London (Letter book, January 11, 1726).

ARMAZINE
(armozeen; Fr. armoisin)

"A silk stuff, or kind of taffety, of an indifferent goodness. It is made at Lyons, and in several places in Italy." East Indian armazines, imported in all colors, were "slighter than those made in Europe and of an inferior quality. Their colours, and particularly the crimson and red, are commonly false, and they have but little gloss, and no brightness at all" (Postlethwayt).

In the nineteenth century, a heavier armazine with ribs was used for curtains, coverlets, and portieres (Harmuth; Havard) while "a strong make of thick plain black corded silk, a kind of taffeta" was used for "scholastic gowns, and for hatbands and scarves" (Caulfeild and Saward).

A 1656 New York order lists "1 armosine cap put in a hat; 3½ yds wide armosine ribbon at 5 st[ivers] a yard" (van Laer, *Jeremias van Rensselaer,* p. 24). A 1763 London advertisement lists "Rich Brocades, Tissues, flowered and plain Sattins, Tabbies, Ducaps, black Armozeens, Rasdumores, Mantuas, &c." (Beck), and "rich Armozed Ground Brocades" were advertised in New England (Earle, *Costume,* p. 65).

A swatch of white "¾ Armozeen" with a slight horizontal rib is in the Lord Chamberlain's accounts, 1754–59 (Public Record Office, LC 9/267). It is thinner and finer than a swatch of ducape pasted below it in the book. Both are in plain weave.

ARRAS

A kind of tapestry. The name of a town in Artois famed for its manufacture of these pictorial wall hangings. "Beautiful Arras-Hangings for a Room" were advertised for sale "at public vendue" in a 1745 *Boston News-Letter* (Dow, *Arts and Crafts,* p. 150).

ATLAS

"A silk-sattin, manufactured in the East Indies. There are some plain, some striped, some flowered, the flowers of which are either gold, or only silk. There are atlasses of all colours" (Postlethwayt). "The German, Dutch, Russian, Polish, and Danish word for satin is *atlas,* and Swedish *atlask;* but a silk stuff wrought with threads of gold and silver, and known by this name, was at one time imported from India" (Beck).

About 1690 at Windsor Castle "the late Queen Mary set up a rich Atlas, and Chintz Bed, which in those times was invaluable, the Chintz being of Masulipatam on the Coast of Coromandel, the finest that was ever seen before that time in England" (Defoe, *Tour,* vol. 1, letter 3). A London advertisement of 1712 specified "a purple and gold Atlas Gown; a scarlet and gold Atlas Petticoat edged with silver; and a blue and gold Atlas Gown and Petticoat" (Malcolm, p. 429).

A swatch of atlas (satin) is in the *Journal für Fabrik* (see Fig. D-27).

AXMINSTER CARPET

A woolen pile carpet (see Fig. D-4) woven in this Devonshire area is described as "a wide, high quality, hand-knotted product" by which "large

Fig. D-4. *Hand-knotted, seamless carpet probably woven at Axminster in Devonshire. (Winterthur Museum.) The pattern for the central medallion of peacocks was adapted from* A New Book of Birds (*London: Robert Sayer, 1765*), *pl. 1.*

seamless carpets like those of Turkey were first produced on English looms" (Nina F. Little, pp. 10, 13). The manufactory was established by Thomas Whitty in 1755. "The warp and shoot are of strong linen, and numerous small tufts of differently-coloured worsted are fixed under the warp and secured by the shoot. The process of weaving

them is tedious: hence the carpets are necessarily expensive, and the whole quantity manufactured is not considerable" (Webster, p. 255). In 1835 the manufactory was moved to Wilton. Machine-made Axminster carpets were not produced until after 1860.

B

BAFTAS
(baffetas)

"A generic term for plain calico of Gujarat [Western India] . . . , varying in quality from coarse to fine. . . . *Baftas* sent to Europe were usually white, but for Asian markets they were more commonly dyed red, blue or black" (Irwin and Schwartz). Baftas were among the cloths imported for printing: *On tirera de l'Etranger des Toiles en blanc, Garas, Baffetas, Guinées & autres de cette nature, pour les peindre ou imprimer* (Kress, S2123).

The word appears on the bottom of a printed textile of about 1775 in the collection of Henry-René D'Allemagne: *Manufacture d' indienne hollandaise de Christ-de-Vries, regié par Dubern et Comp. à Nantes, Bon teint. Baffetas* (D'Allemagne, pl. 56). The fabric was also used in France in the nineteenth century for furnishing: *on faisait des doublures et des tentures d'appartement* (Havard).

About 1745 in Newport, Rhode Island, John Banister ordered "1 Demy Chints Baftaes 6½ yds @ 21 / ." In 1759 James Beekman's factors wrote that they had "sent only twenty Baftaes, demy pieces, printed in England" (2:642).

A swatch of *Baffetas droguetté* of blue silk warp and white cotton weft in a small floral and leaf figure is in the *Journal für Fabrik,* November 1794. The author also speaks of *Baffetas satiné*—on a silk satin ground, "the cotton weft makes the figures."

"Figured Baftha" is in a scrapbook of textiles collected in New Jersey in the 1880s (Fig. D-5). In another of these albums, a swatch of the same cloth is called "Figured India Baftha." Similar coarse cotton cloths printed in red and brown are found as lining materials of several eighteenth-century quilted silk bedspreads in the Winterthur Museum.

BAIZE

A heavy woolen cloth, well felted and usually raised, or napped, on both sides. Dyed brown or green it is used for covering tables, especially billiard tables. Heaton, writing about 1900, noted a difference between bay and baize. "The bay was light, baize is heavy and with a long nap" ("Letter Books of Joseph Holroyd," p. 11n).

BALLASOR

A kind of Indian muslin used for handkerchiefs.

FIG. D-5. *"Figured Baftha from Mary Griscom, 75 years old or 100."* Coarse cotton
cloth printed in red and brown. From a New Jersey scrapbook made in the 1880s.
(Winterthur Museum Library.)

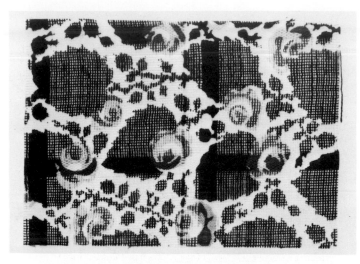

FIG. D-6. *Balzarine, black gauze with printed roses. From* Journal of Design *1 (March–August 1849): 117. (Winterthur Museum Library.)*

BALZARINE
(balzorine)

A light material of mixed cotton and worsted manufactured for women's dresses. Succeeded by barege (Caulfeild and Saward). Many qualities of balzarine brocades were produced on the jacquard loom by using gauze combined with figuring. The *Textile Mercury Dictionary* includes a picture.

Two swatches of balzarine are in the first volume of the *Journal of Design;* one is pink gauze with a pattern of berries edged in black reserved against the background; another is shown at figure D-6.

BANDANNA

"The rich yellow or red silk handkerchief, with diamond spots left white by pressure applied to prevent their receiving the dye. Such handkerchiefs are known in southern India as Pulicat handkerchiefs" (*Hobson-Jobson*). Bandannas were made of washing silk "a yard square, and were both plain and twilled, and kept their colours to the last" (Caulfeild and Saward).

John Holker's manuscript of about 1750 includes examples of resist-printed linen imported from France and said to imitate Indian textiles (see Pl. D-22). After 1800 in England, red or blue spotted handkerchiefs, imitations of tie-and-dye Indian cloths, were printed by the discharge method on cotton cloth. James Beekman placed an order in 1773 for "Spotted red Bandanna" handkerchiefs (Beekman Papers, 2:943). Caulfeild and Saward described the printing process: "A large quantity of Handkerchiefs, dyed Turkey-red, are laid one on the other, and pressed under a perforated plate, when a liquid is poured through the openings, which discharges the colour at those places."

See also Foulard, Indian goods, Lungi, Pullicate.

BARACLADE

The Dutch term for a woolen blanket exported to North America in the seventeenth and eighteenth centuries. Used for clothing as well as for beds (*Textile Mercury Dictionary*).

BARCELONA HANDKERCHIEFS

Handkerchiefs made "of fine twilled silk in plain colors, checks and fancy patterns" (Harmuth). Silk handkerchiefs were apparently made in, or exported from, both Bilbao and Barcelona in Spain. Both "Bilbo" and "Basslonie" handkerchiefs to the value of £37 were lost in the 1760 Boston fire (*Boston Records,* p. 38). James Beekman ordered black Barcelona handkerchiefs and "Cravatts" by the dozen at several prices and by pattern number between 1766 and 1774, as "12 dozen colloured Barcelony handkerchiefs" (2:932).

BARCHENT
(barshent)

"In the fourteenth century a cloth called 'barchent,' which like the English fustian consisted of a linen warp and cotton weft, was woven, and at that time found a widespread market. The early seats of the industry were Ulm and Augsburg, where the famous Fugger family rose to fame on the basis of barchent-weaving" (Daniels, p. 14). Later a strong, twilled cotton fabric, napped on the back and used for cheap dresses, linings, and underwear principally in Germany and Austria (*Textile Mercury Dictionary*).

BAREGE

A dress material of gauze weave with a worsted warp and a silk weft. In London's Great Exhibition of 1851 a prize was awarded in Class 12 (Worsted Stuffs) "for a great variety of light goods of the barege class plain, checked, and brocaded of excellent combinations" (James, Appendix, p. 19). The 1849 *Journal of Design* includes a swatch of "zephyr silk barège" (Fig. D-7). At the 1853 New York industrial exhibition, Abercrombie and Yuill of Paisley, Scotland, received a bronze medal "for the best printed barege long and square shawls" (Dilke, p. 26).

BARLEY CORN
(*Fr. grain d'orge*)

Any cloth woven with a small figure resembling a barley kernel (see Pl. D-38). In eighteenth-century references, the term was applied particularly to fine worsted dress materials. In New York in 1750, "1 ps Barlicornd Everlasting £6.18.0" is listed in Jonathan Holmes's account book (p. 15). Regarding an order for "16 pcs Checked Barle Corns handsom Colloured at 31 /" Thomas Harris of London wrote to James Beekman (1767): "The Hungarian and Barley Corn Stuffs and Prunellas could not be procured in the short Time I had, the Spring Orders having cleared the town of what were on hand before I received your Order" (Beekman Papers, 2:774, 776).

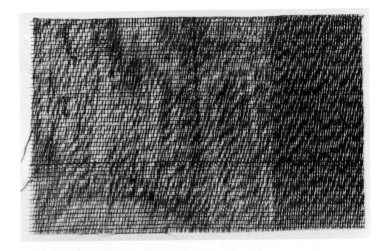

FIG. D-7. *Zephyr silk barege with purple silk warp and purple worsted and white silk twisted together for the weft. From Journal of Design 1 (March–August 1849): 141. (Winterthur Museum Library.)*

BARMILLION
(*bermillion*)

A kind of fustian. First imported from Holland and later woven in the Manchester area, especially between 1670 and 1700; "best white bermillions" were sent from Liverpool to Barbados in 1692 (Wadsworth and Mann, pp. 72n, 113n, 114). In 1650 "22 pcs Bermillions" were imported into Boston (Aspinwall Records, p. 415).

BARRACAN
(*baracan, bouracan*)

A worsted cloth of plain weave listed among New Draperies. "A kind of camblet, of a coarser grain than the common. Wove in a loom with two treddles. The thread of the woof is single, twisted, and spun very fine, and that of the warp is double or tripple. They do not full barracans; they boil them two or three times after they are taken from the loom, to prevent their fraying. Afterwards they

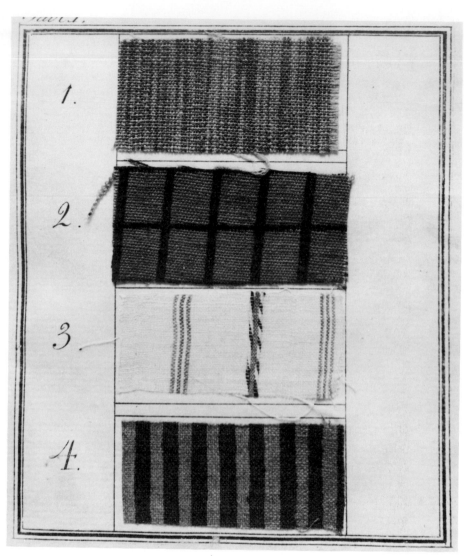

FIG. D-8. (1) *Flamed worsted barracan or camlet with rose and green shaded warp, green weft;* (2) *red worsted barracan with printed black crossbars;* (3) *English brocaded muslin;* (4) *blue and green printed cotton stripe. From* Journal für Fabrik *(February 1793), p. 120.* (Winterthur Museum Library.)

put them into the calendar, to make them smooth. Some are dyed in the piece black, red, blue or brown" (Postlethwayt).

Warp ribbed, as opposed to camlets with weft ribs (Roland de la Platière, *L'Art du fabricant d'étoffes,* p. 27). "Used for cloaks, great coats, and other outward garments, to keep off the rain" (Rolt). Probably the same as paragon but distinct from cotton barragon. The term *barracan* was used frequently in the eighteenth century while *paragon* was used in the seventeenth century.

"Worsted barrigons" were advertised in the *Providence Gazette* on March 24, 1764. In 1772, a proposal for printing by subscription "A Treatise on Weaving" was made by David Valentine of Suffolk County, Long Island. It was to contain "near 300 different Draughts, with full and plain Directions of the Preparations of the Yarn, Warping, and Weaving of Barrogan [here meaning a woolen textile], Tammy, Durant, Paragon, Duroys, Sergedenim, Grogram" (Gottesman, *1726–76,* p. 263).

The 1760 Moccasi manuscript shows London barracans (see Pl. D-55) and others made in Abbeville.

A pattern book dated 1792 at Castle Museum, Norwich, contains swatches in red, turquoise, yellow, green, purple, and blue, woven 28 inches wide and 28 yards to the piece. Swatches of barracans woven in Saxony, one of rose-green shaded warp and green weft and another in red with crossbars printed in black, are in the *Journal für Fabrik* (Fig. D-8).

BARRAGE

"A sort of worked linen made near Caen in three qualities" (Savary des Bruslons). "A linen interwoven with worsted flowers, fabricated in Normandy" (Mortimer). Patterned like silk brocades, these textiles were used for inexpensive dress and furnishing fabrics. They were known to textile dealers in the 1930s and 1940s as *toiles Normande*

and *toiles de Marseilles,* names that probably referred to places of manufacture and export.

Among mixed fabrics shown in the New York industrial exhibition of 1853 were mousseline de laine and barrage. Presumably both fabrics were made with cotton warp and woolen weft by the mid-nineteenth century (Wallis, p. 22).

Six swatches answering this description but without titles are in the Maurepas Papers (see Pls. D-46, D-47, D-48). Others are illustrated in Weigert (pp. 96–98).

A portion of a bed valance made of this material bears a history of ownership in the family of Jean Estienne Benezet, a Huguenot who fled to Philadelphia early in the eighteenth century. The linen-cotton cloth is brocaded with floral motifs in colored worsteds (Winterthur Museum).

BARRAGON

"A description of fustian of a coarse quality, strong and twilled, and shorn of the nap before dyed. It is a cotton textile, and is employed for the clothing of the labouring classes of men" (Caulfeild and Saward). It is not to be confused with barracan, a worsted stuff.

In Aikin's account of Manchester weaving about 1700, "the kinds of fustian then made were herring-bones, pillows for pockets and outside wear, strong cotton ribs and barragon, broad-raced linen thicksets and tufts, dyed, with white diapers, striped dimities, and lining jeans" (p. 158).

John Banister of Newport ordered "cloth collr" and "deep blue" barragons in 1742; and later in the century "Barragons of various figures and colours" were found listed by Earle (*Costume,* p. 53).

Barragons in John Holker's manuscript (swatch nos. 45, 46) are dyed in two shades of brown. He defines them as "napped cotton cloth used for men's clothing and dyed all colors. In the manufacture of these cloths, said to wear as well as wool, two warp yarns were spun together."

BARRAS

A coarse linen fabric originally imported from Holland. In 1696/97 Samuel Sewall wrote that "The Goods . . . are now pack'd up in course Barras, and Markt with Ink No. I. C.11. and left with Mr. Isaac Jones" (Letter book 1:181). Barras was purchased at 4 and 6 shillings by Willing and Shippen of Philadelphia in 1730, as were "2 ps Barras and Hessins." John Banister of Newport purchased "6 Ells Barrass" in 1743.

Three swatches of coarse striped barras "for Shades, Horse Cloths and Coach Cases" are in the circa 1784 Science Museum manuscript (see Fig. D-98).

BARRATINE
(barrateen, barutine, buratin)

An inferior silk fabric made in Persia. "A black barratine mantua and petticoat" were owned by at least one late seventeenth-century colonist in Boston, and "2 silke barrateene under coates" were listed in a 1677/78 Salem inventory (Dow, *Every Day Life,* pp. 71, 268). In 1697 a "baratine body, stomacher, petticoat and forehead clothes" were bequeathed in Philadelphia (Earle, *Costume,* p. 53).

"Buratin," a kind of poplin made of loosely twisted silk warp and coarse woolen weft, was not much used after about 1650 (Havard).

BATAVIA

A fancy French dress silk in twill weave which was fashionable in the 1760s. Nineteenth-century batavias were woven in "a four-shaft twill in all silk, of light make; raw silk, or grege yarns are used for warp and schappe silk for the weft. It is also known as Levantine, and is imitated in cotton" (*Textile Mercury Dictionary*).

Swatches of *Batavia rayé et cadrillé* and *Batavia broché* are seen in figures D-9 and D-10. A swatch book of silks prepared by the Swiss firm Martin Usteri et Fils about 1772 contains a page of batavias (illustrated in Schindler-Ott, p. 18).

The name *batavia* also was applied to swatches of Norwich worsteds in three pattern books in the collection of the Winterthur Museum Library (see Pls. D-62, D-77).

BATH COATING

See Coating.

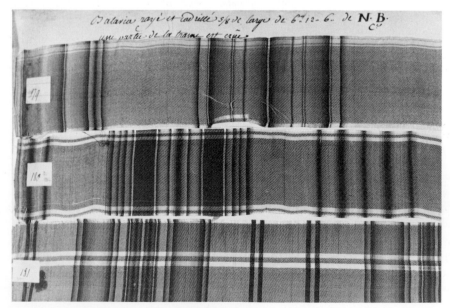

FIG. D-9. *Striped and checked silk batavias. From a French pattern book, ca. 1760. (Warner Archive, Victoria and Albert Museum.)*

Fig. D-10. *Brocaded batavia. From a French pattern book, ca. 1760. (Warner Archive, Victoria and Albert Museum.)*

BATISTE

See Cambric.

BAY
(Fr. bayette; Sp. bayeta)

"A kind of coarse open woollen stuff having a long nap, sometimes frized on one side, and sometimes not frized, according to the uses it is intended for; . . . this stuff is without wale, being wrought on a loom with two treddles, like flannel" (Chambers). Woven in England from the sixteenth century of worsted warp and woolen weft in plain weave; Colchester and Bocking in Essex were towns famous for bay manufacture, together with others in the West of England. *Single, double,* and *minikin* were terms used in grading bays. According to Beawes, "Bocking baise is sold by measure" rather than by the piece. They "are only fit for the Portugal Market; whilst the Colchester Baise [which were finer] are solely vendible in Spain."

Clothing bays were used chiefly for habits of monks and nuns and for lining soldiers' uniforms. "The looking-glass makers also use them behind their glasses, to preserve the tin, or quicksilver, and the case-makers to line their cases" (Chambers). "Much in use by cabinet-makers and upholsterers. By the latter, bays is used to cover carpets, and made to fit round the room, to save them. Bays is used by cabinet-makers to tack behind clothes press chefwood, to throw over the clothes" (Sheraton, *Dictionary*).

According to the Aspinwall Records, double, Manchester, and Barnstaple bays were imported into Boston between 1644 and 1651. The van Varick inventory of 1695/96 includes "41 yards freesd Baays at 4s 6d."

In 1704/5 Thomas Banister of Boston wrote to London about bays, inquiring "after a sort fit for the Indian trade without any Nape with a white stripe through the selvage. If you have any of that sort I have one Customer that trades to Albany that will take off 15 pieces as soon as they arrive . . . , but if you see Cause to send any of these they must be all blews. . . . Next the blews the red sells best and next the Red the purple." Later, Banister says that by bay he means "lo prized blew Broad cloth. And if you please leave out the purple. Those no body Chuses to buy."

On a trip to England in 1767/68, Samuel Rowland Fisher saw at Rochdale, Lancashire, red, blue, and green bays, "fine Drapery Bays & Great Quantitys of Flannels. They are made chiefly of Irish wool & Sent to London white." Red, blue, yellow, scarlet, crimson, and green bays were advertised in the *Providence Gazette* (October 17, December 19, 1778).

Like many other English woolen manufactures, by 1828 cotton was introduced into bay manufacture. "There are a great many baizes of which the warps are made of cotton, and their quantity is rapidly increasing; they are always exported; they have gone to South America for a long while" (Bischoff, 2:177). Writing about 1900, Heaton distinguished between bay and baize: "the bay was light, baise is heavy and with a long nap" ("Letter Books of Joseph Holroyd," p. 11n).

Four swatches of *bayette* in white, black, red, and blue wool, plain weave, made in England *à l'usage des Espagnols en Europe et en Amérique* are in the Maurepas Papers (see Pl. D-49). The Moccasi manuscript of about 1760 includes a swatch of Exeter *Baya osia flanella,* a white, coarse, napped woolen in plain weave (see Pl. D-60). Seven "Broad Bays" are in the Yorkshire pattern book (see Pl. D-98). Swatches of "Long bays" with a hairy surface in brilliant colors and thinner Lancaster and Colchester bays are among the mid-eighteenth-century Berch Papers.

BEARSKIN

"A coarse thick woollen cloth, with a shaggy nap manufactured for . . . overcoats, and very durable" (Caulfeild and Saward). "The articles in which low foreign wool, by admixture with low English wool, is used, are cloths, coatings, bearskins or calmucks, used for greatcoats and carpets" (Bischoff, 2:108).

Arthur Young describes Witney in Oxfordshire as being "very famous for its woollen manufactory, which consists of what they call kersey-pieces, coarse bear-skins and blankets. The two first they make for the North-American market; vast quantities being sent up the river St. Lawrence, and likewise to New-York" (*Southern Counties*).

Bearskin, dreadnaught, and *fearnaught* were American terms for an overcoating cloth of shaggy face (*Textile Mercury Dictionary*).

James Alexander of New York ordered twelve pieces of bearskin at 3 s., 3 s. 6 d., and 4 s. in 1746. In Boston, 1751, a runaway servant wore "a Bearskin Coat, the Body lin'd with red Bayes, and the sleeves with ozenbrig, brown Mohair Buttons on it" (Dow, *Arts and Crafts*, p. 199).

Samples of bearskin, made or dyed at Bean Ing, a woolen manufactory near Leeds in Yorkshire, are in William Gott's pattern book begun in 1815 (Crump, p. 54). They are mentioned in a Leeds directory of 1817 as "Latterly, a large quantity of fancy articles have been made at Leeds, as Swansdowns, Toilinets, Kerseymeres, and a thick, coarse kind of cloth, called bear-skins" (Crump, p. 53).

Eleven swatches of bearskin, dark brown and black heavy shaggy wools, are enclosed in a packet of letters dated 1804 among papers relating to the Nathan Trotter family of Philadelphia.

BEAUPERS

"A woolen fabric of unknown structure, mentioned in seventeenth-century English writings" (Harmuth). A linen fabric of the sixteenth and seventeenth centuries (*Textile Mercury Dictionary*). "Beaupers, the peece conteyning xxv yards" is listed among imported goods in the 1660 Book of Rates (Dow, *Every Day Life,* p. 246). It is also in the 1675 Book of Rates (James, p. 154).

BEAVER CLOTH
(or coating)

A stout woolen cloth with a raised finish resembling beaver fur. That known as patent double cloth was made in 1838 for winter wear; one side was coarse, thick, and warm while the other was very fine (Mann, *Cloth Industry,* p. 197).

Twenty-four swatches of woolen beaver cloth (see Pl. D-99) and three swatches of "Beaver Cloth, for great Coats" (see Pl. D-100) are in the 1770 Yorkshire pattern book.

At the time of the 1853 New York industrial exhibition, T. and W. Carr of Tiverton, England, received a bronze medal "for Patent Wool Beavers, impervious to rain, but perfectly free for perspiration," the Bay State Mills in Massachusetts received a medal "for heavy wool Beaver Cloth, the best exhibited," and August Haussman of Brandenburg, Prussia, received a medal "for fine Cloth for Ladies' Mantles, and fancy double Beaver Cloth; the Beaver Cloths are the best exhibited from Germany" (Dilke, pp. 26, 27).

BEAVERTEEN

Coarse cotton twilled cloth with uncut looped pile. One of the varieties of fustian related to thickset, moleskin, and swansdown. "Of a very soft and pleasant appearance, but is not so impervious to the rain as the barragon" (Perkins, 1833). A lighter texture of moleskin "dyed and printed and then perched on the back to produce a short and soft nap" (Nisbet, p. 139).

Swatches suggested for men's winter wear are shown in figure D-11.

BED

Worsted cloth made in three sizes. In a series of Allegations dating from about 1620, Norwich weavers stated the differences and similarities of certain worsteds as they had been evolved from the fifteenth century:

> The say and piramides may also be affirmed to be that ancient cloth . . . called a bed; the difference only consisting in the breadth and fineness.
>
> For further demonstration, the cloth denominated the worsted, and the cloth called the bed, for the fashion and working were all one, being both of the same draught in the hevill, and both alike wrought with four treadles, yet the one was a fine and a thick cloth, and the other a coarse and a thin, and differed

as much in vein, as a coarse buffyn from a fine piramides. [James, p. 144.]

It has been suggested that "the 'beds' of worsted were . . . the same as say" and that they were used "for curtains and other furniture, such as hangings for the walls" (James, Appendix, p. 4, p. 74).

Bed is also defined as "extra thick worsteds" and "say which served as apparrell" (Jenkins, pp. 28, 256).

See also New Draperies.

BEIDERWAND

A German term used for a type of doublecloth coverlet. The weave is a combination of warp-faced plain weave and weft-faced plain weave. Color and pattern reverse in this construction, as do the weaves. (See Davison and Mayer-Thurman, p. 66; Burnham, pp. 152, 197; Burnham and Burnham, p. 326.)

BELELAIS
(belelacs)

A "silk textile made in Bengal in the manner of taffeta" (Savary des Bruslons). A silk poplin (*Textile Mercury Dictionary*).

BELLADINE

A coarse quality of raw silk "of a very rough nature, yet superior to all for durability" (March, p. 10). "A kind of raw silk which the Levant or Turkey merchants call white silk, and our workmen belladine" (Postlethwayt).

References to belladine as a sewing silk are found for 1746 and 1753: "Three pound of Ballindine all Blew Sewing Silk done up in half pound [skeins], 3 pounds all Black Do., 3 pounds all white Do." and "the Sewing silk was bengall as you desired. belladine would have been finer, but also dearer" (Beekman Papers, 1:12; 2:528); brown, scarlet, green, and crow were other colors ordered.

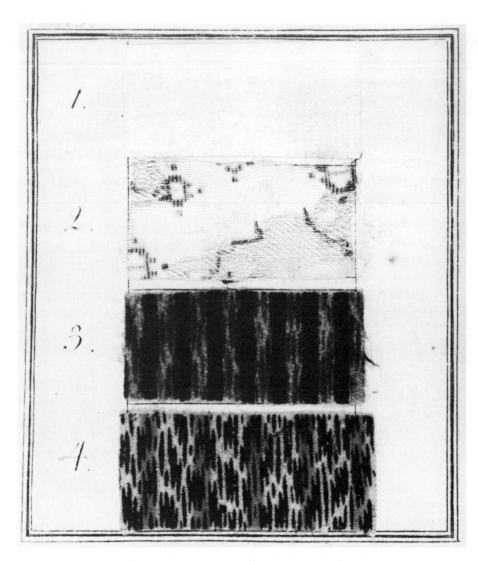

Fig. D-11. (1) *Baffin royal, a linen damask suggested for women's negli-*
gees; (2) a half silk from Lyons with printed blue figures for dresses; (3, 4)
printed Manchester beaverteen. From Journal für Fabrik (*October 1793*),
p. 239. (Winterthur Museum Library.)

BELLE-ISLES

One of the fancy eighteenth-century glazed worsted dress fabrics largely manufactured in Norwich. A swatch with weft float floral sprays in white on shaded warp stripes in brilliant colors is in the Moccasi manuscript of about 1760 (see Pl. D-58). Another swatch is in John Kelly's 1767 pattern book of Norwich worsteds (Fig. D-12). Similar to martinique.

BELZEMINES

Known from twenty-eight swatches as linen silk, watered and striped dress goods. In the letter from Nîmes dated 1750 which accompanies the samples, they are described as *Belzemines ou petite moire* (Fig. D-13). Arthur Young translated the term into "belmozeen," for he described the Duke of Bedford's French bedchamber at Woburn Abbey as "exceedingly elegant; the bed and hangings a very rich belmozeen silk" (*Tour through the North of England*, 1:24). The dressing room was hung with the same cloth.

BENGAL
(*Bengal stripe*)

Any of a variety of goods exported from that region of India. With the restoration of the monarchy in England (1660) and the spread of the fashion for wearing silks and fine muslin, the demand for Bengal textiles increased rapidly, reaching its peak in the 1790s. Europe welcomed Bengal silk goods for their cheapness rather than for quality. Many were of mixed cotton and silk, usually striped. Embroidered muslin piece goods and plain cotton muslins were also imported from the area.

In *The Ancient Trades Decayed, Repaired Again* (1678), we read: "And sometimes is used a *Bangale,* that is brought from India, both for lynings to coats, and for petticoats too; yet our English ware is better and cheaper than this, only it is thinner for the summer" (as quoted in Edward Baines, p. 77). In London, 1680, "Bengalls and Painted Callicoes [were] used for Hanging of Rooms" (OED). In *An Essay on the East India Trade* (1696) Davenant stated, "Tis granted that Bengals and stain'd Callicoes, and other East India Goods, do hinder the Consumption of Norwich stuffs . . ." (p. 31; *Hobson-Jobson*).

For "India Sales at the Store of E. H. Derby, Esq." in Salem, the cargo of the brig *Henry* was divided into Bengal and Madras goods (*Providence Gazette* [February-April 1791]). For Bengals, the following are listed:

> Baftas, sannas, and Cassas—White Cloths proper for Shirting and Sheeting

Fig. D-12. *Worsted belle-isle attached to a page showing the price of warp, shoot, and the various processes in weaving, dyeing, and finishing a piece 32 yards long, 18 inches wide. From John Kelly's pattern book, Norwich, 1767. (Victoria and Albert Museum.)*

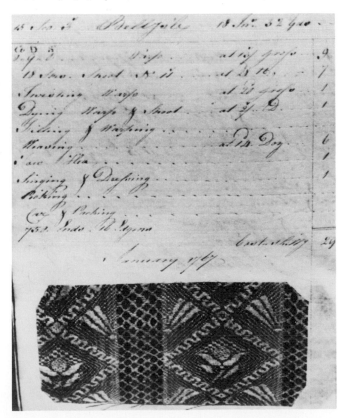

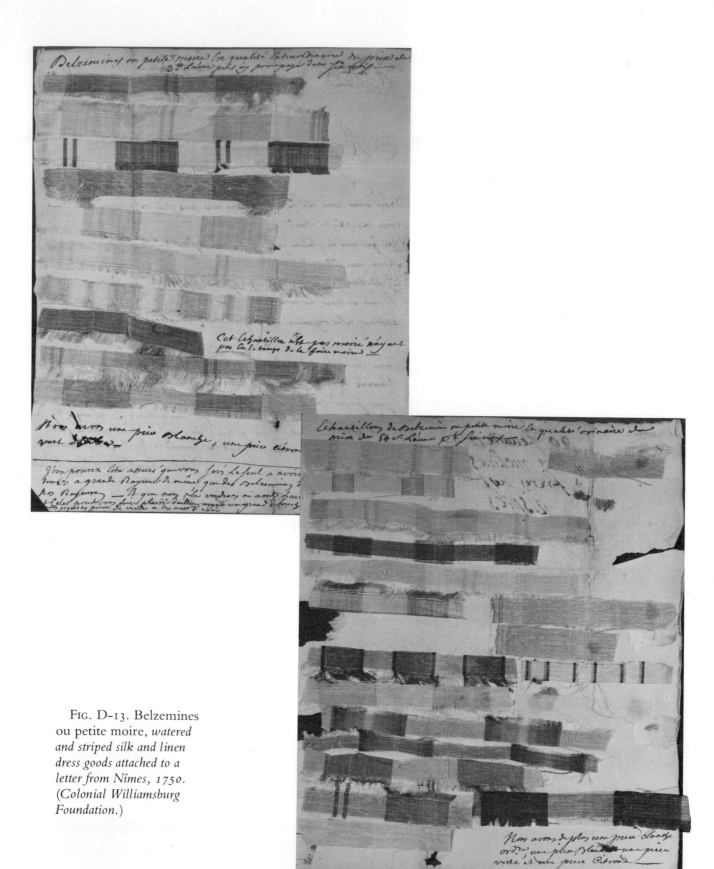

Fig. D-13. Belzemines ou petite moire, *watered and striped silk and linen dress goods attached to a letter from Nîmes, 1750.* (*Colonial Williamsburg Foundation.*)

Dureas, or striped Muslins
Durea Chintz, or painted, striped Ditto
Chintz, a great Variety
Striped Cottons, Jasrenant Muslins, Ditto
    Handkerchiefs

Bengal stripes were striped ginghams from India. Later manufactured in the British Isles, especially at Paisley, Scotland. A great variety of printed stripes made in imitation of Indian cloths were produced in England during the early nineteenth century.

BENGALINE

(1) "A corded silk of Indian make, and possibly origin, slight in texture, manufactured in all colours, considered most appropriate for young ladies' wear in France." (2) "A French-made textile, exceedingly soft, and made of silk and fine wool. It bears some resemblance to poplin but has a much larger cord and more silk in its composition." (Caulfeild and Saward, p. 27.) (3) Lightweight dress goods, woven with silk warp and heavier cotton or woolen filling, forming colored cross ribs; the cheaper grades are all cotton; often also printed (Harmuth).

Bengaline is illustrated in the *Textile Mercury Dictionary,* and a swatch of buff and white *Bengales* is in the *Journal für Fabrik* (Fig. D-14).

BERAMS
(byrams)

A cotton cloth from India. In the sixteenth century, berams were famous as a superior white calico imported by the Portuguese from India; in the seventeenth century, they were "a coarse and inferior calico, usually dyed red, blue, or black for Asian markets" (Irwin and Schwartz). In the eighteenth century, there were "white plain berams, and others striped with colours. The white are about 11 yards long, and about a yard wide; the red are 15 yards long, and something less than a yard wide" (Postlethwayt). A 1727 source specified "some Surat Baftaes dyed blue, and some

Berams dyed red, which are both coarse cotton cloth" (*Hobson-Jobson,* s.v. "Beiramee").

BERGAMO
(bergamot)

A coarse tapestry or wall hanging probably first produced at Bergamo, Italy. Coarse linen or hemp background weave with woolen patterning wefts brocaded in flame (Fig. D-15), flower, scale, or other patterns.

Manufactured with several sorts of spun thread, as flocks of silk, wool, cotton, hemp, ox, cow, or goat's hair. . . . Rouen and Elbeuf, cities of the province of Normandy in France, furnish a considerable quantity of bergamos of all colours, and mixtures of colours some after the manner of the point of Hungary; others with broad stripes, worked with the figures of flowers, birds, or other animals, some with broad and narrow stripes, even, and without figures; others again, which are called China's and Scale's, because they are worked so as to imitate the point of China, and the scales of fishes. [Postlethwayt.]

For a discussion of these hangings, see Thornton, "Tapisseries de Bergame." For two examples of *point de Hongrie* in the Winterthur Museum collection, see Florence M. Montgomery, "A Pattern-Woven 'Flamestitch' Fabric."

BERLINS

Torn-up knitwear remanufactured into cheap woolen cloths. Shoddy and mungo also belong to this category of nineteenth-century goods.

BERLIN WORK

A canvas embroidery worked in worsted yarns copying stitch-by-stitch patterns printed on squared paper. Colored patterns, yarns, and canvas were imported from Germany. This embroidery was especially popular in the 1840s. *See* Pl. D-12.

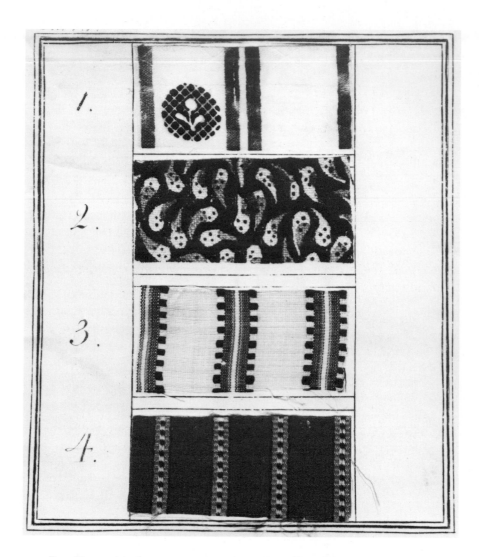

FIG. D-14. (1) *A cross-over (cross-barred and figured muslin) with printed brown stripes and a purple dot; (2) linen printed in purple and brown; (3) Bengal, a corded half-silk in buff and purple; (4) pekin, a corded silk. From* Journal für Fabrik *(September 1794), p. 231. (Winterthur Museum Library.)*

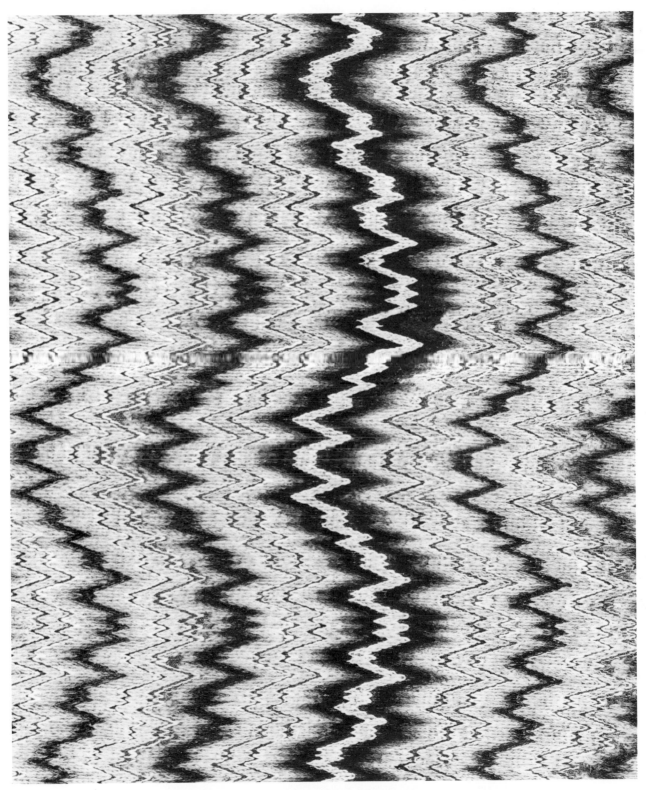

FIG. D-15. *Detail of a remnant of flame-patterned wool on linen tapestry known as bergamo. Made by the Duruflè family, Elbeuf, France, 1700–1725. Extra brocading pattern wefts make the zigzag stripes. The colors of the wools are mustard yellow, brown, dark blue, green, and rose. (Winterthur Museum.)*

167

BETILLES
(bethilles, betteelas)

Muslins, or white cotton cloths woven in southern India. "Betille is somewhat coarse; betille organdy has a round grain, and is very fine; tarnatane betille is very clear" (Postlethwayt). "They were sometimes dyed red, and sometimes striped or flowered with embroidery, [and they were] much in demand in Europe as Neckcloths. The fine grades were sometimes reinforced with thin wire thread" (Irwin and Schwartz).

Thomas Fitch of Boston had difficulty disposing of betilles sent him from London in 1729 (Letter book, June 4).

In 1815, Ackermann published swatches of "new Japanese bettilla muslins," finely woven white cotton with tiny cross-barred patterns, ornamented at the intersections with dots of lilac and bright pink. The colors were carried on the backs of the bars (*Repository* 13, no. 77 [May 1815]: 298).

Mortimer's later nineteenth-century description is of "a thick sort of muslin, the finest resembling cambrick, and the coarser being properly a kind of calico." Harmuth described East Indian betilles as "loosely woven cotton cloth, with white stripes or white window plaids. See Allejeas." In 1915 betilles were "similar to an open texture Swiss muslin; used for waists, etc., in the Phillippines. They come plain, striped, checked or figured" (Harmuth).

BEVERNEU

See Fustian.

BIELEFELD LINEN

In 1833, "the best sort [of linen] manufactured in Germany; and on account of its excellent quality, is preferred both to the Irish and Dutch linens; it is exported to almost every part of the world, but in particular to America. . . . It is exported again from thence to the West Indies and Spanish America in considerable quantities" (Perkins).

BILLIARD CLOTH

Fine quality woolen cloth used to cover billiard tables. In the Lord Chamberlain's accounts of 1755 are listings of billiard cloth "for a table Carpet for Sr T. Robinson's table, Whitehall, 8/4 wide at 20s p. yd" along with other green woolens for "Table Carpets and to Cover Desks," "7/4 wide at 12/0" and "6/4 wide at 10/0" and "7/4 wide Superfine at 24/ p. yd" for "Princess Amelia's Door" (Public Record Office LC 9/267).

A swatch of *Draps de Billard* in green-blue is in the 1807 Aix-la-Chapelle pattern book (p. 22). It is much like cloth found on billiard tables today and was finer and better finished than baize that was often used for covering table and desk tops.

BINDING

A tape or braid. Perkins's 1833 *Treatise on Haberdashery and Hosiery* lists:

> Binding, chintz—is used for binding white dimity and printed furnitures; and the following for binding bed-ticks and mattresses, viz. Blue striped,
> Do. Diamond, otherwise None-so-Pretty
> Common Quality, otherwise worsted binding
> Venetian—is a fine kind of worsted binding used as the binders of Venetian blinds.

See also Quality.

BIRDET
(burdet)

One of the Guinea stuffs, or brightly colored East India goods shipped to London for reexport to Guinea and the West Indies. In the eighteenth century, it was imitated in England in silk and linen plain weave which was given a pressed, or watered, finish.

Lost or stolen goods reported in London newspapers include "a yellow Burdet Coat for a Child of 8 Years old" and "one Sprig'd Callico Gown and Peticoat lin'd with a green, yellow, black and white Burdet and a Petticoat the same as the Linine" (*Post-Boy,* April 10, 1712; *Daily Courant,* October 9, 1717).

Thomas Fitch of Boston ordered "burdetts" with other East India goods. References to "Script & plain Birdet" (1737), and "very nice script Damascus and Chinese Burdet for Waistcoats" (1767) are cited by Earle (*Costume,* p. 57). "New fashion brocaded script Burdet" is listed in the Caine broadside (1754).

A swatch of deep blue silk-linen in plain weave with a watered finish is among the 1730 Alexander Papers. The letter to which it is pasted reads: "1 ps Dove Colour burdet for a tryal; 1 ps olive Do. If you can furnish these cheap I can vent a good many of them, of goodness of pattern annexed."

BIRD'S-EYE

Any cloth woven with a small figure resembling a bird's eye. An East India Company letter of 1662 mentions the inexpensive import: "We formerly received from your parts a Striped or Chequered sort of callicocs, called *Birds Eyes*" (Irwin and Schwartz). Samuel Pepys noted in his diary for 1665: "My wife very fine in a new yellow birds eye Hood, as the fashion is now" (6:102).

In Boston "Three Stuff Gowns, one blue, another green, and the other Birds Eye" were taken by a runaway Irish maidservant in 1751 (Dow, *Arts and Crafts,* p. 199). In 1755 "1 berd Eyd Silk Coat" and "1 Old berd Eyd Worsted Coat" are listed in estate appraisals (New York Appraisements, p. 36).

Swatches of "Bird-eyes, Large figure" and small figure in wool are in the mid-eighteenth-century Yorkshire pattern book (see Pl. D-101).

BLANKET

A white woolen cloth used for bed covers, petticoats, and heavy outer garments. Some were twilled and some were plain weave. Postlethwayt describes their ornamentation for bed covers:

> In order to adorn them, they work stripes of blue or red wool at each end, and a crown at each corner; with this difference, however, that the stripes are worked in the loom; and the crowns are worked with the needle, after the blankets are finished, and before they are sent to the fuller.

A crown motif of a similar sort with *G.R.* above it is worked in blue wool above the brown stripe of a blanket privately owned in Virginia. Others are in the Dr. Samuel Shaw House, Plainfield, Massachusetts; the Bergen County Historical Society, Hackensack, New Jersey (illustrated in Wheeler, p. 26); and Old Sturbridge Village (Fig. D-16).

FIG. D-16. *White woolen blanket with woven border stripe in brown and embroidered crown and G R in blue. The stitching is centered at one end. England, eighteenth century. (Old Sturbridge Village.)*

FIG. D-17. *Rose motif stitiched in colored wools at the corner of a white woolen blanket, probably imported from England, 1800–1850. (Winterthur Museum.)*

FIG. D-18. *Corner of a rose blanket worked by Betsy Reynolds Voorhees, early nineteenth century. (Montgomery County Historical Society, Fort Johnson, N.Y.)*

In the nineteenth century stitched stars or wheels were worked at the corners (Figs. D-17, D-18). Known as "rose blankets," they were commonly imported and have survived in American collections. In 1839 they were described as "blankets . . . generally sold in pairs, or two woven together. These, for beds must be cut, in which case, the edges are sewed over in a very wide kind of button-hole stitch, with red, or other coloured wool, also a kind of circle or star is often worked in the corner with various coloured wool" (*Workwoman's Guide*, p. 200).

Five rose blankets are listed in the 1797 inventory of Aaron Burr's home, Richmond Hill in New York City. In 1830, the bedding warehouse of John K. Simpson in Boston advertised "Rose Point and Duffill Blankets" for sale. A rose blanket with the date 1827 embroidered on it is owned by the Phelps-Hathaway House, Suffield, Connecticut.

The important trade in woolens with the North American Indians and the exact colors and stripes demanded by them are specified in a 1714 letter from James Logan to Edward Hackett:

> These woolens may be so far out of thy way of business as not to be fully known to thee by our names for them. They are 1st. Strowdwater, a cloth . . . blue or red, in purchasing wch a regard must be had not only to the Cloth and Colour but also to the list [selvedge] about which the Indians are Curious [exacting]. This is of the common breadth viz. about 3 fingers with a Stripe or two of White generally. Sometimes in black in ye blue pcs. and always black in ye red.
>
> 2ndly. Duffels of near ye same breadth without any List . . . of the same Colours with the other.
>
> 3rdly. Striped Blankets that are white like other Blankets only towards the ends they have generally four broad Stripes as each 2 red and 2 blue or black . . . they are sold by ye piece containing 15 Blankets for about 3 lbs 10/. [Kidd, p. 43.]

In the 1730s, "5 pr. Indian Blanketts, Black stripe," "25 Indian new fashion blankets," and "10 ps Old fashion duffels or blankets" were ordered by the Livingstons in Schenectady. James and William Miller of Philadelphia advertised that "they have on hand a variety of Articles suitable for the Indian Trade: consisting of Point Blankets, Strouds, Scarlet Cloths, ribbons, &c &c, which they will sell on reasonable terms" (*Dunlap's American Daily Advertiser* [May 14, 1793]).

An order dated November 28, 1805, from Hudson's Bay House, London, is indicative of the magnitude of blanket production:

Gentlemen,

Your Proposals have been received and acceded to . . . You will please to send . . . as early in March as possible, the whole Order to be delivered to our Porters on or before the 23rd of April next without fail . . . Please to observe wherever the Pieces are striped it means all thro' the Piece.

Blankettings
- 4 Ps. Red striped
- 20 " Green do
- 39 " Red & Green do
- 12 " Red striped, Broader, nearly as broad as two stripes of the above.

Duffels
- 2 Ps. White
- 11 " White, Red & Blue Striped
- 11 " " " " & Yellow do

1	Point	125 pairs		
1½	"	142	"	
2	"	151	"	
2½	"	225	"	
3	"	418	"	
3½	"	21	"	
4	"	15	"	
2½	"	17	"	striped Red
2½	"	17	"	" Blue
2½	"	16	"	" Blue, Red & Yellow.

[Plummer and Early, p. 66.]

Black "points" or stripes of a few inches were inserted along the selvedge to denote the barter price in beaver skins.

BLONDINE

One of the fancy eighteenth-century glazed worsted dress fabrics manufactured in Norwich. Three swatches with lace and shaded warp flowers on diamond grounds are in "Patterns of Norwich Manufacture, D. March, 1769" (nos. 336–39) in the Castle Museum pattern books. Two swatches of *Blondina* from Norwich are in the Moccasi manuscript of about 1760 (*see* Pl. D-58).

BOBBIN LACE
(*bone lace*)

A lace worked with thread wound on bobbins or bones. Patterns are produced by entwining threads around pins pierced into a cushion.

BOCASINE
(*bugasin, bugazeen; Fr. boucassin*)

A heavily gummed cloth like buckram used to stiffen and give body to furnishing materials or to clothing. "Bugasines or Callico Buckrams" are listed among imports in the 1660 Book of Rates (Dow, *Every Day Life*, p. 247).

BOCKING

See Bay.

BOLTING
(*boulting*)

Fine worsted cloth used for sifting meal (James, p. 229). The stiff, transparent fabric made of silk in the gum was used for fine sifting in flour mills, for making stencils, and for wig foundations. The term is derived from *bolter*, "a sieve" (*Textile Mercury Dictionary*).

Candace Wheeler used the material for bed hangings commissioned by Lily Langtry:

I suggested a canopy of our strong, gauze-like, creamy silk bolting-cloth, the tissue used in flour mills for sifting the superfine flour. I explained that the canopy could be crossed on the under side with loops of full-blown, sunset-colored roses, and the hanging border heaped with them. That there might be a coverlet of bolting-cloth lined with the delicatest shade of rose-pink satin, sprinkled plentifully with rose petals fallen from the wreaths above. . . . The scattered petals were true portraits done from nature, and looked as though they could be shaken off at any minute. [P. 123.]

BOLTON COVERLET
(or counterpane)

All-white cotton woven with geometrical figures in a looped-pile technique. Some have looped fringe in both inner and outer borders and weavers' or owners' initials and dates.

In his 1767 journal, Samuel Rowland Fisher noted "At Bolton about 12 Miles from Manchester are Woven Cotton Quilts, the same as those done with a Needle and very neat, 65/ to 75/, 12/4th or 3 yds. Square."

Jeremiah Fitch's advertisement seems to describe these coverlets: "English Goods, Cotton counterpanes, some very elegant patterns with and without festoon fringes" (*Palladium* [Boston], May 18, 1810).

Many Bolton coverlets dating from the early nineteenth century are found in American collections. A documented example bearing the name *Col. Henry Rutgers* and the date *1822* was woven in Paterson, New Jersey (illustrated in Schwartz, p. 331). Another example, in a private collection, is woven in a single breadth with the letters of the alphabet and "Philadelphia 1825" woven into the bottom edge. Other examples, probably all imported from Bolton, are found in the Winterthur Museum (Fig. D-19); the John Brown House, Providence, circa 1800; Colonial Williamsburg (this circa 1800 coverlet has pile in two levels); and the Royal Ontario Museum (Fig. D-20); five in the Metropolitan Museum of Art.

The *Textile Mercury Dictionary* describes the weaving technique at "Caddow," a local trade name for coverlets made at Bolton: "Loops are formed in some arranged design. The warp is controlled by two shafts; 2 picks of a fine ground weft are woven in, and then one very thick pick is inserted for figuring. This is pulled into loops." A mid-nineteenth-century pattern for a counterpane of this type is shown and the weaving technique described on page 85 of the Great Exhibition catalogue.

BOMBAZET

Worsted cloth resembling bombazine which could be twill or plain weave and was finished without glaze. Although they had long been woven in other areas, the manufacture of "¾ bombazetts or plainbacks" was introduced into Yorkshire by James Akroyd and Son, of Halifax, in 1813 (James, p. 618).

Bombazets were sold in Orange County, New York, as early as 1802, according to an unidentified merchant's account book owned by a book dealer. In Boston "Bottlegreen, scarlet and black Bombazets; printed crimson, green and scarlet do" were advertised by T. & J. Wiggin, in the *Palladium,* May 8, 1810. "Blue, Chintz, Bombazet and Dimity Curtains" were to be sold at auction from the stock of John Hoburg, a Baltimore upholsterer (*Federal Gazette,* August 9, 1819). Black, slate, blue, crimson, scarlet, green, drab, and purple bombazets are listed among worsted and silk and worsted goods in Forbes's 1827 *Merchant's Memorandum and Price Book.*

BOMBAZINE
(bombazeen)

Introduced into Norwich in the late sixteenth century, this cloth was made of silk warp and worsted weft in 2:1 twill weave. Writing in 1831, Lardner said: "Their manufacture, which once employed a vast number of looms in Spitalfields, has for some time been almost wholly confined to the city of

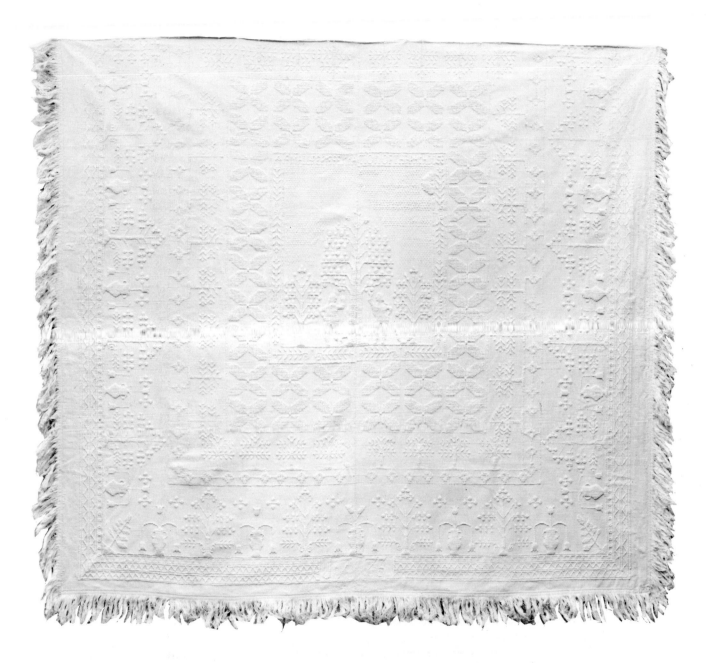

FIG. D-19. *White cotton weft-loop bedspread with figures of Adam and Eve, dated 1773. Probably made in Bolton, Lancashire, although purchased in Pennsylvania. (Winterthur Museum.)*

Fig. D-20. *White cotton weft-loop patterned bedspread, probably made in Bolton, Lancashire, dated 1804. Extra long pile wefts form the inner fringe. (Royal Ontario Museum.)*

Norwich. Bombasins are all woven grey, that is with silk of the natural colour, and they are dyed in the piece after being taken from the loom" (p. 299). Black bombazine for mourning was similar to Norwich crape. More recently, it was made from silk warp and fine botany weft in twill weave.

Samuel Pepys noted in his diary on May 30, 1668: "Up, and put on a new summer black bombasin suit" (9:216). "White bumbasine" curtains are listed in the Wardrobe Room in the 1677 Ham House inventory (Thornton and Tomlin, p. 164). A typical order from James Beekman in 1769 called for "3 pieces Soft black Bembazun, 60 yard at 80/. 85/. 90" (2:806).

A swatch of "Bishop's blue bombazeen for morning dresses," a dark plum-colored silk and wool, is shown by Ackermann (*Repository* 1, no. 2 [February 1809]: 123), and "superfine imperial orange bombazeen for dresses" is yellow silk and orange wool in twill weave (see Fig. D-3). In the Moccasi manuscript, two swatches of bombazine are from London (p. 18) and two are from Exeter.

BOOK MUSLIN

See Muslin.

BORATO

"A similar stuff to Bombazine, or merely another name for some quality of that material" (Beck). In the 1660 Book of Rates, "Bombazines or Boratoes, broad, the single piece, not above 15 yards" are valued at £7 the piece. "Black Hair Borratines" owned by a Norwich merchant advertising in the *London Gazette* may have been the same (May 5, 1698).

See also Norwich goods.

BORSLEY

"A stuff made of combing wool included among others of that description in *Observations on Wool, . . .* 1738" (Beck).

See also Woolen, Worsted.

BOURETTE

Silk dress and furnishing material in plain weave with a rough, knotty surface. The weft yarns were made from coarse outer fibers of cocoons which were carded and spun rather than reeled. A swatch of *Bourette filoselle et Fil,* waste silk and linen, is in the Richelieu Papers (see Pl. D-89).

BOUTONNÉ

A weft-loop weave as found in Bolton coverlets. Also a technique employed by Canadian weavers which uses wefts of colored wools or heavy cottons (Burnham, pp. 182–83; Burnham and Burnham, pp. 159–71). This weaving technique is also found in the textiles woven by the Acadians of Louisiana (Glasgow, p. 341).

BOX CLOTH

Thick, coarse woolen cloth dyed in all colors, although usually in buff. Used for riding habits, coach trimmings, and overcoats (Caulfeild and Saward).

BRAWLES
(braules, brawels)

"A cheap blue-and-white striped cotton cloth, patterned in the loom, classified as a *'guinea stuff'* " (Irwin and Schwartz). These Indian cloths were copied by English weavers at the end of the seventeenth century. Siadder and Chiader brawles were among goods imported by the Dutch from the East Indies between 1686 and 1696 (Kress, S1994). Wearing brawles was prohibited in England from about 1700 (Kress, S2200); however, Earle found brawles advertised with other East Indian goods in colonial newspapers from 1785 to 1795.

BRIDGES SATIN

Satins de Bruges made of silk and linen are included in a long list of mixed goods such as brocatelle (Jacques Savary, 1:101). Made in satin weave, the linen weft was covered by the closely spaced silk warps. It was often striped and used for furnishing and wall hangings. Probably the same as *Imberline*. "The import of raw silk to the southern part of the Low Countries [after 1498] is said to have given rise to the manufacture of half-silks called *satin de Bruges*" (Geijer, p. 162).

BRILLIANT

One of the fancy eighteenth-century glazed worsted dress fabrics largely manufactured in Norwich. According to the *History of the County of Norfolk,* probably written by Richard Beatniffe, "calimancoes, tabinets, brocaded satins, satinets, florettes, brilliants, damasks, and lastings (all worsted goods) were technically called toys, and now are quite superseded by printed cottons" (Beatniffe, 2:59). Swatches of "Brillianetts" with warp-patterned floral sprigs on a white ground are in

FIG. D-21. Brilliantés façonnés, *or brilliants. From a French pattern book, ca. 1760. (Warner Archive, Victoria and Albert Museum.)*

Castle Museum Norwich pattern books dated 1791 and 1792. In these books, they are referred to as brilliants or taboratts. For illustrations of taboratts in the Winterthur Museum's Norwich pattern books, see plates, D-74, D-75, D-76, D-85.

The name may have been adopted from earlier silk dress-goods patterns, for thirty-three French swatches of *Brilliantés façonnés,* striped or checked taffetas with small-scale, warp-faced floral trails, sprigs, or lace are in the Warner Archive (Fig. D-21).

At least five entries for "Brillians," some of them corded, are listed in Willing and Shippen's order book during the 1730s. The firm ordered the pieces by pattern number. Samuel Boardman listed a piece of "flowered Brilliant" of twenty-eight yards in his 1772 account book. The entry follows "prussianett," a dress silk.

In 1872, brilliant was a firm cotton fabric, having a plain ground, with raised figures produced by the threads of the weft; "when viewed in a favorable light, the figures present a very brilliant appearance,—whence its name" (Brown and Gates, p. 49). A swatch of brilliant is in the *Journal of Design* where it is also called "muslinette" (Fig. D-22). A swatch with a similar pattern of pink leaves printed on a white dotted ground is found on page 77 of the same volume.

BRILLIANTINE

About 1835 or 1840, this was known as a very fine weave of silk and cashmere wool. Writing in the twentieth century, Denny described it as a smooth, wiry material the same as alpaca with cotton warp and lustrous wool or mohair filling with little twist. It was made in plain or twill weave and was used for linings, office coats, dusters, and dresses. A heavier quality was called Sicilian cloth.

In the official report of textile manufactures exhibited at the Philadelphia International Centennial Exhibition of 1876, Arlington Mills of Lawrence, Massachusetts, was commended for "a very superior collection of black alpacas, brilliantines, figured mohairs, and Roubaix poplins; all first class goods of their kind, very uniform in width, color, and finish, and being of recent introduction, reflect great credit on the manufacturers" (Group 9, p. 155).

BRITANNIAS
(bretagnes)

Linen fabric of plain weave made in Brittany during the eighteenth century. It was much favored for shirts because of its fine quality. The cloth was also made in Saxony, Silesia, and Perth, Scotland (*Textile Mercury Dictionary*). "The principal market for this article is America, and from thence to the West Indies, where it is used for sheeting and bed-tick in the better families" (Perkins, 1833).

In 1780, 300 pieces of fine linen "Britanias 7½ yards each," costing 59 and 65 stivers per piece, were ordered from Amsterdam, and they arrived at St. Eustatius later that year (Beekman Papers, 3: 986, 1366).

Like book muslin, britannias were folded and packaged in an unusual manner. They were cut in 7½ yard lengths, a size sufficient for two shirts. Many pieces were folded in squares, laid flat, and compressed into bales. For the Spanish trade to South America, the West Indies, and the Canary Islands freight was charged by cubic measurement; a saving of one-third was achieved by not using rolled bundles (Longfield, p. 16).

Fig. D-22. *Cotton brilliant, or muslinet, with a chaplet of rosebuds printed on fancy twilled cloth with a tiny warp-float figure. From* Journal of Design *1 (March–August 1849). 45. (Winterthur Museum Library.)*

BROADCLOTH

Made of carded wool in plain weave and fulled after weaving. Broadcloth was woven on a wide loom and measured 54 to 63 inches in width. Standards of excellence are given by Perkins in 1833:

> They are distinguished from others by their stoutness, and are good in proportion to the fineness and closeness of the weft, the reasonable shortness of the nap, the soft, silky, but not spongy feel, and the goodness of the dye.

Celia Fiennes, a seventeenth-century English diarist, wrote about the process of broadcloth finishing as she observed it at Exeter:

> Then when dry they burle them picking out all knotts, then fold them with a paper between every fold and so sett them on an iron plaite and screw down the press on them, which has another iron plaite on the tope under which is a furnace or fire of coales, this is the hott press; then they fold them exceeding exact and then press them in a cold press; some they dye but the most are sent up for London white. [P. 246.]

The finest broadcloths were made in the West of England where they were known by a variety of names. Broad scarlet cloths called strouds were a specialty of a town of that name where the river water was thought to account for a particularly fine color; medleys, dyed in the wool and with colors mixed before spinning, were made in Gloucester.

Swatches of typical broadcloths are in a Trowbridge clothier's pattern book begun in 1770 and now owned by Samuel Salter and Company of Wiltshire. Two pages from it are illustrated by the International Wool Secretariat in "Wool Through the Ages" and by Ponting in *The Special Characteristics of the West Country Woollen Industry.* Six pattern books that date from 1706 to 1796 are owned by J. and T. Clark, Studley Mills, Trowbridge (Beckinsale, p. xxviii). In 1818 and 1819, the firm produced superfine broadcloths in "claret, corbeau, red, yellow, pink, electorate, woaded and olive ladies."

According to a 1731 manuscript, certain types of broadcloths from Gloucester, Worcester, and Salisbury were shipped to Eastern Mediterranean ports by the Levant, or Turkey, Company (Maurepas Papers). *See also* Levant trade.

Broadcloth was also woven in the North of England, especially in Yorkshire (see Pl. D-102). "The broad cloth, either in its full length of 24 yards, or as a Dozen of 12 to 13 yards, represented the highest grade of Northern fabrics. It was made of the best wool. Next in order of merit came the kersey, which was very little inferior in quality to the broad, but longer and not so wide." The dozens and the kersey "commanded only low prices compared with the high-class fabrics of the West of England. Pennistones, Keighley Whites, and other varieties made in Yorkshire and the North belonged to even lower grades of quality" (Heaton, *Yorkshire Woollen,* p. 145). The eighteenth-century pattern book of Samuel Hill, a Yorkshire clothier, includes swatches of "Broadcloths superfine" (illustrated in Bentley, p. 33). A pattern book inscribed "A. and C. Lindegreen" contains coarse broadcloths and narrow kerseys from the West Riding of Yorkshire (Berch Papers).

Of the excellent properties of broadcloth John Gay wrote in his poem "Trivia: or the Art of Walking the Streets of London, January, 1716":

Nor should it prove thy less important Care,
To chuse a proper Coat for Winter's Wear.
Now in thy trunk thy Doily Habit fold,
The silken Drugget ill can fence the Cold;
The Frieze's spongy Nap is soak'd with Rain,
And Show'rs soon drench the Camlet's cockled grain,
True Witney Broad-cloth with its Shag unshorn,
Unpierc'd is in the lashing Tempest worn;
Be this the Horse-man's Fence; for who would wear
Amid the Town the spoils of Russia's Bear? . . .
That Garment best the Winter's Rage defends,
Whose shapeless form in ample Plaits depends;
By various names in various countries known,
Yet held in all the true Surtout alone;
Be thine of Kersey firm, though small the Cost
Then brave unwet the Rain, unchill'd the Frost.

[Plummer and Early, p. 42.]

Defoe described the importance of English broadcloths and other woolen manufactures in 1728:

Nothing can answer all the ends of dress but good English broadcloth, fine camlets, druggets, serges and such like. These [other countries] must have, and with these none but England can supply them. Be their country hot or cold, torrid or frigid, 'tis the same thing, near the Equinox or near the Pole, the English woollen manufacture clothes them all; here it covers them warm from the freezing breath of the northern bear, and there it shades them and keeps them cool from the searching beams of a perpendicular sun. Let no man wonder that the woollen manufacture is arrived to such a magnitude when in a word it may be said to clothe the world. [*English Commerce,* p. 190.]

The following references to the use of broadcloth in America are characteristic:

Boston, 1691: "Send what may be in your hand, in Norwich stuffs, and an end of good black Broad-Cloth, with suitable Hair Buttons, Calico, Silk and all Trimming" (Sewall, Letter book, 1:118).

Boston, 1693: Margaret Thatcher's inventory lists "1 red broad Cloth Suit of Curtaines and Vallaines with silk Fringe" (SCPR, 13:408).

New York, 1766–85: Typical orders of James Beekman to his London factors included "mens handsome," or "fashionable" blue, brown, black, and "Womens Scarlet in grain" (dyed in the yarn), all of which were to be "well covered" and "well prest" or "Callendered." Samples are attached to orders of 1770 and 1774 (2:725, 751).

Boston, 1783: A coat and vest of "peach-blow" broadcloth with knee breeches of black silk, worn at a Harvard College commencement, are preserved in the Antiquarian House, Plymouth, Massachusetts (Frances Little, p. 81).

Mount Vernon, 1789: George Washington ordered a "suit of cloaths" for his inauguration to be made of broadcloth produced at the Hartford Woolen Manufactory, and Mrs. Washington ordered broadcloth for a riding habit in a color described as "powder smoke" (Frances Little, p. 104).

Boston, 1810: "Black, blue, olive, raven, brown, mixed superfine West of England broadcloths, of the first quality" were offered for sale by T. and J. Wiggin (*Palladium,* May 8).

BROCADE

"A stuff of gold, silver or silk, raised and enriched with flowers, foliages, or other ornaments according to the fancy of the merchant, or manufacturers, who invent new fashions" (Postlethwayt). A "New parcel fine Brocaded Silks with White Grounds, beautifully Flower'd with Lively Colours" was advertised in Boston, 1737 (Earle, *Costume,* p. 65).

In the context of most eighteenth-century textiles brocade referred to textiles with supplementary pattern wefts secured in the main ground weave (Fig. D-23). The supplementary wefts cover only the patterned area and are not carried from selvedge to selvedge. *Barrage* of cotton brocaded with wools, tapizadoe of worsted with polychrome worsted flowers, and numerous silk dress fabrics are brocades in this sense. For further discussion, see Emery. The term *brocade* often refers to any fancy pattern regardless of its actually having been brocaded as described above.

BROCATELLE

Defined in a French dictionary of 1680 as *étoffe de fil et de laine, dont on fait des housses de lit, dont on couvre des chaises et tapisse des cabinets* (Braun-Ronsdorf, p. 23). In the next century, Postlethwayt described this French mixture fabric as "a kind of stuff proper to make hangings, & other furniture. A slight stuff made with cotton, or coarse silk, in imitation of brocadoes. There are some all of silk, & others all of wool."

Brocatelle resembles furniture damask, often with large foliate patterns (Fig. D-24), but it is made with a cotton, linen, or jute filling and silk on the surface in relief or repousseé effect. The Eagle Manufacturing Company of Seymour, Connecticut, received a bronze medal "for Silk Brocatelles and Carriage Drapery of superior quality, perfection in colours and beauty of design" at the 1853 New York industrial exhibition (Dilke, p. 26). For further discussion, see Emery, *Primary Structures of Fabrics*.

The Richelieu Papers include a swatch of *Brocatelle soye et fil* in green and gold made at Avignon in 1736 (see Pl. D-89). A piece of brocatelle woven in 1850 by Daniel Walters and Son of Braintree, Essex, is illustrated at plate 70B of the Connoisseur Period Guides, *Early Victorian*.

FIG. D.-23. *Lilac and white silk brocade with polychrome flowers added by supplementary wefts. France, mid-eighteenth century. Bottom edge turned to show reverse. (Winterthur Museum.)*

FIG. D-24. *Rococo revival armchair of ebonized apple or pearwood; part of a set of furniture probably made by Emmanuel Ringuet Le Prince, New York, ca. 1860 (Metropolitan Museum of Art, gift of Mrs. Douglas Williams.) The handsome rococo revival patterned brocatelle in shades of red, pink, and gold suits this elegant chair with gilt mounts. Note the matching galloon trim.*

BROGLIO
(brolio)

A silk and wool textile woven in small geometric patterns. "New changeable broglios" were advertised in Boston in 1757 (Dow, *Arts and Crafts*, p. 166). Two swatches of *Rich Brolios larghe* are found in the Moccasi manuscript of about 1760 (see Pl. D-54). Made in London, one swatch is yellow and blue silk warp with blue wool weft, and the other is red. A swatch in the Barbara Johnson album has weft-faced geometric designs in brown and white (see Pl. D-34).

BRUSSELS

One of the fancy eighteenth-century glazed worsted dress fabrics largely manufactured in Norwich. Two swatches of *Bruxelles alterna* from Norwich have dark red and blue stripes with warp-faced bands of lace and floral sprigs. They are in the Moccasi manuscript of about 1760 see Pl. D-58).

BRUSSELS CARPET

Woven in a loop-pile technique in 27- to 36-inch-wide strips which were carefully matched for pattern and sewn into larger rugs. The manufacture was introduced at Kidderminster, Worcestershire, about 1720. Charles Partington described them in 1838:

> Brussels carpets are not made in large squares, but in pieces about seven eighths wide. The basis is composed of a warp and woof of strong linen thread; worsted threads are also interwoven, which are formed into loops by means of wires; and these form the pattern, the linen threads not being visible on the surface. When well made they are very durable, and being at the same time elegant, they are at present much in request for the good apartments. [2:28.]

BUCKRAM
(buckeran; Fr. bougran)

In the Middle Ages, a costly fabric (Beck) which was later described as "a coarse cloth made of hemp, gummed, calendered, and dyed several colours. It is put into those places of the lining of a garment which one would have stiff, and to keep their forms. It is also used in the bodies of women's gowns; and it often serves to make wrappers, to cover, or wrap up cloths, serges, and such other merchandizes in, to preserve them, and keep them from the dust, and their colours from fading" (Postlethwayt). Buckram was sometimes made of new cloth but more frequently of old curtains or pieces of sailcloth (Savary des Bruslons).

In Boston, 1722, two men offered their services to "Any Person that has occasion to have any Linnen Cloth made into Buckram, or to buy Buckram ready made, or Calendring any Silk, Watering, Dying or Scouring" (Dow, *Every Day Life,* p. 126).

BUCKSKIN

(1) Fine woolen cloth with a milled and dressed finish showing a distinctive twill. This West of England speciality was "preferred to corded cloth for riding, being fine, smooth, thick, and firm in its texture" (Caulfeild and Saward).

(2) "A kerseymere cloth of very fine texture, embroidered with silk by children. It is remarkably beautiful, is designed for waistcoatings, and is manufactured at Bradford in Yorkshire" (Caulfeild and Saward).

Woven "in an eight-leaf warp satin weave, each warp crossing over six picks and carried under two picks." "It is napped, fulled thoroughly and shorn, the face being finished very smooth" (Harmuth).

BUDOY

A thin, coarsely spun worsted of plain weave with a glazed finish. Swatches in the Yorkshire pattern book are labeled "Durants, or Tammys, or Budoys" (see Pl. D-103).

BUFFYN
(buffiner)

A camlet classed as one of the New Draperies, or lighter worsted cloths, introduced into Norwich in the sixteenth century. By 1579, a complaint against their manufacture was raised: "Of late the use of certain kinds of clothing called new inventions, as Buffiner, Mockadoes, and such like, have grown much in use, to the decay of the use of [broad]cloth" (James, p. 120). At the end of the century, "Grograines, broad or narrow, called Buffines" were described as light in weight and "of delicate texture" (James, pp. 126, 127). About 1620 Norwich worsted weavers alleged that "buffyn, cattalowne, and pearl of beauty, &c., may be affirmed single chamblett, differing only in the breadth" (James, p. 144). For the complete quotation, see New Draperies.

BUNT

"The middle part of a sail, formed into a kind of bag to receive the wind" (Halliwell). "Bed bunts" frequently listed in advertisements probably refer to tightly woven ticking which would encase feathers or straw.

BUNTING

A narrow fabric made of long staple, coarse English wool in an open and plain weave. The name seems to be derived from the German *bunt,* meaning variegated, or gay colored. It was used especially for ships' colors. Bunting is woven with two-ply warps to withstand the strain in weaving and for greater strength when flying in the wind. The spacing between the threads and picks is approximately the same as the diameter of the yarns. With this type of structure, a flag will float in the slightest breeze, and when wet will dry more quickly than an ordinary fabric largely because a greater amount of thread surface is exposed to the air (Priestley, p. 53).

BURDIE

A worsted cloth. Of weaving in the North of England Arthur Young wrote in the 1770s: "Besides broad cloths, there are some shalloons, and many stuffs made at Leeds, particularly Scotch camblets, grograms, burdies, some calimancoes, &c" (James, p. 291).

BURE

A coarse medieval cloth with a long nap, it was used to clothe the poor. According to Paul Rodier, many words are derived from this common textile, such as *burly, burlesque, burratine, burratto, bournous, burros,* and *buron* (p. 32).

BURLAP

Coarse canvas made of jute, piece-dyed or left in its natural color. Low grades were used for gunny sacks and wrapping furniture; a firmer quality with a finish was used for drapery purposes (Denny).

BURNET

A fine woolen cloth of a brown color.

BUSTIAN

A worsted cloth. Bustian and several other seventeenth-century worsteds are cited in the Allegations of Norwich weavers. Bustian is listed in the 1660 Book of Rates among imports and was valued in 1675 at "£2 the single piece, not above 15 yards" (Beck).

See also New Draperies.

C

CADDIS
(caddas)

In France several grades of worsted cloth were called by this name, but in England and America it generally denoted a cheap worsted tape or ribbon. A seventeenth-century London reference cited "Caddas or cruel ribbons, the Dozen Pieces of 26 yards each" (Beck). "Chints caddys @ 7/6" were specified by John Banister of Newport in his 1740 order. In Delaware (1743) "3 Remnants Cadis & Stript Tape" are listed with other bindings and tapes in the Grafton Inventory.

In 1907 Mabel Tuke Priestman, writing in *House Beautiful,* suggested the material for house furnishing: " 'Caddice' is another material which can be utilized for applique. It is 75 cents a yard and 52 inches wide. It is soft and pliable and comes in four colorings, red, rich green, willow-green, and natural linen color. It is especially useful for curtains in a bedroom and when enriched with effective appliques is very decorative" (p. 23).

CADDOW
(caddy)

Randle Holme's 1668 *Academy of Armory* defines this as a coverlet or blanket, a rough woolen covering. In the eighteenth and nineteenth centuries, it was used as a local trade name for coverlets of cotton with coarse pattern wefts drawn up in loops that were made at Bolton in Lancashire.

See also Bolton coverlet.

CAFFARD

An inferior type of damask made of silk and linen, or wool and linen. Lardner's *Cabinet Cyclopaedia* of 1831 says of it:

The French had long since a manufacture in imitation of the old fashioned silk damask, which they called *Cafard* (counterfeit) damask; this, while it had its warp composed of silk, had the shoot of either thread, wool, or cotton, and sometimes even of hair. [P. 295.]

CAFFOY
(caffa, cafoy)

Sixteenth-century references suggest that the fabric was a rich silk (Beck). "A cotton cloth painted in a variety of colors and patterns, made in India for sale in Bengal" (Savary des Bruslons). In England caffoy was made largely in Norwich, the center of worsted weaving, and indeed the weaving of caffoy along with darnex, mockado, and russel figured in a pageant commemorating Queen Elizabeth's visit to Norwich in 1579 (James, p 115).

Caffoy was patterned with wool pile designs in imitation of silk furnishing velvets and damasks. Caffoy furniture is listed in a 1726 inventory of the saloon at Erthig Park, Denbighshire, near Norwich, and caffoy survives on a set of chairs in red wool pile on a yellow silk satin ground (now worn). A curtain valance of the material, which resembles Genoese velvet, is shown at figure 90 by Fowler and Cornforth.

Linen upholstery material with a floral pattern in red, blue, and green wool pile, thought to be caffoy, survives on a set of mid-eighteenth-century chairs at Ham House near London. Wool velvet stamped with a leafy damask pattern covers the walls of the drawing room at Houghton, Norfolk, and house inventories for the room, designed by William Kent (1730–35), note furniture covered with caffoy. The cabinet of another Norfolk house, Felbrigg, is covered with red wool pile damask, perhaps an example of caffoy.

Since wallpapers were frequently made to imitate patterned textiles, it is not surprising to find caffoy wallpapers advertised in London as early as 1720—"a curious sort of Flock work in imitation of Caffaws, and other hangings of Curious figures and colours" (Sugden and Edmondson, p. 40).

CALENDER

Howard's *New Royal Encyclopaedia* of 1788 describes a calender:

> A machine used in manufactories, to press certain woollen and silken stuffs and linens, to make them smooth, even, and glossy, or to give them waves, or water them, as may be seen in mohairs and tabbies [Fig. D-26]. This instrument is composed of two thick cylinders or rollers of very hard and polished wood, round which the stuffs to be calendered are wound: these rollers are placed crosswise, between two very thick boards, the lower serving as a fixed base, and the upper moveable, by means of a thick screw, with a rope fastened to a spindle, which makes it's axis: the uppermost board is loaded with large stones cemented together, weighing twenty thousand pounds, or more. It is this weight that gives the polish, and makes the waves on the stuffs about the roller by means of a shallow indenture or engraving cut into it. [1:425.]

Woolen stuffs made of carded wool received a different finish which is described in Mortimer's *Dictionary* of 1766 at "wool":

> All fulled stuffs are sprinkled over the wrong side, first with gum-water, and, after extension on a large roller, to get out all the creases and inequalities, they are rolled off slowly upon a bar of polished iron, which supports the piece in that state over a large chafing-dish, capable, by its heat, to put the least fibre in motion; and from thence it is carried upon another roller which draws it even by the help

of a wheel or engine for that purpose. And thus the stuff is returned from one to another, at the discretion of the workmen: and this is called dressing or calendering.

CALICO

Cotton cloth of many grades and varieties first made in India and later in the West. Thomas Sheraton gives a broad definition in his *Encyclopedia, 1804–7*:

> In commerce a sort of cloth resembling linens made of cotton. The name is taken from that of Calicut, the first place at which the Portuguese landed when they discovered the Indian Trade. . . . Calicoes are of different kinds, plain, printed, stained, dyed, chintz, muslins, and the like, all included under the general denomination of *calicoes*. Some of them are painted with various flowers of different colours; others are not stained, but have a stripe of gold and silver quite through the piece, and at each end is fixed a tissue of gold, silver, and silk, intermixed with flowers. The printing of calicoes was first set on foot in London about 1676, and has long been a most important article of commerce. [P. 235.]

Rolt's mid-eighteenth-century dictionary supplies the following information:

> Callicoe—one of the general names for the cotton-cloths of India; being a particular kind of cotton, brought from Calicut, and other places, both white and coloured; which was formerly much worn in England for the garments of women and children; but now prohibited to be worn, printed or coloured, otherwise than by needlework, upon account of its prejudicing the woollen and linen manufacturers of Great Britain and Ireland.

To circumvent the prohibition, printers used fustian of linen warp and cotton weft. Not until the various inventions of Hargreaves, Arkwright, and

Crompton made possible the spinning of a strong, fine cotton yarn suitable for warps could an all-cotton cloth be produced to compete with fine Indian calico. The first successes, the necessary legislation for regulating the use of these western calicoes, and the duty to be charged, date from 1774. Swatches of white cotton calico are found in the Hilton manuscript of 1786 (see Fig. D-40).

By 1833 Perkins listed as many as fourteen different kinds of calicoes. Merriam-Webster defines calico as "cheap cotton fabrics with figured patterns."

Seventeenth-century American references probably pertain to Indian calicoes: Edward Wharton's Salem inventory, 1677 / 78, lists "2 calico painted table cloathes" along with shirts and plain tablecloths (Dow, *Every Day Life*, p. 265). An unusual 1684 use of white calico in Boston for bed curtains and chair covers reads: "2 pr. white Calico Curtaines, Valients, tester Clothes and 6 Covers for Chaires." In the same inventory are "2 Calico Side bord Clothes," a "Calico Cuberd Cloth," and "1 Quilt of Calico Colerd and flowred" (Dow, *Every Day Life*, pp. 278–81).

Numerous entries for garments made of calico are found in the 1695 / 96 inventory of Margrita van Varick—nightgowns, neckcloths, aprons, quilted waistcoats, both white and flowered petticoats, handkerchiefs, and "clouts." For furnishing and household use, we find carpets, quilts, "2 stript callico Curtins," "Cullerd callico Curtens," and valances, napkins, pillowbeers, bibs, "children bedds," and "one white Callico blancoate." Another New York inventory of 1757 lists "blew and white Callico window Curtains and Valence" and "blew & white Callico Chimney Cloths Very Old" (New York Appraisements, p. 42).

CALIMANCO
(Fr. calamande, calamandre)

A worsted "stuff . . . [with] a fine gloss upon it. There are calamancoes of all colours, and diversly wrought; some are quite plain; others have broad stripes, adorned with flowers; some with plain broad stripes; some with narrow stripes; and others watered" (Postlethwayt).

An account of about 1802 describes the brilliance of calimancoes, satins, and brilliants:

These were woven in various patterns which were formed in the loom, and were composed of the richest and most brilliant dyes, and variegated by an endless diversity of colours, in the forms of flowers, birds, figures, and fancy subjects, upon the face of the goods. . . . This manufacture was peculiar to Norwich, and the colours employed for it surpassed any others dyed in Europe. [James, pp. 364–65.]

As used for furnishing, "a Handsome Bedstead with Calaminco Curtains, Vallens, Tester & Window Curtains" was offered for sale in Boston, 1729 (Dow, *Arts and Crafts,* p. 108); "1 Easy Chair Coverd with Callimanco" was in the Grafton home in Delaware, 1743; and a sofa covered in "Striped crimson callimanco" was made in Philadelphia, about 1790 (Hornor, p. 267).

Calimanco was far more often used for clothing. A London runaway wore "a Red, Blue and Cynamon strip'd and Spotted Calamanco Wastcoat, and Red Plush Breeches" (*London Gazette,* June 27, 1692); a Boston runaway of 1734 wore "a Green Calliminco Gown, flour'd with white (Dow, *Arts and Crafts,* p. 191). John Banister of Newport ordered scarlet, brown and "Blew emboss'd" calimanco in 1744 and others of Spitalfields make. At Leeds in Yorkshire, Samuel Rowland Fisher ordered "30 ps. Calamancos to be dyd black; 20 ps. ditto to be dyd blue from a neat Mazarine to a light shade; 30 ps. to be dyd Light drabs & Doves . . . all to be 16 Inches wide & 40 Yds in Length to be dyd in the best Manner & double Prest" (1767/68).

In American collections, plain weave glazed calimanco in solid colors of deep indigo, light blue,

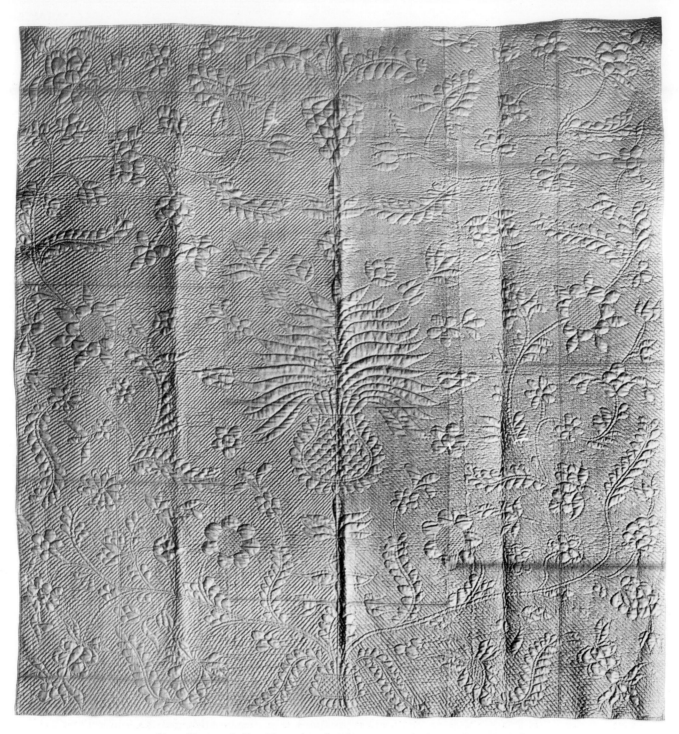

Fig. D-25. *Indigo-blue glazed calimanco quilted coverlet. English or American, eighteenth century. Owned by the Copp family of Stonington, Connecticut. (Smithsonian Institution.)*

green, raspberry red, and pink (often erroneously called linsey-woolsey) is found in coverlets quilted in patterns of large flowers and leaves backed with coarser woolen linings (Fig. D-25). Silk petticoats quilted in more elaborate and finer patterns to calimanco linings of the same color are also known. In some cases, a petticoat has been cut in two and stitched together at the bottom edges to form the center of a coverlet bordered with other material.

Thirty-three swatches of calimancoes dating from 1720 are preserved in the Public Record Office (CO 388/21, no. 209, fols. 150, 151). A swatch of scarlet calimanco is included in James Alexander's 1738 order for textiles (see Pl. D-8). Two London-made swatches are found in the Moccasi manuscript of about 1760. Calimancoes in several grades with spotted, striped, "clouded" (see Fig. D-30), and brocaded patterns are seen in the eighteenth-century Norwich pattern books (see Pls. D-63, D-64, D-79, D-80, D-81).

The proposal of James Popham of Newark, New Castle County, Delaware, to make "Camblets, Callimancoes, Cambletees, plain, striped, and figured Stuffs, Druggets, Sagathies, German Serges, Everlastings, Plushes, &c." was published in a 1770 New York newspaper (Gottesman, 1726–76, p. 262).

CALMUC
(kalmuck)

A name derived from a sheep native to Central Asia. A "twilled woolen made of loose twist yarn, fulled and finished with a long nap, used as winter dress goods" (Harmuth). Two swatches in light and dark brown, coarser than coating, are found in the 1807 Aix-la-Chapelle pattern book (see Pl. D-1).

The material was later imitated in cotton, for "cotton kalmucks and beavers" were listed in Class 11, in Reports of the Juries at the Great Exhibition of 1851.

See also Bearskin.

CAMBRIC
(Fr. batiste)

A fine white linen cloth in plain weave. According to Savary des Bruslons it was

Une sorte de toile de lin, très-fine, & très-blanche, qui se fabrique à . . . Cambray. Les Batistes servent à faire des fichus, ou mouchoirs de col, des garnitures de tête, & d'autres choses semblables pour les femmes. On en fait aussi des surplis, des rochets, des rabats, des manchettes, des cravattes, &c. à l'usage des Ecclésiastiques & de gens du monde.

Visiting Ireland in 1768, Samuel Rowland Fisher "Walkd to John Christy's who shewd . . . great Quantitys of Cambricks made by him at Dundalk & bleached here, some of them very neat & fine, tho no way equal to those imported from France." He added that "several persons from Cambray . . . have the management" of the linen and cambric weaving. In a petition presented by Samuel Crompton, "Cotton Spinner" to the House of Commons, March 5, 1812, it was stated:

The Petitioner's Machine not only removed the pre-existing defects in the art of spinning by being capable of producing every then known description of weft as well as twist of a very superior quality, but gave birth to a new manufacture in this country of fine Cambrics and Muslins, by producing yarns of treble the fineness, and of a much more soft and pleasant texture, than any which had ever before been spun in Great Britain. [Daniels, p. 172.]

A fashionable "Suit of Curtains" was advertised in *The Palladium* (Boston), May 22, 1810: "For sale . . . consisting of 168 yards cambric Chintz; 168 ditto light blue cambrick, for lining ditto with pendent fringe, binding, &c.; gilt Pins, suitable for a drawing room or best chamber—all new, and of the most modern patterns." From 1809 to 1812, swatches of "Morine corded," "Imperial striped," "sea-weed printed," "Jubilee Twill Shawl," and

"Permanent morone [maroon] printed" cambric appeared in Ackermann's *Repository* (see Fig. D-68). By this date, the material was made of fine cotton yarns.

See also Ticking. For "Germain Camebrick for Hankerchives and Aprons," see Fig. D-98.

CAMLET
(*camblet*)

"Of plain weave, . . . woven in many widths, lengths, qualities and in all colors. Some of goat's hair, some partly of silk, or linen, and some entirely of wool; they are made for men's and women's clothing, bed hangings, furniture, and church hangings" (Chambers, Postlethwayt). Worsted camlets became harateens and moreens, grograms and grogrinetts, chinas, or cheneys, when given different finishes. These both Chambers and Postlethwayt describe.

Figured camlets (Fr. *gaufrés*) are "those of one colour, whereon are stamped various figures, flowers, foliages, &c. by means of hot irons, which are a kind of moulds pressed together with the stuff under a press."

Water camlets (Fr. *à Eau*) are "those which, after weaving, receive a certain preparation with water, and are afterwards passed under a hot-press, which gives them a smoothness and lustre."

Waved camlets (Fr. *ondés*) are "those whereon waves are impressed, as on tabbies, by means of a Calender, under which they are passed and repassed several times."

Roland de la Platière in *Art du fabricant d'etoffes* said that camlets with heavy, or coarse, weft yarns, called grosgrains, were suitable for a waved finish similar to modern moiré. Those with finer wefts, more nearly equal in size to the warps, were suited to stamped patterns. He further stated that six threads in each selvedge should be of a different color to indicate that the cloth is made up of yarns dyed before weaving (p. 28).

John Evelyn visited Tours in 1644: "I went to see their manufactures in silk, (for in this town they drive a very considerable trade with silk-worms), their pressing and watering the grograms and camlets, with weights of an extraordinary poise, put into a rolling-engine" (1:111). *See* Fig. D-26.

In his letter book of 1719/20, Samuel Sewall was explicit in his order for bed hangings: "To be Bought. Curtains and Vallens for a Bed, with Counterpane, Head-Cloth and Tester, of good yellow waterd worsted camlet, with Trimming, well made: and Bases, if it be the fashion. A good fine large Chintz Quilt well made. Send also of the same Camlet and Trimming, as may be enough to make Cushions for the Chamber Chairs" (Letter book, 2:105). Newport merchant John Banister's orders from 1739 to 1746 specify "hair," "worsted," "silk and worsted," "double," "single," and "Spitle[fields] make," the colors to be blue, green, scarlet, crimson, cherry, and cloth-colored. Anthony Rutgers's inventory, taken in 1760, included "1 Suit of Green Stampt Camblet Bed Curtains 130/" (New York Appraisements, p. 64).

Abundant examples of camlets are found in merchants' pattern books. Swatches of seven "Broad & Narrow Camblets" are in one of James Alexander's undated orders (see Pl. D-9); cuttings of scarlet and dark blue worsted camlets are attached to a 1738 order to Collinson (see Pl. D-8); and "Green Stampt Camblet" was ordered from William Hunt in 1746 (see Pl. D-11). Listings for silk camlets are found among other silks, as "12 ps Silk Camblets newest fashion good Colours and glossy, all Different Colours" (1737); the cuttings attached to this order have silk warp and worsted weft of different colors. Alexander generally described worsted camlets as "superfine," "narrow," "broad," or "town made."

Fifty swatches of "Superfine Single Cambletts, Common Cullers," "Extra Superfine Double Cambletts," and "Superfine Mixed Cambletts" are found in John Kelly's "Counterpart of Patterns" dated 1763. Camlets made in Amiens, Lille, London, and Norwich are found in the Moccasi manuscript of about 1760 (see Pls. D-54, D-57, D-59, D-62). The Richelieu Papers included camlets made in Holland in 1736 (Lh45d V, p. 24). Winterthur Museum's late eighteenth-century Norwich pattern books include swatches of striped, checked, spotted, and flowered (brocaded) camlets in glazed and unglazed examples of different qualities (see Pl. D-82).

    See also Fig. D-8.

CAMLETEEN
(cambletee, camletine, camletto)

A stuff of "mixcd wool and goat's hair, thread or cotton" (Postlethwayt). A slight camlet, thinner and woven of coarser fibers and yarns. In 1737 James Alexander of New York ordered olive, scarlet, dark blue, dark green flowered, and "1 ps

Fig. D-26. *Cloth is wound on rollers and then crushed under blocks of stone to produce a watered effect in the cloth. From Denis Diderot and Jean d'Alembert,* Encyclopédie, ou dictionnaire raisonné des sciences, des arts et des métiers. . . . Recueil des planches, *11 vols. (Paris: Briasson et al., 1762–72), 11: pl. 130. (Winterthur Museum Library.)*

Dark Dove Colour with white flowers only" and, in 1738, "4 ps figured and stript newest fashion" camleteens. In 1744 John Banister of Newport ordered "Scarlet emboss'd cambleteen, 21 yds. @ 40/." Samuel Rowland Fisher noted the weaving of "common Tammys or Cambletees of the lowest kinds" in Aukland in 1783.

Castle Museum pattern cards and pattern books dating from 1769 to the 1790s contain swatches of spotted, striped, checked, flowered, or brocaded, clouded, or shaded, plain, common, fine, glazed, and unglazed camleteens. Winterthur Museum's Norwich pattern books contain similar types (see Pls. D-66, D-67, D-83, D-84). The Moccasi manuscript contains unglazed examples also from Norwich. Sixteen swatches of coarse checked camleteens, *Camelotillos quadrillados,* are among papers of a vessel seized by an American privateer about 1777 (Polly Papers).

CANTALOON
(catalonia, catalowne; Fr. castelogne)

A bed cover woven of fine wool in Catalonia. The name later was applied to worsteds made in France and England. James quotes from a seventeenth-century Norwich document concerning New Draperies manufactured there:

> Buffyn, cattalowne, and pearl of beauty, &c., may be affirmed single chamblett, differing only in the breadth. . . . To make this buffyn a catalowne, is to twist a thread of one colour with a thread of another, and strike it with [weft of] another colour; to make the same a pearl of beauty, is to make it striped, by colours in the warp, and tufted in the striken. [P. 144.]

An early eighteenth-century English protest against wearing Indian cottons, because their use was seen as a detriment to woolen manufactures, stated:

> All the mean people, the maid servants, and indifferently poor persons who would other-

wise clothe themselves, and were usually clothed in their women's stuffs made at *Norwich and London,* or in *cantaloons* and crapes, &c., are now clothed in calico, or printed linen. [James, pp. 216–17.]

After visiting England's Sturbridge Fair, about 1725, Defoe wrote: "Western goods had their share here also, and several booths were fill'd as full with serges, du-roys, druggets, shalloons, cantaloons, Devonshire kersies, &c. from Exeter, Taunton, Bristoll and other parts west, and some from London also" (*Tour,* vol. 1, letter 1).

The 1715 Elmendorph account book lists "Cantallon 112 yd at 10/ per yd." The 1723 inventory of Mary Hunt, Boston, included 235 yards of cantaloons at 11 shillings a yard (SCPR, 23:152).

Swatches of "cantelloons," "cantoloones," "cantalones," and "cantolunes" are attached to letters dated 1708 to 1711 from Reading, Bath, Stockport, and Haverford addressed to merchants in Bristol. All are rather coarse striped worsteds in a variety of bright colors (see Pl. D-20). Many of them include medley yarns (i.e., yarns of different colors spun together) which were a specialty of West of England weavers. A typical order called for:

> 6 ps Plain black and white
> 1 ps Green Mixture plain
> 1 ps sad blue Oringe and black mixt Plain
> 1 ps crims[on] and white Mixt Plain
> Be sure the Coulrs. be Good if a little vary from the Patterns above.

Postlethwayt said of the city of Bristol in Somersetshire that it had "also some considerable manufactures of woollen stuffs, particularly cantaloons, which are carried on chiefly by French refugees."

CANTERBURY

In the seventeenth and eighteenth centuries a brocaded dress fabric made of silk warp and cotton weft (*Textile Mercury Dictionary*). Canterbury was a silk weaving center at the peak of production in the late seventeenth century (Thornton, *Baroque and Rococo Silks,* p. 62n).

CANTON

Known from the 1786 Hilton manuscript as a ribbed cotton cloth—the warp passes over several weft threads to form the cords. In the nineteenth century, the following canton cloths were manufactured:

Canton crape, a highly finished fabric "made with fine silk or cotton warp and heavier filling, forming light cross ribs." "Made of Canton silk [it] is heavier than crepe de chine" (Harmuth). A dress material made in various plain colors (Caulfeild and Saward).

Canton flannel, a 2/2 twilled soft cotton fabric with a long nap; bleached, unbleached, or piece-dyed in plain colors. Used for sleeping garments, interlinings, overcoat pockets, household purposes, and diapers (ca. 1900).

Canton linen, commonly called grass cloth. Fine, translucent fabric made of ramie (china grass) which looks like linen. Bleached or dyed blue. Formerly sold in oriental shops for lunch cloths, doilies, blouses. Plain-weave (Denny).

CANTOON

"A fustian with a fine cord visible on one side, and a satiny surface of yarns running at right angles to the cords upon the other side. The satiny side is sometimes smoothed by singeing. The stuff is strong, and has a fine aspect" (Webster, p. 962). The material was used for sails and the clothes of laboring men. A draft for "Cantoon back Satinet" is in John Hargrove's 1792 weavers' book. In the twentieth century, when dyed "a fawn or drab hue," it was used for "men's riding and sporting suits" and occasionally for ladies' jackets (Nisbet, p. 137).

CANVAS

Postlethwayt writes of various kinds of canvas:

(1) A very clear unbleached cloth of hemp or flax wove very regular in little squares. It is used for working tapestry [needlepoint] with the needle, by passing the threads through the intervals of squares. There is coarse, middling, and fine canvas.
(2) A coarse cloth of hemp, unbleached, somewhat clear, which serves to cover women's stays, also to stiffen men's cloaths, and to make some other of their wearing apparel.
(3) A very coarse cloth of hemp, unbleached, which serves to make towels.
(4) A sort of very coarse cloth made of hemp, very strong and very close, which serves to make sails for shipping.

Writing in 1833, Perkins says of different kinds of canvas:

Green canvass, alias green bolting, is used for windoe blinds, the covering of meat-safes, &c. Yellow canvass, otherwise yellow bolting—used by children at schools for samplers. Rug canvass—is an article used as a ground for the working of fancy worsteds or yarn, for the various ornamental squares, circles, &c. intended to be placed on tables and sideboards, &c. to prevent their being scratched, or damaged. It is also used for the base of hearth-rugs.

CARLOWNE

A sixteenth- to seventeenth-century worsted textile.

CARPMEAL
(carptmeal)

A town in Lancashire where cheap woolen cloth of that name was made from the Middle Ages.

CARRELL
(*carrolle, currelle*)

Because this material is listed in the 1570 book of drapery belonging to the hall at Norwich, it may be assumed that it was made wholly or in part of worsted (Beck).

CASHMERE

Made of the hair of the Kashmir goat, this is one of the fabrics made in imitation of the coveted twill-tapestry shawls from India and was especially fashionable from the last years of the eighteenth century. "A closely woven, soft, fine, and light dress fabric made with single cotton or wool warp and fine Botany filling in a 2-1 weft face twill" (Harmuth). Two pieces of "Cachmere" from Hargreaves and Company are in the *Journal of Design* for 1849 (1:108, 115). Both are printed on twill-woven cloth.

In the Great Exhibition, London, 1851, "His Royal Highness Prince Albert exhibits in Class xii. . . . Cashmere brocade fabrics . . . composed of silk warp, and weft of wool, shorn from the Cashmere goats, in Windsor Park. . . . the first made from Cashmere wool, grown in this country, and as one amongst innumerable manifestations of the deep and active interest which His Royal Highness has ever taken in promoting and encouraging the manufactures of this country" (James, Appendix, p. 23).

"A specimen of cashmere furniture, printed with copper rollers, in the chintz style, in ten colours," exhibited in the New York industrial exhibition of 1853 was noted as being "admirable, in the clearness and distinctness of the large masses of colour. The design is of the floral type usually adopted for furnitures" (Wallis, p. 30).

See also Angola, Cassimere, Cassinet.

CASHMERE ATLAS

"All-wool, highly finished weft satin dress goods, the filling is finer and of slacker twist than the warp" (Harmuth).

CASHMERETTE

A twilled, soft, and lustrous cotton fabric, often lightly napped, made to imitate cashmere.

CASSIMERE
(*kerseymere*)

A medium-weight twilled woolen cloth of soft texture. This fabric was patented by Francis Yerbury of Bradford in 1766 and developed in the late eighteenth century. Patent records show that two species were manufactured, "one quilled in the weaving with a flat whale, the other with a round one, which may be directed to any point, the threads of both chain and shoot crossing each other in a transverse manner" (Beckinsale, p. xxvii).

Plain varieties, competitors of broadcloth, were used for clothing and furnishing and were "soon diversified by the introduction of fancy varieties, patterned and sometimes mixed with silk, cotton, or mohair for coats and waistcoats" (Mann, "Textile Industries," p. 161).

Alexander Hamilton in his "Report on the Subject of Manufactures" to the House of Representatives in 1791 wrote of "a promising essay, towards the fabrication of cloths, cassimeres, and other woollen goods" which at that time was "going on at Hartford, in Connecticut. Specimens of the different kinds which are made, in the possession of the Secretary, evince that these fabrics have attained a very considerable degree of perfection" (p. 128). Whether the officer met by Henry Wansey in Hartford in 1794 wore cassimere of American manufacture is a question: "At breakfast with us the first morning, was an American officer, in his uniform; it was a blue coat of superfine cloth, with scarlet facings and cuffs; a buff cassimere waistcoat and breeches" (p. 69).

In *Household Furniture* (1808), George Smith recommended cassimere for draperies and wall coverings: "These Draperies for Drawing Rooms should be made of satin or lustring, with under-curtains of muslin or superfine cassimere" (p. 1). "For Eating Rooms and Libraries, a material of more substance is requisite than for Rooms of a lighter cast; and for such purposes superfine cloth, or cassimere, will ever be the best; the colours as fancy or taste may direct; yet scarlet and crimson will ever hold the preference" (p. xii). "In this Design the whole decoration is after the antique. The mantles on the walls are meant to be real, and of satin, muslin, or superfine cassimere" (p. 29).

"West of England Cassimeres, of the first quality" in "black, blue, buff, olive, raven, brown, and mixed superfine Yorkshire cloths and Cassimeres" were offered for sale by T. & J. Wiggin in Boston (*Palladium,* May 8, 1810).

At the New York industrial exhibition of 1853, fancy printed cassimeres woven in Lowell, Massachusetts, appeared "to suit a large class of buyers, particularly for the western markets, as being at once low in price and showy in character." Also exhibited were woven cassimeres made at the Melville Manufacturing Company, Melville, Massachusetts: "The Jacquard has been lately introduced into use in the production of figure patterns in fancy cassimeres. . . . The pattern being woven, the goods are slightly fulled afterwards, and the result is satisfactory when too defined a figure has not been attempted. In small patterns the fulling process breaks down the forms, and thus gives, when finished, an agreeable variety to the surface" (Wallis, pp. 16, 19). The Salisbury Woolen Company of New York received a bronze medal "for Silk and Wool Cassimeres of superior finish" at the 1853 New York industrial exhibition (Dilke, p. 28).

A dozen fancy cassimeres are presented in the *Journal für Fabrik,* 1792–94, in hand-colored engraved plates and in swatches (see Fig. D-97). Some are woven, some printed, some have small amounts of silk, and some have cotton warps. "A Persian kerseymere, worked in tambour" for waistcoats is shown in Ackermann's *Repository* (see Pl. D-88) as well as "light sage green or cream-colored kerseymere breeches" and a "Child's Dress of nankeen or buff kerseymere, of the Highland order" which were fashionable in 1810, and "light-coloured double-milled cassimere pantaloons"

which were used for men's walking dress in 1809 (*Repository* 3, no. 18 [June 1810]:388; 2, no. 7 [July 1809]: 46).

Swatches of "Fine twilled flannel," "diment uniform," and "Double Milld. Buff" cassimere are in a pattern book dated 1798/99 (Public Record Office, c/113/16). Swatches of *Casimir croisé Simple, Casimirs côtelés,* and cassimeres of three qualities are in the Aix-la-Chapelle pattern book of 1807.

CASSINET
(cassenet, cassinette, kerseynette)

A light mixed cloth, a modification of cassimere, with the warp of cotton, and the weft of very fine wool, or wool and silk, in twill weave. In American manufacture, cassinet was a coarse variety of satinet and did not aim at fineness of texture; cassinets were frequently called negro cloths (Arthur H. Cole, pp. 199, 201).

CASTORINE

A dress fabric of wool and beaver fur made for winter wear (Fig. D-27).

CATALOWNE

See Cantaloon.

CATGUT

An open linen or cotton fabric of plain weave in which the warp and the weft are twisted and stiffened. It was used for embroidery. John Penn's 1788 sale of household goods included "3 silk blinds and 2 catgut ditto, in mahogany frames."

CATGUT GAUZE

A special form of gauze weaving in which there is a double crossing of the warp ends between each pick (*Textile Mercury Dictionary*). The fabric was used for stiffening dresses, coat sleeves, and for

FIG. D-27. *Swatches of castorines: (1, 2) heavy, hairy goods; (3, 4) smooth and felted; (5) a swatch of half silk (atlas); and (6) a swatch of printed cotton. From* Journal für Fabrik *(November 1792), pl. 1. (Winterthur Museum Library.)*

the foundation of bonnets (Perkins). A fashionable headdress, "The Ranelagh Mob; or the Hood from Low Life," was described in the *London Chronicle,* 1762: "This is a piece of gauze, minionett, catgut, or Leicester web, which is clouted about the head, then crossed under the chin, and brought back to fasten behind, the two ends hanging down like a pair of pigeons tails" (Malcolm, p. 338).

CAUNGEANTRIE

One of the New Draperies developed in Norwich in the sixteenth century. "A stuff, chiefly of one colour, but intermixed with another of less body, so that the colour seemingly changes according to the position in which it is viewed" (Du Cange).

See also Chambray, Changeable fabrics.

CHAGRIN

See Shagreen.

CHALLIS
(challie)

A soft wool, or wool-cotton cloth, plain, printed, or figured.

> About the year 1832, the article called "Challis" was introduced [at Norwich], certainly the neatest, best, and most elegant silk and worsted article ever manufactured: it was made on a similar principle to the Norwich crape only thinner and softer, composed of much finer materials, and instead of a glossy surface as in Norwich crapes, the object was to produce it without gloss, and very pliable and clothy. The best quality of "Challis" when finished with designs and figures (either produced in the loom or printed) was truly a splendid fabric, which commanded the attention of the higher circles, and became a favourite article of apparel at their fashionable resorts and parties. [James, p. 436.]

It was twill woven and "printed in coloured flowers on a white ground, which has the effect of vel-

vet painting" (Caulfeild and Saward). The name may derive from a cloth called "Shalli," meaning twill, made of the finest mohair yarn and woven in Angora, Asia Minor (James, p. 462n).

CHAMBRAY

A type of gingham, plain in color and weave, often having a colored warp and white filling. It may be "made from any color as you may wish, in the warp, and also in the filling; only have them differ from each other" (Bronson, p. 21).

In 1812 "11 cases of cotton goods, consisting of chambrays, stripes, checks, Plaids, Shirting and bedticks" were offered for sale by Ralph Smith, Jr., of Rhode Island (*Federal Gazette and Baltimore Daily Advertiser,* February 13, 1812).

Thin silk and cotton "Chamberry muslins" in brown and white, green and purple, and black are dated 1807 and 1808 in the Johnson album.

CHANGEABLE FABRICS

Plain weave fabrics with warp of one color and weft of another. Chambray, caungeantric, and modern Oxford cloth used for men's shirts are included among these textiles.

Of three silk gowns stolen in Boston, 1710/11, one was "changeable colour, a second flowr'd and the third stript"; a "changeable colour'd silk" petticoat was also taken (Dow, *Every Day Life,* p. 68). In Virginia "a remarkable piece of fine silk mantua, changing from red to green" was advertised in 1767 (Virginia Records).

CHARCONNAE
(charkhanar, cherconnae, cherconnee)

Striped or checked cloth of mixed silk and cotton from India. Thomas Fitch, merchant and upholsterer of Boston, ordered "Cherconees bright Colours" in June 1724 and subsequently "red and white and no Sad Colours" (Fitch letter book).

Fig. D-28. *Six swatches of linen checks of patterns favored by Germans living in Pennsylvania and found in that area. Blues and browns predominate in color. (Winterthur Museum, gift of Mrs. Edgar H. Sittig.)*

CHAUTAR
(*chowtar, chowter*)

Plain white calico imported from India and used for shirting. "Modern . . . *chotari* has four threads in each warp and weft, and the seventeenth-century *chautars* may have been the same" (Irwin and Schwartz; see also *Hobson-Jobson*).

CHECK

A fabric made of any fibers in plain weave with colored warp and weft stripes intersecting at right angles to form squares (Fig. D-28). Checks may also be printed. Checked linen had many household uses; one found in the 1695/96 van Varick inventory is for "one feather bedd, coverd with Checkerd linnen." A wide variety of furniture checks were made, especially in the Manchester area, and became popular about 1750 or 1755.

In Boston in 1760, "Scarlet and Crimson Check for Bed Curtains" was advertised (Dow, *Arts and Crafts,* p. 167). In 1762 James Boswell recorded in his London journal that he had "a handsome tent-bed with green and white check curtains [which] gave a snug yet genteel look to my room, and had a military air which amused my fancy and made me happy." In New York in 1768, "Saxon blue, green, yellow, scarlet, and crimson furniture checks" were for sale (*American Wing Handbook,* p. 130).

In John Holker's manuscript of about 1750, swatches 1 to 9 of blue-and-white linen-and-cotton checks were made in the Manchester area "for home consumption and for export, especially to the colonies. They were used for sailors' blouses, children's clothing and linings." Swatches 10 through 17, "Furniture Checks" in bolder patterns, woven in a variety of colors with large white fields, were "made and sold in Manchester for curtains and chair coverings" (see Pl. D-23). In these examples, for the most part colored cotton threads form the checks, although number 11 has a weft of scarlet wool. Number 12 has broad green checks in combination with red lines; number 13 has scar-

let checks banded by indigo; number 14 tan edged with red; number 16 tan with red and blue. A typical material for slipcovers, number 17 has bold green checks. In 1795 John Aikin wrote about furniture checks of this type: "An application of the lighter open striped checks to bed-hangings and window-curtains forty years since introduced the making of furniture checks, which have almost set aside the use of stuffs in upholstery" (p. 160).

Holker includes three swatches of "Handkerchief Checks" in his manuscript and says that they are made entirely of linen in "Manchester and surrounding towns," and that they "were extensively sold at home, abroad, and in the colonies." A full piece included five dozen handkerchiefs. One example has dark red and blue checks with wide borders of lighter blue; number 78 has the addition of red between the broader blue stripes. Characteristic are a greater predominance of blue and smaller white fields than in the household and furnishing checks.

Ten swatches of checks woven at the Arkwright Mill in Rhode Island, about 1810, are illustrated by Frances Little (p. 124, fig. 19).

Tweed houndstooth checks used for jackets and skirts are woven in 2/2 twill generally in two colors.

See also Fig. D-98.

CHELOS
(*chelloes*)

Inexpensive cotton cloth from India with red, blue, or black stripes, patterned in the loom (Irwin and Schwartz). *Chelles* were checked and were used for trousers of slaves (Savary des Bruslons).

In 1739 Philip Schuyler of Albany specified "20 Ps Challoes, not Challaes of 10 yds but Challoes of 18 yds of ab. 17 or 18/." Nine years later Hermanus Bleecker listed "12 Chelloes, Blue—18 yds at 19/." In 1767 James Beekman's factor wrote: "We have sent you ten Chelloes of a finer sort than you wrote for being smaller checks and much better cloth than the lower, and cheaper than they have been for some time" (2:912).

FIG. D-29. *Dark red worsted stamped, by means of an engraved metal roller, in a pattern imitating a palmate woven silk damask. (John Brown House, Providence, Rhode Island.) Worsteds with this finish were known as harateen and moreen, and possibly as china or cheney in the eighteenth century. Such textiles, widely imported into the colonies for furnishing, are frequently found listed in upholsterers' advertisements, bills, and estate inventories. Examples of cheney woven in red, blue, green, and gold are known in American collections where they were used for furnishing.*

CHENEY
(cheyney, china)

A worsted furnishing material dyed red, green, blue, yellow, or purple and sometimes watered. The name may derive from the French *chaîne*, meaning warp. The fabric was related to harateen and moreen although not now clearly distinguishable, and no documented example of the material has been found. *See* Fig. D-29.

By 1651 Henry Landis, Boston shopkeeper, stocked "Cheny," "Double Cheny," and "Tamy Cheny"; and in 1660 a Salem merchant, Edward Wharton, had "1 cheny sad Collrd. uper woemans coate" (Dow, *Every Day Life,* pp. 83, 263).

Other references note its use for furnishings.

Cambridge, Massachusetts, about 1640: "Philop & Cheny curtaines in graine with a deep silke fring on the vallance, and a smaller on the Curtaines, and a Coverlett sutable to it, made of Red Kersie, and laced with a greene lace, round the sides and 2 downe the middle" (Morison, p. 31).

Boston, 1724: "best Clean well water'd Orange Coloured Norwich chainys with pretty good lace binding and breed Suteable" (Fitch letter book, June 24).

Albany, 1739: "2 ps blew China for bed Curtins @ 19/2 ps red do & 2 ps green do" (Philip Schuyler to Samuel Storke).

Boston, 1746: "A fashionable crimson Damask Furniture with Counterpain and two Sets of Window Curtains, and Vallans of the same Damask. Eight Walnut Tree Chairs, stuft Back and Seats covered with the same Damask, Eight crimson China Cases [slipcovers] for ditto, one easy Chair and Cushion, same Damask, and Case for ditto" (Dow, *Arts and Crafts,* p. 111).

New York City, 1754: "1 cord Bedstead, Teaster, Rods & Suit of red China Curtains £3.5.0. 3 prs window Curtains & Chimney Vallens of Old blew Cheany £0.12.0" (New York Appraisements, p. 26).

John Banister's Newport records of 1739 show that ingrain colors were more expensive and that harateen was more costly:

16 Ps green Waterd Cheney	22/	17.12.–
6 Ps blew Ditto	22/	6.12.–
10 Ps Mock Crimsons	26/	13.1.–
2 Ps Crimson Ingrain Cheney at	34/	3.8.–
2 Ps Crimson Ingrain Harrateens	48/	4.16.–

CHERRYDERRY
(charadary, carridary)

Striped or checked woven cloth of mixed silk and cotton imported from India from the late seventeenth century (Irwin and Schwartz). In Boston, 1728, a runaway servant wore a "narrow striped Cherrederry gown, turned up with a little flowered red and white callico, stript homespun quilted petticoat, plain muslin apron" (Dow, *Arts and Crafts,* p. 187).

About 1760, the cloth was imitated in the Manchester area: "the silk branch was attempted in cherry derry's and thread satins" (Butterworth, p. 64). In 1767 both Indian and English cherryderrys were sold by Kearny and Gilbert of Philadelphia (*Pennsylvania Chronicle,* April 20).

Eight swatches of English cherryderrys of silk warp and cotton weft in tobines, checks, and stripes are in the Holker manuscript of about 1750 (see Pl. D-24). They were used for women's dresses and handkerchiefs.

CHEVERETT
(chiverett)

One of the fancy eighteenth-century glazed worsted dress fabrics largely manufactured in Norwich. The name may have derived from the word *chevron.* The 1730–34 ledger of Philadelphia merchants Willing and Shippen specifies "1 ps Cheveret 12 yds @ 6/," "1 ps Cheveret 26 yds @ 3/2," and "1 ps Cheverets 27 yds @ 6/."

A swatch woven in a small yellow and black diamond figure in Norwich is in the Moccasi manuscript (see Pl. D-57). Another woven in a zigzag pattern in pink and blue is in the Kelly pattern book, 1767.

CHINÉ

A term used in dyeing whereby the threads, warp, weft, or both, are dyed or printed before weaving with resulting clouded or flame effects. For a description of how it was made, see *Le Dessinateur* by Joubert. A Manchester firm was commended at the Great Exhibition of 1851 "for a very admirable range of Chiné goods produced from combinations of worsted, cotton, silk, and linen, with printed warps" (James, Appendix, p. 19).

See also Clouds, Hooping, Lustring, Sarcenet.

CHINTZ

A word derived from *chitta,* meaning "spotted cloth" (Irwin and Brett, p. 1). In seventeenth-century India, the word referred to a specially designed painted or printed cotton which was sometimes glazed (Beer, p. 9). The technique of madder-mordant painting in India is described by P. R. Schwartz with documentation from eighteenth-century French sources in Irwin and Schwartz, *Studies in Indo-European Textile History.*

Chintz was used in the colonies for clothing and furnishings. For example, in New York, Margrita van Varick's inventory of 1695/96 included a "chint" petticoat, a waistcoat, seven "mantells" and a "flowerd Carpet."

In England the madder-mordant technique was adapted for wood-block printing on cloth about 1676. By 1754 beautiful patterns in a wide range of vegetable colors were being printed, and in London

> Mr. Sedgwick, a very considerable trader in printed goods, had the honour to present to Her Royal Highness the Princess of Wales, a piece of English chintz, of excellent workmanship, printed on a British cotton (that is of linen warp and cotton weft) which being of our own manufacture, her Royal Highness was most graciously pleased to accept of. Her Royal Highness added, that it was preferrable to any Indian chintz whatsoever. [*Gentleman's Magazine,* as quoted in James, p. 223n.]

Twenty-nine swatches of English block-printed textiles dated to 1726, the earliest documented examples known, are among the Alexander Papers; from about 1750, there are thirteen examples of English block-printed textiles in the Holker manuscript, swatches 88 to 100 (illustrated in Florence M. Montgomery, *Printed Textiles,* Figs. 8–14b).

Indicative of the wide variety of chintzes imported into America is the advertisement of George Bartram in the *Pennsylvania Chronicle* for September 7, 1767: "A very large and neat assortment of prints, consisting of dark and light, single and double purple cottons, calicoes and linens, dark and light chintzes and chintz cottons of the newest and handsomest patterns, best china blue and crimson ground furniture, calico, with blue and red striped ditto for trimmings."

A collection of 76 eighteenth-century Indian painted and resist-dyed textiles, probably made for the French market, and 74 French block-printed cottons (known as *indiennes*) are owned by the Cooper-Hewitt Museum. Many are in brilliant unfaded condition. Eleven other Indian examples are illustrated in "The Josephine Howell Scrapbook" (Brett).

See also Fig. D-64.

CIRCASSIAN

Originally a material of mohair yarns in a fancy twill weave, later a mixture of wool and cotton, made to imitate fashionable cashmere shawls. In 1813, Ackermann suggested wool circassian cloth "for dresses of various descriptions, and also for the coat *à la surtout*" (*Repository* 10, no. 59

[November 1813]: 302). The twill-woven swatch illustrated is beige wool with a shawl figure printed in green and red. Swatches of "Col'd Circassians" are in a merchant's invoice book in the Essex Institute, Salem, circa 1830.

Circassian was also the name given to a dress fashion: "A figured double twilled jonquil sarsnet, adapted for the Circassian robe and Austrian tunic" shown by Ackermann (*Repository* 3, no. 16 [April 1810]: 270).

CIRÉ CLOTH
(sear cloth)

Waxed cloth used for wrapping textiles to keep out moisture.

CIRSAKAS

See Seersucker.

CLOUDS

Fabrics with clouded, or shaded, effects produced by dyeing or printing warp threads in different colors prior to weaving. Especially beautiful shaded or clouded floral patterns for dress silks were made in this technique during the eighteenth century (see Fig. D-31).

"Fine Cotton and Worsted clouded Waistcoats" were advertised in Boston in 1749 (Dow, *Arts and Crafts,* p. 161). In 1738 Mary Blair of Boston owned a "clouded stuff Bed with a Chince quilt lin'd w'th Silk" (SCPR, 34:157).

Twelve swatches of silk clouds made in Spitalfields and dated 1784/85 are in the Warner Archive (T380-1972). From the 1790s, swatches of clouded worsteds from Norwich include camlets without glaze, *Callemandres rayés à Flammes Fins* (see Pl. D-65), and *Tabourets rayés et nuancés* (see Pl. D-74). Clouded calimancoes are also found in the Norwich pattern books (Fig. D-30).

Compare Chiné, Hooping, Lustring. *See also* Fig. D-64.

COACH LACE

Borders and tapes for trimming coach and carriage upholstery. They are similar to furniture braids, livery tapes, and gartering. Nineteenth-century tapes made by William Marsh of Quincy, Massachusetts, had raised velvet figures woven in stylized floral and Greek key patterns (Frances Little, illus., p. 88; present location of sample cards is unknown).

COATING

Thick, heavy woolen cloth with a long nap. In 1739 James Alexander ordered blue and red coating as well as duffels and blankets; naps and bearskins, at about the same price, were listed adjacent to "coatens" in 1716. Two swatches of brown and black coating of finer quality than the adjacent examples of calmuc are in the 1807 Aix-la-Chapelle pattern book (see Pl. D-2).

FIG. D-30. *Clouded calimancoes. From a Norwich pattern book, ca. 1785. (Winterthur Museum Library.)*

Ladies in the Dress of the Year 1795.

Fete at Frogmore, in honour of her Majesty's Birth Day.

Engraved for Gedge's Ladies own Memorandum Book.

Ladies of Distinction

Euston Hall in Suffolk the Seat of His Grace the Duke of Grafton.

in the fashionable Dresses of the Year.

A Clouded French Satin Gown.
ten yards. seven shillings a yard.
given me by Mrs Woodhull.
made at Kensington July 1795.

A Blue Canterbury Muslin
One guinea.
made at Kensington June 1795.

29

Bath coating, a specialty of that town, was described as "a thick kind of double raised baize . . . used for women's petticoats, and a winter article; it is also to be had in nearly all colours, and such goods are used for cloaks" (Perkins). "Light baize of great width and long nap"; Bath flannel and Bath beaver were related goods (Harmuth).

About 1765 in New York, "brown, blue, and scarlet new-fashioned Bath coating" and "scarlet, blue, claret colour and grey mixt Bath beaver coatings" were advertised (Singleton, *Social New York,* p. 231). In Boston, 1769, "two very good plain & Knapt Bath Beaver Surtouts of a light mixt Colour one very large the other suitable for a Boy of 12 years" were lost (Earle, *Costume,* p. 243). According to Ackermann, "great-coats are in general worn of olive, olive brown, dark bottle green superfine cloth, or superfine Bath coating" (*Repository* 3, no. 14 [February 1810]: 122).

COBURG

First introduced in 1843, a few years after Queen Victoria's marriage to Prince Albert of Saxe-Coburg-Gotha, as a lighter description of paramatta cloth. It was a 2 / 1 twilled dress material of silk warp and worsted weft. However, in 1851 "coburgs in cotton warp, wefted with worsted" were part of the Great Exhibition (James, Appendix, p. 19). "They can be had in all colours and are chiefly used for coat linings and for dresses by the lower orders, who always employ them for mourning" (Caulfeild and Saward). Swatches of "Stone-Drab Saxony Coburg" and "Scarlet Aus-

Opposite: FIG. D-31. *A scrapbook page with a sample (bottom left) of "A Clouded French Sattin Gown . . . made at Kensington in 1795." The material is black and green striped with shaded white, pink, and green spots. Included on the page are plates from fashion magazines of that year and a swatch of "Blue Canterbury Muslin." From the Barbara Johnson album. (Victoria and Albert Museum.)*

tralian Coburg" are in the *Journal of Design* for 1852 (6:48). Coburgs were also printed.

See also Orleans, Paramatta.

CODRINGTON

In 1849, " 'Madonnas,' 'Albert cords,' 'Californias,' 'Cassinetts,' [and] 'Codringtons' " were all "goods of a fancy character, consisting of mottled and mixed wefts, silk stripes and figured goods, silk mixture grograms, cords, &c., to which a great variety of fancy names were given, no way indicative of the character or description of cloth" (James, p. 529). A fancy alpaca (*Textile Mercury Dictionary*). Salisbury Manufacturing Company won a bronze medal "for silk warp Codringtons, for style of fabric" at the 1853 New York industrial exhibition (Dilke, p. 28).

COGWARE

Narrow, coarse woolen cloths fulled and raised like frieze and made in several parts of England from the fourteenth century onward. They are also listed with other coarse woolens such as Kendals and carpmeals (Strutt). "Worsteds called also cogwares, or vesses and old hames, made at Norwich, are mentioned in the statutes as early as the eighth of Edward II" (Strutt, as quoted in James, p. 44).

COLNE

A valley in the West Riding of Yorkshire where "Colne serges, a heavy narrow stuff" were made (James, p. 364).

COPPERPLATE PRINTING

A technique related to intaglio printing with engraved metal plates on paper. By using copper sheets of up to 36 inches square, a yard of cloth could be printed in a press before shifting the cloth

and recoloring the plate. This monochrome technique, confined to red, blue, purple, or sepia, permitted finer linear effects than did woodblocks. Without copyright laws, artists' designs were freely copied and often embellished with flowers and foliage drawn by textile designers. Adapted designs from print sources included classical ruins, exotic birds, chinoiserie, patriotic subjects (Fig. D-32), the theater, and nursery themes.

Copperplate printing in England dates from 1756, at which date the technique was brought from Ireland by Francis Nixon of Drumcondra to the London area. Characteristically English patterns, as opposed to the better known French toiles de Jouy, have been identified by means of large pattern books with textile designs printed on paper, many bearing unmistakably English factory names. Widely available and apparently cherished, readily identifiable English textiles have survived in the United States in larger quantities than in England. Prints were used for both dress and furnishing.

The research of Peter Floud and Barbara Morris on English textile printing resulted in exhibitions held at the Cotton Board, Colour Design and Style Centre, Manchester, 1955, and the Victoria and Albert Museum, London, 1960. *See also* Florence M. Montgomery's *Printed Textiles.*

About 1760 Philip Bell of London made a tester bedstead for George Washington with "a neat cut Cornish," or pierced cornice. The bed was to be hung with "Chintz Blew Plate Cotton furniture," and, according to English custom, a coverlet, four chair seats, festoon curtains, and "2 Neat cut window Cornishes" were all covered in the same material (Fede, p. 18).

Aside from furnishing fabrics, copperplates were used for printing a great variety of handkerchiefs. Some illustrated fables, moral scenes, or alphabets for children; others illustrated popular pleasures and pastimes of the day, cartoons, maps, and historical subjects and heroes, many of which were aimed at the American market.

The technique developed in the early nineteenth century into continuous cylinder printing.

CORD

Stout, heavy woolen, or cotton and woolen, fabric woven with a raised cord or ridge running in the warp. Between 1810 and 1813, J. and T. Clark, Studley Mills, Trowbridge, "went in extensively for cords—Bedford, Regent, Union, Princes and Oxford" (Beckinsale, xxviii).

The manufacture of Bedford cord, first made in Bedford, England, was also claimed by New Bedford, Massachusetts, where it was being made in 1845. The fabric, which simulates pile cloth corduroy, was made first in worsted yarn and later in cotton and wool. Until recently much of the material sold today as piqué was really Bedford cloth (*American Fabrics Encyclopedia*, p. 200). Pictures, patterns, and diagrams of Bedford cord are given in Nisbet (pp. 110–25).

Queen cord is stout, ribbed cotton trousering. In 1784 James Beekman ordered "8 pieces Corduroys" and "8 pieces Queens Cord" which he specified should be "handsome Olive and fashionable Colours. different prices" (3:1115).

CORDUROY

"A kind of coarse, durable cotton fabric, having a piled surface, like that of velvet, raised in cords, ridges, or ribs" (Merriam-Webster). It was made with an extra weft for the pile. The character of corduroy has not changed greatly since the late eighteenth century. The name derives from *"Corde du roi,* the king's cord" (Beck). Just how it differed from queens cord can only be conjectured. According to Perkins, it was made either twilled or plain in several qualities, "olives, drabs, slates, fawns, and white."

Opposite: Fig. D-32. *William Penn's treaty with the Indians as shown on a copperplate-printed textile, England, ca. 1785. From a print after the painting by Benjamin West. (Winterthur Museum.)*

Neither Holker nor Aikin used the name, although they mentioned a great variety of cotton velvets made in the Manchester area as "strong cotton ribs and barragon, broad-raced lin[en] thicksets and tufts" (Aikin, p. 158). James Beekman first referred to it by name along with jeans, dimities, pillows, and velverets in a London order for goods dated 1784, his first order after the Revolution (3:1115).

On December 5, 1789, the *Providence Gazette* ran the advertisement of a corduroy weaver:

Manufactures. Notice is hereby given, to Town and Country, that by the Middle of January next there will be ready to engage or take in Work for Customers, a Person that can weave, cut and singe, all Kinds of Corderoys. He likewise can weave Velverets, twilled or plain Thicksetts, Denims, Fustians, Jeans, Royal Rib, Cottonet, Ribbed Sattin, by Length or Breadth, Florentines, ribbed or plain, &c.

As Specimens of his Work can be the only Recommendation, these may be seen at Mr. Lewis Peck's Shop, where the Person may be spoke with.

Emery defined corduroy as "cotton weft-pile fabric ribbed in the warp direction, the pile produced by cutting the vertically aligned floats of a supplementary (pile) weft" (p. 176).

COSSA
(cassa, cossae, kassa)

Plain muslin or *toile de mouseline unie & fine, que les Anglois raportent des Indes Orientales* (Savary des Bruslons). The following appear in James Beekman's orders during the second half of the eighteenth century:

4 pieces ⁶/₄ Cossae Muslin 20 yard from 65/. to 90/
6 pieces " " " Striped " 65/. to 90/
2 pieces " " " Cross Band " 86/. and 90/
2 pieces " " " Needle work flowered "

While in England in 1767/68 Samuel Rowland Fisher ordered "2 Ell w'd Cossees—60/."

COTTON

A term used to designate certain woolen cloths from at least the fifteenth century, so one must be cautious in reading the term. Wadsworth and Mann suggested that "the explanation of the use of the word cotton may lie in the fact that it had also the sense of nap or down, and the process of raising the nap of woollen cloths was called 'cottoning' or frizing" (p. 16). At the end of the sixteenth century, Manchester was "eminent for its woollen cloth or Manchester cottons" (Daniels, p. 7n). An act of 1609 concerned "kendals and other coarse things of the like nature and made of the like coarse wool, and differing in name only, called cogware, coarse cottons and carptmeals," and in 1620, exports to Europe "included woollen goods like Manchester, Welsh and 'northern' 'cottons,' linsey wolseys and kerseys . . ." (Wadsworth and Mann, pp. 16n, 21).

Butterworth wrote in 1822 of

Kendal cottons, a manufacture which has subsisted now near five centuries, . . . made entirely of wool, and that of the coarsest kind. Like the Welsh cottons, they are manufactured both frized and plain, and are used chiefly for negro clothing in America, and the West Indies, though some are worn at home by the poor or labouring husbandmen, and various conjectures have been offered respecting the origin of the name, but the most probable is, that it is a corruption of the word coating. [P. 60.]

COTTONADE

Originally plain, also serge, or twill woven, all-cotton fabric made with single yarns and heavy filling. Made in solid colors, checks, stripes, plaids, etc. and used for dress goods, tablecloths, and, with the stronger grades, trousers (Harmuth). Coarse, heavy cotton fabric, an imitation cassimere (*Textile Mercury Dictionary*). Among the Acadians of Louisiana, cottonade was "the general clothing weight fabric," falling in the blue-white-brown color range (Glasgow, p. 341).

COUTI

Known from fifteen swatches of brightly colored silk / linen striped dress goods in a 1772 letter from Nîmes and said to be "an article very much in fashion everywhere today" (Fig. D-33).

COUTIL

See Ticking.

COUTY

Known from seven swatches in the Moccasi manuscript to be a linen or cotton fabric (see Pl. D-61). One swatch is labeled "per mobili." Just how couti (q.v.) and couty relate to coutil (*see* Ticking) is not understood.

CRANKY

In northern British dialect, cranky meant checkered (Halliwell). As a textile, it may have referred to a checked cloth woven in the Manchester area. References to cranky hair and flock mattresses are in Thomas Chippendale's accounts. Crankies are mentioned in Virginia merchants' records. In 1786, T. T. Byrd was billed £1.16.0 for "a Wool Cranky Matrass," perhaps a woolen check or a cotton check filled with wool flock (Armistead-Cocke Papers, Box 2, folder 6).

CRAPE

"A light, transparent stuff, in the manner of gauze; made of raw silk, gummed and twisted on the mill;

wove without crossing and much used in mourning" (Chambers). Other crapes were made of worsteds and sometimes mixed with silk.

In March 1695, Thomas Banister noted in his order book the shipment of "8 peices of embroydred Crapes at 26 / per peice" and "1 peice Silke Crape Narrow Stript at 30 /." On July 20, 1695, he wrote to his London factor: "Black crapes sell very well . . . but send no cloth crapes. Let them be a good black and let them be as little woole as you can." By cloth crapes Banister meant those made entirely of wool.

Of eight swatches of crapes included in James Alexander's 1736 order, some are all wool and some silk and wool; he requested that they be "black and white, nothing blewish" (see Pl. D-9). Newspaper advertisements of 1755 specified "Silk Crape, Widow's Crape, Cyprus and Hat Crape" (Earle, *Costume*, p. 97).

In the nineteenth century, many new kinds of crape were invented. In 1822 Stephen Wilson patented his British crape (number 4714) "employing two wefts of worsted on a common worsted or other warp, these wefts being spun from five to seven times harder than for ordinary weaving and having their twist in opposing directions" (Warner, p. 636). In the same year, embossed crape was first patented—"a plain, thin silk gauze, stiffened with shellac and embossed with various patterns by being passed over a heated revolving copper cylinder on the surface of which the desired design was engraved" (Warner, p. 285). Denny describes several other new kinds of crape, "a general term covering many kinds of crinkled or uneven materials":

(1) Hard twisted yarns in right and left twist, warp or filling, or both which kink up when released from the loom. Includes georgette. (2) Alternate groups of warp yarns, some wound on separate beam or held slacker than the rest, forming crinkled stripes as in seersucker or Austrian shade cloth. (3) Treatment with chemicals to produce blistery or creped surface. Includes plissé. (4) Engraved rollers

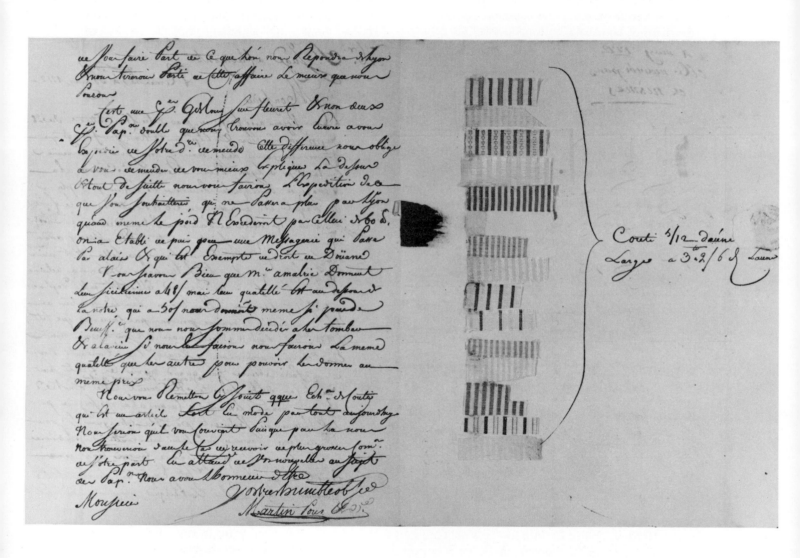

FIG. D-33. *Fifteen swatches of couti pasted to a letter from Nîmes dated 1772. (Colonial Williamsburg Foundation.)*

or grooves plus chemicals produce a fabric like Kimono crepe. (5) Heat and engraved rollers produce mourning or hard crepes which are woven from hard-spun silk in the gum.

The 1797–1809 trader's book includes the following notations: "Crapes—the usual price of this article is 16,000 reas or $17.50 per piece and the colours ought to be blue, rose, white, yellow, &c. some plain and some figured" (see Fig. D-96). In Boston on April 24, 1810, "1 case coloured Canton Crapes of a very superior quality—sage, lilac, white, pink, slate, buff, yellow, different shades of blue, drab, &c." were advertised for sale in the *Palladium*. In the John R. Latimer papers for 1815, "Black Canton Crape" and "Coloured ditto viz. lilac, pink, white, blue, nankeen, orange, crimson" are listed.

A swatch of merino crape in pink silk and gray wool, a plain weave for ladies' autumn dresses, is in Ackermann's *Repository* for 1809, and a swatch of Chinese crape in pale blue silk twill is in that of 1812 (2, no. 8 [August 1809]: 132; 7, no. 42 [June 1812]: 370).

See also Norwich crape.

CRETONNE

In the eighteenth century, a "white cloth with warp of hemp and weft of linen made in Normandy" used for curtains, table linen, and men's and women's shirts (Savary des Bruslons). Early in the twentieth century, Harry Nisbet wrote:

> Crepe fabrics are also sometimes printed with decorative designs, and sold as a light and cheap material known as "cretonne," which is employed extensively as loose coverings for furniture; also antimacassars, covers, curtains, hangings, and for many other similar household articles. Cretonnes are usually printed on both sides of the fabric, with a design and colour scheme of a different character on each side, to make them quite reversible.[P. 103.]

In 1919, *Good Furniture,* a magazine published in Grand Rapids, defined cretonne as "a term applied to a variety of printed designs on linen, cotton, and mixtures of either with other coarser fibres, such as jute and hemp—either hand-blocked or machine-printed" (p. 217). Samples of post-World War I nursery prints entitled "The Navy," "Aviation," and "The Infantry" showed boys engaged in military activities. The article pointed out that the printing effects achieved were possible because of cretonne's "softer surface and a certain irregularity of light and shade playing across its twisted threads. The pigments not only soak in deeper on a softer surface, but the irregular distribution of the colors produces something of the charm and quality of antique tapestry designs" (p. 223).

CREWEL

Loosely twisted, fine two-ply worsted yarn especially suited to embroidery as it easily pulled through cloth. The worsted men "likewise deal in crewels, which are the ends of the warps of worsted or yarn cut out of the loom" (Mortimer). In London "Caddas or cruel ribbons" were taxed in 1640 (Beck). In Boston in 1736, a haberdasher sold "Crewels in Shades" (Dow, *Arts and Crafts,* p. 156). Beck cites a poem of 1784: "With here and there a tuft of crimson yarn / Of scarlet cruel in the cushion fix'd."

Ann Pollard Rowe has written the most recent comprehensive study of this embroidery.

CROCUS
(*crocas*)

Coarse sacking, as gunny or burlap. Crocus is among linens listed in eighteenth-century custom house regulations reprinted in Postlethwayt's appendix. This coarse cloth was used for servants' and slaves' summer clothing, especially in the southern colonies.

CRYSTAL

"A very fine wide Durant, termed Crystal (Spanish *crystalla,* transparent) is exported, always white, for Nuns' Veils" (Booth). "Dress goods, made with fine silk warp and wool filling which form alternate fine and heavy (often irregular) ribs" (Harmuth).

CUBICA

A fine, thin worsted serge, usually red; a very fine kind of shalloon. It was used for lining coats and dresses. "A very fine shalloon, always unglazed, has the Spanish name of Cubica. It is chiefly exported to Catholic countries to be made into gowns for the ecclesiastics, and is therefore dyed black, blue, carmelite brown, &c., according to the several orders of Friars" (Beck, p. 297). James cites from a long list of worsted manufactures of Bradford in 1857: "4/4 Plainbacks or Cubicas of one Twill. 4/4 Shalloons or Cubicas of two Twills" (p. 532).

CULGEE

A rich figured silk worn as a turban or sash, hence a figured Indian silk. A 1696 definition reads: "There is two sorts of Indian Silk called Culgees, the one is Satten, the other is Taffety, they are stained with all sorts of colours. They are much used for Handkerchiefs, and for Lining of Beds, and for Gowns for both Men and Women" (OED). "A Piece of White Culgee Sattin, flowered with Blue, Scarlet, and Orange Colours" was advertised among stolen goods in the London *Post Man* (December 27, 1701).

The Wistar Letter book contains orders for "2 doz Silk Culgee handker. blue Ground with Small White Spotts" and "2 doz. of Silk Culgee, one blue ground & Large White Spotts, the Other Red Ground at 30/" (December 4, 1766).

Three swatches of Wiltshire culgeed flannels are in the mid-eighteenth-century Berch Papers (see Pl. D-13). They are fine woolen fabrics with crude discharge patterns which go through to the other side of the cloth, thus making them reversible.

The printing technique of these western woolens is not clearly understood, but like many other textiles they were undoubtedly made to imitate the Indian materials.

CULLEN
(colleyn, coleyne)

Refers to fabric from Cologne in Germany.

CUTS

Blankets woven in pairs and cut in two after weaving. Webster said that they were made "of the best tail wool" and used for seamen's hammocks.

See also Witney.

CUTTANEE
(cotonis, cuttance)

"An important [seventeenth-century] Gujarati export cloth of mixed silk-and-cotton with satin weave, usually striped and sometimes interspersed with flowers. Much in demand for the making of quilts, which were popular in England" (Irwin and Schwartz). According to a Royal African Company letter of 1678, cuttanees (probably plain woven cotton) were imported for printing in England: "Cuttannees, a sort stamped in England with flowers" (Wadsworth and Mann, p. 131). About 1719 "Striped, Floured and Wrought Cuttannees" were among prohibited East India goods (Kress, S2200). In this century, "cuttance" is defined as a "fine heavy and stout silk satin of East India, with bright colored woven stripes and cotton back; used for upholstery" (Harmuth).

CYLINDER PRINTING

A technique employing engraved copper cylinders, each inked with a different color, by which

FIG. D-34. *A design derived from Audubon's* Birds of America *and printed with copper cylinders. (Winterthur Museum, gift of Victoria and Albert Museum.)*

cloth was continuously printed (Fig. D-34). Invented as early as 1783 by Thomas Bell, a Scotsman, it was first used for furnishing fabrics about 1810. At first only one metal cylinder was cut, generally inked in red, and other colors were added by surface printing methods. By about 1835, with the development of large printing presses, many cylinders, each inked in a different color, could be controlled. A pantograph which etched the designs in several repeats across the surface of the roller reduced production costs considerably.

CYPRUS
(cypress)

A light, transparent material of silk and hair resembling crape and used for mourning dress, especially as a hatband. It is thought to have originally been imported from Cyprus. "Cobweb lawn, or the very finest lawn, is often mentioned with cyprus" which may once have been a sheer, creped linen material, according to Beck.

A 1613 English inventory lists white, green, and black cyprus garters (Ingatestone, p. 5). In Boston "1 flowered Cyprus handkerchief" is listed in the 1723 inventory of Mary Hunt (SCPR, 23: 152).

Twelve yards of the "broadest Cypres gause" were imported into Virginia in 1773 (Norton, p. 331).

FIG. D-35. *Silk damask dress, probably English, traditionally thought to have been worn at the Mischianza ball held by British officers in honor of Sir William Howe, Philadelphia, 1778. (Philadelphia Museum of Art.)*

D

DAMASK

A reversible patterned fabric made from several fibers, or combinations of fibers, and used as table linen, clothing (Fig. D-35), and furnishings. "Damask is patterned by the contrast between the warp-float and weft-float faces of a satin weave" or "the patterning can be effected by contrast between the two faces of uneven twill as well as satin" (Emery, p. 134). Flowers and other figures appear in relief above the ground (Fig. D-36).

On July 21, 1695, Thomas Banister of Boston ordered "mock damasks and the best worsted damasks you can get and silk stuffs but the newest fashion." In Boston newspaper advertisements, we find in 1732 "a fine new Silk Damask Quilt and Quilted Cushion of the same"; in 1734, "Gentlemens Night Gowns and Banjans, made of Worsted Damasks, Brocaded Stuffs, and Callamancoes"; and in 1762, "Yellow and crimson Silk Damask Window Curtains, compleat" (Dow, *Arts and Crafts,* pp. 109, 155, 120). "Womens best Damask Worsted Shoes in fashionable colours, viz: Saxon blue, green, pink colour, and white" were advertised in 1751 (Earle, *Costume,* p. 225).

In the Boston fire of 1760, Sarah McNeal sustained heavy losses of silk damasks valued at £6 a yard as compared with brocaded silks at £9 and silver tissue at £11:

> 27 yards blew English Dammask
> 18 yards green ditto
> 16 yards Cloath ditto
> 27 yards dark blew ditto
> 12 yards Ash ditto
> 11 yards Red ditto
> Remnants of difrent Coulers

FIG. D-36. *Green wool damask woven in floral and leaf pattern. England, late seventeenth / early eighteenth century. (Colonial Williamsburg Foundation.)*

She also listed damask dresses in crimson, blue, sand-color, green, white, and "one Grey English Damask Gound Quite new"|(*Boston Records,* pp. 37, 41). *See also* Fig. D-64.

It is not always possible to judge from inventory descriptions, except perhaps by the value, whether a damask was all silk, a combination of silk and worsted, or entirely worsted. From inventories, however, it is clear that American upholsterers followed English furnishing practices and used the same material throughout a room for bed and window curtains and upholstery. In Thomas Chippendale's accounts, silk-upholstered furniture was provided with more practical cases, or slipcovers, made of worsted in the same color, for ordinary use. In a 1746 Boston advertisement slipcovers were provided for damask-covered backstools and an easy chair: "A fashionable crimson Damask Furniture with Counterpain and two Sets of Window Curtains, and Vallans of the same Damask. Eight Walnut Tree Chairs, stuft Back and Seats covered with the same Damask, Eight crimson China [cheney] Cases for ditto, one easy Chair and Cushion, same Damask, and Case for ditto" (Dow, *Arts and Crafts,* p. 111).

A 1770 Boston advertisement offered "12 Mohogony carv'd frame Chairs with crimson damask bottoms; 2 crimson damask Window Curtains and window Cushions"; and one of 1773 specified "A very rich Silk Damask Bed, with Window Curtains, Chairs, and an easy Chair, all in the newest Taste. A large Sopha and ten Chairs covered with the best crimson Silk-Damask, and four large Window Curtains of the same. A small Sopha and five Chairs of the same Damask, in the Chinese Taste" (Dow, *Arts and Crafts,* p. 126). In New York in 1784, "Rich yellow silk and worsted damask...a sofa, twelve chairs, and three window curtains of sky-blue silk and worsted damask stuffs garnished and fringed" were advertised (Gottesman, *1777–99,* p. 147). Earlier residents had possessed "A Great Cheer Covered with blew worsted Damask, Old" and "Crimson worsted Damask window Curtains" (New York Appraisements, 1757, 1760, pp. 42, 76).

Documented swatches and patterns of damasks are found in other records. Four "Silk Damasks, ½ yard Wide from 18d to 20d yard" of worsted weft and silk warp, circa 1720, are in the Weavers' Company manuscript. Large-scale patterns for Spitalfields silk dress damasks are preserved in the Print Room of the Victoria and Albert Museum. *See also* Spitalfields.

Of a swatch of fine dark green wool damask, Holker commented: "this material is made in all colors; much used for gentlemen's dressing gowns, it wears well. The luster is achieved by means of hot pressing." Of a swatch of Spitalfields red silk and wool damask, he said: "This material is made in all colors for furnishing" (Holker manuscript, nos. 111, 112).

Late eighteenth-century swatches of *Sattins de lit fins* and *très fins* (actually of damask weave), some in two colors, are in a Norwich pattern book at Winterthur (see Pl. D-68), and Norwich fine and superfine bed damasks are in the Kelly pattern books. Swatches of red and blue worsted *Bed Damasco* are in the Moccasi manuscript (see Pl. D-56).

A mid-nineteenth-century Irish linen damask tablecloth and napkins presented to the Earl of Clarendon are illustrated by Yapp at "Textile Fabrics," (pls. 24, 25), along with other plates showing characteristic patterns of 1850 to 1875.

DARNEX
(dornick, dornix)

A cloth of linen warp and woolen weft probably first made in Flanders at Tournay (Du. *Dorneck*), and brought to Norwich by Flemish weavers in the sixteenth century. The fabric "came in several classes, [and] the term probably embraced a whole range of rather coarse, comparatively large-patterned upholstery materials that were readily distinguishable even if their patterns varied considerably" (Thornton, *Interior Decoration,* p. 109). In Scotland "dornick" was a linen fabric of damask weave and generally listed among the napery of a household (definition, courtesy of Margaret Swain).

FIG. D-37. *Printed mousseline de laine. From* Journal of Design 1 *(March–August 1849): 73. (Winterthur Museum Library.)*

"Tapestry or Dornex hangings of what sort soever made in England whereof any part wool . . . 10d. per yard" are listed in the mid-seventeenth-century Book of Rates (Thornton, "Tapisseries," p. 88). It was used for hangings (see Pl. D-95), carpets, vestments, coverings, cushions, coverlets, and coarse clothing.

Abbott Lowell Cummings in his inventory study for *Bed Hangings* found little mention of the material after 1700. In the nineteenth century, it was defined as a sort of checked table linen.

The 1638 disposition of Mistress Glover's belongings stated that "shee had 3 sorts of Hangings, one of tapestry and striped hangings, and greene darnicke" (Morison, p. 32). William Paine's inventory of 1660 includes "2 darnick carpetts," probably for bed or table covers, and a schoolmaster owned an "old darnkell coverlet" (Dow, *Every Day Life,* pp. 261, 45). Ebenezer Savage, first native-trained upholsterer of Boston, owned six pieces of "darnix" valued at 48s. 4d. per piece at the time his inventory was taken in 1684 (SCPR, 9:264).

DELAINE

A fine woolen fabric, first called *mousseline de laine,* or muslin of wool, developed by the French. It "began to come into demand" in England about 1835, "being a fabric composed of worsted weft and cotton warp. . . . These kinds of stuffs being particularly adapted for printing colours upon, have added much to the ornamental character of worsteds" (James, pp. 476, 634). Delaines were also warp printed.

Noted for their "cheapness, durability and sightliness" (Arthur Cole, 1:326), swatches of delaines are in many sample books. "Pale red for Delains" is the caption for a swatch found in a dye receipt book kept by Samuel Dunster of Johnston, Rhode Island, in 1844. Eight examples of printed delaines are in the *Journal of Design* of 1849 (Fig. D-37). "Old Southampton Odds and Ends," a scrapbook dating from the 1880s at Winterthur Museum, contains a piece of "Old Fashioned Delaine." In a pattern book prepared at Old Pacific Print Works, Lawrence, Massachusetts, 1874, are printed delaines of several kinds and qualities; some have paired and some single warps, others are printed on fancy cloth with a tiny float figure. Both plain and twill weaves are present (Fig. D-38).

Delaines are commonly found in "Log Cabin" pieced quilts in which the wiry, hard cloth never lies quite flat and assumes a slightly tubular appearance.

FIG. D-38. *Swatches of woolen delaines woven with paired warps, dated 1874. At left is a paisley pattern printed in red, yellow, green, and black; at right are two black and green samples. From a sample book inscribed "Delaines Book" from Old Pacific Print Works, Lawrence, Massachusetts. (Cooper-Hewitt Museum, gift of Frederick J. Whitehead.)*

DENIM

"Washable, strong, stout twilled cotton cloth, made of single yarn, and either dyed in the piece or wóven with dark brown or dark blue warp and white filling; used for overalls, skirts, etc." (Har-muth). The term probably derives from *Serge de Nismes,* a twilled woolen cloth made in France; by the late eighteenth century, it was also made of wool and cotton.

In Providence, Rhode island, a German redemptioner ran away wearing a "blue and white Kersey Shirt and Sergedenim Breeches" (*Providence Gazette,* April 29, 1786). "Sergedenim" and "searge de-nim" were advertised in Boston and Hartford newspapers in the 1770s (Earle, *Costume,* p. 213).

Single, double, and striped cotton denims were manufactured in the Lancashire area. Swatches dating from 1786 are in the Hilton manuscript (Fig. D-39).

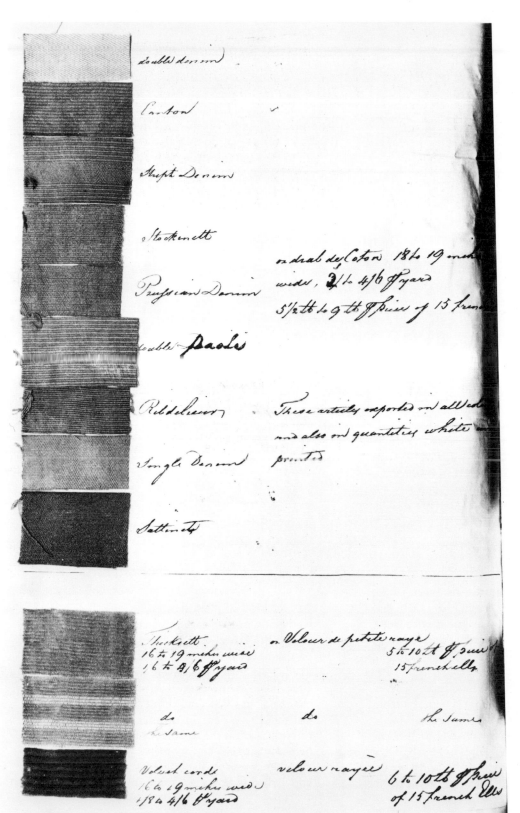

FIG. D-39. *Swatches of denims, stockinette, double paoli, satinet, thickset, and velvet cords, all cotton textiles typical of those produced in the Manchester area. From the Hilton manuscript, 1786. (Public Record Office.)*

217

DENMARK SATIN

"Stout English worsted satin, dyed black and finished with a high luster; used for slippers" (Harmuth). Forbes listed it among worsted and silk-and-worsted goods in 1827.

See also Amens, Everlasting.

DESOY

A stout twilled silk, first known as sergedesoy. It was frequently used in the eighteenth century, especially for men's coats and waistcoats (Earle, *Costume,* p. 98). "No serges of silk can be found mentioned until recent times, when serge du soy was in the last [eighteenth] century sold as a dress material, and more recently as a lining" (Beck).

DIAMANTINE

One of the fancy eighteenth-century glazed worsted dress fabrics largely manufactured in Norwich. A swatch of pink, blue, and white, fine diamond-pattern glazed worsted from Norwich is in the Moccasi manuscript of about 1760 (see Pl. D-57). An identical pattern is in the John Kelly pattern book of 1767.

DIAPER

A kind of dimity; a linen fabric (sometimes with cotton) woven with lines crossing to form diamonds with the spaces variously filled with lines, a dot, or a leaf (OED). The name is derived from the place of its first fame, Ypres in Flanders. Twill weave.

Willing and Shippen of Philadelphia ordered "Clouting, Napkin & Tabling Diaper" from England in the 1730s. Of "Six coarse diaper Breakfast Cloths" sent to his wife, Deborah, Benjamin Franklin wrote from London in 1758: "They are to spread on the Tea Table, for no body breakfasts here on the naked Table, but on the Cloth set

a large Tea Board with the Cups" (*Franklin Papers,* 7:381). In Providence, 1786, "1 Set Diaper Bed Curtains, old" were inventoried in the "Little Bed Room Chamber" of Joseph Brown.

Two mid-eighteenth-century swatches of linen / cotton diaper woven on a harness loom and used for "summer waistcoats, bodices and petticoats" are in the Holker manuscript. Swatch number 63 is a simple diaper pattern; in swatch number 64, lozenges center two dotted patterns in alternate weft rows. Three swatches of "Flowered Cotton Diaper" (*basin à fleurs brochées;* swatch nos. 65–68) are woven with stylized floral and leaf patterns of large scale centered in lozenges (see Pl. D-25). Of these, Holker says that different patterns and qualities are used for petticoats and furnishing.

At plate 12 of "Miscellany" in the third volume of plates, Rees gives the "draught and cording of looms" for diapers. Other nineteenth-century drafts for "diaper and Pint work—16 leafe" and "Rose Diment Diper" are in the Struble weaving book at the Metropolitan Museum of Art (Margaret E. White).

DIMITY
(Fr. *basin*)

The term refers to any of a number of harness-loom patterned fabrics. According to a 1696 draper's handbook,

A finer kind of plain dimity, "single Wove," was made in two varieties, with and without a nap; the latter kind, which was the finest, "is used only for to Work Beds on," or, when dyed, "to foot stockings with or to line Breeches." Among the varieties which were cut there was flowered dimity of several patterns and two degrees of fineness [one called tufts], made on the treadle loom, and used for men's waistcoats and women's petticoats. . . . Another variety, also called striped dimity, was "cotton flowered with several sorts of coloured satin stripes, but it is not properly a dimity." [Wadsworth and Mann, p. 114.]

In 1739 Philip Schuyler of Albany ordered "12 ps fine Tuft dimothy of 24 yds" (p. 99).

According to Rees, writing in the early nineteenth century,

Dimity is a kind of cotton cloth originally imported from India, and now manufactured in great quantities in various parts of Britain, especially in Lancashire. Dr. Johnson calls it dimity, and describes it as a kind of fustian. The distinction between fustian and dimity, . . . seems to be this; that the word fustian is used to express a common tweeled cotton cloth of a stout fabric, upon which no ornament is woven in the loom; but which is most frequently dyed after being woven. Dimity is also a stout cotton cloth of a similar fabric; but is ornamented in the loom, either with stripes or fanciful figures, and when woven is seldom dyed, but commonly bleached of a pure white. The striped dimities are the most common, as they require less labour in weaving than the others, and the mounting of the looms being more simple, and consequently less expensive, they can be sold at much lower rates. For the plans of mounting both kinds, as generally practised by weavers, see the article Draught and Cording. [12: n.p.; see also plates 4 and 12 of "Miscellany" in the third volume of plates.]

From about 1750 to 1825, common varieties of dimity differed from the thin corded muslin (often printed with sprigs) known as summer dress goods. Bedspreads called dimity are like seersucker with puckered stripes; "they are lightweight, wash well, and are used in hospitals and other institutions" (Denny). Three definitive articles by Hazel E. Cummin elaborate on this information and illustrate examples of striped and checked dimities from American collections (Fig. D-41).

The following kinds of dimity were offered for sale in the Caine broadside (1754):

Two ps superfine stript corded Dimity
One ps fine flower'd ditto
One ps fine flower'd & diamond ditto
One ps ditto small diamond ditto
One ps fine flower'd yard wide ditto
One bundle Women's Dimothy Caps
One bundle fine Dimothy Stomagers [stomachers].

Twenty years later, "very fine corded Dimothy for Breeches" was advertised (Dow, *Arts and Crafts,* p. 184).

Twelve "Satton Dimotys" of linen with brightly colored silk stripes are preserved in the Weavers' Company manuscript and date from about 1720 (see Pl. D-97). This was probably the kind of lining material described in a London advertisement: "A stript Blue and White Silk Night Gown lin'd with Yellow Silk Dimity" (*Post Man,* August 2, 1715).

Six swatches of corded dimities are preserved in the Hilton manuscript (see Fig. D-75). They have herringbone and tobine stripes and date from 1786. The same manuscript has two plain and striped India dimities and two figured dimities (Fig. D-40). Two swatches of striped and bird's-eye dimities of linen and cotton, and one of linen with colored silk weft, are in the Richelieu Papers (Lh45 I, p. 108); they were woven at Nantes and date from 1736. Rouen swatches (1737) called *Futaines et Basins* were woven in diamond and ribbed patterns (Lh45c, p. 30).

Eight swatches in the Holker manuscript indicate that the term *dimity* covered a wide variety of cotton cloth from fine bird's-eye (swatch 63) to large flowered patterns (see Pl. D-25) and stripes (swatches 69–71). All were sturdy and serviceable, as well as attractive for furnishing and clothing.

In 1812 Ackermann presented a swatch of stamped dimity, "an entirely new article for white beds and other furniture . . . it wants no lining,

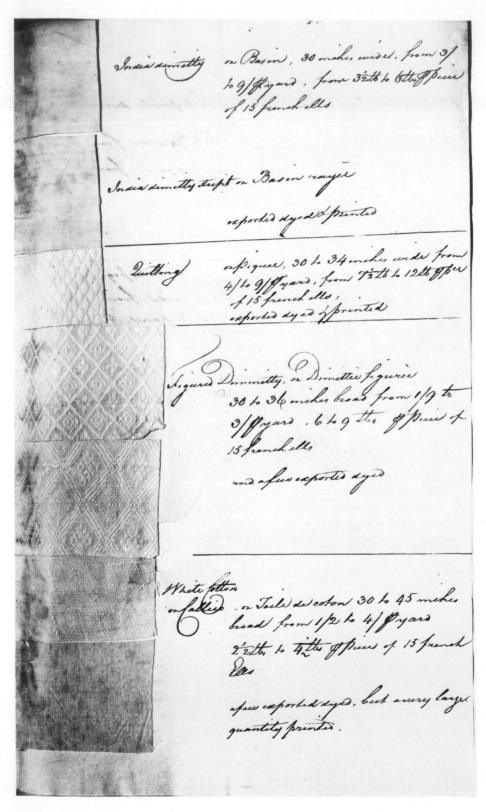

FIG. D-40. *Swatches of dimity, quilting, and calico. From the Hilton manuscript, 1786. (Public Record Office.)*

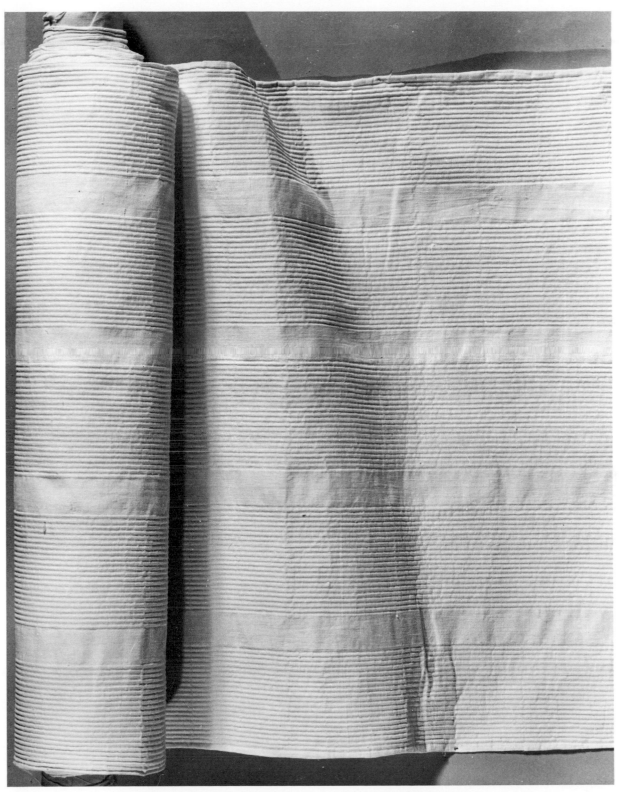

FIG. D-41. *Striped cotton dimity, 23 inches wide. Made in England, ca. 1800.*
(Copp Collection, Smithsonian Institution.)

and is sold by the piece at a very reasonable price" (*Repository*, 8, no. 47 [November 1812]: 304). The swatch, in fine twill stripes, is embossed with a leaf pattern.

DINOY

One of the fancy eighteenth-century glazed worsted dress fabrics largely manufactured in Norwich. James Beekman's London agent wrote in 1766, "I have sent you a new kind of Stuffs called Figured Dinoys in the room of Cheverets which Latter being much the same Nature and Quality with Checked Hungarians there are few made" (Beekman Papers, 2:770).

DOBBY

A small-figured union (mixed-fiber) material made of cotton and worsted. About 1815,

> Mr. James Akroyd, Junior, . . . introduced . . . a species of stuff termed "dobby," from being woven by the aid of a wood machine with that appellation placed across the loom, and in use to the present period for weaving coat linings of cotton warp and worsted weft. . . . [It resembled] a figured wildbore. The figures, at first, were mostly a small diamond or lozenge, designated bird's eye, but there was a capability of great range of figure, being woven with from sixteen to nineteen healds, so that, eventually, the figures consisted of flowers and other patterns and devices of a small kind, not exceeding a sixpence in size. [James, p. 374.]

The dobby loom, still in use today, controlled small, multiharness patterns and probably preceded the jacquard attachment. For descriptions, see Fox, *Mechanism of Weaving*.

DOESKIN

New in Gloucestershire in the late 1830s, doeskin was developed from fancy woolen cassimeres. Of different qualities in thickness and color, it was used for clerical garments, riding trousers, and naval officers' uniforms. The name was also given to a twilled cotton fabric napped on one side which was used for backing artificial leather and for sport coats.

A swatch of black Irish doeskin in twill weave is in the *Journal of Design* (5:119).

At the New York industrial exhibition of 1853, Middlesex Company of Lowell, Massachusetts, displayed, among other woolen goods, beaver cloths, cassimeres, and doeskins "manufactured entirely of native wool" (Wallis, p. 16).

DOMESTICS

Cotton goods, shirting, and sheeting made in the United States.

DOMET
(domett)

"We have latterly introduced a great deal of cotton with the woollens, making an article called dometts, and another article called domett baize, which has superseded woollen baize" (an 1828 account cited in Bischoff, 2:178). In 1833 domet was used chiefly by the poorer classes as well as for shrouds and the lining of coffins (Perkins). Later cotton varieties were woven in warp stripes in plain weave and finished with a nap on both sides to be used for pajamas and shirts.

A strong, heavy twilled cotton cloth with a raised face on both sides, either gray or bleached (*Textile Mercury Dictionary*). It was used by dressmakers as wadding.

DOREA
(doorea, doria, doriya)

A warp striped or checked fabric of mixed silk and cotton from India. Offered for sale at auction on July 4, 1695, were "several pieces of very fine Thread Stripe Muslins in single pieces. 20 yards each, being the Bale of Dorees bought at the East-

India House last Sale" (*London Gazette*). According to a 1699 description,

> *Doreas* depends much on fancy as to the works and stripes, but it is essential to their value that they be most of them of a fine thread clear and thin, and the stripes of as great variety as you can, some single, some double, or treble or more stripes, some small, some a little larger stripes and other checkered, and some finely wrought with flowers between the stripes, which you call *Jamdennies*. [Quoted in Irwin and Schwartz.]

Four examples of mid-eighteenth-century doreas included in the Berch Papers accord with seventeenth-century descriptions. "Doreas agabannas" are embellished with embroidered flowers in natural-colored silk (see Pl. D-14). Compare Alacha, Charconnae, and Cherryderry.

By the late 1780s, Manchester muslins made in imitation of Indian goods were manufactured as cheaply as imported goods, and doreas were among those no longer requested by the East India Company (Michael Edwards, p. 44).

DORROCK

"A coarse linen fabric used for common household wear, nearly resembling diaper, and ornamented with squares. It derives its name from the town of Dorrock, in Scotland, where it was manufactured for table-cloths" (Webster, p. 951).

DORSETTEEN
(dorsettee, dorsettine)

Finely woven worsted cloth with an additional silk weft. In 1767 Samuel Rowland Fisher noted in his journal the manufacture in Norwich of "Dorsitteens—16 Ins. at 24 / to 30 / " and "broad" at "65 / to 75 / ." In 1769 James Beekman ordered "26 pieces Dorsattes. or Irish silk camblet 26 yard at 25 / . Vizt. 10 black and white, 4 blue and white. 4 blue and yellow, 4 brown and white. 4 brown and yellow"

(2:806). Old stock listed in the Philadelphia inventory of merchant Samuel Neave included "2 ps Venetian Poplin, Dorsetees, Camblet. The Poplin & Dorsettees are unsaleable. Some of the Camblets have been long in the House and cost high and some are a little Moth Eat."

Swatches of silk-and-worsted dorsetteen are in Castle Museum pattern books dated 1769 and 1792 and among the midcentury Berch Papers.

DOWLAS

"A coarse linen, very commonly worn by the lower classes. . . . This, with the kindred fabric of lockram, was once imported from Brittany in large quantities. . . . [but with] the destruction of several very profitable French manufactures," following the Revolution of 1689, England encouraged the manufacture of dowlas and lockram at Hamburg, and it is from Germany that many came to America. In the nineteenth century, the name was applied to a "strong calico made in imitation of the linen fabric" (Beck).

The Aspinwall Records of seventeenth-century imports to Boston include "20 yds dowlas," "1 fardle doulas cont[aining] 4 pces," "nineteen hund ells Dowlas," and "4 bales doulas" (pp. 412–30). Earle records a 1688 New Hampshire order for "as many yards of Doulas as will make a dozen shirts" (*Costume*, p. 101). In Philadelphia, 1688, dowlas was used for sheets and the cases of a feather bolster and pillows (Moon inventory). Samuel Rowland Fisher ordered "¾ Dowlas and ⅞ wh[ite] Checkt Dowlas" with other coarse cloths in 1767/68; the next year James and Drinker of Philadelphia offered "White Russia Dowlas or ravens duck" for sale (*Pennsylvania Chronicle,* December 4, 1769).

Manufacture continued in the nineteenth century. John Admanson, Dundee, Scotland, won a bronze medal "for improved Canvass, Dowlas, and striped, plain and unbleached imitation Russia Sheeting" at the 1853 New York industrial exhibition (Dilke, p. 26).

DOZENS

Coarse woolen cloths about twelve yards in length. The term was used especially in two areas of England; an undyed cloth known as Devonshire kersey, or Devon dozen, was made in that West Country area from about the middle of the sixteenth century. Heaton writes of Yorkshire manufactures in the eighteenth century: "The broad cloth, either in its full length of 24 yards, or as a Dozen of 12 to 13 yards, represented the highest grade of Northern fabrics. Next came the kersey, which was very little inferior in quality to the broad, but longer and not so wide" (*Yorkshire Woollen,* p. 145n). "Another manufacture of surprising extent, is the Yorkshire coarse cloths, called double dozens, and kerseys" (Postlethwayt).

In 1629 each Englishman preparing to sail for New England was expected to provide himself with clothing which included "1 suit of Nordon dussens or hampshire kersies lyn'd the hose with skins, dublets with lynen of gilford or gedlyman kerseys" (Dow, *Every Day Life,* p. 61).

DRAB
(Fr. drap)

Thick, stout, closely woven overcoating, which was heavy and expensive; also an undyed cloth of gray-beige color. A London runaway took with him "a new great loose-body'd Drab Coat, value 50s, a close body'd superfine Drab Coat, a lightish Colour, with a Collar lined with a slip of Scarlet Velvet, value 4£" (*Daily Post,* January 23, 1721). Swatches of drab are in the early eighteenth-century cloth book of Usher and Jeffries, Wiltshire County Record Office (Mann, *Cloth Industry,* p. 312).

DRABDEBERRY
(Fr. drap de Berry)

A woolen cloth. "A light drabdeberry Cloth Coat and Wastcoat" were advertised in London in the late seventeenth century (*Post-Boy,* December 30, 1699).

DRAB STYLE
(in calico printing)

The color palette produced by dyeing cloth printed with different mordants in a bath of quercitron which was derived from the American oak of that name. It produced a variety of colors from yellow through buff, tan, and olive to brown. Printed textiles in this style were fashionable from 1799 to 1806 (Floud, "Drab Style," p. 238).

DRAFT

A woolen material with a small geometric pattern. Edward Wharton's Salem inventory of 1677/78 lists "1 large draft lite collrd, 14s" and others at 12 and 10 shillings. The same inventory lists "oringe collrd worsted draft" and "24 yards flowered silk draft" at two shillings a yard (Dow, *Every Day Life,* p. 263). Booth links draft to amens and everlasting patterned with small weft figures.

DRAWBOY

Technically, all fabric woven on a draw loom. The name applied particularly to figured and quilted cotton goods woven in Manchester:

> Owing to the greater variety of patterns attempted in figured goods, a more complicated loom became necessary, as well as the employment of a boy to manipulate the treadles for the raising and lowering of the warps which was required in the weaving of such goods. The goods produced were consequently known by the name of draw-boys. [Daniels, p. 74.]

Aikin, also writing of Manchester, stated "as figures made with treadles are confined to a scanty range, beyond which they grow too complicated, the workmen had recourse to the use of draw-boys, which gave name to a new and important branch of trade" (p. 159). The loom attachment called a drawboy is described in *Arts and Manufactures:*

> A most ingenious piece of mechanism, which retained the name of the *draw-boy,* because it performed his work. It consisted of a half wheel, the rim or periphery of which was grooved, so as to catch into the various strings required to be pulled down. This half-wheel travelled along a rack, or toothed bar, oscillating, at the same time, from right to left, and drawing down particular cords as required to form the pattern, thus removing all possible chance of mistake by depressing the wrong handle. [P. 372.]

Butterworth's description is similar:

> The machine is situated in a small square frame, not larger than a chair, which stands at the side of the loom, and cords from all the different healds, are conducted from the loom down to this frame, where they are arranged in order. Each cord has a knot, answering to the handle, which the boy pulled in the common draw loom; and there is a piece of mechanism actuated by the treadles, which at every stroke, selects the proper cord, and draws it down so as to raise the healds belonging to it. The next time it changes its position and takes another cord, and so until the whole number of cords have been drawn, and the pattern completed. [P. 142.]

James wrote that "Halifax [noted for worsted manufactures] and some other places also engaged in the making of figured stuffs, 'drawboys' . . . which, in a degree but very clumsily, performed what has since been so easily and wonderfully accomplished by the Jacquard engines" (p. 264). Webster mentions drawboys among worsted fabrics called everlastings or lastings.

Earle found "Fine Figured Drawboys for Womens Coats with Fringe" listed in a Boston newspaper of 1750 (*Costume,* p. 101). Samuel Boardman of Wethersfield ordered a piece of drawboy from New York in 1772.

DRESDEN

A fancy silk and worsted dress fabric. "Dresdens and dresdenetts" and "Dresdens Barlicorns" were advertised in Boston in the 1760s (Dow, *Arts and Crafts,* pp. 167, 170). Two swatches of London dresden, fine worsteds with small warp-float patterns in silk, are in the Moccasi manuscript of about 1760 (see Pl. D-53). A swatch of "check Dresden" with warp-float stripes is in the John Kelly pattern book of 1767.

DRILL
(drilling)

A heavy linen cloth. "Drilling & pack duck" are listed among imports in the 1660 Book of Rates (Dow, *Every Day Life,* p. 251). A later reference describes drill as a three-thread cotton or linen twilled cloth, either in white or colors. By 1833 drills formed "part of the uniforms of the army and navy, in the summer months, [which] tends to render them a staple article for the tailor during that season" (Perkins). Lightweight drill was called "jean" or "middy twill," and khaki-colored drill was called "khaki." According to the 1854 report of George Wallis on American manufactures, goods of excellent quality were woven in United States mills, especially by the Amoskeag Company, Manchester, New Hampshire. These consisted of "ducks, tickings, denims, drillings, sheetings, and cotton flannels of varied width and quality," some of which obtained prize medals in the Great Exhibition of 1851 (Wallis, p. 10).

Both brown and white drills were ordered from London by James Beekman in 1784 (3:1181). References to drill are found in Chester County, Pennsylvania, inventories between 1770 and 1849 (Schiffer, *Inventories,* p. 234).

DROGUET

A group of fancy French silks used for ladies' and gentlemen's clothing in the eighteenth century (Fig. D-42). According to Joubert, author of *Le dessi-*

Fig. D-42. *Droguet woven in dark blue and white silk by an apprentice weaver of Lyons, 1840. (Collection of Mrs. Rockwell Gardiner.)*

nateur pour les . . . étoffes de soie (1765), several kinds can be distinguished: *Droguets lisérés, satinés, lustrinés & Peruviennes & Prusiennes.* Swatches of *Peruviennes* and *Prusiennes* (see Fig. D-84) in a French pattern book of about 1763 are characterized by small pattern units.

The following description suggests a damask weave: *Droguet satiné—cette étoffe, qui est à-peu-près la même que le Damas, avec cette différence que dans le Damas c'est un satiné, qui fait le fond, et le gros-de-Tours le sujet, au lieu que dans le Droguet satiné, c'est le satiné qui fait fleur par un poil et le gros-de-Tours ou Taffetas fait le fond* (Joubert, p. 9).

Droguet is defined in this century as a "silk textile created in the 18th century with a small pattern unit produced by various means. The motifs may, for instance, be formed by floats of a flushing warp above a ground weave. In *droguets lisérés,* wefts of different colours may be used, to form figures in weft floats, or in fine tabby they may interlace with ends of a flushing warp" (Burnham, p. 200).

The Richelieu Papers of 1736 contain sixteen swatches of *droguets de Soye dont les hommes se sont habillés pendant l'Eté* and eleven swatches of droguets (Lh45b II, pp. 63, 70).

In 1870 *Godey's Lady's Book* suggested droguets for dresses: "The silk droguets have colored patterns which look exactly like designs in raised silk embroidery" ([January 1870]: 107).

"A sort of stuff, very thin and narrow, usually all wool and sometimes half wool and half silk; having sometimes the whale [rib] but more usually without, and woven on a worsted chain [warp]" (Chambers). Defoe noted that about 1725 the town of Devizes in Wiltshire,

has lately run pretty much into the drugget-making trade, and great quantities of druggets are worn in England, as also, exported beyond the seas, even in the place of our broad-cloths, and where they usually were worn and exported; but this is much the same as to the trade still; for as it is all a woollen manufacture, and that the druggets may properly be called cloth, though narrow, and of a different make, so the makers are all called clothiers. [*Tour,* vol. 2, letter 4.]

Elsewhere, Defoe referred to the making of druggets and shalloons, "and such slight goods."

Patterns produced by George Wansey in 1695 and preserved in the Wiltshire Record Office show that drugget was "a less closely woven species of cloth, popular because of its lighter weight" (Mann, "Textile Industries," p. 159).

Twilled druggets "were once commonly known in trade as corded druggets, but when of linen warp and woollen weft as threaded druggets, and were particularly a Devonshire manufacture" (Beck). A London tailor advertised "Drugget and Stuff Suits of Cloaths lined with Shalloon for £3 10s. and with Silk Shagreen or Sattinet for 3£10s., likewise fine Spanish or Silk Druggets lined with Shalloon or Durance for 4£15s or with Silk Shagreen or Sattinet for 6£15s" (*Post Man,* July 11, 1706).

Although druggets were imported from England, they were also made in America. A 1721 account of weaving in Massachusetts states: "In this Province there are all sorts of Common manufactures. The inhabitants have always worked up their own wool into coars Clothes, druggets and serges; but these, as well as their homespun linen, which is generally half cotton, serve only for the use of the meanest sort of people" (Tryon, p. 78).

Advertisements for fugitive slaves and servants in colonial New Jersey specified the clothes they wore, which included a "brown colored homespun drugget coat," a "suit of light gray homespun drugget cloth," and a "blue gray homespun drugget coat" (Tryon, p. 202). A New York widow's wardrobe (1682) included "colored drugget petticoats with gray . . . [and] with white linings" and one with "pointed lace linings," perhaps meant in the sense of trimmings (Earle, *Costume,* p. 26). The van Varick shop inventory lists striped and flowered drugget, and the Elmendorph account book has "5ps Culld. [colored] Drugt.," "Cloth Drugt.," and two pieces of black drugget at different prices. In 1739 Philip Livingston ordered "fine drogets—all good cloath colours." "Corded drugget" was advertised in 1760 (Dow, *Arts and Crafts,* p. 167).

Among the Richelieu Papers are swatches of a plain green woolen drugget made for the Levant trade at Marseilles (Lh45 I, p. 13), and a linen/wool with weft stripes in black, blue, red, and white made at Saint-Lo (Lh45c IV, p. 92). From Holland are swatches of *Droguets ou Silesies* (plain and striped), *en mosaique,* and *à Fleurs* (lozenge patterns) (see Pl. D-92). All are dated 1736. Midcentury swatches of plain and corded Berkshire druggets are in the Lindegreen pattern book in the Berch Papers.

The Moccasi manuscript of about 1760 contains *Droghetti di Silesia* from Elbeuf and Rheims, *Droghetti osia Duroyelluies* (duroys) and *Droghetti cordati* from London (see Pl. D-55) and Exeter (see Pl. D-59).

By the second quarter of the nineteenth century usage had changed.

> Druggets are very wide, being sometimes two yards, and sometimes four yards. They are chiefly employed to lay over another carpet, to preserve it when the room is in daily use, and only removed for company. Sometimes druggets alone are laid, and when of a handsome brown or marone colour look exceedingly well. They should be very tightly stretched on the floor, so as not to present a wrinkle to view. [*Workwoman's Guide,* p. 202.]

"A coarse cloth made of Felt, and printed in various patterns and colours, not only employed as a carpet and to underlie carpets—to preserve them from being cut and worn, and to render them softer to the tread—but also employed as linings for rugs made of skins" (Caulfeild and Saward).

DUCAPE

"A plain-wove stout silken fabric of softer texture than *Gros de Naples.* Its manufacture was introduced into this country by the French refugees of 1685" (Beck).

In New York, James Alexander ordered rich green, pink, yellow, white, light blue, cinnamon, plum, and "dark cloth colored" ducapes in 1760. "Black and cloth-coloured ducapes" together with "striped and cloth-coloured lutestrings and mantuas" were similarly marketed in Philadelphia by Kearny and Gilbert (*Pennsylvania Chronicle,* April 20, 1767).

A wedding gown of brown ducape is noted in colonial America, 1770 (Earle, *Costume,* p. 102). Two years later a piece of "green Ducape, striped and sprigged" was woven in London from silk raised by Mrs. Stiles in New Haven, Connecticut (Frances Little, p. 143).

Six mid-eighteenth-century swatches of ducape in shades of light brown and buff included in the Berch Papers are finely corded and watered. A swatch of buff silk, plain weave, horizontally ribbed, is preserved in the Lord Chamberlain's accounts, 1754/59 (Public Record Office LC 9/267); it is a little heavier than a swatch of armazine pasted above it in the book. Another swatch with matching trimming is found in the Barbara Johnson album (see Pl. D-35). Swatches of watered ducape from Spitalfields dating from 1784/85 are preserved in the Warner Archive.

See also Sarcenet.

DUCK

Strong, thick linen cloth, finer and lighter than canvas. So called because its glazed surface sheds water. Late nineteenth-century Irish ducks, made in white, or unbleached, and in black, brown, blue, gray, and olive colors, were used for laborers' blouses. Heavy grades of duck were used for tents, awnings, boat sails, tarpaulins, aprons, and belts in machinery; lighter weights for outing suits, middies, physicians' coats, cooks' coats, and trousers (Denny). More recently duck has been made of cotton. References to ravensduck and Russia duck are common in American records.

DUFFEL
(duffle)

Heavy, napped woolen cloth. Duffels arriving in Boston in 1645 were probably those made in England, dyed and finished in Flanders or Holland, and transshipped to the colony (see Pl. D-21). The Aspinwall Records list "one pack cont 10 duffls of 500 flem[ish] ells a pce. one pack 12 pcs of leiden Doffles cont 27 flem els a piece . . . one pack 12 Duffl. 27 ells a pce" (p. 395).

To Americans probably the most interesting description of duffel is found in Robert Plot's 1677 account of Witney, a town in Oxfordshire where duffels were made:

> These Duffields . . . otherwise called Shags, and by the Merchants, Trucking-cloth [barter cloth]; they make in pieces about 30 Yards long, and one Yard ¾ broad, and dye them Red or Blue, which are the Colours that best please the Indians of Virginia and New England, with whom the Merchants truck them for Bever, and other Furrs of several Beasts, &c.; the use they have for them is to apparel themselves with them, their manner being to tear them into Gowns of about two Yards long, thrusting their Arms through two Holes made for that Purpose, and so wrapping the rest about them as we our Loose-coats. [P. 284.]

About 1725 Defoe wrote that Witney "Duffield Stuffs" were not only worn by the North American Indians but were "much worn even here in winter" (as quoted in Beck, p. 106). In the next century, Booth defined duffel as "a stout milled Flannel, but of greater breadth and differently dressed. It may be either perched or friezed and is sold of all colours." Beckinsale called them "cheap utilitarian cloths with a thick shaggy nap always in demand for overcoats and seamen's garments" (p. xxviii).

As early as 1686, Bostonian Samuel Sewall ordered "Six peces of blew Duffals good Deep blew" (Letter book, 1:32). In New York, James Alexander (1739) and Gerard Beekman (1747) both ordered blue and red duffels.

Swatches of blue, green, and red duffels dating from 1746–52 are among the London Public Record Office documents (HCA 32/125). Swatches of London and Exeter duffels are included in the Moccasi manuscript (see Pls. D-53, D-60).

In the early nineteenth century Witney duffels were "supplied white and drab, and in various colours, such as rose, green, blue, and yellow; or striped in two, three or four colors" (Plummer, p. 100).

See also Witney.

DUNGAREE

"A strong coarse calico with multiple warps and wefts woven mainly in the Goa region of India, usually dyed brown" (Irwin and Schwartz). Navy-blue dungareelike jean or denim was made into sailors' clothes. Mortimer describes the characteristic material of yarn-dyed weft and white warp woven in twill weave.

DUNJARS

Probably originally an Indian textile, later imitated in England. Seven swatches of English "Dunjars half yd. broad at 25 pr. yd." from about 1720 are thin striped silks with coarser filling yarns,

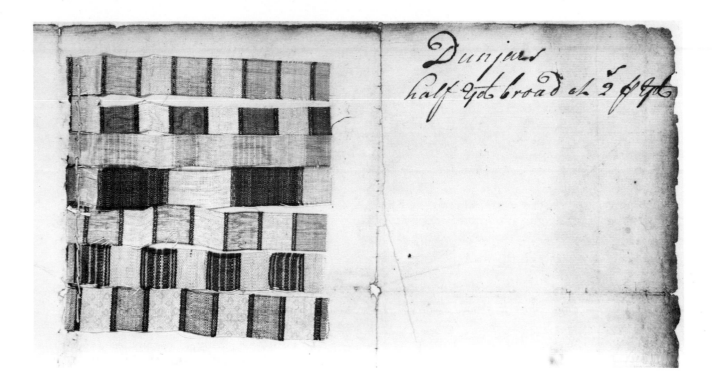

sometimes watered and patterned (Fig. D-43). In
1725 Peter Faneuil ordered "1 New Striped Dun-
jar 28 yards at 20d" (Rothstein, "Calico Campaign," p. 17n).

FIG. D-43. *Striped dunjars, some of them watered
and patterned, ca. 1720. From the Weavers' Company
manuscript. (Public Record Office.)*

DURANCE
(durant)

"Durance or Duretty, with thred or silk" was listed
among imports in the 1660 Book of Rates. As
manufactured in England a century later, it was a
glazed worsted of plain weave, finer than tammy.
Its name denoted its enduring quality like everlasting and perpetuana. By 1836, it was little used in
England but "exported, in considerable quantities,
to Spain and Portugal" (Booth). Of the finish after
weaving, Beck wrote:

> Both Tamies and Durants were hot-pressed
> and glazed, but the former were kept at the
> full width of the cloth, while the latter were
> creased, that is, they were folded, selvedge to
> selvedge, which leaving a marked line, . . .
> running lengthwise along the middle of the
> piece.

English durance is related to French *duroi*
(Cummin, "Tammies and Durants"). However,
swatches in the Moccasi manuscript make it clear
that durance and duroy were two different materials (see Pls. D-54, D-55). A swatch of blue white
twilled and glazed, or hard pressed, wool from
Exeter is called *Durante osia Lustrina* and is included
on the same page with six duroys, also from Exeter (see Pl. D-60).

Durance and duroy, both imported into
America, were used generally for gentlemen's
clothes lined with shalloon. In 1767 at Leeds, Samuel Rowland Fisher noted that "Fine Tammys or
more properly fine Durants, black & Drabs" cost
33 shillings, while at Durham durance cost from
24 to 31 shillings. In London he ordered "20 ps
Clo[th] Col[ore]d Durrants—33/6, black, green,
blue, and pink." A 1766 order for blue, brown,
and drab durance at 33 shillings is in the Wistar

Letter book, Philadelphia. In 1784 James Beekman ordered "20 pieces fine Durants 30 yard at 32 / ." The colors he specified were black, blue, pink, green, white, and brown (3:997). Samuel Boardman ordered the same colors from New York in 1772.

Six swatches of "Durants, or Tammys, or Budoys . . . finished in common colours" are in the eighteenth-century Yorkshire pattern book. All are thin, coarsly spun, highly glazed worsteds (see Pl. D-103).

DURELLE

See Grandrelle.

DUROY

A lightweight worsted material generally used for men's clothing. From six swatches in the Moccasi manuscript, it can be determined that Exeter duroys were woven in solid colors, in two-color stripes, and two-color figures without glaze (see Pl. D-60). London duroys were of plain weave in solid colors and glazed (see Pls. D-54, D-55).

The anonymous author of "A Short Essay upon Trade," 1741, tells of a scheme to manufacture more woolen goods:

> I don't see how it [the price of combing wool] will advance again, unless the royal family, which is large, and occasion many birth-days, should think proper, at least once a year, to wear worsted stuffs, which may be embellished in such a manner as to appear splendid, and by that means bring them into a fashion; and also if the gentlemen would wear duroys, or other worsted stuffs during the summer . . . , it would not only render them fashionable at home, but likewise in all our Colonies abroad. [James, p. 235.]

A 1716 entry for "1 ps Duroys—£3.2.6" is in Mary Elmendorph's account book, Kingston, New York. Frequently this material was specified for suits: in New York, 1734, Robert Livingston ordered "6 ps Duroyce with buttons and mohair Suitable"; in Newport, 1745, "14 yds Duroy for Coat & Breeches @ 14 /" (Banister Papers, p. 702); in 1759, George Washington ordered "A Light Summer Suit made of Duroy by the measure" (Earle, *Costume,* p. 41). On the other hand, "figured duroys for women's wear" were advertised in the *Providence Gazette,* October 31, 1767. More curious are the "fifty pieces of striped duroys, and also forty-four pieces of figured duroys" that the East India Company sent to China for the Mandarins' dress in 1811 (James, p. 380).

Eleven swatches of double duroys, either solid or two colored, glazed and in plain weave from the West Riding of Yorkshire are in the Lindegreen pattern book among the Berch Papers. Eight swatches of *Duroys fins* are found in a Norwich pattern book (see Pl. D-69). Others from London are found in the Moccasi manuscript where they are related to druggets, *Droghetti osia Duroyelluies* (see Pl. D-55).

DUVETYN
(Fr. duvet, meaning down)

Late nineteenth- and twentieth-century dictionaries define duvetyn as a "soft woolen fabric with spun silk or mercerized cotton back in twill weave; fine, downy nap is raised with an emery cylinder. Used for coats, suits, dresses, and millinery trimmings" (Denny). "A very soft French fabric, made of worsted warp and two-ply silk (tussah) filling in four harness twill weave, the filling covering the face. A fine downy nap is raised with an emery cylinder; used for coats, dresses. The cheaper grades are similar to the pocket velvet" (Harmuth).

In the Aix-la-Chapelle pattern book of 1807 are forty-seven swatches of *duvet double & simple sur cotton, à double face,* and *sur laine* (see Pl. D-3) which follow these descriptions, if not the weaving technique. They are woven of brilliant wools "in imitation of English manufactures" for waistcoats.

E

ECORCE
(Fr. écorce d'arbre)

A bast fiber halfway between silk and linen (Savary des Bruslons). Cloths made of it were first imported from India and included *Guingans, Millas, Cherquemolles, Fotalangées* (striped), and *Pinasses* and *Biambonnées* made entirely of écorce fiber. French imitations in cotton enriched with silk may have rivaled English goods such as the half-silks referred in the 1720 Weavers' Company manuscript. *See* Alacha, Tobine.

Five swatches called "écorce," of cotton with additional colored silk warp stripes are in the Maurepas Papers (see Pls. D-38, D-39, D-40).

See also Dunjars.

ELATCHES

See Alacha.

EMBOSSING

The term may refer to either (1) the process of impressing patterns on worsted cloth, particularly camlet, to imitate expensive silk damasks, or (2) printing colored patterns on white serge or flannel.

(1) According to an early eighteenth-century English pamphlet, the stamping or impressing of fabrics had been practiced for some time. In defense of the "Right of the Leather-Guilders, Hair-shag-Embossers, and the Company concerned in Flowering, Damasking and Embossing by Hot Rowls," the pamphleteer wrote: "Weavers in Spittle-Fields have made moulds, presses, &c. and Embossed Flowers and Figures of various Colours on Hair-Shags and other commodities" (Kress, S2470). In 1716 John Blanch wrote that "much flower'd imboss'd Cloth" was being sent to Flanders and that "we come short of no foreign Countrey in the nicest Curiosity of its Manufacture" (Kress, S2724). This method of finishing "is to pass the cloth over a hot brass cylinder, on which are engraved various flowers, or other fancy figures. While passing over this cylinder, the cloth is pressed by two wooden rollers, and thus its surface is indented with those figures. This sort is called Embossed Moreen" (Booth).

A particularly handsome piece made by this process bears a pattern of carnations and a butterfly stamped on bright raspberry-red worsted (Fig. D-44). Formal foliate patterns dyed in the same red, deep blue, or green were used for furnishing and upholstery (Fig. D-45). More common, and generally on coarser cloth, is the outlined damask pattern called "harrateen" in the Holker manuscript (swatch nos. 109, 110); it is printed on gold and on green worsted. Of these Holker says "the wavey pattern is achieved by means of a hot copper cylinder." The full repeat of this type of pattern which measures nearly 36 inches is known from the headcloth of a bed at Ham House near London. *See* Cheney.

A later description of a related embossing technique is given by Perkins: "Silk is Embossed by passing the plain stuff between rollers, the surfaces of which contain the desired pattern, on one cylinder raised, and on the other sunk, so that the eminences of the one coincide with the depressions in the other" (p. 139). Also writing in the 1830s, Lardner states:

> This process has of late been very extensively employed for ornamenting waistcoat patterns, producing a very rich and tasteful appearance; but it can be more appropriately applied to ribands or other fabrics which are not much exposed to friction; the inequalities of surface are otherwise found to be unfavorable to the durability of the material. [P. 298.]

FIG. D-44. *Watered red worsted embossed with pattern of flowers and butterflies, 1750–75. From a set of bed hangings that belonged to Daniel and Sarah (Peele) Saunders of Salem, Mass., who were married in 1770. (Essex Institute.)*

OPPOSITE

FIG. D-45. *Green worsted stamped or embossed with a heavy palmate pattern in imitation of a lace-patterned silk furnishing damask of the 1720s. From the reverse of a lighter green calimanco quilted coverlet. (Winterthur Museum.)*

FIG. D-46. *Samples of embossed serge in red, pink, gold, green, and blue. From a pattern book dated 1769. (Castle Museum.)*

FIG. D-47. *Pocketbook made of embossed serge printed in red, gold, and green. England, ca. 1760. (Colonial Williamsburg Foundation.)*

(2) The process of printing colors on white cloth is identified by a swatch of "Embosd serge Devonshire" with a brown and red dotted leaf and floral pattern printed in surface colors on white twill which is in the Lindegreen pattern book among the Berch Papers (see Pl. D-17). Seven similar although untitled printed patterns are in a 1769 Norwich pattern book (Fig. D-46). A swatch of Silesian *gedrückter Flanel* is preserved among the municipal papers of Cracow (illustrated by Endrei). A larger piece printed in sage-green, orange-red, and mustard-gold on white wool twill is in a pocketbook (Fig. D-47).

Several references to pieces of embossed serge are in the Elmendorph account book in 1716. Robert Livingston ordered embossed serge "Yallow ground and blak flours" and "gay flowers" in 1734. In 1716 James Alexander ordered "6 ps Emboised or flowered flannel" which were to be black and white, yellow and red, blue and black, black and red, red and blue, and red and white. A 1750 New York inventory lists "2 Emborst Sarge Petty Coats" (New York Appraisements, p. 6). The Joshua Fisher and Sons ledger of 1784 lists "1 ps Embossed Serge purp & wt, 37 yds - 2/11" and "2 ps red and yellow ditto, 73 yds at 3/" which indicates the kind printed in colors, while the mention of "1 ps Embossed Serge, 36 1/2 – 3/" and "1 ps Scarlet ditto – 18" probably referred to the kind stamped with a metal cylinder.

ERMINETTE

In the early nineteenth century, Ackermann suggested erminette in imitation of fine, soft cashmere shawl material: "A new, elegant, and much approved fabric for ladies' winter dress, combining the warmth of the Vigonia and Angola cloths with the lightness and flexibility of an Indian shawl" (*Repository* 12, no. 72 [December 1814]: 368). He showed a swatch of lightweight olive drab wool in plain weave and well milled.

An earlier fabric—erminetta—is described by Earle as a "thin stuff for summer wear." "Genteel Linen and Cotton Erminettas" were advertised in Boston in 1751 (*Costume*, p. 106).

ESTAMENE
(estamin; Fr. étamine)

Fine, lightweight worsted cloth. The French *estame* and Italian *stame* signify worsted, but "*estamine* is not only a thin worsted fabric, for wear, but such a tissue as is used for separating flour from its bran, or for purifying liquors, whether that cloth be made of worsted, linen yarn, hair, or any other substance" (Booth).

French swatches of *étamines* dating from 1736 are in the Richelieu Papers (Lh45 I, pp. 94, 95, 99, 101). Two swatches of *estamines con fiori ed a flame* are in a Castle Museum pattern book dated 1769.

By the late 19th century estamine was described as a coarse description of Woollen Bunting or Canvas, more or less transparent. It is employed as a dress material, and intended to be worn over a contrasting colour. The threads are of a fluffy character, and the material is to be had in a bright but dark blue, navy blue, russet and other shades of brown, in black, cream colour, maroon, and sage green. Etamine is also woven with stripes of velvet, embroidered, and in plaited woven stripes; and it is also produced in cotton. [George Cole.]

See also Stamin, Stammet, Tammy.

ESTERET

See Starret.

EVERLASTING
(lasting)

A stout, closely woven worsted stuff, dyed black and other colors, and much used for ladies' shoes. It was described about 1800 as "a stout fabric only eighteen inches wide, with double warps, (sometimes of three threads,) and single weft, made with a five heald twill. There were different sorts of lastings as prunelles wrought with three healds. Also serge de Berry, a variety heavier, and woven with seven healds" (James, p. 362). By 1836 "lasting" was "woven either with a double tweel, or a satin tweel, in which latter case it is called Den-

FIG. D-48. *Swatches of everlastings. From an eighteenth-century folding pattern card.* (*Public Record Office.*)

mark Satin. It is also figured and a very fine sort, of various patterns, is exported to the continent; which, being chiefly used for Church furniture, is called Amen, or Draft" (Booth).

James Alexander of New York ordered "1 ps Scarlet Everlasting 20 yds Dimond Wove" in 1740 and "2 ps Black Barley cornd" and plain everlastings in 1760. James Beekman ordered everlastings, or lastings, in black, brown, and "handsome Cloth blues" (2:714). "Scarlet, pink, blue and green everlastings" were advertised in the *Providence Gazette,* October 8, 1763.

In 1767 Samuel Rowland Fisher noted in his journal "At Halifax are Sold great Quantitys of Plain & figur'd Lastings which are made in the Country round the Town & brought to Markett White." These can be documented by twelve swatches of "Everlastings, com[mon] quality, but good sort" found in the Yorkshire pattern book of 1770 (Atkinson, p. 17) (see Pl. D–101). Other fig-

ured and flowered everlastings are on an eighteenth-century folding pattern card (Fig. D-48). Amens, moreens, and shalloons are included on the same card (see Fig. D-1).

About 1810, everlastings were "an article extensively used for light summer coats in the [United] States" (James, p. 373). Webster wrote, "it is made of various patterns, plain, twilled, or figured, and is distinguished by different names, according to the figures and quality; as Prunella, Amens, Florentina, and draw-boys" (p. 946).

In the Moccasi manuscript, swatches of London *Double* and *Migliori Eternelles* have small weft-patterned figures (see Pl. D-54). The *Journal für Fabrik* has a swatch of black wool everlasting in satin weave made in Saxony for men's trousers (April 1792, p. 282). Twelve swatches of the fabric are found in a late eighteenth-century Norwich pattern book in the Winterthur Museum Library.

See also Perpetuana.

F

FEARNAUGHT
(fearnought)

A thick cloth with a long pile, also called *dread-naught* and *fearnothing*. Earle notes advertisements for runaway slaves wearing "fearnothing" jackets, 1752 and 1753. Greatcoats and "Red Breeches, or Fear-nothing Trousers" are found in Boston advertisements for 1747 (Dow, *Arts and Crafts,* pp. 160, 197).

FENTS

"A technical term denoting the ends of calicoes, of various descriptions, tacked together. The name is likewise given to the ends of imperfectly printed cambrics, which are sold by weight, and used for patchwork quilts" (Caulfeild and Saward).

FERRANDINE
(farendon)

Originally an all-silk textile. "A light cloth of which the warp is entirely of silk and the weft of wool or of hair, linen or cotton. It is a kind of slight moire or *poux de soie*" (Postlethwayt). Translating the work of Savary des Bruslons, Postlethwayt used the word *moire,* the French word for mohair, rather than moiré, as we now call watered silks. He likened ferrandine also to *poux de soie* which, in this case, may have referred to padua say or padua serge. Ferrandine was a fabric of plain weave and light in weight (Braun-Ronsdorf, p. 22).

Black, green, and "bluish" are listed in Jacques Savary's *Le Parfait Négociant* (1:338). Its use for light curtains is mentioned by Havard. In 1684/85 in Salem "6 yd ¾ wosted Farenden at 20d" is mentioned (Dow, *Every Day Life,* p. 271). The 1695/96 New York inventory of Margrita van Varick's estate lists "two black farrentine Mantuas, one black farrendine petticote."

Burail was a similar slight moiré infrequently used for furnishing (Havard).

FERRET

A tape, ribbon, or binding. Edward Wharton's inventory, Salem, 1677/78, lists red and green ferrets (Dow, *Every Day Life,* p. 266). Thomas Banister of Newport ordered "blew and green ferrets" in 1699. James Alexander's 1739 order specified both "round" and "flat ferrett Laces."

A 1754 reference lists "waistcoats . . . edged and trimmed with black ribbands and ferreting" (OED). In Boston, 1762, "Cotton and Silk Ferrit Laces, also Black and Colour'd Silk Ferrits" were advertised (Earle, *Costume,* p. 110). In 1766 Philadelphia, "4 Groce 6d Silk ferrets. 2 black 2 Red 2 Green 4 blue" were ordered (Wistar Letter book). "Venetian blinds strung with ferret" are recorded in 1836 (OED).

FERRET SILK

"Ignorantly, or improperly called spun silk, and sold as such in manufacture, is much inferior to spun silk, though much smoother; it is made from burs, and the bags the worms die in, it is fine and soft, has a flat appearance like cotton, and wears but very indifferently" (March, p. 38). Ferret tapes and ferreting may have been made from this poor-grade raw silk.

FIGURETTO

A costly fabric listed in the 1660 Book of Rates among exports:

Figurettoes { with Silk or Copper, narrow, the piece, 15s. broad, the piece, £1.10.0 [Beck.]

In 1745 John Banister ordered "5 fine dyed Figurettes 20 yds no. 1 @ 16/" and "5 superfine [Figurettes] 20 [yds no.] 2 [@] 18/."

FILLETING

A kind of tape. Diaper filleting, colored filleting, and "a percell of Red filit & tape" are listed in a Salem inventory of 1684 (Dow, *Every Day Life*, pp. 272, 273).

FILOSELLE

The trade name for a spun silk thread suitable for use with the needle and formed of very lightly united strands (Chambers). Savary des Bruslons writes of its inferior quality and the articles made from it:

> *Bourre de soie, qu'on appelle aussi* Filoselle, *ou* Fleuret. *C'est la partie de soie qu'on rebute au dévidage des cocons; on la file & on la tire avec la carde ou le peigne, après qu'on a dévidé la fine soie de dessus les cocons.*
>
> *La Bourre de soie se file, & se met en échevaux, de même que la bonne soie, & entre dans la composition de plusieurs sortes d'étoffes; elle s'emploie aussi à fabriquer des bas, des gants, des padoues [ribbons], des ceintures, des aiguillettes, des lacets, du cordonnet.* [S.v. "Bourre de Soie."]

Furnishing fabrics made of silk and filoselle are in the Richelieu Papers (see Pl. D-90).

FINGRAM
(fingrom)

"A course kind of serge principally made at Stirling" (Defoe, *English Tradesman*, 2:283). According to an account of 1735, "at Aberdeen and countries adjacent, large quantities of our own coarse tarred wool are manufactured into coarse serges called fingrams" (James, p. 221n).

Two pieces "colour'd Fingrims" valued at 26 shillings are listed in the 1693 inventory of James Lloyd (SCPR, 13:267). In May 1728 Thomas Fitch of Boston ordered shalloons and fingrams from London (Letter book).

FLANNEL

Made of woolen yarn "slightly twisted in the spinning, and of open texture, the object in view being to have the cloth soft and spongy, without regard to strength. . . . All the sorts are occasionally dyed, though more usually sold white. Flannels are bleached by the steam of burning sulphur, in order to improve their whiteness" (Beck).

Swatches of Silesian, English, and printed flannel dating from 1690, among the municipal papers of Cracow, are illustrated by Endrei ("Tissus d'usage," p. 25). Two swatches of white Exeter flannel are in the Moccasi manuscript (see Pl. D-60).

See also Culgee, Embossing.

FLORENCE

A lightweight taffeta dress silk (Fig. D-49). Joubert describes both batavia and florence taffeta (p. 18). "Thrie yards of sky colloured florence Cessnutt [sarcenet]" and "Tuo yards of Yallow florence Cessnutt" were inventoried in the Wardrobe Room at Ham House in 1677 (Thornton and Tomlin, p. 163). A swatch of Nîmes and six of Avignon manufacture are found in the Richelieu Papers for 1736 (Lh45 I, p. 51; Lh45 V, p. 36). Others are found in the Warner Archive (Figs. D-50, D-51).

The Avignon firm of Thomas Brothers was awarded a bronze medal "for coloured Florences, for perfection in colour and manufacture" at the 1853 New York industrial exhibition (Dilke, p. 28). In the fifteenth century, florence was a coarse woolen cloth.

See also Lustring, Plunket.

FLORENTINE

"A silk stuff, chiefly used for men's waistcoats . . . made striped, figured, and plain; the last being a twilled fabric. Two other stuffs are known under this name; one composed of worsted, used for common waistcoats, women's shoes, and other

140.

Figured Lustrings or Sarsnetts, are also a saleable article when chosen favor= =ably, they are now worth 1000 reas or $1.25 per covedor, which is equal $1.67 per yard, the colours ought to be light and airy, and the Silks something like the annexed patterns; which are called Florence Legere, are 7/12 Ell wide. — Sattins also of much such figures will answer.

Plain Sarsenetts, are a good article, colors ought to be light blue, Green, White, Rose &c.

articles; the other, made of cotton, resembling jean, and generally striped, is used for making trousers" (Waterston). A twilled silk, thicker than florence (Caulfeild and Saward).

James Beekman ordered black florentine from London in 1784 (3:1018); black, blue, and green silk florentines were offered for sale in the *Providence Gazette,* November 11, 1786. In 1794 Henry Wansey noted while traveling in Connecticut that "at one house where I stopped, a young woman told me that herself and sister had last year raised silk enough to make eighteen yards of florentine" (p. 71). In Boston, "Black silk Florentine for vests"

FIG. D-49. *"Florence Legere," samples of fancy, thin silks comparable to lustrings and sarcenets which could be bought profitably in Canton for sale in the United States. From a trader's book kept between 1797 and 1809. (Rhode Island Historical Society.)*

and "printed Florentines for pantaloons" were offered for sale in *Palladium* (May 8, 1810).

Swatches are in the Warner Archive (see Pl. D-96). Swatches of Norwich worsted florentine are in a Castle Museum pattern book dated 1791.

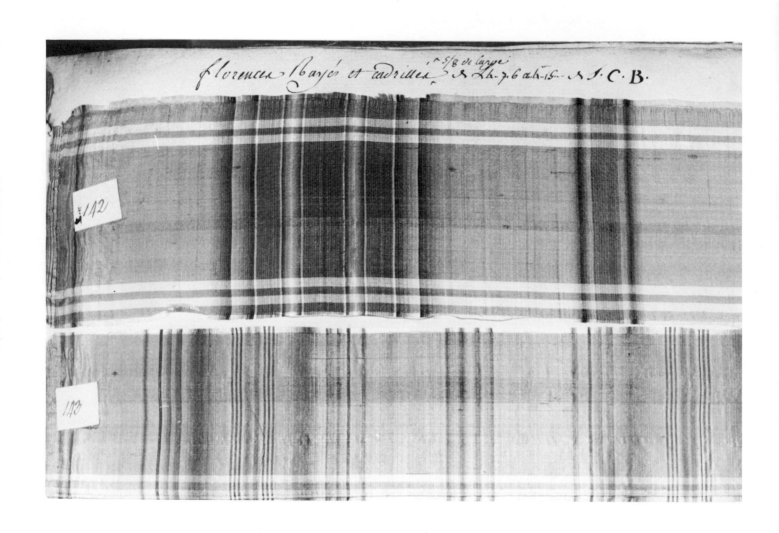

FIGS. D-50, D-51 opposite. *Striped, checked, and broacaded silk taffeta called florence. From a French pattern book ca. 1760. (Warner Archive, Victoria and Albert Museum.)*

FLORETTA

One of the eighteenth-century glazed worsted dress fabrics largely manufactured in Norwich. Most of the late eighteenth-century Castle Museum and Winterthur Museum pattern books include swatches of "Floretts," "Florettas," *"Fleurets fins"* (see Pl. D-70), and "Florattas," or "Toys," woven in small lozenge and zigzag patterns in two colors. Likewise, Kelly's "Counterpart of Patterns" contains swatches (nos. 47–62). Others are found in the Moccasi manuscript (Pl. D-57).

An Albany, New York, reference of 1748/49 lists

4 Florets Blue & White
4 Do   Black & White
3 Do   Red & White
1 Do   Cherry & White. [Bleecker Papers.]

Floretta is also the English term for French *fleuret* or waste silk. "All silks cannot be spun and reeled; either because the balls have been perforated by the silkworms themselves; or because they are double or too weak to bear the water; or because they are coarse &c. Of all this, together they make a particular kind of silk called floretta; which, by being carded, or even spun on the distaff or the wheel, in the condition it comes from the ball makes a tolerable silk" (Chambers).

See also Filoselle.

FLUSHING

With blanketing and coating, a class of heavy broadcloth made at Witney, Oxfordshire, in the early nineteenth century. In 1828, "another article approaching to blankets, called flushings or bearskins" were "made chiefly of English wool" (Bischoff, 2:175).

In 1825 Philadelphia merchants Wistar, Siter, and Price ordered "3 pc. Blue Witney flushing, close sheared exactly similar to Bath Coating but very stout & fine Indigo" (Plummer, p. 251).

FOREST CLOTH
(*forest white*)

A coarse, cheap broadcloth related to frieze, kersey, and pennystone. In 1749 Gerard Beekman of New York wrote to his father in London:

> I have not yet Sold any of your Cloaths but hope as the Season advances Shall be Able to sell them. Had they bin Cours broad Cloaths or Common forrist Cloths from about 3/ a yard to 3/6 a yard some or other Light mixt Coulers would have sold much Sooner, and for greater advance, for those you have Sent are what we call plains and too high priced. [1:89.]

Later Beekman orders called for "Sorted Russet Collours" and "fashionable colours." "A large assortment of fine, super and superfine black, blue, scarlet, brown, mixt and cloth coloured forrest and broadcloths, with rattinets and shalloons suitable to ditto" for lining materials were offered by George Bartram for sale in Philadelphia (*Pennsylvania Chronicle,* September 7, 1767). Joshua Fisher and Sons' ledger lists forest cloth as late as 1783/84.

FORFARS

A common unbleached linen sheeting principally used for wrapping and towels. Often linked with hessian or barras. "Hessia and Forfar are very coarse linens, used for various purposes, as straining on sofas, &c." (Webster, p. 951).

FOULARD
(Fr. foulas)

Three silk handkerchiefs in the Holker manuscript, circa 1750, identify this material as printed (see Pl. D-26) or checked twill. Holker says that such materials were bought in Paris as Indian merchandise, although of English manufacture, for women's dresses and were called *foulas*. The checked examples in brilliant colors were made in "Spitalfields, one of the principle suburbs of London."

FRIEZE

A coarse napped woolen cloth. In 1662 Thomas Fuller wrote of frieze as a coarse cloth manufactured in Wales "than which none warmer to be worn in winter, and the finest sort thereof very fashionable and gentile" (Beck). David Booth's 1836 description of the finish corresponds to that of Duhamel du Monceau in *Descriptions des arts et métiers* of 1765:

In the Friezing, or Frizing of woollen cloth the hairs of the pile are twisted into each other so as to form little raised naps, or burrs, which are thickly and regularly spread over the surface of the cloth. This effect is produced either by working with the hand, or by a Friezing Machine. In either case the cloth is stretched on the Friezing Table and, having its surface moistened with a thin solution of honey or other glutinous substance, the pile is twisted into little knobs by the semicircular motion of the Friezer or Crisper, which is a board incrustated with a kind of cement made of glue, sand, &c. The cloth is gradually taken from the Friezing table by means of a wooden roller, beset with short wire points in the manner of Cards. Every sort of woollen cloth, or of woollen and worsted, may be Friezed; but worsted cloths, having no pile, cannot admit of that operation. [P. 183.]

A passage from John Dyer's long poem *The Fleece,* 1757, tells of the warmth of the "kindly" fleece:

In webs of Duffield woof,
Their limbs, benumb'd, enfolds with cheerly
   warmth,
And frize of Cambria, worn by those, who
   seek,
Through gulphs and dales of Hudson's wind-
   ing bay,
The beaver's fur, though oft they seek in vain.

Thirty pieces of frieze were imported into Boston as early as 1651, according to the Aspin-wall Records (p. 427). In 1745 John Banister ordered light drab, pearl, "green twill'd or blue" frieze. In Boston 1757, "a Saxon blue frize Jacket Lin'd with baize, slash sleeves . . . a brown Fustian Jacket, a pair of scarlet everlasting Breeches . . . one white cotton and Linen and one Woolen check'd Shirt" were worn by a runaway black servant (Dow, *Arts and Crafts,* p. 201). James Beekman of New York ordered eighty-four pieces of frieze in "handsome sorted Russet Collours" in 1766 (2:709). His subsequent orders specified the same colors.

Swatches of four friezed broadcloths in the eighteenth-century Yorkshire pattern book show the curled finish (see Pl. D-100).

FRISÉ

A late nineteenth-century pile fabric, usually mohair, of uncut loops. Designs may be produced by contrast of cut and uncut loops, by different colored yarns, or by printing the surface. Denny says it was used for upholstery and illustrates one example.

FUGERE
(*fugeere*)

A kind of canvas made in Germany. The name is possibly derived from the Augsburg family of Fugger.

"One role brod sheeting fugeere canvas cont. 138 yds at 21d yd" was shipped from Boston to Taunton, Massachusetts, in 1688 (Watkins).

FULLING

A process of scouring and pressing whereby woolen goods were cleansed of grease and thickened into a compact finished material (Frances Little, p. 34). "The object of fulling is to work the fibres so that the surface may not show the naked transverse threads, but form a felted mass, fulling being really only a kindred process to felting" (Beck).

FURNITURE CHECK

See Check.

FUSTIAN

A general term covering a large category of linen and cotton, or, later, all-cotton textiles. Fustians, probably made partly of wool, were imported into England under the names of places where they were manufactured—Amsterdam, Augsburg, Milan, Naples, Prussia, Venice, and holmes (Ulm), jean (Genoa), barmillion, and beverneu.

Fustians made in Norwich from about 1336 were a worsted article: "Soon after this Norwich . . . became the most flourishing city in all England, by means of its great trade in worsteds, fustians, freezes, and other woollen manufactures" (Bloomfield as quoted in Beck). Wadsworth and Mann stated that the first Walloon and Dutch immigrants, arriving in 1554, "brought to Norwich the making of 'fustians of Naples,' in part . . . a worsted stuff" (p. 19). The same authors cite a petition giving the date of the first manufacture of cotton and linen fustians in Lancaster:

> About twenty yeeres past [ca. 1601] diverse people in this Kingdome, but chiefly in the Countie of Lancaster, have found out the trade of making of other Fustians, made of a kind of Bombast or Downe, being a fruit of the earth growing upon little shrubs or bushes, brought into this Kingdome by the Turkie Merchants from Smyrna, Cyprus, Acra and Sydon, but commonly called Cotton Wooll; and also of Lynnen yarne most part brought out of Scotland, and othersome made in England, and no part of the same Fustians of any Wooll at all. [P. 15.]

In the eighteenth century, Lancashire became the center of cotton and linen manufacture which formed an important part of England's textile export trade to the colonies and other European countries. "The main production between 1670 and 1700 was of jeans, pillows, stripes and barmillions; tufts were being made by 1674" (Wadsworth and Mann, p. 113n). Their manufacture in and around Manchester is corroborated by Aikin who says "the kinds of fustian then made [ca. 1700] were herring-bones, pillows for pockets and outside wear, strong cotton ribs and barragon, broad-raced linen thicksets and tufts, dyed, with whited diapers, striped dimities, and lining jeans" (p. 158). "These were succeeded by . . . goods figured in the loom with draw boys, and at later periods by cotton velvets, quiltings, counterpanes, corded dimities, velveteens, and strong fancy cords" (Butterworth, p. 66).

Of the many varieties made, John Holker includes in his manuscript swatches of barragon, jean, pillow, silveret, and thickset. Wadsworth and Mann distinguished two kinds of fustian—"those with a plain and those with a cut and raised surface—a difference depending both on weaving and finishing" (p. 113). Fustians with a "cut and raised surface" probably resembled those mentioned by John Banister: "I sent you Invoice of goods for the Spring but omitted Figurd or Tufted Fustian" (December 17, 1739).

In the early nineteenth century, Rees defined fustian as "a species of coarse, thick twilled cotton, generally dyed of an olive, leaden, or other dark colour." He illustrated eighteen fustian drafts, "the most common fabrics of the fanciful varieties of this article," including corduroy, jean, pillow, thickset, velveret, and velveteen.

The following American references show the use of fustian for clothing and furnishing:

Boston, 1650: Fustians were imported (Aspinwall Records, p. 418).

Salem, 1684: "3 fustian wescoats" are listed in an inventory (Dow, *Every Day Life,* p. 282).

Boston, 1687: Samuel Sewall wrote in his letter book, "I have two small daughters who begin to goe to schoole: my wife would intreat your Lady to pleasure her so far as to buy for her, white Fustian drawn, enough for curtins, wallen, counterpaine for a bed, and half a duz. chairs, with four threeded [ply] green worsted to work it" (1:44).

Boston, 1736: "A fine Fustian Suit of Curtains, with a Cornish and Base Mouldings of a beautiful Figure, drawn in London, on Frame full already worked; as also enough of the same for half a dozen Chairs" was advertised (Dow, *Arts and Crafts,* p. 110). Another reference to embroidered fustian is found in the same volume.

Boston, 1749: "A Woman's Fustian Petticoat, with a large work'd Embroider'd Border, being Deer, Sheep, Houses, Forrest, &c., so worked" (p. 176).

New York, 1784: James Beekman ordered "16 pieces dyed Pillows or fustians . . . brown and olives" (3:1115).

G

GALLOON

A tape or ribbon. Caulfeild and Saward's nineteenth-century definition of two kinds of galloon may well apply to earlier periods as well:

One is a strong, thick gold lace, with an even selvedge at each side. It is woven with a pattern in threads of gold or silver, on silk or worsted, both plain and watered, and is employed in uniforms and on servants' livery hats. The other is of wool, silk, or cotton combined with silk or worsted, and is used for trimming and binding articles of dress, hats, shoes, and furniture.

GAMBROON

A union fabric described by James: "[About 1834] another fabric came into the market . . . under the singular name of gambroons, . . . the yarn being composed of separate threads of cotton and worsted twisted together. These stuffs were adapted for men's coats, &c." (p. 445). The fabric is also described as a twilled linen cloth made for linings.

GARLICK
(*garlits, garlix, gulick, gulix*)

A linen cloth first imported from Goerlitz, Silesia. It could be fully or partially bleached: "There are several sorts, the first is a blew whiting, and ell-wide garlits, which is of a browner whiting" (OED). A linen cloth named after Jülich (Du. *Gulik;* Fr. *Juliers*), a German town 16 miles northeast of Aachen. The fabric is the same as garlix (Wilson, pp. 8, 46, 52).

"Garlick Holland" and "double fold Garlix" in various widths such as "7–8," "3-qrs," and "yard wide" are specified in American records from the late seventeenth century. Thomas Fitch commented on the material at some length:

Very course 3 / 4 Garlets not being serviceable wont sute our People, though we certainly have enough that are poor. Yet they don't wear Garlets but homespun Linnens, or rather cotten and linnen cloth that is very durable though not so white. Those that buy Garlets therefore are for a sort that will wear and look pretty well and so decline buying courser than [pattern] No. 1772. [April 2, 1726.]

In 1756 Pomeroys of London wrote to James Beekman: "The 7/8 Garlix we esteem remarkably cheap, being of the best fabrick and very fine. We believe the Yard wide Garlix will give you full content" (2:549); in the following year, they wrote: "We have usually sent you the strong 7/8 Garlix with the red mark calld Loyds Garlix" (2:629); and again, "The Yard wide garlix now sent are of the tandem sort As very few tight bound garlix are now imported. . . . Our customers approve that sort, as they can examine into them" (2:632).

Garlick was one of the most commonly imported materials and presumably a good household textile. In 1760, a claim was made for two garlick aprons and garlick of various widths lost in the Boston fire (*Boston Records,* p. 1).

See also Holland.

GARTERING

Tape or braid tied around the calf of the leg to support stockings. Similar to coach lace and furniture braids and tapes. In 1736 Mary Alexander of New York received from Peter Collinson in London twenty-one samples of woolen tapes, some mixed with linen or a little silk, woven in plain or twill weave in bright colors (see Pl. D-10).

GAUZE

A thin, light, transparent fabric woven in a crossed-warp technique (Emery, p. 189). By extension, any sheer, open fabric. Silk gauze was woven at Spitalfields until the 1760s when Paisley "became the centre of a flourishing gauze manufacture" (Beck).

The van Varick inventory of 1695/96 lists "2 chimnie cloths of Crimson gaze; 6 window curtaines ditto - £6:10:0." The Norton Papers of Virginia in 1768 list "6 yrds handsome flower'd Gauze Ell wide" (p. 72); and in 1772 "12 yards of neat spriged Gause undressed, 4 yards of a sort" (p. 218). "Plain, striped and flowered silk gauze" were offered for sale by George Bartram (*Pennsylvania Chronicle,* September 7, 1767).

GEORGIAN CLOTH

A lightweight broadcloth fashionable in 1806 and after (McClellan, *1800–1870,* p. 439). In 1811 and 1812, Ackermann suggested gray Georgian cloth for women's riding habits and in "a pale lead or olive tinge" for evening dress (*Repository* 6, no. 36 [December 1811]: 358; 7, no. 42 [June 1812]: 355).

GHENTING
(*genting*)

A kind of linen made in the Flemish town of Ghent. A Salem inventory of 1684 lists "171 yd. Genting in 20 pls [parcels] & Severll. Remnts. at 18d" among coarse linens (Dow, *Every Day Life,* p. 274). In the 1854 Caine broadside, Boston, "one ps. stript bordered genting Handkerchiefs" is listed with cambric and lawn which are fine, thin linens.

See also Holland.

GHENTISH HOLLAND

See Holland.

GIMP

"An open work trimming, used on both dress and furniture, and in coach lace making. It is made of silk, worsted, or cotton twist, having a cord, or a wire running through it. The strands are plaited or twisted, so as to form a pattern. The French word Passementerie has much superseded that of Gimp, in reference to the finer sorts used for dress" (Caulfield and Saward).

"Black, blue, green, scarlet, yellow, cloth coloured and white, broad and narrow gimps, with a variety of silk trimmings" were advertised by George Bartram in the *Pennsylvania Chronicle* (September 7, 1767).

GINGERLINE

Cloth of ginger color listed among the materials supplied to the North American Indians in the seventeen century (Earle, *Costume,* p. 114).

GINGHAM

In India probably first made of cotton and Tussur silk. A striped cloth woven with multiple-stranded warps and wefts and noted for toughness of texture. In the West, it was a cloth of pure cotton woven with dyed yarns often in stripes and checks (Irwin and Schwartz, pp. 40, 64).

In 1670 "2,000 pieces of striped *Ginghams* according to pattern now sent" were ordered from Bengal along with "10,000 coloured *Ginghams,* 10 yards long, full yard wide, most Graies, even collours, free from Rowes, and of best sorts" (quoted in Irwin and Schwartz).

Richard Grafton's Delaware inventory (1743) lists "4½ yds Striped Gingham @ 2.9."

Gingham manufacture was well established in America by the mid nineteenth century when George Wallis reported that "the manufacture of ginghams is now carried on to a large extent, particularly at South Hadley, opposite to Holyoke, and at Clinton, Massachusetts. The goods are admirable, though light in quality, of good dye, and the colours generally put in with good taste. This, however, depends so much upon the market or class of customers for which the goods are intended, that justice to the manufacturer always demands caution in pronouncing as to the fitness or non-fitness of decoration, even in its simplest forms. . . . The Glasgow Mills Company [South Hadley] contributed [to the New York industrial exhibition of 1853] a very satisfactory assortment of dress ginghams, handkerchiefs, gala plaids, and white and coloured cotton yarns" (Wallis, p. 12).

GLANNEN

A woolen cloth similar to flannel. In Randle Holme's seventeenth-century *Academy of Armory,* the term is listed with other woolen cloths.

GORGORAN
(*gorgoron, gorgoroon*)

"Heavy East Indian silk cloth having stripes woven in two kinds of weaves" (Harmuth). *Gourgouran—* *étoffe de soie richement brochée qu'on tirait des Indes, et dont on faisait des rideaux* (Havard). From a source dated 1760 Havard cites *Lits de cramoisi, dont un à la polonoise, avec des rideaux de gourgouron pareille.* "British East India Company supercargoes used both *gorgoroon* and *gorgoron* to refer to a material later called *grogram*" (Lee-Whitman, p. 28).

GOSHEE

Possibly a silk / cotton fabric made in China or India (Lee-Whitman, p. 28).

GOSSAMER

A rich silk gauze, nearly as open as common gauze, but at least four times as thick and strong. It was used for veils and dresses (Perkins).

Swatches of gossamer silk, satin, and gauze are in Ackermann's *Repository* for 1809 and 1810. "A mazarine and orange flowered gossamer silk, adapted for full dress" and made of silk and wool is recommended for "Circassian or Polish robes, and worn with satin or crape slips" (3:57).

GOWNS

Fancy cottons woven in the Manchester area apparently for dresses. "Gowns striped across with cotton in a variety of patterns and colours were introduced sixty years ago [1735], and had a considerable run" (Aikin, p. 160). Such cottons probably are represented in the Manchester pattern books although without being named.

GRANDINE

One of the fancy eighteenth-century glazed worsted dress fabrics largely manufactured in Norwich. Two swatches of grandine with stripes, shaded floral sprigs, and lace bands in warp patterns are in the Moccasi manuscript (p. 23). Four swatches of *Grandines à Fleurs Brochés Fins* with shaded flowers and lace on diaper grounds are in a Norwich pattern book of the late eighteenth century (see Pl. D-71).

GRANDRELLE
(*grandrill, grandurelle*)

Twilled or plain cotton—or linen and cotton—material characterized by a ply yarn spun of different colored strands. In the nineteenth century, grandrill was described as a "dark grey material made of cotton and employed for the making of stays; a description of coarse Jean" (Caulfeild and Saward).

Remnants of "Grand Durells, qt. 36 yds @ 3/ " were part of the estate of Thomas Hysham, 1751 (New York Appraisements, p. 7). In the following year at Boston "Grandurals for Mens or Womens wear" were advertised (Dow, *Arts and Crafts,* p. 163). "A complete assortment twilled and plain Grandurells, of every colour and kind" were advertised in *Palladium,* May 8, 1810.

A swatch with warp of brown and white linen and cotton yarns spun together and weft of linen is in the Holker manuscript (no. 61). Holker says that this material was used for men's summer clothing and that it was exported in considerable quantities to the colonies. "Durells for chair bottoms" were advertised in a 1768 Virginia newspaper.

GRANITE CLOTH

A late nineteenth-century piece-dyed worsted dress material with a hard, pebbly surface produced by an irregular wide twill.

GRAZET

A silk and worsted dress material, often with warp of one color and weft of another. In 1719 Claudius Rey wrote of flowered grazets:

> Those women which were formerly clothed with Woorsted Damasks, Plain and Flower'd Russels, and Flower'd Calimancoes and Fine Stuffs from 15d to 20d per Yard (these were all Woollen Stuffs) besides those Half-Silks and Half-Woorsted, such as Flower'd Grezates, Woorsted Satinets, &c. are now generally clothed with the cheapest Callicoes, and with the best of printed Linnens. [P. 11.]

The 1695/96 van Varick inventory includes "8 remnents Canterbury grasset qt 81½ yd" and "9¾ yds Black grassett." Both plain and striped grazets are listed in Willing and Shippen's Philadelphia ledger dated 1730–34 (p. 95). Joshua Fisher and Sons of Philadelphia ordered "10½ yds Hair Grazet at 10/" in 1784 (p. 106).

Swatches of grazet dating from the second quarter of the eighteenth century are in the Alexander Papers (see Pl. D-9).

GRENADINE

An open silk or silk and wool textile used for dresses. Braun-Ronsdorf called it a lightweight fabric of a silk/wool mixture, plain or figured, similar to barege, while Peuchet, circa 1800, called it a superfine barracan.

An 1869 source said "From its being a grenadine, not a shining silk, a common error prevails that it is of thread [linen yarn]" (OED); and in 1890 a reference is made to "very light and transparent woollen materials of the kind that used to be called barege, mousseline-de-laine, and grenadine" (OED). Later writers relate grenadine to marquisette, both woven in leno, or gauze, weave. Denny refers to a cotton curtain fabric of leno construction with swivel dots or figures in white or colors.

Dresses of lilac, violet, and pearl gray grenadine are mentioned in *Godey's Lady's Book,* August 1870. In September of the same year: "the lowest price grenadine is the all wool in square meshes; then there is the silk and wool canvas grenadine, a more expensive goods, and cooler than all wool" (p. 292). Starched grenadine "with a thread drawn in" was used for Shaker women's caps at New Lebanon in 1872 (Gordon, pp. 24, 178). The dull rather than shiny appearance of the fabric is due to the silk threads used in weaving: "A silk thread

OPPOSITE

FIG. D-52. *Silk/wool grenadine printed with brown roses and polychrome sprays. From a New Jersey scrapbook, 1880s. (Winterthur Museum Library.)*

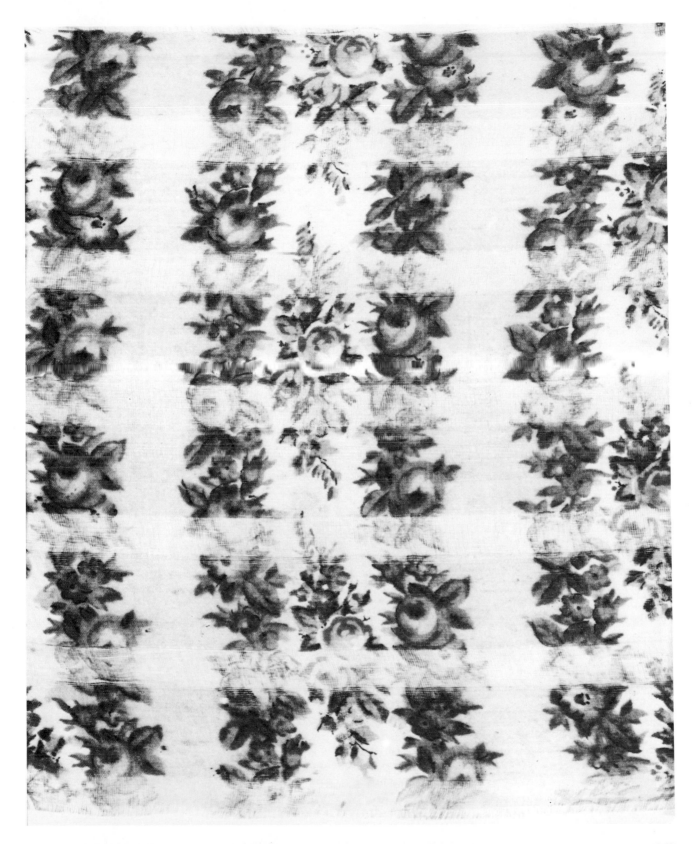

249

formed by doubling two or more ends of poil, and then throwing them in a direction opposite to that of the individual poil ends. The composition is like that of organzine, but grenadine is three or four times more tightly twisted" (Burnham, p. 66).

A piece of silk and wool grenadine dating from the 1880s is shown at figure D-52. Plain black gauze "Pineapple grenadine" is in another album of the same date (Winterthur Museum Library). "Thin curtains are now made of a material known as Russian grenadine, with insertions and edgings of Cluny lace. Others of Saxony lace have all the appearance, at a little distance, of applique." (*Carpet Trade and Review,* April 1, 1883, p. 43.)

GROGRAM

A silk and worsted, or mohair, cloth listed among New Draperies. Woolen yarn called grogram was imported from Turkey for its manufacture. A London reference of 1641 cites "Grogram or Mohair Yarne" and "Chamlets or Grograms" (Beck). In 1650, "six pcs Turkie grograine" were imported into Boston (Aspinwall Records, p. 415).

According to Earle, "A stitcht Grogram doublett" was owned by a Maryland colonist in 1638; at about the same time John Winthrop, governor of Massachusetts Bay, wrote that he was sending "a piece of Turkey Grogram, about ten yards, to make you a suit"; in 1733 Governor Belcher ordered from his London tailor "a yellow grogram suit work't strong as well as neat and curious" (*Costume,* pp. 120–21). In 1654 Jeremias van Rensselaer brought "A Turkish grosgrain suit" and other clothing to the colonies for trading purposes (van Laer, *Jeremias van Rensselaer,* p. 14). "Worsted plad water'd grograms" for men's clothing are mentioned in New York in 1745 (Singleton, *Social New York,* p. 190); and in Boston "One ps dark gray rich hair Grogram" is listed in the 1754 Caine broadside. Hair grogram was also made into women's gowns.

Two swatches of brown and tan silk and wool corded grogram accompany James Alexander's 1760 order. Ten grograms, coarse ribbed worsteds

with water markings, are in the eighteenth-century Yorkshire pattern book. They differ little from the moreens in the same book, although the moreens are not watered. "Grograms or Russell Cords" were manufactured at Bradford, Yorkshire, as late as 1857 (James, p. 532).

Chambers described silk grograms as "a sort of stuff, all silk; being in reality no more than a taffety, coarser and thicker than ordinary." Six "Figured Grograms," of silk warp and worsted weft, are among the Berch Papers. They have small geometric patterns of zigzags, grouped dots, and lozenges (see Pl. D-15) and are very similar to two swatches of London *gros grain faconné* in the Moccasi manuscript (see Pl. D-53).

GROGRINETT

A fine watered camlet probably manufactured in Norwich. Four mid-eighteenth-century swatches labeled "Super fine Grogrinetts, 22 to 24 In, 30 yds" are in the Berch Papers (see Pl. D-16). The cloth is finer than moreen, harateen, or grogram.

GROS DE NAPLES, GROS DE RHINE, GROS DE TOURS

Silk textiles of plain weave with a corded effect. Havard calls them *Taffetas à gros grain, uni, plus épis que l'ordinaire.* Perkins describes gros de Naples as "a plain stout silk; it is the staple of silks; but of which there are, of course, many qualities, and in all colours." "The usual name for a cannelé [ribbed fabric] that has only two picks of weft moving together" (Burnham, p. 53).

At the 1853 New York industrial exhibition, gros de Naples manufactured by Von der Muhill won a bronze medal "for beauty in Colours, perfection in manufacture and cheapness," and honorable mention for black gros de Rhine silks was given to Milson and Clark of Manchester and to Jules Staubli of Zurich (Dilke, pp. 28, 29).

Among the Richelieu Papers dating from the 1730s are two swatches of gros de Naples made in Holland and two of gros de Tours woven in Genoa, one of which is plain and the other with

FIG. D-53. *Silk* Grosdetour rayé et cadrillé. *From a French pattern book, ca. 1760.*
(Warner Archive, Victoria and Albert Museum.)

warp faced satin flowers on a gros de Tours ground (Lh45d V, pp. 11, 42). Others of French manufacture are illustrated by Weigert at plates 46, 47, 48, 93, and 94. The Warner Archive includes circa 1760 swatches of striped and checked gros de Tours and gros de Naples (Fig. D-53).

GROS DES INDES

According to Lardner's *Cabinet Cyclopaedia* of 1831, a material "formed by using different shuttles with threads of various substances for the shoot, whereby a stripe is formed transversely to the length of the goods" (p. 298).

GROSGRAIN

Any textile of plain weave wherein the weft yarns are heavier than the warps to give a corded effect. This category includes textiles of worsted, silk, or combinations of fibers as grogram, gros de Naples, and gros de Tours.

Swatches made in Holland, and now in the Richelieu Papers are inscribed *Camelottes—les uns sont à gros grain; les autres avec grain plus fin* (Lh45d V, pp. 24, 25). The Moccasi manuscript contains two swatches of grosgrain in blue and brown silk, two swatches of *gros grain façonné* in pink and dark blue silk and wool with a small lozenge figure (see Pl. D-53), and two swatches of flowered grosgrain in pale blue and olive silk and wool with a petaled figure (p. 15); all were of London manufacture.

In the nineteenth century, grosgrain was described as having "a variation in the texture, caused by the warp threads passing over two of the shoots at once, taking up one only: this often finishes the edge of a riband" (Fairholt). Caulfeild and Saward described grosgrain as "a stout black silk, having a fine cord like that of Rep. The colour is dull, and therefore very suitable for mourning." Denny stated it was a "firm, stiff, closely woven, corded fabric. The cords are heavier and closer than those in poplin, more round than those in faille."

GUINEAS
(*Guinea stuff, Guinea cloth*)

Cheap, brightly colored Indian cottons imported by the East India Company to sell on the Guinea Coast, and to plantation owners in the West Indies as cheap clothing for slaves. "They were mostly striped or chequered cloths, much admired on account of the brightness of their colours and the fact that the dyes were non-fugitive" (Irwin and Schwartz, p. 12).

The Maurepas Papers of about 1743 state that "Cotton cloths called guineas, dyed green, blue, maroon, etc. were manufactured in Holland for sale in Spain as *hollandilles*" (see Pl. D-49). Somewhat later in the century Mortimer describes a shipment of Guinea stuffs for South America: "The assortment of a hundred pieces to be as follows: 30 pieces deep blue, 20 pieces pale blue, 15 pieces parrot green, 15 pieces orange, 10 pieces musk, 5 pieces yellow, and 5 pieces flesh colour." Early in the nineteenth century, Thomas Cooper wrote of western imitations: "In dyeing cotton, the light shades are usually dyed first: very full blues are seldom wanted unless for Guineas, which require to be so deep that the coppery hue is perceptible on casting your eye along the piece" (p. 270).

A 1728 order to Samuel Baker lists "12 ps. Guinea Stuffs" (Ten Eyck Papers); and in 1734 Robert Livingston ordered "100 ps best Guinea Stuffs."

Indiennes ou Guinées found in the Richelieu Papers for 1736 are coarse printed cottons exported from Marseilles (see Pl. D-93). The reverse trade is shown by swatches of coarse striped cotton cloths made in Africa and brought to New Jersey in the nineteenth century (Fig. D-54).

See also Berams, Birdet, Brawles.

GULICK
(*gulix*)

See Garlick, Holland.

FIG. D-54. *Swatches of coarse cotton stripes "Woven on the coast of Guinea Africa by the negroes brought to this country in the winter of 1800 . . . the Mate boarded at the farmhouse where Wm. Carpenter now lives and presented the above to the lady of the house." From a New Jersey scrapbook made in the 1880s. (Winterthur Museum Library.)*

GUNNY

Coarse cloth made in India of jute fiber to be used for sacks and to cover bales.

GURRAH
(garat)

Plain cotton cloth made in northeast India (Irwin and Schwartz). It was used in England and France in the eighteenth century for coarse printing (Wadsworth and Mann, p. 163). A memoir of about 1758, probably written in Rouen, stated *on a cherché en France à imiter les Garats, sorte de Toile des Indes la plus adaptée à l'impression* (Kress, S4130). It was also used for table linen and other household purposes. For swatches of gurrah, see John Forbes Watson, 8: nos. 297, 299, 300, 302, 306.

GUZZEE
(guzzy, Fr. guzenis)

An ordinary plain white calico similar to baftas and gurrahs.

H

HAIRBINE

A silk and worsted material, which probably contained some mohair, used for men's clothing. In 1737 Robert Livingston ordered "Light coloured hairbines" from London, and in the following year "1 ps. Olive Colour hairbine with buttons & mohair Suitable."

Swatches of "lead Colr," olive, brown, and blue / black in silk and wool are in the Alexander Papers of June and November 1738 (see Pl. D-8); black and white hairbines are in his papers of 1739. Two swatches of Norwich silk and wool *Camelotto osia arbines soprofini in seta* are in the Moccasi manuscript (p. 24). A pattern book with Italian captions in the Castle Museum contains over one hundred swatches of *Hairbines mezzo Setta*. As late as May 1792, striped *Harabini* in yellow and brown, and black and brown, are shown in the *Journal für Fabrik*.

HAIRCLOTH

Made of the long mane and tail hairs of horses on a linen, cotton, or woolen warp and used for sacks and sieves, for stiffening clothing, and for upholstery. The term may also refer to cloth containing mohair yarn.

In 1739 James Alexander of New York ordered "3 doz hair cloaths for Skirts of men's Coats." In the following year John Banister of Newport ordered "13 doz. hair cloths for Shapes, 12 flatts at 17/6."

In the 1760s Thomas Chippendale billed clients for parlor, dining room, and library chairs covered in haircloth which in two instances he specified as crimson and green (Boynton, pp. 40, 46, 90). George Hepplewhite's *Guide* of 1789 suggests that "Mahogany chairs should have the seats of horsehair, plain, striped, chequered, &c. at pleasure" (p. 2). Deborah Franklin wrote from

Philadelphia in 1765 that the dining room chairs had been covered in "a plain Horsehair and look as well as Paddozway [paduasoy]" (Franklin Papers, 12:296). In addition to plain satin and satin stripe upholstery haircloth which has survived, an empire-style child's chair in the Connecticut His-

torical Society, Hartford, is covered with a floral sprig pattern. Black was the most popular color followed by green, but examples in blue-green and gold, red and white, and two shades of green on a red ground are known in American collections (Fig. D-55).

FIG. D-55. *Haircloth woven in red and two shades of green. Removed from an American empire settee of about 1825. (Winterthur Museum.)*

HAIRCORD
(haircord muslin)

A kind of dimity. The name is derived from the stripe which is of narrow width and resembles a small cord or hair (Perkins). "A very fine kind of cotton cloth, the threads running the long way, and presenting the appearance of fine cords" (Caulfeild and Saward). It was used for infants' robes and dresses in the nineteenth century.

HALF THICKS

Coarse woolen cloth. Defoe wrote of "Those [foreigners] whose Clothing was of coarse Duffells, Wadmill, Halfthicks, and in general a kind of the coarsest Kersies, but a degree or two above Blankets; or perhaps the meanest of our Dozens, and what we call Yorkshire Cloths" (*English Commerce,* p. 182). About 1725 on his northern tour, Defoe found Rochdale in Lancashire "very considerable, for a sort of coarse goods, called half-thicks and kersies, and the market for them is very great" (*Tour,* vol. 3, letter 8).

In Brandon and Dolbear's journal, Boston 1739, are listed

> a piece plain blue half Thicks
> a piece knapt blue   "   "
> a ps. green knapt half Thicks

The Philadelphia inventory of Samuel Neave, 1774, lists:

> 4 ps plain wt Halfthicks
> knapped   "
> 6 ps plain purple Halfthicks
> 18 ps knapd ditto

A few of these are a little touch'd [by moth?] on the outside.

George Bartram advertised blue, green, and red half thicks along with flannels, duffels, and other woolen goods in the *Pennsylvania Chronicle,* September 7, 1767.

Swatches of twill-woven Yorkshire half thicks are among the Berch Papers.

HAMMERCLOTH

"The ornamental cloth, often fringed, which was formerly hung over the driver's seat or box of a coach, now used only on coaches of ceremony" (Merriam-Webster). By extension this may have been a protective and ornamental covering for a piece of furniture. "A green hammer cloth laced with gold" is listed in Lord Botetourt's inventory of the "Chamber over the Dining Room" (Botetourt manuscripts).

HANDWARPES

Sixteenth-century cloth of worsted warp and woolen weft fulled after weaving and made at Coggeshall in Essex. Sometimes called coxsalls. The cloth was related to bay.

HARATEEN
(harrateen)

A worsted furnishing material frequently mentioned as dyed green, red, yellow, blue, or "Cloath Coulered." Related to cheney, moreen, and camlet, it was among the important Norwich manufactures. Harateen is one of the most frequently listed materials for furnishing and upholstery in inventories prior to about 1750, after which it began to lose its popularity to washable materials. In 1726, Thomas Fitch urged harateen—his first mention of it—on a customer: "I concluded it would be difficult to get Such a Calliminco as you propos'd to Cover the Ease Chair, and haveing a very Strong thick Harratine which is vastly more fashionable and handsome than a Calliminco I have sent you an Ease Chair Cover'd wth sd Harrateen wch I hope will Sute You" (Jobe, p. 34n).

Four pieces of harateen are found in the Holker manuscript of about 1750 (see Pl. D-27). John Holker described numbers 107 and 108 as "a kind of woolen mohair [*moire*] made in Norwich. The waved pattern is made by means of a hot press, the use of which is little understood in France. This material is used for furnishing"; two coarser swatches of harateen (nos. 109, 110) cost two shillings less per yard. They are described as "the same material as no. 107 and no. 108 but coarser [*plus commun*]. The wavy pattern is here achieved by means of a hot copper cylinder." Large pieces of harateen resembling these latter swatches, with full widths and repeats of about forty inches, show that the meandering stamped pattern was intended to imitate the outlines of formal foliate patterns in silk damask furnishing fabrics. The wavy lines are exactly repeated on either side of a central longitudinal axis.

In fabrics with weft yarns coarser than the warps a watered effect was generally achieved by doubling the material lengthwise along the selvedges and submitting it to great pressure (or by pressing two full widths superimposed on one another). The yarns were thereby forced and flattened against each other. On the other hand, the additional linear pattern in the swatches shown in plate D-27 could only have been made with an engraved roller, as Holker stated, which would have been costly. A pattern achieved by this method, in the Essex Institute, Salem, includes sprays of flowers and butterflies in a style not unlike wood-block printed fabrics of the period (see Fig. D-44).

In the latter part of the eighteenth century, harateen was produced in the West Riding of Yorkshire and "an ancient manufacturer" described it as "a coarse stuff, woven plain; something between a tammy and moreen" (James, Appendix, p. 229).

In 1735 "a Field Bedstead and Bed, the covering Blew Harrateen" were sold at "Publick Vendue" in Boston; "A Coach [couch] Bed with all the Furniture, viz, a beautiful Suit of red Harriteen Curtains, double Valians, a Tester and Head Cloth" were offered for sale there in 1757 (Dow, *Arts and Crafts*, pp. 110, 115). Losses in the 1760 Boston fire included sets of green, crimson, and "Cloath Coulered" harateen curtains, green and red easy chairs covered in harateen, and the "Head of a yellow Harrateen Bed" (*Boston Records*, p. 40).

John Banister in 1739 listed the following fabrics in his accounts:

16 Ps green Waterd Cheney [at]	22/
1 Ps blew Ditto	22/
10 Ps Mock Crimson	26/
2 Ps Crimson Ingrain Cheney	34/
2 Ps Crimson Ingrain Harrateen	48/
[Note the greater cost.]	

In the following year, Banister ordered a "Sett of green Harrateen bed Curtains" and another of crimson.

In New York as late as 1768, "Worsted Damasks, Moreens, Harrateens, and Chineas [cheney]" were all stocked by upholsterer Joseph Cox (Gottesman, *1726–76*, p. 136). In 1760 Thomas Duncan of that city had "Yellow Harriteen Bed Curtains & Vallins" with "Window Curtains of the Same" and "7 Black walnutt Chaires old with Harriteen Seats" (New York Appraisements, p. 76).

For further explanations, see Cummings, s.v. "mohair." It should be noted that harateen is incorrectly defined as a linen material in the OE and several other dictionaries.

HARDEN
(hurden)

A coarse cloth made from hemp or tow fibers used from the sixteenth century for sheets, towels, tablecloths, bags, and work smocks (Beck). Samuel Rowland Fisher noted in his 1767 journal that "Between Settle & Lancaster are Made all the Hardons & Sacking." At that time he ordered the material in three different widths.

The Workwoman's Guide (1838) suggests its use in putting up beds. "Large sheets of coarse brown paper pasted together in lengths should be laid over the beds to catch the dust. Some persons lay hurden or coarse linen between the head of the bed and these sheets of paper" (p. 193).

HARESBACK

A woolen cloth finished with a springy, horizontally teased surface. A swatch in light gray is included with fine flannels, cassimeres, coatings, and bays in a "Standards" book of 1798/99 (Public Record Office, CME / C113 / 16).

HARLEQUIN
(harlekin)

One of the fancy eighteenth-century glazed worsted dress fabrics largely manufactured in Norwich. Swatches of brightly colored small checked worsteds from Norwich are in the Moccasi manuscript (p. 24), and fifteen swatches of "Corded Harliquins, 18 Ins: 32 yds" are in the 1763 Kelly book. Swatches are also in a Norwich pattern book (DMMC 65 x 695.1).

HENRIETTA

A cloth of silk and wool first made about 1660 and named in honor of Henrietta Maria, queen consort of Charles I of England. In the nineteenth century, it was a material used for mourning, "the warp composed of spun silk, and the weft of fine Saxony wool" (Caulfeild and Saward). It was a lightweight cashmere of high finish.

HERNANI

A French dress goods which Harmuth said was lighter than grenadine and made of silk and wool. In the *Journal of Design,* written at the time of the Great Exhibition of 1851, the wide mesh hernani was described as "a novelty of this season"; "formerly it could only be purchased in black, now it is to be had in all the most delicate and desirable colours" (p. 493). Nearly twenty years later *Godey's Lady's Book* repeated these comments (February 1870).

Possibly the name *hernani* was given to this cloth following the first performance of Verdi's opera of that name in 1844.

HERRINGBONE

Any textile woven in a zigzag pattern resembling chevrons or the bones of a herring. Diagrams of herringbone weaves are illustrated at figures 10, 11, and 12 and a wool and cotton herringbone blanket woven in Ontario about 1855 is illustrated at figure 138 all in Burnham and Burnham.

In a John Banister order of 1745, "Herinboun" was listed along with fustians such as barragon, jean, and pillow. A coarse, sturdy herringbone twill of linen warp and cotton weft "used for pockets in clothing" is in the Holker manuscript.

HESSIAN
(hessen)

"A coarse hempen cloth, the name is most probably indicative of its origin" (Beck). Hessian and forfars were two qualities of the commonest unbleached sheeting and principally used for packages (Perkins).

"Dutch Barras and Hessens Canvas" are listed under linen goods in the 1660 London Book of Rates (Beck). "Barris and Hessins" are specified in Willing and Shippen's 1730–34 ledger (p. 141). In Joshua Rowland Fisher's order of 1767 from Philadelphia, both brown and white, or unbleached and bleached, "Hessons" were listed with sailcloth, Russia sheeting, osnaburg, dowlas, and other coarse cloths.

HOLLAND

Linen cloth. Once specifying the country of manufacture for a wide variety of linen goods, "holland" later became the generic name for linen cloth, often of fine quality. Linen goods made elsewhere were also sent to Holland to be bleached. According to Chambers,

> The principal mart or staple of this cloth is at Haerlam, whither it is sent from most other parts as soon as wove, there to be whitened the ensuing spring. That manufactured in

Frizeland is the most esteemed, and called frize holland. It is the strongest and the best coloured of any of that fineness. It is never calendered, nor thickened as the rest; but is imported just as it comes from the whitster.

Governor Stuyvesant (b. 1602) was christened in an "infant shirt, of fine holland, edged with narrow lace" (Watson, *Annals of New York,* p. 152). In a 1668 Dorchester, Massachusetts, inventory "A White Holland Apron with a Small Lace at the bottom" is listed (Earle, *Costume,* p. 47). In 1731 a Boston resident lost a "blew strip'd holland Waistcoat" (Dow, *Arts and Crafts,* p. 173). In 1760 "18 shifts one dozn of them very fine hollan" were lost in the Boston fire (*Boston Records,* p. 41).

James Beekman ordered "¾ wide dark blue and white striped Holland" and brown holland (2:834, 945). In 1758, by which time hollands were made in the Manchester area, his London agents asked for clarification of his order:

> We cannot tell what you mean by yard wide Cotton Strip[e]s at 12½ per Ell neither could our Agent in Manchester. We sell Cotton Warps or hollands at about 12d or 12½ per yard but they are but ⅞ wide or rather 13/16. We wish you would send us a pattern of it and then you may depend on them. [2:612.]

Swatches 21 to 24 (see Pl. D-28) in the Holker manuscript, called cotton holland or cotton warps, explain Beekman's "Cotton Strip[e]s." Holker says that, in addition to linen warp yarns, cotton, in shades of blue, red and blue, tan, dark red, and so on, form the colored warp stripes. Similar striped fabrics from Rouen, called *siamoises,* of linen warp and cotton weft are found in several swatch books (see Pls. D-41, D-42, D-43). Holker claimed the English goods to be superior in pattern, in wear, and in their suitability to calendering or lustering. Swatches of striped and checked hollands in the Science Museum manuscript (ca. 1784), are accompanied by the comment that several were worn "instead of our English Worsted Stuffs" (see Figs. D-98, D-99).

In the nineteenth century holland was

unbleached and made in two descriptions— the glazed and unglazed. The former is employed for carriage or chaircovers and trunk linings; the latter for articles of dress— men's blouses, women's and children's dresses, and many other purposes. A description of Holland [shade holland] is employed for window roller blinds, made in cotton as well as linen. They are highly glazed and sized, so as to be less influenced by dust, and are made in white, blue, buff, green, and in stripes of different colours. [Caulfeild and Saward.]

Lord and Taylor's 1881 catalogue listed holland spring window shades in white, green, blue, drab, brown, and painted (p. 162).

Ghentish holland was used for sheeting. In 1707 Samuel Sewall wrote to England "The rest [of the goods to be sent] in Ghentish Holland, a round-thredded Holland, not Kentish: about 4s. an Ell, or 3.6d" (Letter book, 1:360).

Garlick, gulick, gulix, or guilick holland, very fine and white, was chiefly used for men's shirts. Defoe's tradesman's wife (1726) wore "Muslin from foreign trade; as likewise her Linen, being something finer than the man's, may perhaps be a Guilick-Holland" (*English Tradesman,* p. 403). Thomas Fitch ordered "Gulick shirting holland ...white and strong" and later requested "4 ps of fine Gulick holland" to be sent "with the first Parcells of Garlix" (Letter book, July 18, 1726), and December 26, 1727.

Tufted holland was presumably related to tufted fustian, for in 1691 Samuel Sewall requested from London "a piece of good Tufted Holland, fine and thick" (Letter book, 1:118).

See also Hooping.

HOLMES

A kind of fustian. "The two kinds most used in England [in the sixteenth century] were those of Ulm and Genoa—or as they were universally known, 'Holmes' and 'Jean' or 'Jeans' fustians" (Wadsworth and Mann, p. 19).

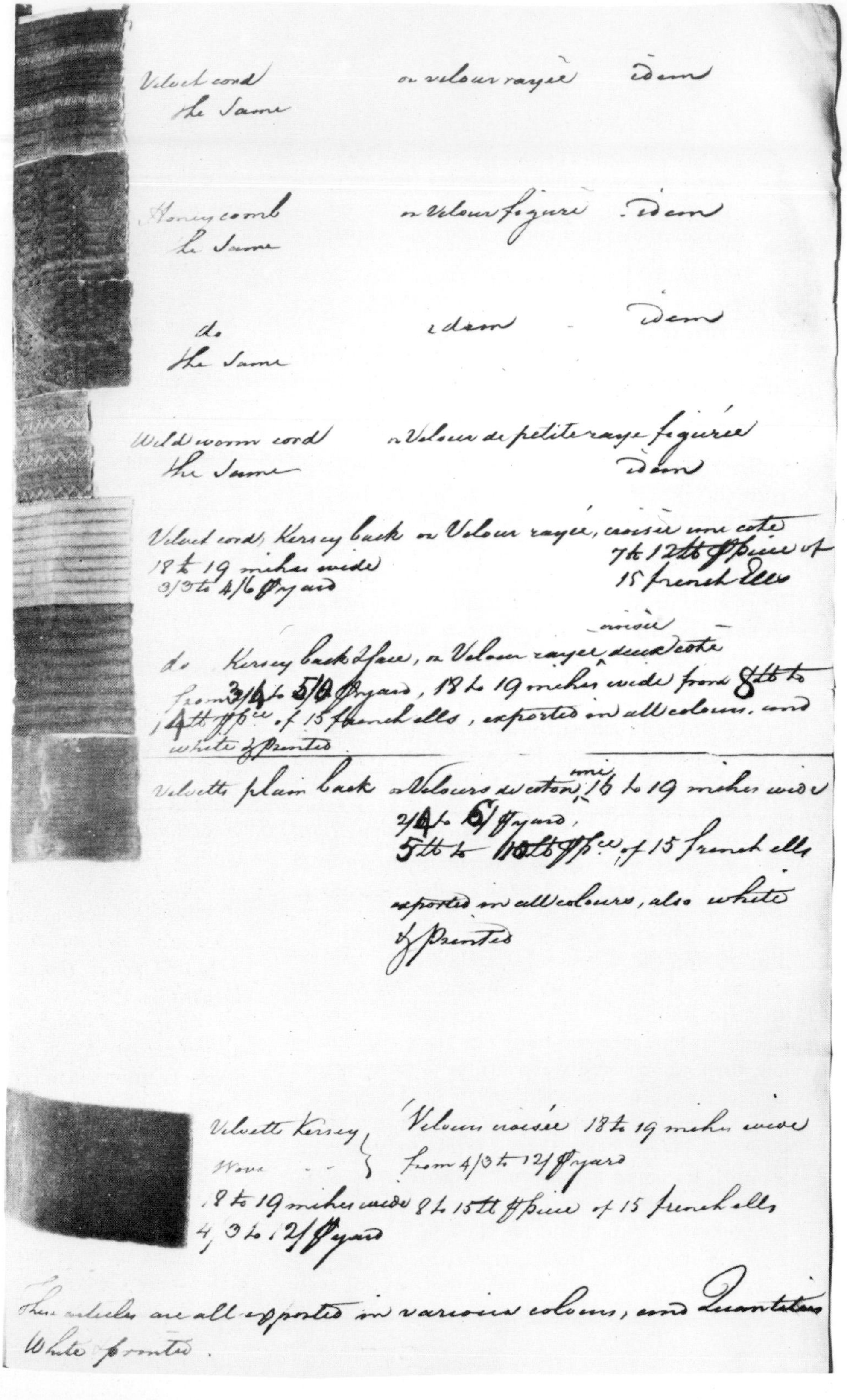
Velvet cord — or velour rayée — idem
the Same
Honeycomb — or Velour figuré — idem
the Same
do — idem — idem
the Same
Wildworm cord — or Velour de petite raye figurée
the Same — idem
Velvet cord, Kersey back or Velour rayée, croisée une cote
18 to 19 inches wide — 7 to 12 ll per piece of
3/3 to 4/6 per yard — 15 french Ells
do Kersey back & face, or Velour rayée, croisée deux cote
from 3/4 to 5/6 per yard, 18 to 19 inches wide from 8 ll to
14 ll per pce of 15 french ells, exported in all colours, and
white & printed
Velvetts plain back or Velours de coton, uni 18 to 19 inches wide
2/4 to 5/ per yard,
5 ll to 10 ll per pce of 15 french ells
exported in all colours, also white
& printed
Velvett Kersey Wove — Velours croisée 18 to 19 inches wide
from 4/3 to 12/ per yard
18 to 19 inches wide 8 to 15 ll per piece of 15 french ells
4/3 to 12/ per yard
These articles are all exported in various colours, and Quantities
White & printed.

FIG. D-56. *Swatches of cotton-pile textiles: velvet cord, honeycomb, wildworm cord, and velvet kerseys. "These articles are all exported in various colours, and Quantities, White & printed." From the Hilton manuscript, 1786.* (Public Record Office.)

HONEYCOMB

A kind of cotton velvet with a fancy pattern that is known from two swatches in the 1786 Hilton manuscript (Fig. D-56).

HOOPING
(hooping holland)

A linen textile which Earle suggests was used for petticoats into which reeds or bones could be run to stiffen them (*Costume,* p. 137). "Hooping Hollands" were advertised in Boston in 1750 (Dow, *Arts and Crafts,* p. 163). The Holker manuscript contains three swatches of hooping (see Pl. D-29). The top swatch has a chiné, or warp-printed, stripe. According to Holker, they were sold for ladies' paniers.

HOUNSCOT
(hanscott, hounscoat, hunscoat)

A say, or light worsted cloth classed among New Draperies and named after the town Hondschoote in Flanders where they were made beginning in 1374. "The cloths resembled a traditional worsted in that both warp and weft were prepared from combed wool. There followed a particular method of warp-sizing and weaving after which the cloths were lightly fulled and then given a smooth finish by calendering" (Coleman, p. 422). Black or white English "hounscot says" were shipped to Spain and the Spanish West Indies in the eighteenth century.

See also Anacoste.

HOUSEWIFE'S CLOTH OR COTTON

"A middle sort of linen cloth between fine and coarse, for family uses" (Chambers). "Wiggon or housewife cotton" was advertised in the *Pennsylvania Chronicle, and Universal Advertiser,* December 4 and 11, 1769.

See also Dowlas.

HUCKABACK
(huck, hugabag)

"A linen for towels with raised figures" (Beck). Updating the French-English vocabulary prepared by CIETA in 1964, Dorothy Burnham (p. 72) gave the following: "A self-patterned weave with a tabby ground with small all-over motifs in offset rows formed by warp floats on one face and weft floats on the other." The floats give the cloth greater absorbency.

The linen sold at Warrington, near Liverpool, "is generally speaking a sort of table linnen, called huk-a-back or huk-a-buk; 'tis well known among the good housewives so I need not describe it" (Defoe, *Tour,* vol. 3, letter 10). The term probably derives "from the linen towelling at one time ped-

Fig. D-57. *Linen napkin woven in a huckaback diamond pattern. Owned by Mary Pauline Lentilhon, ca. 1835–40; probably United States. (Winterthur Museum.)*

dled by traveling 'hucksters' in the British Isles" (Emery, p. 125, diagram at fig. 218).

Orders in the Beekman Papers from 1757 to 1770 include "narrow Russia hucaback," "Rusha diaper or huckaback" and "20 pieces Huckaback, and 20 pieces Rushia diaper 17 Ells each at 11d per Ell." The draft for "English huckabag" is included in John Hargrove's 1792 weaver's book.

An example of huckaback woven in Guilford, Connecticut, is illustrated by Frances Little in *Early American Textiles* at figure 2-d. Tablecloths are illustrated by Burnham and Burnham, pages 128 and 129. *See also* Fig. D-57.

HUMHUM
(hammam, hamoene)

Plain cotton cloth of thick, stout texture woven in Bengal. In 1767, Samuel Rowland Fisher ordered "6/4 Humhums—30/," and Philadelphia merchants Kearny and Gilbert advertised this cloth in the April 20 and 27 issues of the *Pennsylvania Chronicle.*

It has also been suggested that humhum resembled modern turkish toweling, that it was a coarse India cotton found only in wealthy homes, and that it was used for general utility purposes such as toweling (Larson, p. 29).

HUNGARIAN

One of the fancy eighteenth-century glazed worsted dress fabrics largely manufactured in Norwich. Both striped and checked hungarians were ordered by Albany residents in 1754 (Ten Eyck Papers). James Beekman was specific in his order of 1766: "22 pieces yard wide Checked Hungarian, quantity 30 yard @ 29/ Vizt. 6 pieces black and white and 16 pieces dark brown ground and bright Colloured Checks" (2:774). Jonathan Holmes's New York account book lists "1 piece Stripd Diamond Hungarian Cambliteen."

I

IMPERIAL

A name given to several kinds of cloth as:

Imperial satin—closely woven cotton fabric.
Imperial serge—another name for perpetuana, or lightweight twill of worsted and wool.
Imperial shirting—bleached cotton shirting.
Imperial tape—stout cotton tape. [Harmuth.]

Two swatches of plain woolen and two of mixed colors called *Imperiali* and made in Rheims are in the Moccasi manuscript (p. 38). "Cerulean blue Imperial Gauze, calculated for evening or dinner parties," in a plain spaced weave of pale blue silk with white cotton warp cords, is in Ackermann's *Repository* (7, no. 40 [April 1812]: 250).

INDERKINS

In 1696: "a sort of Cloth of no great use . . . [and] only proper for Towels, it is a coarse narrow Cloth which comes from Hamborough . . . it is made of the worst of Hemp" (OED). Perhaps hinderlands, inderlins, and "imperlings blew or red" are all names for coarse German linens.

INDIAN GOODS

Anglo-Indian commerce in textiles began with the founding of the East India Company in 1600. This trade has been comprehensively discussed by John Irwin in Irwin and Schwartz, *Studies in Indo-European Textile History*.

Of the trade in Indian goods Macpherson says:

It was about this time [1670] that the wear of the flimsy muslins from India was first introduced into England: before which time our more natural and usual wear was cambrics, Silesia lawns, and such kind of fine flaxen linens, from Flanders and Germany, in return for our woollen manufactures of various kinds, exported to these countries in very considerable quantities. [2:540.]

During the last quarter of the seventeenth century, English weavers protested the stream of imported Indian goods which they considered detrimental to their own manufactures. Typical of the complaints is one published in 1678:

Instead of Green Sey that was wont to be used for Childrens Frocks, is now used Painted, and *Indian*-stained, and Striped Calico; and instead of a Perpetuana or a Shalloon to Lyne Mens Coats with, is used sometimes a Glazened Calico, which in the whole is not above twelve pence cheaper, and abundantly worse. For either Perpetuana or Shalloon will wear out two Coats, or when it hath worn out one Coat, it will serve for one use or other afterwards for children. [*Ancient Trades Decayed, Repaired Again,* p. 16.]

Long lists of Indian imports were published in pamphlets, among them "A Particular of the Silks . . . which came from the East–India . . . with the Rates at which they were sold at the late Sale at the East–India House" (Kress, S2180); "An Extract from the Dutch Printed Cargoes of the several Sorts of Goods Following, By them Imported from the East–Indies between the Years 1686 and 1696 Inclusive, Viz. Silks, or Goods mixed therewith, Callicoes and other Goods Painted, Stained, Printed or Coloured There" (Kress, S1994); and about 1701, "A List of Several Sorts of Silks and Callicoes usually imported from the East–Indies, Persia and China, Prohibited to be used in England, by the Bill Entituled, An Act for Restraining the Wearing of all Wrought Silks, Bengals Dyed, Printed or Stained Callicoes" (Kress, S2200). In addition eighty names of Indian goods "From a Tract Protesting against Foreign Importations That Was Printed about 1700" are listed in *Dutch and Flemish Furniture* by Esther Singleton (p. 293).

The anticalico campaign of 1719–21 which again brought forth a flood of pamphlets, has been discussed by Natalie Rothstein in "Calico Campaign." In her article, she illustrates swatches of some of the English imitations of Indian goods made at that time which have been preserved in the London Public Record Office (see Pl. D-97 and Fig. D-43).

Samples of printed handkerchiefs made in imitation of Indian goods were resist-printed in two shades of red or in indigo (see Pl. D-22). Holker explained that in London the English printed fine linen cloth (Fr. *batiste*) from Cambray, Valenciennes, and St. Quentin for home consumption as well as for export to Europe and the colonies. The import tax paid when the white cloth was imported was rebated when the printed handkerchiefs were exported.

John Aikin, writing of Manchester manufactures, said "the tying and dying of silk handkerchiefs is brought to perfection, so as to imitate those imported from India; and the variety of printed handkerchiefs here, both cotton and linen, is scarcely to be enumerated" (p. 160). Handkerchiefs described as "Paistwork," probably referring to the resist paste used in printing them, were advertised in the *Boston Gazette* on May 26, 1755 (Dow, *Arts and Crafts,* p. 164). In 1770 James Beekman ordered "10 dozen blue and white paste linnen Handkerchiefs at 11 / " and "5 dozen red and white [handkerchiefs] at 12 / " (2:930). For silk handkerchiefs made in imitation of Indian goods, *see* Foulard.

Despite legislation prohibiting the sale, use, and wear of printed calicoes, they could be brought to England for reexport, and many other kinds of Indian textiles were manufactured on order for markets in North Africa, Turkey and the Levant, West Africa, and the slave plantations of the West Indies. This trade, including that to the American plantations is described in *Trade Goods* by Alice B. Beer.

Direct trade with the East by the United States after the Revolution is documented by many surviving merchants' records and newspaper advertisements in port cities. One such notice, "India Sales at Salem at the Store of E. H. Derby, Esq.," ran in the *Providence Gazette* from February to April 1791:

> [from Bengal:]
> Cargoe of the Brig Henry lately arrived from Bengal, Madras, and Isle of France: consisting of a large and valuable Assortment of India Goods, as follow, viz.
>> Baftas, Sannas, and Cassas—White Cloths proper for Shirting and Sheeting
>> Dureas, or striped Muslins
>> Durea Chintz, or painted, striped Ditto.
>> Chintz, a great Variety
>> Striped Cottons, Jagrenant Muslins, Ditto Handkerchiefs.
> [from Madras:]
>> Ginghams, Blue Cotton Handkerchiefs
>> Long Cloths of a superior Quality, suitable for Shirting
>> Madras Patches, beautifully figured
>> Camboys, or blue and white Striped Cottons
>> Moreas, or plain white Cloths
>> Madras Cambricks
>> Ditto handkerchiefs with borders. Book Muslins, Ditto handkerchiefs, a great Variety
>> A quantity of China Silk Handkerchiefs, etc. etc.

Imported Indian colored cottons for the African trade included

> striped, checked and plain, in endless variety, every pattern being known by a different title. Guinea stuffs, . . . bejutapauts, negannepauts, nicconnees, tapseils, brawls, chelloes, romals and more than twenty other varieties mentioned in the Custom House Accounts were all coarse cottons in different colours, patterns and lengths, exported under their Indian names. Their bright colours, which were as brilliant after washing as before, took the negroes' fancy, and without great advantages in design or price it was difficult to compete with them. [Wadsworth and Mann, p. 151.]

In 1835 Edward Baines described the cotton manufactures of India:

> Bengal is celebrated for the production of the finest muslins; the Coromandel coast, for the best chintzes and calicoes; and Surat, for strong and inferior goods of every kind. The cottons of Bengal go under the names of casses, amans, and garats; and the handkerchiefs are called Burgoses and Steinkirkes. Tablecloths of superior quality are made at Patna. The basins, or basinets, come from the Northern Circars. Condaver furnishes the beautiful handkerchiefs of Masulipatam, the fine colours of which are partly obtained from a plant called chage, which grows on the banks of the Krishna, and on the coast of the Bay of Bengal. The chintzes and ginghams are chiefly made at Masulipatam, Madras, St. Thomé, and Paliamcotta. The long cloths and fine pullicats are produced in the presidency of Madras. The coarse piece-goods, under the names of baftas, doutis, and pullicats, as well as common muslins and chintzes, are extensively manufactured in the district of which Surat is the port. [P. 75.]

In the 1870s, with the express purpose of stimulating the manufacture of imitations of Indian goods that could be sold at a profit in England, John Forbes Watson published a seventeen-volume work entitled *Collection of Specimens and Illustrations of the Textile Manufactures of India*. Hundreds of swatches of cloth identified by fiber content and place of manufacture in India are included in these books. For anyone unfamiliar with Indian geography and the language, it is difficult to find names comparable with those which appeared in American newspaper advertisements in the eighteenth and early nineteenth centuries.

The reader is referred to N. N. Bannerjei's *Cotton Fabrics of Bengal* and the book known as *Hobson-Jobson*. I have included in this catalogue only those Indian textiles most frequently found in merchants' records and for which a meaningful definition could be ascertained.

See also Guineas.

INGRAIN

Scarlet dye (kermes), long thought to be a grain, was actually obtained from the bodies of insects. The term may refer to the color scarlet or to cloths dyed in the yarn before weaving. The latter were considered superior to piece-dyed goods.

In 1774 James Beekman ordered "8 pieces womens 7/4 Scarlet in grain [broad cloth] . . . to be well covered & pressed" (2:751). In 1789 George Washington wrote about "superfine American Broadcloths": "As to the colour, I shall leave it altogether to your taste; only observing, that, if the dye should not appear to be well fixed, & clear, or if the cloth should not really be very fine, then (in my judgment) some colour mixed in grain might be preferable to an indifferent (stained) dye" (Frances Little, p. 104).

INGRAIN CARPET

"Double-cloth carpets, i.e. carpets composed of two cloths of different colours woven together in such a way that first one and then another appears on the surface, thus forming a pattern" (King, "Textiles," *Early Georgian,* p. 119). They were made in narrow strips perhaps 36 inches wide and then sewed together and were also called Kidderminster, two-ply, and Scotch carpets (Page, p. 19). "Three-ply ingrain . . . was not invented until 1822 in Kilmarnock, Scotland, and was first made in New England at Thompsonville, Connecticut, by the Hartford Manufacturing Company in 1833" (Nina F. Little, p. 11) (Fig. D-58).

INKLE
(incle)

A tape or braid used for trimming dresses and bed curtains, for garters, stays, and apron strings. Inkle was made in great variety. Earle cites "rich inkle lustring" made of silk (*Costume,* p. 142); another source states "one bundle 3 ps silk and incle Bed-Lace" (Caine broadside). Fairholt says that it "was generally of a yellow colour, but sometimes striped blue and pink, or blue and red" and "was worn by the humbler classes as a trimming." It was made in England from the mid-seventeenth century (Beck).

Inkle belonged to a large category of smallwares. Aikin wrote of the inkle loom developed by the Dutch and probably brought to Manchester in the mid-eighteenth century: "Upon the introduction of Dutch looms . . . inkle, tapes and filleting, which had before been made in frames or single looms, were now . . . wrought in these new engines" (p. 157). Inkle was also a kind of linen thread.

IRISH STITCH

"A straight stitch on canvas worked in zigzag lines, often in gradations of colour" (Swain, *Historical Needlework,* p. 122), more commonly known today as bargello, Florentine, or Hungarian stitch.

The 1693 Boston inventory of Margaret Thatcher lists two carpets, a cushion, and a couch of Irish stitch work (SCPR, 13:408). In the 1761

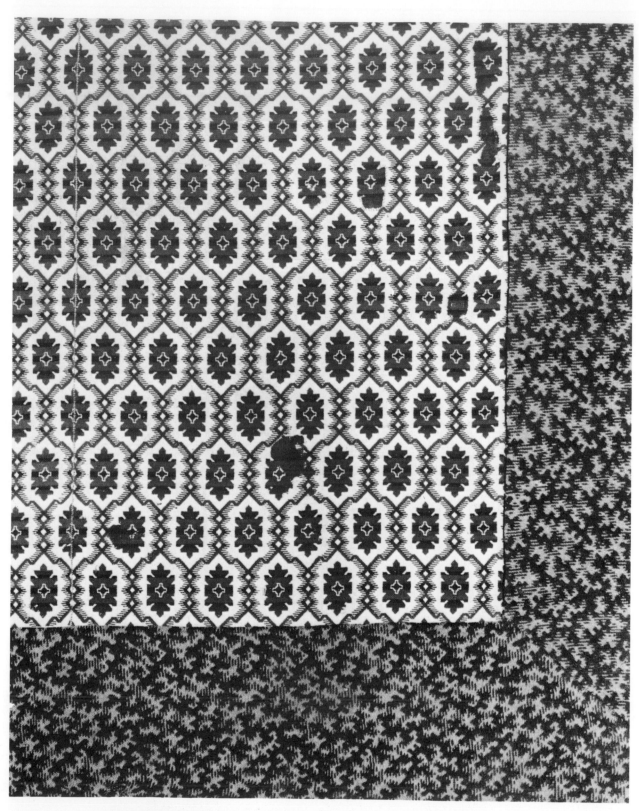

Fig. D-58. *Ingrain carpet with attached border. The field is olive, light green, dark green, and white. The border is light and dark green. England or Scotland, 1820–40. (Winterthur Museum.)*

FIG. D-59. "Table Cloath" worked primarily in Irish stitch by Mary Oothout in the New York area and dated "September the 9 1759." (Winterthur Museum.)

FIG. D-60. *Irish terries made of silk and worsted by William Fry and Company, Dublin, for curtains and upholstery. From G. W. Yapp, ed.,* Art Industry: Furniture, Upholstery, and House-Decoration (1879; *reprint ed., Westmead, Farnborough, Hants.: Gregg International Publishers, 1972), pl. 73.*

Boston inventory of Joseph Richards "2 Irish stitch'd cusions" and "3 Holland Pillow coats" (possibly slip cases for the needlework) are listed (SCPR, 58:323).

Irish stitch table covers, upholstery, men's and women's pocket books, hand fire screens, house-wives, and book covers in flamelike patterns worked in worsted crewels survive in American collections (Fig. D-59).

IRISH STUFFS

According to the Holker manuscript, these were woven largely in Norwich, and some at Spital-fields, of silk warp and worsted weft for women's

dresses. The swatches shown have narrow satin stripes or checks (see Pl. D-30).

IRISH TERRIES

Manufactured by William Fry and Company of Dublin, "famous manufacturers of poplins, tabi-nets, and other beautiful tissues" (Fig. D-60). The patterns are described as "elegant diapers formed of the elements of styles more or less remote." Of the material Yapp says that it "has a peculiar rich-ness and metallic lustre which render it admirably fitted for upholstering purposes, and it is consid-erably cheaper than stuffs composed of silk alone" (illustrated at Yapp, "Textile Fabrics," pl. 73). *See* figure D-60.

J

JACONET
(*jaconot*)

A thin, closely woven cotton textile, thicker than muslin, slighter than cambric, and thinner than nainsook. "It is the thickest of the soft muslins, employed for dresses, neckcloths, and infants' clothes" (Caulfeild and Saward). Glazed jaconets were dyed in various colors. First made in India, many varieties of the material were developed in France.

By the late 1780s, Manchester manufactures rivaled inexpensive Indian cotton goods, such as doreas, "Ballasore handkerchiefs, jaconets, and checked and striped muslins," and could be sold more cheaply (Michael Edwards, p. 44).

In 1768 and 1771, Virginia merchants ordered "Jacquonot Muslin" and "fine Jakernet Muslin" (Norton Papers). "Striped Scotch Jaconot Mus-lin" is shown in Ackermann's *Repository* (8, no. 45 [September 1812]: 180). The swatch is fine cotton with paired cords of slightly heavier yarn.

At the 1853 New York industrial exhibition, a bronze medal "for superiority of fabric" was awarded to Hadley Falls Mills in Massachusetts for its "Cambrics, Jaconets, Brilliants, and Lawns"; Hartmann et Fils of Münster received a medal "for style, execution, and beautiful effect on Jaconets, Bareges, &c." (Dilke, p. 27). It was further reported that Hadley Falls Mills used number 90 yarn, the finest spun in the United States in the mid-nineteenth century, to manufacture "lawns, or jaconets, chiefly for printing" (Wallis, p. 12). Swatches of printed jaconets are in the *Journal of Design* (5:107, 139).

JACQUARD

About 1801 Joseph Marie Jacquard (1752–1834) invented the weaving apparatus that bears his name. It was not a loom but an appendage employing wire needles and a series of punched cards, not unlike a piano roll, which mechanically selected the warp threads and raised them when

270

necessary. The services of a drawboy who manipulated the warp cords according to the weaver's directions were thereby eliminated. During the nineteenth century, this attachment was widely used in coverlet weaving in the United States and Canada (Fig. D-61).

JAMDANEE
(*jamdany*)

"Muslin, brocaded in white or coloured silk or cotton, usually with floral pattern" (Irwin and Schwartz). It was like dorea, sometimes woven of mixed cotton and silk, and was an expensive fabric. Swatches are in John Forbes Watson (7: swatch nos. 253–54); other specimens are preserved in the Indian section at the Victoria and Albert Museum (Irwin and Schwartz).

JEAN

A linen / cotton, twilled cloth of the fustian group. In the sixteenth century, "the two kinds [of fustians] most used in England were those of Ulm and Genoa—or as they were universally known, 'Holmes' and 'Jean' or 'Jeans' fustians; Milan fustian was much dearer, and the so-called 'fustian of Naples' was a costly article" (Wadsworth and Mann, p. 19). Perkins wrote in 1833:

> Jeans are made of cotton, and are twilled; are made in white and in many colours, also striped. Satteen Jeans are made of the same material, but of a very superior kind, not twilled but exhibiting a soft and smooth face; they are considerably stronger than the for-

OPPOSITE
FIG. D-61. *Jacquard double-weave coverlet, "Hempfield Railroad." Blue wool and white cotton. Woven about 1850 to commemorate the Hempfield Railroad which ran from Wheeling, West Virginia, to Washington, Pennsylvania. (Smithsonian Institution.) Initially the railroad was to have continued through Hempfield Township to Greensburg, Westmoreland County, Pennsylvania, but the Hempfield Township segment was never built.*

mer, and are to be had in white, black, and many colours; when coloured, they are usually prepared for summer trousers, in which case they are calendered.

In 1629/30 "11 yards of wt. English ieans" were supplied to the Massachusetts Bay Company store (Dow, *Every Day Life,* p. 240); and in 1650 "19 peecs Jeines fustian" were imported into Boston (Aspinwall Records, p. 414).

About 1730, Willing and Shippen imported "Superfine Jane." Between 1766 and 1784 James Beekman's orders specified "white Jeans," while Samuel Rowland Fisher requested "15 ps dy'd Jeans sorted—the Col[or]s all neat drabs, doves, and Leads, no Olives" (Journal, 1767/68).

Jeans are included among fustians in John Holker's manuscript. Swatches 47 to 50 show material "dyed in shades of brown for men's clothing"; swatch 50 is of a finer grade used for "gentlemen's clothing and officers' greatcoats." Swatches 73 to 76 show "white jeans," or bleached varieties, used for men's and women's clothing and the coarser varieties used for trouser and waistcoat linings. Some resembled those brought from India.

A swatch of "Striped Twill Jean" with printed blue pinstripes, fashionable in 1810 for men's waistcoats and trousers, is found in Ackermann's *Repository* (3, no. 18 [June 1810]: 398). Rees includes a draft for "Double jean" among fustians in his *Cyclopaedia.*

JERSEY

Randle Holme's *Academy of Armory* defines jersey as "the finest wool taken out of other sorts of Wool by Combing it with a Jersey-Comb." The knitting of stockings and other worsted articles was long a staple industry of Jersey, one of the Channel Islands. "One fine Knit Jersey Night Gown" and "3 pair of Knit Jersey Breeches" were advertised in the *London Gazette* in 1693 (OED). "Jersey is still the local name for worsted in Lancashire" (Beck). Since about 1835, the word has been a synonym for a knitted shirt or sweater.

K

KENDAL

A Westmoreland town known for green woolen cloths sometimes called Kendal cottons or Kendal greens. During the Middle Ages, Kendal cloths were included with kerseys, friezes of Coventry, cogwares, Welsh cloths, and carpmeals which were free from taxation if valued below a certain figure (Strutt). Later they were made in Kent and were known as Kentish Kendals (Fairholt). Kendals were made of the coarsest kind of wool, and like Welsh cottons, they could be either frized or plain (Butterworth, p. 60).

In 1575 a minstrel wore "a side gown of Kendal green," a long hanging robe of coarse green woolen cloth or baize (Fairholt). A nobleman seeking diversion during the reign of Henry VIII disguised himself as Robin Hood and "attended by twelve noblemen all apparelled in short coats of Kentish Kendal," burst in upon the queen and her ladies (Beck). A cloth called *Lincoln green* was also worn by archers and by Robin Hood. A poem written in 1601 reads in part: "All the woods / Are full of outlaws, that in Kendall green / Follow'd the outlaw'd Earl of Huntington" (Beck).

KENTING

A fine, closely woven linen cloth that was largely manufactured in the county of Kent. It was used for household purposes such as napkins, tablecloths, and jelly strainers. Twelve yards of "Stript Kentin" and two "kenting aprons" are listed in the 1723 inventory of Mary Hunt (SCPR, 23:155). A 1742 Boston inventory lists "1 Suit Strip'd Kentg. Curtains & Vallens" (Cummings, p. 28).

In 1767 James Beekman's factors wrote, "[by] the Kenting lawns you wrote for from 18 to 28 [shillings] we suppose you meant swiss or Siletia

lawns, which being dear [we] have omitted. We esteem the french clear lawns to be much cheaper" (2:912). In 1769 Beekman ordered "6 pieces Clear Kenting Lawn," "6 pieces flowered," "6 pieces Striped," and "6 Kenting or Muslin Needle work Aprons" and in the following year "10 dozen bordered kenting handkerchiefs" (2:921, 931).

Apparently kenting was finer than Ghentish holland which was used for sheeting. Samuel Sewall distinguished between the two in a 1707 letter which is quoted at Holland.

KERSEY

A cheap, coarse woolen cloth of twill weave classed among Old Draperies. The word came originally from the East Anglian town of that name. An act of 1552 enumerated various kinds of kerseys, such as ordinary, sorting, Devonshire (called washers or wash-whites), checks, dozens, and straits (Strutt, p. 210). In earlier centuries, a piece measured 16 to 18 yards in length and less than a yard in width, but by the eighteenth century, many kerseys were over 40 yards in length. They were made of short-stapled native wool, fulled less heavily than the traditional broadcloth, lighter in weight, narrower, and cheaper (Coleman, p. 421).

Savary des Bruslons described them in the early eighteenth century: *Carsay, creseau, étoffe de laine croisée, qui est une espèce de grosse serge à deux envers, couverte de poil des deux cotés. Les carsayes se tirent presque tous d'Angleterre, & d'Ecosse, ou ils sont aussi appellés Kersey. Cette étoffe se fabrique particulièrement dans la Province de Kent. Il y en a de gros & de fins, quelquefois blancs, & quelquefois teints en différentes couleurs.*

Kersey possessed admirable qualities for keeping out wet and cold and was, therefore, in great demand throughout many parts of Europe, especially among the poorer classes. It was used for overcoats, and large quantities were turned into garments for the armies of Europe (Heaton, "Holroyd and Hill," p. 10). Watchet kerseys were named after the West Country town on Bridgwater Bay where they were made.

In Yorkshire woolen manufacture the traditional cloth was the kersey, a well-milled narrow cloth in which no attempt was made to obtain the completely felted surface that was the distinguishing feature of broadcloth (Ponting, *South-West England*, p. 15). In Yorkshire, kerseys were also known as Northern Dozens.

The following references indicate the kinds of kersey made and the uses to which they were put:

Boston, 1650: "5 pcs course broades & one kersey, one pack | pce course broade & 1 pce of stuffe. one pack cont. one pce Kersey & some other course cloth" (Aspinwall Records, p. 412).

Boston, 1666: "Pieces of Kersie wrought for chayers & stooles" were listed in Richard Hicks's inventory at £1.10.0 (SCPR, 5:11).

Maryland, 1721: "The Inhabitants wear the like Cloathing and have the same furniture within their houses with those in this Kingdom. The slaves are cloathed with Cottons, Kerseys, flannels, & coarse linnens, all imported" (Tryon, p. 98).

William Bliss of Chipping Norton, England, received a bronze medal "for Kersey Checks for horse clothing, the best exhibited" at the 1853 New York industrial exhibition (Dilke, p. 26).

Sixteen swatches of olive and black felted Yorkshire kerseys are in the Lindegreen pattern book among the mid-eighteenth-century Berch Papers. A swatch of kersey is also in the Yorkshire pattern book of about 1770 (see Pl. D-102). Cotton kerseys of Lancashire manufacture are shown with cotton velvets and velvet cords in the 1786 Hilton manuscript (see Fig. D-56).

KERSEYMERE

See Cassimere.

KERYABADS

In the late seventeenth century, an Indian cotton cloth. "A good quality plain white calico, much in demand for the English home market on account of its exceptional length and breadth" (Irwin and Schwartz).

KIDDERMINSTER CARPET

Ingrain strip carpet made at Kidderminster and other towns in Worcestershire from about 1735 and very generally exported to America.

See also Ingrain carpet.

KIDDERMINSTER STUFFS

Identified from swatches in the mid-eighteenth-century Berch Papers as diamond-and-chevron patterned worsteds (see Pl. D-17), inferior in quality to Norwich goods.

KILMARNOCK CARPET

Double-cloth, ingrain carpet woven in Kilmarnock, Scotland.

KINCOB

Same as medieval cammocca, an Eastern damask or brocade (*Hobson-Jobson*). Malcolm quoted a 1712 advertisement in the *Spectator* for an "Isabella coloured Kincob Gown flowered with green and gold" (p. 429). The fabric was imported from India.

L

LADINE

One of the fancy eighteenth-century glazed worsted dress fabrics largely manufactured in Norwich. In New York, James Beekman ordered "12 pieces 16 Inch wide Laydines quantity 26 yard at

FIG. D-62. *Swatches of ladines, brightly colored striped worsteds. From a Norwich pattern book, ca. 1794. (Winterthur Museum Library.)*

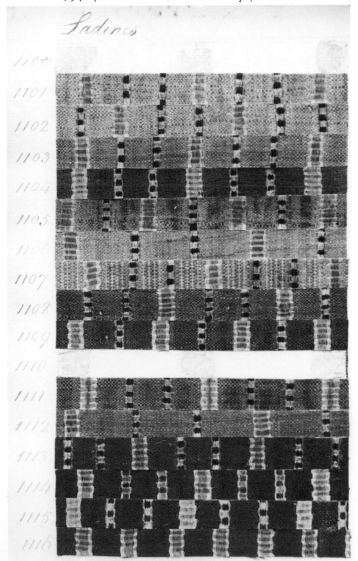

24/. narrow Stripes and dark bright colours" in 1770 (2:816).

Two swatches of Norwich ladines with bright dotted warp float stripes are in the Moccasi manuscript (p. 23). The Castle Museum pattern book of F. Tuthill et Fils contains swatches of ladine camleteens; other swatches are in a Norwich pattern book at Winterthur Museum (Fig. D-62).

LAMPARILLA

A slight camlet made in Flanders and largely shipped to Spain and its colonies. Various kinds were manufactured—some plain, some with small flowers, and others striped. According to Savary des Bruslons they were called *nompareilles* in France because they were without parallel in width, being the narrowest woven.

In 1654 Jeremias van Rensselaer brought to New Netherland "200 yds. nonpareil" for trading (van Laer, *Jeremias van Rensselaer,* p. 14). "Lamparillas, half silk and half worsted" were listed among goods transmitted to the Spanish West Indies in the early nineteenth century (James, p. 209n).

Two swatches of glazed worsted *sanspareille* from Lille, one black and gray mixed and the other green, plain weave, are in the Moccasi manuscript of about 1760 (see Pl. D-61).

Compare None-so-pretty.

LAMPAS

The name applied to Indian painted and resist-dyed textiles made for the most part on the Coromandel coast (Savary des Bruslons). *Lampasses* are also listed among *Chites* (Indian cotton textiles) in a 1762 French merchant's manual (*Manuel historique*).

Some writers equate the term with medieval

diaper weaving. In the West the term was applied to a great variety of drawloom patterned fabrics that were expensive, generally made of silk, and some with additions of metallic threads. The name may have been adopted from the Indian cottons to promote the sale of these western silks.

In the nineteenth century, Havard defined lampas as a silk, generally with large patterns, imported from China or Persia and made in Lyons successfully for a century. The satin ground is shinier than that of damasks. It is made of double warp and weft yarns of which the weft binding yarn may be cotton. Most date from the nineteenth century and are mechanically woven.

The 1964 definition for lampas established by CIETA in Lyons has been updated (Burnham, p. 82):

> Term used exclusively for a figured weave in which a pattern, composed of weft floats bound by a binding warp, is added to a ground weave formed by a main warp and a main weft. The ground weave is variable. The weft threads forming the pattern may be main, pattern, or brocading wefts; they float on the face as required by the pattern, and are bound by the ends of the binding warp in a binding which is ordinarily tabby or twill and is supplementary to the ground weave. . . . The essential ingredient of a lampas weave is *a secondary or binding warp* to bind the wefts that form the design.

LASTING

See Everlasting.

LAWN

A delicate linen used for shirts, handkerchiefs, ruffles, and aprons. For "six yards of good ruff-lawn well worked with cutwork, and edged with good white lace" Queen Elizabeth paid 60 shillings in 1586 (Beck). "Cobwebb Lawnes" are listed among exports in the 1660 Book of Rates (Dow, *Every Day Life,* p. 255).

In 1686 Samuel Sewall of Boston ordered "Six Duz. of Lawn sive Bottoms, not of the Largest size, all to be bordered with reed [red] Leather, for the white Leather rots the Lawn, being dressed with Allome" (Letter book, 1:33). The 1754 Caine broadside includes superfine, spotted, and "fine plain Lawn." While in Paisley, Scotland, in 1767, Samuel Rowland Fisher noted in his journal, "Lawns; flower'd & strip; clear; long lawns; and cambricks." "An assortment of plain, flowered, netted, sprigged, striped, spotted and openwork lawn for aprons; flowered and sprigged lawn in aprons with flowered and striped borders" were advertised for sale in the *Providence Gazette,* June 1, 1768.

In 1784 John, Lord Sheffield wrote of lawns:

> The consumption of this article is greater than that of cambric, and it is a question, whether coarse kinds of it can be had on better terms in Flanders, France, or Britain. Large quantities are made at St. Quintin, and in that part of the continent, and also in Scotland; but the finer kinds are run into England from France and Flanders. In America fine long lawns were substituted where cambricks could not be had. [P. 52.]

In the nineteenth century, "Lawn closely resembles cambric, only thinner and finer. There are various cloths called Lawns, which are really muslins made of cotton, such as French Lawn and Victoria Lawn, which is a thick make of book muslin, in black and white, used for dress linings" (Caulfeild and Saward). Bishop lawn is "a soft, sheer cotton fabric, similar to Swiss muslin, but finer and closer, and has a bluish tint" (Brown and Gates, p. 52).

LEMONEE

A kind of East Indian goods ordered by Thomas Fitch in 1724 with sousaes, calicoes, charconnaes, and longcloths. He specified that it be "of a pretty lively colour."

LENO
(leneau)

A gauze weave in which warp yarns arranged in pairs cross and recross one another between picks of weft. A structure in which rows or areas of gauze weave are separated by, or combined with, areas of plain weave (Emery, p. 192).

A white "raised corded leno . . . frequently worn over coloured sarsnet or satin slips" is shown in Ackermann's *Repository* for 1810 (4, no. 20 [August 1810]: 119).

LEVANTINE

"A stout and very rich faced twilled silk, quite soft; its face and back vary in shade; for instance, if the face be of blue black, the back will be a jet, and vice versa. It is never seen in colours; it is made for dresses" (Perkins). A later author described levantine as a "Four-leaf, double-faced, closely woven silk serge, having single or ply warp. Comes mostly in solid colors, but also in stripes" (Harmuth).

Two swatches of black levantines are on a sample card sent to Benjamin Shreve in 1819. They are described as "particularly handsome ribbed fabric, similar to that seen in clothing of the period, and very much like that used on the backgrounds of some American silhouettes" (Crossman, p. 246).

LEVANT TRADE

Late seventeenth-century trade to eastern Mediterranean ports was controlled by the Levant, or Turkey, Company incorporated during Queen Elizabeth's reign. The Maurepas Papers give a full account of the trade in textiles; one manuscript, dated 1731, describes the broadcloths woven in Gloucestershire, Worcestershire, and Salisbury which were sent to London to be napped, sheared, and dyed in as many as sixteen colors—red, wine, violet, sky-blue, and the various greens, with a few called "pearl" and "aurora." These, together with cinnamon, wormwood, orange, lemon, and sea-green broadcloths, known as "Persian colours," were taken by merchants from Smyrna and Aleppo far into the interior of Asia (Mann, *Cloth Industry,* p. 19). Important for this dictionary is the statement in the Maurepas Papers that the four qualities of English woolen cloth described were similar to those which the British exported to the American colonies: *à peu près de la même qualité que ceux qui s'envoyent à la nouvelle Angleterre, la nouvelle York et les autres Isles de l'Amérique.*

According to Postlethwayt, "by the indefatigable endeavors and profound policy of their great minister Colbert" it "was not long before woolen manufactories of divers kinds [were established] in France, *façon d'Angleterre,* or of the English method of fabrication." "The great Colbert took these measures: he first informed himself of the several sorts of the British manufactures sold in every foreign market, whereof he had pieces and patterns brought him; and he erected particular works for the making those very goods" (see Postlethwayt, s.v. "France").

In 1708 specifications and regulations for the weaving and the grades of wool to be used in these cloths were imposed by the French government. They were known by the names *aboucouchou, Londres, Londrins, mahoux, nims,* and *seizains.*

Rordansz, writing in 1819, specified nine colors for these French cloths: "The fine cloth which the Tunisians have chiefly made use of for many years past, has been of French manufacture; they esteem the colour rather than the quality of the cloth; bales should be assorted as under." He further says: "The Moors always entertained a favourable opinion of English manufactures, and the French, to humour them, gave their cloth the name of *Londras,* wishing to make the Moors believe it was manufactured in London."

Arthur Young, traveling in France in the late 1780s, observed that the *"Londrins,* of which at all these towns I took patterns, are a very light, beautiful, well-dyed bright cloth that have had, and deservedly, from quality and price, the greatest success in the Levant; I saw the wool they are made of, and should not have known it from a good

specimen from the South Downs of Sussex"
(*Travels in France,* p. 304).

Four swatches of *mahout* in two different
qualities and in different colors are in the 1807 Aix-
la-Chapelle pattern book (see Pl. D-4).

See also Londres, Londrin.

LINDIANA

A fabric named "in compliment to the all-popular
Jenny." The *Journal of Design,* published in 1849,
includes a swatch of light blue silk and worsted
lindiana in plain weave (1:42).

LINEN

Cloth of many grades and weaves made from flax
fibers. Postlethwayt made the following state-
ments about imported linens: "England is served
with fine linnen from Holland, and countries adjacent to it, and with cambrics, and other sorts of
linnen from Holland and France. England and the
British Plantations are served with great quantities
of middling and low-priced linnens of divers sorts,
from Silesia, and other parts in the upper and lower
circle of Saxony." The kinds of linen goods
imported are detailed in the 1660 Book of Rates:

Linnen Cloth
    Calicoes, fine or course
    Cambricks " " "
Canvas
    Dutch Barras and Hessens Canvas
    French or Normandy Canvas, and Line
      narrow, brown or white
    Franch Canvas and linebroad for tabling
    Packing canvas, guttings, and Spruce
      canvas
    Poledavies
    Spruce, Elbing, or Quinsborough canvas
    Stript or tufted canvas with thread
    Stript, tufted or quilted canvas with silk
    Stript canvas with copper
    Vandelose or Vittery canvas
    Working canvas for cushions narrow;
      broad; the broadest sort.

Damask
    Tabling of Holland making
    Towelling and Napkening of Holland
      making
    Tabling of Silesia making
    Towelling and Napkening of Silesia
      making
Diaper
    Tabling of Holland making
    Towelling and Napkening of Holland
      making
    Napkins of Holland making
    Tabling of Sletia making
    Tabling and Napkening of Sletia making
Lawns
    the half piece; the piece
    voc. Calico lawns
    voc. French lawns
    voc. Sletia lawns
Flanders Holland cloth
    Flemish cloth
    Gentish cloth
    Isingham cloth
    Overisils cloth
    Rouse cloth
    Brabant cloth
    Emden cloth
    Freeze [Friesland] cloth
Brown Holland
Bagg Holland
British
Cowffeild cloth or plats
Drilling and pack duck
Ebling or Damask cloth double ploy
Hambrough and Sletia cloth broad, white or
    brown
    Hamborough cloth narrow
    Hinderlands, Middlegood, headlake, and
      Muscovia linen, narrow
Irish cloth
Lockrams
Treager, great, and narrow or common
    dowlas
    broad dowlas
Kinsters

Ozenbrigs
Soultwich
Polonia, Ulsters, Hannovers, Lubeck, narrow Slotia, narrow Westphalia, narrow Harford, plain napkening, and all other narrow cloth of high Dutchland and the East Countrey, white or brown.
All Linen of Germany or high Dutchland and Silesia . . . broad Strasborough or Hamborough linen
Twill and ticking of Scotland. [Beck.]

Postlethwayt's Appendix A lists for Custom-House business are similar:

Isingham
Gentish
Hollands $\begin{cases} \text{Bag} \\ \text{Gulix} \\ \text{Alcumore} \end{cases}$
Borelaps
Headen rolls
Hinderlinds
Osnaburgs, distinguished by a catherine wheel and the word osnaburg stamped round it
Hammels
Hartfords
crocus
Dutch barras
Hessens canvas
Drillings
Dowlas $\begin{cases} \text{single} \\ \text{double} \end{cases}$
Garlix
Lubeck duck
Blue paper Silesia's
Holland's duck
Russia sail cloth

An extraordinary list of linen items is included in the 1770 inventory taken at the Governor's Palace, Williamsburg:

Linnen
26 Pillow cases
 2 pr very large fine Sheets
17 pr lesser fine do

18 ½ pr Servants do
 4 Damask long Dinner table cloths
 6 Doz. Napkins to Do
 4 Damask long table Cloths
 3 ½ doz Napkins to do
 4 long Diaper table cloths
 4 Middle Cloths to do
 5 doz. Napkins to do
 2 long Damask table cloths
 4 doz. Napkins to do
 1 large Damask table cloth
 1 Middle cloth to do
 1 doz. Napkins to do
 6 Fine damask table cloths
 6 doz. Napkins to do
 2 Damask table cloths
 2 doz Napkins to do
30 Dinner table cloths & 5 doz odd Napkins
36 Breakfast cloths
12 Servants table cloths
 2 ½ doz fine diaper tea Napkins
35 Damask do
 3 doz. fine diaper Towels
27 Huckaback do
64 Brown Rubbers
 5 Round Towels
 2 Coarse dresser cloths.
[Botetourt manuscripts.]

In the last years of the eighteenth century, U.S. Secretary of the Treasury Alexander Hamilton proposed collecting a duty on coarse varieties of linen:

Flax and Hemp. Manufactures of these articles have so much affinity to each other, and they are so often blended, that they may with advantage be considered in conjunction. Sailcloth should have 10 per cent duty. 7½ per cent for drillings, osnaburgh, ticklenburghs, dowlas, canvass, brown rolls, bagging, and upon all other linens, the first cost of which at the place of exportation does not exceed 35 cents per yard. [P. 256.]

See Beck for a list of imported linens and a history of linen manufacture in the British Isles.

LINSEY-WOOLSEY

A coarse cloth made of linen warp and woolen weft. "A coarse woollen manufacture first constructed in the parish of Linsey in Suffolk" (Fairholt). Defoe, describing a home in *The Complete Tradesman,* wrote: "The Hangings, suppose them to be ordinary Linsey-Woolsey, are made at Kidderminster, dy'd in the country, and painted, or water'd at London; the curtains—suppose of Serge, from Taunton and Excester; or of Camblets, from Norwich; or the same with the Hangings, as above" (p. 404).

Beginning in the seventeenth century, governors of American colonies reported on the home weaving of linsey-woolsey. A Mr. Denton living in New York, 1670, reported: "They sowe store of Flax, which they make every one Cloth of for their own wearing, as also woollen Cloth, and Linsey-woolsey" (Tryon, p. 68). John Fanning Watson later wrote of colonial New Yorkers' clothing: "Their petticoats of linsey-woolsey, were striped with gorgeous dyes. . . . they were all of their own manufacture, of which circumstance, as may well be supposed, they were not a little vain. The gentlemen of those days, were well content to figure in their linsey-woolsey coats—domestic made, and bedecked with an abundance of large brass buttons" (*Annals of New York,* p. 170). In 1767, it was reported, "there is a general Manufactory of Woolen carried on here and consists of two sorts, the first a coarse cloth entirely woolen, ¾ of a yard wide; and another a stuff which they call Linsey Woolsey. The Warp of this is Linen and the Woof Woolen" (O'Callaghan, 1:734).

Perkins described a broader variety of "Linsey, or linsey woolsey": "This article is in white, blue, blue and white mixed, blue and red mixed, and striped, of various colours. It is made of thread [linen] and wool. The white is used for women's petticoats, and the coloured for aprons."

Traditionally, in America, the name linsey-woolsey has been incorrectly given to woolen coverlets with large floral and feather quilted patterns. These coverlets have a surface of all-worsted cloth (glazed camlet or calimanco) dyed deep indigo blue, light blue, raspberry red, pink, deep green, etc.; the underside of coarser unglazed wool is frequently gold. Probably some of these coverlets were imported already quilted; others, with the reverse side made of a variety of striped or plain woolen pieces, may have been quilted in America using new material only on the surface.

Fifteen "Old Linsey woolen Patterns" are in a textile scrapbook assembled in New Jersey in the late nineteenth century (p. 43). Despite the label, none of the swatches contains any linen yarn. Some have warp and weft of different colors; some are twills.

LIST CARPET

Similar to rag carpet, the weft often consists of selvedges (lists) cut from textiles, thus providing the name given to this kind of carpeting in the eighteenth century (Fig. D-63). Warp yarns could be of homespun flax or tow.

Samuel Rowland Fisher saw list carpet being made at Leeds in 1783. List carpeting for stairs, imported from London and Bristol, was advertised in the *Boston Gazette* in 1761 (Dow, *Arts and Crafts,* p. 119).

LOCKRAM

Linen cloth of various qualities first made in Locronan, Brittany, from which the name was derived. In the seventeenth and eighteenth centuries, it was often associated with dowlas which cost somewhat more:

4 pecs of Lockrom of 11d or 12d Ell
2 pec of Dowlace of 15d Ell
2 " of " 1 of 18d and one of 20d.
[Sewall, Letter book, 1:31.]

It was used for coarse clothing, household articles, and uniforms, as may be seen from a letter written by Charles I (1642) to his nephew, Prince Rupert: "Great quantities of cloth canvass and Locherame" could be had in Cirencester, Stroud, and other towns nearby "for supplying ye great necessities Our Souldiers have for Suits" (Ponting, *South-west England,* p. 143).

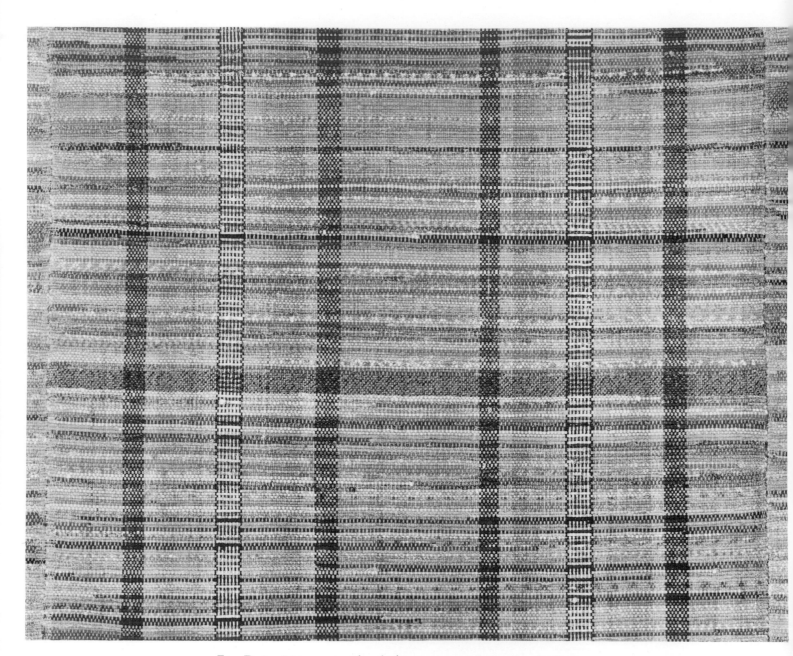

FIG. D-63. *List carpet with polychrome warp stripes and weft of cotton strips of cloth. Late nineteenth or early twentieth century. Possibly similar to eighteenth-century list carpets. (Winterthur Museum.)*

As early as 1629/30, it was stocked at the Massachusetts Bay Colony storehouse (Dow, *Every Day Life,* p. 240), and large quantities were imported throughout the remainder of the century. A dozen lockram napkins and a tablecloth are listed in the 1647 inventory of William Clarke of Salem, Massachusetts.

LONDRES

Fulled woolen cloth manufactured especially in Languedoc in imitation of West of England broadcloths and used in the Levant trade. Government regulations for the kinds of wool, number of warp threads, breadths, lengths, and factory stamps are specified in Savary des Bruslons. Different grades were known by the names *Draps Londres, Londres larges,* and *Londres.*

Swatches of several grades and widths of londres woven in Marseilles in 1736 are in the Richelieu Papers (Lh45 I). One is called *Drap Saisin rouge de Garence pour le Levant,* another *façon d'Angleterre;* twenty undated swatches, most of which are red, of *Draps Londres large de Manufacture Royalle de Marseilles* are in another volume (Lh40).

LONDRIN

Fulled woolen cloth manufactured especially in Languedoc in imitation of West of England broadcloths and used in the Levant trade. Government regulations for *premiers Londres* and *seconds Londrins* are given in both Savary des Bruslons and Diderot. Finer Spanish wool and a greater number of threads per inch in the warp accounted for its superior quality in comparison with londres.

Four swatches of *Draps Londrins* in two shades of green, black, and wine red are in the 1807 Aix-la-Chapelle pattern book (see Pl. D-5). Of these cloths, the author says, "the manufacture at Aix was commenced about 40 or 50 years ago. They have been especially favored in this country as much for the quality of the goods as for the lively colors and modest price."

Three letters with 48 swatches of *Londrina Seconda* in bright colors from Carcassone are in the Textile Study Room of the Metropolitan Museum of Art. Colonial Williamsburg owns a pattern card with eleven swatches of *Londrins Seconds* dating from the mid-eighteenth century.

See also Levant trade.

LONGCLOTH
(long ells, long lawn)

Any cloth woven in unusually long pieces.

"The ordinary, staple cotton-cloth of Coromandel trade, especially esteemed in Europe on account of its length (usually about 37 yards). . . . It was usually exported white, but it could also be bought blue or brown" (Irwin and Schwartz). A 1724 Boston order called for "a parcell long Cloths of 2 Colour'd handsome large Flowers or branches and some smaller ditto pretty good cloth but very neat Flowers pretty showy to look like Chints" (Fitch, Letter book). The next year the same merchant ordered "Long Cloth Callicoes, 18 yds. long of two Colours and good figures."

In the sixteenth century, woolen longcloth was regulated at 28 to 30 yards by 63 inches and weighed 80 pounds, while short cloths were five yards shorter and weighed only 64 pounds (Heard, p. 82). Of woolen longcloth, Defoe says that "fine flannels, and long cloths for the Turkey Trade, call'd Salisbury Whites were made in that West-of-England town" (*Tour,* vol. 1, letter 3).

Like serge, "long ells" were twilled cloths of worsted warp and woolen weft. In 1824 they were described as "an article which formed the chief manufacture of Devonshire, [and] cost in production, the piece containing in length twenty-five yards, thirty inches wide, weight twelve pounds, the following: Worsted warp, 4¼ lbs. at 2/2 [at] £0.9.2 . . . Short wool weft, 8½ lbs. at 1/3 [at] 0.10.7½ . . . Weaving and finishing [at] 0.4.5 [totaling] 1.4.2½" (James, p. 398). Swatches of Devonshire longcloth are found in the Berch Papers; some are corded and some twill woven.

LORETTO

"Damascus Lorettos & Burdets for fine west-coats" were advertised in Boston 1767 (Earle, *Costume,* p. 254). In 1771 James Beekman ordered from Robert and Nathan Hyde of Manchester (3:1419):

4	pieces Super Silk Moreens	133¼ yds.	2/2
2	pieces Super Silk Brunswicks	77 yds.	3/
2	pieces Super Silk Lorettos [No.] 1	75½ yds.	3/3
1	pieces Super ditto [No.] 2	28½ yds.	3/6
1	piece Super Silk Damask	31½ yds.	2/9

"Lorrettas, Moreens and Brunswicks" are also grouped together in the Hyde pattern book of the same date, although no captions are connected to the swatches.

LOTORINE

See Lutherine.

LOUISINE

Lightweight, silk fabric woven "with twice as many warp ends than fillings to the square inch" (Harmuth). Usually each pick crossed two warps at once to form warp ribs. "A very thin plain silk material, suitable for children's wear, and for slight summer costumes. It is a kind of Surah silk, or Sicilienne, and is to be had in all colours, and also woven in small checks and stripes" (Caulfeild and Saward).

LUNGI
(*lungee*)

The garment or material used by Indians for loincloths. "The body is of small blue and white checks, the selvage is composed of various colored stripes and a narrow red stripe is running length-wise in the middle" (Harmuth). The word is often linked with romal.

"Silk Lungees at 1/" and "Herba and Cotten Lungees at 3s 6d" were imported into London about 1700 (Kress, S2180).

See also Romal and Fig. D-88.

LUSTER
(*lustre*)

A shiny silk and worsted dress material similar to poplin. In 1840 the main articles manufactured from "Alpaca wool consist of Alpaca lustres, which are dyed, and Alpaca mixtures, which are undyed, and both are made of cotton or silk warp" (James, p. 458). Plain, checked, figured, and "Lustre Orleans (Spanish Proportions)" are mentioned by James (pp. 527, 532).

In Ackermann's *Repository* "a fawn-coloured lustre for evening half dress" is made of silk and wool (see Pl. D-88), and "a bright geraneum lustre for evening wear" is a finer textile (*Repository* 7, no. 38 [February 1812]: 122). Purple, ruby, and brown lusters of 1819 are in the Barbara Johnson album.

LUSTRENE

In the eighteenth century, a woolen cloth with a smooth finish produced by hard pressing. In the Moccasi manuscript a swatch of Exeter *Durante osia Lustrine* is pale bluish-white wool twill that has been hard pressed; *lustrine unita* is somewhat coarser (see Pl. D-60).

In the late nineteenth century, lustrene was a smooth cotton fabric of satin weave used for lining the sleeves of men's overcoats. The yarns were treated with lead solution and polished with heat and pressure, giving them a peculiar smoothness (Denny). Another definition says the weave was twill and that the yarns were mercerized.

Lustrene, a figured silk or wool satin, made in France had flowered patterns produced with an extra warp; the back was plain. Havard defines it as a flowered silk stuff made in Genoa and called by that name because of its shine and brilliance.

Swatches of warp-patterned silk lustrenes used for men's suitings are in an invoice from Terret Frères, Lyons, to M. Juge, Clermont, May 3, 1778 (Rothstein, "European Silks," pl. 10).

LUSTRING
(lutestring)

A light, crisp plain silk with a high luster. "A taffeta which had been stretched and, while under tension, smeared with a syrupy gum. This dressing was dried with the aid of a small brazier and gave the material a glossy sheen. Lustrings were mostly plain, striped, changeable, or decorated with white patterns, but they could have large patterns similar to those on other silks" (Thornton, *Baroque and Rococo Silks,* p. 27, pls. 84B, 86A, 91B).

Beck says that the cloth was introduced into England "by the French refugees who fled here after the revocation of the Edict of Nantes [1685] In the fourth year of William and Mary the importation of this and the kindred fabric alamode was practically stopped by the heavy duties then imposed upon all such stuffs of foreign manufacture, and in the same year the persons engaged in the manufacture in this country were incorporated by charter under the title of the Royal Lustring Company." By Act of Parliament in 1698 the company was to "enjoy the sole use, exercise, and benefit of making, dressing, and lustrating of plain black alamodes, renforcez, and lustrings in England and Wales for fourteen years to come." Lustring, "woven in England from the late 17th century by the Royal Lustring Company, . . . was primarily a black material" (Rothstein, "Nine English Silks," p. 16). The black hood worn by Defoe's tradesman's wife was "a thin English Lustring" (p. 403).

Of brocaded lustrings, G[odfrey?] Smith says in *The Laboratory; or, School of Arts,* 1756, that they "are either upon a plain or figured ground;

the design must be open and airy, composed of various sorts of flowers, carelessly disposed and garnished; care must be taken to prevent . . . the expense of workmanship and yet to make as great a show for the money as possible." Two watercolor patterns and matching brocaded silks of 1747 and 1748 which fit this description are shown by Rothstein at figures 4 and 6 of "Nine English Silks."

In London, early in the nineteenth century, George Smith suggested the material for furnishing: "Where the stands [of fire screens] are wholly mahogany, the mounts may be covered with lustring in flutes, with tassels to suit" (*Household Furniture,* p. 20). In 1809 Rudolph Ackermann described bed curtains "of blue satin, lined with white lutestring, and trimmed with a narrow gold edging" (*Repository 1, no. 5 [May 1809], 334*).

In 1698 Samuel Sewall of Boston ordered "A piece of flowerd Lutestring qt. between 36 and fourty yards, with Trimming, to make Gowns and petticoats for my daughters" and in 1706 "Eight yards black flowerd Lutestring or Damask. Let the flowers be of Herbs or Leaves; not of Animals, or artificial things." In 1714 he ordered "A good strong black Silk Damask, or Lutestring Flowered (no Silk Grass to be in it:) To make two Jackets, and two pair of Breeches" (Letter book, 1:203, 338; 2:37).

Swatches of "plain midling blue lustring" and "green ½ Ell Lustring" are attached to James Alexander's orders to Collinson in London dated 1735 and 1737. In other orders, Alexander requested "1 ps yellow & white changeable," "2 ps. plain green not changeable," and black "two-thread" and "three-thread" lustrings.

See also Pl. D-8.

Dress patterns in "brown pink and stript" and "blue and white checker'd" lustrings are in the 1754 Caine broadside. John Norton of Virginia ordered pink and white "shot" (warp printed, or *chiné*) lustrings in 1770 (p. 330). Ten years later, fashionable colors in lustrings sold in Newport included "Plum, Pink, Flystale, Cinnamon and Laylock

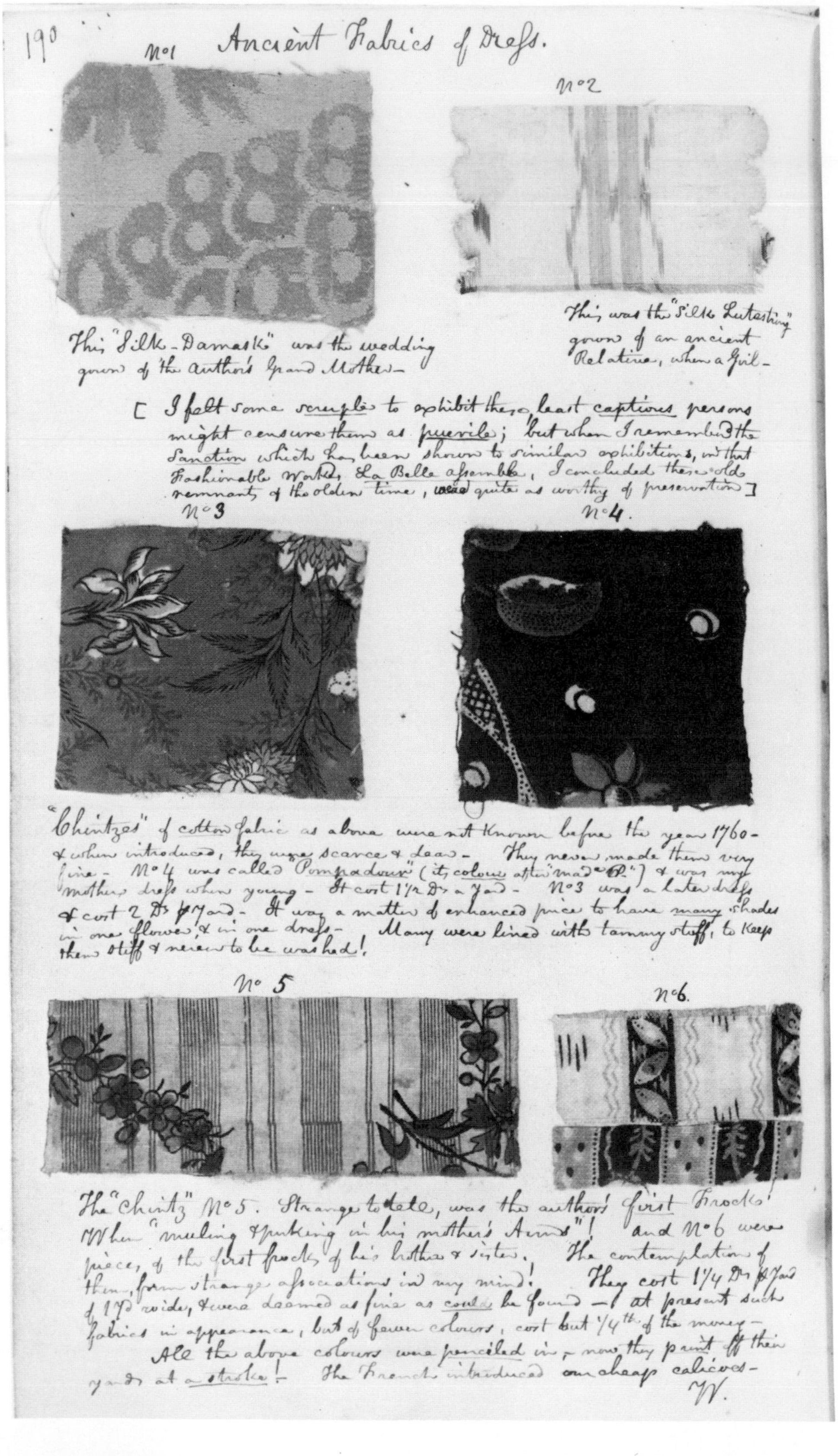
190
Ancient Fabrics of Dress.
No 1
No 2
This "Silk-Damask" was the wedding gown of the author's Grand Mother—
This was the "Silk Lutestring" gown of an ancient Relative, when a Girl—
[I felt some scruples to exhibit these, least captious persons might censure them as puerile; but when I remembered the sanction which has been shown to similar exhibitions, in that Fashionable Works, La Belle assemblée, I concluded these old remnants of the olden time, were quite as worthy of preservation]
No 3
No 4.
"Chintzes" of cotton fabric as above were not known before the year 1760— & when introduced, they were scarce & dear— They never made them very fine— No 4 was called "Pompadour" (its colour after Madme P.) & was my mother's dress when young— It cost 1½ Ds a Yard— No 3 was a later dress & cost 2 Ds pr Yard— It was a matter of enhanced price to have many shades in one flower, & in one dress— Many were lined with tammy stuff, to keep them stiff & never to be washed!
No 5
No 6.
The "Chintz" No 5. Strange to tell, was the author's first Frocks! When "mewling & puking in his mother's Arms"! and No 6 were pieces of the first frocks of his brother & sister. The contemplation of them, form strange associations in my mind! They cost 1¼ Ds pr Yard of 1½ wide, & were deemed as fine as could be found — & at present such fabrics in appearance, but of fewer colours, cost but 1/4th of the money—
All the above colours were pencilled in, now they paint off their yards at a stroke! The French introduced our cheap calicoes—
W.

FIG. D-64. *Silk lustring with warp-printed, clouded stripes worn by "an ancient Relative, when a Girl" (top right). Other "old remnants of the olden time" are a silk damask and four printed cotton chintzes, the bottom three of which were worn by children. Probably English, 1770–90. From the manuscript copy of John Fanning Watson's* Annals of Philadelphia, *p. 190. (Library Company of Philadelphia.)*

[lilac]" (Earle, *Costume,* p. 154). In 1784 black, white, light pink, light purple, green, garnet, light blue, and brown lustrings were ordered by James Beekman in New York (3:1115).

In 1786 "Mrs. Foot [of Connecticut], from silk of her own raising, had made [in England] twelve yards of lutestring, three quarters of a yard wide, and the next year, eight yards of black satin" (Frances Little, p. 143).

Among "Ancient Fabrics of Dress" in John Fanning Watson's manuscript for *Annals of Philadelphia* is a shaded or clouded lustring from "the Silk Lutestring gown of an ancient Relative, when a Girl" (Figs. D-64, D-65).

In a trader's book kept between 1797 and 1809, swatches of figured lustrings or sarcenets from Canton are also called "Florence Legere" (see Fig. D 49).

LUTHERINE

A glossy, stiff material. In 1744, patent number 611 was issued for a method of combing wool with silk to be used instead of mohair yarn for "lutherines, rufferines, princes stuff, or prunellas which was chiefly used in making clergymen's gowns" (Warner, p. 637).

Silk "lotorine" was used to line a coach sold by John Curlett and Son's Extensive Coach Factory, a Baltimore firm from 1814 to 1823.

LYONS

The largest and most prestigious silk-weaving center in France during the eighteenth century. Histories of Lyons silk manufacture are given in all standard French sources. For a recent account, see *Baroque and Rococo Silks* by Peter Thornton.

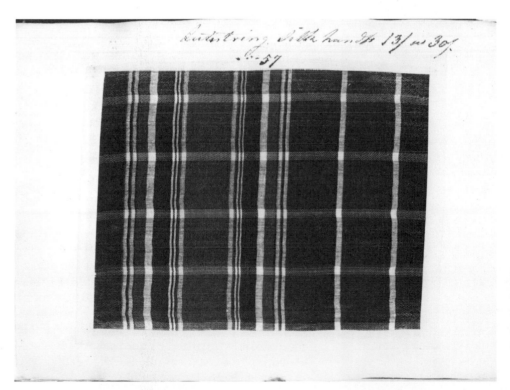

FIG. D-65. *Silk lustring. Made in India. Plain weave in shades of red with yellow and white stripes and bands. From Handkerchief pattern book. Paper in the book is watermarked 1787. (Cooper-Hewitt Museum, gift of Mrs. Samuel S. Walker.)*

M

MACKINAW

"A thick blanket, at one time distributed to the Indians of the north-west [territory] by the United States government." In 1824 an order for blankets was placed by Wistar, Siter, and Price of Philadelphia: "50 prs. Mock Mackinaw or 2d qulty Witneys[,] 15 prs. Green d[itt]o. are wanted by 1st March at Philadelphia, must be in Liverpool by Middle Jany" (Plummer, p. 251).

FIG. D-66. *Macramé. From S. F. A. Caulfeild and Blanche C. Saward,* Dictionary of Needlework *(London: L. Upcott Gill, 1882), p. 335, fig. 1.*

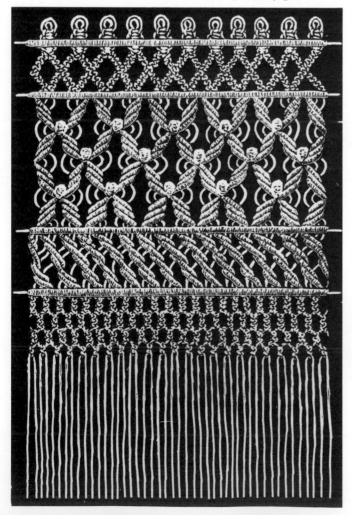

About 1900 the material was defined as a heavy napped woolen fabric sometimes mixed with cotton which was used for lumbermen's jackets and overcoats. The two sides might differ in color and design.

MACRAMÉ

A kind of knotted lace or fringe made with stiff thread. This work is known in nineteenth- and twentieth-century revivals of Italian knotted points (*Punto a Groppo*). It was much used for ecclesiastical linen, church vestments, and other trimming from the end of the fifteenth to the seventeenth century. Directions and pictures are given in Caulfeild and Saward (Fig. D-66) and in de Dillmont.

MADAPOLAM

A kind of cotton cloth named for the East India Company village where it was sold. As with many cotton textiles originally exported from India to England, by 1900 the trade had been reversed, and madapolam was a staple export from England to India.

MADDER
(Fr. garance)

A red vegetable dye derived from *Rubia tinctorum,* a plant native to Asia Minor. It was used for dyeing wool, silk, and cotton until the last quarter of the nineteenth century when it was supplanted by synthesized alizarin. In India, cotton cloths painted by hand with mordants (metallic oxides or minerals such as alum and iron) produced fast colors when dipped in a madder bath. In the west, woodblocks, one for each color, were used for printing the mordants. In madder-mordant printing, colors ranged from red to purple as well as dark brown in varying shades.

MADRAS

Goods exported from that part of India. In a *Providence Gazette* advertisement from February to April 1791, "India Sales at the Store of E. H. Derby, Esq." in Salem are divided into Bengal and Madras goods. For the latter he lists the following:

> Ginghams, Blue Cotton Handkerchiefs
> Long Cloths of a superior Quality, suitable for Shirting
> Madras Patches, beautifully figured
> Camboys, or blue and white striped Cottons
> Moreas, or plain white Cloths
> Madras Cambricks
> Ditto handkerchiefs with borders.
> Book Muslins, Ditto handkerchiefs, a great variety.

In the 1830s and 1840s, "large, bright-coloured handkerchiefs, of silk warp and cotton woof, which were formerly exported from Madras, and much used by the negroes in the West Indies as head-dresses" were known by the name of *Madras* (*Hobson-Jobson*). More recently the name has been applied to bright checked and plaid cotton cloth imported from India for men's jackets and trousers and women's dresses and skirts. The dyes used were not entirely fast, causing this material to be called bleeding madras.

MAHOUT

See Levant trade.

MANCHESTER COTTON

In the sixteenth century, a coarse, cheap woolen stuff like frieze.

MANCHESTER GOODS

By the mid-seventeenth century, Manchester was well known for many kinds of cotton and linen / cotton cloth including Manchester velvets, or cotton velvets, and smallwares such as inkles, tapes, and filleting (Fig. D-67).

Evidence of the cloth produced around Manchester is found in the 1767/68 journal notations of Samuel Rowland Fisher of Philadelphia: "The Checks, Stripes, Bed Ticks & Bunts, Fustians, Jeans, Thicksetts, Corded & Figur'd Dimotys &c. are made all around the Town to the Distance of about 12 or 15 Miles."

The Holker manuscript is of great importance for documenting Lancashire manufactures. It includes swatches of over a dozen cotton and linen fabrics made in the area. Supplementing Holker are John Aikin's *Description of the Country . . . round Manchester* (pp. 157–69) and a lively account by Streat and Leutkens.

See also Fustian.

MANCHESTER VELVETS

Cotton velvets including thickset, velveret, and corduroy. Holker's manuscript includes seven swatches of cotton velvets dyed in shades of brown. Of them he said that many patterns and qualities were manufactured in Manchester and its environs and that they had begun to supplant Utrecht velvets made partly of wool. Dyed all colors except scarlet, which did not "take" on cotton, they were made of the finest yarns imported from Jamaica or the French islands. Holker further related that the secret of their manufacture was jealously guarded, and only with infinite pains and almost insurmountable difficulties, even at peril of his life, was he able to bring to France the swatches included in his book. He added that these velvets improved in appearance with wear; his trousers made of the material wore for three years and outlasted others two to one.

Streat and Leutkens wrote: "Cotton velvets whose fame spread far beyond England soon after 1760—they were what the Continent meant by 'Manchester goods'—evolved from fustian weaving" (p. 25).

Hundreds of swatches of plain, fancy, and printed cotton velvets, many intended for men's

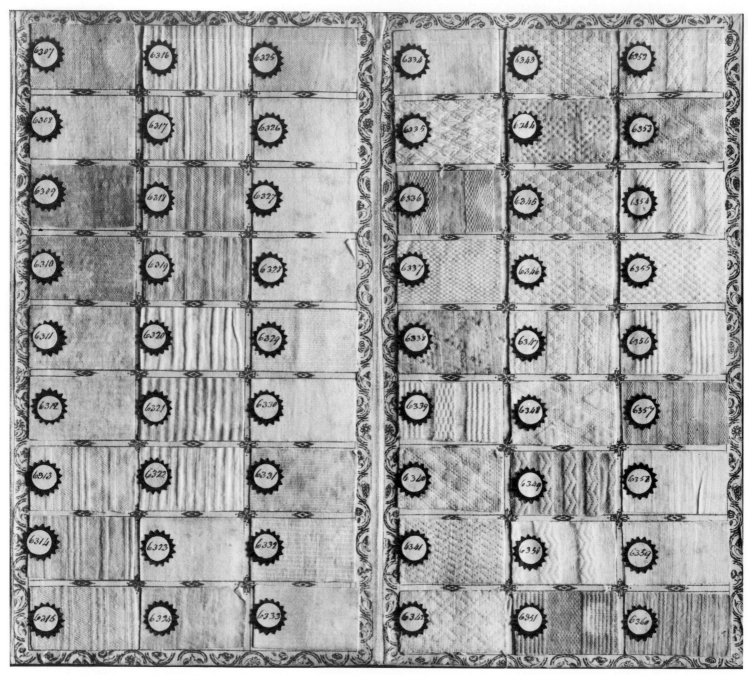

FIG. D-67. *Two pages of typical cotton Manchester goods. From a folding pattern card prepared by Thomas Smith in 1783. (Winterthur Museum Library.)*

waistcoats, are found in Manchester pattern books of the late eighteenth century in the collections of Colonial Williamsburg, Cooper-Hewitt Museum, and Winterthur Museum (see Pl. D-37).

Thirty Rouen imitations of Manchester velvets in superfine and channeled, or corduroy, examples that date from about 1760 are in the Moccasi manuscript (see Pl. D-51). They may have been woven at Holker's *Manufacture Royalle de velours et draps de coton,* established in 1752. Checked, striped, and medley swatches are presented in gray, fawn, blue, black, and dark green. The pile of these fine cotton textiles was intended to give them the sheen of expensive silk fabrics.

Samuel Boardman of Wethersfield, Connecticut, bought a piece of "Manchester Velvet of 16 yds at 6/8" in 1772.

See also Honeycomb.

MANTUA
(manto)

A silk of plain weave, heavier than taffeta. "Originally a gown or sacque open to display the petticoat; then the outer mantle or cape, and finally a stuff for the making of mantuas" (Earle, *Costume,* pp. 155–56). In 1758 the town of Mantua was described as "a Place of Good Trade: their Silk Manufacture particularly has a great Reputation all over Europe; it is from this City those glorious Italian Silks called Mantuas take their name, which our Countrymen find more Difficulty in imitating than any other" (Beck).

In 1726 Defoe described the tradesman's wife "not dressed over fine." "Her Gown, a plain English Mantua-silk, manufactur'd in Spittle-fields. Her Petticoat the same" (p. 403). "A rose-coloured paduasoy Mantua, lined with a rich mantua silk of the same colour" was stolen in London in 1731 (Malcolm, p. 432).

Although generally used for dresses, mantua was occasionally mentioned as a furnishing material. In 1808 John Rea of Philadelphia wrote to Thomas Jefferson about curtains for Monticello: "I sent this morning by the mail stage a trunk con-

taining 4 window draperies. . . . They are made of the best crimson mantua which I hope will give satisfaction." Jefferson later ordered a coverlet to match (Kimball and Kimball, p. 268).

From 1737 to 1760, James Alexander ordered mantua silks in black and white, black, yellow, pink, light blue, and brown. A swatch of "green mantua" is attached to the copy of his 1738 order. Seven mid-eighteenth-century swatches of changeable mantuas of different colors in warp and weft are in the Berch Papers. A piece of gray-blue taffeta is attached to the manuscript of John Fanning Watson's *Annals of Philadelphia* (Frances Little, p. 148). Watson says that this mantua was woven in England from silk raised in Lancaster County, Pennsylvania, and was fashioned into a court dress for Queen Charlotte in 1770.

MARBLE CLOTH
(Fr. marbre)

Several kinds of cloth made to resemble the veining of marble. From the twelfth to the sixteenth centuries, Norwich was famous for *marbrinus,* or *marbre,* a novelty worsted. Later imitated at Salisbury and Wilton in the West Country where medleys were a specialty. In the late nineteenth century, the name was applied to a book cloth made of cotton and usually paper lined. At another time, a dress goods of silk and wool was "woven with a mottled face in various colors, produced by multi-colored weft" (Harmuth).

See also Medley cloth.

MARCELLA
(Marseilles, marsella)

Although no documented examples have survived, during the eighteenth century Marseilles seems to have been a center, or at any rate the port of export, for fine quilted petticoats and coverlets. The earliest quilts were made from two layers of cloth closely stitched by hand with pattern areas raised by being stuffed through the coarser backing. The "Marcels bed and canopy—cost 20

FIG. D-68. *Fashionable summer dress materials: (1) book muslin, (2) nainsook, (3) cambric muslin, and (4) marcella chintz or shawl-pattern muslin. The angular sprigs on three of these patterns were printed in imitation of fine twill-woven cashmere shawls then at the height of fashion. From Repository 2, no. 7 (July 1809): 60. (Winterthur Museum Library.)*

guineas" imported via England by Eliza Pinckney of Charleston about 1745 was undoubtedly of this handstitched kind (Ravenel, p. 113). A toilet, or dressing, table of the late 1760s draped to match the hangings on a state bed at Hopetoun House in England had a petticoat of "some brocaded silk or crimson silk damask fringed at Bottom, the top covered with Marseils or other fine Quilting made to the Shape" (Coleridge, p. 154).

At a later date, marcella was imitated in loom-woven patterns of double cloth with an extra heavy cording weft between the layers. *Transactions of the Society for the Encouragement of Arts, Manufactures and Commerce* (London, 1783) states that a premium was offered for imitating "Marseilles quilting" in the loom:

> When the proposition was first made in the Society, of offering a premium to encourage the making in the loom, an imitation of that Species of Needlework, long known by the name of Marseilles Quilting, it was almost rejected as visionary and impossible; but the laudable spirit of enterprize, which has always distinguished this Society, determined them to publish the premium, and the consequence has justified the venture. The manufacture is now so thoroughly established and so extensive, being wrought in all the different materials of Linen, Woollen, Cotton, and Silk, that there are few persons of any rank, condition or fix, in the Kingdom, and . . . within the extent of British Commerce, so greatly is it exported, who do not use it in some part of their cloathing; so that we may safely say if the whole fund and revenue of the Society had been given to obtain this one article of Trade, the national gain in return should be considered as very cheaply purchased. [Royal Society of Arts, p. 36.]

In 1784 Joshua Fisher and Sons of Philadelphia ordered marcella by the yard along with a piece of twenty yards of "White Mock Marseilles" which they ordered by pattern number. "White Marseilles 4-qr. and 9-8ths Quilting, bordered and

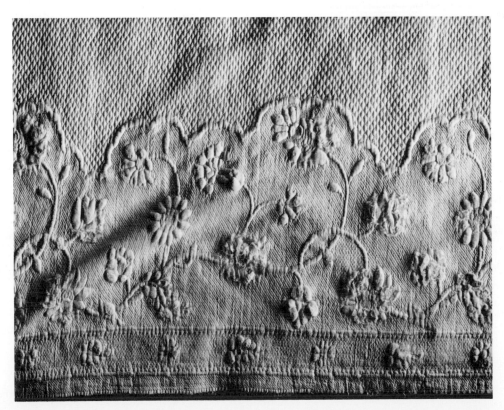

FIG. D-69. *Quilted petticoat border woven in the loom rather than hand stitched. Probably once called Marseilles, it is characteristic of Manchester goods of the late eighteenth century. (Colonial Williamsburg Foundation.)*

plain" were offered for sale in the *Providence Gazette,* May 28, 1785.

Examples of loom-woven petticoats in white cotton, preserved at Colonial Williamsburg, probably date from the third quarter of the eighteenth century (Fig. D-69). After that time, jacquard-woven quiltings were widely used for men's waistcoats, and dozens of fine-patterned quilted materials are found in late eighteenth- or early nineteenth-century merchants' pattern books in the Colonial Williamsburg, Cooper-Hewitt, and Winterthur collections. Ackermann presents several swatches of marcella in white and in printed patterns for summer waistcoats. One example has a small shawl pattern printed in gold and brown on white cotton cloth with a woven rib (Fig. D-68). *See also* Fig. D-3.

Patterns of bed quilts are known from the catalogues of the Great Exhibition of 1851 and those held in Paris in 1867 and 1878. "Counterpanes of snow-white Marseilles" were included in Lord and Taylor's 1881 catalogue "in preference to the various fancy colored bed-coverings in use the last few years. . . . A fine light quality of Marseilles is now used, and new patterns are still in graceful flower and leaf designs" (p. 152).

In 1892 George Cole described marcella as "a stiff corded cotton fabric, used principally for ladies' white dresses and vests. Marseilles quilts are woven of very fine yarn in large, embossed figures."

Marcella is known today in the stiff-bosom shirts and ties of men's formal dress, sometimes called piqué.

MARRYMUFF

A coarse common cloth (Fairholt). "Piramides or Maramuffes, both broad and narrow, are shown amongst stuffs [worsteds] in the Charter of Charles I. to the City [of London], 1641" (Beck).

"Kerry-Merry-Buff" is "a kind of material of which jerkins were formerly sometimes made. The phrase seems to have been proverbial, and is often used jocularly" (Halliwell).

MARSEILLES

See Marcella.

MARTINIQUE

One of the fancy eighteenth-century glazed worsted dress fabrics largely manufactured in Norwich. Two swatches with shaded lozenges centering a small leaf and narrow zigzag stripes are in the Moccasi manuscript (see Pl. D-58). John Kelly's 1763 pattern book includes swatches of martiniques with lozenges, floral sprigs, and weft stripes matching those in the warp (Fig. D-70).

See also Belle-isles.

MATELASSÉ

A term applied to a silk or woolen textile which has a raised figure or flower on the surface and appears to have been machine quilted. The word is derived from the French *matelasser,* to quilt or wad. "Very fine descriptions" of silk matelassé were produced in the 1880s for dresses, mantles, and opera cloaks; others made of wool were used for mantles and jackets (Caulfeild and Saward).

According to the CIETA definition, matelassé is a double-woven textile with a quilted appearance. A wadding weft is used to increase the relief.

See also Marcella.

MECKLENBURGH

One of the fancy eighteenth-century glazed worsted dress fabrics largely manufactured in Norwich. Hugh H. Wentworth advertised "new fashioned Mecklenburg stuffs" imported from Bristol in the *New Hampshire Gazette,* July 29, 1763. "Mecklenburgs worsted Flowers—28 / " and "ditto Silk Flowers" were noted by Samuel Rowland Fisher as Norwich manufactures in his 1767–68 journal.

Swatches of late eighteenth-century mecklenburgh with fine shaded stripes and

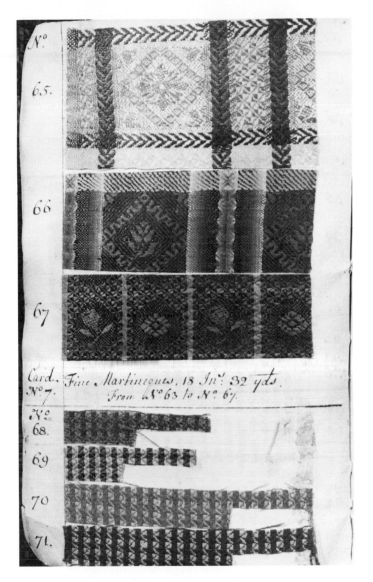

FIG. D-70. *Fine worsted martiniques (nos. 65–67) and "esteratas" (nos. 68–71) from John Kelly's "Counterpart of Patterns," 1763. (Victoria and Albert Museum.)*

brocaded flowers are found in a Norwich pattern book (see Pl. D-72); sample 361 includes strawberries. Two other swatches, in a pattern book of F. Tuthill et Fils, were available in pieces 16 inches wide and 26 yards long (Castle Museum).

MEDLEY CLOTH

Woolen cloth made with fleece-dyed yarns of mixed colors. Also known in the 1630s and 1640s as Spanish cloth, because of the admixture of fine imported Spanish wool; it was "a well-made material of a lighter weight than other cloth" (Mann, *Cloth Industry,* p. xv). About 1725, Defoe considered these West of England cloths a "truly noble manufacture" and described "this trade of fine Spanish medley cloth, being the mix'd colours and cloths, with which all the gentlemen and persons of any fashion in England, are cloth'd, and vast quantities of which are exported to all parts of Europe." Of Trowbridge and Bradford, Defoe says that they "are the two most eminent clothing towns in that part of the vale [of Avon] for the making of fine Spanish cloths, and of the nicest mixtures" (*Tour,* vol. 2, letter 4).

Medleys were imitated by piece dyeing woven white woolens before fulling. These were called "say-dyed" cloths.

See also Marble cloth.

MERCOOLEES
(merculees)

"A good plain white calico, woven in [north India]. Shipped to London in large quantities, and sometimes bought for transforming into chintz" (Irwin and Schwartz).

MERINO

Cloth woven from the wool of the merino sheep. Rudolph Ackermann was lavish in his praise of George III who had introduced merino sheep ("these useful animals") into England in 1786 and of the monarch's "unwearied and patriotic effort for their increase and diffusion" (*Repository* 1, no. 3 [March 1809]: 189). The tipped-in swatch of "Anglo-Merino cloth" is described as a "new and curious article, which may be had of various colours [here peach colored]," "the closest imitation of the real India [cashmere] shawl fabrique ever produced in this country," "nearly as fine as muslin in its texture, and highly elegant in its appearance for full dress or evening wear." Ackermann's *Repository* presents other swatches of merino crape in gray wool and pink silk, plain weave (2, no. 8 [August 1809]: 132); in gray and black for intermediate mourning habits (4, no. 24 [December 1810]: 372); and in pale blue and white with a gauze stripe (8, no. 43 [July 1812]: 53). *See also* Pl. D-88.

George Smith (1826) recommended using merino damask for dining room window curtains, for "drapery . . . continued over the piers" of three windows in drawing rooms, with muslin glass curtains beneath, and for a sofa. He says that it "makes up beautifully, not requiring a lining."

Merino for waistcoats "is made of very superior wool, with a liberal quantity of silk, and is of a most unique texture," according to Perkins writing in 1833.

MESSINET
(missinet)

Silk and worsted dress material manufactured in Norwich and Spitalfields (see Pl. D-31). Two swatches of London manufacture found in the Moccasi manuscript are changeable silk and worsted materials of plain weave, one in blue/pink; the other in purple/pink.

Messinets were advertised in the *Boston News-Letter* (December 18, 1760) and were among worsted goods advertised by Kearny and Gilbert (April 20, 1767) and by James and Drinker (December 4, 1769) in the *Pennsylvania Chronicle and Universal Advertiser*.

MILDERNIX

A kind of sailcloth. The word is a variant of medrinacks, a coarse canvas used by tailors to stiffen doublets and collars (OED). Quarter, half, and full yard-wide "medrinix" are listed in the shop inventory of George Corwin, Salem, 1684/85 (Dow, *Every Day Life*, pp. 274, 275).

Mildernix and poldavy, a related coarse linen, "whereof sails and other furniture for the shipping and navy" were made, were first manufactured in England about 1590 (Beck).

See also Sailcloth.

MINIKIN BAY

A superior grade of bay.

MINIONET
(mignonette, minott, minuet)

A kind of thin lawn. "Minuet Aprons" (Earle, *Costume*, p. 48) and "Scotch minionet lawn" (Beekman, 2:648) are noted in the 1740s and 1760s. John Penn's 1788 inventory listed curtains made of "minionet gauze" for a stained field bed. Directions for making plain "Mignonette Netting," a kind of narrow bobbin lace for curtains and window blinds, are given by Caulfeild and Saward (p. 361).

MOCKADO
(moquette, moucade)

A wool velvet once classed with New Draperies. Mockado, moquette, and moucade may all be derived from French *mosquets* and English "Musketta carpetts" mentioned by Peter Thornton as imported from Anatolia and found listed in English inventories (*Interior Decoration*, p. 109). From paintings it can be determined that some were patterned with prayer niches (mosque carpets?). Possibly the European fabrics were made in imitation of these exotic weaves and given the names to promote their sale (see Fig. D-71).

According to Roland de la Platière both the warp and weft of moquette were linen but coarser than that used for Utrecht velvets. The pile was formed by an extra warp of wool. Moquettes were made plain or figured or were stamped with patterns after weaving. They were used for furniture and for carpeting.

A "mock velvet" is listed in an inventory of 1582 as "redd mockadowe," along with others of black and red, and "blewe and browne." In a pageant honoring Queen Elizabeth, upon the occasion of her visit to Norwich in 1579, tableaus "illustrative of the principal parts of its manufactures" were presented which included the weaving of "tuff mockado" along with russel, darnex, and caffoy (James, p. 115).

Double, single, and "tuft" mockadoes are listed in the 1641 Book of Rates (James, p. 118). Beck conjectured that mockado was "a fabric either of woollen or silk on which a pattern was formed with loops, which being afterwards cut, in the same way that velvet was sheared, left the pattern in pile. This might then be a showy stuff of no great value."

Savary des Bruslons relates *mocade* to moquette and *peluche* (plush) and mentions its use for common furnishings like wall hangings, side chairs, armchairs, stools, table covers, portieres, and carriages. Havard equates *mocade* with moquette and describes four kinds: (1) tapestry or wall coverings—those with the heaviest pile; (2) *Pied-court* woven in smaller patterns for seat furniture; (3) *Communes* woven in checks and stripes for cushions, stools, benches, and traveling cases; and (4) *Tripes* woven in a single color or a stripe, and sometimes stamped or embossed (*gauffré*) in imitation of Utrecht velvets. Havard illustrates a seventeenth-century pattern for moquette by Jean Berain, designer to the king.

Carpeting was related to upholstery fabric called mockado, and in 1741 patent number 578 was granted to Ignatius Couran of London, merchant, John Barford of Wilton, upholder, and William Moody of Wilton, clothier, for their "new invention of making carpeting commonly called French carpeting or Moccadoes and in France *moucades* or *moquets*" (Mann, "Textile Industries," p. 181).

In much of present-day weaving, mockado is woven in two layers, face to face. After weaving, the pile is cut in the middle between the two grounds.

The Moccasi manuscript contains two swatches of *Mocchetta unita denominata trippa* from Abbeville (see Pl. D-52). A similar swatch from Lille is called *Mocchetta goffrata* and is similar to a swatch of *Veluto d'Utrech* also with a stamped pattern placed just above it in the manuscript (see Pl. D-62).

See also Tripp, Velvet.

MODENA
(Fr. modesne)

One of the "stuffs mixed with goat's-hair, wool, thread, and cotton" (Postlethwayt). According to Harmuth's modern definition, modena was a lightweight Italian dress goods made of a mixture of silk waste, cotton, and wool.

In the 1730s Willing and Shippen of Philadelphia ordered "1 ps modena 30 yds" and "3 Ps. Silk and worsted modenas," the latter by number and probably from a pattern card. In 1739, among other silks, John Banister ordered "1 Ps Modena best Ingr[ain] Persian" and "1 ps rich Modena Ingr. ½ Ell Mantua" and other pieces in cherry, blue,

FIG. D-71. *Mockado (wool moquette) probably made in France
in the seventeenth century. (Cooper-Hewitt Museum.)*

green, and white. In this reference, the word *modena* seems to be used as an adjective to indicate an Italian silk, since Banister links it with persian, a thin silk, and mantua, a heavy silk. Here ingrain refers to yarn dyed before weaving, an indication of better quality goods.

MOHAIR
(Fr. moire)

Cloth made from the wool of the Angora goat imported by the Turkey Company trading in the Levant. A 1699 London pamphlet refers to "Grogran or mohair yarn, . . . being generally the product of exchange of our coarsest English woollen cloth" (James, p. 180). From notes kindly furnished by Natalie Rothstein of the Victoria and Albert Museum, it can be determined that mohair, as a furnishing material, was high priced and, when mixed with silk, cost more. Peter Thornton argued that mohair was a silk fabric (*Interior Decoration,* p. 116). We cannot be certain of the weave, but the esteem in which it was held can be judged by the fact that in several instances slipcovers, or cases, made of less expensive materials such as serge, check, and printed linen were made for furniture upholstered in mohair.

Camlets made from mohair yarn were given various finishes: plain, watered (i.e., pressed smooth and lustrous), waved (i.e., folded and submitted to pressure), and figured (i.e., stamped between metal plates or cylinders engraved with patterns). James writes of manufactures made in the mid-nineteenth century from mohair yarn as

> many kinds of camblets which, when watered, exhibit a beauty and brilliance of surface unapproached by fabrics made from English wools. It is also manufactured into plush, as well as for coach and decorative laces, and also extensively for buttons, braidings and other trimmings for gentlemen's coats. Besides it is made up into a light and fashionable cloth suitable for paletots and such like coats, combining elegance of texture with the advantage

of repelling wet. A few years since Mohair striped and checked textures for ladies' dresses, possessing unrivalled glossiness of appearance, were in request; but of late these have been superseded by Alpaca. . . . Also, large quantities of what is termed Utrecht velvet, suitable for hangings and furniture, linings for carriages, are made from it abroad. Recently, this kind of velvet has begun to be manufactured at Coventry, and it is fully anticipated that the English made article will successfully compete with the foreign one in every essential quality. [P. 465.]

Moire, the French word for mohair found grouped in several dictionaries under more nearly phonetic spellings such as *mohère, mouaire,* and *mohaire,* was originally used to designate the fabric made of angora wool. Gradually, however, *moire* was applied more particularly to French ribbed silks and the word *moreen* to English worsteds (Havard; Cummin, "Moreen"; Cummings, p. 30). Both silks and worsteds, with a weft of greater thickness than the warp, could be given a waved look if folded selvedge to selvedge and submitted to great pressure.

In Boston "a yellow Mohair Bed lined with a Persian of the same Colour, and six Chairs of the same Mohair, little the worse for wear" were advertised in 1737, and "A very rich and handsome Crimson Mohair Bed and Chairs" were advertised in 1760 (Dow, *Arts and Crafts,* pp. 110, 119). In 1765 Benjamin Franklin wrote to his wife Deborah from London: "The blue Mohair Stuff is for the Curtains of the Blue Chamber. The Fashion is to make one Curtain only for each Window. Hooks are sent to fix the Rails by at Top, so that they might be taken down on Occasion" (*Franklin Papers,* 12:62).

In keeping with London custom, the furniture and hangings in Peter Faneuil's Boston bedroom matched: "Yellow Mohair Bed . . . 6 Chairs, a Great Chair, 2 Stools, Window Curtains and Cushons all the same" and valued at £180 in his 1743 inventory (SCPR, 37:111).

For articles of clothing, a London advertisement offered a "red Mohair Gown and Petticoat lined with a red Lutestring" (*Post-Boy,* October 10, 1709).

The word *mohair* in connection with caffoy and flock wallpapers, as used in eighteenth-century English inventories, may refer to the use of chopped wool to form the pile surface (Fowler and Cornforth, p. 132).

See also Moiré, Moreen.

MOIRÉ

A silk fabric with a pronounced grain, or rib; a kind of *gros de Tour* but not as strong. Some were given a waved finish like tabbies (Savary des Bruslons). Beck quotes Andrew Ure's description of the process whereby a waved finish is imparted to cloth:

> These silks are made in the same way as ordinary silks, but always much stouter, sometimes weighing, for equal surface, several times heavier than the best ordinary silks. They are always made of double width, and this is indispensable in obtaining the bold waterings, for these depend not only on the quality of the silk, but greatly on the way in which they are folded when subjected to the enormous pressure in watering. They should be folded in such a manner that the air which is contained within the folds of it should not be able to escape easily; then when the pressure is applied the air, in trying to effect its escape, drives before it the little moisture which is used, and hence causes the watering. Care must also be taken so to fold it that every thread may be perfectly parallel, for if they ride one across the other the watering will be spoiled. The pressure used is from 60 to 100 tons.

The Richelieu Papers include two swatches of plain *moirés* and one of *moiré gauffrée* with a fine floral pattern stamped on a ribbed silk. They were made in Holland and are dated 1736. A swatch of Avignon manufacture in the same book is called *Moire menu grain soye et filoselle* (common ribbed moiré of silk and floss silk) in brilliant yellow (see Pl. D-89).

MOLESKIN

A napped cotton material or fustian with the pile cut short before the material is dyed. Harmuth wrote that it is "made with one set of warp and two sets of filling, of the same yarn, spun two picks on the face and one pick on the back, the former combined with alternate warp ends, forming a modified satin weave. The back filling is combined with every warp end forming a three-end weft twill."

Like barragon it was used for working men's clothes, as a foundation for some artificial leather, and for lined sport coats. Moleskin is listed under vestings in Charles Forbes's *Merchant's Memorandum.*

MOMIE CLOTH
(*mummy cloth*)

An unbleached, plain woven, heavy linen or cotton made in imitation of the ancient cloth and used for embroidery grounds, waistcoats, towels, and dresser runners in the late nineteenth century. A swatch of momie "cloth from Egypt," an unbleached linen, is found in a New Jersey scrapbook made up in the 1880s (Winterthur Museum Library). Patterns printed on momie cloth are in an 1883 receipt book from Old Pacific Print Works, Lawrence, Massachusetts (Fig. D-72). Some are textured by tiny floats in the plain weave; others are printed in two shades of brown with a different pattern on the reverse. Momie cloth of "cotton warp and woollen weft, or else a silk warp and woollen weft" looked like "very fine Crape" (Caulfeild and Saward). The crinkled, lusterless black cloth was suitable for mourning.

MONK'S CLOTH

Worsted cloth worn by monks in medieval England was woven 12 yards in length and 45 inches in width. In the nineteenth century, the name was given to rough canvaslike drapery material made of heavy cotton yarns containing some flax, jute, or hemp in 2 × 2 basket weave. Friar's cloth was a 4 × 4 weave and Druid's cloth 6 × 6 or 8 × 8.

MONTEITH

A printed cotton handkerchief with white dots on a colored ground. Similar to bandanna.

MOORFIELDS CARPET

A hand-knotted woolen pile carpet. Thomas Moore's factory at Chiswell Street, Moorfields, Devonshire, was probably founded before 1757, the year in which he competed with Thomas Whitty of Axminster for a premium offered to hand-knotted carpet weavers by the Royal Society of Arts (Tattersall and Reed, p. 44). Both men employed the turkish knot for their pile carpets.

William Bingham of Philadelphia owned "one of Moore's most expensive patterns" according to Henry Wansey who visited him in 1794 (Wansey, p. 105).

MOQUETTE

See Mockado.

MORDANT

A metallic oxide or mineral used in conjunction with madder, quercitron, or other dyes in the colorfast printing and dyeing of cloth. "Metallic salts with an affinity for both fibers and dyestuffs . . . improved the colorfastness of certain dyes" (Adrosko, p. 4).

MOREA
(moree)

"One of the categories of staple cotton-cloth woven on the Coromandel Coast, usually of superior quality and much in demand in Europe as a substitute for linen cloth. It was also used for chintz-making" (Irwin and Schwartz). "Raw Morea" silk is listed among imports in the 1660 Book of Rates (Dow, *Every Day Life,* p. 253).

As imitated in the Manchester area, it was a muslin much used in the African export trade. Silk warps were introduced into moreas for dress goods (Aikin, p. 160). Striped swatches are found in issues of the *Journal für Fabrik* for February 1792 (Fig. D-73), July 1792, and October 1795, where they are said to be of Swiss or of Lyons manufacture.

MOREEN

A worsted cloth which generally was given a waved or stamped finish. In 1836 David Booth described the various finishing processes and types of moreens:

> Moreens are plain stout cloths, of worsted, the weft of which, in comparison with the warp, is a very thick thread. They are woven white and then dyed of any requisite colour, but their distinguishing characteristic is acquired in the process of Watering, by which the surface assumes a variety of shades, as if the cloth were covered with a multitude of waving and intersecting lines. This effect is thus produced: the piece, or web, of cloth is folded, from one end to the other, in triangular folds, without attending to regularity, and being thus reduced to a comparatively small length, it is put upon a roller and rolled under a calender of very great weight. When taken out, the strong threads of the weft are found to have impressed lines upon both surfaces, which are variously waved in consequence of the foldings above described. As it is only intended to have one side waved, the

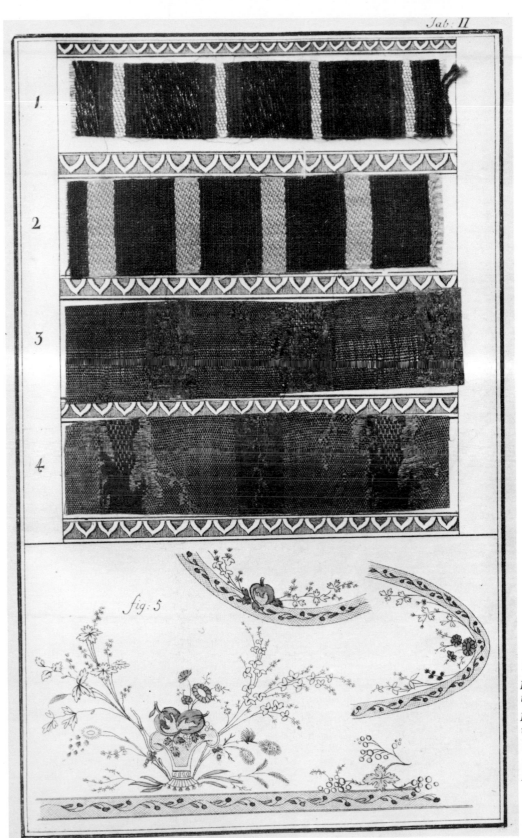

FIG. D-73. (*1,2*) *Half-silk Moreas oder Lustrines;* (*3,4*) *pekins, striped half-silks with trailing floral patterns;* (*5*) *printed patterns for needlework. From* Journal für Fabrik (*February 1792*), *p. 155. (Winterthur Museum Library.)*

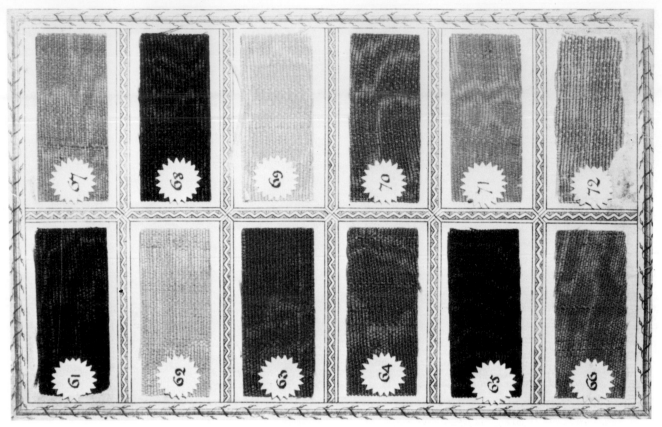

FIG. D-74. *Swatches of moreens from an eighteenth-century folding pattern card. (Public Record Office.)*

web is made up, for the press, with pasteboards between each second fold, so as to allow one side of the web to be wholly without the pasteboards. The web is then hot-pressed and that side, which was covered with pasteboard, comes out glazed, while the other remains Watered. [A sample of glazed pasteboard used for pressing is in the Moccasi manuscript (see Pl. D-60).]

When it is wanted to be creased, it is folded, in the first instance, selvage to selvage. Another operation is to pass the cloth over a hot brass cylinder, on which are engraved various flowers, or other fancy figures. While passing over this cylinder, the cloth is pressed between two wooden rollers, and thus its surface is indented with those figures. This sort is called Embossed Moreen.

"The name of this stuff was formerly Moireen, which gives its origin more distinctly. It is an imitation of moire in commoner materials for purposes of upholstery" (Beck). "The French speak of *la moire ondée,* which our manufacturers have chosen to call Watered Moreen" (Beck). The word *moreen* "is a corruption of *moiré,* which was the French adaptation of the English word mohair" (Gloag). In the first half of the eighteenth century, "Kidderminster [in Worcestershire] was the seat of the moreen and damask manufacture and all sorts of bed furniture and hangings" (James, p. 255).

As an increasing variety of washable furniture fabrics became available after the American Revolution, moreens fell from fashion. They were revived in the nineteenth century, however, and beginning about 1811 were manufactured largely in Yorkshire (James, p. 373). Nineteenth-century moreens may be distinguished from eighteenth-century examples by the more even spinning of the yarns and by harsh colors such as orange. The stamped floral patterns lack the finesse and variety found in earlier pieces.

In the Beekman Papers, moreen is mentioned in a wide variety of colors in the 1770s, including black, Saxon blue, Saxon green, and pea green. Brown, yellow, crimson, garnet, pink, and purple are specified in the 1774 New York advertisement of Woodward and Kip (*American Wing Handbook,* p. 130). Sir Francis Bernard, governor of Massachusetts, owned in 1770 "1 Mohogony four Post Bedsted, with Crimson Moreen Furniture, and 2 Window Curtains; 1 Mohogony four post Bedsted with yellow Moreen Furniture, and 2 Window Curtains; 1 Sett of yellow bottom Chairs" (Dow, *Arts and Crafts,* p. 125). "Five crimson moreen drapery window curtains, with laths, cornices, and three yellow ditto" were offered for sale in Philadelphia in 1779 (Prime, *1721–1785,* p. 213).

In *Household Furniture* (1808), George Smith suggested "superfine cloth, or cassimere, for the draperies of dining rooms and libraries" and added that "where expense is an object undressed morine of a fine quality will form a good substitute." He also mentions the suitability of moreen trimmed with worsted fringe for breakfast parlors (pp. xii, 2). In the October 30, 1810, *Palladium,* James Foster of Boston advertised: "Scarlet embossed Moreen for Curtains[,] Grey [embossed moreen for curtains,] Green Moreen for Cushings[, and] Green and Crimson Bindings."

Included in the "stock in trade" of Baltimore upholsterer John Hoburg were scarlet, watered crimson, drab, orange, yellow, blue, green, and black moreens (*Federal Gazette and Baltimore Advertiser,* August 9, 1819).

Ten swatches of "fine flower'd Mooreens" without pattern are in the 1770 Yorkshire pattern book (see pl. 104). Of about the same date in the Berch Papers are watered "Supr fine Moreens" in black and dark green. Moreens in brilliant yellow, turquoise, and scarlet appear along with olive, brown, and purple in a 1791 Castle Museum pattern book. Eleven others (swatch nos. 61–72) are pasted to an eighteenth-century folding pattern card (Fig. D-74).

MOROCCO CLOTH
(leather cloth)

According to a report of the New York industrial exhibition of 1853, this cloth is

A most perfect imitation of morocco, by the application of a preparation of caoutchouc, or gutta percha, to the surface of plain woven or twilled cotton cloth. The surface is corrugated in imitation of morocco, and is coloured and varnished so as to present all the external appearance of that kind of leather. The elasticity is perfect, showing no tendency to crack, and so far as time has at present tested its durability, this appears to be satisfactory. Its cost is less than one-third that of morocco, and from the width of the cloth, it cuts to much greater advantage in the covering of articles of furniture, for which, as well as carriage linings, particularly railway carriages, it is coming largely into use. [Wallis, p. 23.]

MOUSSELINE DE LAINE

See Delaine.

MULL

A shortened form of mulmul. Soft, fine white cotton imported from India from the seventeenth century. "A staple commodity of Bengal often embroidered with floral motives for the English market, where it was in demand for peticoats" (Irwin and Schwartz). Dutch traders distinguished between fine, common, and flowered. Muslin handkerchiefs, also known as mallemolles, were sometimes bordered with gold or striped with gold and silk. Savary des Bruslons wrote: *Les femmes s'en servent en France à mettre sur leur col & à cacher une partie de leur gorge, soit par modestie, soit pour ornement.*

Mull was later woven in Europe, especially in Switzerland. This "very thin and soft variety of Muslin [was] employed for morning dresses, and for trimmings. Mull Muslin is finer than Nainsook, is of a pure white colour, and has a perfectly soft finish" (Caulfeild and Saward). Thomas Fitch of Boston requested "good fine Muslins call'd Mullmulls" from London (Letter book, May 28, 1728).

MUNGO

Remanufactured wool made from felted rags. It was considered inferior to shoddy made from worsted rags. Tradition has it that the name arose when "one of the dealers in the newly-discovered material was pushing the sale of a small quantity, when doubts were expressed as to its likelihood to sell, to which the possessor replied, 'It mun go,' meaning, 'It must go' " (Beck).

MUSLIN

A fine cotton textile first made in India. Tavernier, a seventeenth-century merchant and traveler, wrote of the "calicuts [muslins sold in Calcutta] made so fine you can hardly feel them in your hand, and the thread, when spun, is scarce discernible." About 1670 muslins imported by the East India Company displaced "cambrics, Silesia lawns, and such kind of flaxen linens of Flanders and Germany" (Beck). Mortimer listed twenty-five "species" of East India muslins imported from the time of William and Mary at 15 percent duty. Bannerjei (1898) listed thirteen East India muslins and noted that "special names are given to other muslins made in Dacca, according to their patterns."

Not until the invention of the mule-jenny in 1779 were fine cotton yarns suitable for successful muslin weaving spun in England and Scotland. By 1833 Perkins could list twenty-five different kinds of muslins in his *Treatise on Haberdashery*.

A particularly interesting American reference is the one in Margrita van Varick's 1695/96 inventory to "a sett of white floward muslin curtens." After the 1760 Boston fire a resident submitted a claim for "a suit of very fine muslin Curtains for a field Bed" (*Boston Records,* p. 60).

Samples of "Narrow Striped Muslin," "small cross band," red and white "Turkey Stripe," and a printed sprigged pattern are in a Beekman order dated 1774 (Beekman Papers, 2:945–46).

Nine swatches of muslin cord in the 1786 Hilton manuscript resemble swatches of dimities shown above them but have heavier cotton cords in twill stripes (Figs. D-75, D-76).

See also Mull.

Book muslin (book calico) is a name derived from the booklike form in which some of the finer calicoes were folded and marketed in India. John Irwin cited a 1608 reference which says that a book "containeth 14 English yards."

In 1707 Thomas Banister of Boston, who understood this method of folding cloth, ordered "50 or 60 ps of Broad blew Calicoes, vulgerly called Book calicos, being folded broad." In 1754 book muslins could be purchased in Boston "ell wide" and "yard wide" (Caine broadside). On his 1767–68 trip to England, Samuel Rowland Fisher ordered in Newcastle "Patterns to be all very small & chiefly running figures or Spriggs to be callenderd not glazd & each Ps divided in two & folded Book fashion." During the Revolution when Providence merchants tried to establish trade with France, they discovered that textile terms were not universally understood:

> All the Dictionaries in the World could not translate the names of the goods ordered. Order a French Merchant to ship a piece of *Mousseline de Livre,* but no Manufacturer in Europe would be able to furnish him, and he would write in answer that it was not to be found, unless some American were to tell him that a piece of Goods called *ourgandi* answers to Book Muslin, except in the folding it. [Hedges, p. 253.]

Perkins, referring to English-made muslin in 1833, wrote: "The chief markets for it is in America, and the West Indies; where in particular, the checked sort is used for sailors' shirts, and the striped for curtains, trousers, jackets, &c." He adds:

> [It is] made in three distinct kinds, viz. hard, soft, and lawn book. The hard is so called, from its being stiffened or dressed; the soft,

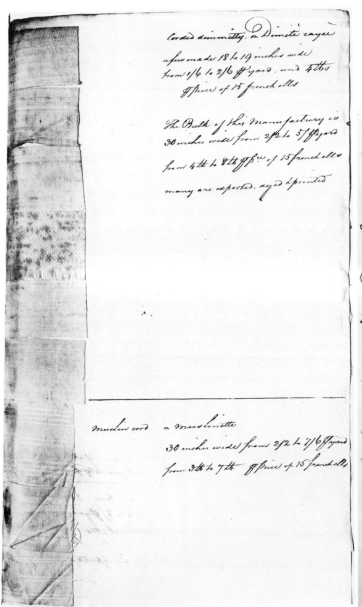

FIGS. D-75, D-76. *Swatches of corded dimity, muslin cord or muslinet, and sateen. From the Hilton manuscript, 1786. (Public Record Office.)*

October, 1809.—Vol. 2.

The Repository

Of Arts, Literature, Commerce, Manufactures, Fashions, and Politics.

MANUFACTURERS, Factors, and Wholesale Dealers in Fancy Goods, that come within the scope of this Plan, are requested to send Patterns of such new Articles, as they come out; and if the requisites of Novelty, Fashion, and Elegance, are united, the quantity necessary for this Magazine will be ordered.

R. Ackermann, 101, *Strand, London.*

from its being perfectly undressed; and, for a further distinction, it is called the imitation of India. The lawn book is made to imitate the French clear lawn; it is less clear than the hard book, and much stiffer: it is also called widows' lawn, mourning muslin, and is used for widows' caps, cuffs, collars, and frills. The India Book is an exquisitely fine article, folded, ornamented, and numbered the same as the original India.

Webster said that "Buke muslin (erroneously written book) is a plain, clear muslin . . . woven for working in the tambour" (p. 961).

"Clear 6-Quarter Book Muslins, for Caps, Aprons and Handkerchiefs, cross-barred and striped Muslins, for Gowns and Aprons; and jaconet bordered Muslin Handkerchiefs" were offered for sale at the store of Brown and Francis (*Providence Gazette,* May 2, 1789).

A dozen swatches of plain, figured, brocaded, and printed muslins are found in the *Journal für*

OPPOSITE

FIG. D-77. *Swatches of (1) corded muslin; (2) Brazilian corded sarcenet for robes, pelisses, and spencers; (3) pomona green shawl print in imitation of Indian silk; and (4) printed book muslin for evening wear. From* Repository 2, no. 10 (October 1809): 277.

Fabrik from 1792 to 1795 (see Figs. D-8, D-81); others are included in Ackermann's *Repository* from 1809 to 1815. In this period of their greatest popularity they were recommended for dresses, shawls, and window curtains. The *Repository* includes a swatch of "rose-coloured printed book muslin, best calculated for the ball-room or evening party" which "must be worn over white sarsnet, satin, or glazed cambric." This pale pink swatch is loosely woven in plain weave with a small black printed figure (Fig. D-77, no. 4). A similar swatch in yellow with a black "shawl" figure is found in the same volume (see Fig. D-68).

MUSLINET

A fancy cotton dress material suggested for "morning wraps, jackets, frocks and high gowns." Swatches in stripes, brocades, and small figures, sometimes with printed motifs and additions of colored silk threads, are in the *Journal für Fabrik* from 1792 to 1794 (see Fig. D-97) and in Ackermann's *Repository* in thin white cotton with chevron stripes. Later, muslinet was defined as "a thick variety of muslin, resembling a brilliant, which is used for infants' clothing and for dressing gowns" (Caulfeild and Saward).

See also Fig. D-75.

N

NAINSOOK

A fine white cotton muslin of plain weave made in imitation of an Indian cloth, and described by G. S. Cole as made plain, striped in the warp, and in small damasked checks. It was used as a summer fabric, principally for the making of white dresses, aprons, infants' wear, and lingerie. In this century, it is described as a soft-finished white cotton fabric with a polish on one side, lighter in weight than longcloth and more highly finished; not so closely woven as cambric but heavier than batiste (Denny).

Ackermann presents a swatch of white "Striped muslin or Nainsook" with heavier warp cords for morning dress in 1809 (see Fig. D-68). A pinafore made of white nainsook muslin is shown in *Godey's Lady's Book,* February 1870 (p. 396, fig. 7).

Nainsook was advertised as a foundation cloth

for window shades by F. J. Kloes and Company, New York, in 1886: "There are many grades of goods used for shade foundations, among the finest of which are Lonsdale cambric and a lightweight nainsook, that is employed for transparent effects" (Bishop and Coblentz, p. 82).

NANKEEN

A cotton cloth of plain weave originally sold at Nankin in China and made from a yellow variety of cotton "of the same yellow tinge which it preserves when spun and woven into cloth" (Edward Baines, p. 31n). At least by the mid-eighteenth century, in the Manchester area it was made of ordinary cotton dyed yellow. Swatch number 62 in Holker's manuscript is nankeen suitable for men's waistcoats and trousers which he says wears very well.

With the entry of United States ships into the East India trade after the American Revolution, the importation of nankeens increased to the point that "their price was almost a standard of exchange" (Earle, *Costume,* p. 166). The term *nankeen* was applied to a large variety of cotton goods sold in Canton.

Rhode Island merchants directed their supercargoes to purchase yellow, white, deep blue, and black nankeens (Weeden, pp. 242, 271). "Prices Current at Canton," written in 1807 for Benjamin Shreve of Boston, states: "The Yellow Nankeen is made from the Cotton in its natural state of colour, never having been dyed, and the colour improves and grows darker and more beautiful by age. Blue Nankeens are not quite so fine as the above but are considerably in demand and the consumption in the United States is by no means small" (Crossman, p. 23).

Henry Wansey wrote of nankeen, nankinet, and other cotton manufactures on May 31, 1794:

> Went with a party to see Dickson's cotton manufactory at Hell Gates, about five miles from New York. . . . In one shop I saw twenty-six looms at work, weaving fustians, calicoes, nankeens, nankinets, dimities, etc.

and there are ten other looms in the neighbourhood. They have the new-invented spring shuttle. They also spin by water, using all the new improvements of Arkwright and others. Twelve or fourteen workmen from Manchester. All the machinery in wood, steel, and brass, were made on the spot from models brought from England and Scotland. [P. 82.]

Swatches of fancy colored dress nankeens in striped and herringbone patterns, some with additions of silk, are in the *Journal für Fabrik* from 1792 to 1795. These nankeens are of western manufacture.

Similar "yellow-tan to rose-tan to medium brown" cotton called *nankin* or *coton jaune* was made by the Acadians in Louisiana (Glasgow, p. 339).

NAPS

A heavy woolen material with napped "surface twisted into little knots by a napping machine advertised from 1726" (Mann, *Cloth Industry,* p. 50n). Scarlet and green "Knaps" were advertised in 1746 in New York (Gottesman, *1726–76,* p. 266); and James Alexander of that city placed an order in the same year for blue, green, scarlet, and "Cloth Colrd" naps each at two different prices. George Bartram offered "an assortment of coarse and fine, wide and narrow, naps and plains" in the *Pennsylvania Chronicle,* September 7, 1767.

NECONNEE
(nicconnee, nickanee)

A cheap Indian striped calico, patterned in the loom, and bought mainly for the slave markets. Irwin suggested that it may have been the same as modern nakhuna with white warp and the weft striped in various colors (Irwin and Schwartz). Savary des Bruslons said they were blue and white striped. They are found grouped with other Guinea stuffs such as brawles, tapsels, and anabasses. Western imitations were made of cotton and wool (Wadsworth and Mann, p. 151).

NEGRO CLOTH

A coarse homespun fabric used for clothing slaves in the West Indies and the southern colonies. Inexpensive grades of cloth were also imported for the same purpose. A 1745 invoice of John Banister of Newport lists fifteen yards of negro cloth at 8 shillings a yard. *See also* Niger cloth.

NEW DRAPERIES

During the second half of the sixteenth century, new kinds of manufactures were developed in East Anglia made of worsted yarn spun from combed, long-staple wool; others were part worsted and part carded, short-staple wool. In general they were lighter in weight than old woolens such as frieze and kersey and were suitable for wear on warm days or in hot climates. They needed little or no fulling or elaborate finishing. *Barracan, bay, bombazine, calimanco, grogram, mockado, perpetuana, rash, say, serge, shalloon,* and *stammet* are some of the names given to them (Coleman, p. 418). A manuscript dated 1592 preserved in the Lansdowne collection gives the names, weights, and values of twenty-nine New Draperies which are listed and described by James (pp. 125–27).

By the close of the reign of James I (d. 1625), other types of worsted cloth had been invented. These are described in allegations prepared by the worsted weavers of Norwich:

> A buffyn, a catalowne, and the pearl of beauty, are all one cloth; a peropus and paragon all one; a saye and piramides, all one; the same cloths bearing other names in times past. The paragon, peropus, and philiselles may be affirmed to be double chambletts; the difference being only, the one was double in the warp, and the other in the weft. Buffyn, cattalowne, and pearl of beauty, &c., may be affirmed single chamblett, differing only in the breadth. The say and piramides may also be affirmed to be that ancient cloth, mentioned in the said statute, called a bed; the difference only consisting in the breadth and fineness. . . .

> To make of . . . [the] worsted a stamin, was but to make it narrower and thinner in the stay; to make the bed a say, which served for apparel, was to make the same much narrower and finer; this cloth hath continued its name and fashion till this day; but, now lately, by putting the same into colours, and twisting one third of one colour with another colour, being made narrow, it is now called piramides.

> From worsted are derived, in another line, other cloths.

> A worsted was wrought with four treadles; to make thereof a bustian, is to weave with three of the same treadles; to make the same a double chamblet, is to use the two right foot treadles; to make it single, is to use the two left foot treadles; to make this a philisello, a peropus, a paragon, or a buffyn, is but to alter the breadth, and to make them double, treble, or single in the striken [weft, or shoot]; and to make this buffyn a catalowne, is to twist a thread of one colour with a thread of another, and strike it with another colour; to make the same a pearl of beauty, is to make it striped, by colours in the warp, and tufted in the striken. [James, p. 144; also in Beck.]

In addition to these worsted and part-worsted textiles, Dutch and Walloon weavers fleeing Spanish rule in the Netherlands brought to the area the art of mixing linen and silk with combing wools. Among these goods can be listed alapeen, anterne, bombazine, darnex, drugget, frizadoe, grogram, hair camlet, and poplin. For a complete list, see Kerridge, page 29.

NIGER CLOTH

A labeled swatch is in the Noska pattern book of 1860. White and brown cotton yarn is twill woven with blue cotton yarn. The cloth may have been developed from the coarser, homespun negro cloth. *See also* Negro cloth.

NILLAES

A "striped cloth of mixed Tussur silk and cotton, occasionally flowered" (Irwin and Schwartz). Imported from Bengal in 1679, most prized were "the sort that are finest and most Glossy and striped with the lightest colours as hair colour, sky colour and the like, but those that are Red and Tauny ground striped with black are not vendible" (quoted in Irwin and Schwartz). In London in 1767 Samuel Rowland Fisher ordered fifteen pieces of nillaes at 17 shillings each along with other Indian goods.

NONE-SO-PRETTY

A term applied generally to tapes or ribbons. Willing and Shippen of Philadelphia ordered them by the gross in the 1730s, and Samuel Rowland Fisher recorded in his 1767/68 journal "20 doz Nonsoprettys—no Greens nor Yellows." In Boston, "None-so-Pretty Tapes" were offered in 1771, as were, in the following year, "Blue & white, Red & white, Green & white Furniture checks with None-so-Prettys to match." In 1886 a Rhode Island store dating from the eighteenth century had an old box labeled "None-so-Prettys" that contained "rolls of strong brown linen braid about three-quarters of an inch wide, with little woven figures, white, red, or black dots or diamonds" (Earle, *Costume,* pp. 173–74). Perkins (1833) lists among bindings "Blue Diamond, otherwise None-so-Pretty."

Havard defines *nompareille* as a very light and narrow camlet or a ribbon of silk.

See also Lamparilla.

NORWICH CRAPE

The black fabric adopted for official court mourning in the eighteenth century and worn by the clergy. It was made of silk warp and worsted weft, twill woven like a bombazine with the worsted thrown to the right side.

In 1737 James Alexander ordered "black and white Norwich mourning Crape" at six different prices.

About 1819 a new crape was introduced at Norwich and soon was woven in Yorkshire as well. This was a glossy fabric made of silk warp and worsted weft in plain weave which differed from bombazine in being "tamet woven," that is without "wale," and both sides were alike. These were woven in gray and afterward dyed in colors for ladies' dresses (James, pp. 386–87). Thomas Webster remarked that it was "difficult to say how this came to be designated a crape, as it is a very different fabric from the usual crapes" and it "is distinguished from bombazin chiefly in not being twilled" (p. 972).

NORWICH GOODS, OR STUFFS

A general term for worsteds manufactured in East Anglia and marketed at Norwich. Known since the sixteenth century as New Draperies, the most flourishing period of their manufacture occurred during the middle of the eighteenth century when foreign trade included all of Europe, the Baltic ports, Russia, China, the Levant, the West Indies, Spanish America, and the North American colonies.

Names for the various kinds of Norwich stuffs, including those made entirely of worsted yarns, wool and worsted, and silk and worsted mixed, are particularly difficult to identify. Many novelty titles were used, and when the sale of a material languished, it was given a new name in the hope of captivating buyers (Fuller).

Postlethwayt said of the county of Norfolk:

Its manufactures are, generally speaking, sent to London, though they export considerable quantities also to Holland, Germany, Sweden, Norway, and other ports of the Baltic and Northern Seas. They consist in great variety of worsted stuffs, as says, bays, serges, shalloons, &c. in which they carry on a vast trade; and are lately come to weave druggets, crapes, and other curious stuffs: of all which it is said, this city vends to the value of no less than £100,000 a year.

More pattern books survive with swatches of fancy worsted cloths than of any other type of eighteenth-century fabric. In this highly organized trade, English merchants sent out sample books filled with an incredible variety of brilliantly colored patterns neatly numbered for ease in ordering. Among these pattern books are two prepared by John Kelly in the 1760s for Spanish and Portuguese trade and now in the Victoria and Albert Museum. Others in the Nordiska Museet, Stockholm, were collected by Anders Berch, an economist. Similar books are owned by the Castle Museum at Norwich. Several others, probably dating from the 1790s, now at Winterthur Museum, had long been owned by the Philadelphia Textile Institute and, presumably, were once used by a merchant of that city. The Moccasi manuscript also contains swatches of Norwich goods (see Pls. D-56, D-57, D-58, D-59).

Camlets, worsteds without glaze, were woven in striped, shaded, spotted, sprigged, changeable, and brocaded patterns. Camleteens, narrower and thinner than camlets, were also produced in great variety. Worsted damasks, sometimes called bed satins, were woven in single colors or in two contrasting shades.

Within the large category of calimancoes were striped, flowered, and checked patterns and others bearing names such as dresdens, martiniques, and espolinados (names penned in the pattern books probably invented to appeal to certain markets). Others indicate small allover patterns: florettas, esteretts, cheveretts, diamantines, and harlequins. Other groups with white lace bands woven on colored grounds with polychrome brocaded flowers were called batavia, blondine, grandine, mecklenburgh, russeline, and taboratt or brilliant.

NOYALLS
(nowells, noyales, noyles)

A strong, unbleached canvas made of hemp. This sailcloth was first made at Noyal and at various places in Brittany in France (OED; Savary des Bruslons). Noyalls canvas was imported into Boston in 1650 (Aspinwall Records, p. 422) and is listed in Boston inventories of 1660 and 1684 (Dow, *Every Day Life*, pp. 258–60, 271, 274).

OATMEAL CLOTH

Made of cotton, linen, and wool with a pebbled face resembling an oatmeal cake. These thick, soft, and pliant cloths were available in all colors (Caulfeild and Saward). Fancy oatmeal cotton cloths were woven in diamond designs and stripes, but uncolored. Some were used for embroidery in crewels and silks; a thin quality was used for dresses, and a thicker one for upholstery.

OLD DRAPERIES

The long history of woolen manufacture in England is told by several writers. Royal encouragement and protection granted to foreign weavers, dyers, and fullers to settle in England fostered the manufacture. According to Beck (s.v. "cloth") in the fourteenth century "manufactures of fustians were settled at Norwich, baizes at Sudbury, broad cloths in Kent, kerseys in Devon, friezes in Wales, cloths in Worcestershire, Gloucestershire, Hampshire, Sussex, and Berkshire, coarse cloths in the West Riding of Yorkshire, and serges at Colchester and Taunton. Many of these manufactures became permanent in these places." An act passed in 1376 stated "that no subsidy be paid on our own woollen manufactures 'till they be fulled, which was to be performed before they should be exported.' " This was "the first of many efforts to foster the manufacture by making it compulsory that the finishing processes should be performed at home." "The textile manufactures were now firmly established" (Beck, pp. 70, 71).

See New Draperies for the next major development.

OLDHAM
(old hame)

A coarse worsted named for a town in Norfolk where it was made from the fourteenth century. The term may imply that the fabric "had long and of *old* time been made at Home," that is to say in England, as compared with a foreign manufacture (James, p. 44). Oldham is also the name of a wool town in Yorkshire.

ORANGELIST

A 1¾-yard-wide baize dyed in fancy colors and exported from England chiefly to Spain. It is also described as a coarse woolen lining material. The name implies that the selvedges had orange stripes.

ORGANDY

A fine, sheer cotton fabric of plain weave; a thin, transparent, wiry muslin that can be dyed, printed, or white. Savary des Bruslons compares it to betilles.

See also Muslin, esp. book muslin.

ORLEANS

A dress material of plain weave. The warp is of thin cotton "and the weft of worsted, which are alternately brought to the surface in the weaving. There are some with a silk warp; others are figured, and others have double warps. They are durable in wear, are dyed in all colours, as well as in black, and measure a yard in width" (Caulfeild and Saward, p. 373).

Of lighter, less expensive dress materials developed in the late 1830s such as orleans, coburg, paramatta, luster, and poplin made with cotton warps, James writes that this manufacture "has imparted a new character to the worsted industry, enabled the manufacturer to suit the requirements of the age by producing light and elegant stuff goods, rivalling in cheapness articles from cotton, and in brilliancy and delicacy those of silk. . . . [The] prevailing taste, . . . became year by year more evident for light, elegant, and cheap articles of dress, which lacking the wearing qualities of former stuffs were yet more showy and attractive" (p. 471).

ORRICE
(orris)

A kind of heavy ribbon or gimp trimming, sometimes woven with gold and silver, and used in the seventeenth and eighteenth centuries for trimming dresses and furnishings. The word later included "nearly every description of upholstery galloons," especially those used for saddle and coach trimmings (Beck). Willing and Shippen imported "Orrice and worst'd Raines" (horse reins?) in the 1730s.

Samples of mid-eighteenth-century brilliant red and green silk orrice in various widths, which the Lord Chamberlain purchased from Tempest Hey, silk-lace maker, are reversible silk ribbons with lozenge patterns in weft floats (Public Record Office LC9/267). The Lord Chamberlain's accounts include a variety of other ribbons, "binding," and "chair lace" made partly of "crewel" (worsted) or cotton and silk.

OSNABURG
(oznabrig)

Coarse, unbleached linen or hempen cloth first made in Osnabrück, Germany. It was commonly used for trousers, sacking, and bagging. Made of cotton in the nineteenth century in blue and white or brown and white, stripes, checks, or solid colors, it was used for overalls and farmers' clothing in the United States.

A "Brown Ozenbridge Jacket and Breeches" were worn by a runaway slave in Boston, 1704 (Earle, *Costume*, p. 174). Blue and "blue Holland" osnaburgs appear in Mary Elmendorph's account book in 1715 and 1737 at Kingston, New York. A 1728 order specified "fine white ozenbs" (Ten Eyck Papers).

In Boston "22 yds. Ozenbriggs to pack . . . [a piece of flowered damask] in @ 4/6" were charged in the Brandon and Dolbear journal of 1739. In 1740 John Banister of Newport wrote his agent: "As to the small Canvas, I never expect to sell it unless at a very low advance, it being not fit for anything but what ozenbrigs will doe better for." A claim was made after the Boston fire of 1760 for "2 Large Underbeds of Oznagr" (*Boston Records*, p. 73).

In 1747 Gerard Beekman of New York ordered "Three Pieces good Ossinbrig" to be bought in Newry, Ireland (1:34). In 1757 James Beekman's London agent wrote of the difficulties in getting osnaburgs from Germany: "Our Ships from Bremen being frozen up by the late severe winter could supplie You only with half of Your Osnabrigs, and our ships from Ostend not being yet arrivd have sent You but Half of Your quantity" (2:632). Again in 1760 he wrote "Our hambrough ships not being yet arrived could not complie with Your tendem Sletias nor Your osnabrigs at 7 3/4" (2:647). By the 1770s, Beekman's orders generally specified Scotch osnaburgs.

George Bartram advertised "Scotch, German and Lancashire oznabrigs" in the *Pennsylvania Chronicle*, September 7, 1767. The 1770 inventory of the Governor's Palace in Williamsburg lists "Oznabrigs intended to paste the Paper on in the Supper Room" which were, apparently, to strengthen the wallpaper (Botetourt Manuscripts).

The Milledgeville Manufacturing Company in Georgia was awarded a bronze medal for "Osnaburghs, for weight and durable qualities" at the 1853 New York industrial exhibition (Dilke, p. 27).

Osnaburg sold today in dry-goods stores is coarse cotton muslin with brown flecks simulating the rough fibers of unbleached muslin.

OVERSHOT

A term used in coverlet weaving to describe supplementary or pattern weft yarns of a contrasting color and usually of heavier weight which float over the tabby ground (Fig. D-78).

FIG. D-78. *Detail of overshot coverlet found in Saugerties, New York, and dated 1773. Probably woven in the Hudson Valley, possibly near Albany. Made on a four-shaft loom of white cotton and dark blue wool, this is the earliest dated example known in America. (Winterthur Museum.)*

P

PADUA SAY, OR PADUA SERGE

A worsted or mixed wool and worsted cloth of twill weave. Padua serge ordered about 1720 for the great front curtain of the Hampton Court playhouse cost 2s. 9d. per yard as compared with 2s. 3d. for Norwich paragon, and 3s. 4d. for crimson ingrain paragon for the window curtains (Rothstein, "Calico Campaign," p. 17).

In the *Household Books of Lord William Howard,* 1633, "five yeardes of Padua saye for a peticote for my Ladie" cost 21s. 8d. (Beck).

In Salem, Massachusetts, one piece of "padaway searge" was valued at £2 15d. in the 1677/78 inventory of Edward Wharton (Dow, *Every Day Life,* p. 263). "An easy Chair coverd with a blue Padua old," was part of the estate left by Ruth Mills in 1738 (SCPR, 34:176).

PADUASOY
(padaway, pattisway, poudesoy)

A rich and heavy silk tabby with a self-colored pattern and usually brocaded. It was generally corded and was the heaviest of dress silks. Savary des Bruslons called it *pout,* or *pou de soie:* "A strong, closely woven silk fabric of a quality between a *gros-de-Naples* and a *gros-de-Tours.*"

Sir William Pepperell (1696–1759) ordered from London at the time of his daughter's marriage,

> *Silk* to make a woman a full suit of clothes, the ground to be white padusoy and flowered with all sorts of coulers suitable for a young woman—another of white watered *Taby* and *Gold Lace* for trimming of it; 12 yards of Green Padusoy; thirteen yards of Lace. [Wharton, p. 203.]

James Alexander's 1737 order for "a ps of 20 yds padissoi 6/9 yd." included the request that "it

be Soft being for hoods for friends, of the same breadth with the ps of two thried Lustring." "Rose colour'd Padusoy" and "Padusoy ribbons" were for sale in Boston in 1754 (Caine broadside).

In 1765 Deborah Franklin informed her husband, Benjamin, that the dining room chairs had been covered in "a plain Horsehair and look as well as Paddozway" (*Franklin Papers,* 12:296).

A watercolor pattern for a paduasoy is illustrated at figure D-79.

Poult-de-soie, a related late nineteenth-century corded silk, was made of silk and alpaca yarn and had a shiny surface.

PALAMPORE
(palamposh)

A mordant-painted and resist-dyed Indian cotton cloth with arborescent and floral patterns. The word is derived from Persian and Hindi *palangposh,* a bedcover. A palampore was composed of a single chintz panel; the word first appeared in English East India Company records in 1614 (Irwin and Brett, p. 27). Palampores with histories of eighteenth-century ownership are found in American museums and historical societies (Fig. D-80). The 1702 inventory of Mary Ritchards lists "1 Pallampore and 4 small Boxes—15/8."

PAOLI

One of the fancy eighteenth-century worsted dress fabrics largely manufactured in Norwich. Striped, shaded, flowered, and brocaded examples are found in a 1791 Castle Museum pattern book. Late eighteenth-century Lancashire weavers also made a cotton cloth of this name. A ribbed cotton swatch of "double Paoli" in the 1786 Hilton manuscript is related to denim and other twills (see Fig. D-39).

Fig. D-79. *Watercolor pattern for "A Paduasoy with a backshot broacaded with gold and one colour" made by Spitalfields designer James Leman and dated May 12, 1721. (Victoria and Albert Museum.)*

Possibly the fabric was named for Corsican patriot Pasquale Paoli (1725–1807) who was much lionized in England.

PARAGON

A coarse worsted or camlet that was sometimes watered. "A stuff, plain or embroidered, used for common wear in the seventeenth century" (Earle, *Costume,* p. 176).

In allegations written in 1618 to prove that the New Draperies were essentially the same as older types of worsted fabrics, the weavers of Norwich stated that "the paragon, peropus, and philiselles may be affirmed to be double chambletts; the difference being only, the one was double in the warp, and the other in the weft" (James, p. 144).

"Hangings for a Room of Green Paragon" are listed in a 1674 London newspaper. "Two white Printed Parragon Window Curtains" are mentioned in the *London Gazette,* April 22, 1689. About 1720 Norwich paragon at 2s. 3d. a yard and very fine crimson ingrain paragon at 3s. 4d. were ordered for window curtains at the Hampton Court playhouse. Padua serge for the great front curtain cost 2s. 9d. per yard (Rothstein, "Calico Campaign," p. 17).

"One Turkie Paragon" was imported into Boston in 1650 (Aspinwall Records, p. 415), and "4 pr. parogon bodys and Stomachers" and "6 parogon Chaires" are listed in a Salem inventory of 1684 (Dow, *Every Day Life,* pp. 272, 277). "Parragon curtain and vallaines and bedstead and curtain rods and Tester cloath" were listed in the 1693 inventory of William Lash (SCPR, 13:199). Before the mid-eighteenth century, paragon was

OPPOSITE

FIG. D-80. *Palampore, painted and resist-dyed cotton cloth. Made on the Coromandel Coast of India in the first half of the eighteenth century. History of ownership in the Augustine Boyer family of Kent County, Maryland. (Winterthur Museum, gift of Miss Gertrude Brincklé.)*

supplanted by harateen, moreen, and worsted damask for furnishing.

Barracan and paragon, both worsteds, may have been the same. Possibly some of the finer examples pictured at barracan were intended for clothing, while coarser varieties were for furnishing. (See Thornton, *Interior Decoration,* p. 114.)

PARAMATTA

A cloth developed from eighteenth-century Norwich bombazine of silk warp and worsted weft generally dyed black. Paramatta was first made with cotton warp and woolen weft, but by 1856 it was made of silk and worsted. Coburg was a similar cloth, and they were both woven in 2/1 weft faced twill. They were used for mourning and for raincoats.

A swatch of blue and beige silk and wool flowered damask in the *Journal of Design* for 1851 (5:no. 30) is described as follows: "The Paramatta is a somewhat new manufacture, the use of which is largely spreading, and, with other fabrics, superseding printed goods to some extent. The present specimen is remarkable for its softness, fineness, lustre, and durability."

Paramatta, the name of a town in New South Wales, was the port from which fine merino wool was exported.

PARIS CORD

"A thick rich silk with fine small ribs running across. This was first brought from France, and the genuine has the cord all silk. An imitation is made here [England], and some of this has the cord of cotton. It is much used in making waistcoats and stocks" (Webster, p. 970).

PASSEMENTERIE
(passements)

Narrow wares or trimmings including laces, galloons, gimps, fringes, braids.

PATCH

Possibly the same as panches, an Indian printed cloth, or possibly derived from Indian pitcharies (modern *pachedi* or *pichodi*) "coloured calicoes . . . with a plain field of either white, red, blue or maroon, plain borders and wide crossborders" (Irwin and Schwartz). Advertisements in the *Providence Gazette* include the following: "A fine assortment of calicoes, chintz and patches" along with "best copperplate curtain furniture" (April 17, 1773); two gowns stolen, "one of them a dark striped patch" (December 19, 1778); "London chintzes and Calicoes. Patch and purple Cotton Shawls" (May 27, 1797); "India Chintzes and Calicoes, in Patches and Pieces of the newest patterns" (October 22, 1791). In 1791 Elias Hasket Derby of Salem advertised "Madras Patches, beautifully figured" in the same newspaper.

PATNA

A place name given to painted cotton cloth from northeast India. A letter of 1700 in the India Office Archives states "The Pattana chints with white grounds now grow into demand again, as the Painting will be brisk and lively colours and not too full of work" (as quoted in Irwin, p. 45).

In a 1770 order to London for a great variety of cottons and linens, James Beekman specified "20 pieces Chintz Patana 12 /or 14 /" (2:930).

PATOLA
(patole, patolo)

A type of silk cloth from western India, "the warp and weft being tie-dyed before weaving according to the pre-determined pattern" (Irwin and Schwartz).

PEARL OF BEAUTY

A kind of camlet related to buffyn and catalowne in the allegations of Norwich weavers of about 1620. There it is said that to make this camlet "a pearl of beauty, is to make it striped, by colours in the warp, and tufted in the striken [weft]" (James, p. 144).

See also New Draperies.

PEELING
(pealong, pelang, pelin)

A kind of silk satin made in China. Peelings, first imported by the Dutch, were brought back by 1681 in English East India Company ships:

> The Silks which the Company commonly bring in are the main part of them Taffaties and other plain or striped Silks and Pelongs, such as are not usually made in England but imported from France, Italy and Holland; where lately when Pelongs were scarce, many were made and imitated at Harlem and from thence imported into England. [Warner, p. 631.]

Savary adds that they were "made in white or colors, plain, figured and in several qualities."

From 1766 to 1784 the Beekmans ordered black, white, and brown "Pealong Sattins," some "small figured" or "spotted." Samuel Boardman ordered "1 ps Black pelong—30 yards @ 6/6" in 1772 from New York.

In the 1770s John Norton of Virginia ordered "bright pink" and "handsome blue . . . peeling satins" (p. 212); and a "green Peeling Satin Quilted Petticoat" (p. 190); but more interesting are the four luxurious "white Quilted Peeling Child Bed Basket and Pin Cushions well and Safe Packed up or the Sattin will mildue and spot" (p. 218).

Ackermann suggested white peeling satin to wear under a thin material such as imperial crape or Spanish gauze for dresses (*Repository* 2, no. 4 [April 1809]: 258).

PEKIN

A painted or embroidered silk fabric, generally with floral designs, imported from China and imitated in France from about 1760. Havard cites rooms in which it was used for wall hangings and upholstery.

The name was also applied to silk dress goods woven in alternate satin and velvet stripes. The satin stripes were replaced by gauze in pekin gauze. Swatches are found in issues of the *Journal für Fabrik* for February 1782 (see Fig. D-73), September 1794 (see Fig. D-14), February 1795, and June 1795 (see Fig. D-81). The OED cites an 1891 reference to "striped brocade or pekin, having on the silken stripes flowers in old rose."

PELISSE

A lightweight broadcloth used for women's clothes, especially the cape fashionable in the second half of the eighteenth and in the nineteenth centuries. It was generally a soft twill-woven cloth, thinner than cassimere. George Palmer advertised it among "Fall and Winter Goods" in the *Columbian Centinel* (Boston) October 28, 1812. Swatches are in the pattern book of William Gott of Leeds begun in 1815 (Crump, p. 309).

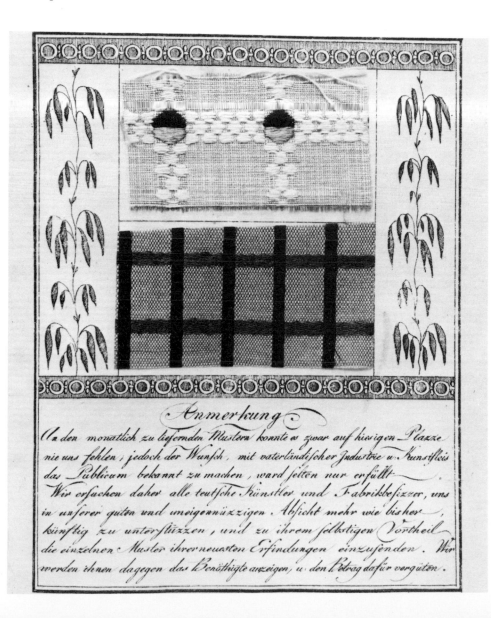

Fig. D-81. (*Top*) *Brocaded muslin of Swiss manufacture.* (*Bottom*) *A pekin half-silk.* From Journal für Fabrik (*June 1795*), *p. 469.* (*Winterthur Museum Library.*)

PENELOPE CANVAS

"A description of cotton canvas made for Berlin woolwork, in which the strands run in couples, vertically and horizontally, thus forming squares containing four threads each. It is less trying to the eyes of the embroiderer than ordinary canvas, as there is little counting to do; and the squares are large compared with the single threads of the latter" (Caulfeild and Saward).

PENNYSTONE
(penniston, penestown)

A coarse woolen cloth taking its name from a town in the West Riding of Yorkshire where it was first made. Pennystones were always sold in the white and were therefore also known as forest whites. Some varieties were friezed, or given a napped finish. Regulations for the length, breadth, and weight of a piece were established as early as 1551 (Beck).

By the mid-eighteenth century they were dyed; Beekman's orders to merchants in Liverpool and Bristol specified the colors red, blue, and green.

PERCALE
(perkale)

A fine cotton cloth originally from India where it was sold white or dyed blue. Measuring just over a yard, "percallaes" were used in India as one of the ground cloths for painted chintz (Irwin and Brett, p. 8).

Percale was manufactured in England in 1670 and in France in 1780 (Caulfeild and Saward). Ackermann comments on the material in 1816: "Perkale, as they call cambric muslin, is now almost the only thing worn in the morning costume: you must not, however, fancy that this proceeds from a wish to encourage English manufacture, but partly from a love for novelty, and partly because it is less expensive than cambric, and equally fashionable" (*Repository,* 2d ser., 1, no. 5 [May 1816]: 306). Printed percales were used for shirting.

PERCALINE

A highly finished and dressed percale in plain weave sold in solid colors for lining, stiffening, and bookbinding. Some varieties received a moiré finish. It was used for a type of appliqué called Elysée work, described by Caulfeild and Saward in 1882, with floral designs "cut out of light colored sateen cloth, laid upon dark sateen and ornamented with embroidery stitches in colored filoselles."

PEROPUS
(parapes, perapos)

A stuff of combing wool or mixed silk and wool; a kind of camlet. Ash-colored, green, and watered peropuses are listed in seventeenth-century English inventories (Beck).

According to John Taylor, the water poet, writing in 1624 in his *Praise of Hempseed,* it and several other fabrics were mixed with linen:

> Alas! what would our silk mercers be,
> What would they do, sweet Hempseed, without thee?
> Rash, taffeta, paropa, and novato,
> Shag, filizetta, damaske, and mochado.
> [Beck.]

See also Mockado.

PERPETUANA
(perpcheana, perpets)

A durable woolen fabric given "a defensive, artificial selling name" similar to everlasting, durance, and sempiternum (Coleman, p. 425). Like serge, it was made of combing and carding wool mixed together in a twill weave, as distinct from everlasting composed of combing wool (Beck). As one of the lighter New Draperies it was described in 1613: "There are some merchants that deal in stuffs termed new drapery, especially in perpetuanas, which are now grown to great use and traffic, but not likely to continue long by their falsehood" (James, p. 134).

In 1678 an English pamphleteer commented on the increased popularity of calicoes imported from India at the expense of woolen goods:

> This [woolen] trade is very much hindered by our people who do wear many foreign commodities instead of our own. Instead of green sey, that was wont to be used for children's frocks, is now used painted and India stained and striped calicoes, and instead of a perpetuano or shalloon to line men's coats with, is used sometimes a glazened calico which in the whole is not above twelve shillings cheaper, and abundantly worse. [*Ancient Trades Decayed, Repaired Again.*]

In the next century Postlethwayt wrote that "Perpetuanas designed for the Spanish West-Indies are commonly sent in assortments of 40 pieces, viz. 15 green paroquet, 15 pieces blue, 5 musc-colour, 5 black."

Perpetuanas were received at the Massachusetts Bay Company storehouse as early as 1629/30 (Dow, *Every Day Life,* p. 240). For bed hangings a 1648 English reference mentions "a counterpane to the yellow perpetuana bed" (OED); and in Virginia 1653, "curtains of red perpetuana" (Frances Little, p. 211). In the Wharton inventory of 1677/78 are "3 yrds. red perpetuana" and "1 perpetuance under pettecoate" (Dow, *Every Day Life,* pp. 265, 266).

Preserved among municipal papers in Poland is a swatch of perpetuana dated 1690 and described: *Une étoffe très mince, bien pressée, faite de laine peignée teinte en masse, à armure sergé 2/2, quelque peu moins foulonnée que l'Englische Cronrasche, son voisin dans la collection* (Endrei, "Tissus d'usage," p. 27).

In the Richelieu Papers a swatch of *Perpetuelle à carreaux* from Rheims, 1736, has a small lozenge pattern woven in yellow and tan wool (Lh45b, p. 96). A swatch of *Perpetuanne ou Drap de Silesie* in beige wool with white lozenges centering four dots; and a swatch of the same pattern in red-brown are found in another volume without date (Lh40, swatch nos. 8 and 9; Weigert, pls. 165, 166). "Perpetuanas—English Everlastings" in red, black, and

shades of olive green are found in the Berch Papers. They are woven in fine weft-float patterns and date from 1753.

See also Everlasting.

PERSIAN

A thin plain silk, principally used for linings in coats, petticoats, and gowns in the eighteenth century. Silks from Persia were the most highly esteemed of all Eastern fabrics, and the name *Persian* may first have been given to English imitations to promote their sale. In 1782 the anonymous English author of *The Contrast* declared of them: "Indeed, we cannot conveniently do without slight Silks, such as Persians, Sarsnets, Modes, and Sattins for cloaks" (p. 20).

In 1831 Lardner categorized silk textiles:

> The plainest mode of silk-weaving takes the name of Persian, sarsnet, gros-de-naples, ducapes, &c., varying only in the thickness of the fabric, or the quality of the material of which it is composed, and not at all differing in the arrangements of its interlacings.
>
> The quality first mentioned [Persian] is exceedingly flimsy in its texture, and has of late nearly gone out of use, its place being taken by the description next in quality, sarsnet. This which used to form the substance of garments, is now most usually employed for lining them, giving place in its turn, as regards its former more dignified uses, to gros-de-naples. This last is made of stouter and harder thrown organzine silk, and is put together with more care and labour, containing a greater number of threads, both warp and shoot, in a given surface. Ducapes are likewise plain-wove stout silks, but of softer texture than the last. [P. 296.]

Persian silks were imported by the East India Company to London and then, in turn, to the colonies. "Persian silke" is listed in a Salem inventory of 1684/85 (Dow, *Every Day Life,* p. 271); and in Boston Samuel Sewall noted in his diary for 1724

FIG. D-82. Persanne Rayé à Bouquet, *checked silk taffeta or Persian with a pot of flowers painted in one square. From a French pattern book, ca. 1760. (Warner Archive, Victoria and Albert Museum.)*

"My wife wore her new Gown of Sprig'd Persian" (7:332).

In 1737 James Alexander of New York ordered red, white, and blue Persians, and by 1760 additional colors such as rose, pink, and black were specified. "Lemmon colour'd" and green can be added from the Caine broadside of 1754. A Beekman order for "Persian taffatys" in 1770 included black, green, blue, and striped (2:931). Whether these were made in the East or in England cannot be determined. In 1778 Sally Wister of Philadelphia recorded in her journal, "put on a new purple and white striped Persian, white petticoat, muslin apron, gauze cap and handkerchief" (p. 58). The Warner Archive includes a swatch of *Persanne Rayé à Bouquet* (Fig. D-82).

For a state bed George Smith suggested that the furniture should be of lilac silk, embroidered border and lining, with rose-coloured Persian; the counterpane the same" (*Household Furniture,* p. 6).

See also Taffeta.

PERUVIAN
(Peruvienne)

A fancy eighteenth-century silk dress material. A silk woven of threads of two different colors in such a way as to present two sides of different shades (Havard). Like prusianett it was reversible.

See also Droguet.

PETERSHAM

"A very thick, shaggy kind of woollen cloth, of a dark navy blue colour, employed for men's overcoats, and what are called 'pilot coats,' suitable for seafaring purposes, or for wear in very severe weather" (Caulfeild and Saward).

At the New York industrial exhibition of 1853, cheaper imitation petershams "with a curled surface," made in New England by a felting process, were judged "superior to even the general run of common cloths for overcoats" (Wallis, p. 17).

PHILIP AND CHENEY

A worsted material; Philip was later dropped from the name. Beck cites the following reference from the *Household Books of Lord William Howard:* in 1624 "10 yeards of crimson in grain chamblet, phillip and china, 40s," and in 1627, "15 ycardes of waterd Phillip and Cheyney for Sir William Howard's children, 27s. 6d."

See also Cheney.

PHILISELLE

A seventeenth-century worsted cloth made in Norwich; a kind of double camlet.

See also New Draperies.

PILLOW

A common, plain fustian. A 1696 draper's handbook defines "Pillow fustian" as "exceeding strong for Wast-Coats and for Lining of Breeches, but many will not use them for either, because they think them too thick, it being double wove; . . . some are Brown, those are always dyed sad colour for men's Frocks" (Wadsworth and Mann, p. 114).

"Twelve pieces plain dyed Pilloes" at prices ranging from 24 to 32 shillings a piece in "sorted midling brown and olives" were ordered in 1767 by James Beekman; in 1770 he ordered "24 pieces Olive Coloured Pillows . . . and handsome browns" (2: 837, 842). In contrast, in 1768 Samuel Rowland Fisher ordered in Manchester "neat drabs, doves, and Leads, no Olives" which were the same colors he specified for jeans and velverets.

John Holker's manuscript contains two swatches of pillows in brown linen and cotton, or all cotton, in three qualities (swatches 42–44). They are twilled and have a soft pile. Holker states that the all-cotton variety with mechanically spun warp and weft yarns had superior wearing qualities and was suitable for the clothing of workmen, domestic servants, and hostlers. Pillow of finer quality and bleached (swatch 44) encased feather beds, pillows, and bolsters.

PILOT CLOTH

Heavy, stout, and coarse navy blue twilled woolen fabric finished with a nap. Used by seamen.

See also Petersham.

PINTADO

In sixteenth-century Portuguese texts, the word applied to cheap block-printed cotton cloth made in India (Irwin and Brett, p. 1n). But in the following century, the words *pintado* and *chintz* indicated the rich arborescent and floral cottons of fine quality mordant-painted and resist-dyed in India.

From about the middle of the seventeenth century, explicit directions and actual patterns to appeal to the western market were sent by East India Company merchants to their agents. In 1657 an order was placed for "Chints or Pintadoes 1,000 pieces . . . Pintadoe Quilts that may match the works of ye Chints, 300" (Irwin and Brett, p. 27). The 1660 London Book of Rates lists "Pintadoes or Callecoe cubbard clothes" (Dow, *Every Day Life,* p. 252).

For the remainder of the century, sales in England for clothing and furnishing were enormous. Several laws were enacted for the protection of the English weaving industry, and in 1720 "the Use and Wearing in Apparel" of imported chintz, and also its "use or Wear in or about any Bed, Chair, Cushion, or other Household furniture" were prohibited (Irwin and Brett, p. 5).

See also Palampore.

PIQUÉ

A name derived from a French verb, *piquer,* meaning to quilt. White cotton piqués in imitation of hand-quilting were woven in the loom from about the third quarter of the eighteenth century, and examples appear in issues of the *Journal für Fabrik* for March 1794, December 1794, and September 1795.

Later definitions describe piqué as a stout, strong cotton dress goods woven in either cross-rib effects or in figures. Uses for piqué included infants' coats, carriage robes for summer, cravats, trimmings, skirts, vests, and dresses (Denny). Men's dress clothes—white ties, vests, and stiff-bosomed shirts—are made of piqué. Pictures of modern "piqués or toilet welts," "matelassé fabrics," and "toilet quilting fabrics," all related, are discussed in detail by Nisbct (pp. 413–72).

Tiny swatches of a white piqué from Rouen are attached to two 1779 invoices among the John

FIG. D-83. *Pink silk satin piqué. From an apprentice weaver's book, Lyons, 1840. (Collection of Mrs. Rockwell Gardiner.)*

Holker, Jr., Papers in the Library of Congress. Dozens of similar patterns are found in merchants' swatch books of the late eighteenth century. A nineteenth-century example is shown at figure D-83.

See also Manchester goods, Marcella.

PIRAMIDES

A fine, narrow worsted made with yarns of two colors twisted together.

See also New Draperies, Say.

PLAID

A twill or plain woven cloth with a pattern of intersecting stripes in both the warp and weft. The patterns may also be printed.

A typical "Scotch Pload," shown in the Holker manuscript (see Pl. D-32), was worn by Scots, particularly the mountain men, and by members of the Scottish Regiments serving in England. It was also made into men's dressing gowns. A 1738 Boston newspaper advertised "Banjans made of Worsted Damask, Brocaded Stuffs, Scotch Plods and Calliminco" (Earle, *Costume,* p. 51).

Both summer and winter fashions in silk plaids are found in a sample book from the Warner Archive. George Wilson of Hawick, Scotland, received a bronze medal "for Shepherd Plaids, Tweeds, and Travelling Plaids, superiority of Shepherd Plaids, and excellence of other articles" at the 1853 New York industrial exhibition (Dilke, p. 28). Indeed, plaids have never been long out of fashion for blankets, scarves, neckties, ribbons, and clothing.

PLAINBACK

A worsted manufacture introduced into Yorkshire about 1813. It was the predecessor of merino but was stouter. Of single warp and weft, the name is derived from the fabric's twilled face but plain back (James, p. 374).

See also Bombazet, Bombazine.

PLATILLA

A very fine, well-bleached linen first made in Silesia and later in France. According to Savary des Bruslons it was exported primarily to Spain, the Spanish West Indies, and the Guinea coast. In 1833 Perkins wrote that they were "put up in the very same way as *Cholets.* On the slip [label?] near the end of the piece is a silver paper with the inscription *Platilles Royales.*" Others were called *bocadillos* or *platilles simples.*

Two "peices of course Plattillous" valued at £3.02.06 were listed in a 1693 Carolina inventory (Baldwin). "White Platillas; dyed do." were advertised in the Boston *Palladium* on May 8, 1810.

PLUNKET

One of a group of coarse woolen cloths including "azures, blues, sorting-cloths, short cloths, coloured and white" which in 1605 were "distinguished from the fine cloths by a blue selvedge or edging on both sides of the list" (Strutt). In the fifteenth century such coarse cloths included, in addition to plunkets, "turkins, celestrines, packing-whits, vesses, cogware, worsteds, florences, bastards, kendals, sayling-ware with crewil lists, and frise-ware" (Beck). Beck suggests that the word derives from the French *blanchet* ("blanket").

PLUSH
(Fr. peluche)

Wool velvet. A kind of stuff with a velvet nap or shag on one side "composed of a weft of a single woolen thread, and a double warp, the one wool, of two threads twisted, the other goats-hair. Some plushes are made entirely of worsted and others composed wholly of hair" (Chambers). Plush was made in all colors and was used for breeches, waistcoats, and winter jackets (Savary des Bruslons). It was frequently used for furnishing and occasionally for altar frontals and pulpit cloths.

In Boston in 1741 a runaway servant wore "a pair of orange colored plush breeches" (Dow,

Every Day Life, p. 66). "Green, blue and red Hair Plush" were advertised in the *Providence Gazette* on February 21, 1789.

A specialty of France, plush was woven in that country beginning in the late seventeenth century. Swatches of plush characteristic of Amiens manufactures of about 1762 are preserved in the Archives de la Somme (Havard). From "among the fashionable articles for gentlemen's wear," Ackermann includes in his *Repository* a swatch of red "plush, manufactured from mohair, some of which are made in imitation of fur, others rival an article of the same nature made with silk" (see Pl. D-87). Silk plush had a longer pile than silk velvet.

Marx and Weigert of Berlin received an honorable mention for their "Stamped Furniture Plushes" at the 1853 New York industrial exhibition (Dilke, p. 29). In 1883 the Hartford Silk Manufacturing Company showed "black silk plush" and announced that soon it would have "full lines of the same in red, blue, old-gold, olive and other popular shadings. The introduction of upholstery plushes in these colors by an American house will be quite an event, and orders are already being recorded." (*Carpet Trade and Review* 14, no. 2 [January 15, 1883]: 35).

POINTS

Heavy woolen blankets used for barter. According to Plummer, who wrote of the blanket industry at Witney, "they are usually dyed some bright colour or colours and have short stripes, 4¼ inches long woven into the edge of the cloth at right angles to the selvedge near the corner. Half-points had stripes of 2½ inches in length" (p. 99). In the 1780s point blankets were first made at Witney for the Hudson Bay Company: "Soon the Indians understood that the short coloured bars, called points, at the edge of a blanket near the end represented an exchange or barter value of the same number of beaver skins. A bar half the normal length represented half a point, and was worth half a skin or an imperfect one" (Plummer and Early, p. 40).

In 1815, in answer to a request for prices and qualities from members of the Hudson's Bay House, John Early wrote from Witney:

The articles mostly shipped of our goods to the United States are as follows:—

Best	2½ point Blankets,			19/6 per pair.	
Com.	2½	"	"	13/6	"
Best	3	"	"	25/6	"
Com.	3	"	"	19/	"
Best	6/4 Stripd. Duffills		23 Blankets	£10.15.0 p. p ce.	
Com.	6/4	"	" (light)	28 "	£10.10.0 "
Best	7/4	"	"	16 "	£10.10.0 "
Com.	"	"	" (light)	20 "	£10.10.0 "

Our usual credit is 6 months or allow 5 per cent for cash. [Plummer, p. 244.]

POISEE

Sprigged or flowered satin, painted or printed in China (Lee-Whitman, p. 32ff.).

POLDAVY
(*poldavis*)

A kind of sailcloth. Named for Polle-Davy, a town in lower Brittany where it was first woven. In 1645 "20 pcs. poll Davis" were imported into Boston, as were "10 pcs poule Davis" in 1648 (Aspinwall Records, pp. 404, 406).

See also Sailcloth.

POMPADOUR

A blue-green color, a shade of pink, or a pattern of floral sprigs associated with Mme de Pompadour, mistress of Louis XV.

A remarkable document of sprigged chintz printed on a plum-colored ground is preserved in John Fanning Watson's manuscript for *Annals of Philadelphia*. Of it he wrote "No. 4 was called 'Pompadour' (its colour after 'Made P.') & was my mothers dress when young. It cost 1½ Drs a Yard." A deep purple-red swatch from a "Pompadour broad-Cloth Riding Dress" dated 1760 is in the Barbara Johnson album.

PONGEE

"A thin soft clothing and curtain fabric of Chinese origin woven from uneven threads of raw silk and possessing a characteristic ecru or tan color; also an imitation of this fabric" (Merriam-Webster). Early in the nineteenth century, this fabric was dyed other colors as well, for in Canton (September 27, 1815) it could be purchased in yellow, buff, pink, light blue, white, straw, and black; and in "Prices Current at Canton" (1807), a trader wrote that pongee is a peculiar kind of silk, very strong and wears a great while, that it may be had of all colors and of different qualities. He recommended its use for cloak and coat linings (China Trade Records).

POPLIN
(*Fr. papeline*)

A lightweight dress goods. According to Lardner "Poplins and Lustres are composed partly of silk and partly of worsted, with a somewhat larger portion of the former material than enters into the composition of bombasin.... Poplins were manufactured of exceedingly fine qualities in Dublin" (p. 299). The fine silk warps completely covered the coarser worsted wefts for a corded, or ribbed, effect. Savary des Bruslons describes poplin as: *une étoffe assez légère, dont la chaine est de soie & la treme de fleuret ou filoselle. Il s'en fait de plaines, de figurées & de toutes couleurs. Grisettes, ne sont que de veritables Papelines.*

According to Webster, "Dublin is the place where they are made of the first quality. Superb patterns have been manufactured for court dresses, in gold and silver, on white, pink, and azure grounds, with flowers, and of every variety of colour" (p. 972).

In 1754 Beekman's London agent wrote: "Inclosed are 3 Patterns of Venetian Poplins 42 yards 16 Inches at 43 /. they are much in wear here and we have different Colours" (Beekman Papers, 2:535). Richard Wistar of Philadelphia ordered in 1766 "2 ps Yard Wide Corded Poplin, brown Ground & Yellow Silk Stripes, the Other Some What upon the Purple Colour." Samuel Rowland

Fisher saw "Venetian Poplins, some Sattin Stripes" at Kidderminster in 1767.

James Alexander frequently ordered poplins and on occasion retained a piece of the cloth which he was sending to London for a sample (see Pl. D-9). In the copies of his orders for 1736, June 1738, and 1739 there are fourteen swatches of silk and wool poplins in color combinations of blue/gold, green/red, yellow/brown, white/black, yellow/red, and white/red. In addition, one 1760 order without swatches includes brown/orange, brown/green, and brown/pink. Twelve swatches of plain and striped poplin made in Nîmes in 1736 are among the Richelieu Papers (Lh45 I, pp. 50, 51). The Moccasi manuscript of about 1760 contains London-made *Poupline larghe* in black and in a polychrome silk stripe with pink wool weft (see Pl. D-53). A swatch of "silver grey figured poplin . . . for evening dress, when the change of mourning takes place" is found in Ackermann's *Repository* for 1810 (4, no. 24 [December 1810]: 372). It is woven with a white silk warp and gray woolen weft in a fine lozenge pattern.

The fabric is often linked with tabinet.

PRESSING

Thomas Webster's mid-nineteenth-century definition of the process for woolen cloth reads:

> The cloth being doubled and laid in even folds, a leaf or sheet of glazed pasteboard is inserted between each fold of the cloth; it is then laid in the press, and covered with thin wooden boards, in which are placed iron plates properly heated; and on the whole the top of the press is brought down, with the degree of force judged necessary to give it the proper gloss. [P. 943.]

A sample of glazed pasteboard used for pressing is in the Moccasi manuscript (see Pl. D-60).

See also Moreen.

PRINCE'S EVERLASTING

Patent number 1437 was granted to Joshua Bennett in 1784 for "Prince's everlasting union" made of worsted, mohair, and silk (Warner, p. 637).

PRINCE'S LINEN

A cheap linen fabric. John Banister specified twenty-five ells of prince's linen as an inside wrap for printed calicoes and chintzes in 1739. George Bartram listed prince's linen with dowlas in his advertisement in the *Pennsylvania Chronicle,* September 7, 1767.

James Beekman's London agent, "having just landed a fresh sortment of princes linnen" supplied him with "ten pieces finer than those sent . . . by Livingston." The fabric cost 8 pence per ell throughout the period 1766 to 1784 (2:549).

PRINCE'S STUFF

A silk and worsted cloth patented in 1744 (number 611) by which wool was combed with silk to be used instead of mohair yarn for "lutherines, rufferines, princes stuff or prunellas which was chiefly used in making clergymen's gowns" (Warner, p. 637). Prince's stuff, however, was known earlier in the century, for "a Rutherine or Princes-Stuff black Wastcoat, only the Body lin'd and that with strip'd Dimmity" was advertised in the *London Gazette,* December 3, 1713.

PRINCETTA

A Norwich manufacture begun in the late 1830s and made of silk warp and worsted filling. In 1844, it was described as "a sharper handling cloth than a paramatta" (James, p. 528).

PRUNELLA

One of the worsted textiles made at Norwich. In 1727 James Scottowe advertised in the *Norwich Gazette* that he had "neat woven whims flowered in the loom with silk up or worstead [i.e., bro-

FIG. D-84. *Silk* Prusiennes *with small warp-faced sprigs. From a French pattern book, ca. 1760.* (*Warner Archive, Victoria and Albert Museum.*)

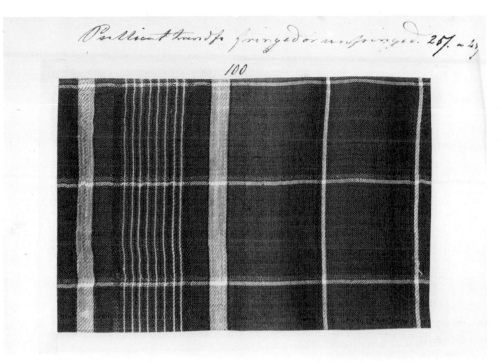

Pulliat hand. fringed or unfringed. 25 . ~ 25

100

FIG. D-85. *Silk pullicat handkerchief, twill weave in red with green and white stripes and bands. Made in India. From Handkerchief pattern book. Paper in the book is watermarked 1787. (Cooper-Hewitt Museum, gift of Mrs. Samuel S. Walker.)*

caded] on a white prunel at reasonable rates" (Warner, p. 284). *See* Prince's stuff.

In the 1660s a worsted prunella petticoat was owned in Virginia, and a Boston resident in the early 1690s owned a "Blacke Prunella Gowne and Petticoat." By 1740 prunella was used for women's shoes, and by 1772 "Strong rich black silk and Hair Prunella [was used] for Clergymens Coats and Waistcoats" (Earle, *Costume,* pp. 192–93). Until recent times it has been used for academic gowns and judges' robes as well. Not all prunellas were black. The *Mercurius Publicus* (London), May 31, 1660, records the loss of "A white Dimity Bag wrought with red Worsted, having therein a pink-coloured silk Prunella Petticoat, laced round with one broad silver lace, and two up before, with linnen and other necessaries." In 1767 Samuel Rowland Fisher ordered "9 ps drab Prunellos and blue Prunellos." A May 26, 1779, *New Jersey Gazette* advertisement listed "7 yards of prunella, the warp orange colour, and the filling blue." James Beekman's orders from 1766 to 1784 were generally for black, white, and colored, some of which were "narrow striped."

Modern definitions suggest that it was a 2/1

warp faced twill; some was made with cotton filling in a satin weave. It resembled lasting.

PRUSIANETT

A fancy eighteenth-century silk dress material; a reversible, small-patterned silk with the warp forming the pattern. Similar to a droguet. Joubert said of it: *C'est une modification encore de la Peruvienne, elle se fait par le moyen d'un poil qui, par l'industrieuse mécanique du métier, fait dessin des deux côtés de l'étoffe, c'est à dire, qui n'a point d'envers.* French samples are found in the Warner Archive (Fig. D-84). *Prusienne* was also a changeable fabric with a weft of a third color (Havard).

In 1772 Samuel Boardman of Wethersfield, Connecticut, ordered "1 Piece prusinett, No. 17— 28 yds." from New York.

PULLICATE
(*pullicat*)

A colored cotton or silk handkerchief, originally made at Pulicat, a town on the Madras coast (Fig. D-85). From about 1785 the fabric was imitated in England largely for South American markets. Harmuth described it as "pale-orange colored."

Q

QUALITY

A binding tape made of worsted, silk, or cotton in several grades (see Pl. D-36). In the nineteenth century, it was used especially for carpet binding. James Beekman's 1769 order to Bristol is typical:

> 26 gross fine worsted Quality at 6/6. Vizt. 6 black, 2 red, 1 pinck, 1 Scarlet, 4 browns, 1 yellow, 6 dark blue, 2 light blue, 2 Saxon green, 1 dark green
> 33 gross fine shoe quality at 4/9. Vizt. 8 black, 8 cloth blues, 1 light blue, 1 Saxon blue, 1 Saxon green, 1 yellow, 2 pinck, 1 Scarlet, 2 green, 8 dark sorted cloth colours. [2:875.]

In 1764 Beekman's London agent wrote that "the finess does not make it dearer 'tis the Colour and may have as fine as you please. I imagine you want it of same kind as the green, blue and yellow etc. are, of which are generally finer than Cloths and Drabbs, the latter being made stouter for Taylors, and the other is calculated more for Milliners and Ladys use" (2:762–63).

"3 Ps Silk quallitys @ 8/" were inventoried with "Gallune" and "Broad & Narrow ferrit" in Delaware in 1743 (Grafton).

QUEENS CORD

Stout, ribbed cotton trousering. In 1784 James Beekman ordered "8 pieces Corduroys" and "8 pieces Queens Cord" and specified they should be "handsome Olive and fashionable Colours. different prices" (3:1115).

R

RADZIMIR
(radsimir, rasdimore)

"A very rich description of silk textile, especially designed for Mourning, and otherwise known as Queen's Silk, her Majesty [Queen Victoria] having always patronised it. It is a kind of silk serge, and the name is synonymous with the French *Ras de St. Maur,* by which a silk dress material was designated in the last century, when it was much in fashion" (Caulfeild and Saward). Weigert said that eighteenth-century "Ras de Saint-Maur" was made entirely of silk, or of silk and *fleuret* (fine wool), or of wool warp and silk weft. It was dyed black.

In February 1763, it was advertised in the *British Chronicle* among "a very great assortment of Rich Brocades, Tissues, flowered and plain Sattins, Tabbies, Ducaps, black Armozeens, Rasdumores, Mantuas, &c." (Beck).

RANTER

A worsted fabric made in the early eighteenth century.

RASH
(rasse; Fr. ras, meaning smooth)

A cloth of combing and carding wool mixed. Like serge, it was usually twill woven and is found mentioned among New Draperies. Rashes covered a wide variety of woolen goods—some were close cropped, without nap, others were shaggy. Silk rashes and silk and wool mixtures were also made.

"Ten cloth rashes" were shipped to Boston in 1648 (Aspinwall Records, p. 407). Samuel Sewall found that "black Rashes" which he had had for three years "were not vendable" in 1698 (Letter book, 1:208).

Swatches in the Richelieu Papers of 1736 and 1737 made in Holland and in France are twilled, lightweight cloths in white and in colors.

RATTEEN
(ratine)

A thick woolen stuff, twill woven "on a loom with four treddles, like serges that have the whale or quilling. There are some rateens prepared like [broad]cloths, others left simply in the hair [i.e., not sheared]; and others where the hair or nap is frized" (Postelthwayt). Ratteens were chiefly manufactured in France, Holland, and Italy, and mostly used in linings; "the frize is a sort of coarse rateen; the drugget, a rateen half linen, half woollen" (Chambers). "Drugget, Baize, Frieze, and other coarse cloths are known in commerce by the general name of rateens" (Booth, p. 182).

A runaway Negro slave "wore a green Ratteen Coat, Waistcoat, and Breeches" in Boston in 1746 (Dow, *Arts and Crafts,* p. 197). In 1757 and 1759, Albany merchants ordered "Knept [napped] Scarlet Ratten," "Good Green Do.," and "Dark gray Ratteen" from James Beekman in New York (2:659, 665).

Benjamin Dolbeare's 1787 Boston inventory lists the following furnishing ratteens: "1 Crimson rateen Easy Chair," "1 [crimson rateen] bed with 6 window Curtains," "6 black Walnut Chairs with ratteen bottoms."

In the Richelieu Papers dated 1736, five swatches of *Ratines de Beauvais* used for *"habillement des Paysans . . . et pour Juppons de femmes," "Juppons de dessous pour les Dames,"* and *"Redin-*

gottes d'hommes" are white, or white with blue stripes, heavy and woolly (Lh45 I, p. 43); one swatch of *Ratine à poil* and sixteen swatches of friezed ratines from Holland are in another volume (Lh45 V, p. 23). Ratteens from Rouen, Abbeville, London, and Holland (see Pl. D-53) are in the Moccasi manuscript.

See Revêche.

RATTINET
(ratinet)

A thinner, lighter ratteen similar to shalloon. Both materials were generally used for lining clothes and are frequently found advertised in late eighteenth-century newspapers as "Best London superfine Broad Cloths, with rattinets to match" (Gottesman, 1777–99, p. 135). In the Boston *Palladium* for May 8, 1810, T. and J. Wiggin offered "black and blue Rattinets." One of James Beekman's orders called for "handsome cloth browns." Samuel Rowland Fisher and Arthur Young both visited Romsey, about ten miles north of Southampton, which they described as an important center for the manufacture of both shalloons and rattinets. Fisher noted that rattinets of the best kind were sold white.

A pair of green rattinet window curtains were among the household effects left by Sarah Arnold of Fort George, New York, in 1772 (Arnold inventory). "Buff Colour'd Rattinet" was used to line silk window curtains in the drawing room at Mersham-Le-Hatch, owned by Sir Edward Knatchbull, a customer of Thomas Chippendale in the late 1770s (Boynton, p. 102).

RAVENSDUCK

A coarse canvas or sailcloth.

RENFORCE

A slight silk. In the year 1692 the Company of Alamode, Renforce and Lustrings was incorporated in London (Warner, p. 630). In 1698 the firm

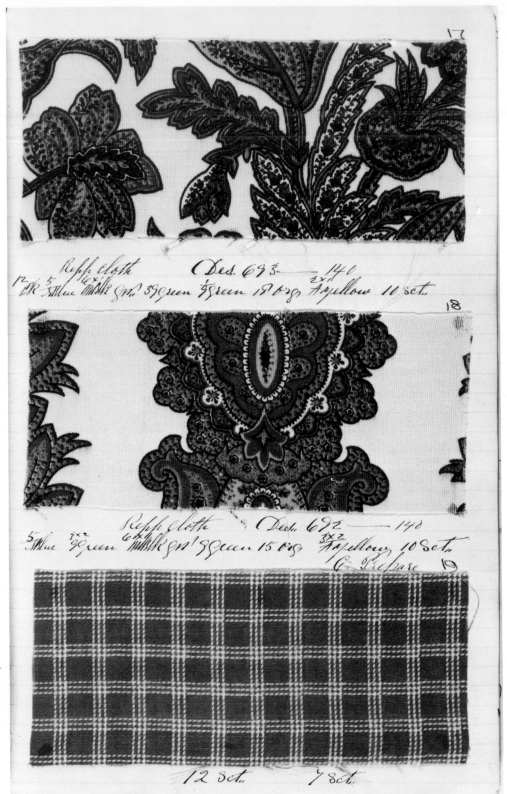

FIG. D-86. Two swatches
of "Repp Cloth" dated 1871.
Wool, plain weave with paired
warps, loosely woven. Presumably the lowest untitled
swatch is a delaine made of
wool in plain, loose weave.
From a sample book inscribed
"Delaines Book," from Old
Pacific Print Works, Law-
rence, Massachusetts. (Cooper-
Hewitt Museum, gift of Frederick J. Whitehead.)

"obtained an act of parliament . . . that they enjoy the sole use, exercise, and benefit of making, dressing, and lustrating, plain black alamodes, renforcez, and lustrings, in England and Wales for fourteen years" (Macpherson, 2:701).

In France the word was used in connection with velvets (*panne*) by Savary des Bruslons and Roland de la Platière.

REP

Cloth of plain weave with a ribbed effect achieved by means of heavier weft yarns covered with finer, more numerous warp yarns (Fig. D-86). Beck distinguishes rep as having heavier wefts as compared with cords which have heavier warps. Reps were made of silk, wool, or silk and wool.

Robert Albrecht of Chemnitz, Saxony, was awarded a bronze medal "for Upholstery Materials of superior execution, in Silk Brocade and Silk and Woolen Reps" at the 1853 New York industrial exhibition (Dilke, p. 26).

REVÊCHE

A "plain woven, soft French wool cloth of English origin, having a long nap, often curled [or frized], on one side. Later made in twilled serge weave, with a soft, spongy, fulled body" (Harmuth).

Richelieu Papers, dated 1736, contain a swatch of loosely woven white flannel in plain weave called *Revêche de Beauvais pour mettre derrière les glaces de Miroir,* a use cited by Thomas Sheraton for English flannel.

ROANNES

The English name for linen cloth made in Rouen from the fifteenth century (OED). Harmuth described it as a textile made of cotton and linen used for bedding.
See also Rouen.

ROLL

A cloth traditionally rolled rather than folded. It is often found mentioned as brown rolls, which may refer to unbleached linen. In 1767/68, Samuel Rowland Fisher ordered "36 Brown Roles @ 5d" together with other coarse cloths like hessian, sailcloth, dowlas, brown sheeting, and osnaburg.

ROLLER PRINTING

See Cylinder printing.

ROMAL
(*rumal*)

A handkerchief imported from India; a cover or decorative piece. Silk, cotton, and Serunge romals were prohibited in England at the end of the seventeenth century (Kress, S2200).

One "peece fine Romalls qt. 115 Hancher [handkerchief] neck cloths at 2/" was sent from Boston to Taunton in 1688 (Watkins) Samuel Boardman listed "1 Piece Silk Lunge Romall Handkr. No. 30, qt. 15" in his 1772 account book. Benjamin Wister ordered the following romals from London in 1789:

  40 pieces India Cotton Romals, blue and white—if at or under 11/ Send double the Quantity
  30 pieces do do do red mixt—if at or under 11/ Send 2/3rds more
  10 pieces do do do large red Check'd
   8 pieces best Red Silk Pullicat Romals
  18 pieces Lungee narrow Stripd do in 16 a piece. Send none but red Striped.

A pattern book containing a fascinating variety of ninety-five handkerchief swatches, mounted on paper watermarked "London 1787," is preserved in the Cooper-Hewitt Museum. The samples range from sturdy checked linens to delicate muslins, some with additions of silk and others entirely of silk. Although not identified by place of manufacture, the silk and cotton romals, lungis (Fig. D-87), pullicates, and lustring silk handkerchiefs were probably imported from India for the English market.

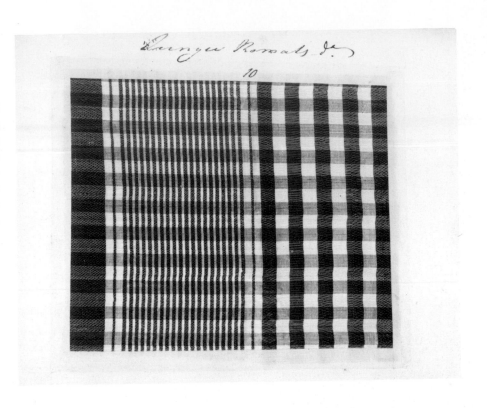

FIG. D-87. *Lungi Romal handkerchief of silk, plain weave with red and white stripes and bands. Made in India. From Handkerchief pattern book. Paper in the book is watermarked 1787. (Cooper-Hewitt Museum, gift of Mrs. Samuel S. Walker.)*

ROSETTA

Glazed worsted twill. A swatch in rose color found in the eighteenth-century Yorkshire pattern book is identified as "16 inches 27 yds, warp double yarn, at 31s. pr. ps. com. colours" (see Pl. D-103).

"One Gown and Petticoat of a Blue Rosetta Silk, the Petticoat flounced" were stolen in London (*Daily Courant,* September 3, 1715).

ROUEN

In the manufacture of cotton goods, the northern French city of Rouen was the counterpart of Manchester. A wide variety of textiles were produced and are known from sample books and manuscripts (see Pls. D-50, D-51, D-91, D-94). They can readily be compared to English manufactures, for there can be no question of the commercial rivalry between the two nations and the extensive smuggling carried on in order to procure patterns.

Among the most important Rouen manufactures were siamoises. First woven of silk and cotton, from about 1693 they were made of linen warp and cotton weft in stripes and checked patterns. Figured and sprigged patterns in linen and cotton in the Richelieu Papers resemble fancy Norwich calimancoes of worsted; in fact one example is captioned *façon de calmande* (Weigert, pl. 84).

During the eighteenth century, the finest, most expensive silk textiles were produced in Lyons where the best designers were commissioned. In general Rouen copied their patterns in less expensive silk-and-cotton combination fabrics. Of them the Maurepas Papers say: *Les Étoffes soye et Cotton de Rouen sont faites dans le même gout que celles en soye des manufactures de Lyon, tant en uni qu'en figuré et en Broché* (see Pls. D-44, D-45, D-46, D-47, D-48).

Another large group of less expensive textiles known to dealers earlier in this century as *toiles Normande* or *toiles de Marseilles* once were called *barrage.* The patterns of wool brocaded flowers on linen/cotton cloth also follow styles found in Lyons dress silks.

Imported East Indian fabrics such as cherryderrys, messinets, and dimities were imitated by weavers of Rouen just as they were by English weavers.

Fig. D-88. *Mention of green rugs occurs over and over again in eighteenth-century records. This fragment of a tufted green wool rug may be an example of the kind imported to the colonies. (Winterthur Museum.)*

RUFFERINE

A silk and worsted textile made in Norwich in the eighteenth century.

See also Prunella.

RUG
(rugg)

A coarse wool cloth with a shagged or friezed finish used as garments by the poorer classes and, doubtless, as bed coverings. For its history, see Beck.

From James Alexander's records, it is clear that rugs were a kind of cloth rather than floor carpets. He ordered, in 1746, 2-yard and 2¼-yard widths in several qualities: "24 8/4 Spotted Rugs at 6/6," "24 8/4 Green [rugs at] 14/," and "12 9/4 [rugs at] 16/" (Fig. D-88)

RUSSEL
(rushell)

A worsted damask woven in solid colors, two colors, or brocaded. In *The Weaver's True Case* (1719), women's dresses are described: "Our Country Farmers Wives, and other good Country Dames [are clothed] with woorsted Damasks, flower'd Russels, and flower'd Calimancoes, and the meanest of them with plain woorsted Stuffs" (p. 39).

Philip Benezet, merchant of Philadelphia, wrote in 1771 of "3/4 wide Callemancoe, which you call Russells" (Cox, p. 106). In finishing, these fabrics were "hot-pressed, or calendered to give the lustrous appearance of satin" (Caulfeild and Saward).

By far the most complete descriptions of the types of russels imported into New York are found in the Alexander Papers:

June 7, 1737

1 piece Green flowered Rushell 30 yds 40/
1 full blue flowered   Do
2 olives flowered   Do
1 brown flowered   Do
1 Drab flowered   Do

1 Black with a white flower Do
1 Blue with a white flower   Do
1 Green with a white flower Do
1 Light Olive with a white flower Do.
. . . By flowered & flowers I don't mean Sprigs but by flowered I mean Large running flowers of Same Colour as this is & by a white flower I mean Large running white flowers thro the whole ps.

June 1, 1738

1 ps flowered Rushell Red ground with a white & green flower
1 ps flowered Do. Colour like pattern annexed [no swatch] and flowers of same Colour
3 ps more a little Different
1 ps flowered Do. blue ground & white flowers
1 ps green ground & white flowers
1 ps purple ground & white flowers
1 ps black ground & white flowers
1 ps deep olive ground & white flowers
1 ps Deep Cinamon ground & white flowers
1 ps blue with a blue flower
1 Do. green with a green flower
1 ps Scarlet flowered Rushell with a Scarlet flower
3 ps of Brocaded Rushells near to the pattern but each ps Different
Let all be large new fashioned patterns.

June 23[, 1738,] pr Langden

3 ps Green flowered Rushell Large figures
3 ps blue   Do
1 ps Scarlet flowered Rushell, white ground. Scarlet, green, blue & yellow flowers mixt.
1 Do Scarlet ground white flower.

Opposite the first two items of the third order Alexander pinned swatches of light and dark blue worsted damask and one of green and olive (see Pl. D-8).

Swatches of black and olive glazed russels are found in the eighteenth-century Yorkshire pattern book (see Pl. D-103; see also Atkinson, p. 18).

Russels were used in the colonies for banyans, or men's dressing gowns, women's shoes (much more durable than silk brocade), bed and window curtains, and upholstery. A "double gown, one side silk stuff the other russel" was stolen in Boston, 1710/11 (Dow, *Every Day Life,* p. 68). The estate of Isaac Smith of Boston, probated in 1787, had the following furnishings which, presumably, all matched:

1 Easy Chair, green russell	£3.0.0
6 mahogany Chairs, russell bottoms	4.10.0
4 window Curtains	4.0.0
1 Set green russell Curtains, for Bed, Tester, &c.	4.0.0
	[SCPR, 86:100.]

A definition of about 1800 calls russel "a kind of lasting, manufactured of double warp and single weft, and with a fine should twill like the calimanco which it resembled in all respects except being stouter, having a double warp" (James, p.

362). By the 1880s, it was sometimes corded (russel cord) and "employed for making summer coats, scholastic gowns, lawyers' bags, &c. It is a mixture of cotton and wool, the cord being of cotton; and it washes well" (Caulfeild and Saward). Some were figured and made with silk warps for dresses.

RUSSET

A coarse woolen cloth dating from the Middle Ages which was worn by certain religious orders and the lowest classes of people. A kind of coarse homespun "sheepe's russet cloth, [was] called friers' cloth or shepheard's clothing" (Fairholt). In the eighteenth century, it was largely manufactured in Yorkshire.

RUTHERING

See Prince's stuff.

S

SAGATHY
(sagathee)

A slight woolen stuff of twill weave; a kind of serge or ratteen, sometimes mixed with a little silk. A "led-coloured saggathe coat and wastecoat" are referred to in 1712 (OED). In 1752 "a light cloth-colour'd Sagathy coat lined with Lead colour'd Allapine" was worn by a Philadelphia runaway (Earle, *Costume,* p. 210). Samuel Rowland Fisher noted "Silk Sagathys - 75/" among Norwich manufactures in his 1767/68 journal. James Beekman's orders generally specified blue, brown, and black sagathy. Those listed in Samuel Neave's 1774 inventory were "much eat."

Harmuth says it was "woven in four-leaf twill with a white warp and colored filling and given a high finish with the calendar." Swatches of London manufacture in brown and dark blue, twill

weave with a fleck of white twisted in the yarns are found in the 1760 Moccasi manuscript, as are two swatches of Exeter manufacture twill woven in gold and brown-and-white mixed (see Pl. D-59). A Castle Museum pattern book dated 1769 has swatches of green, blue/orange, and tan/white.

SAILCLOTH

The 1590 preamble to an act of Parliament states that "the cloths called mildernix and powel-davies, whereof sails and other furniture for the navy and shipping are made, were heretofore altogether brought out of France and other parts beyond sea, and the skill and art of making and weaving of the said cloths never known or used in England" (Beck).

FIG. D-89. *Twilled silk sarcenets. From a pattern book in the Warner Archive, 1810– 20. (Victoria and Albert Museum.)*

SALEMPORE
(salampore)

A staple cotton cloth woven on the coast of South India. It varied widely in quality and price; "the usual dimensions were 16 x 1 yard, thus coming between *Morees* and *Longcloth.*" It was "exported in large quantities to Europe from 1660 onwards" (Irwin and Schwartz).

In 1728 Thomas Bayeux of New York ordered "3 ps Selampores 162 yds at £2.10.0."

SAMITE

A medieval silk, interwoven or embroidered with gold, and richer and heavier than cendal. In the early seventeenth century, it was a kind of half silk with a lustrous satin finish (Michel).

SARASA

Printed cotton fabric from India, Thailand, and Java (batik). See Seika, *Mukashi-watari sarasa,* whose three volumes contain color illustrations showing a variety of patterns including floral, figural, and bird designs, geometrics, stripes, and checks. Techniques are illustrated by examples of tie-dyeing, "pinned" work, and resist printing, along with hand-painted and block-printed types. For illustrations of four pages, see Paula D. Preston, "A New Acquisition and the East India Trade," *New-England Galaxy* 9, no. 1 (Summer 1967): 59–63.

SARCENET
(sarsnet; Fr. armoisin)

A thin, transparent silk of plain weave. The name is derived from the Latin *Saracenus,* "from first having been woven by Saracens, probably in Spain." Beck suggested that it was not used extensively until the fifteenth century and probably displaced "the older kindred fabric cendal." Thicker than persian, sarcenet was woven twilled, as well as plain, and in all colors (Perkins). Sarcenet is listed in the seventeenth-century Ham House inventories in wide variety—changeable, clouded, florence, persian, and striped—where it was used for sun blinds, protective bed and furniture cases, and wall curtains in front of finer materials (Thornton and Tomlin, pp. 21, 52, and *passim*).

"Women's Sarsnet Quilted Patticoats 4 yards wide, Persian and Taminy Ditto" were advertised in a 1753 Boston newspaper (Earle, *Costume,* p. 183). In 1760 James Alexander ordered black and white and purple and white sarcenet handkerchiefs, and Kearny and Gilbert advertised a "Variety of figured, checked, striped and plain sarsnet and other ribbons" in the *Pennsylvania Chronicle,* April 20, 1767. In 1766 James Beekman ordered bright green, white, black, and "Sky Blue figured" sarcenets; "the figured Sarcenet to be Small Sprigged or flowers. as those Spotted or Dotted will not Sell" (2:773). Swatches of "Figured Lustrings or Sarsnetts" are found in a trader's book kept between 1797 and 1809 (see Fig. D-49).

Swatches of a great variety of fancy small-patterned sarcenets for ladies' dresses appear in the monthly issues of Ackermann's *Repository* during the second decade of the nineteenth century (see Fig. D-77). Swatches of twilled sarcenets are included in a sample book in the Warner Archive (Fig. D-89). Two swatches of green twill with small patterns dating from 1820 are preserved in a Public Record Office manuscript (BT 1/49).

See also Persian.

SATEEN

An irregular twill weave in which the satin effect is produced by predominant weft threads. Sateen often refers to a cotton material. (Emery, pp. 111, 137.)

See also Fig. D-76.

SATIN

"A kind of silken stuff, very smooth, and shining, the warp whereof is very fine, and stands out; the woof coarser, and lies underneath: on which

FIG. D-90. *Swatches of fine brocaded satins. Swatch no. 140 is a brocaded tappizadoe. From John Kelly's "Counterpart of Patterns," 1763. (Victoria and Albert Museum.)*

depends that gloss, and beauty, which is its price" (Chambers). In 1831 Lardner wrote:

> Satin is a twill of a peculiar description: the soft and lustrous face which it exhibits is given by keeping always a very large proportion, frequently even as much as seven out of every eight threads of the warp, visible, or as it is called, floating above the shoot. Satin is always woven with the face downwards, the labour of the weaver being thereby abridged, because it is easier to raise seven eighths of the warp with every cast of the shuttle. [P. 296.]

Emery's modern definition is similar:

> a *simple float-weave* structure. It is like *uneven twill* in having *dissimilar* faces, with warp-floats on one face and weft-floats on the other; but differs in that the diagonal alignment of floats is intermittent. The points at which floats are bound are dispersed so that successive wefts never bind or are bound by adjacent warps. The pattern of the dispersal of binding points can vary, as well as the float span; but the binding of floats is always single. [P. 108.]

The warp threads are ordinarily much finer than the weft threads and more numerous to the square inch so that they conceal the weft and make an unbroken, smooth, and lustrous surface.

Many worsted satins are found in the Norwich pattern books (see Pl. D-73). Some have additions of polychrome brocaded motifs and others are really damasks in one color or two but named "Bed Sattins."

The following satins were listed in the warehouse inventory of Boston merchant James Lloyd in 1693: "Gold colour'd flowered sattin, seed colour'd flowerd ditto, white sattin, sattin flowerd with gold, red sattin gold and silver, yellow flowerd sattin, sattin spotted blew, yellow plaine sattin" (SCPR, 13:267).

Extensive listings and some swatches of silk satins are found in the 1828–31 papers of James W. Latimer who ordered "China Sattins" in "sky blue, white very clear, white Pearl cast, brown, and green"; "Damasked ditto" were to be crimson, green, purple, sky blue, and gold.

Pattern books in the Warner Archive are rich in brilliant satins of Spitalfields manufacture for both spring and fall seasons. Some are figured, some have warp-printed motifs, and others are striped.

See also Figs. D-3, D-31, D-96.

Fig. D-91. *Worsted cloth identified from Norwich pattern books as "Brocaded Sattin" (actually a two-color damask) with floral centers brocaded in red, pink, yellow, and brown. (Winterthur Museum.)*

SATINET
(*satinette, sattinade*)

"A very slight, thin sort of sattin, chiefly used by the ladies for summer night-gowns, &c. and ordinarily striped. The word is a diminutive of sattin" (Chambers). "Sattinnett checks" (1768) and "Cross barred" and "Rich Striped Satenet" (1770) are among Beekman's orders (2:796, 815). In the 1786 Hilton manuscript, a swatch of twilled cotton satinet resembling denim is included (see Fig. D-39).

In Massachusetts by about 1810, satinet "was made of cotton-mill warps and of a woolen filling so overlying the former as to produce a cloth that could be finished like an all-wool fabric. These goods originally were substantial, and they speedily displaced serges and cheap cassimeres for outer garments of medium grade" (Clark, 1:564). Satinets were manufactured by 1825 in Paterson, New Jersey (Schwartz, p. 331). The fabric has also been described as an inferior kind of satin, sometimes a stout cotton satin with napped and shorn face and napped back.

From swatches of black worsted in satin weave found in a Norwich pattern book of 1794 in the Winterthur Museum Library, it can be determined that some satinet was made of wool. It resembled lasting and poplin. Beekman ordered "Settinet Lasting," probably meaning a worsted (3:1292).

For a discussion of satin, sateen, and satinet, see Emery (pp. 137–38).

SAXE GOTHA

John Banister ordered one 36-yard piece of this cloth at 9 shillings a yard in 1745, and, in another invoice, "4 ps Saxe Gotha—141 yards 22/6." The character of this cloth is unknown, but since much linen and hempen goods came from Germany in the eighteenth century, it probably was a kind of linen.

SAXONE

An inexpensive dress material with silk warp and linen weft. Three striped swatches from a circa 1760 French pattern book in the Warner Archive are described as silk and linen tabbies with tobine patterns made by shafts and warp floats in silk (Rothstein, "The English Market for French Silks").

SAXONY

Wool first obtained from Saxony in the early years of the nineteenth century and used for woolen as opposed to worsted goods. About 1835, "with inventions in spinning, new fabrics also sprung up. Lately a new article, termed Saxon camblet, though woven plain like a wildbore, had been produced. These, afterwards designated Saxonies, were altogether constructed of worsted" (James, p. 445).

Saxony for women's dresses—"The weft is made from the finest Saxony wool and the warp from the finest Australian wool, both combed by hand"—was shown at the Great Exhibition of 1851 (James, Appendix, p. 19).

SAY
(*saye*)

A thin woolen stuff, or serge, of twill weave. In the fifteenth century, says made in the Norfolk area were high-quality worsted cloths; lighter, cheaper cloth was introduced during the following century. Say, to designate a woolen cloth, is probably derived from the Dutch word *saai* meaning wool or woolen cloth (Beck).

The warp threads of silk says may have been sized to give them a sheen, a preparation given to Bocking bays in the eighteenth century and to imitations of them manufactured in Yorkshire (Pilgrim, p. 260).

In both the 1660 and 1671 books of rates, imported says are listed as:

Sayes, Double Sayes, or Flanders serges, the piece, containing 15 yards   £9.0.0

Double Say or Serge, the yard   0.9.0
Mil'd Says, the piece   6.0.0
Hounscot Say, the piece, containg
    24 yards   6.0.0
       [Dow, *Every Day Life,* p. 253; Beck.]

In 1728, say was "a very light crossed stuff, all wool; much used abroad for linings, and by the religious for shirts; and with us, by the Quakers, for aprons, for which purpose it is usually dyed green" (Chambers). About the same time Defoe, writing of English cloth worn in Italy, noted that the clergy wear black bays while "the Nuns are vail'd with fine Says, and Long Ells" (*English Commerce,* p. 184).

Like shalloons, about 1800 says were "full-twilled stuffs, that is twilled on both sides." They were "woven with a four heald twill, but the warp and wett for says were heavier to make a stouter stuff, and they were also usually fabricated from wool of a superior quality, and made 42 inches wide, and 42 yards long. . . . They were largely exported to Spain, Portugal, and the Italian States to make priests' attire. Both says and shalloons were made heavier at the commencement of the century, than at present" (James, p. 362).

Cloths "dyed in the say," or piece, were dyed before being fulled. A swatch of *Draps Sayes,* twill-woven and piece-dyed in red is in the Aix-la-Chapelle pattern book of 1807.

As early as 1629/30, green and yellow says were received at the Massachusetts Bay Company storehouse. The 1677/78 Salem inventory of Edward Wharton lists "1 greene say frock" while another Salem inventory in the same year lists "3 silk say under pettecoates lite collrd" (Dow, *Every Day Life,* pp. 240, 262, 263). Samuel Rowland Fisher noted in his journal at Sudbury in 1767/68 the weaving of worsted "Says or Burial Crapes chiefly for the Italian trade."

SCOTCH CARPET

Double-cloth ingrain carpet woven in Scotland.
See also Ingrain carpet.

SCOTIA SILK
(*Scotia washing silk*)

Made in early nineteenth-century Scotland of mixed cotton and silk. In 1809 Ackermann suggested it for pelisses and dresses and remarked that it cost half as much as pure silk (*Repository* 1, no. 4 [April 1809]: 256; no. 5 [May 1809]: 328).

SEERHAND MUSLIN

A muslin between nainsook and mull "particularly adapted for dresses, on account of its retaining its clearness after washing" (Webster, p. 961).

SEERSUCKER
(*cirsaka, sirsaka*)

An Indian striped fabric of mixed silk and cotton exported to England from the end of the seventeenth century. The name is a corruption of the Persian *shir-o-shakhar* meaning "milk and water," a term found in sixteenth-century inventories and dictionaries (Cummin, "Early Seersucker"). As in England, an exotic name was adopted for a native manufacture, and both Paulet and Joubert describe *cirsakas* which can be identified with eighteenth-century swatches in the Musée Historique des Tissus at Lyons (Wiederkehr, pp. 90–98). The background weaves varied from tabby for summer goods to twill for autumn and satin for winter. The patterns resembled droguets.

Three pairs of seersucker window curtains were owned by William Trent of New Jersey in 1726. Thomas Hunt of Boston owned "1 pr. of searsucker Curtains and Vallens" in 1734 (Cummings, p. 36). Both bed curtains and petticoats of Indian calico were lined with seersucker in the 1730s and 1740s.

Cummin illustrated a piece of silk and cotton striped Indian seersucker brought to Salem about 1800, which she described as having "alternate stripes of pale gray-blue fleuret silk, with rippled stripes of pure white cotton. The ripples are formed by weaving with the cotton warps in looser tension than the silk" ("Early Seersucker"). The *Jour-*

nal für Fabrik presents swatches of sircicas in gold and white striped silk/cotton in broad and narrow stripes and another with brown silk warp and brown cotton weft twisted with yellow and light blue silks (June 1794, p. 70; May 1795, p. 387).

Seersucker in this century was woven with two warp beams, on one of which the yarns were held under slacker tension to form the crinkled effect: "For the crinkle portion, an extra beam is necessary, and there is very little weight used upon such beam, so that as the reed forces the picks into the cloth it also pulls down a certain amount of yarn, which extra yarn creates the crinkle in the fabric" (Bennett, p. 154).

The word seersucker is used today in the sense of a striped cotton, or synthetic blend, with a puckered surface.

SEGOVIENNE

A hairy twilled flannel made of fine Spanish wool from Segovia. A cloth of this name was used for upholstery from the fourteenth century and was especially popular in the seventeenth century (Havard).

Two swatches are found in the Journal für Fabrik where they are suggested for children's wear and everyday clothing. One is printed in brown on an orange ground, the other in black on a pea-green ground (September 1792); another in brown and orange on a bright yellow ground (February 1794). These swatches resemble the brilliant striped waistcoat materials in the 1807 Aix-la-Chapelle pattern book which also includes a piece of Spanish wool fleece called segovienne.

SEMPITERNUM
(sempiterne, sempiternille)

"A twilled woolen stuff, resembling serge, . . . deriving its name, like lastings and perpetuanas, from its durable qualities" (Beck). In England it was made largely in the environs of Colchester and Exeter and came to be imitated in France at the end of the seventeenth century: Il y avoit déja quelque tems que les Ouvriers François s'étoient appliqués à imiter diverses petites étoffes de fabriques étrangères, entr'autres les bayettes, les sempiternes ou perpetuanes & les anacostes (Savary des Bruslons). Generally shipments to Spanish America included an assortment of 40 pieces: "15 pieces parrot green, 15 pieces sky blue, 5 musc, and 5 black" (Savary des Bruslons). Sempiternum for a "cubbord cloth with silke fringe" is listed in the 1647 inventory of William Clarke of Salem, Massachusetts.

A swatch of green English sempiternum in twill weave is found in the Maurepas Papers dated 1743 among Etoffes d'Angleterre, à l'usage des Espagnols en Europe et en Amerique (see Pl. D-49).

SERGE

A twilled cloth with worsted warp and woolen weft woven on a four-treadle loom. Developed with other New Draperies, it was lighter and narrower than broadcloth and of better quality than kersey. It was distinguished in the seventeenth century as being middleweight, cheap, and hard wearing (Heaton, Yorkshire Woollen, p. xvii). Chambers gave a detailed description of the processes necessary to prepare the fibers for weaving; to size the warp; to full, pick, wash, and dry on a tenter the woven piece; to dye, sheer, and press the finished cloth.

Many different kinds and qualities of serge were woven, and many were named for the place of their manufacture. The keen commercial rivalry between the two countries led the French to make serges in imitation of English cloth—some were named Serges façon de Londres "to render them more esteemed"—whereas the English made serges called Serge de Nismes, later abbreviated to denim. On the other hand, Samuel Rowland Fisher "viewed the Manufactures" of "German serges" at Devizes in the West of England in 1767, and swatches of serge de Nims and serge de Rome are included in Samuel Hill's mid-eighteenth-century pattern book (Atkinson, p. 17).

In William Paine's estate (1660) "one bedsteed, Curtaines & vallens of red searge" which probably matched "2 red cloath chaires with fringe" were inventoried in the hall chamber (Dow, *Every Day Life,* p. 263). A 1677 Salem inventory lists "1 sad collrd. woemans searge coate" and "1 black fine searge upper pettecoate" (Dow, *Every Day Life,* p. 261). The van Varick inventory of 1695/96 contains several listings for serge:

14 yards read Sarge at   4.6d
7¼ yard Sarge denim   9.0
a Suit sarge Curtaines & vallance.
Silke fringe   £6.0.0
6 Scarlet Sarge curtaines & vallance   4.10.0
1 greene Sarge chimnie cloth with
    fringe   1.0.0

An especially interesting use of serge in furnishing is found in Thomas Chippendale's 1778 bill to Sir Edward Knatchbull for "48 Yds Buff Serge in Bags to the Window Curtains" which were apparently the protective covers for silk curtains (Boynton, p. 103).

From the Beekman Papers, it can be seen that even in the eighteenth century cloth names were not always precisely understood by merchants and their English factors. In 1760 Peach and Pierce of Bristol wrote: "You will Observe in the Long Ells (which we take to be what you mean by Serges folded up as Shalloons) we are afraid the Maker has not been exact in Colours so that if you do not like them dispose of them on Our Accounts" (2: 616). In 1766 Beekman ordered "6 pieces Serge or Long Ells. quantity 30 yard at 30 l. 4 green and 2 blues" as well as scarlet and white serges at 18 or 20 shillings a yard. Shalloons were listed separately and cost 36 shillings a yard. By comparison, German serges in the same order cost 3 shillings a yard (2:709).

Swatches of 1716 preserved in the Archief Brants, Amsterdam, show serge to be a fine smooth cloth of rich, bright colors—pink, cream, tawny, light and golden brown, yellows, whites, and blacks. These were sold in pieces of 30 to 40 yards, and half or three-quarters of a yard wide (Wilson, p. 38). Three swatches in the Maurepas Papers (1743) show two shades of brown and white

twill-woven wools, made in England and used *à doubler les habits* which cost 30 shillings a yard (see Pl. D-49). "The Dutch substitute cotton goods dyed in the same colors as these serges which they call hollandilles" (Maurepas Papers).

In the Moccasi manuscript, Exeter serges are presented in eight red swatches of different qualities and prices (see Pl. D-60). For twilled white London serge, see plate D-53; for colored serge, see plates D-54, D-55.

Embossed serge is described under Embossing. From merchants' orders it is not always possible to distinguish between the two different techniques—(1) the impressing of wools with patterns and (2) the printing of wools in colors with woodblocks. However, there is no question that Robert and Peter Livingston ordered the latter in 1734: "6 ps Imbost Sarges, Yellow ground and blak flours," and two years later "1 ps Imbost Sarge with yallow flowr." Lively color descriptions are also found in the Beekman Papers for 1767 and 1768: "6 pieces Emboss Serge black and red, quantity 32 yard at 13d" and "yellow and red," "yellow, red and green mixed," and "red, green and white" (2:864, 870). Two floral "printed stuffs" of 1762 and 1763 are included in the Johnson album which may be examples of embossed serge. The Berch Papers also have swatches of embossed serge (see Pl. D-17).

More than a dozen swatches of slight, twilled silks called *serge de Soye* are found in the Berch Papers at different prices.

In the first half of the twentieth century, serge made entirely of worsted was the standard material of men's best blue serge suits.

SHAG

In the eighteenth century, a heavy worsted material with a long nap, related to duffel, coating, and blanket. The term once applied to a cloth made of inferior silk; in 1671 Edmond Booth petitioned to manufacture "a rich Silk Shagg . . . made of a Silke Waste, hitherto of little or no use, and shagged by

Tezell or Rowing Cards, like as English Bayes, Rowed Fustians or Dimatyes" (Warner, p. 400).

Shag was imported into Boston from the mid-seventeenth century, and by about 1700 "tawny, murry, & liver-culler shagg" were ordered by Major John Pyncheon of Springfield, Massachusetts (Earle, *Costume,* p. 215). Scarlet, purple, black, drab, dove, and light, "midling," and full green shags are listed in James Alexander's orders of 1735 and 1738. In 1739 John Banister received hair shags dyed in colors of copper, green, drab, scarlet, and blue. In 1767/68 at Leeds, Samuel Rowland Fisher saw "worsted Shags all Colours 20/ to 21/" and in Coventry "Hair Shaggs" and "Worsted Shaggs."

In England we read in 1703 of "Red shag breeches striped with black stripes" (Beck); in Boston (1741) "A blue shagg great coat" was worn by a runaway manservant (Dow, *Arts and Crafts,* p. 195). Waistcoats and petticoats were also made of shag.

Swatches of scarlet and white (actually buff) hair shags in the Yorkshire pattern book are close-cropped worsted velvets (see Pls. D-101, D-103). Swatches in dark blue and black are stamped with small geometric patterns.

SHAGREEN

A spotted silk taffeta made in all colors, especially black. The pebbled surface resembled sharkskin. It was used for lining clothes.

Willing and Shippen (1730s) ordered "4 Ps. Mantua and Shagreens." In 1740 an order for a suit of three-pile black velvet specified a "lining of the best double shagrine of a dark gold colour, if that not to be had some other good lining silk of that colour" (Earle, *Costume,* p. 39).

A swatch of shagreen made in Genoa is in the Richelieu Papers for 1736. A green swatch is included in the Alexander Papers (1737).

In the nineteenth century, a strong cotton book cloth, heavily sized and finished to resemble leather, was given the name *chagrin.*

SHALLOON

A cheap twilled worsted. Listed among New Draperies developed in the sixteenth century, shalloons were also known by the name of *rasses* (James, p. 123) or *rashes.* Booth writes that "worsted yarn is manufactured into calamancoes, shalloons, bombazets and other light stuffs, of which the threads are visible, not being covered with a pile." He adds that in finishing, shalloons could be either "hotpressed or unglazed."

In 1769 Arthur Young noted that at Romsey "near 500 hands are employed in making those Shalloons which are called Rattinets" (*Southern Counties,* p. 207). From the early eighteenth century, shalloons were also manufactured in Yorkshire and shipped from Bristol, although those marketed in London were of better quality.

Unglazed "Supr Fine Shalloons provided for St. Petersburg, rough pattns for Dyer's use only" and twenty-two finished swatches, all in bright colors, are in the Yorkshire pattern book on a page dated 1750 (see Pl. D-103). Also made in the north are swatches in red and blue in the Holker manuscript (see Pl. D-33). Twenty examples of Devonshire shalloons, glazed and twill woven, are in the mid-eighteenth-century Berch Papers.

The weaving of shalloons changed little over the centuries, for in 1801 they were again defined as "full-twilled stuffs, that is twilled on both sides, made of single warp and weft, woven with four treadles in a variety of qualities. . . . This class of goods formed the materials for female dresses. Large amounts were dyed scarlet and forwarded to Turkey" (James, p. 362).

One of the materials most commonly imported into America, shalloons were used for the lining of clothing. James Alexander specified "10 ps good London Shalloons" in blue, black, red, green, olive, and "other good Cloathe Colours for a tryal" in 1737. A 1739 Rhode Island invoice of John Banister included a bale of 20 pieces of shalloons and another bale with blue, green, black, mock scarlet, and "Cloth Coloured" shalloons. James Beekman's 1769 order specified "34 pieces

Shalloons at 29/. 12 sorted handsome cloth browns, 10 cloth blues, 2 red, 4 black, 6 Russett colours" (2:875). One writer, however, found them unsatisfactory: "Silk waistcoats and Breeches are soon destroyed by shalloon linings from friction, silk linings, or fine cloth faceings substituted, would turn out to much better effect" (March, p. 42).

Although shalloons were not generally used for bed hangings, the following references are of interest: in Virginia, 1730, "curtains of yellow shalloon" (Frances Little, p. 240); in New York, 1757, "a Small four post bedstead with Green Shalloon Curtains" (New York Appraisements, p. 42); in Hadley, Massachusetts, 1796, "Friday put on a blue Shaloon (Shalloon—a thin losely woven twilled worsted stuff) to quilt for my mother" (Phelps Diary, p. 301).

SHODDY

A reclaimed wool, especially that obtained by garnetting or pulling apart soft rags from worsteds or from knitted or loosely woven woolens (Merriam-Webster). "Made from old woolen stockings or rags, shredded or picked by hand or machine, to render the yarn or threads suitable for spinning into yarn a second time; or to give a fiber that can be woven or felted in with a wool or cotton warp" (Megraw). It was distinguished from mungo by length of fiber and by the superior quality of fabrics manufactured from it.

"Benjamin Law . . . first wove a piece of cloth from shoddy in 1813" (Beck). To judge from samples in the 1860 Noska pattern book, cloth containing shoddy yarn was not necessarily of poor quality.

See also Berlins.

SHOT

A term used to describe textiles made partly of silk. A textile shot with silk in the Johnson album has white silk warp yarns alternating with red wool warps and a weft entirely of red wool. Thus the textile is about one-third silk, soft, and yet lustrous. Beck includes cloths of different colored warp and weft such as caungeantrie at this word. Chambray is another.

SIAMOISE

A large group of linen and cotton goods, some with additions of wool or silk. First woven of silk warp and cotton weft, they were made in imitation of the magnificent garments worn by ambassadors of the King of Siam upon the occasion of their visit to the court of Louis XIV in 1684, and again in 1686 (Savary des Bruslons).

From about 1722, siamoises woven of linen warp and cotton weft formed one of the most important manufactures of Rouen. Their similarity to English worsteds, especially to striped camlets, is unmistakable, and doubtless these less expensive fabrics were made in the hope of capturing from England the bulk of the trade with Spain, including the more important West Indies and South American colonies.

In writing of the manufactures of Normandy, Savary des Bruslons includes under the name *siamoise* a wide assortment of cloths such as checks and stripes woven entirely of linen, linen and wool, or cotton and linen. Striped siamoises made of linen and cotton were used for inexpensive coverings, summer slipcovers, bed covers, and hangings from 1737 (Havard).

Eight striped or checked swatches from Rouen dated 1737 are in the Richelieu Papers (see Pl. D-94); others are from Meslay and Nantes. Sixteen swatches of linen and cotton stripes and checks dated 1743 are in the Maurepas Papers (see Pls. D-41, D-42, D-43).

Striped, checked, and brocaded *Chamoisa* (possibly the Italian writer's attempt at the French word *siamoise*) made of cotton and colored silks at Rouen are found in the Moccasi manuscript (see Pl. D-50). Twenty or more years later than the cotton/linen siamoises known from the Richelieu and Maurepas papers, the manufacture at Rouen may have included silk and cotton thin dress goods like Moccasi's *chamoisa*. Both kinds of textiles are listed in the French *Manuel historique* of 1762.

Twenty-seven swatches of siamoises are found in two invoices dated 1779 among the John Holker, Jr., Papers. These swatches of white, or partially bleached, cotton and cotton/linen cloth probably came from the royal manufactory established in 1752 by Holker's father at Rouen. As French consul-general at Philadelphia, the younger Holker purchased cloth for the United States government and on his own account. Except for one piqué (machine quilted), one *cannelé* (ribbed), and one fine blue and white check, the swatches are plain woven, indicating that the term *siamoise* was also applied to such goods.

Siamoises pour Meubles were advertised together with dimities and fustians by a Paris upholsterer who supplied Thomas Jefferson (1790) (Marie Kimball, "Jefferson's French Furniture," p. 124).

A swatch of siamoise appears in the *Journal für Fabrik* as late as March of 1796 (p. 238). The pattern is a fancy broken stripe. Silk/cotton siamoises with printed floral patterns continued to be manufactured throughout the nineteenth century for furnishing and summer dresses (Braun-Ronsdorf, p. 22).

See also Rouen.

SILESIA
(sleazy, slesia; Fr. silesie)

Thin, slight, twilled linen cloth (made near Hamburg) which has given its name to the word *sleazy*. In a broad sense silesia referred to many grades and patterns of linens, unbleached or dyed in colors and later imitated in cotton. It was used for household purposes, for the lining of clothing, and more recently for window roller-blinds. Both small diaper and larger weft-float floral patterns were made, but all were apparently coarse and low priced.

A piece of "Slesy Holland" is listed in a 1684 Salem inventory (Dow, *Every Day Life,* p. 275). In 1759 London factors wrote to James Beekman:

"All our hambrough linens are considerably dearer. We have sent You the lowest Clouting diapers we could procure, but have been obligded to omitt the quadruple Sletias You wrote for" (2: 644). At another time Beekman was sent tandem silesia, a kind folded to permit inspection of the piece. In supplying an Albany customer in 1785, Beekman substituted a piece of tandem silesia for the lowest priced Irish linen ordered (3:1292). In addition to brown quadruple silesias, Samuel Rowland Fisher ordered "6 ps printd Silesias red Bengall Stripe—36/," according to his journal of 1767/68.

The Lonsdale Company of Providence received a bronze medal "for coloured Silesias, for fineness of fabric and superiority in the colouring and finish" at the 1853 New York industrial exhibition (Dilke, p. 27).

Woolen cloths also woven in Silesia were imitated, especially in France. Woolen *droguets* or *silesies en mosaique* and *silesies à fleurs* from Holland are seen in plate D-92.

SILK

Cloth woven from the shiny, smooth filaments reeled from cocoons, especially those produced by the silkworm *Bombyx mori*. A wide variety of imported raw silks and silk goods are listed in the London 1660 Book of Rates:

> Bridges [Bruges] silk, Ferret or Floret silke, Fillozell or Paris silke.
> Granado. Silke black & colours.
> Naples. Silke, black & colours.
> Organzine, Pole & Spanish, Raw China, Raw Silke, short and long,
> Raw Morea, Satin Silke, Sleave Silke,
> Silke Nubbs or Husks,
> Throwne Silke. [Dow, *Every Day Life,* p. 253.]

Silks advertised in Boston in 1765 included "Yellow-ground Brocades, white figured Tabby; brown Padusoy; green mantua Silks; black, coloured, plain, flowered and spotted Sattens; pelong ditto; large fringed Barcelona Handkerchiefs; Ballandine Silk; Padusoy Satten; Sarsenet and figured Ribbons" (Dow, *Arts and Crafts,* p. 171).

Silks were always high-cost, luxury articles; their sheen was imitated in chintz by glazing and in worsteds by pressing.

See Burnham (p. 125) for definitions of silk yarns (cordonnet, crepe, grenadine, organzine, poil, and tram). For the history of silk culture and weaving, see Beck.

See also Lyons, Spitalfields.

SILKEEN

"About 1779, Charles Taylor developed a fustian velvet which, because of its silken sheen, went by the name of silkeen, a material with printed ribs and untouched ground, which then was dyed a different colour" (Luetkens, p. 26).

SILVERET
(Fr. sayette)

A half-silk mixed with cotton or wool. In his manuscript, John Holker said of a swatch of light brown silk and cotton twill called silveret that it was used for men's clothing (swatch 53). In the Moccasi manuscript two swatches of London manufacture have pink silk warps with blue wool weft and purple wool weft, both in twill weave (see Pl. D-53). Silveret was sold in New York as early as 1750 (Holmes account book, p. 15), and it was advertised in Philadelphia on April 20, 1767, by Kearney and Gilbert.

SINCHAW
(synchaw)

A silk imported from China from the late eighteenth century. "Prices Current in Canton," 1807, describes it as "a firm thick even Kind of Goods, handsome and measured 30 Yards or nearly that and weigh 44 Tub or 42 to 43, varying in length about a yard and in weight as above. Cost about 15½ to 16½ $ pr ps. Much used in the U. States" (China Trade Records).

"Changeable Senshaws, mostly blue and green, red and green, black and red, green and yellow" were ordered from John R. Latimer of Philadelphia in 1815.

In 1819 Pickering Dodge gave Benjamin Shreve samples of silks obtained from Eshing, a Chinese silk merchant, as a purchasing guide. Dodge listed the kinds of silk available: "Synchaws, Lustrings, Sarsnets, Bonnet silks, Ponges, Crapes, Sewings, Satins, Levantines or twilled silks, Florentines, Camblets, Pelong Satins, Black and Check'd Hkfs and Nankins" (Crossman, fig. 211).

SLUYER
(schleier)

Linen cloth first woven in Silesia. It was made fine and bleached like cambric or left "in the brown" (unbleached).

SMALLWARES

Tapes and narrow bindings of cotton, linen, silk, or worsted, plaited sash cord, braid, etc. (Beck). Writing about Manchester in 1795, Aikin stated that "to the manufactory of laces, inkles, tapes, and filleting, was early added that of divers kinds of bindings and worsted small wares" (p. 162).

SOUSAE
(soosey)

A cloth of silk, or mixed cotton and silk, imported from India. It was usually about a yard wide and varied from 10 to 20 yards in length. Sousaes were much in demand in England at the turn of the eighteenth century; typical orders included checks, small stripes, and "white and black stripes" (Irwin and Schwartz).

Thomas Fitch ordered India goods in May 1724: "Send more low priced Callicoes and Garlets or Narrow Susey or Lemonees if reasonable but nothing high cost will turn to account." A month later his letter book reads: "If at the Fall

Sale these following goods are to be bought reasonably, please to buy me some persian Taffety, a good parcell of narrow Susees narrow strip'd as many black and white as may be, none crossbarrd, a good parcell of Lemonies, charconees and long cloths glazed not too much white." Although black and white striped "sooseys" were the most common, another of Fitch's orders, September 22, 1727, added "white with other Colours, all narrow stripes."

SPANISH CLOTH

In the seventeenth century, it was "well known that the real superfine cloth everywhere must be entirely of Spanish wool, and therefore often called Spanish cloths" (Macpherson, 2:538). Finer and more expensive than broadcloth, some Spanish cloths were made of a mixture of colored yarns spun together which were called medleys. In *A Plan of the English Commerce* Defoe wrote: "by Spanish Cloth I mean the fine medley Cloths . . . which are mix'd with Spanish Wool in the Making" (p. 183). Spanish cloths were a West of England specialty in the seventeenth and eighteenth centuries. They were imported into Boston from about 1650 (Aspinwall Records).

Woolen cloths were made especially for the Spanish market and for the Spanish colonies in South America and the West Indies in a wide range of colors and in different qualities. In the mid-seventeenth century, they included the following:

Cloths in 20 pieces, 19 brown and 1 black
Sempeternas, in 40 pieces, the following colours, viz.
>>15 pieces of parrot green, 15 pieces of sky blue,
>>>5 pieces of musk, 5 pieces of black
Serges, all brown, or sorted like the sempeternas
Estaminas, wide and well calendered, brown and green.
Serges, fine, of a scarlet colour
Says, white and black, well calendered
Bombazeen, double, brown and greenish

Serges of Hoogwet, half white and half black, very fine and well calendered.
Bays of Colchester, the 100 pieces assorted as follows,
>>viz. 20 pieces black, 15 pieces parrot green, 15 pieces sky blue, 12 pieces of the best yellow, 10 pieces scarlet, 10 pieces red, 8 pieces violet, 5 pieces very white, 5 pieces caracucha.
>>>>>>>>[Mortimer.]

SPITALFIELDS

The center of silk weaving on the outskirts of London. It became important after the revocation of the Edict of Nantes in 1685 when Huguenot weavers fled France to settle there. In the mid-eighteenth century Wyndham Beawes wrote:

This county [Middlesex] has few Manufactures out of its Metropolis [London], though some of Spital-fields, &c. are very extensive, and brought to great Perfection; so that I may venture to assert, that our Artisans now equal if not exceed the French in the Beauty of their Silk Fabrick, and still continue their wonted Superiority in the Woollen ones. [P. 622.]

Samuel Curwen of Boston recorded his impression of the area in 1776 and 1777:

Walkt out with Mr. D. and Bourne to Spital fields with a letter from I[saac] S[mith, merchant of Boston] to a Mr. Dalbear, with whose son, accompanying us, we were admitted to the looms of the workers in Sattins, Taffaties, modes, lutestrings, pessions [Persians], Brocades and Velvets, whom we saw at work. To describe them is beyond my ability, though clear enough in idea, the flowered brocade was wrot by no less than 36 shuttles and an apparatus of Threads. [1:178.]

Some nine hundred watercolor patterns and *mises en carte* drawn by Spitalfields designers are owned by the Victoria and Albert Museum. From them the styles for fashionable dress silks can be plotted for the first sixty years of the eighteenth century. Many of the patterns are reproduced in Peter Thornton's *Baroque and Rococo Silks* and in articles by him and by Natalie Rothstein, who is preparing a book about the Spitalfields silk industry based on the archive.

Unlike patterns for eighteenth-century dress silks which were brought out twice a year, furnishing damasks were much more traditional in style and continued in use for decades. Among the patterns of Anna Maria Garthwaite, Spitalfields designer, only one furnishing damask is included (Fig. D-92).

STAINBOULIFRIES

"A manufacture of silk and cotton, watered on one side, and suitable for Ladies' Gowns" was advertised in the Boston *Palladium* on May 4, 1810.

STAMIN
(stamfortis, stamyn)

Cloth name derived from the Italian *stame* meaning both a worsted yarn and a warp. Stamin was one of the many New Draperies made of lighter worsted yarn, or part worsted and part carded yarns, for which Norwich was noted. "The name probably came from the French *estamine,* the original of another stuff, once well known, called Tammy, and the equivalent of serge" (Beck). Hazel E. Cummin discussed the etymology of the word in "Tammies and Durants."

STAMMEL

A kind of worsted cloth commonly of a red color and used for breeches, petticoats and gowns in the seventeenth century (Beck).

Halliwell cited *Times Curtaine Drawne,* 1621:

But long they had not danc'd, till this yong maid,
In a fresh stammell petticote array'd,
With vellure sleves, and bodies tied with points,

Began to feele a looseness in her joynts.
[Beck.]

"Blew stammels" are listed in the 1693 warehouse inventory of James Lloyd, merchant of Boston (SCPR, 13:267).

STAMMET

A lightweight worsted, or part-worsted cloth made in the Norwich area from the sixteenth century.
See also Estamene, Stamin, Tammy.

FIG. D-92. *Watercolor design for a furniture damask by Spitalfields designer Anna Maria Garthwaite, dated 1743. (Victoria and Albert Museum.) Note that the pattern is intended to fit a balloon-shaped chair seat.*

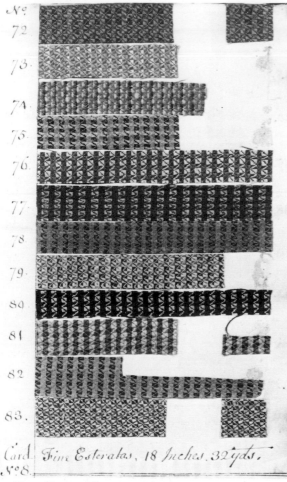

Fig. D-93. *Fine worsted "esteratas," or starrets. From John Kelly's "Counterpart of Patterns," Norwich, 1763. (Victoria and Albert Museum.)*

STARRET
(esteret)

One of the fancy eighteenth-century worsted dress fabrics largely manufactured in Norwich. "Starretts for Gowns and Banyans" were advertised in Boston 1735 (Earle, *Costume,* p. 51), and "5 ps yd wide Starretts" were ordered with other worsteds by John Banister of Newport in 1739. Starrets imitated silk textiles and some were mixed with some silk; Peter Fanueil's 1743 inventory lists "6¼ yds. of Silk Staret" (SCPR, 37:113).

Two swatches of *Norwich Esteretes* are in the Moccasi manuscript of about 1760. Fine zigzag patterns are shown woven in two and in four colors (see Pl. D-57). John Kelly's "Counterpart of Patterns," Norwich 1763, presents sixteen swatches of "Esteratas, 18 Inches. 32 yds" woven in three colors in interrupted zigzags of small figure (Fig. D-93; see also Fig. D-70, nos. 68–71).

STOCKINETTE

Known from the 1786 Hilton manuscript as a twilled cotton cloth similar to denim (see Fig. D-39). Two drafts for stockinette are found in John Hargrove's 1792 weaver's book.

STOCKINGETTE CLOTH

A woven cloth made with rubber warp, "otherwise known as Jersey, or Elastic Cloth differing in their widths" (Caulfeild and Saward).

STRAITS
(streits)

Light, narrow woolen cloth. Like kerseys, straits were half as wide as broadcloth and weighed less.

STRIPES

Woolen cloth with striped selvedges made in Gloucestershire in the 1820s for the East India Company trade with China. The fabric was very flimsy although made of Spanish wool (Mann, "Textile Industries," p. 167). Any cloth woven with colored stripes in the warp or weft.

STROUD

A woolen cloth woven and dyed, especially red, on the River Stroud in Gloucestershire. About 1725 Defoe wrote:

Gloucestershire must not be pass'd over, without some account of a most pleasant and fruitful vale which crosses part of the country, from east to west on that side of the Cotswold, and which is call'd Stroud-Water; famous not for the finest cloths only, but for dying those cloths of the finest scarlets, and other grain colours that are any where in England; perhaps in any part of the world. [*Tour,* vol. 2, letter 6.]

Another early writer says, "the water here is found by experience to be very proper for red or scarlet dyes, also black; in both which they do drive a mighty trade. The water here is run through an iron mine which is the reason it dyes red the better" (as cited by Ponting in *South-West England,* p. 145). According to recent analysis the fine scarlet color of strouds was achieved from cochineal dyed on a tin mordant. For the most part, these woolen cloths were shipped from Bristol to the colonies twice a year. As early as 1705 Thomas Banister ordered "2 ps of red strouds and 2 of blew & 6 ps of half thicks."

Strouds, duffels, and blankets, which the North American Indians traded for beaverskins, were made to their exact specifications, as shown in the letter book of James Logan in 1714:

> These woolens may be so far out of thy way of business as not to be fully known to thee by our names for them—They are 1st Strowd water a cloth about 4d broad about 4/ p yd blue or red in purchasing wch a regard must be had not only to the Cloth & Colour but also to the list [selvedge] about which the Indians are Curious [i.e., exacting]. This is of the common breadth viz. about 3 fingers with a Stripe or two of white generally. Sometimes in black in ye blue pcs. and always black in ye red. 2ndly. Duffels of near ye same breadth wthout any List for 20d to 2 sh or 2/2 (but that's too high) of the same Colours with the other.
> 3rdly Striped Blankets that are white like other

Blankets only towds the ends they have generally for broad Stripes as each 2 red and 2 blue or black near—they are full 2 yds long or better and above 6/4d wide some near 7/4 they are sold by ye piece containing 15 Blankets for about 3 lbs. 10/.

In the following year, 1715, Logan again emphasized that "ye fashion as well as fineness" must be regarded. He specified the lengths and the colors of the selvedges; in blue blankets, for instance, "an even stripe of white about half an Inch in breadth but if some could be had wth two handsome white stripes and somewhat narrower, it would doe better and be ye more engaging for Variety" (Kidd, pp. 53, 54).

Undoubtedly for the Indian trade Robert Livingston ordered in 1737:

> 4 ps Red Strowds black Salvidge
> 4 ps   Do.   Blue, white Narrow Stripe
> 5 pr. Indian Blankets, 20 in a ps.

For the account of Arent Stevens of Schenectady, he ordered:

> 2 ps Blue Strouds, with narrow Stripe
> 2 ps Red Strouds, Best with black Salvedge
> Indian Blanketts, Black stripe.

In 1755 the *Histoire et commerce des colonies angloises* said of the New York trade in strouds with the Indians: *"Les marchandises du plus grand débit parmi les sauvages sont les strouds et autres sortes de laineries"* (Butel-Dumont, p. 145).

See also Duffel, Witney.

STUFF

A general term for worsted cloths. In 1833 Perkins listed the following kinds:

> Stuff—is twilled or plain, is made of common wool, and may be had of black and every colour.
> Merino—is nothing better than a superior stuff, in the ordinary qualities, but in the

higher walks they are splendid goods, in the production of which the French bear the palm,—approximating as they do to the imitation of cashmere.

Shalloons—are loosely made stuffs for lining skirts of coats and liveries; may be had in all colours.

Lastings, Prunella, and Florentine—are three kinds of goods generally in black, are both figured and plain, and principally used for shoes.

Tammies—are highly glazed plain stuffs, may be had in all colours, and in white; and were originally used for women's petticoats.

Calimancoes—are the same goods as the above, but have broad stripes of the same colour, somewhat raised above the ordinary surface, and which run warpwise. were originally manufactured in the Netherlands.

Moreens—are for furniture; generally watered, and may be had figured; are ¾ths wide, lengths from 28 yards, and of all colours. This article verges upon upholstery, in which trade these goods are to be met with in very superior makes, advancing from the common article here named to the most costly and superb imitation of the original damask, and recognized under a multitude of names.

Camblets—are made of closely twisted worsted yarn. Until within a very few years, they were principally used for military and naval cloaks, but now are rarely in demand, save for the East India trade.

Plaids—are all more or less made in imitation of the Scotch national costume, of which none are so good as the original. The Scotch plaid is a coarse and very strong article, and each distinct pattern is the badge of its clan; it is also called tartan.

In addition to the worsteds listed above, Webster listed Denmark satin, ratteen, bombazet, tammy or durance, calimanco, cubica, serge, mousseline de laine, challis, etc. (p. 946).

SWANSDOWN

A waistcoat material described by Perkins in 1833 as "originally made of wool and a small quantity of silk, but latterly with a large quantity of cotton instead of silk." Swansdowns and toilinets were fancy woolen textiles, or cotton and wool, developed in the early nineteenth century. Samples of pink, salmon, scarlet, light blue, and apple-green swansdown yarns are in William Gott's pattern book begun in 1815. "Both [swansdown and toilinet] were popular for waistcoats for many years, especially with horsy men—grooms, huntsmen and coachmen" (Crump, p. 55).

SWANSKIN

A fine woolen cloth of plain weave related to flannel and bay. Defoe's tradesman's wife wore (1726) "Her Inner-petticoats, Flannel and Swanskin, from Salisbury and Wales" (p. 403). A piece of "saxon Green Swan Skin bays" is listed in Jonathan Holmes's account book in 1750. "Blue and white," "Cotton Stripes or Swanskins," and "white Swanskin fine" were listed in the Caine broadside of 1754; and "42 yds English Swanskin" and "24 this Countrey" were lost in the Boston fire of 1760 (*Boston Records,* p. 39). "Cotton Stripes or Swanskins" and "Plain & Spotted Swanskins" are noted in Samuel Rowland Fisher's journal of 1767/68 at Kendall near Lancaster. In New York "A Parcel of Swanskin Blankets, 9-4, and 10-4 wide, of the first Quality" were for sale in 1770 (Gottesman, *1726–76,* p. 269). Swatches of worsted swanskin are found in a Castle Museum pattern book dated 1791.

In the late eighteenth century, the name *swanskin,* or *swansdown,* was also given to a fleecy cotton cloth. Sometimes called ironing cloth, it was also used for printers' blankets, for heavy underclothing, gaiters, and jackets. "A description of calico stuff, one side of which is fleecy, the fibres being pulled to the surface and forming a nap, and somewhat resembling Swansdown feathers. Tightly and closely woven, similar to 'Cricketing,' but of a commoner description of quality, and may be had both white and unbleached. In America it is sometimes employed in lieu of flannel" (Caulfeild and Saward).

SWISS LACE
(Swiss Brussels)

A machine-made imitation of sixteenth-century Swiss lace largely produced in Nottingham of coarse cotton (see Fig. D-94). "Employed in upholstery for window curtains, wall paper preservers, behind washstands, and for short blinds." "Some new kinds have been produced in broad stripes, alternately coloured with designs, and white of the ordinary openwork description" (Caulfeild and Saward). Charles Eastlake had "seldom seen a better material , , , worked in two or three small but well-defined patterns" and in design "infinitely superior to the ordinary muslin curtain, on which semi-naturalistic foliage and nondescript ornament is allowed to meander after an extravagant and meaningless fashion" (p. 92).

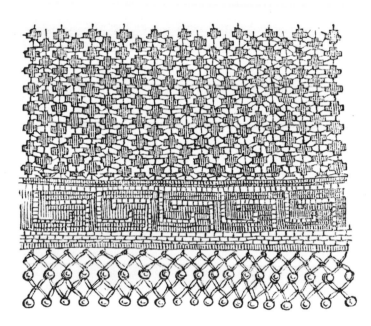

FIG. D-94. *"Swiss Lace" for summer curtains. From Charles Locke Eastlake,* Hints on Household Taste *(London: Longmans, Green, 1868), p. 92. (Winterthur Museum Library.)*

T

TABBY

A plain silk, slightly heavier than lustring and stronger and thicker than taffeta. A cloth woven in a plain weave. Many were given a watered or waved finish. The process is described in a 1758 dictionary:

> Tabbying, is the passing a silk or stuff under a calender, the rolls of which are made of iron or copper, variously engraven, which, bearing unequally on the stuff, render the surface thereof unequal, so as to reflect the rays of light indifferently, making the representation of waves thereof, as on a tabby. It is performed without the addition of any water or dye; and furnishes the modern philosophers with a strong proof, that colours are nothing but appearances. [Barrow, 2:303.]

As shown in figure D-44 flowers could be engraved on rollers of this kind and probably were used to emboss tabby as well as worsted moreen (see Embossing); Samuel Pepys commented in his diary "My wife extraordinary fine today in her Flower tabby suit, bought a year and more ago, before my mother's death put her into mourning, and so not worn till this day—and everybody in love with it; and indeed she is very fine and handsome in it" (March 26, 1668, 9:134).

In the next century, the material was defined as "a coarse kind of Taffeta, thick, glossy, and watered by pressure between the rollers of a cylinder, and the application of heat and an acidulous liquor. . . . The beautiful description of silk called *Moiré* is a Tabby; and worsted stuffs, such as moreen, are likewise Tabbies" (Caulfeild and Saward).

From 1737 to 1760 James Alexander of New York ordered white, blue, green, gray, ash, "Dove," and "Lead" colored tabbies. Swatches, attached to the copies of several orders, are ribbed silks with coarser weft than warp yarns. In 1759 George Washington ordered from London "A Salmon Coloured Tabby of the Enclosed Pattern to be made in a sack & coat" (Earle, *Costume,* p. 41).

Tabbies could also be ornamented with brocading, and a pattern for one drawn by Spitalfields designer Anna Maria Garthwaite in 1752 is preserved in the Victoria and Albert Museum with a matching silk panel (Rothstein, "Nine English Silks," figs. 7, 7a).

Fourteen swatches of ribbed silk "Tabbys, Richest Sort. ½ Ell wide, 8 / 6 pr Yd." in different colors, followed by seven of the "Cheap Sort— 7/6," are in the Berch Papers.

TABINET

A kind of poplin, once extensively manufactured in Ireland, with silk warp and woolen weft. It was usually woven in diaper patterns and used mostly for window curtains (Beck). Tabinet often received a watered, or tabbied, finish. A silk and linen tabinet with flowers on a watered ground woven by J. Stillwell and Company, London, in 1843 is shown in Morris, "Textiles," *Early Victorian Period* (pl. 70A). Engraved illustrations of patterns by William Fry and Company of Dublin are shown in Yapp's *Art Industry* (pls. 35, 49, "Textile Fabrics").

OPPOSITE
FIG. D-95. *Swatches: (1,2) a furniture chintz in a brown animal-skin pattern with blue shading resembling a twill; (3) a French striped tabinet; and (4) a silk cotton toilinet with pink and black stripes to be worn for evening or full dress with a bodice of velvet or satin. From Repository 13, no. 73 (January 1815): 57. (Winterthur Museum Library.)*

Howe and Stevens, Boston dyers, described tabinet in 1864: "plain or figured Irish poplin . . . made of silk and cotton, plain, striped, or figured, and is never used for any other purpose than for bed and window curtains, and for covering sofas, chairs, ottomans and coach linings. It is very much used for drawing and sitting-room walls, instead of paper, paint, or tapestry, and when used for this purpose it is not put on tight and flat like paper or tapestry, but fluted, and has a magnificent appearance" (p. 41).

Lighter varieties were used for dresses, and in 1815 Ackermann presented a swatch of dark blue, green, and black striped silk woven with a green wool weft "calculated for morning or domestic wear" (Fig. D-95).

TABLING

Table linen such as diaper, barleycorn, and damask. In England the tops of fine tables and chests of drawers were customarily protected with fitted leather covers, of which one remains in Ham House. In America, to judge from portraits such as those by Ralph Earl, tables were covered with green cloth sometimes trimmed with fringe. Jonathan Holmes's account book of 1749–54 lists "1 ps silk and worsted tablin" which may have been a fine covering of this sort (p. 27).

TABORATT
(tabaret, tabouret)

(1) Shaded and striped worsteds found in several late eighteenth-century Norwich merchants' sample books (see Pls. D-74, D-75, D-76, D-85). Their

patterns have warp shaded floral sprigs and fine tobine dots woven on solid-colored backgrounds (see Pl. D-58). A 1749 Boston advertisement lists "Worsted Tabaritts the newest fashion. In Imitation of a rich Brocaded Silk" (Earle, *Costume,* p. 243). *See also* Brilliant.

(2) By the end of the century, the material, now used for furnishing, was defined as "a stout satin-striped silk [with] broad alternate stripes of satin and watered material, differing from each other . . . in colour; blue, crimson, or green satin stripes are often successively divided by cream-coloured Tabby [watered] ones" (Caulfeild and Saward). In a March 1797 order from Henry Thompson (of Baltimore?) to "Messrs. Wilsons, Cabinet-makers, Upholsterers, Appraisers & Undertakers" of London are specified:

> 73¾ yds of Barre[d] Taberay for 3 festoon
>   window Curtains
> 62½ yds of Tammy to line   Do
> 64 yds of   silk quality Binding
> 13 yds of   plain silk fringe gimp head

George Smith in *Household Furniture* (1808) recommends: "In elegant Drawing Rooms, plain coloured satin or figured damask assumes the first rank, as well for use as for richness: lustring and tabarays the next; the latter, however, makes but indifferent drapery" (p. xii). A plate in Ackermann's *Repository* of 1812 presents "a beautiful French scroll sofa adapted for the drawing-room, which may be made of rose-wood, with gold ornaments, and covered with rich chintz or silk tabouret, corresponding with the other parts of the furniture" (8, no. 44 [August 1812]: 113). An undated London trade card of "Smith & Compy, Furniture Printers & Manufacturers of Damasks, Silk Taborets & Moreens" is used as a bill to itemize "319 Yards Crimson & Drab stripe Tabarett" and "60 yds Rich Gold color Silk Gimp" (Heal collection).

By 1864 taboratt was manufactured in the United States made of silk and cotton, plain, striped, or figured. It was "never used for any other purpose than for bed and window curtains, and for covering sofas, chairs, ottomans, and coach linings. It is very much used for drawing and sitting-room walls . . . and has a magnificent appearance. Tabaret (tabberea some call it) curtains are always lined with tammy . . . always the color of the curtains. . . . Crimsons, ambers, drabs, greens, and blues are the prevailing colors for tabarets" (Howe and Stevens, p. 41).

TABYREAN
(taborine)

"A fabric of silk and worsted especially adapted for the American market, was manufactured in considerable quantities in Hampshire in the early nineteenth century and generally sent to Philadelphia" (Warner, p. 330). Yorkshire "tab moreens" were "a lower quality of moreen and made in an unscoured state" (James, p. 390). The name suggests a moreen which has received a tabby, or watered, finish, or a cloth of mixed silk (tabby) and wool. The 1803 estate inventory of Joseph Hopkins, New York, lists tabyreans in pink, green, crimson, mulberry, black, and blue.

TAFFETA
(taffety)

In seventeenth-century trade with Bengal, the term covered a wide variety of silk and silk/cotton goods, many of them striped or checked, among which were alachas, seersuckers, sousaes, and charconnaes (Irwin and Schwartz, p. 47). Together with other East India goods Thomas Fitch ordered from London "Persian Taffetys, as few whitish ones as may be, if none t'would be best; bright reds, gold Colours, bright greens, peach bloom and other good colours" (May 20, 1727).

Most European taffetas were plain woven silks with weft threads slightly thicker than warp and related to tabby, alamode, Persian, sarcenet, and lustring. According to Savary des Bruslons:

> Taffetas are made in all colors. Some are glossy, some changeable, some striped with

"French or Italian Goods.

Of Silk Goods the manufactures of France and Italy, will always answer at this market, & they will also at all times take the lead of the British Manufactures of the same kind, as they are generally more fanciful, or have a greater display of taste, and, as the raw material of itself is so much more valuable in England, than it is in either of the other countries.

Satins this article is always demanded, the colours ought to be crimson, Rose, Green, White, Purple, light Blue, Black, & other handsome & fashionable colours, the present prices of the same quality as the annexed samples, are 1800 reas or $2..0 the covedo of 27 Inches nearly they are the French Sattins of 4/24 Ell wide.

Taffetas or Lustrings, this kind of goods is also in demand, and the present prices are 800 reas or 75 Cents per covedo, equal to about $1..0 per yard for such as are in quality like the annexed patterns — they are sometimes higher, the colours ought to be much the same as the Sattins.

Crapes, the usual price of this article is 14000 reas or $17..50 per piece and the colours ought to be, blue, rose, white, yellow, &c. some plain and some figured, but mostly plain — a few Crape robes may also answer.

FIG. D–96. Satins, taffetas or lustrings, and crapes.
From a trader's book kept between 1797 and 1809. (Rhode Island
Historical Society.)

silk, gold or silver; others are flamed [warp-printed], checked, flowered, or with patterns called *point de la Chine* and *de Hongrie.* Many others have names, dictated by fashion or by the fancy of the manufacturers, so bizarre that it would be both useless and difficult to give them all, aside from the fact that their names rarely last through the year in which they were created. . . . Most taffetas are used for women's summer dresses, for linings, scarves, headdresses, canopies for beds or easy chairs, window curtains, bedspreads and other furnishings.

Paulet said that taffetas are all alike, wherever they are woven, except for their measurements and for the number of silk yarns in the warp and the weft. He further included *les Gros-de-Tours, les Gros-de-Florence, les Gros-de-Naples, les Gourgourans, les Pous-de-Soie, les Pekins, les Moëres unies sur soie & sur fil, les Bours du Levant, les Papelines & toutes autres Etoffes du même genre* which differ only in name and in the use of a little more silk in the warp, the weft, or both (p. 4).

Of taffetas Webster wrote in 1845 that they have "usually a remarkably wavy lustre, imparted by pressure and heat, with the application of an acidulous fluid to produce the effect called watering" (p. 969).

For the most part, James Beekman ordered black taffetas, and his agents sent Indian, Persian, or English depending upon the price; in 1771 the "India China taffaties havin fallen ten shillings per piece" in price and the "Spittlefeilds taffaties being so much inferior on quality" were omitted from his shipment (2:933). Other orders requested bright blues, bright green, brown, narrow striped, and English taffetas—"not Stiffned" (2:910). After the American Revolution direct trade between China and the United States resulted in the importation of great quantities of silks. Typical of the newspaper advertisements is one in the *Providence Gazette* for "Fresh Goods" from Canton which included silks, satins, lustrings, taffetas, and ribbons (June 8, 1793).

TAFFICILA

See Tapsel.

TAMMY

A strong, lightweight worsted of plain weave and open texture, often glazed. The name is one of several derived from the Italian *stame* meaning both a worsted yarn and a warp. The etymology of the word is discussed in Hazel E. Cummin, "Tammies and Durants" (p. 153). Peuchet, writing in 1801, found the English tammies superior: "the long, shiney fibers make a beautiful cloth which takes a lustrous finish" (*Vocabulaire*). More recently tammies were made with cotton warp and worsted weft.

Green, yellow, claret, and especially red and blue tammies are listed in seventeenth-century American inventories. James Beekman's annual, or semiannual, orders from New York included black, white, brown, green, blue, yellow, red, pink, and striped tammies.

Tammy was used for bed and window hangings, for ladies' petticoats and dresses, for the linings of men's coats, and as strainer cloths, or sieves. At a county ball held in York, England, as late as 1808, "comprising the rank and fashion of the north, the ladies were attired in tammy dresses, and very gay they appeared" (James, p. 363). In the manuscript for *Annals of Philadelphia,* author John Fanning Watson says that many chintz dresses "were lined with tammy stuff, to keep them stiff & never to be washed!" (p. 190).

Thomas Chippendale's bills to Sir Edward Knatchbull in the 1770s include "3 spring Curtains of Green Tamy Complete," and "166 yds fine Tammy Lining" for "Drapery Window Curtains" (Boynton, "Mersham-Le-Hatch," pp. 99, 100). A charge of six pence was made by the London Society of Cabinet-makers in 1803 for "Putting on the Tammy with braid, ea. side" of a horse fire screen and "Putting on the Tammy or Shalloon with braid on each side of each panel of a Folding Fire Screen" (London Book of Prices).

Eight swatches of *Tamise viré semplici* and *doppie viré,* some mixed with a little silk, are in the Moccasi manuscript of about 1760. Made at Amiens, the colors are brown, blue, green, and red (p. 9); for two swatches of twilled *Tamine osia Etamine* from London in black/blue and pale blue/white, see plate D-54; for swatches of Yorkshire tammies, see plate D-103.

TANDEM

A kind of linen cloth first made in Germany. In the *Boston Gazette* (December 31, 1754), it was advertised as "just imported from London . . . 3-4th and yard wide garlixs, tandems, hollands, cambricks." A circular from Hamburg printed in the *Pennsylvania Gazette* of November 26, 1783, listed "German cloth of every quality and colour . . . Silesia linens, . . . Rough dowlas, Quadruple tandems, Brown Silesias."

A 1757 letter to James Beekman from London agents indicates that tandem referred to a method of rolling a bolt of cloth: "The Yard wide garlix now sent are of the tandem sort As very few tight bound garlix are now imported, and believe You will find them very cheap. Our customers approve that sort, as they can examine into them, the tandem Sletias now sent are of the same sort sold You in August last" (2:632).

TANJIB
(tanjeeb)

A plain cotton cloth, usually of superior quality, from Bengal. It was exported in large quantities to England at the end of the seventeenth century. Special orders were sometimes embroidered in silk chain-stitch for dresses and petticoats (Irwin and Schwartz). Savary des Bruslons added that the material was also embroidered with cotton and that handkerchiefs were made of it.

TAPIZADO

A brilliantly colored worsted with polychrome brocaded flowers produced at Norwich in the eighteenth century. Examples are found in the Moccasi manuscript of about 1760 (see Pl. D-56), in John Kelly's pattern books dated 1763 and 1767 (see Fig. D-90), and in other merchants' pattern books in the Castle and Winterthur museums (see Pls. D-77, D-86).

TAPSEL
(tapseel, topseile, tafficila)

A cheap striped cloth made in western India which can be grouped with Guinea stuffs such as brawles, neconnees, and anabasses. Made of mixed silk and cotton patterned in the loom, tapsels were imitated in the West during the eighteenth century. Savary des Bruslons defines the cloth as coarse cotton ordinarily striped with blue.

John Banister's 1739 invoice book lists "6 Narrow Tapsuls 14 Yds o/o."

TAUNTON

A broadcloth first made in the town of that name in Somersetshire. Specifications for its measurements and weight were established in the second half of the sixteenth century.

TAURINO

A kind of cloth made of sheep's wool and cattle hair in New York frontier settlements during the eighteenth century (Tryon, p. 204).

TERRINDAM
(turundam)

"Plain muslin, usually of superior quality, woven chiefly in Dacca [India]" (Irwin and Schwartz).

TERRY CLOTH

A cotton fabric with a looped pile surface made by a supplementary warp, used especially in the manufacture of Turkish towels. First made of silk in

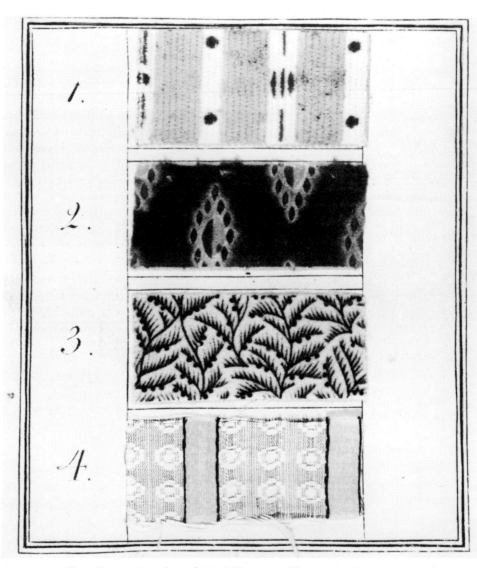

FIG. D-97. *Swatches of (1) thickset, or ribbed, printed cotton; (2) velveret, or printed napped cotton; (3) twilled and printed woolen cassimere; (4) silk and cotton muslinet of Swiss manufacture. From* Journal für Fabrik *(October 1794), p. 308. (Winterthur Museum Library.)*

1841 and of worsted in 1845, terry cloths were successfully woven of cotton yarns in 1848. In 1864 they were manufactured in Paterson, New Jersey.

THICKSET

A kind of cotton fustian or velvet made either plain or flowered (Fig. D-97). Swatches 51 and 52 in John Holker's manuscript resemble fine-wale corduroy; one is linen/cotton, the other all cotton, and both are dyed brown. A wide variety of cotton velvets, including two of thickset (one striped), are in the Hilton manuscript of 1786 (see Fig. D-39).

In 1759 James Beekman of New York ordered thicksets with shalloon, buttons, and mohair for lining and trimming, and in 1766 he ordered 16 pieces of 24 yards each in five different grades of "sorted Olives" (2:662, 862). A runaway black slave wore "a lightish-colour'd Thickset Coat, a blue Ratteen Jacket with Cuffs to the Sleeves, a blue Broad Cloth Jacket without Sleeves, Flannel Shirt, stript Flannel Trowsers" (Dow, *Arts and Crafts,* p. 203). "A great variety of cotton and worsted thicksetts" were offered for sale in the *Providence Gazette,* December 18, 1762.

See also Beaverteen.

THUNDER AND LIGHTNING

A heavy woolen cloth, probably rain repellent. A "Thunder and Lightning Coat; otherwise German Sarge" is listed in a *Virginia Gazette* of 1757 (Earle, *Costume,* p. 89).

TICKING
(ticken; Fr. coutil)

Linen twill. According to John Holker's manuscript, this material was used for the aprons worn by distillers, brewers, and waiters (swatch no. 31). Savary des Bruslons stated that army tents were made of ticking and that it served to enclose feathers in mattresses, bolsters, and pillows. Samples of blue and white and tan and white striped linen *coutil,* included in a letter from Lyons dated 1775, are in the collection of Colonial Williamsburg (1971-173).

Superfine ticking (Holker's swatch no. 32) was woven in a herringbone pattern to line garments, for women's stays, and for hunters' gaiters. Like so many other linen textiles, these were later made of cotton.

Bed ticking and coarser "Ticking for Flock Beds" of English make, Flanders bed tickings, and Hamborough "ticken" for "Wascoates and Breeches" are found in a Science Museum manuscript of about 1784. Fine qualities with a variety of colored stripes were also used for shoes (Figs. D-98, D-99).

In 1854 Wallis reported: "Tickings are extensively manufactured, and often form a department in the large cotton establishments in the New England States. The manufacture of them, with checks, stripes, &c., also form a considerable item in the home industry of Pennsylvania" (p. 13). Writing of goods of this class contributed at the New York industrial exhibition of 1853, Wallis said: "it is scarcely possible to conceive a firmer or better made article, and the traditionary notion that really good tickings can only be manufactured from flax receives a severe shock when such cotton goods as these are presented for examination" (p. 13).

TICKLENBURG
(tichlingburg)

A coarse, rough cloth made of hemp or linen. Like osnaburg, which was less coarse, it was named after the German town where it was once made. Samuel Rowland Fisher ordered "10 ps supperband Ticklenburgs at 10d" and "7 ps underband Ticklenburgs at 9¾" in London, 1767.

Alexander Hamilton recommended a 7.5 percent duty on ticklenburgs imported into the United States in 1790, as well as on other linen goods such as drill, osnaburg, dowlas, canvas, brown roll, and bagging (p. 256).

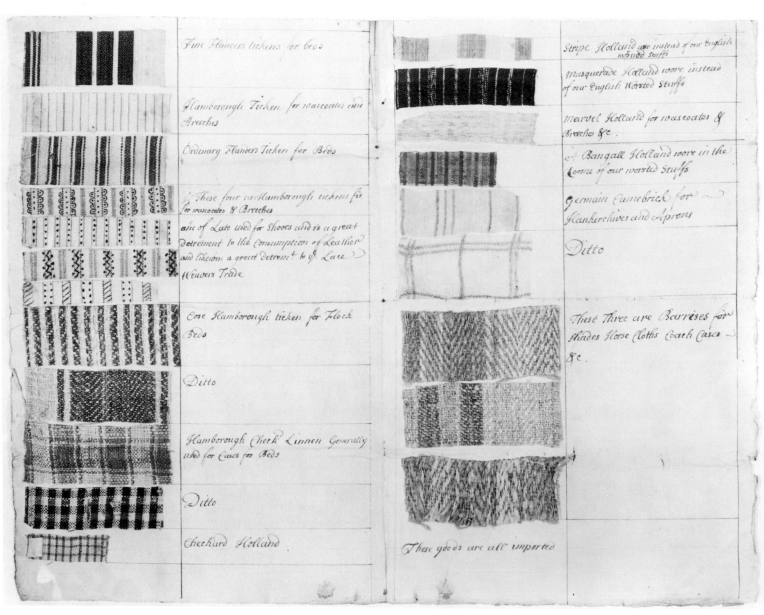

Fine Flanders tickens for beds

Hamborough Ticken for wascoates and Breeches

Ordinary Flanders Ticken for Beds

These four are Hamborough tickens fit for wascoates & Breeches

are of Late used for Shooes and is a great detreiment to the Consumption of Leather and likewise a great detremt to of Lace Weavers Trade

Cose Hamborough ticken for Flock Beds

Ditto

Hamborough Check Linnen Generally used for Cases for Beds

Ditto

Checkurd Holland

Stripe Holland are instead of our English worsted stuffs

Masquerade Holland wove instead of our English Worsted Stuffs

Marvel Holland for wascoates & Breeches &c.

A Bangall Holland wove in the Loome of our worsted Stuffs

Germain Camebrick for Hankerchives and Aprons

Ditto

These Three are Beurrises for Shades Horse Clothis Coach Cases &c.

These goods are all imported

FIGS. D-98, D-99 OPPOSITE. *Linen goods of the late eighteenth century from Hamburg, Flanders, Bengal, Germany, and England used for bed ticks, horse cloths, coach cases, men's coats, breeches, waistcoats, and women's shoes. (Science Museum, London.)*

364

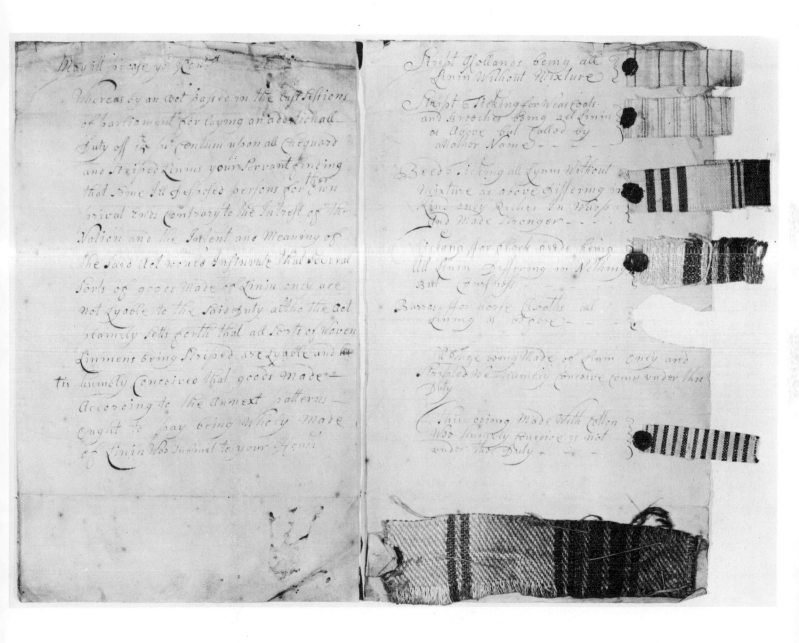

May itt please y^e Hon^bl

Whereas by an Act passed in the last Sessions
of Parliament for laying an additionall
Duty off 15 p^r Centum upon all Cheqward
and Striped Linins your Servant finding
that some ill disposed persons for their
privat ends Contrary to the Intrest of the
Nation and the Intent and Meaning of
the said Act would Insinuate that severall
sorts of goods Made of Linin only are
not lyable to the said Duty altho the Act
Expressly setts forth that all sorts of woven
Linnens being Striped are lyable and itt
tis humbly Conceived that goods Made
According to the Annext patterns
ought to pay being Wholly Made
of Linin Wee Submit to your Hon^rs

Right Hollands being all
Linin Without Mixture

Right Ticking for Wastcoats
and Breeches being all Linin
as Above but Called by
another Name

Beed Ticking all Linin Without
Mixture as above Differing in
Name only Richer in Warp
and Made Stronger

Ticking for Cloak bags being
all Linin Differing in Nothing
But Coursness

Barracan for horse Cloaths all
Linin as Above

All these being Made of Linin only and
Striped Wee humbly Conceive comes under this
Duty

These being Made With Cotton
Wee humbly conceive is not
under this Duty

TIFFANY

A thin transparent silk. Under seventeenth-century Massachusetts sumptuary laws, tiffany hoods were forbidden to folk of modest fortune (Earle, *Costume,* p. 245). Like cyprus and crape, black tiffany was used for mourning. "Hat band Crapes and Tiffiny" were among articles lost in the 1760 Boston fire (*Boston Records,* p. 38).

Beck cites "bird-eyes tiffany" in 1711: "The piece of luxury . . . was the tablecloth and napkins, which were all tiffany, embroidered in silk and gold, in the finest manner, in natural flowers. It was with the utmost regret that I made use of these costly embroidered napkins, which were as fully wrought as the finest handkerchief. . . . You may be sure that they were quite spotted before dinner was over."

In 1791 at a Charleston, South Carolina, ball honoring President Washington "the ladies and dresses were really superb—painted tiffany and silver twice was quite common . . . the most elegant . . . was a tiffany gown and coat—with a border a quarter deep of the most superb painted tiffany . . . in festoons the flowers very small but very distinct. They seemed to be made of foil spangles and painting so that it was extremely brilliant" (Ott, p. 181).

Another kind of tiffany was made of fine flax and was related to cobweb lawn. Randle Holme in the *Academy of Armory,* 1688, called it a housewife's cloth made of hemp or flax.

Tiffany of open weave and stiffened with gum was used for artificial flowers in the late nineteenth century.

TILLET
(tillot, tilleting)

A coarse cloth used as a wrapper for goods being shipped. A shipping charge for tilleting often is found itemized at the bottom of eighteenth-century invoices. The material was also used for awnings, tents, and barge, cart, and wagon covers. Possibly the same as tilt.

According to Whittock's 1837 *Book of Trades,* "the tillet, or little cloth, for encasing glazed stuffs intended for a foreign market, was the first approach towards pattern floor-cloth painting" (p. 246).

TILT

Largely made at Witney for use as awnings and wagon, barge, and horse covers. They were made of coarse unscoured yarns "in which the grease was left to increase [their] resistance to rain" (Plummer, p. 5n). Possibly the same as tillet.

TIRETAINE
(tariton)

A coarse linsey-woolsey, or all-wool cloth, which Beck relates to tartan; a 2/2 twill of linen warp and low quality woolen weft. In France it was associated with *bure, poulangy, berluche, belinge,* or *belingue,* all coarse cloths (Braun-Ronsdorf, p. 24). A swatch among the Richelieu Papers called *Bellingues ou tirtaines* is a heavy wool and linen cloth made in Picardy and dated 1737 (Lh45c IV, p. 101).

TISSUE

A rich fabric used for altar frontals, expensive dresses, coronation chairs, and other luxury purposes. The weaves often included silver and gold threads. Technically tissue was made with two sets of warp threads and at least two sets of shafts, and with one or more pattern wefts controlled by the figure harness of a drawloom. G[odfrey?] Smith's *Laboratory* describes the patterns as "commonly drawn with large ornamental flowers and leafs . . . ; the groundwork is frequently filled up with mosaick-work of one sort or other." He added that small silk flowers may be introduced to such designs (Thornton, "Silk-Designer's Manual," p. 16).

In London, stolen coronation robes and other clothing belonging to the Countess Dowager

Effingham in 1760 included "a silver tissue petticoat" and "a white tissue flowered Sack and Petticoat" (Malcolm, p. 444). In that same year "14 yds Silver Tushsue at £11" were lost in the Boston fire (*Boston Records,* p. 37). In 1758 Benjamin Franklin wrote to his wife, Deborah: "There is a better Gown for you of flower'd Tissue; 16 Yards, of Mrs. Stevenson's Fancy, cost 9 Guineas; and I think it a great Beauty. There are no more of the Sort, or you would have had enough for a Negligee or Suit" (*Franklin Papers,* 7:382). (See Pl. D-87.)

Although a few seventeenth-century English inventories list bed hangings of rich tissue and other cloths with metal threads, they are not found in colonial records.

See Lampas.

TOBINE

A wide variety of dress materials from fine silks to silk and worsted, and linen and cotton combinations that have warp-float patterns of small flowers or intermittent stripes and dots.

G[odfrey?] Smith's *Laboratory* includes them in a list of flowered silks: "There are likewise lutestring tobines, which commonly are striped with flowers in the warp, and sometimes between the tobine stripes with brocaded sprigs. Some have likewise a running trail with the colour of the ground as other lutestrings" (p. 41). P. A. De Brissac, a London designer, listed in his 1760 account book "Rich tobine for the same number of cords as a former tobine which was nothing but rose buds and leaves" and a "D[ark] G[round] Chints Tobine." "A brocaded lustring Sack with a ruby-coloured ground and white tobine stripes," "a pink and white striped tobine Sack and Petticoat," and a "garnet-coloured lustring Nightgown, with a tobine stripe of green and white" are mentioned by Malcolm in the chapter "Anecdotes of Dress" (p. 348).

Two swatches of tobines in silk and worsted dating from about 1720 are preserved in the Weav-

ers' Company manuscript (see Pl. D-97). The watercolor pattern for a brocaded tobine designed by Anna Maria Garthwaite in 1747, together with a dress woven from it, are shown in Rothstein, "Nine English Silks" (figs. 3, 3a). Many striped tobines, although not always named, are found in the Warner Archive. In 1746 James Alexander attached to the copy of his order to William Hunt three cuttings of white linen with intermittent blue cotton stripes (see Pl. D-11). The Holker manuscript contains swatches called tobine messinets which are made of fine worsted patterned in silk (see Pl. D-31). Seven worsted and six silk and worsted patterns woven in tobine stripes are in a Norwich pattern book among the Berch Papers of about 1750 (see Pl. D-18). Both Spitalfields and Norwich manufactures are specified.

TOILINET
(tollanette)

Made of silk and cotton warp with woolen filling. The fabric could be plain, figured, or printed and was similar to cassimere. Swatches are found in the monthly fashion magazines *Journal für Fabrik* and Ackermann's *Repository* from 1793 to 1815 (see Fig. D-95). Toilinets were used for dresses but more especially for waistcoats.

The most brilliant patterns are found in the Aix-la-Chapelle pattern book of 1807 (see Pl. D-6). Made of cotton and wool they include small figures or stripes in silk and imitate English manufactures.

TOY

A general term for fancy worsted dress goods made in Norwich. In March 1695 "4 ps Worsted toys at 19/6 p ps" are listed in Thomas Banister's Boston order book (p. 32).

See also Floretta, which was apparently the same.

TRIPP
(*Fr. Trippe*)

A kind of moquette or velvet stuff of woolen pile and warp of goat's hair. It was made plain or striped. Also, by means of relief-carved metal rollers, tripps could be stamped with floral or geometric patterns in the manner of ciselé velvets. A 1641 source notes "Naples Fustian Tripp, or Velvet" which was probably a cotton textile (Thornton, *Interior Decoration,* p. 356, n. 60).

Two swatches of *Mocchetta unita denominata trippa* from Abbeville are in the Moccasi manuscript (see Pl. D-52). One is red with a stamped pattern; the other is woven in a geometric figure in red, green, and white on a black ground.

TUFTS

A kind of fustian or cotton velvet related to thickset and made in the Manchester area. Black, gray, blue, green, and red tufts are mentioned in letters of 1738–42 written by a Bolton middleman (Wadsworth and Mann, p. 264–67). "Tufted fustian" was advertised in the *Pennsylvania Journal* on October 20, 1748.

TULLE

Silk bobbin net first produced in France toward the end of the eighteenth century. Beck gave the history of this material and the related zephyr, illusion, and blonde nets.

TURKEY WORK

Also called setwork and Norwich work. (See Upholstery, Fig. 3.) A woolen pile fabric made in imitation of Turkish carpets for use as upholstery and table and floor carpets especially during the seventeenth century. It was worked on a loom mounted with strong hempen warp threads to which rows of colored worsted yarns were tied by hand. The knots of wool, generally the same as for Turkish rugs (known as Ghiordes), were held in place by one or more weft shoots of hemp. The knots were later clipped to form an even pile. As durable as carpets, Turkey work was particularly well suited to seating furniture which received hard wear. With its floral patterns and bright tacks and fringe for trimming, it was decorative as well.

A particularly handsome piece is described in London's *Kingdom Intelligencer,* January 20, 1661:

> A very faire new and large Turkey Carpet, about 6 yards long and three yards broad, the ground white and the workes four true Lovers Knots with a July flower in the middle, the square which the four Knots make, wherein the flowers standes about five inches, the Border round about the Carpet is flower work very large.

In 1686, a South Carolina merchant owned "12 rich new backes and seats of Turkey work for chear[s]" valued at £10 (as quoted in Baldwin). Capt. George Corwin of Salem owned a Turkey work carpet, and the following chairs, by 1694:

> 9 turkey worke chaires without backs, 5 s. each
> 4 ditto wth. Backs at 8 s. each
> 6 low Turkey worke dito with Backs, 8 s. each. [Dow, *Every Day Life,* p. 276.]

In 1691/92 Samuel Sewall made a note to "Write to Cousin Hull, for Saml. Gardener, two small Bibles with cases Turkey Covers" (Letter book, 1:131).

TWILL
(*tweel*)

A kind of weave producing a diagonal effect in the finished cloth. Twills are "float weaves characterized by a diagonal alignment of floats for which a minimum of three warp groupings is essential. . . . Adjacent wefts never float over or under the same group of warps, and for each successive passage of the weft the warp grouping is stepped one warp beyond the previous grouping" (Emery; for illustrations of various types of twill weaves, including diamond, herringbone, and bird's-eye, see Emery, pp. 92–105; see also Burnham, pp. 154–60).

Savary des Bruslons claimed that twill-woven cloths wore better than those of plain weave. Webster generalized that

> Tweeled or twilled cloth is a description of figure-weaving depending upon the arrangement of threads that compose the warp and the weft. . . . When twilled cloth is composed of silk, it is called satin; when of cotton, fustian or jean; when it is composed of woollen, it is called serge, or kerseymere; and in linen it is distinguished by various names. . . . Cloths may be twilled on one side or on both sides, as shalloon; and they may be made, by various dispositions of the loom, to exhibit the different stripes and figures seen in dimity, diaper, and damask. [P. 935.]

U

UNION

A nineteenth-century term for cloth woven from a combination of yarns, as linen/cotton, silk/cotton, or wool/cotton.

V

VALENCIA

A waistcoating material with a cotton warp and "silk warp for the silk pattern, and the weft is worsted of British wool. There are often imitations of silk patterns from Spitalfields, and form a very showy manufacture" (Webster, p. 972). It closely resembled toilinet.

Ackermann's *Repository* recommended silk-striped valencia for waistcoats in 1809 (1, no. 3 [March 1809]: 186).

VANDELAS
(vandale)

A kind of strong, coarse canvas used especially for sails, manufactured in the district of Brittany formerly called *Le Vandelais* (OED).

VELURE
(velour)

Derived from the French word *velours* meaning velvet. The term seems to have been used for a wide variety of pile fabrics. The 1660 Book of Rates lists single and double velure among exports. By 1892 it denoted "a cotton curtain fabric, woven with a coarse stiff pile on the terry cloth principle, alike on both sides, and dyed in solid colors" (George S. Cole).

Six mid-eighteenth-century velures in the Berch Papers are corded and have uncut pile in floral patterns.

VELVERET

A cotton pile fabric, often ribbed like corduroy, and largely made in the Manchester area from about 1750. James Beekman of New York ordered velverets by pattern number from Manchester, Bristol, and London from about 1767 to 1784. Like thicksets (see Fig. D-97), they were worn by men and generally were requested in brown, black, and "dark olive," although one order specified "Pompedore" and crimson (2:834).

"Velverets began [in the 1770s] to be stamped with gold spots and figures by the ingenuity of Mr. Mather. . . . An attempt was made to stamp the pile of velverets in figures by heated rollers, as linseys and harrateens had formerly been done for bed-furniture; but without success. . . . The former deficiency as to finishing the cotton velvets and thicksets put the manufacturers upon several methods to remedy that defect . . . [and] soon raised velverets, which were made as a middle species between velvets and thicksets" were perfected (Aikin, pp. 161–63).

Samuel Rowland Fisher ordered "Six half ps neat dove & Lead Col[ore]d Velveretts" while at Manchester in 1767. He asked the merchant to "Be particular in the Cols of these as the Sale depends upon them. No Olives—3/3 to 3/9." On September 7 of the same year, George Bartram advertised "Black, blue, olive and cloth coloured cotton velvets and velverits" in Philadelphia (*Pennsylvania Chronicle*).

VELVET

A pile fabric made of silk, wool, or cotton fibers. It is an extra-warp woven-pile structure whereas velveteen is an extra-weft structure (Emery, p. 175).

Among the Lord Chamberlain's accounts of 1754–59 are swatches of silk Genoa velvets of fine quality in red, purple, black, and green silk, the last designated as "2 yds to Cover a Card Table." Dutch velvets in the same accounts are coarser and cheaper in price (Public Record Office, LC 9/267).

Utrecht velvet is a stout velvet which, according to Roland de la Platière, was made of linen warp and weft with pile of goat's hair in solid colors or striped, embossed with patterns or printed. It was used for upholstery and coach linings.

In the Moccasi manuscript of about 1760 are swatches of *Veluto d'Utrech* in gold with a cut-pile pattern and *Mocchetta Goffrata* with a stamped pattern made at Lille (see Pl. D-62). Twenty swatches of flowered and plain wool velvets of Spitalfields manufacture in gold, scarlet, tan, black, green, and raspberry have cut or uncut pile as well as voided areas (see Pl. D-19).

See Manchester velvets for cotton velvets.

VELVETEEN

Cotton velvet. According to Emery it has an extra-weft woven-pile structure (p. 175). In 1776, a new kind of goods called "velvateens," patent number 1123, was claimed to be an improvement "on velvarets, far superior" (Warner, p. 637). In 1833 the fabric was of much greater substance than cotton velvet and could be had of every possible color, including white and black (Perkins).

VENETIAN

A closely woven woolen cloth having a fine twilled surface, used as a suiting or dress material. Venetians were developed from twilled cassimeres in the West Country about 1840 (Mann, p. 193). Also a tape or braid used for venetian blinds and upholstery binding.

VENETIAN CARPET

The names *Venetian carpet* and *striped Venetians* were applied to carpeting made with brightly colored warp stripes of wool and a weft of linen or hemp (Fig. D-100). They were woven on a two-harness loom in the home but were also imported from the late eighteenth century to America. Webster

FIG. D-100. *Striped Venetian carpet, English or American, early nineteenth century. The vegetable-dyed, polychrome wools are characteristic of the color palette used before synthetic dyes were developed. (Collection of Florence M. Montgomery.)*

commented that "the warp is so thick as to cover entirely the woof" and adds that "Venitian carpeting is used chiefly for bedrooms and stair-carpets, the dust adhering less to them than to others" (p. 255).

VERMILLION

A kind of cotton cloth. The first document concerning the cotton manufacture of England is contained in Lewis Roberts's *Treasure of Traffic*, 1641:

> The town of Manchester buys the linen yarn of the Irish in great quantity, and weaving it, return the same again in linen into Ireland to sell. Neither does her industry rest here, for they buy cotton wool in London, that comes from Cyprus and Smyrna, and work the same into fustians, vermillions and demities, which they return to London where they are sold, and from thence, not seldom, are sent into such foreign parts, where the first materials may be more easily had for that manufacture. [Butterworth, p. 65.]

VESTING

Waistcoat material. A late eighteenth-century pattern book, stamped "J. Jh. Clerc Fils & Cie. de Paris," contains 286 samples of striped vestings and other wool/cotton textiles, some with a little silk and possibly intended for dresses. Checks, stripes, quiltings, and dotted and herringbone patterns are represented, unfortunately without identification or date.

The greatest variety and most colorful assortment of materials used for gentlemen's vests is presented in the 1807 Aix-la-Chapelle pattern book—*Piquet & Trips en Laine, Toillinettes, Wolstrips, Côte Transparente* (see Pl. D-7), and two qualities of *Duvet*. Others are found in the *Journal für Fabrik* and Ackermann's *Repository*. The following list of vestings is presented in Forbes's *Merchant's Memorandum and Price Book* published in Boston in 1827:

Toilenet
Valencia Ass[orte]d
Swansdown   do.
Moleskin
Marseilles—white
      Assd. Fancy
      Plain Silk
      Strip'd do
      Fig'd do
      Silk Velvet

A comparable list is presented by Perkins in 1833 under waistcoatings with the additions of silk, quiltings (another name for marcella), and merino.

A fancy mid-nineteenth-century English alpaca fabric was called California vesting: "Soon after 1849, Mr. White [of Huddersfield] produced the gold coloured twists needed to make the California vestings, which became seasonable articles at the time of the gold discovery in that State" (Warner, p. 254).

See also Duvetyn, Toilinet.

VIRGINIA CLOTH

A homespun and homewoven cloth made in Virginia. Andrew Burnaby in *Travels through the Middle Settlements in North America,* in 1759 and 1760, wrote "their manufactures are very inconsiderable. They make a kind of cotton cloth which they clothe themselves with in common, and call it after the name of their country [Virginia]" (Tryon, p. 98). A mixture of tow and cotton used for servants' wear (Frances Little, p. 67n).

VITRY

A kind of light durable canvas once made at Vitre, a town in Brittany. A 1757 reference says "Holland's duck, or vitry, is whilst in use, more pliant, and less apt to split" (OED). It can be related to vandelas and noyalls. "Vittrey at 14d" is listed in the 1660 inventory of William Paine with poldavy, noyalls, and lockram, all heavy utility cloths (Dow, *Every Day Life,* p. 259).

W

WADMAL
(wadmel, wadmill, wadmol, wednel)

A rough woolen cloth used principally for lining horse-collars and for rough clothing. "Wadmoll mittens" and "a woadmell petticoat" are cited by Earle (*Costume*, pp. 253–54), and "wadmoll" stockings and waistcoats by Dow (*Every Day Life*, pp. 253, 257). For earlier references, see Beck.

The material was occasionally used in less important English rooms for furnishing (Thornton, *Interior Decoration*, p. 115).

"*Vadmal* [is] a word which in the Scandinavian languages remains the common term for domestically produced woollen fabrics" (Geijer, p. 69).

WAHRENDORP

Although Perkins (1833) defined this fabric as "a very fine bleached linen principally exported to America and the West Indies by way of Bremen and Hamburg," earlier references link it with "Brown Hessians," a coarse, unbleached material (*Providence Gazette,* January 21, 1797). In 1751, "5 Remnants of Warendorps qt. 26 yards @ 7/6" and in 1762 "3 Remnants Warendorps, 25 yds. 8/" are listed in New York appraisements. Three pieces "Warrendorps linen each 46 ells" are listed in the 1728 New York inventory of Thomas Pavel at the Winterthur Museum Library.

WASHER
(wash-white)

Cheap, narrow woolen cloth resembling kersey but only half thickened or half-fulled. That made in Devonshire, sometimes called Devonshire impenetrable, was famous.

WATERING

A technique used for finishing cloths of plain weave with a heavier weft than warp to give them a watered, or waved, look.

Swatches in the Holker manuscript are watered harateens of which Holker states: "The wavey effect is achieved by means of a hot press, the use of which is little understood in France" (see Pl. D-27). Two swatches of black and dark green superfine moreens and ten swatches of superfine grogrinetts of finer weave, also with watered patterns, are in the Berch Papers.

Silk textiles like taffeta with heavier weft threads than warp were called moiré when folded and pressed or when two pieces were pressed against each other. Diderot shows the great press weighted with stones under which the rolled pieces of cloth were placed (see Fig. D-26). The result is a textile with a shimmering or wavey appearance.

See also Embossing, Moreen, Pressing.

WEB

A thick, warm woolen cloth manufactured, along with flannels, in Montgomeryshire, Merionethshire, and part of Denbighshire during the 1790s (Banks, p. 63).

WELSH COTTON

A loosely woven woolen cloth resembling flannel. Macpherson referred to a 1566 statute which states that "the trade in Welsh woollen cloth and lining, commonly called Welsh cottons, frises, and plains, had for a long time been considerable" in Shrewsbury, a town near the Welsh border.

The Aspinwall Records show the importation of Welsh cottons into Boston as early as 1650.

See also Cotton (to designate woolen cloth).

WIGAN

A cotton cloth woven in the Lancashire town of that name. "7/8 yard and 6/4 wigon or house-wife cloth" was advertised by James and Drinker in the *Pennsylvania Chronicle, and Universal Advertiser* (December 4, 1769). Kearny and Gilbert's advertisement in the same paper (April 20, 1767) offered a "variety of Wigan and Manchester checks."

In the nineteenth century, it was known as a calico. "In quality they are soft, warm and finished; but are stout and heavy. . . . They are made for sheetings, amongst other purposes, and measure from 2 to 3 yards in width" (Caulfeild and Saward). Samples of thick calicoes, called longcloths and wigans, woven by hand, are included in the 1851 *Crystal Palace Exhibition Illustrated Catalogue* (no. 1195). Harmuth called wigan "a heavily starched, open cotton canvas, used for interlining, usually gray or black. The bleached grades are used for shirts."

WILDBORE

A worsted made stouter and closer woven than a tammy but finished without glaze. "Marone Ribb'd Wildbores" were advertised in Salem in 1784 (Earle, *Costume*, p. 257). About that time Samuel Rowland Fisher, at Wortley near Leeds, noted in his journal: "Benjamin North makes Durants, Tamys, Wildboars, Cambletts & Calamanco's."

James Akroyd of Halifax manufactured "18-inch lastings, calimancoes and wildbores, called Little Joans, very similar to modern buntings, in the last quarter of the 18th century" (Warner, p. 236). Among Yorkshire worsted manufactures made in 1843 are "Wildbores or Bombazets," 16 to 17 inches wide and 28 yards long, sold for 11 to 18 shillings per piece (James, p. 495).

In the *Providence Gazette,* "Wildbore, and other Stuffs for Womens Gowns" were offered for sale on January 1, 1791, and "Wildbores, striped and plain" on November 19, 1791.

WILDWORM CORD

A kind of cotton velvet with a zigzag cord known from a swatch in the 1786 Hilton manuscript (see Fig. D-56).

WILTON CARPET

A type of strip pile carpeting. A patent was granted in 1741 to make at Wilton "French carpeting" which differed from Brussels carpeting in having cut pile. Webster described the difference:

> When the wires upon which the loops are formed are drawn out, the worsted loops are cut through with a sharp knife, and then they form a pile in the manner of plush or velvet. The basis is linen. This manufacture was introduced into this country through the exertions of Lord Pembroke; and they have the advantage of being executed in very beautiful designs. In the *Royal Wilton* the pile is raised higher than in the common Wilton. [P. 255.]

Hand-knotted carpets were made at Wilton after 1835 when the Axminster factory and operation moved to Wilton.

WILTON CLOTH

Woolen cloth made in Wilton, Wiltshire. From 1766 to 1784 James Beekman ordered it by the piece at prices ranging from 3s. 6d. to 4s. 6d. a yard in "handsome brown Cloth colours," "handsome different colours," and green. Whatever the nature of Wilton cloth, apparently it was being copied in homespun by Rhode Island weavers as early as 1765. In that year Gerard G. Beekman wrote to Evan and Francis Malbone: "I should be much Obliged to you if [you] Could Procure me Enough homespun Cloth that is of good Couler and fine for Two Coats and Wa[s]te Coats for myself and friends use. am informed it may be had very good with you and also the same Quantity of what is made in Immitation of Wilton Only of a mixture of black and white, Such as the Inclosed Sample which Came from your place (or better if you can)" (1:489–90).

WINCEY
(winsey)

A word derived from linsey-woolsey. Very durable and used by the poorer class of people; "there is a quantity of oil in the common qualities, accompanied by a disagreeable odour" (Caulfeild and Saward). A reference to a suit of green wincey is in *Godey's Lady's Book,* January 1870, p. 105.

WITNEY

A heavy, loose woolen cloth, or coating with a nap made at Witney in Oxfordshire. In 1677, Robert Plot records that blankets were made at Witney of "ordinary and middle" wool. When mixed with "the courser Locks of Flecce-wool, a sort of Stuff they call Duffields" is made. "Of their best Tail-wool they make the Blankets of 6 Quarters broad, commonly called Cuts, which serve Seamen for their Hammocs; and of their worst they make Wednell [wadmol] for Collar-makers, Wrappers to pack their Blankets in, and Tilt-cloths for Barge-men."

Arthur Young, traveling in the late 1760s, says of the town:

> Witney is very famous for its woollen manufactory, which consists of what they call kersey-pieces, coarse bear-skins, and blankets. The two first they make for the North American market; vast quantities being sent up the river St. Lawrence, and likewise to New-York. Their finest blankets . . . are exported to Spain and Portugal; but all are sent to London first. [*Tour through the Southern Countries,* p. 130.]

Witney duffels were "exported to Virginia and New England, for cloathing the Indians" (Postlethwayt). In 1716 a Boston newspaper listed "True Witney broadcloth, with its shag unshorn"

(Dow, *Every Day Life,* p. 83). The loss of a "Great Coat of Red Whitney with red velvet Cape" was reported in a colonial newspaper of 1736 (Earle, *Costume,* p. 88).

WOOD-BLOCK PRINTING

The printing of cloth by means of mordants, that is to say metallic oxides or minerals, which when dipped in dye such as madder or quercitron caused a chemical reaction to take place and fixed the colors in the fibers. A separate block and a different mordant, or strength thereof, were required for each color.

William Sherwin of West Ham, near London, probably the first calico printer in England to use the fast-dye technique, was granted a patent in 1676 "for a new way for printing . . . and stayning" calico. Documented examples dating from 1726 are found in the Alexander Papers, and thirteen especially handsome midcentury pieces in the full chintz color palette are included in the Holker manuscript. Later eighteenth- and nineteenth-century changes in fashion have been documented by Peter Floud and Barbara Morris from factory records.

WOOLEN

Cloth made of carded short-staple wool fibers. After weaving, the cloth was fulled or shrunk to make it denser and heavier. Broadcloth was England's traditional fine woolen manufacture. The soft fluffy fibers of carded wool were also suitable for knitting.

WORSTED

Lightweight cloth made of long-staple combed wool yarn. The name was derived from the village of Worstead near Norwich, a center for worsted weaving. The smooth, shiny fibers were suitable for embroidery and indeed were synonymous with the word *crewel,* or crewel yarn.

In 1738 a "Manufacturer of Northampton-shire" listed the various kinds of woolen and wor-sted fabrics (as well as mixed goods) then being manufactured (*Observations on British Wool*):

The first, viz. is Combing Wool.

Says
Borsleys
Shalloons
Spanish Crapes
Bur[y]ing Crapes
Tamys
Purnellows [prunella]
Sattannets
Harrateens
Cheneys
Serges
Sagathies
Duroys
Durants
Ranters
Buntings
Boulting Cloths
Swathing Bands
Serge Denim
Camblets
Camblettees
Calimancoe plain
Calimancoe flower'd
Damasks
Russets
Everlasting
Cantiloons
Worsted Plus
Quarter Diamond
Bird's Eye and Diamond
Grogram
Paragon
Cadis
Gartering
Quality Binding
Stockings
Caps
Gloves
Breeches Knit.

With many other sorts of Plain and Figur'd Stuffs.

The following Goods are made of Combing Wool and Carding Wool mix'd together, the Combing is the Warp or Webb; the Carding is the Woof or Shoot, viz.

Bays
Broad Rash
Cloth Serge
German Serge
Long Ells
Druggets plain
Druggets corded
Flannel
Swan Skin
Suinco Bays or Wadding
Perpetuanas

The following Goods are made with Long Wool and Silk, Mohair, and Cotton mix'd, viz.

Norwich Crapes
Silk Druggets
Hair Plush
Hair Camblet
Stockings
Spanish Poplins
Caps and Gloves
Venetian Poplins
Alapeens
Anterines
Silk Sattenets
Bombasines

And divers sorts of different Stuffs, both figur'd, clouded, spotted, plain and strip'd, too tedious to name. [James, p. 226.]

A similar list for 1772 is found in Bischoff (1:186):

General Estimate of the Yorkshire Woollen Manufacture, Easter 1772

Annual Amount of the Manufacture of Clothing or Short Wool [i.e., woolens] Broad cloths, narrow cloths, bays, ker-seys, half thicks, blankets, hose, Colne serges, and plains, penistones, kerseys, hats, horse sheets, and coverlets

£1,869,700.15.7½

Annual Amount of Combing Wool [i.e., worsteds]

Shalloons, callimancoes, russels, tammies, single camblets or camblettees, prunells, and moreens, all made of single yarn; everlastings, figured and flowered amiens, scrgcs dc Nismes and serges de Rome, whose warps are of double yarn, and various other articles

£1,404,000.0.0

In the records of James Akroyd and Son of Halifax in Yorkshire, the transition from hand-loom weaving to jacquard patterns and finally to mechanical weaving is detailed. With experimentation, new combination fabrics appeared every few years as listed below:

1798.   Calimancoes, plain and ribbed; lastings; prunelles.
1803.   Serges de Berri; shalloons; russells; wildbores.
1811.   Moreens; says; duroys.
1813.   3/4 bombazetts or plainbacks.
1819.   Bombazines and Norwich crapes.
1822.   Camblets; toborines; fancy russells; dobbies.
1824.   Damasks.
1826–27. French merinoes, and full twills.
1834.   French figures—a damask made 6/4 wide, of single worsted warp, and fine English or merino weft, wrought by jacquard engine, and producing a most beautiful and exact design.
1836.   Alpaca figures.
1838–40. Figured orleans, on a similar principle to the French figures, only substituting cotton warp, producing a light fabric, and a great and agreeable variety of figure. [James, p. 618.]

See also New Draperies, Norwich goods, Stuff, Woolen.

Z

ZACARILLA

"Far thinner even than mull, and when used, it is for the purpose of dresses" (Perkins).

ZANELLA

Serge made with cotton warp and worsted filling, used for linings and umbrella covers.

Bibliography

The extensive bibliography of textiles indicates that through the centuries a remarkable number of people have been interested in cloth for a wide variety of reasons. Charles Du Cange wrote of their Latin names; F. W. Fairholt, James Malcolm, James Planché, and Joseph Strutt wrote histories of English dress. John Dyer wrote a long poem about wool; James Boswell and Samuel Sewall noted fabrics in their diaries as did Benjamin Franklin and Thomas Jefferson in their letters.

In addition to standard early encyclopedias such as those of Nathan Bailey, Ephraim Chambers, Samuel Johnson, and Abraham Rees, commercial dictionaries and encyclopedias are extremely useful for the identification of textile terms no longer familiar to us. Of these, by far the most important is Jacques Savary des Bruslons's *Dictionnaire universel de commerce* (1723–30). Between 1751 and 1755 much of this was translated and published in English by Malachy Postlethwayt with comparisons made to English patterns of trade and goods produced, a work owned by Lord Botetourt of Williamsburg. Later publishers like Richard Rolt based their work on Savary des Bruslons and Postlethwayt but omitted their lengthy comments. In 1783 Thomas Mortimer enlarged Wyndham Beawes's *Lex Mercatoria* of 1752. David Macpherson's four-volume *Annals of Commerce* (1805), which includes the work of Adam Anderson up to 1760, is exhaustive.

English county histories contain particulars of the kinds of cloth woven in an area. Daniel Defoe, in his extensive travels (ca. 1725), and Arthur Young, half a century later, described weaving centers throughout the British Isles. Later authors concerned themselves with specialized types of manufacture such as *The Trowbridge Woollen Industry* (1951) by R. P. Beckinsale, *The Witney Blanket Industry* (1934) by Alfred Plummer, and *The Yorkshire Woollen and Worsted Industries* (1920) by Herbert Heaton. John James's *History of the Worsted Industry* contains all the important documentation prior to 1857, and James Bischoff's *Comprehensive History of the Woollen and Worsted Manufactures* (1842), a compilation of works by earlier writers, describes wool processing, spinning, weaving, and finishing and gives a great deal of information on the commerce of wool. More recent research on wool and worsted has been done by Ephraim Lipson and by Kenneth G. Ponting of the Pasold Research Foundation.

Five books include the most important information about Manchester, the center of British cotton weaving: *A Description of the Country . . . round Manchester* (1795) by John Aikin, *History of the Cotton Manufacture* (1835) by Edward Baines, *Early English Cotton Industry* (1920) by George W. Daniels, and the splendid economic study *The Cotton Trade and Industrial Lancashire* (1931) by Alfred Wadsworth and Julia de Lacy Mann. The period 1780–

1815 is covered in *The Growth of the British Cotton Trade* (1967) by Michael Edwards.

Textiles are included in general books about American manufactures such as J. L. Bishop's *History of American Manufactures* (1864), Victor S. Clark's *History of Manufactures in the United States* (1929), and R. M. Tryon's *Household Manufactures* (1917). More specialized are *Textile Industries of the United States* (1893) by William R. Bagnall and *American Wool Manufacture* (1926) by A. H. Cole. These books are especially important for textile technology and economic history.

For the technical aspects of weaving and finishing in eighteenth-century France, Diderot's *Encyclopédie* and the several sections on textiles by different authors in *Descriptions des arts et métiers,* published by the Royal Academy of Sciences, Paris, are invaluable although difficult for English-speaking readers. The Oxford *History of Technology,* edited by Charles Singer and others, includes long sections chronologically arranged with many illustrations on fiber and textile processing. The comprehensive study of weaving techniques made by Irene Emery for *The Primary Structure of Fabrics* is recommended for those more interested in this aspect of textiles. Dorothy K. Burnham's recent *Warp and Weft* is a valuable contribution to the understanding of techniques. It includes the international vocabularies established by members of the Centre International d'Etude des Textiles Anciens in Lyons.

Design and ornament and the changes in fashion which occurred in the patterns of expensive silk brocades can be studied in standard textile books and museum publications. Representative is Adele Coulin Weibel, *Two Thousand Years of Textiles* (1952). The finest work on the history of European silk weaving, with emphasis on the great centers of Spitalfields and Lyons, is Peter Thornton's *Baroque and Rococo Silks* (1965).

Several writers have attempted textile dictionaries. E. E. Perkins's *Treatise on Haberdashery* (1833) was written for the young merchant starting in trade. Despite its limitation in the number of words included, William Beck's *Draper's Dictionary* (1882) is invaluable for its references to the use made of materials over long periods of time. Editors of the *Oxford English Dictionary* relied extensively on Beck's work, but unfortunately the historical references are inadequate and a great many words are not to be found.

Grace G. Denny, Louis Harmuth, and Robert H. Megraw, writers in this century, often fail to suggest the changes in the character of a textile over time. The *Dictionary of Needlework* by S. F. A. Caulfeild and Blanche Saward is in effect a dictionary of textiles as well and is especially useful for nineteenth-century terms. Editors of *Textile Mercury,* a Manchester trade publication, published the *Mercury Dictionary* in 1950, a useful book but unfortunately now out of print. *CIBA Review,* published since 1937 by the Swiss color chemical firm, contains many popular, well-illustrated articles on the historical aspects of textile production in all countries. A fine recent survey is *A History of Textile Art* (1979) by Agnes Geijer.

This study of textile importation and use in the British colonies of North America and the United States would have been infinitely more difficult without the six volumes of newspaper advertisements on the arts and crafts compiled by George Francis Dow, Alfred Coxe Prime, and Rita Susswein Gottesman. They include advertisements of the textiles stocked by cabinetmakers, upholsterers, tailors, dressmakers, embroiderers, and importers, as well as the shop goods of dry-goods merchants, haberdashers, garment cleaners, undertakers, and those who sold at "Publick Vendue." For Rhode Island, I made a study of the textiles advertised in the *Providence Gazette* from 1762, the year it began publication, to 1800. Seventeenth- and eighteenth-century English textile references are taken largely from London Newspaper References, which are extracts from notices in London newspapers in an eleven-volume typescript in the Metropolitan Museum of Art Library.

Also helpful are the articles by Hazel E. Cummin on calimanco, dimity, moreen, and seersucker published in *Antiques* which were the first systematic studies concerned with antique domestic textiles. Abbott Lowell Cummings's *Bed Hangings* contains a glossary of textile terms assembled from American wills and inventories and other sources.

As an example of the usefulness of inventories for the study of textiles, as well as many other household furnishings, portions from the 1770 inventory of the Governor's Palace compiled from the Botetourt Manuscripts in the Virginia State Library by the staff at Colonial Williamsburg are cited below. Large pieces of cloth, apparently stocked for use as required together with clothing materials to be made up or remnants from garments previously used, were inventoried in the first storeroom along with tea, spices, sugarloaves, sieves, brushes, kitchen utensils, and tools:

> 1 ps Holland—3 ps Sheeting
> 11¾ yds coarse Irish Linen—
> 17 yds do 12 yds do—13½ yds Huccoback

10 Yds holland Sheeting—2 Yds worstead gauze—1 ps Morees—1 ps fine Damask Napkining—21 damask breakfast Cloths—2 ps Oznabrigs

37 yds Oznabrigs—76 yds & ¼ do

4 ps checkt Handkerchiefs—

7 Checkt Handkerchiefs—

8¼ yds brown Holland—5½ yds printed Cotton—1 Woman's Cotton Gown

5 small remnants of white Flannel

1 ps crimson Shalloon—1 ps br. Fustian

18¾ yds do—8½ yds crimson Shag

21¼ yds crimson Cloth & a remnant of Livery Lace—17 yds light colld do

9 yds do for great Coats—25¼ yds do

16¼ do 7 yds deep green Cloth

8 yds light cold do—20½ yd blue plains

8¼ green do—2 ps & 18¾ yds Russia Drab—1 Bale unopen'd contg 3 ps green & 3 ps blue plains—

11 Men's Castor Hats—23 pr coarse thread Hose—23 pr worstead do

25 pr Yarn do—4 Parcels of worstead & 3 of Metal Buttons—1 paper & a piece of Pins—19 pieces of white Tape—

2 ps green ferriting—6 cut pieces of Ribband of difft Sorts—37 hks Mohair of different Sorts—7 Bunches of Cruels

32 hks & a Ball of Silk—12 Bunches Thread—1 doz thread Laces—

16 papers of thread & 2 doz thread waist coat Buttons—2 small brown Linen bags—a dble body Girth—

(For another portion of this inventory, see dictionary entry at Linen.)

For Boston I relied primarily on the glossary compiled from "old letters, wills, inventories of estates, court records, and . . . newspapers" by Alice Morse Earle in *Costume of Colonial Times* (1894). *Every Day Life in the Massachusetts Bay Colony* by George Francis Dow includes a glossary and several important seventeenth-century inventories. The Aspinwall Records of 1644 to 1651 list over forty-five different kinds of cloth imported. The Boston Records include claims made for textiles lost in the fire of 1760.

Among eighteenth-century American merchants' records providing incontrovertible proof of the kinds of textiles brought to East Coast ports are the Beekman Papers, readily referred to in bound volumes published by the New-York Historical Society. Together with the Alexander Papers they present a broad picture of New York textile imports with many letters about the goods, the times, and the shipping details. The New York Appraisements contain household inventories and the seven-page inventory of textile merchant Thomas Hysham.

For Philadelphia, the 1728–37 ledger of Willing and Shippen was helpful. Receipts, invoices, orders, ledgers, journals, and daybooks among the Wistar Papers list textile imports from about 1760 to 1820. Two ledgers of Joshua Fisher and Sons, 1784–88 and 1792–97, contain typical entries, but more interesting is the journal kept by his son, Samuel Rowland Fisher, during trips to England in 1767/68 and 1783/84 when he visited textile weaving centers and ordered goods to be sent to Philadelphia.

An unusually complete record of fifty years of textile importing and merchandising is found in the Banister Papers which include the Boston letter book of Thomas Banister (1695–1712) and the invoice and letter books of John Banister of Newport covering the period 1739–46. For Virginia, I found useful *John Norton and Sons, Merchants of London and Virginia, . . . 1750–1795.*

Several bibliographies with long lists of design books are useful to the textile specialist. Among them are the published catalogues of the Metropolitan Museum of Art and the Winterthur Museum libraries. Peter Ward-Jackson's *English Furniture Designs of the Eighteenth Century* covers the work of Daniel Marot, William Hogarth, Thomas Chippendale, Thomas Sheraton, George Hepplewhite, and many others. For the first quarter of the nineteenth century, Rudolph Ackermann's *Repository* is valuable, both for the textile swatches included and for his comments and colored prints of fashionable furniture and furnishings. The most up-to-date bibliography for the Victorian period is by Jeremy Cooper.

Any study of window curtain and bed hanging styles and the arrangement of rooms in America must be based on English custom as shown in drawings, prints, and paintings. One-hundred-fifty years of British rule undeniably disposed the colonists toward English precedents; London remained the style center as well as the principal trading center for exported goods long after the American Revolution. The Connoisseur Period Guides, Tudor through early Victorian, are arranged by topic (architecture, furniture, textiles, etc.) and are excellent introductions to the styles. Peter Thornton's *Seventeenth-Century Interior Decoration in England, France, and Holland* summarizes his extensive research at the Victoria and Albert Museum in recent years. The changing uses of rooms and the social workings and protocol of princely residences are described in Mark Girouard's *Life in the English Country House*. Useful for prints and paintings that detail the international flavor of interior design are *Werken van D. Marot*, Wilhelm Kurth's *Die Raumkunst im Kupferstich des 17 und 18 Jahrhunderts*, and *An Illustrated History of Furnishing* by Mario Praz.

Early photographs of some original upholstery are in Percy Macquoid and Ralph Edwards's *Dictionary of English Furniture: From the Middle Ages to the Late Georgian Period*. Eighteenth-century pattern books such as Thomas Chippendale's *Director* and drawings assembled in Peter Ward-Jackson's *English Furniture Designs of the Eighteenth Century* record fashionable furniture styles and show the correct contours of stuffing and the methods of tacking. Chippendale's accounts to clients, published by Lindsay Boynton in *Furniture History*, trace his work from design concept to reality. Denis Diderot and Jean d'Alembert's *Encyclopédie* makes explicit the methods and tools employed by upholsterers. Thomas Sheraton's and George Hepplewhite's books, among others, gave recommendations for the kinds of furnishing materials suited to various rooms. For years John Fowler and John Cornforth visited public and private homes in England, and *English Decoration in the Eighteenth Century* (1974) reflects their concern to document all aspects of decorating, room arrangement, upholstery, and bed and window curtain treatments.

For the nineteenth century, there are superb collections of pattern books in the Metropolitan Museum of Art and Winterthur Museum; however, one can begin a study with the *Pictorial Dictionary of British Nineteenth-Century Furniture Design*, which contains small cuts from many of the important design books arranged according to type—see especially "Bedroom Furniture," "Chairs," "Couches," "Window Cornices with Drapes," and "General Views." John Cornforth's *English Interiors, 1790–1848* gives a pictorial record of room views, many of them in color.

Some French designs popularized by Pierre de la Mésangère in the irregular issues of *Meubles et objets de goût* (1802–35) were borrowed by London publisher Rudolph Ackermann for *A Series Containing Forty-four Engravings of Beds, Sofas, Ottomans, Window-Curtains, Chairs, Tables, Book-Cases, &c.* (1823) and for the monthly issues of his *Repository* (1809–28). Thomas Hope, wealthy designer and collector amateur who published *Household Furniture and Interior Decorations* in 1807, was a friend of Charles Percier and was influenced by Percier's work on buildings and interiors for Napoleon. Percier and Pierre F. L. Fontaine, in turn, published *Recueil de décorations intérieures* in 1812. Henry Havard's four-volume *Dictionnaire de l'ameublement* (1887), a compendium of French interior decoration, is illustrated with contemporary prints and paintings and includes definitions of materials, especially those used for drapery and upholstery.

The long history of nineteenth-century eclectic revival styles is found in pattern books. Such information is fortified by the records of Gillow and Company, a London and Lancaster firm in business from 1731 until the early years of this century. Of great practical value is James Arrowsmith's *Analysis of Drapery* (1819) with instructions for measuring material and cutting the parts of curtains; *The Workwoman's Guide* (1838) focuses on cutting and sewing done in the home. Richard Charles's *Three Hundred Designs for Window-Draperies, Fringes, and Mantle-Board Decorations* (1878) serves as a summary of revival styles. Sources for curtains, especially French but including English and American as well, are suggested in Samuel Dornsife's "Design Sources for Nineteenth-Century Window Hangings," a survey of books collected by the author, many of which are part of the Dornsife Collection of the Victorian Society in America at the Athenaeum of Philadelphia.

The transmittal of styles from one country to another was greatly fostered by international fairs beginning with the Crystal Palace in 1851 and the New York industrial exhibition in 1853.

The midcentury *Industry of All Nations: The Art Journal Illustrated Catalogue* of the Crystal Palace exhibition shows designs in every medium including patterned fabrics, upholstery materials, and carpets, as well as cornices and bed hangings. Many pictures of objects in the exhibition were incorporated by G. W. Yapp into *Art Industry and House-Decoration* (1879). Pictorial catalogues of later fairs, such as the 1876 centennial in Philadelphia and the 1893 World's Columbian Exposition in Chicago showed similar interests. Kenneth W. Luckhurst's *The Story of Exhibitions* appraises their significance.

The reform movement pioneered by John Ruskin and championed by William Morris was popularized by Charles Locke Eastlake in *Hints on Household Taste* (London, 1868; and five American editions in the 1870s). Following Eastlake's dictates, upholstery and furnishings were simplified both in England and in America. For books on the aesthetic taste, the arts and crafts movement, japonism, and later styles, one must turn to the works of architect-designers who published room views with complete furnishings.

The differences are enormous between richly appointed houses of England and the smaller early American homes with a few rooms used for a variety of household activities. Only through the study of household estate inventories can an accurate picture of American furnishings be recreated. The *American Wing Handbook* (1942), R. T. Hanes Halsey and Elizabeth Tower's *Homes of Our Ancestors,* Abbott Lowell Cummings's *Bed Hangings* and his *Rural Household Inventories, . . . 1675–1775,* and Margaret Schiffer's *Chester County Inventories, 1684–1850* are all useful in this regard. Susan Prendergast Schoelwer's "Form, Function, and Meaning in the Use of Fabric Furnishings" is an exemplary inventory study of the period 1700 to 1775 for Philadelphia County. The Botetourt inventories in the Virginia State Library formed the basis for the 1981 reinterpretation of the Governor's Palace at Colonial Williamsburg. *A Documentary History of American Interiors from the Colonial Era to 1915* by Edgar Mayhew and Minor Myers brings together information about style periods and all aspects of interior furnishing including textiles and floor coverings.

Another tool for recreating historic house interiors are craftsmen's bills to clients. Nicholas Wainwright's study of the John Cadwalader papers resulted in *Colonial Grandeur in Philadelphia.* Similar studies of letters, including orders, were made by Marie Kimball for Lansdowne, the White House, and Monticello. Benjamin Franklin's letters are frequently cited. Similarly useful is Margaret Klapthor's essay "Benjamin Latrobe and Dolley Madison Decorate the White House, 1805–11." Documentation from paintings, drawings, and prints by American artists is important. Harold Peterson's *Americans at Home: From the Colonists to the Late Victorians* is well known. John Singleton Copley's portraits are also explicit in upholstery details; these may be seen in Jules Prown's book about the artist.

For nineteenth-century historic houses, there are American publications, although it must be noted that Americans continued to use English and French sources for window curtain and bed hanging patterns. By the end of the Civil War, Andrew Jackson Downing's *Architecture of Country Houses* (1850) had sold over 16,000 copies. In a chapter entitled "The Treatment of Interiors," he included room views in the current revival styles and a section on window curtains. Downing was influenced by Thomas Webster's *An Encyclopaedia of Domestic Economy* (1845), which contains a chronologi-

cal account of bed styles and window curtains, and by John Claudius Loudon's *An Encyclopedia of Cottage, Farm and Villa Architecture and Furniture* (1833).

In *Modern Dwellings in Town and Country Adapted to American Wants and Climate* (1878), H. Hudson Holly presented the Queen Anne style as then known in England and mentioned reform designers and theorists as well as leading architects. For the interiors, he illustrated suitable curtains made in horizontal bands sometimes serving as portieres to curtain alcoves or as room dividers.

Domestic economy, homemaking, home furnishing, and good taste were the subjects of many books. Known as "how-to" books they included Catharine Beecher and Harriet Beecher Stowe's *The American Woman's Home* (1869), Charles Wyllis Elliott's *The Book of American Interiors* (1876), Clarence Cook's *The House Beautiful* (1877), Harriet Spofford's *Art Decoration Applied to Furniture* (1878), Ella Rodman Church's *How to Furnish a Home* (1883), Laura Holloway's *The Hearthstone; or, Life at Home* (1883), and Almon Varney's *Our Homes and Their Adornments; or, How to Build, Finish, Furnish, and Adorn a Home* (1883).

Periodicals such as *Godey's Lady's Book* (1830–98) and *Hearth and Home* (1868–75) influenced taste. *Practical Decorative Upholstery* by Frank A. Moreland (1890) with methods of measuring, cutting, and hanging bed and window curtains should be as helpful in restoration work as it was in its own day. Jane Nylander's *Fabrics for Historic Buildings* (2d ed., 1980) is an excellent guide to fabric patterns and houses.

The ideals of supporters of the arts and crafts movement were expressed by Clarence Cook in *House Beautiful* and especially by Gustav Stickley in *Craftsman Homes* (1909) and in his magazine *The Craftsman* (1901–16). Drawings of interiors with complete furnishings, and more particularly sections on needlework and stencil patterns, show simple motifs for ornamenting a variety of home furnishings. David Hanks included upholstery fabrics and carpets in his *Decorative Designs of Frank Lloyd Wright.*

Paralleling modest craftsman and prairie homes in date were the lavish mansions built in Newport, in New York City, on Long Island, and in the beaux arts style called American renaissance. In the 1890s and thereafter, many revival styles patterned now after Italian, French, and English grand rooms of the baroque and renaissance past were created. Edith Wharton and Ogden Codman's *Decoration of Houses* (1897) belongs to this age. Photography, newly introduced, recorded the interiors of many of these houses, and several collections of photographs have been published. See, for example, *The Tasteful Interlude* by William Seale, *Beaux-Arts Estates* by Liisa Sclare and Donald Sclare, and *New York Interiors at the Turn of the Century in 131 Photographs by Joseph Byron*.

Working about the same time, Candace Wheeler, a member of Louis Comfort Tiffany's creative Associated Artists, wrote *Principles of Home Decoration* (1903), and fashionable interior designer Elsie de Wolfe wrote *The House in Good Taste* (1913). Other writers were concerned with antiquarianism and the colonial revival style, and the early photographs published by Mary Northend in *Colonial Homes and Their Furnishings* (1912) are especially valuable for documenting that trend in furnishing practices.

Each book, manuscript, and photographic collection cited has been helpful in some way, but most useful are the swatches preserved in pattern books and letters (described in the bibliography). They enable us to link definitions to actual textiles and textiles to furnishing practices. With modern photography and relatively inexpensive reproduction processes, the character of the textiles can now be shown.

ACKERMANN, RUDOLPH. *The Repository of Arts, Literature, Commerce, Manufactures, Fashions and Politics.* 1st ser. 14 vols. London: R. Ackermann, 1809–15.

Monthly volumes containing fabric swatches for furnishing and especially fashionable dress materials. A second (14 vols., 1816–22) and third (12 vols., 1823–28) series were published from 1816 to 1828 under the title *The Repository of Arts, Literature, Fashions, &c.* but do not contain fabric swatches.

——————. *A Series Containing Forty-four Engravings of Beds, Sofas, Ottomans, Window-Curtains, Chairs, Tables, Book-Cases, &c.* London: R. Ackermann, 1823.

ADAM, ROBERT. *The Works in Architecture of Robert and James Adam.* 2 vols. London: Printed for the authors and sold by T. Becket, 1773–76. Reprint ed., introduction by Robert Oresko, London: Academy Editions; New York: St. Martin's Press, 1975.

ADROSKO, RITA J. *Natural Dyes in the United States.* Washington, D.C.: Smithsonian Institution Press, 1968.

AIKIN, JOHN. *A Description of the Country from Thirty to Forty Miles round Manchester.* London: John Stockdale, 1795.

Aix-la-Chapelle pattern book. Library, Musée des Arts Décoratifs, Paris.

Seventy-one swatches of woolen and combination cloths ranging from Levant goods, billiard cloth, serge, cassimere, and other vestings, to coarse, hairy coating and calmuc are found in a manuscript dated 1807 with the title "Echantillons des manufactures de la ville d'Aix la Chapelle." Prices, measurements, fibers, and countries where sold are stated. Included at the back of the book are thirteen wads of unspun French, German, Portuguese, and Spanish wool fibers of the kinds used in their manufacture.

From the introduction (translated from the French): "Only within the last few years have the cloths been dyed in the wool. . . . Many weavers have begun to use carding and spinning machines, but the majority still employ hand labor. Trade in these goods with the Levant began about 40 or 50 years ago and has been especially favored by the beauty and brilliance of the colors, and the modesty of their price. The cloths have been shipped to Prussia for over a century; commerce with Sierre le grand has been particularly favorable. Cassimeres have been profitably manufactured since English imports were prohibited. Fashionable goods, made largely in imitation of English manufactures, began about two years ago. The sale of *Woltrips* [striped wools], *Duvets, Côtes transparentes* [coating?], *toilinettes* and *piquets en laine* [both gentlemen's fancy vestings] is already considerable and increases daily."

Alexander Papers. New-York Historical Society, New York.

Pinned to copies of their letters to English agents are tiny pieces of cloth of the kinds and colors James and Mary Alexander, merchants of New York, ordered from London. Ranging in date from 1726 to 1760, the orders document the remarkable variety of textiles being shipped to New York.

"Soon after his arrival in America [ca. 1715] Alexander married the widow of a prosperous merchant named Provoost. His wife had continued her first husband's business after his death with much success, and her second marriage did nothing to interfere with it" (*Dictionary of American Biography*). Much of the Alexanders' business was in haberdashery, or what today we call notions. Always insistent upon receiving fashionable goods, they ordered expensive silks and worsteds, as well as plain, utilitarian materials. Orders are surprisingly numerous for accessories such as gloves, shoes, fans, and handkerchiefs; crewels, sewing silks, pins, and needles for embroidery; tassels, fringe, cord, and braid for window and bed curtains; and laces, ribbons, gimp, and buttons for trimming clothes.

Two narrow cuttings of glazed worsted damask, identified as russels, are of particular interest in a 1738 order, for in other manuscripts this material is called "Bed Sattin." To a single sheet dated 1726 from David Barclay of London are pasted twenty-eight strips of English block-printed cottons. Mordant printed with madder in shades of purple, red, and brown, they are important stylistically in the study of English textile printing and show the dependence of English printers on floral patterns imported at that time from India.

English copperplate-printed bed curtains which survive in American collections are frequently found bordered and ornamented with block-printed floral or scroll patterns. Printed vertically (i.e., parallel to the selvedges), they were cut into strips for this purpose. Typical patterns are shown in an order to David Barclay dated 1749, a few years prior to the first copperplate printing of textiles.

These papers and the Beekman Papers (q.v.), also in the New-York Historical Society, afford remarkable documentation for textile importation into the port of New York during the eighteenth century.

ALLEMAGNE, HENRY RENÉ D'. *La Toile imprimée et les Indiennes de traite.* 2 vols. Paris: Gründ, 1942.

All Sorts of Good Sufficient Cloth: Linen-Making in New England, 1640–1860. North Andover, Mass.: Merrimack Valley Textile Museum, 1980.

American Fabrics Encyclopedia of Textiles. Compiled by Editors of *American Fabrics.* 2d ed. Englewood Cliffs, N.J.: Prentice-Hall, 1972.

[*American Wing Handbook*]. R. T. H. Halsey and Charles O. Cornelius. *A Handbook of the American Wing.* 7th ed. revised by Joseph Downs. New York: Metropolitan Museum of Art, 1942.

The Ancient Trades Decayed, Repaired Again. Wherein are Declared the Several Abuses That Have Utterly Impaired All the Trades in the Kingdom . . . Written by a Country Trades-man. London: Dorman Newman & T. Cockerel, 1678.

ANDREWS, ALFRED. "Some Nineteenth-Century Windows." *Antiques* 50 (1946): 90.

Arkwright Mill, R.I. Sample book of checked fabrics, assembled in 1816. Rhode Island Historical Society, Providence.

Armistead-Cocke Papers. Gwen Library, William and Mary College, Williamsburg, Va.

ARNOLD, SARAH. Inventory, New York, 1772. Original in New-York Historical Society, New York. Joseph Downs Manuscript and Microfilm Collection, M-1, Winterthur Museum Library.

ARROWSMITH, JAMES. *An Analysis of Drapery; or, The Upholsterer's Assistant, Illustrated with Twenty Plates to Which is Annexed a Table, Showing the Proportions for Cutting One Hundred and Thirty Various-Sized Festoons.* London: M. Bell, 1819.

Art Journal. *See The Industry of All Nations, 1851.*

[Arts and Manufactures]. *The Useful Arts and Manufactures of Great Britain.* London: Society for Promoting Christian Knowledge, 1846.

ASHTON, LEIGH. *Samplers.* Plymouth, England: Mayflower Press, printed for the Medici Society, 1926.

[Aspinwall Records]. *A Volume Relating to the Early History of Boston Containing the Aspinwall Notarial Records from 1644 to 1651.* Boston: Municipal Printing Office, 1903.

ATKINSON, FRANK, ed. *Some Aspects of the Eighteenth-Century Woollen and Worsted Trade in Halifax.* Halifax, Yorkshire: Halifax Museums, 1956.

A new and expanded edition of Herbert Heaton, ed., "The Letter Books of Joseph Holroyd (Cloth-Factor) and Sam Hill (Clothier)," 1914 (q.v.). See pp. 16–18 for a full description of the Yorkshire pattern book (q.v.) owned by Mrs. George Stansfeld.

BAGNALL, WILLIAM R. *The Textile Industries of the United States.* Cambridge, Mass.: Riverside Press, 1893.

BAILEY, NATHAN. *An Universal Etymological English Dictionary.* 27th ed. London: Duncan, Robertson & Shaw, 1794.

BAINES, EDWARD. *History of the Cotton Manufacture in Great Britain.* London: H. Fisher, R. Fisher & P. Jackson, [1835]. Reprint ed., London: Frank Cass, 1966.

BAINES, THOMAS. *Yorkshire Past and Present: A History and a Description of the Three Ridings of the Great County of York . . . with an Account of its Manufacturers . . . including an Account of the Woollen Trade of Yorkshire by E[dward] Baines.* 2 vols. in 4. London: William Mackenzie, 1871–77.

For Edward Baines's article on the woolen trade, developed from a paper read in 1858, see vol. 2, pp. 629–96.

BALDWIN, AGNES L. "Inventories of Estates in Carolina, 1690–1700" and "Inventories and Merchants' Lists, 1670–90." Typescript owned by Florence M. Montgomery. From "Wills, Inventories, and Miscellaneous, 1692–93," South Carolina Archives, Columbia. Works Progress Administration typescript copies, Charleston County Library, Charleston, S.C.

BANERJEI, N. N. *Monograph on the Cotton Fabrics of Bengal.* Calcutta: Bengal Secretariat Press, 1898.

Banister Papers. Letter book and papers of Thomas Banister of Boston, 1695–1712. Letter books of John Banister, grandson of Thomas, Newport, R.I., 1739–50. Originals in Newport Historical Society. Joseph Downs Manuscript and Microfilm Collection, M-191, Winterthur Museum Library.

[BANKS]. *Filature, commerce, et prix des laines en Angleterre, ou correspondance sur ces matières, entre MM. Banks, Arthur Young.* Paris: Cuchet, 1790.

BARNES, EDMUND. Color or dye receipt book, 1829. Cooper-Hewitt Museum, New York.

    Inscribed: (on cover) "Blackford Bridge near Bury, Spt. 7, Edmund Barnes" and (at back) "Edmund Barnes, Providence." Swatches of roller-printed textiles printed with various color receipts. One page is signed "Dover" (New Hampshire).

BARRON, JAMES. *Modern and Elegant Designs of Cabinet and Upholstery Furniture.* London: W. M. Thiselton, [1814].

BARROW, JOHN. *Dictionarium Polygraphicum.* 2 vols. London: C. Ilitch, 1758.

BAUMGARTEN, LINDA R. "The Textile Trade in Boston, 1650–1700." In *Arts of the Anglo-American Community in the Seventeenth Century,* edited by Ian M. G. Quimby, pp. 219–73. Charlottesville: University Press of Virginia, 1975. *See also* Linda Baumgarten Berlekamp.

BAYEUX, THOMAS. Papers. State Library, Albany, N.Y.

BEARD, GEOFFREY, ed. "The Harewood Chippendale Account, 1772–77." *Furniture History* 4 (1968): 70–80.

[BEATNIFFE]. *A General History of the County of Norfolk, Intended to Convey All the Information of a Norfolk Tour.* 3 vols. London: Longman, Rees, Orme, Brown & Green, 1829. Vol. 2, *Norwich.*

    Probably written by Richard Beatniffe (d. 1818).

BEAWES, WYNDHAM. *Lex Mercatoria Rediviva; or, The Merchant's Directory.* 4th ed., enlarged by Thomas Mortimer. London: J. Rivington & Sons, T. Longman, B. Law, et al., 1783.

BECK, S. WILLIAM. *The Draper's Dictionary: A Manual of Textile Fabrics.* London: Warehousemen & Drapers' Journal Office, [1882].

BECKINSALE, R. P., ed. *The Trowbridge Woollen Industry as Illustrated by the Stock Books of John and Thomas Clark, 1804–24.* Devizes, Wiltshire: Headley Bros., 1951.

Bed Ruggs, 1722–1833. Exhibition catalogue. Introduction by William L. Warren, catalogue by J. Herbert Callister. Hartford, Conn.: Wadsworth Atheneum, 1972.

BEECHER, CATHARINE E., and HARRIET BEECHER STOWE. *The American Woman's Home.* New York: J. B. Ford; Boston: H. A. Brown, 1869.

[Beekman Papers]. White, Philip L., ed. *The Beekman Mercantile Papers, 1746–1799.* 3 vols. New York: New-York Historical Society, 1956.

BEER, ALICE BALDWIN. *Trade Goods: A Study of Indian Chintz in the Collection of the Cooper-Hewitt Museum of Decorative Arts and Design, Smithsonian Institution.* Washington, D.C.: Smithsonian Institution Press, 1970.

BENDURE, ZELMA, and GLADYS PFEIFFER. *America's Fabrics.* New York: Macmillan Co., 1946.

[BENNETT]. *A Cotton Fabrics Glossary.* Boston: Frank P. Bennett, 1914.

BENTLEY, PHYLLIS. *Colne Valley Cloth from the Earliest Times to the Present Day.* London: Curwen Press for the Huddersfield and District Woollen Export Group, 1947.

    The Yorkshire pattern book (q.v.) owned by Mrs. George Stansfeld is described; swatches of long bays and broadcloths are illustrated in color.

Berch Papers. Nordiska Museet, Stockholm.

    Collected during the 1750s, the papers provide especially rich documentation for English textiles commonly exported to Sweden and probably characteristic of our own colonial imports. Staple woolens and worsteds from the West of England and Norwich areas are found. Among silks are good quality dress fabrics; although fashionable, high-priced London brocades are lacking. Textile trade with the East is represented largely by Indian cotton dress goods, some with colored silk stripes and others embroidered. The papers include:

    (a) Pattern book containing over 100 cotton velvets, velures, veluretts, and silk damasks, satins, tabbies, ducapes, grograms, mantuas, and serge.

    (b) Pattern book of English worsteds with titles in Swedish, several dated 1753 and inscribed "Norwich."

    (c) Pattern book of English worsteds with titles in English.

    (d) Pattern book (inscribed on cover "A. and

C. Lindegreen") contains woolens and worsteds from Yorkshire, Berkshire, Wiltshire, Somersetshire, Devonshire, Essex, Kidderminster, Lancaster, Colchester, Norwich, and Spitalfields.

(e) Over 150 loose pages of miscellaneous textiles including East Indian cotton materials and some French wools.

Anders Berch (1711–74) was a pioneer in the fields of Swedish law and economics and held the second European chair for the study of economics at Uppsala University. He was the author of *Theatrum oeconomico mechanicum*.

For a fuller notice of Berch's interests, see Elisabet Stavenow-Hidemark, "The Berch Collection of Textiles," *CIETA*, no. 49 (1979): 21–24. The Nordiska Museet plans to publish the entire collection.

BERLEKAMP, LINDA BAUMGARTEN. "The Textile Trade in Boston, 1650–1700." Master's thesis, University of Delaware, 1976. *See also* Linda R. Baumgarten.

BISCHOFF, JAMES. *A Comprehensive History of the Woollen and Worsted Manufactures.* 2 vols. London: Smith, Elder, 1842. Reprint ed., London: Frank Cass, 1968.

BISHOP, JOHN LEANDER. *A History of American Manufactures from 1608 to 1860.* 2 vols. Philadelphia: Edward Young, 1864. Reprint ed., St. Clair Shores, Mich.: Scholarly Press, 1976.

BISHOP, ROBERT, and PATRICIA COBLENTZ. *The World of Antiques, Art, and Architecture in Victorian America.* New York: E. P. Dutton, 1979.

[BLACKIE AND SON]. *The Cabinet-Maker's Assistant.* London: Blackie & Son, 1853. Reprint ed., *The Victorian Cabinet-Maker's Assistant,* introduction by John Gloag, New York: Dover Publications, 1970.

BLAIR, ALICE. Inventory, 1738. Original in Probate Records, Suffolk County, Mass. Suffolk County Courthouse, Boston. Joseph Downs Manuscript and Microfilm Collection, M-121, Winterthur Museum Library.

BLAKELY, EDWARD T. *History of the Manufactures of Norwich.* Norwich: Jarrold & Sons, [ca. 1850]. Original in Victoria and Albert Museum, London. Joseph Downs Manuscript and Microfilm Collection, M-188, Winterthur Museum Library.

BLEECKER, HERMANUS. Papers, mid-eighteenth century. AV9902-133, State Library, Albany, N.Y.

BLOMEFIELD, FRANCIS. *An Essay towards a Topographical History of the County of Norfolk.* 5 vols. Firsfield: n.p., 1739–75.

BLYTHE, G. K. *The Norwich Guide.* Norwich: n.p., [ca. 1850]. Original in Victoria and Albert Museum, London. Joseph Downs Manuscript and Microfilm Collection, M-888, Winterthur Museum Library.

BOARDMAN, SAMUEL. Account book, Wethersfield, Conn., 1772. Old Academy Museum, Wethersfield.

Boardman ordered textiles from New York.

Book of Rates, 1660. *See The Statutes of the Realm.*

BOOTH, DAVID. *An Analytical Dictionary of the English Language.* London: Simpkin, Marshall, 1836.

[Boston Records]. *A Volume of Records Relating to the Early History of Boston. Accounts of Losses Sustained by the Fire of 1760.* From *Original Papers in the Office of the City Registrar.* Boston: Municipal Printing Office, 1900.

BOSWELL, JAMES. *London Journal, 1762–63.* London: Heinemann, 1951.

Botetourt manuscripts. Virginia State Library, Richmond. Included in *Inventories of Four Eighteenth-Century Houses in the Historic Area of Williamsburg.* Williamsburg. Colonial Williamsburg Foundation, n.d.

BOYNTON, LINDSAY. "Thomas Chippendale at Mersham-Le-Hatch." *Furniture History* 4 (1968): 81–104.

BOYNTON, LINDSAY, and NICHOLAS GOODISON. "Thomas Chippendale at Nostell Priory." *Furniture History* 4 (1968): 10–61.

BRANDON, JOSEPH, and BENJAMIN DOLBEAR. Journal, Boston, 1739–48. Joseph Downs Manuscript and Microfilm Collection, 55 x 549 Winterthur Museum Library.

Brandon and Dolbear were dry-goods merchants.

BRAUN-RONSDORF, M. "Mixture Fabrics of Later Times." *CIBA Review* 12 (1960): 16–28.

BRETT, KATHERINE B. "The Josephine Howell Scrapbook." *Needle and Bobbin Club Bulletin* 56 (1973): 20–34.

BRIDGENS, RICHARD. *Furniture with Candelabra and Interior Decoration.* London: William Pickering, 1838.

BRIGHTMAN, ANNA. "Window Curtains in Colonial Boston and Salem." *Antiques* 86 (1964): 184–87.

—————. *Window Treatments for Historic Houses, 1700–1850.* Preservation Leaflet Series, no. 14. Washington, D.C.: National Trust for Historic Preservation, 1968.

BRONSON, J. and R. *The Domestic Manufacturer's Assistant and Family Directory in the Arts of Weaving and Dyeing.* Utica, N.Y.: Printed by W. Williams, 1817. Reprint ed., *Early American Weaving and Dyeing: The*

Domestic Manufacturer's Assistant and Family Directory in the Arts of Weaving and Dyeing, introduction by Rita J. Adrosko, New York: Dover Publications, 1977.

BROTHERS, SAMUEL. *Wool and Woollen Manufactures of Great Britain: A Historical Sketch of the Rise, Progress, and Present Position.* London: Piper, Stephenson, & Spence, 1859.

BROWN, C. M., and C. L. GATES. *Scissors and Yardstick; or, All About Dry Goods.* Hartford: C. M. Brown & F. W. Jaqua, 1872.

BROWN, JOSEPH. Inventory, Providence, 1786. Probate Records, Providence, Rhode Island, City Hall.

BROWN, RICHARD. *The Rudiments of Drawing Cabinet and Upholstery Furniture.* 2d ed. London: J. Taylor, 1822.

BURNHAM, DOROTHY K. *Warp and Weft: A Textile Terminology.* Adapted and expanded from Vocabulary of Technical Terms, 1964, with permission of the Centre International d'Etude des Textiles Anciens. Toronto: Royal Ontario Museum, 1980. *See also* CIETA, *Vocabulary of Technical Terms.*

BURNHAM, HAROLD B., and DOROTHY K. BURNHAM. *Keep Me Warm One Night: Early Handweaving in Eastern Canada.* Toronto and Buffalo: University of Toronto Press, in cooperation with the Royal Ontario Museum, 1972.

BURNS, GEORGE C. *The American Woolen Manufacturer: A Practical Treatise on the Manufacture of Woolens, in Two Parts.* Central Falls, R.I.: E. L. Freeman, 1872.

> The two parts form a complete work on the American way of manufacturing more comprehensive than any yet issued. Illustrated with diagrams of various weavings and twelve samples of cloth for explanation and practice.

BURR, AARON. Inventory, New York, 1797. In "The Furnishing of Richmond Hill in 1797: The Home of Aaron Burr in New York City." *New-York Historical Society Quarterly* 11 (1927): 17–23.

BURY, HESTER. *A Choice of Design, 1850–1980, Fabrics by Warner & Sons Limited.* Catalogue for a traveling exhibition 1981–82. Braintree, Essex: Warner and Sons, 1981. *See* Warner Archive.

[BUTEL-DUMONT, GEORGES MARIE]. *Histoire et commerce des colonies angloises.* Paris: Le Breton et al., 1755.

BUTTERWORTH, JAMES. *The Antiquities of the Town, and a Complete History of the Trade of Manchester.* Manchester, England: C. W. Leake, 1822.

> The account of cotton manufactures is based largely on the 1795 work by John Aikin (q.v.).

CAINE, HENRIETTA MARIA. "Catalogue of Goods to be Sold by Publick Vendue." Broadside, 1754. Massachusetts Historical Society, Boston.

CARY, JOHN. *An Essay on the State of England in Relation to Its Trade.* Bristol: W. Bonny, 1695.

Castle Museum. Pattern books. Norwich, England.

> (a) Four folding pattern cards containing 337 worsted swatches with titles written in English, ca. 1790. Cover marked "H."

> (b) Folio pattern book of large worsted swatches with titles written in English, ca. 1790.

> (c) Pattern book of 698 worsted swatches with titles written in Italian. Marked "D. March, 1769." Includes seven pieces of printed flannel pasted in at the back of the book.

> (d) Pattern book of 823 worsted swatches with titles written in French, ca. 1790. Marked "F. Tuthill & Fils, Norwich."

> (e) Pattern book of worsted swatches marked "Charles Tuthill, Norwich," ca. 1790. (Note: This corresponds exactly to a pattern book inscribed "Booth and Theobald" in the Joseph Downs Manuscript and Microfilm Collection, 65 x 695.5, Winterthur Museum Library.)

> (f) Pattern book of worsted swatches marked with an anchor and "I H S B, No. 40, Beoan 9 May 1791/to Decr. 1791."

> (g) Order book containing worsted swatches dated 1792.

> (h) Order book containing worsted swatches dating from 1794–99. *See also* Norwich worsted pattern books.

CAULFEILD, S. F. A., and BLANCHE C. SAWARD. *Dictionary of Needlework.* London: L. Upcott Gill, 1882. Reprint ed., *Encyclopedia of Victorian Needlework,* New York: Dover Publications, 1972.

CHAMBERS, EPHRAIM. *Cyclopaedia; or, An Universal Dictionary of Arts and Sciences.* 2 vols. London: D. Midwinter, J. Senex, et al., 1741.

CHARLES, RICHARD. *The Cabinet Maker: A Journal of Designs for the Use of Upholsterers, Cabinet Makers, Decorators, Carvers, Gilders, and Others.* London: E. & F. Spon, 1868.

————. *Three Hundred Designs for Window-Draperies, Fringes, and Mantle-Board Decorations.* London: R. Charles, 1874.

CHARLESTON, R. J. "An Eighteenth-Century Weaver's Pattern-Book." *Needle and Bobbin Club Bulletin* 36 (1952): 27–43.

> The pattern book is inscribed "Timothy Bent his Book. 1788" (the latest certain date is 1795) and

is in the possession of the Blaise Castle House Museum at Henbury, near Bristol. Pattern drafts are given for more than sixty-six weaves with swatches from finished goods. Illustrated are four blue and white and two "self-coloured" figured linens.

CHEROL, JOHN A. "Designed for Another Age: Decorative Arts in Newport Mansions." *Antiques* 118, no. 3 (September 1980): 498–501.

—————. "Kingscote in Newport, Rhode Island." *Antiques* 118, no. 3 (September 1980): 476–85.

CHILD, JOSIAH. *The Interest of England Considered in an Essay on Wool.* London: Walter Kettilby, 1694.

[China Trade Records]. Records concerning ships sailing from Salem and Boston to China, 1784–1823. Prices current at Canton, 1807. Originals in the Essex Institute and the Benjamin Shreve Papers, Peabody Museum, Salem, Mass. Joseph Downs Manuscript and Microfilm Collection, M-108, Winterthur Museum Library. *See also* Carl L. Crossman, *The China Trade,* and Latimer Papers.

CHIPPENDALE, THOMAS. *The Gentleman and Cabinet-Maker's Director.* London, 1754; 2d ed., 1755; 3d ed., 1762. Reprint of 3d ed., New York: Dover Publications, 1966.

CHURCH, ELLA RODMAN. *How to Furnish a Home.* New York: D. Appleton, 1883.

[CIETA]. Centre International d'Etude des Textiles Anciens. *Bulletin de Liaison.* Lyons, 1955–.

—————. *Vocabulary of Technical Terms. Fabrics. English, French, Italian, Spanish.* 2d ed. Lyons: Centre International d'Etude des Textiles Anciens, 1964.

For the revised and expanded edition of this work, see Dorothy K. Burnham, *Warp and Weft.*

CLARK, VICTOR S. *History of Manufactures in the United States.* 2 vols. New York: McGraw-Hill Book Co. for the Carnegie Institute of Washington, 1929.

CLARKE, WILLIAM. Inventory. Salem Quarterly Court Files, vol. 1, leaf 81. From *Probate Records of Essex County, Massachusetts,* vol. 1 (1635–64), pp. 65–67. Salem, Mass.: Essex Institute, 1916.

Clerc, J. Jh., Fils & Cie. de Paris. Pattern book, late eighteenth century. Cooper-Hewitt Museum, 1936.29.4, New York.

Two-hundred eighty-six swatches of vestings and wool/cotton textiles, some with a little silk. Patterns include checks, stripes, quiltings, dots, and herringbones.

CLOUZOT, HENRI. *Le Métier de la soie en France.* Paris: Devambez, 1914.

COLBY, AVERIL. *Quilting.* London: B. T. Batsford, 1972.

COLE, ARTHUR HARRISON. *The American Wool Manufacture.* 2 vols. Cambridge, Mass.: Harvard University Press, 1926.

COLE, GEORGE S. *A Complete Dictionary of Dry Goods.* Chicago: W. B. Conkey Co., 1892.

COLEMAN, D. C. "An Innovation and Its Diffusion: The 'New Draperies.'" *Economic History Review,* 2d ser., 22 (1969): 417–29.

COLERIDGE, ANTHONY. "James Cullen, Cabinet-Maker at Hopetoun House." *Connoisseur* 163 (1966): 154–60.

The Connoisseur Period Guides. *See* Ralph Edwards and L. G. G. Ramsey.

The Contrast; or, A Comparison between our Woollen, Linen, Cotton, and Silk Manufactures. London: J. Buckland & W. Robson, 1782.

COOK, CLARENCE. *The House Beautiful: Essays on Beds and Tables, Stools and Candlesticks.* New York: Scribner, Armstrong, 1877.

Excerpts reprinted in Hugh Guthrie, ed., *Late Victorian Decor from Eastlake's Gothic to Cook's House Beautiful* (q.v.).

COOPER, GRACE ROGERS. *The Copp Family Textiles.* Smithsonian Studies in History and Technology, no. 7. Washington, D.C.: Smithsonian Institution Press, 1971.

COOPER, JEREMY. "Victorian Furniture: An Introduction to the Sources." *Apollo* 95 (1972): 115–22.

COOPER, THOMAS. *A Practical Treatise on Dyeing and Calicoe Printing.* Philadelphia: Dobson, 1815.

CORNFORTH, JOHN. *English Interiors, 1790–1848: The Quest for Comfort.* London: Barrie & Jenkins, 1978.

—————. "The Victoria Mansion, Portland, Maine." *Country Life* 167 (March 27, April 3, 1980): 926–29, 1014–17.

COX, RUTH YVONNE. "Textiles Used in Philadelphia, 1760–75." Master's thesis, University of Delaware, 1960.

CRAWFORD, M. D. C. *The Heritage of Cotton.* New York: Grosset & Dunlap, 1924.

CROSSMAN, CARL L. *The China Trade.* New York: Charles Scribner's Sons, 1972.

Silk samples from Eshing given by Pickering Dodge of Salem, Mass., to Benjamin Shreve in 1819 as a purchasing guide are discussed on page 245 and illustrated in color at figure 211. The swatches are preserved in the Peabody Museum, Salem, and include "Synchaws, Lustrings, Sarsnets, Bonnet silks, Ponges, Crapes, Sewings, Satins, Levantines or twilled silks, Florentines, Camblets, Pelong Satins, Black and Check'd Hkfs and Nankins." Of swatches numbered to 48 some are missing. *See also* China Trade Records *and* Latimer Papers.

CRUMP, W. B. *The Leeds Woollen Industry, 1780–1820.* Leeds: Thoresby Society, 1931.

————. The 1815 pattern book of dyer William Gott (q.v.) is described.

The Crystal Palace Exhibition Illustrated Catalogue: London, 1851. Introduction by John Gloag. Reprint ed., New York: Dover Publications, 1970.

————. An unabridged reprint of *The Industry of All Nations, 1851* (q.v.).

CUMMIN, HAZEL E. "Calamanco." *Antiques* 39 (1941): 182–83.

————. "Camlet." *Antiques* 42 (1942): 309–12.

————. "Colonial Dimities, Checked and Diapered." *Antiques* 38 (1940): 111–12.

————. "Moreen—A Forgotten Fabric." *Antiques* 38 (1940): 286–87.

————. "Tammies and Durants." *Antiques* 40 (1941): 153–54.

————. "What was Dimity in 1790?" *Antiques* 38 (1940): 23–25.

Note: In addition to the articles above, three short notes on Miss Cummin's research were also published: "A Dimity of 1737," *Antiques* 39 (1941): 255–56; "Early Seersucker," *Antiques* 38 (1940): 231–32; and "A Note on Nankin, Colonial Calico," *Antiques* 41 (1942): 197.

CUMMINGS, ABBOTT LOWELL, comp. *Bed Hangings: A Treatise on Fabrics and Styles in the Curtaining of Beds, 1650–1850.* Boston, Mass.: Society for the Preservation of New England Antiquities, 1961.

CUMMINGS, ABBOTT LOWELL, ed. *Rural Household Inventories: Establishing the Names, Uses, and Furnishings of Rooms in the Colonial New England Home, 1675–1775.* Boston: Society for the Preservation of New England Antiquities, 1964.

[CURWEN]. Oliver, Andrew, ed. *The Journal of Samuel Curwen, Loyalist.* 2 vols. Cambridge, Mass.: Harvard University Press, 1972.

DANIELS, GEORGE W. *The Early English Cotton Industry with Some Unpublished Letters of Samuel Crompton.* Manchester: At the University Press, 1920.

DAVENANT, CHARLES. *An Essay on the East India Trade.* London, 1696.

DAVIDSON, MARSHALL B. *The American Wing: A Guide.* New York: Metropolitan Museum of Art, 1980. *See also American Wing Handbook.*

DAVIDSON, RUTH BRADBURY. "Upholstery Fabrics for Antique Furniture." *Antiques* 56 (1949): 57.

DAVISON, MARGUERITE PORTER. *A Handweaver's Pattern Book.* Chester, Pa.: Printed for the author by John Spencer, 1971.

DAVISON, MILDRED, and CHRISTA C. MAYER-THURMAN. *Coverlets.* Chicago: Art Institute of Chicago, 1973.

DE BRISSAC, P. A. Account book, London, 1760–62. Joseph Downs Manuscript and Microfilm Collection, 59 x 2, Winterthur Museum Library.

————. De Brissac designed block- and copperplate-printed textiles, tissues, tobines, brocades, mantuas, striped satins, tabbies, ribbons, etc.

DECKER, PAUL. *See* Paul Dohme.

DE DILLMONT, THÉRÈSE. *Encyclopedia of Needlework.* 1870. Mulhouse: Brustein, 1890. Reprint ed., Philadelphia: Running Press, 1972.

DEFOE, DANIEL. *The Complete English Tradesman.* London: Charles Rivington, 1726.

————. *A Plan of the English Commerce.* London: Charles Rivington, 1728.

————. *A Tour through the Whole Island of Great Britain, Divided into Circuits or Journies.* 2 vols. London: Printed for Peter Davies, 1727.

DENNY, GRACE GOLDENA. *Fabrics and How to Know Them.* 3d ed. Philadelphia: J. B. Lippincott Co., 1928.

DEVILLE, JULES. *Dictionnaire du tapissier critique et historique de l'ameublement français.* Paris: Ch. Claesen, 1878–80. Winterthur Museum Library.

DIDEROT, DENIS, and JEAN D'ALEMBERT. *Encyclopédie, ou dictionnaire raisonné des sciences, des arts et des métiers, par un Société de Gens de Lettres.* 17 vols. Paris: Briasson et al., 1751–65. *Recueil de planches.* 11 vols. Paris: Briasson et al., 1762–72. Reprint ed., *A Diderot Pictorial Encyclopedia of Trades and Industry,* edited and introduction by Charles Coulston Gillispie, 2 vols., New York: Dover Publications, 1959.

DILKE, [C. WENTWORTH]. "Special Report." In *New York Industrial Exhibition: General Report of the British Commissioners.* London: Harrison & Son, 1854.

DIX, JAMES. Papers. Society of Friends Library, London.

[DMMC]. Joseph Downs Manuscript and Microfilm Collection, Winterthur Museum Library.

DOHME, PAUL. *Paul Decker's Fürstlicher Baumeister in Siebenundfünfzig Tafeln.* Berlin: Ernst Wasmuth, 1885.

DOLBEARE, BENJAMIN. Inventory, Boston, 1787. Original in the Massachusetts Historical Society, Boston. Joseph Downs Manuscript and Microfilm Collection, Ph-438, Winterthur Museum Library.

DORNSIFE, SAMUEL J. "Design Sources for Nineteenth-Century Window Hangings." In *Winterthur Portfolio 10,* edited by Ian M. G. Quimby, pp. 69–99.

Charlottesville: University Press of Virginia, 1975.

DOW, GEORGE FRANCIS. *The Arts and Crafts in New England, 1704–1775; Gleanings from Boston Newspapers.* Topsfield, Mass.: Wayside Press, 1927.

——————. *Every Day Life in the Massachusetts Bay Colony.* Boston: Society for the Preservation of New England Antiquities, 1935.

DOWNING, ANDREW JACKSON. *The Architecture of Country Houses.* New York: D. Appleton, 1850.

The furniture section is reprinted in *Furniture for the Victorian Home* (q.v.).

DOWNS, JOSEPH. *American Furniture: Queen Anne and Chippendale Periods.* New York: Macmillan Co., 1952. Reprint ed., New York: Bonanza Books, 1977.

——————. "Authentic Draperies Reconstructed from Old Pictures." *Fine Arts* 18 (1932): 17–21.

——————. "Early American Interiors with Contemporary Window Hangings." *Antiques* 50 (1946): 240–44.

——————. "Neo-Classic Draperies from Original Designs." *Fine Arts* 18 (1932): 29–32.

DRESSER, CHRISTOPHER. *Principles of Decorative Design.* 1873. Reprint. New York: St. Martin's Press, 1973.

DU CANGE, CHARLES DU FRESNE. *Glossarium ad scriptores mediae et infirmae latinitis, 1678.* 1883–87. Reprint ed., Graz, Austria: Akademische Druck-u, Verlagsanstalt, 1954.

DUDLEY, J. G. "A Paper on the Growth, Trade, and Manufacture of Cotton." *American Geographical and Statistical Society Bulletin* 1 (1852).

DUHAMEL DU MONCEAU, HENRI-LOUIS. *Art de friser ou ratiner les étoffes de laine.* Paris: L. F. Delatour, 1766. From *Descriptions des arts et métiers,* Winterthur Museum Library.

——————. *L'Art de la draperie, principalement pour ce qui regarde les draps fins.* Paris: H. L. Guerin & L. F. Delatour, 1765. From *Descriptions des arts et métiers,* Winterthur Museum Library.

DUNSTER, SAMUEL. Color books or dye receipt books, 1828–58. Rhode Island Historical Society Library, Providence.

Some of the eleven books contain swatches of roller-printed textiles. Dunster worked in La Grange, Philadelphia Co., Pa.; Philip Allen & Sons Printworks, Coventry, R.I.; Sprague's, Cranston, R.I.; Clays Printworks, Johnston, R.I.; and Cocheco Printworks, Dover, N.H.

Dye receipt book. Rhode Island, 1858–59. Joseph Downs Manuscript and Microfilm Collection, 69 x 211, Winterthur Museum Library.

Included are about 200 samples of printed cottons.

DYER, JOHN. *The Fleece: A Poem in Four Books.* London: R. & J. Dodsley, 1757.

EARLE, ALICE MORSE. *Costume of Colonial Times.* New York: Charles Scribner's Sons, 1894. Glossary. Reprint of 1924 ed., Detroit: Gale Research Co., 1975.

——————. *Two Centuries of Costume in America, 1620–1820.* 2 vols. New York: Macmillan Co., 1903. Reprint ed., 2 vols., New York: Arno Press, 1968.

EASTLAKE, CHARLES LOCKE. *Hints on Household Taste.* London: Longmans, Green, 1868; 2d ed., 1869; 3d ed., 1872; 4th ed. rev., 1878. American publication, edited by Charles C. Perkins, Boston: J. R. Osgood, 1872; 2d ed., 1874; 3d ed., 1875; 4th ed., 1876; 5th ed., 1877; Boston: Houghton Mifflin Co., 1879. Reprint of 4th British ed., 1878, New York: Dover Publications, 1969.

EDWARDS, MICHAEL M. *The Growth of the British Cotton Trade, 1780–1815.* New York: Augustus M. Kelley, 1967.

EDWARDS, RALPH. *The Shorter Dictionary of English Furniture.* London: Country Life, 1964.

EDWARDS, RALPH, and L. G. G. RAMSEY, eds. *The Connoisseur Period Guides.* 6 vols.; *The Tudor Period, 1500–1603; The Stuart Period, 1603–1714; The Early Georgian Period, 1714–1760; The Late Georgian Period, 1760–1810; The Regency Period, 1810–1830; The Early Victorian Period, 1830–1860.* London: The Connoisseur; New York: Reynal, 1958. Reprint ed., 6 vols. in 1, New York: Bonanza Books, 1968.

For references to the chapters on textiles in these volumes, see Donald King and Barbara Morris.

ELLIOTT, CHARLES WYLLYS. *The Book of American Interiors.* Boston: J. R. Osgood, 1876.

ELMENDORPH, MARY. Account book, 1715–90, Kingston, N.Y. State Library, Albany, N.Y.

EMERY, IRENE. *The Primary Structures of Fabrics.* Washington, D.C.: Textile Museum, 1966.

ENDREI, WALTER G. "English Kersey in Eastern Europe with Specific Reference to Hungary." *Textile History* 5 (1974): 90–99.

——————. "Tissus d'usage quotidien aux 16e–18e siècles." *Bulletin du Liaison, Centre International d'Etude des Textiles Anciens* 16 (1962): 17–29.

Three swatches of English, Silesian, and printed flannel are illustrated from a collection of forty swatches that were used as established standards of quality in Breslau, 1684–90.

English Chintz. London: Her Majesty's Stationery Office, 1955.

   Illustrated with pieces in the Victoria and Albert Museum collection. Published to accompany the 1955 exhibition catalogue, *English Chintz: Two Centuries of Changing Taste* (q.v.).

English Chintz: English Printed Furnishing Fabrics from Their Origins until the Present Day. Catalogue of a loan exhibition at the Victoria and Albert Museum, 1960. London: Her Majesty's Stationery Office, 1960.

English Chintz: Two Centuries of Changing Taste. An exhibition assembled by the Victoria and Albert Museum at the Cotton Board, Colour Design and Style Centre, Manchester. London: Her Majesty's Stationery Office, 1955.

English Printed Textiles, 1720–1836. London: Her Majesty's Stationery Office, 1960.

   Illustrated with pieces in the Victoria and Albert Museum collection. Published to accompany the catalogue of the 1960 exhibition of *English Chintz: English Printed Furnishing Fabrics from Their Origins until the Present Day* (q.v.).

English Wool Trade: Selected Tracts, 1614–1715. London: Gregg Press, n.d.

   A collection of six rare works republished from originals in the Goldsmiths' Library of Economic Literature, University of London: "John May, 1613"; "S[mith], W. gent. The Golden Fleece, wherein is related the riches of English wools in its manufactures . . . London, 1656"; "Fortrey, Samuel"; "Carter, William"; "Reasons humbly offered"; "Haynes, John, 1715."

[Essex Institute]. Invoice book, 1828–31. No. 129,931, Essex Institute, Salem, Mass.

   Contains a great variety of current fashions in English roller-printed cotton textiles (largely dress fabrics) together with an occasional piece marked "French" or "domestic." Included but not named are wools, wool plaids, wide-wale corduroy, green shag, stamped moreen, wool damask, and hair-cloths. It was assembled by an unidentified American importer selling to auction houses and commission merchants, several doing business in Philadelphia. Comments about the goods such as "a fair article as to quality" and "rather light goods and not well assorted as to colors" record fashions of the times.

EVANS, JOAN. *Pattern: A Study of Ornament in Western Europe from 1180 to 1900.* 2 vols. Oxford: Clarendon Press, 1931.

[EVELYN, JOHN]. Bray, William, ed. *Memoirs of John Evelyn . . . Comprising His Diary, from 1641 to 1705–6 and a Selection of His Familiar Letters.* 5 vols. London: Henry Colburn, 1827.

EVELYN, JOHN. *The Diary of John Evelyn.* Introduction and notes by Austin Dobson. 3 vols. London: Macmillan, 1906.

FAIRHOLT, F. W. *Costume in England: A History of Dress from the Earliest Period till the Close of the Eighteenth Century.* London: Chapman & Hall, 1846. Glossary.

   Especially useful for the earlier periods, including armor.

FAIRLIE, SUSAN. "Dyestuffs in the Eighteenth Century." *Economic History Review,* 2d ser., 17 (1965): 488–510.

FEDE, HELEN MAGGS. *Washington Furniture at Mount Vernon.* Mount Vernon, Va.: Mount Vernon Ladies' Association of the Union, 1966.

FIENNES, CELIA. *The Journeys of Celia Fiennes.* Ca. 1697. Reprint ed., London: Cresset Press, 1949.

Fielding Pattern Book. *See* Manchester Goods.

FISHER, JOSHUA, AND SONS. Ledgers, 1784–88, 1792–97. Originals owned by Henry Austin Wood. Joseph Downs Manuscript and Microfilm Collection, M-664, Winterthur Museum Library. *See also* Samuel Rowland Fisher.

FISHER, SAMUEL ROWLAND. Journals and ledgers, 1767–68, 1783–84. Originals owned by Miss Sarah A. G. Fisher. Joseph Downs Manuscript and Microfilm Collection, M-296, Winterthur Museum Library.

   The journals kept by Fisher on two visits to England are referred to frequently. The Quaker merchant of Philadelphia was the son of Joshua Fisher and grandfather of Joseph Wharton, founder of the Wharton School of Finance and Commerce, University of Pennsylvania. *See also* Joshua Fisher and Sons.

FISKE, PATRICIA L., ed. *Imported and Domestic Textiles in Eighteenth-Century America.* Proceedings of the 1975 Irene Emery Roundtable on Museum Textiles. Washington, D.C.: Textile Museum, 1975.

FITCH, THOMAS. Letter book, 1723–33. Massachusetts Historical Society, Boston.

   The letter books and account books of Fitch and his son-in-law, Samuel Grant, Boston upholsterers, are discussed in Brock Jobe, "The Boston

Furniture Industry, 1720–1740" (q.v.).

FLOUD, PETER. "The Drab Style and the Designs of Daniel Goddard." *Connoisseur* 139 (June 1957): 234–39.

FORBES, CHARLES P. *Merchant's Memorandum and Price Book.* Boston: John Marsh, 1827.

FOWLER, JOHN, AND JOHN CORNFORTH. *English Decoration in the Eighteenth Century.* London: Barrie & Jenkins; Princeton, N.J.: Pyne Press, 1974.

FOX, THOMAS W. *The Mechanism of Weaving.* London: Macmillan, 1922.

FRANKLIN, BENJAMIN. *The Papers of Benjamin Franklin.* Vols. 1–14, edited by Leonard W. Labaree. Vols. 15–20, edited by William B. Willcox. New Haven and London: Yale University Press, 1959–.

FRANKLIN, WILLIAM. *See* Charles Henry Hart, ed., "Letters from William Franklin to William Strahan."

FULLER, THOMAS. *Worthies of England.* 1662. Abridged edition by John Freeman. London: George Allen & Unwin, 1952.

Furniture for the Victorian Home; Comprising the Abridged Furniture Sections from A. J. Downing's Country Houses of 1850 and J. C. Loudon's Encyclopedia of 1833. Watkins Glen, N.Y.: American Life Foundation, 1978.

GEIJER, AGNES. *A History of Textile Art.* London: Pasold Research Fund in association with Sotheby Parke Bernet, 1979.

A General History of the County of Norfolk. N.p.: Printed by John Stacy, 1829. Original in the Victoria and Albert Museum Library, London. Joseph Downs Manuscript and Microfilm Collection, M-888, Winterthur Museum Library.

GILBERT, BARBARA L. "American Crewelwork, 1700–1850." Master's thesis, University of Delaware, 1965.

GILL, CONRAD. *The Rise of the Irish Linen Industry.* Oxford: Clarendon Press, 1925.

Gillow Records. Joseph Downs Manuscript and Microfilm Collection, M-1425 through M-1525, Winterthur Museum Library.

 The cabinetmaking, interior decorating, and upholstering firm of Gillow and Company (later Waring and Gillow, Ltd.) of London and Lancaster, England, was active from 1731 into the 1900s. The largest portion of the surviving records are in the Westminster City Libraries, London, and are an incomparable source for study of the firm's business practices and craft organization. Many drawings made for clients are in the Lancaster City Library and in the Victoria and Albert Museum, Department of Prints and Drawings.

GILROY, CLINTON G. *The Art of Weaving, by Hand and by Power.* New York: G. D. Baldwin, 1844.

————. *The History of Silk, Cotton, Linen and Wool, and Other Fibrous Substances: Including Observations on Spinning, Dyeing and Weaving.* New York: Harper & Bros., 1845.

GIROUARD, MARK. *Life in the English Country House: A Social and Architectural History.* New Haven and London: Yale University Press, 1978.

————. *The Victorian Country House.* Rev. and enl. ed. New Haven and London: Yale University Press, 1979.

GLASGOW, VAUGHN L. "Textiles of the Louisiana Acadians." *Antiques* 120, no. 2 (August 1981): 338–47.

GLOAG, JOHN. *A Short Dictionary of Furniture.* London: George Allen & Unwin, 1952.

Godey's Lady's Book (title varies), 1830–98. Volumes 1–125 published in Philadelphia, the rest in New York.

GORDON, BEVERLY. *Shaker Textiles Arts.* London and Hanover, N.H.: University Press of New England with the cooperation of the Merrimack Valley Textile Museum and Shaker Community, 1980.

GOTT, WILLIAM. Pattern book, 1815. University of Leeds, Yorkshire.

 Contains 71 swatches of dyed woolen cloth and yarn with corresponding receipts and 100 swatches of blended or mixture cloths. *See also* W. B. Crump, *Leeds Woollen Industry.*

GOTTESMAN, RITA SUSSWEIN. *The Arts and Crafts in New York, 1726–1776: Advertisements and News Items from New York City Newspapers.* New York: New-York Historical Society, 1938.

————. *The Arts and Crafts in New York, 1777–1799: Advertisements and News Items from New York City Newspapers.* New York: New-York Historical Society, 1954.

————. *The Arts and Crafts in New York, 1800–1804: Advertisements and News Items from New York City Newspapers.* New York: New-York Historical Society, 1965.

GRAFTON, RICHARD. Inventory, January 16, 1743. New Castle County Inventories, Public Archives Commission, Hall of Records, Dover, Del.

GRANT, SAMUEL. Account book, 1737–60. American Antiquarian Society, Worcester, Mass.

 The letter books and account books of Thomas Fitch and his son-in-law, Samuel Grant, Boston upholsterers, are discussed in Brock Jobe, "The Boston Furniture Industry, 1720–1740" (q.v.).

Great Exhibition catalogue. *See The Crystal Palace Exhibition Illustrated Catalogue: London, 1851.*

GUTHRIE, HUGH, ed. *Late Victorian Decor from Eastlake's Gothic to House Beautiful.* Library of Victorian Culture. Watkins Glen, N.Y.: American Life Foundation, 1967.

Edited excerpts reprinted from Charles Eastlake, *Hints on Household Taste* (q.v.), and Clarence Cook, *The House Beautiful* (q.v.).

HALLIWELL, JAMES ORCHARD. *A Dictionary of Archaisms and Provincial Words, Obsolete Phrases, Proverbs, and Ancient Customs, from the Fourteenth Century.* 1847. 2 vols. London: Thomas and William Boone, 1852.

HALSEY, R. T. HAINES, AND ELIZABETH TOWER. *The Homes of Our Ancestors.* Garden City, N.Y.: Doubleday, Page, 1925.

[HAMILTON, ALEXANDER]. *Report of the Secretary of the Treasury on the Subject of Manufactures, Made the Fifth of December, 1791.* Printed by order of the House of Representatives. Philadelphia: Joseph R. A. Skerrett, 1824.

Handkerchief pattern book. Cooper-Hewitt Museum, 1936.46.1, New York.

Ninety-five swatches of textiles from India mounted in a book on paper watermarked "London 1787." Linen check, cotton, and silk/cotton romals; lungi romals; rosetta; lustring silk and pullicate handkerchiefs are included.

HANKS, DAVID A. *The Decorative Designs of Frank Lloyd Wright.* New York: E. P. Dutton, 1979.

HARGROVE, JOHN. *The Weavers Draft Book and Clothiers Assistant.* Baltimore: I. Hagerty, 1792. Reprint ed., introduction by Rita J. Adrosko, Worcester, Mass.: American Antiquarian Society, 1979.

First book about weaving printed in the United States. Adrosko judges the fifty-two drafts to be a compilation of patterns then known to John Hargrove of Baltimore. Among the patterns presented are bird's-eye, cord, denim, diaper, dimity, ducape, "English Huckabag," fustian, jean, M's and O's, muslinet, satinet, stockinette, thickset, velveret, and worm.

HARMUTH, LOUIS. *Dictionary of Textiles.* New York: Fairchild Publishing Co., 1915.

This edition and those of 1920 and 1924 were revised for *Fairchild's Dictionary of Textiles* (1959) edited by Stephen S. Marks (q.v.); for a later revision (1967), see Isabel B. Wingate.

HARRINGTON, VIRGINIA D. *The New York Merchant on the Eve of the Revolution.* New York: Columbia University Press, 1935.

HART, CHARLES HENRY, ed. "Letters from William Franklin to William Strahan." *Pennsylvania Magazine of History and Biography* 35 (1911): 415–62.

HARTE, N. B., and K. G. PONTING. "Essays in Honour of Miss Julia de Lacy Mann," in *Textile History and Economic History.* Manchester: Manchester University Press, 1973.

HAVARD, HENRY. *Dictionnaire de l'ameublement et de la décoration, depuis le XIIIe siècle jusqu'à nos jours.* 4 vols. Paris: Maison Quantin, [1887].

HEAL, AMBROSE. *London Tradesmen's Cards of the Eighteenth Century: An Account of Their Origin and Use.* London: B. T. Batsford, 1925.

[Heal Collection]. Ambrose Heal Collection of English Trade Cards, 1660–1850. Originals in British Museum, London. Joseph Downs Manuscript and Microfilm Collection, M-230, Winterthur Museum Library.

HEARD, NIGEL. *Wool, East Anglia's Golden Fleece.* Lavenham: Terence Dalton, 1970.

Hearth and Home. Edited by D. G. Mitchell and Harriet Beecher Stowe. Vols. 1–9, December 26, 1868, to December 25, 1875 (weekly). New York: Pettengill, Bates.

HEATON, HERBERT. "The American Trade." In *The Trade Winds: A Study of British Overseas Trade during the French Wars, 1793–1815,* edited by C. Northcote Parkinson, pp. 194–226. London: Published for the Thoresby Society by George Allen & Unwin, 1948.

————. "Yorkshire Cloth Traders in the United States." *Thoresby Society Publications* 37 (1945): 225–87.

————. *The Yorkshire Woollen and Worsted Industries, from the Earliest Times up to the Industrial Revolution.* 2d ed. Oxford: Clarendon Press, 1965.

HEATON, HERBERT, ed. "The Letter Books of Joseph Holroyd (Cloth-Factor) and Sam Hill (Clothier)." County Borough of Halifax, *Bankfield Museum Notes,* 2d ser., no. 3 (1914).

HEDGES, JAMES B. *The Browns of Providence Plantations.* Cambridge, Mass.: Harvard University Press, 1952.

HEISEY, JOHN W., comp. *A Checklist of American Coverlet Weavers.* Edited and expanded by Gail C. Andrews and Donald R. Walters. Prepared for the Abby Aldrich Rockefeller Folk Art Center. Williamsburg, Va.: Colonial Williamsburg Foundation, 1978.

HEPPLEWHITE, GEORGE. *The Cabinet-Maker and Upholsterer's Guide.* London, 1788, 1789, 1794. Reprint of 3d ed., 1794, introduction by Joseph Aronson, New York: Dover Publications, 1969.

"High Wages Bring Opportunity to American-Printed Fabrics." *Good Furniture* 12 (1919): 216–24.

Hilton manuscript, 1786. Public Record Office, BT6/111, 112, London.

Swatches of cotton goods presented in evidence before the negotiations of Eden's Treaty with France. Included are examples of calico, denim, dimity, muslin, paoli, sateen, thickset, velvet, and others.

[*Hobson-Jobson*]. HENRY YULE AND A. C. BURNELL. *Hobson-Jobson: A Glossary of Colloquial Anglo-Indian Words and Phrases, and of Kindred Terms, Etymological, Historical, Geographical and Discursive.* Edited by William Crooke. London: John Murray, 1903.

Holker manuscript. Musée des Arts Décoratifs, Paris.

This folio sample book contains more than 115 examples of printed chintzes, silks, calendered wools, checks, plaids, and cotton velvets, with handwritten comments about their manufacture. It provides rare documentation for eighteenth-century English textile terms. The manuscript entitled "Livre d'échantillons" was prepared by John Holker, a Lancashireman familiar with textile production. It was presented by Marc Morel, inspector for cotton manufactures in Rouen, to M. de Montigny of the Royal Academy of Sciences.

The report, prepared about 1750, describes the various kinds of textiles manufactured in Lancashire of linen thread, linen and cotton, silk and cotton, wool and cotton, and all cotton. Also detailed are their English names, their widths and lengths, and their value in English money reduced to the French equivalent.

A more complete discussion of the manuscript is found in Florence M. Montgomery, "John Holker's Mid-Eighteenth-Century *Livre d'échantillons*" (q.v.).

HOLKER, JOHN, JR. Papers. Library of Congress, Washington, D.C.

Volume 7, folios 1232 and 1233, contain swatches of *cannelé, picqué, siamoises,* and *toile* pasted to invoices dated 1779.

HOLLOWAY, LAURA C. *The Hearthstone; or, Life at Home.* Philadelphia: Bradley, Garretson; Chicago: Wm. Garretson, 1883.

HOLLY, H. HUDSON. *Modern Dwellings in Town and Country Adapted to American Wants and Climate with a Treatise on Furniture and Decoration.* New York: Harper & Bros., 1878. Reprinted in *Country Seats and Modern Dwellings: Two Victorian Domestic Architectural Stylebooks by Henry Hudson Holly.* Introduction by Michael Tomlan. Watkins Glen, N.Y.: Library of Victorian Culture, 1977.

HOLME, RANDLE. *The Academy of Armory; or, A Display of Heraldry.* 1649.

The original manuscript dated 1649, now in the British Museum, London, was published in part by Holme in 1688 (book 1, chap. 1, through book 3, chap. 13); the same part was printed again in 1701 by the Booksellers of London and Westminster. The second part (book 3, chap. 14, through book 4, chap. 13) was edited by I. H. Jeayes and published in London for the Roxburghe Club, 1905.

HOLMES, JONATHAN. Account book, 1749–54. Joseph Downs Manuscript and Microfilm Collection, 71 x 71, Winterthur Museum Library.

HOLROYD, JOHN BAKER, earl of Sheffield. *Observations on the Commerce of the American States.* 6th ed. London: J. Debrett, 1784.

HOMERGUE, JOHN D', AND P. S. DUPONCEAU. *An Essay on American Silk.* Philadelphia: John Grigg, 1830.

HOPE, THOMAS. *Household Furniture and Interior Decoration, Executed from Designs by Thomas Hope.* London: Longman et al., 1807. Reprint ed., New York: Dover Publications, 1971.

Hopewell Cotton Works. Pattern book, East Nottingham Township, Chester County, Pa., 1828. Chester County Historical Society, West Chester, Pa.

Contains swatches of checked and striped materials used for clothing and household purposes.

HOPKINS, JOSEPH. Inventory, New York, 1803. Joseph Downs Manuscript and Microfilm Collection, 54.106.33, Winterthur Museum Library.

HORNOR, WILLIAM MACPHERSON, JR. *Blue Book: Philadelphia Furniture, William Penn to George Washington.* Philadelphia, 1935. Reprint ed., Washington, D. C.: Highland House Publications, 1977.

HOWARD, GEORGE SELBY. *The New Royal Encyclopaedia, and Cyclopaedia; or, Complete Modern and Universal Dictionary of Arts and Sciences.* 3 vols. London: Alexander Hogg, 1788.

HOWE AND STEVENS. *Treatise upon Dyeing and Scouring, as Adapted to Their Family Dye Colors.* Boston, 1864.

HOWELL, JOSEPHINE. Scrapbook. Cooper-Hewitt Museum, New York.

Contains swatches collected by Jacques Martin of Paris: 76 eighteenth-century Indian painted and resist-dyed textiles, probably made for the French market, and 74 French block-printed cottons, known as *indiennes*.

HOWLAND, RICHARD H. "Three Victorian Mansions: Camden." *Nineteenth Century* (Winter 1979): 40–44.

HYDE, ROBERT AND NATHAN. Pattern book, 1771. *See* Manchester pattern books.

INCE, WILLIAM, AND JOHN MAYHEW. *The Universal System of Household Furniture*. London, 1762. Reprint ed., London: Alec Tiranti; Chicago: Quadrangle Books, 1960.

The Industry of All Nations 1851. The Art Journal Illustrated Catalogue. London: George Virtue, 1851. Reprint ed., *The Crystal Palace Exhibition Illustrated Catalogue, London 1851*, introduction by John Gloag, New York: Dover Publications, 1970.

[Ingatestone]. Inventories of Ingatestone and Thorndon Halls, 1572, 1608, and 1613. Transcripts made by Olwen Hall. Friends of Historic Essex, 1968. Mimeographed.

International Wool Secretariat, London. Articles reprinted from *Wool Knowledge: The Journal of Wool Education*. London, 1959–61. "Making Wool Fabrics"; "Warp and Weft"; "Wool in Fabric and Fashion"; "Wool in History"; "Wool Through the Ages"; "Woollens and Worsteds."

IRWIN, JOHN. "The Etymology of Chintz and Pintado." *Journal of Indian Textile History* 4 (1959). Published in Ahmedabad, India.

IRWIN, JOHN, AND KATHARINE B. BRETT. *Origins of Chintz*. With a catalogue of Indo-European cotton paintings in the Royal Ontario Museum, Toronto, and the Victoria and Albert Museum, London. London: Her Majesty's Stationery Office, 1970.

IRWIN, JOHN, AND P. R. SCHWARTZ. *Studies in Indo-European Textile History*. Ahmedabad, India: Calico Museum of Textiles, 1966. Glossary.

JACOBS, BERTRAM. *Axminster Carpets (Hand-Made), 1755–1957*. Leigh-on-Sea, England: F. Lewis, 1970.

JAMES, JOHN. *History of the Worsted Manufacture in England: With Introductory Notices of the Manufacture among the Ancient Nations, and during the Middle Ages*. London: Bradford, 1857. Reprint ed., London: Frank Cass, 1968.

JENKINS, J. GERAINT, ed. *The Wool Textile Industry in Great Britain*. London and Boston: Routledge & Kegan Paul, 1972.

JOBE, BROCK. "The Boston Furniture Industry, 1720–1740." In *Boston Furniture of the Eighteenth Century*, edited by Walter Muir Whitehill, pp. 3–48. Charlottesville, Va.: University Press of Virginia, 1974.

JOHNSON, BARBARA. Album, England, 1746–1823. Victoria and Albert Museum, T219–1973, London.

A scrapbook of fashionable clothing materials worn by Englishwoman Barbara Johnson (1738–1825). Included are fashion prints and a wide variety of swatches dated 1746 to 1823.

JOHNSON, SAMUEL. *A Dictionary of the English Language*. 6th ed. 2 vols. London: J. F. & C. Rivington, 1785.

JOUBERT DE L'HIBERDERIE. *Le Dessinateur pour les fabriques d'étoffes d'or, d'argent et de soie*. Paris: Sebastien Jorry, Bauche, Brocas, 1765. From *Descriptions des arts et métiers*, Winterthur Museum Library.

JOURDAIN, MARGARET. "Window Curtains of the Eighteenth Century." *Country Life* (1946): 668–69.

Journal für Fabrik, Manufaktur, Handlung und Mode. 35 vols. Leipzig: Voss & Leo, 1791–1808. (Monthly.)

Contains swatches of fashionable textiles imported from England and France, as well as German textiles. The Winterthur Museum Library has a partial run from 1792 to 1796 and July through December 1800.

The Journal of Design and Manufactures. 6 vols. in 3. London: Chapman & Hall, 1849–52.

Illustrated with over 800 engravings and about 200 swatches.

JOY, EDWARD T. *English Furniture, 1800–1851*. London: Sotheby Parke Bernet Publications, Ward Lock, 1977.

KARLSON, WILLIAM. *Stat och Vardag i stormaktstidens herremanshem*. Lund: C. W. K. Gleerups Forlag, 1945.

Kelly Books. Victoria and Albert Museum, London.

(a) "Book of Patterns manufactured by Mr. John Kelly of Norwich, 1767."

(b) "Mr. J. Kelly's Counterpart of Patterns from No. 1 to No. 239, sent to Spain and Portugal by John Kelly of Norwich, 1763."

These two small books contain swatches of glazed worsted dress and furnishing fabrics for which Norwich was famous. They are the earliest dated pattern books known which contain identified swatches of fancy worsteds.

KERRIDGE, ERIC. "Wool Growing and Wool Textiles in Medieval and Early Modern Times." In *The Wool Textile Industry in Great Britain*, edited by J. Geraint Jenkins, pp. 19–33. London and Boston: Routledge & Kegan Paul, 1972.

KIDD, KENNETH E. "Cloth Trade and the Indians of the Northeast during the Seventeenth and Eighteenth Centuries." Toronto: Royal Ontario Museum Annual, 1961.

Letters are cited from the James Logan Papers in the Historical Society of Pennsylvania, Philadelphia, in particular from Logan's letter book, 1712–15, with reference to woolens imported for trade with the Indians.

KIMBALL, FISKE, AND MARIE KIMBALL. "Jefferson's Curtains at Monticello." *Antiques* 52 (1947): 266–68.

KIMBALL, MARIE G. "The Furnishings of Governor Penn's Town House." *Antiques* 19 (1931): 375–78.

———. "The Furnishings of Lansdowne, Governor Penn's Country Estate." *Antiques* 19 (1931): 450–55.

———. "The Original Furnishings of the White House." *Antiques* 15 (1929): 481–85; 16 (1929): 33–37.

———. "Thomas Jefferson's French Furniture." *Antiques* 15 (1929): 123.

KING, DONALD. "Textiles." In *The Tudor Period, 1500–1603,* The Connoisseur Period Guides, edited by Ralph Edwards and L. G. G. Ramsey, pp. 101–12. New York: Reynal, 1958.

———. "Textiles." In *The Stuart Period, 1603–1714,* The Connoisseur Period Guides, edited by Ralph Edwards and L. G. G. Ramsey, pp. 119–32. New York: Reynal, 1958.

———. "Textiles." In *The Early Georgian Period, 1714–1760,* The Connoisseur Period Guides, edited by Ralph Edwards and L. G. G. Ramsey, pp. 119–32. New York: Reynal, 1958.

———. "Textiles." In *The Late Georgian Period, 1760–1810,* The Connoisseur Period Guides, edited by Ralph Edwards and L. G. G. Ramsey, pp. 107–16. New York: Reynal, 1958.

KING, THOMAS. *See The Upholsterers' Accelerator.*

KJELBERG, PIERRE. "Le Catalogue descriptif complet du lit empire." *Connaissance des arts* 182 (1967): 79–85.

———. "Le Lit tel qu'il était exactement au temps de Louis XV." *Connaissance des arts* 132 (1963): 78–87.

KLAPTHOR, MARGARET BROWN. "Benjamin Latrobe and Dolley Madison Decorate the White House, 1809–11." Contributions from the Museum of History and Technology, bulletin 241, paper 49. Washington, D.C.: Smithsonian Institution, 1965.

Kress Library of Business and Economics. *Catalogue Supplement, 1473–1848.* Boston: Baker Library, Harvard Graduate School of Business Administration, 1967.

The following entries are listed in the catalogue supplement. Originals are in the collections of the Kress Library of Business and Economics, Harvard University, unless otherwise noted.

[Kress, S1866]. "The Weavers Answer, to the Objections Made by the Lustrings Company." [London, 1695.] Broadside.

[Kress, S1994]. "An Extract from the Dutch Printed Cargoes of the Several Sorts of Goods Following, By them Imported from the East-Indies between the Years 1686 and 1696 Inclusive, Viz. Silks, or Goods mixed therewith, Callicoes and Other Goods Painted, Stained, Printed or Coloured There." London?, 1697?. Broadside.

[Kress, S2123]. Le Comte, Louis Daniel. *Memoirs et Observations, Topographical, Physical, Mechanical, Made in a Journey through the Empire of China, and Published in Several Letters.* Translated from the French edition. 3d ed., rev. London, 1699. Original in Harvard University Library.

[Kress, S2180]. "A Particular of the Silks, and a Specimen of the Toyes and Handicraft Wares, which came from the East-India, on the Ships Martha, Sarah and Dorothy; with the Rates at which they were sold at the late Sale at the East-India House." London?, 1700?. Broadside.

[Kress, S2200]. "A List of Several Sorts of Silks and Callicoes usually imported from the East-Indies, Persia and China, Prohibited to be used in England, by the Bill Entituled, 'An Act for Restraining the Wearing of all Wrought Silks, Bengals Dyed, Printed or Stained Callicoes.'" London, 1700?. Broadside.

[Kress, S2470]. "Reasons Humbly Offered Against the Passing a Bill for the Encouragement of an Invention of Damasking, Striking and Fixing Colours into All Sorts of Stuffs, Cloth, and Raising and Embossing Flowers of Various Colours on the Same." N.p., 171–?. Broadside.

[Kress, S2495]. Marperger, Paul Jakob. *Ausfürliche beschreibung des Hanffs und Flachs und der daraus verfertigten Manufacturen. . . .* Leipzig: J. F. Gleditsch & Son, 1710.

[Kress, S2724]. [John Blanch]. *Speculum commercii; or, The History of Our Golden Fleece.* London: R. & J. Bonwick, 1716.

[Kress S4130]. "Mémoire sommaire de la communauté des marchands-merciers-drapiers-unis de la ville de Rouen, sur la tolérance du port & usage des toiles peintes, teintes & imprimées." Rouen?, 1758?.

KURTH, WILHELM. *Die Raumkunst im Kupferstich des 17*

and 18 Jahrhunderts. Stuttgart: Julius Hoffmann, 1923.

Ladies Dictionary. London: Printed for J. Dunton, 1694.

LAMBERT, MISS. *The Ladies' Complete Guide to Needle-Work and Embroidery*. Philadelphia: T. B. Peterson & Bros., [1859].

LA MÉSANGÈRE, PIERRE DE. *Meubles et objets de goût*. 2 vols. Paris: Pierre de La Mésangère, au Bureau des Dames, [1802–35].

    A series of color plates showing furniture and decorative objects which appeared irregularly between 1802 and 1835. An important source for window arrangements of the first part of the nineteenth century.

LAMONTAGNE, ROLAND, ed. *Textiles et documents Maurepas*. Ottawa: Editions Lemeac, 1970.

LARDNER, DIONYSIUS, ed. *The Cabinet Cyclopaedia: A Treatise on the Origin, Progressive Improvement, and Present State of the Silk Manufacture*. London: Longman et al., 1831.

LARSON, CEDRIC. "Cloth of Colonial America." *Antiques* 39 (1941): 28–30.

Latimer Papers. Winterthur Museum Library and Library of Congress.

    The papers of the Latimer family are largely concerned with the China trade. A bill of lading dated 1807 for nankeens and sinchaws sent to James R. Latimer from Canton includes ten swatches of changeable silks. Other papers include orders for sewing silk, sarcenet, pongee, silk florentine, etc. For Winterthur holdings see Joseph Downs Manuscript and Microfilm Collection, 60 x 1.9–14, 60 x 27. *See also* Carl L. Crossman, *The China Trade*.

LATOUR, A. "Colbert and the French Wool Manufacture." *CIBA Review* 67 (1948): 2437–76.

LEE-WHITMAN, LEANNA. "The Silk Trade: Chinese Silks and the British East India Company." *Winterthur Portfolio: A Journal of American Material Culture* 17 (1982): 21–41.

LIPSON, EPHRAIM. *The History of the Woollen and Worsted Industries*. London, 1921. Reprint of 2d ed., London: Frank Cass, 1965.

————. *A Short History of Wool and Its Manufacture (mainly in England)* Cambridge, Mass.: Harvard University Press, 1953.

LITTLE, FRANCES. *Early American Textiles*. New York: Century Co., 1931.

LITTLE, NINA FLETCHER. *Floor Coverings in New England before 1850*. Sturbridge, Mass.: Old Sturbridge Village, 1967.

LIVINGSTON, ROBERT. Order book, 1734–39. Livingston Papers, State Library, Albany, N.Y.

LOGAN, JAMES. Letter book, 1712–15. James Logan Papers, Historical Society of Pennsylvania, Philadelphia.

    See also Kenneth E. Kidd, "Cloth Trade and the Indians of the Northeast."

[London Book of Prices]. *The Cabinet-Makers' London Book of Prices, and Designs of Cabinet Work*. Rev. ed. London, 1803.

[London Newspaper References]. H. A. Scott Extracts from notices in London newspapers referring to seventeenth- and eighteenth-century fine and decorative art objects. Gleaned from the Burney Collection, British Museum, London, 1937. Typescript, 11 vols., no. 159, Ex8. Metropolitan Museum of Art Library, New York.

LONGFIELD, A. K. "Irish Linen for Spain and Portugal: James Archbold's Letters 1771–79." In *Proceedings of the Royal Irish Academy*, vol. 76, sec. C., no. 2, pp. 13–26. Dublin: Royal Irish Academy, 1976.

Lord and Taylor Catalogue of Silks, Dress Goods, Cloths, . . . Carpets, Upholstery, Etc. New York, 1881. Reprint ed., *Clothings and Furnishings: Lord and Taylor, 1881*, Princeton, N.J.: Pyne Press, 1971.

LOUDON, JOHN CLAUDIUS. *An Encyclopedia of Cottage, Farm and Villa Architecture and Furniture*. London: Longman et al., 1833.

    The furniture section is reprinted in *Furniture for the Victorian Home* (q.v.).

Loudon Furniture Designs from the Encyclopedia of Cottage, Farmhouse, and Villa Architecture and Furniture, 1839. Introduction by Christopher Gilbert. East Ardsley, Wakefield, Yorkshire, and London: S. R. Publishers and The Connoisseur, 1970.

LUCKHURST, KENNETH W. *The Story of Exhibitions*. London and New York: Studio Publications, 1951.

LYNN, CATHERINE W. *Wallpaper in America: From the Seventeenth-Century to World War II*. New York: W. W. Norton, 1980.

MCCLELLAN, ELISABETH. *Historic Dress in America, 1607–1800*. Philadelphia: G. W. Jacobs, 1904.

————. *Historic Dress in America, 1800–1870*. Philadelphia: G. W. Jacobs, 1910.

MCCLELLAND, NANCY. *Duncan Phyfe and the English Regency*. New York: William R. Scott, 1939.

MCCULLOCH, J. R. *A Dictionary, Practical, Theoretical, and Historical of Commerce and Commercial Navigation*. 2 vols. Philadelphia: T. Wardle, 1840.

MACARTNEY, CLARENCE E., and GORDON DORRANCE. *The*

Bonapartes in America. Philadelphia: Dorrance, 1939.

MACPHERSON, DAVID. *Annals of Commerce*. 4 vols. London: Nichols et al., 1805.

Includes *Historical and Chronological Deduction of the Origin of Commerce* (1764) by Adam Anderson.

MACQUER, PHILIPPE DE. *Dictionnaire raisonné universel des arts et métiers*. 5 vols. Paris: P. F. Didot, 1773.

MACQUER, PIERRE JOSEPH. *L'Art de la teinture en soie*. Paris, 1763. From *Descriptions des arts et métiers*, Winterthur Museum Library.

————. *The Art of Dying Wool, Silk, and Cotton*. London: R. Baldwin, 1789.

MACQUOID, PERCY, AND RALPH EDWARDS. *The Dictionary of English Furniture: From the Middle Ages to the Late Georgian Period*. 3 vols. London: Country Life; New York: C. Scribner's Sons; 1924–27.

MADIGAN, MARY JEAN SMITH. *Eastlake-Influenced American Furniture, 1870–1890*. Exhibition catalogue. Yonkers, N.Y.: Hudson River Museum, 1973.

————. "The Influence of Charles Locke Eastlake on American Furniture Manufacture, 1870–90." In *Winterthur Portfolio 10*, edited by Ian M. G. Quimby, pp. 1–22. Charlottesville: University Press of Virginia, 1975.

MALCOLM, JAMES PELLER. *Anecdotes of the Manners and Customs of London during the Eighteenth Century*. London: Longman et al., 1808.

See especially chapter 8, "Anecdotes of Dress and of the Caprices of Fashion."

MALTON, THOMAS. *A Compleat Treatise on Perspective*. 2d ed. London: Robson, 1778.

MALYNES, GERARD. *Lex Mercatoria*. London: Adam Islip, 1622.

Manchester pattern books.

A good many pattern books and long folding pattern cards prepared in Manchester, long the center of cotton weaving, have survived. In his history of Manchester, James Butterworth (q.v.) wrote of their use:

> The pattern cards of Manchester goods sent out to the continent by the leading houses engaged in the foreign trade, have presented specimens of near two thousand different kinds, varying in strength and fineness, from the coarse and heavy fabrics, to the finest and most delicate muslins, and in colour from the richest chintz to plain and self-coloured grounds; some figured in the loom, some chequered and others plain, yet all, or the greatest part of them, composed entirely of cotton. [P. 66.]

The following are in the Joseph Downs Manuscript and Microfilm Collection, Winterthur Museum Library:

(a) Book of 431 swatches of printed cottons, velvets, dimities, quiltings, cords, diapers, etc., dated 1783. Prepared by Thomas Smith. 65 x 698.

(b) Folding card of 138 swatches prepared by Nathaniel and Joshua Gould, 1775–85. 65 x 699.

(c) Book of 430 swatches. Probably Manchester, late eighteenth century. 65 x 700.

(d) Book of 431 swatches dated 1783. 77 x 110. (Identical to a book at Colonial Williamsburg.)

Another is owned by the Metropolitan Museum of Art, New York: a long folding pattern card with 492 swatches which contains examples of linen checks, including several probably used for furniture covers, stripes, some mixed with wool, cotton, or silk, fustians, corduroys, velvets, and figured dimities, some of them probably once known as drawboys. The card was prepared for "Benjamin and John Bower, Manchester, April 1st, 1771, Pr the Brigantine Havannah, Capt. Nicholson." (Similar books are owned by the Cooper-Hewitt Museum.)

A weaver's pattern book kept by Jeremiah or Jeremy Fielding of Manchester from 1775 to 1778 is owned by the Merrimack Valley Textile Museum, North Andover, Massachusetts. Swatches tipped into the book are not identified, but they closely resemble the goods shown in merchants' pattern books. Drafts for the following types of Manchester goods, always with some of the weaver's comments, include:

Barragon
Cord without Cuting. Note: This seems like Cordery without cutting with a fine Chain Between and Floats over 6 Ends.
A Cord chain'd on both sides.
Everlasting Cord. This has a fine chain on both sides and the tuft Floats over 8 ends. Invented by Thomas Nicols.
Elliots Cord; Grand Brittish Cord; Rodney Cord.
Kings Cord. This has a plain Backside and under the Tuft is a fine chain. And it floats over 5 ends.
Dimons [Diamonds] with a rose in the middle.

Fustian. All sorts of Fustions that will cut one and one are called Velveteens.

Hearing bone. Note: You must Draw into the heals as it is figured.

Jeans, double, single, Double Jean'd Thicksetts.

Pillow

Plain Back. This has a plain Backside and a chain under the Tuft and Floats over 8 Ends.

Pocketing

Pokes of Pillows; Pokes of Seven Shafts.

Ribs, double ribs, Royal ribs.

Satenet

Stockenet

Stripes

Thicksett, Macarony or Diced Thicksett, Floating Thicksetts. This has a plain Back side and plain under the Tuft and Floats over 5 Ends.

Thicksetts Turned. The one Tuft is on the face side and the other on the Backside. Quarrel'd Thicksett.

Ticks

Twills

Velverat, Chain'd Back'd Velverat, Diced Velverat.

Velvet, cotton printed; ribbed; plain colors and printed.

Velveteens, single Bound, double Bound, Jean Back, chain'd Back, hunney Comb.

Wild Worm, Wild Worm and Cord.

A pattern book of the firm of Robert and Nathan Hyde, Manchester, is privately owned. The firm run by the two brothers seems to have been important in American trade before the Revolution. James Beekman ordered quantities of stripes, checks, cotton gowns, pillows, dimities, bunts, velverets, and handkerchiefs, as well as silk damasks and haberdashery from them between 1767 and 1771. Nathan Hyde visited in New York in 1769 and "received repeated favors during his residence" from the Beekmans (see Beekman Papers, 2:840). Unfortunately, the numbers of the Hyde pattern book ranging from 1,010 to 1,559, do not match Beekman's 1771 order where pattern numbers are listed in the hundreds, indicating that he used an earlier book. The Hyde pattern book, dated 1771, is inscribed with the brothers' names and lists the types of goods which they were prepared to export:

Robert & Nathan Hyde, Manchester, 1771
A list of Goods that are Manufactured & Exported by Robert & Nathn. Hyde of Manchester, Viz.

Checks & Stripes of all Sorts
Cotton & worsted Furniture Checks
Printed & Check Hkfs of all Sorts
Linen & Cotton Hollands & Ginghams
French & Cotton Stripes of all Sorts
Bed Ticks & Bed Bunts
Turkey Stripes & Cotton Gowns
Silk Damascus, Soosees, & Burdets
Lorrettas, Moreens, & Brunswicks
Silk Starretts, Chinces & Ginghams
Cotton Velvets, Velverets & Vellures
Fustians, Jeans, Pillows & Thicksetts
Cotton Sattinetts, & Denims for Breeches
Corded & figur'd Dimothys
Dutch Cords, Jeanetts & White Jeans
Cotton Counterpanes, & Drawboys
Marseilles Quilts for Beds & Pettycoats
Garters, Quality Bindings, & tapes of all Sorts
Coat Bindings, Shoe Bindings, & Laces of all Sorts
Bed Lace, Livery lace, & Coach Lace
White & Colour'd threads of all Sorts
Buttons, twist, & Hair of all Sorts
Silk Knee Garters, Silk Ferrets &
Silk Laces, of all Sorts
Castor & felt hatts of all Sorts
Worsted & Hair Shags & Plushes
Worsted, Cotton, thread & Silk Stockings.

MANN, JULIA DE L. *The Cloth Industry in the West of England from 1640 to 1880.* Oxford: Clarendon Press, 1971.

————. "Textile Industries since 1550." In *A History of Wiltshire,* vol. 4, edited by Elizabeth Crittall, pp. 148–82. London: Oxford University Press, 1959.

————. "A Wiltshire Family of Clothiers: George and Hester Wansey, 1683–1714." *Economic History Review,* 2d ser., 9 (1956–57): 241–53.

See also Wadsworth, Alfred P., and Julia de L. Mann, *The Cotton Trade and Industrial Lancashire, 1600–1780.*

MANN, JULIA DE L., ed. "Documents Illustrating the Wiltshire Textile Trades in the Eighteenth Century." In *Wiltshire Archaeological and Natural History Society,* vol. 19. Devizes, Wiltshire: Hereford Times, 1964.

Manuel historique, géographique et politique des négocians, ou encyclopédie portative de la théorie et de la pratique du commerce. 3 vols. Lyons: Jean-Marie Bruyset, 1762.

MARCH, R. *A Treatise on Silk, Wool, Worsted, Cotton, and Thread.* London: Printed for the author, 1779.

MARKS, STEPHEN S., ed. *Fairchild's Dictionary of Textiles.* New York: Fairchild Publications, 1959.

A revised edition of the 1915, 1920, and 1924 editions of Louis Harmuth, *Dictionary of Textiles* (q.v.). A new edition of *Fairchild's Dictionary of Textiles* appeared in 1967, edited by Isabel B. Wingate (q.v.).

[MAROT]. *Werken van D. Marot, Opperboumeester van Zyne Majiesteit Willem den Derden Konig van Groot Britanje.* Amsterdam, [1707?].

MARPERGER, PAUL JAKOB. *Tuchmacher Handwerks: Beschreibung des Tuchmacher Handwerks, und der aus groß und fein sortirter wolle verfertigten tuecher.* Dresden and Leipzig, [1720?].

Maurepas Papers. Joseph Downs Manuscript and Microfilm Collection, Winterthur Museum Library.

(a) Reports on the possibility of selling cloth from Rouen in Spain and the West Indies, 1743. 62 x 14.1–6.

Includes 64 swatches of French textiles which closely parallel English manufactures. The swatches identify the *toileries* or inexpensive textiles being produced at Rouen, the center of cotton manufacture in France. Many were made in imitation of imported Indian silk-and-cotton goods—striped, chevron, checked, and lozenge patterns; floral patterns which required a draw loom; linen and cotton stripes called siamoises; tobines; and cottons brocaded with floral sprigs in brightly colored wools. The last sheet presents nine swatches of West of England wools used for clothing by the Spanish both at home and in South America. Parallels to these patterns are found in English half-silks, striped calimancoes and camleteens, and the great variety of cotton goods woven in Manchester during this period.

(b) Reports on English cloth manufacture and the Levant trade, 1731. 62 x 15.1–5.

Four kinds of woolen cloth made for the Levant trade are described as similar to those which the British export to their North American colonies.

The swatches are illustrated in color and described in *Textiles et documents Maurepas,* edited by Roland Lamontagne (q.v.) with an introductory essay by Florence M. Montgomery entitled "Les matières textiles au XVIIIe siècle." *See also* Robert F. Metzdorf, ed., *Historical French Documents . . . from the Archives of Jean-Frederic Phelypeau Comte de Maurepas.*

MAYHEW, EDGAR DE N., and MINOR MYERS, JR. *A Documentary History of American Interiors from the Colonial Era to 1915.* New York: Charles Scribner's Sons, 1980.

MECRAW, ROBERT H. *Textiles and the Origin of Their Names.* New York: Printed for the author, 1906.

Mercury Dictionary. See Textile Mercury Dictionary.

[MERRIAM-WEBSTER]. *Webster's Third New International Dictionary of the English Language: Unabridged.* Springfield, Mass.: C. & G. Merriam Co., 1966.

MESSER, JOYCE P., ed. *Textile Samplebooks and Swatches in the Merrimack Valley Textile Museum.* North Andover, Mass.: Merrimack Valley Textile Museum, 1971. Addenda, 1972.

American and European factory records, scrapbooks, dye receipts, etc., of the nineteenth and twentieth centuries.

METCALF, PAULINE C. "The Interiors of Ogden Codman, Jr., in Newport, Rhode Island." *Antiques* 118, no. 3 (September 1980): 486–97.

Metropolitan Museum of Art. Samples, circa 1740, no. 156. 415 Ec 4 F.

Three letters with 48 swatches of *Londrina Seconda* from Carcassonne.

———. Sample book, circa 1800, no. 156. 415 T52 Q.

Contains 1,385 swatches of floral silks, velvets, trimmings, and furnishing and dress fabrics.

———. *Handbook. See American Wing Handbook.*

Metropolitan Museum of Art Library Catalogue. 25 vols. Boston: G. K. Hall, 1960.

METZDORF, ROBERT F., ed. *Historical French Documents of the Eighteenth Century . . . from the Archives of Jean-Frederic Phelypeau Comte de Maurepas.* Sale catalogue no. 2092, lots 67, 72. New York: Parke-Bernet Galleries, 1962.

MICHEL, FRANCISQUE. *Recherches sur le commerce, la fabrication et l'usage des étoffes de soie, d'or et d'argent et autres tissus précieux en occident, principalement en France pendant le Moyen-Age.* 2 vols. Paris: Imprimerie de Crapelet, 1852.

Moccasi manuscript. Bibliothèque Forney, 677.064, Paris.

Woven textiles of circa 1760 from France, England, and Holland were assembled in a manuscript book presumably written to instruct Italian merchants or as a record of textile production. The title reads: *Manifatture di Francia, Inghilterra ed Olanda. Mostre raccolte viaggiando dal Signor Moccasi, mercante di panni e nel suo ritorno verso il 1760 presentate al Conte Bogino.* Inscriptions and ornamental flourishes are penned in red and black inks with birds, animals, and flowers incorporated in the initial letters or as tailpieces.

Dress and furnishing fabrics in silk, wool, cotton, linen, and combinations thereof are included. Especially important for this study are the manufactures of London, Norwich, Leeds, and Exeter. In general the fabrics represent those in everyday use. Of the two weaving centers producing the most costly, fashionable brocades—Spitalfields and Lyons—no mention is made. Many of the swatches are tiny.

MONTGOMERY, CHARLES F. *American Furniture: The Federal Period.* New York: Viking Press, 1966. Reprint ed., New York: Bonanza Books, 1978.

MONTGOMERY, FLORENCE M. "Antique and Reproduction Furnishing Fabrics in Historic Houses and Period Rooms." *Antiques* 107 (1975): 164–69.

_____. "English Textile Swatches of the Mid-Eighteenth Century." *Burlington Magazine* 102 (1960): 240–43.

_____. " 'Fortunes to be Acquired': Textiles in Eighteenth-Century Rhode Island." *Rhode Island History* 31 (1972): 52–63.

A study of merchants' and shopkeepers' advertisements for textiles found in the *Providence Gazette,* 1762–1800.

_____. "John Holker's Mid-Eighteenth-Century *Livre d'échantillons.*" In *Studies in Textile History in Memory of Harold B. Burnham,* edited by Veronika Gervers, pp. 214–31. Toronto: Royal Ontario Museum, 1977.

_____. "Les Matières textiles au XVIIIe siècle." Introduction to *Textiles et documents Maurepas,* edited by Roland Lamontagne, pp. 33–60. Ottawa: Editions Lemeac, 1970.

_____. "A Pattern-Woven 'Flamestitch' Fabric." *Antiques* 80 (1961): 453–55.

_____. *Printed Textiles: English and American Cottons and Linens, 1700–1850.* New York: Viking Press, 1970.

_____. "Room Furnishings as seen in British Prints from the Lewis Walpole Library." Part 1, "Bed Hangings." *Antiques* 104 (1973): 1068–75; part 2, "Window Curtains, Upholstery, and Slip Covers." 105 (1974): 522–31.

_____. "1776—How America Really Looked: Textiles." *American Art Journal* 7 (1975): 82–92.

_____. "Stylistic Change in Printed Textiles." In *Technological Innovation and the Decorative Arts,* edited by Ian M. G. Quimby and Polly Anne Earl, pp. 257–76. Charlottesville: University Press of Virginia, 1974.

MOON, JOHN. Inventory of shop goods, Philadelphia, 1688. Joseph Downs Manuscript and Microfilm Collection, 56 x 12.6, Winterthur Museum Library.

MORELAND, FRANK A. *Practical Decorative Upholstery; Containing Full Instructions for Cutting, Making and Hanging All Kinds of Interior Upholstery Decorations.* Boston: Lee & Shephard; New York: C. T. Dillingham, 1890. Reprint ed., *The Curtain-Maker's Handbook,* introduction by Martha Gandy Fales, New York: E. P. Dutton, 1979.

MORISON, SAMUEL ELIOT. "Mistress Glover's Household Furnishings at Cambridge, Massachusetts, 1638–1641." *Old-Time New England* 25 (1934): 29–32.

MORRIS, BARBARA. "Textiles." In *The Regency Period, 1810–1830,* The Connoisseur Period Guides, edited by Ralph Edwards and L. G. G. Ramsey, pp. 107–16. New York: Reynal, 1958.

_____. "Textiles." In *The Early Victorian Period, 1830–1860,* The Connoisseur Period Guides, edited by Ralph Edwards and L. G. G. Ramsey, pp. 113–28. New York: Reynal, 1958.

MORTIMER, THOMAS. *A New and Complete Dictionary of Trade and Commerce.* London: Printed for the author, 1766.

MUSÉE DES ARTS DÉCORATIFS. *Des Dorelotiers aux passementiers.* Paris: Union Centrale des Arts Décoratifs, 1973.

"Muster Karte von Iermesût, Scalli, Cettari, Cutni und Scamalagia. Nach Ostindischer Art des Benedict Codecasa, K.K.P., Landebefugter Seidenzeig Fabrikant in Wien 2." Joseph Downs Manuscript and Microfilm Collection, 62 x 32, Winterthur Museum Library.

A late eighteenth-century sample book of 272 swatches of striped silk and cotton materials patterned after Indian goods.

NARES, ROBERT. *A Glossary; or, Collection of Words, Phrases, Names, and Allusions to Customs, Proverbs, Etc. . . .* Rev. ed. London, 1905. Reprint ed., Detroit: Gale Research Co., 1966.

NEAVE, SAMUEL. Shop and house inventory, Philadelphia, 1774. No. 38, Will Book Q 37, Register of Wills, City Hall, Philadelphia, Pa.

New Jersey scrapbooks. Salem County, N.J., 1880–89. Joseph Downs Manuscript and Microfilm Collection, 73 x 291, 75 x 9.1–3, Winterthur Museum Library.

A group of four similar albums containing examples of dress and furnishing materials, among them English chintzes and copperplates, a few Indian textiles, homespun woolens, and household checks, some of which date from the late eighteenth century. Many are designated as materials for wedding dresses. Some are described as "ancient" or "75 or 100 years old." There is frequent overlapping among the books of the same materials and the same women's names. It is remarkable that four such books prepared by members of this South Jersey Quaker community should survive.

[New York Appraisements]. "Appraisements made by Christopher Bancker and Brandt Schuyler, begun in New York ye 25th of May, 1750 and with Joris Brinckerhoff ye 26th of April, 1753." Appraisal Book 66, New York estates, ships overdue, etc. Joseph Downs Manuscript and Microfilm Collection, 53.190, Winterthur Museum Library.

New York Industrial Exhibition: General Report of the British Commissioners. London: Harrison & Son, 1854.

    See especially "Special Report of Mr. [C. Wentworth] Dilke" and "Special Report of Mr. George Wallis."

New York Interiors at the Turn of the Century in 131 Photographs by Joseph Byron from the Byron Collection of the Museum of the City of New York. Text by Clay Lancaster. New York: Dover Publications, 1976.

NICHOLSON, PETER, and MICHAEL ANGELO NICHOLSON. *The Practical Cabinet-Maker, Upholsterer, and Complete Decorator.* London: H. Fisher, Son & P. Jackson, 1826. Reprint ed., Brooklyn Heights, N.Y.: Beekman Publishers, 1973.

Niles' Weekly Register (title varies). 76 vols. Baltimore, 1811–49.

NISBET, HARRY. *Grammar of Textile Design.* 3d ed. New York: D. Van Nostrand, 1927.

NORTHEND, MARY H. *Colonial Homes and Their Furnishings.* Boston: Little, Brown, 1912.

[NORTON, JOHN]. Frances Norton Mason, ed. *John Norton and Sons, Merchants of London and Virginia, being the Papers from Their Counting House for the Years 1750 to 1795.* Richmond, Va.: Dietz Press, 1937.

Norwich worsted pattern books. Joseph Downs Manuscript and Microfilm Collection, Winterthur Museum Library.

    (a) Pattern book containing 510 Norwich worsteds with titles written in French, circa 1785. 65 x 695.1.

    (b) Pattern book containing 2,140 worsteds with a few titles written in German. A torn label on the cover of the book reads "Copy of a Pattn.

Book sent to C O." The back of the cover is marked ICH. Paper watermarked 1794. 65 x 695.2.

    (c) Pattern book containing 685 worsteds with titles written in English. Includes a written list of prices and notes that the patterns were sent to D. Callaghan, *chez Louis Preiswerk, Bâle* (1794); Mr. Collins (1794); Messrs. Wm. Fox and Sons, Cheapside, London (1795); and Nethropp & Harris, Copenhagen (1797). 65 x 695.3.

    (d) "Counter, 1788" containing 4,240 swatches of worsteds without titles. 65 x 695.4.

    (e) Pattern book containing 852 worsteds. Bears the inscription "Booth and Theobald, Norwich" (1790–1810). The arrangement and numbering of swatches corresponds exactly to a book inscribed "Charles Tuthill" which is in the Castle Museum, Norwich. Paper watermarked 1801. 65 x 695.5.

    (f) Pattern book containing 1,884 worsteds with English titles, circa 1785. 65 x 695.6.

    See also Castle Museum.

Noska pattern book. Merrimack Valley Textile Museum. A book of workmen's clothing samples prepared for Charles Noska, Mannayunk, Pa., 1860. It includes swatches of Niger cloth, Pokeno [Pocono] cotton rib, dimity, and shoddy.

NYLANDER, JANE C. *Fabrics for Historic Buildings.* 3rd ed. Washington, D.C.: Preservation Press, National Trust for Historic Preservation, 1983.

Observations on British Wool, and the Manufacturing of It in This Kingdom . . . , by a Manufacturer of Northamptonshire. London: Printed by H. Kent for the author, 1738.

O'CALLAGHAN, EDMUND BAILEY. *The Documentary History of the State of New York.* 4 vols. Albany: Weed, Parsons, 1849–51.

"Old Southampton Odds and Ends." Joseph Downs Manuscript and Microfilm Collection, 75 x 130, Winterthur Museum Library.

    A scrapbook assembled in Long Island, N.Y., in the twentieth century, which contains samples of wool, lace, linen, etc., woven in the eighteenth and nineteenth centuries.

[OED]. *Oxford English Dictionary: Being a Corrected Reissue . . . of a New English Dictionary on Historical Principles.* 13 vols. Oxford: At the Clarendon Press, 1933.

OTT, JOSEPH K. "Rhode Islanders in Charleston: Social Notes," *South Carolina Historical Magazine* 75, no. 3 (July 1974): 180–83.

Pacific Printworks, Lawrence, Mass. Dyers' receipt books, 1853–ca. 1890. 48 vols. Cooper-Hewitt Museum, gift of Frederick J. Whitehead, 1945–55–1–48, New York.

PAGE, RUTH. "English Carpets and Their Use in America." *Connecticut Antiquarian* 19 (1967): 16.

PARTINGTON, CHARLES F. *The British Cyclopaedia of the Arts, Sciences, History, and Biography.* 10 vols. London: William S. Orr, 1838.

Pattern book, possibly England, 1800–1825. Joseph Downs Manuscript and Microfilm Collection, 69 x 216, Winterthur Museum Library.

> Included are printed cottons, woven linens, silk ribbons, net, baize, wool, velvet, gauze, vestings, nankeen, florentine, moreen, broadcloth, coating, cassimere, sinchaw, chambray, cambric, and leno.

PAULET, J. *Art du fabriquant d'étoffes de soie.* Paris: L. F. Delatour, 1773–76. From *Descriptions des arts et métiers,* Winterthur Museum Library.

PENN, JOHN, JR. Broadside of household goods offered for sale, Philadelphia, 1788. Joseph Downs Manuscript and Microfilm Collection, 55.512, Winterthur Museum Library.

> For further discussion, see "Inventory of the Household Effects of John Penn, Jr., 1788," *Pennsylvania Magazine of History and Biography* 15 (1891): 373–75.

PERCIER, CHARLES, and PIERRE F. L. FONTAINE. *Recueil de décorations intérieures, comprenant tout ce qui a rapport à l'ameublement . . . composé par C. Percier et P. F. L. Fontaine.* Paris: Chez les auteurs, 1812.

PERKINS, E. E. *A Treatise on Haberdashery and Hosiery.* London: Thomas Hurst, 1833.

PERSOZ, JEAN FRANÇOIS. *Traité théorique et pratique de l'impression des tissus.* 4 vols. Paris: V. Masson, 1846.

PETERSON, HAROLD L. *Americans at Home: From the Colonists to the Late Victorians.* New York: Charles Scribner's Sons, 1971. Originally published under the title *Americans at Home.*

PEUCHET, JACQUES. *Dictionnaire universel de la géographie commerçante, contenant tout ce qui a rapport à la situation et à l'étendue de chaque état commerçant.* 5 vols. Paris: Blanchon, 1799–1800.

—————. *Vocabulaire des termes de commerce, banque, manufactures, navigation marchande, finance mercantile et statistique.* Paris: Testu, 1801.

[Phelps Diary]. THOMAS ELIOT ANDREWS, ed. "Diary of Elizabeth Porter Phelps." *New England Historical and Genealogical Register* 120 (1966).

[Philadelphia Centennial Exhibition]. United States Centennial Commission. *International Exhibition, 1876, Official Catalogue.* Rev. ed. Philadelphia: John R. Nagle for the Centennial Catalogue Co., 1876.

Philadelphia: Three Centuries of American Art (1676–1976). Philadelphia: Philadelphia Museum of Art, 1976.

Pictorial Dictionary of British Nineteenth-Century Furniture Design. Introduction by Edward T. Joy. Woodbridge, Suffolk: Baron Publishing for the Antique Collectors' Club, 1977.

PILGRIM, JOHN E. "The Cloth Industry in East Anglia." In *The Wool Textile Industry in Great Britain,* edited by J. Geraint Jenkins, pp. 252–68. London and Boston: Routledge & Kegan Paul, 1972.

PLANCHÉ, JAMES ROBINSON. *A Cyclopaedia of Costume or Dictionary of Dress; Including Notices of Contemporaneous Fashions on the Continent to George the Third.* 2 vols. London: Chatto & Windus, 1876–79.

—————. *History of British Costume.* London: Charles Knight for the Society for the Diffusion of Useful Knowledge, 1834.

—————. *A Complete View of the Dress and Habits of the People of England: From the Establishment of the Saxons in Britain to the Present Time.* By Joseph Strutt. New and improved edition by J. R. Planché. London: H. G. Bohn, 1842.

PLOT, ROBERT. *The Natural History of Oxfordshire.* Oxford: Printed at the Theater; London: S. Millers, 1677.

PLUMMER, ALFRED. *The Witney Blanket Industry: The Records of the Witney Blanket Weavers.* London: George Routledge & Sons, 1934.

PLUMMER, ALFRED, and RICHARD E. EARLY. *The Blanket Makers, 1669–1969.* London: Routledge & Kegan Paul, 1969.

Polly Papers. Suffolk County Courthouse, file no. 102538, Boston, Mass.

> The American schooner *Polly* seized the cargo of a prize ship. Among papers pertaining to this (ca. 1777) court case are fifty swatches of English calimancoes, camlets, and camleteens with titles written in Spanish.

Pondicherry Company, Bridgeton, Maine. Swatches and drafts of woolen cloth woven at mills in Maine, Massachusetts, New Hampshire, and West Virginia, 1896–1913. The collection includes the finishing room ledger from Pondicherry which was used as a scrapbook. Merrimack Valley Textile Museum.

PONTING, KENNETH G. "Clothiers' Pattern Books." *Journal of Industrial Archeology* 2 (1965): 147–49.

> Eighteenth- and early nineteenth-century pat-

tern books, dye receipts, and business records of West of England clothiers, many of whom specialized in broadcloths. These records are owned by the firms of J. T. & J. Clark and Messrs. Samuel Salter and Company of Trowbridge; the Wiltshire Record Office; the Archeological Society Library, Devizes; the Bath Public Library; and the Public Record Office, London.

—————. *A History of the West of England Cloth Industry*. London: Macdonald, 1957.

—————. *The Special Characteristics of the West Country Woollen Industry*. London: International Wool Secretariat, 1956.

—————. *The Woollen Industry of South-West England*. Bath: Adams & Dart; New York, Augustus M. Kelley, 1971.

POSTLETHWAYT, MALACHY. *The Universal Dictionary of Trade and Commerce Translated, from the French of the Celebrated Monsieur Savary . . . with Large Additions*. 2 vols. London: J. & P. Knapton, 1751–55.

PRAZ, MARIO. *An Illustrated History of Furnishing from the Renaissance to the Twentieth Century*. New York: George Braziller, 1964.

PRENDERGAST, SUSAN MARGARET. "Fabric Furnishings Used in Philadelphia Homes, 1700–1775." Master's thesis, University of Delaware, 1978. *See also* Susan Prendergast Schoelwer.

PRESTON, PAULA D. "A New Acquisition and the East India Trade." *New-England Galaxy* 9, no. 1 (Summer 1967): 59–63.

PRIESTLEY, GEORGE. "The Production of Flags and Bunting." In *Warp and Weft* (reprinted from *Wool Knowledge* [the Journal of Wool Education]), pp. 53–56. London: International Wool Secretariat, 195?.

PRIESTMAN, MABEL TUKE. "What You Can Do with Appliqué." *House Beautiful* 22 (1907): 23–24.

PRIME, ALFRED COXE. *The Arts and Crafts in Philadelphia, Maryland, and South Carolina, 1721–1785*. Topsfield, Mass.: Wayside Press for the Walpole Society, 1929.

—————. *The Arts and Crafts in Philadelphia, Maryland, and South Carolina, 1786–1800*. Topsfield, Mass.: Wayside Press for the Walpole Society, 1932.

PRITCHARD, MIRIAM ELEANOR. *A Short Dictionary of Weaving*. New York: Philosophical Library, [1956].

PROWN, JULES DAVID. *John Singleton Copley*. 2 vols. Cambridge, Mass.: Harvard University Press for the National Gallery of Art, 1966. Vol. 1, *America, 1738–1774*. Vol. 2, *England, 1774–1815*.

Public Record Office, London.

(a) Counterpart of pattern book to Jno. Hynes, 1764 (C217/70). Contains 260 swatches of amens, bird's-eye, shalloon, lasting, wool velvet, and moreen.

(b) The Lord Chamberlain's accounts, especially "Patterns and Rates," 1754–1759 (LC9/267). Includes swatches of Genoese and Dutch silk velvets, satin, armazine, camlet, ducape, harateen, holland, moreen, serge, tammy, ticken, and a great variety of braids, bindings, and cords.

(c) "Standards" book, 1799 (CME C113/16). Has swatches of haresback, cassimere, livery, drapery bay, flannel, shalloon, and coating.

(d) HCA 32/125 contains swatches of duffels, long ells, says, serge, shalloon, and sagathy dating from 1746 to 1752.

(e) Hilton manuscript, (q.v.)

Most of the above references were provided by Natalie Rothstein, assistant keeper in the Textile Department, Victoria and Albert Museum, London, who has worked extensively in the records.

RALEY, ROBERT L. "Interior Designs by Benjamin Henry Latrobe for the President's House." *Antiques* 75 (1959): 568–71.

RAMSAY, G. D. *English Overseas Trade during the Centuries of Emergence*. London: Macmillan, 1957.

—————. *The Wiltshire Woollen Industry in the Sixteenth and Seventeenth Centuries*. London: Oxford University Press, 1943. Reprint ed., London: Frank Cass, 1965.

RAVENEL, HARRIOTT HORRY. *Eliza Pinckney*. New York: Charles Scribner's Sons, 1896.

REATH, NANCY ANDREWS. *The Weaves of Hand-Loom Fabrics*. Philadelphia: Pennsylvania Museum, 1927.

Recueil de draperies d'Hallavant mis au jour et augmenté par Osmont et Dezon. Paris: Rotonde du Temple, [ca. 1815?].

REES, ABRAHAM. *The Cyclopaedia; or, Universal Dictionary of Arts, Sciences, and Literature*. 41 vols. and 6 vols. of plates. Philadelphia: Bradford, Fairman, et al., 1810–24.

Repository. See Ackermann.

REY, CLAUDIUS. *Observations on Mr. Asgill's Brief Answer to a Brief State of the Question between the Printed and Painted Callicoes*. London: W. Wilkins, 1719.

Richelieu Papers. Bibliothèque Nationale, Paris.

A complete record of French and foreign textile manufacture between 1732 and 1737 is presented in eight folio volumes of textile swatches which were assembled by Armand de Viguerot du Plessis, duc de Richelieu (1696–1788).

They formed part of a 52-volume collection in his library referred to as "Records of Our Time." After Richelieu's death, the entire collection was purchased for the king's library and is now housed in the Cabinet des Estampes, Bibliothèque Nationale.

Seven of the volumes are alike in size (Lh45 to Lh45F, nos. 1–7, of which nos. 6 and 7 contain ribbons). In a single volume of smaller size (Lh40) entitled "Fashionable materials from 1720–35," the swatches are arranged chronologically, whereas in the other books prices are given as well as the date and place of manufacture.

A representative selection of the swatches is described in the beautifully illustrated book *Textiles en Europe sous Louis XV* by Roger-Armand Weigert (q.v.) which includes an English preface by Valerie C. Sutton.

RITCHARDS, MARY. Inventory, **1702**. New Hampshire Provincial Probate Records, vol. 4, pp. 166–69. New Hampshire Division of Records Management and Archives, Concord, N.H.

RODIER, PAUL. *The Romance of French Weaving*. New York: Frederick A. Stokes, 1931.

ROLAND DE LA PLATIÈRE, JEAN-MARIE. *L'Art de préparer et d'imprimer les étoffes en laines, suivi de l'art de fabriquer les pannes ou peluches, les velours façon d'Utrecht et les moquettes.* Paris: Moutard, 1780. From *Descriptions des arts et métiers*, Winterthur Museum Library.

————. *L'Art du fabricant de velours de coton, précedé d'une dissertation sur la nature, le choix, et la préparation des matières, et suivi d'un traité de la teinture et de l'impression des étoffes.* Paris: Moutard, 1780. From *Descriptions des arts et métiers*, Winterthur Museum Library.

————. *L'Art du fabricant d'étoffes en laines rases et sèches, unies, et croisées.* Paris: Moutard, 1780. From *Descriptions des arts et métiers*, Winterthur Museum Library.

ROLT, RICHARD. *A New Dictionary of Trade and Commerce*. London: T. Osborne, J. Shipton, et al., 1756.

RÖRDANSZ, C. W. *European Commerce; or, Complete Mercantile Guide to the Continent of Europe*. Boston: Cummings & Hilliard, 1819.

ROTH, RODRIS. *Floor Coverings in Eighteenth-Century America*. Washington, D.C.: Smithsonian Press, 1967.

ROTHSTEIN, NATALIE. "The Calico Campaign of 1719–1721." *East London Papers* 7 (1964): 3–21.

————. "The English Market for French Silks." *Bulletin de Liaison du Centre International d'Etude des Textiles Anciens*, no. 35 (1972): 32–42.

Salesman's order book from France dating from circa 1763–64, including gold and silver batavias, brocades, grograms, lustrings, Peruvians, painted sarcenets, satins, and tissues.

————. "European Silks: Historical and Domestic." *Apollo* 105 (1977): 468–72.

————. "The Introduction of the Jacquard Loom to Great Britain." In *Studies in Textile History in Memory of Harold B. Burnham*, edited by Veronika Gervers, pp. 281–304. Toronto: Royal Ontario Museum, 1977.

————. "Nine English Silks." *Needle and Bobbin Club Bulletin* 48 (1964): 4–35.

————. "Silks for the American Market." *Connoisseur* 166 (1967): 90–94; 166 (1967): 150–56.

————. "The Warner Archive." *Bulletin de Liaison du Centre International d'Etude des Textiles Anciens*, no. 36 (1972): 25–28.

ROWE, ANN POLLARD. "Crewel Embroidered Bed Hangings in Old and New England." *Bulletin, Museum of Fine Arts, Boston* 71 (1973): 102–66.

Royal Society of Arts. *Transactions of the Society for the Encouragement of Arts, Manufactures, and Commerce: With the Premiums Offered in the Year 1783*. Vol. 1. 3d ed. London: C. Spilsbury, 1806.

SAVARY, JACQUES. *Le Parfait Négociant, ou instruction générale pour ce qui regarde le commerce des marchandises de France et des pays étrangers*. Paris: Jean Guignard fils, 1675.

SAVARY DES BRUSLONS, JACQUES. *Dictionnaire universel de commerce*. 1723–30; 6th ed., 5 vols., Geneva: Les Frères Cramer & C. Philibert, 1750–65. *See also* Malachy Postlethwayt.

A Scheame of the Trade as it is at present carried on between England and France in the Commodities of the native Product and manufacture of each Countrey, Calculated as Exactly as possible in Obedience to the Comand of the Right honoble. the Lords Comrs. for the Treaty of Comerce with France and humbly tendred to their Lordships, 29th November, 1674. Original at Harvard School of Business Administration, Cambridge, Mass. Joseph Downs Manuscript and Microfilm Collection, M-257, Winterthur Museum Library.

SCHIFFER, MARGARET B. *Chester County, Pennsylvania, Inventories, 1684–1850*. Exton, Pa.: Schiffer Publishing, 1974.

──────. *Historical Needlework of Pennsylvania.* New York: Charles Scribner's Sons, 1968.

SCHINDLER-OTT, M. "Zurich Silks in Past Fashions." *CIBA Review* 119 (1957): 17–20.

SCHLESINGER, ARTHUR M. *The Colonial Merchants and the American Revolution, 1763–76.* New York: Columbia University Press, 1918.

SCHOELWER, SUSAN PRENDERGAST. "Form, Function, and Meaning in the Use of Fabric Furnishings: A Philadelphia Case Study, 1700–1775." *Winterthur Portfolio: A Journal of American Material Culture* 14 (1979): 25–40.

SCHUYLER, PHILIP. Miscellaneous manuscripts, vol. 5, Schuyler Papers, State Library, Albany, N.Y.

SCHWARTZ, ESTHER I. "Notes from a New Jersey Collector: Early Commercial Weaving in Paterson." *Antiques* 74 (1958): 329–32.

Science Museum manuscript, ca. 1784. London.

> Twenty-seven swatches of linen barras, cambric, holland, and ticking used to show examples of the types of imported goods subject to duty were sent with a petition to Parliament in connection with an act introduced in 1784 and repealed in 1861 (Act 24, George III, Session 21, chapter 40).

SCLARE, LIISA, AND DONALD SCLARE. *Beaux-Arts Estates: A Guide to the Architecture of Long Island.* New York: Viking Press, 1980.

[SCPR]. Probate Records, Suffolk County, Mass. Originals in Suffolk County Courthouse, Boston. Joseph Downs Manuscript and Microfilm Collection, M-109 (1628) through M-180 (1852), Winterthur Museum Library.

SEALE, WILLIAM. *Recreating the Historic House Interior.* Nashville: American Association for State and Local History, 1979.

──────. *The Tasteful Interlude: American Interiors through the Camera's Eye, 1860–1917.* New York: Praeger Publishers, 1975.

SEIKA, YAMAGA. *Mukashi-watari sarasa* [Early imported sarasa]. 3 vols. Kyoto, Japan, [1917].

SEWALL, SAMUEL. *Diary of Samuel Sewall, 1674–1729.* In *Collections of the Massachusetts Historical Society,* 5th ser., vols. 5–7. Boston: Published by the society, 1878–79, 1882.

──────. *Letter-Book of Samuel Sewall.* In *Collections of the Massachusetts Historical Society,* 6th ser., vols. 1 and 2. Boston: Published by the society, 1886, 1888.

Sheffield, third earl of. *See* John Baker Holroyd.

SHERATON, THOMAS. *The Cabinet Dictionary.* London: W. Smith, 1803. Reprint ed., edited by Charles F. Montgomery, introduction by Wilford P. Cole, New York: Praeger Publishers, 1970.

──────. *The Cabinet-Maker, Upholsterer and General Artist's Encyclopedia.* London, 1804–7.

──────. *The Cabinet-Maker and Upholsterer's Drawing-Book.* Various editions, London, 1791–1802. Reprint of 1793 ed., introduction by Joseph Aronson, New York: Dover Publications, 1972. Reprint of 1802 ed., edited by Charles F. Montgomery and Wilford P. Cole, introduction by Lindsay O. J. Boynton, New York: Praeger Publishers, 1970.

──────. *Designs for Household Furniture.* London: T. Taylor, 1812.

SHURTLEFF, NATHANIEL B., ed. *Records of the Governor and Company of the Massachusetts Bay in New England.* 5 vols. Boston: William White, 1853–54.

SIMPSON, JOHN K. Billhead, Boston, 1830. Joseph Downs Manuscript and Microfilm Collection, 60 x 15.4, Winterthur Museum Library.

> Simpson owned a bedding warehouse.

SINGER, CHARLES, et al., eds. *A History of Technology.* 5 vols. Oxford: At the University Press, 1954–58.

SINGLETON, ESTHER. *Dutch and Flemish Furniture.* London: Hodder & Stoughton, 1907.

──────. *Social New York under the Georges, 1714–1776.* New York: D. Appleton, 1902.

SKEAT, WALTER W., and A. L. MAYHEW. *A Glossary of Tudor and Stuart Words.* Oxford: Clarendon Press, 1914.

SMITH, GEORGE. *The Cabinet-Maker and Upholsterer's Guide.* London: Jones, 1826.

──────. *A Collection of Designs for Household Furniture and Interior Decoration.* London: J. Taylor, 1808. Reprint ed., edited by Charles F. Montgomery and Benno M. Forman, introduction by Constance V. Hershey, New York: Praeger Publishers, 1970.

SMITH, G[ODFREY?], comp. *The Laboratory; or, School of Arts.* 2d ed. London: Printed for H. D. Symonds, J. Wallis, et al., 1756.

SMITH, WALTER. *Art Education, Scholastic and Industrial.* Boston: J. R. Osgood, 1873.

──────. *Industrial Art.* The Masterpieces of the Centennial International Exhibition, vol. 2. Philadelphia: Gebbie & Barrie, 1876.

Spitalfields silks. Victoria and Albert Museum. This archive of some 800 watercolor patterns of English silks by Spitalfields designers in the first half of the eighteenth century has been owned by the museum since the mid-nineteenth century. Many are reproduced in Peter Thornton's *Baroque and Rococo Silks* (q.v.) and in articles by him and by Natalie Rothstein in the *Needle and Bobbin Club Bulletin. See also* Jean-Michel Tuchscherer.

SPOFFORD, HARRIET PRESCOTT. *Art Decoration Applied to Furniture.* New York: Harper, 1878.

The Statutes of the Realm. 9 vols. in 10. London: George Eyre & Andrew Strahan, 1810–22. Vol. 5 (1819), pp. 184–202, contains the Book of Rates, 1660.

STICKLEY, GUSTAV. *Craftsman Homes.* New York: Craftsman Publishing Co., 1909. Reprint ed., *Craftsman Homes: Architecture and Furnishings of the American Arts and Crafts Movement,* New York: Dover Publications, 1979.

STILLIE, T. A. "The Evolution of Pattern Design in the Scottish Woollen Textile Industry in the Nineteenth Century." *Textile History* 1 (1970): 309–31.

Over thirty swatches of Scottish woolens are illustrated.

STOKES, I. N. PHELPS. *Iconography of Manhattan Island.* New York: Robert H. Dodd, 1926.

STOKES, J. *The Complete Cabinet Makes and Upholsterer's Guide.* London: Dean & Munday, [1829].

STREAT, E. R., and CHARLOTTE LEUTKENS. "Manchester: The Origins of Cottonopolis." *CIBA Review,* no. 2 (1962): 2–33.

STRUTT, JOSEPH. *A Complete View of the Dress and Habits of the People of England, from the Establishment of the Saxons in Britain to the Present Times, Illustrated by Engravings taken from the Most Authentic Remains of Antiquity.* London: J. Nichols, 1796. Glossary.

SUGDEN, ALAN VICTOR, and JOHN LUDLAM EDMONDSON. *A History of English Wallpaper: 1509–1914.* London: B. T. Batsford, 1925.

SWAIN, MARGARET H. "The Furnishing of Holyroodhouse in 1668." *Connoisseur* 194 (1977): 122–30.

———. *Historical Needlework: A Study of Influences in Scotland and Northern England.* London: Barrie & Jenkins, 1970.

SWAN, ABRAHAM. *The British Architect; or, The Builder's Treasury of Stair-Cases.* Various editions, London: Printed for the author, 1745, 1748, 1750, 1758; Philadelphia: R. Bell for J. Norman, 1775. Reprint of 1758 ed., New York: DaCapo Press, 1967.

SWAN, SUSAN BURROWS. *Plain and Fancy: American Women and Their Needlework, 1700–1850.* New York: Holt, Rinehart & Winston, 1977.

———. *A Winterthur Guide to American Needlework.* New York: Crown Publishers, 1976.

"En Tapetserarbok fran Karl Johan-tiden." Circa 1835. Ms. no. 815, Villa Rosendals Museum, Stockholm.

Facsimile ed., *An Upholsterer's Hand Drawn Design Book from the Time of Karl Johan.* Stockholm: Kung. Husgerådskammaren Marek, 1979.

The original belonged to F. J. Pettersson. While probably dating from about 1835, some of the watercolor designs for curtains are closely related to designs by Osmont and Hallavant of the period 1810 to 1820 and to the work of Percier and Fontaine (q.v.), and to that of La Mésangère (q.v.).

Die Tapezierkunst in Allen Stielen. Berlin: Verlag von Ernst Wasmuth, 1895.

TATTERSALL, C. E. C., and STANLEY REED. *A History of British Carpets.* Leigh-on-Sea, England: F. Lewis, 1966.

Temple-Newsam House. *The Golden Age of English Furniture Upholstery, 1660–1840.* Catalogue of an exhibition held August 15 to September 15, 1973, in the Stable Court Galleries. Text by Karin M. Walton. Leeds: Temple-Newsam House, 1973.

Ten Eyck Papers. State Library, Albany, N.Y.

[*Textile Mercury Dictionary*]. *The Mercury Dictionary of Textile Terms.* Compiled by the staff of *Textile Mercury.* Manchester: Textile Mercury, Tillotson's (Bolton), [1950].

THATCHER, MARGARET. Inventory, Boston, 1693. Original in Probate Records, Suffolk County Courthouse, Boston. Joseph Downs Manuscript and Microfilm Collection, M-113, Winterthur Museum Library.

Théorie de la fabrication des étoffes de soie. Cours de Joannes Alexandre Hardouin, élève de la classe particulière de Jules Meunier, professeur de mise-en-carte à l'Ecole Royale des Beaux-Arts de Lyon, 1840. Owned by Mrs. Rockwell Gardiner, Stamford, Conn.

The student's name and "40" of the date are in script; the remainder of the title is printed.

THOMPSON, HENRY (possibly of Baltimore, Md.), bill to, from Messrs. Wilson, The Strand, London, 1797. Original in Maryland Historical Society, Baltimore. Joseph Downs Manuscript and Microfilm Collection, Ph 1104, Winterthur Museum Library.

THORNTON, PETER. "Back-Stools and Chaises à Demoiselles." *Connoisseur* 815 (1974): 98–105.

———. *Baroque and Rococo Silks.* New York: Taplinger Publishing Co., 1965.

———. "An Eighteenth-Century Silk-Designer's Manual." *Needle and Bobbin Club Bulletin* 42 (1958): 7–31.

———. "The Furnishing of Mersham-le-Hatch." *Apollo* 91 (1970): 266.

——————. "Room Arrangements in the Mid-Eighteenth Century." *Antiques* 99 (1971): 556–61.

——————. "The Royal State Bed." *Connoisseur* 195 (1977): 136–47.

——————. *Seventeenth-Century Interior Decoration in England, France, and Holland.* New Haven and London: Yale University Press, 1978.

——————. "Tapisseries de Bergame." *Pantheon, Internationale Zeitschrift für Kunst* 18 (1960): 85–91.

THORNTON, PETER K., and MAURICE TOMLIN. "The Ham House Inventories." *Furniture History* 16 (1980): 1–194.

THROOP, LUCY ABBOT. *Furnishing the Home of Good Taste.* New York: McBride, Nast, 1912.

TIDBALL, HARRIET. *Thomas Jackson, Weaver: Seventeenth- and Eighteenth-Century Records.* Lansing, Mich.: Shuttle Craft Guild, 1964.

Based on a mid-eighteenth-century American weaver's manuscript owned by the Cooper-Hewitt Museum, New York. In connection with its publication, samples of cloth were woven following Jackson's specifications for patterns, colors, and fibers. These are on file at the museum and include barleycorn, damask, diaper, huckaback, M's and O's, and shag petticoats.

TOLLES, FREDERICK B. *Meeting House and Counting House: The Quaker Merchants of Colonial Philadelphia, 1682–1763.* Chapel Hill: University of North Carolina Press, 1948.

TOMLINSON, CHARLES, ed. *Cyclopaedia of Useful Arts, Mechanical and Chemical, Manufactures, Mining, and Engineering.* London and New York: George Virtue, [1854].

Trader's book, 1797–1809. Rhode Island Historical Society, no. C736, Providence, R.I.

Lists articles which will sell profitably in the United States and describes those preferred in "Marseilles, Barcelona, Canton, Manilla, India in General, Bengal, Leghorn, Trieste, Rio de Janeiro, the River Plate, Salvador, and Pernambuco." Twenty swatches of "Figured Lustrings and Sarsnetts" from Canton and more than thirty "Sattins" and "Taffetas or Lustrings" from France and Italy are pasted into the book.

Transactions of the Society for the Encouragement of Arts. See Royal Society of Arts.

TRENT, WILLIAM. Inventory, "Late of Nottingham in the County of Burlington in the Western Division of the Province of New Jersey, 1726." Original in Office of Superior Court, bound volume, 1211–1216C, 1433–1448C. New Jersey State House Annex, Trenton. Joseph Downs Manuscript and Microfilm Collection, Ph 184.1,2, Winterthur Museum Library.

Trotter Family Papers. Joseph Downs Manuscript and Microfilm Collection, 61 x 88.4, Winterthur Museum Library.

Contains eleven samples of bearskins (dark brown and black, heavy, shaggy wools) and ten samples of changeable silks. Found among papers of 1805–10 at 36 North Front Street and brought to Cleevegate, Chestnut Hill, Philadelphia, home of William Henry Trotter. Probably belonged to Nathan Trotter.

TRYON, ROLLA MILTON. *Household Manufactures in the United States, 1640–1860.* 1917. Reprint ed., New York: Johnson Reprint Corp., 1966.

TUCHS CHERER, JEAN-MICHEL, ed. *Etoffes Merveilleuses du Musée Historique des Tissus, Lyon.* 3 vols. [Tokyo]: Gakken, 1976.

The Upholsterers' Accelerator: Being Rules for Cutting and Forming Draperies, Valances, &c., Accompanied by Appropriate Remarks. Also Containing a Full Description of the New System Which will Greatly Facilitate and Improve the Execution. By an upholsterer of forty-five years' experience. London: At the Architectural and Scientific Library, Bloomsbury, [ca. 1840]. 37 plates.

Barbara Morris attributes this work to one Thomas King, ca. 1833 ("Textiles," *Early Victorian,* pp. 118–19.)

URE, ANDREW. *Dictionary of Arts, Manufactures, and Mines.* London: Longman, Orme, et al., 1839.

VAN LAER, ARNOLD J. F., ed. and trans. *Correspondence of Jeremias van Rensselaer, 1651–1674.* Albany: University of the State of New York, 1932.

VAN LAER, ARNOLD J. F., ed. *Van Rensselaer Bowier Manuscripts: Being the Letters of Kiliaen van Rensselaer, 1630–1643.* Translated by Mrs. Alan H. Strong. Albany: University of the State of New York, 1908.

VAN VARICK, MARGRITA. Inventory, New York, 1695–96. Original in New York Court of Appeals, Albany. Joseph Downs Manuscript and Microfilm Collection, Ph 441, Winterthur Museum Library.

Includes the "apprisement of ye Shopp goods." Two issues of the *Winterthur Newsletter* (8, nos. 2 and 3 [February 26 and March 26,' 1962]) were devoted to this inventory.

VARNEY, ALMON C. *Our Homes and Their Adornments; or, How to Build, Finish, Furnish, and Adorn a Home,*

. . . the Whole Being Designed to Make Happy Homes for Happy People. Detroit: J. C. Chilton, 1883.

VIAUX, JACQUELINE, comp. *Catalogue matières: Arts-décoratifs, beaux-arts, intérieures.* 4 vols. to date. Paris: Société des Amis de la Bibliothèque Forney, 1970–.

Victoria and Albert Museum. *See* Barbara Johnson album, Kelly Books, Spitalfields silks, *and* Warner Archive.

Virginia Records. Notes on textiles advertised in Virginia newspapers and found in Virginia inventories. Compiled by Mildred Lanier when she was curator of textiles, Colonial Williamsburg Foundation, Williamsburg, Va.

WADSWORTH, ALFRED P., and JULIA DE L. MANN. *The Cotton Trade and Industrial Lancashire, 1600–1780.* Manchester: At the University Press, 1931. Reprint eds.; Manchester: At the University Press, 1965; New York: Augustus M. Kelley, 1968.

WAINWRIGHT, NICHOLAS B. *Colonial Grandeur in Philadelphia: The House and Furniture of General John Cadwalader.* Philadelphia: Historical Society of Pennsylvania, 1964.

WALLIS, GEORGE. "Special Report." In *New York Industrial Exhibition: General Report of the British Commissioners.* London: Harrison & Son, 1854.

[WANSEY, HENRY]. DAVID JOHN JEREMY, ed. *Henry Wansey and His American Journal, 1794.* Philadelphia: American Philosophical Society, 1970.

WARDEN, A. J. *The Linen Trade.* London: Longman, Green, et al., 1864.

WARD-JACKSON, PETER. *English Furniture Designs of the Eighteenth Century.* London: Her Majesty's Stationery Office, 1958.

Warner Archive, Victoria and Albert Museum, London.

Warner and Sons, Ltd., of Braintree, Essex, a silk weaving firm, in 1972 disposed of many of its early patterns and books from other companies. Of the 58 lots sold through Christie's, the Victoria and Albert Museum acquired about 20 swatch books, as well as watercolor designs and point-papers for many brocades and fancy silks. Together with the earlier Spitalfields watercolors (q.v.) in that museum, it is now possible to study two centuries of silk patterns, the weaving of which was always in the forefront of fashion. Few of these are referred to in this book because they are generally unnamed (and indeed unnameable in their fantastic variety) and are referred to as tobines, tissues, figured satins, or winter and spring patterns.

Since 1979 Warner and Sons has exhibited its remaining historical collection of some 30,000 items in a warehouse in Braintree which is open to scholars by appointment. Selected items from this collection, including sample lengths of textiles and pattern books with swatches, were shown in a traveling exhibition during 1981 and 1982. A catalogue accompanied the exhibition. *See* Hester Bury, *A Choice of Design, 1850–1980, Fabrics by Warner & Sons Limited.*

WARNER, FRANK. *The Silk Industry of the United Kingdom, Its Origin and Development.* London: Drane's, [1921].

WATERSTON, WILLIAM. *Cyclopaedia of Commerce.* London: H. G. Bohn, 1847.

WATKINS, WALTER KENDALL. "An Invoice of Fabrics, etc. Shipped from Boston to Taunton in 1688." *Old-Time New England* 23 (1932): 84.

WATSON, JOHN F. *Annals and Occurrences of New York City and State, in the Olden Time.* Philadelphia: Henry F. Anners, 1846.

WATSON, JOHN FANNING. Manuscript for *Annals of Philadelphia,* published in 1830. Copies owned by the Historical Society of Pennsylvania and the Library Company of Philadelphia.

Contains swatches of "Ancient Fabrics of Dress": five examples woven in England from silk raised near Philadelphia in the 1770s, three worn at the Meschianza Ball, 1778, and eight "specimens" of brocaded silks dating from the 1720s and 1740s.

WATSON, JOHN FORBES. *Collection of Specimens and Illustrations of the Textile Manufactures of India.* 17 vols. London: India Museum, 1873–80. Victoria and Albert Museum and Cooper-Hewitt Museum libraries.

————. *Collection of Specimens of the Textile Manufactures of India.* 2d ser. London: India Museum, 1872–77. Cooper-Hewitt Museum.

————. *The Textile Manufactures and the Costumes of the People of India.* London: George Edward Eyre & William Spottiswoode, 1866.

WAXMAN, LORRAINE. "French Influence on American Decorative Arts of the Early Nineteenth Century: The Work of Charles-Honoré Lannuier." Master's thesis, University of Delaware, 1958.

Weavers' Company manuscript. Public Record Office, CO388/21. London.

Twenty-two swatches of the earliest documented striped, checked, and flowered calimancoes are found in "Samples submitted to the Commissioners for Trades and Plantations by the Weavers'

Company, 1719–20." Other worsteds which differ little from later Norwich manufactures are called simply stuffs. Cloths made of part silk and part cotton, linen, or worsted include "Satton Dimotys," "Tobines," "Elatchs," and "Dunjars."

    These pages were prepared by the Weavers' Company in defense of their manufactures against the then popular painted calicoes imported from India. The weavers' campaign led to the act of 1721 which prohibited the sale, use, and wear of painted calicoes in England. A fuller account and description of the swatches is in Natalie Rothstein, "The Calico Campaign of 1719–1721" (q.v.).

The Weavers' True Case. London: W. Wilkins, 1719.

WEBSTER, THOMAS. *An Encyclopaedia of Domestic Economy.* New York: Harper & Bros., 1845.

WEEDEN, WILLIAM B. "Early Oriental Commerce in Providence." *Proceedings of the Massachusetts Historical Society,* 3d ser., 41 (1908): 236–38.

WEIBEL, ADELE COULIN. *Two Thousand Years of Textiles: The Figured Textiles of Europe and the Near East.* New York: Pantheon Books, published for the Detroit Institute of Arts, 1952.

WEIGERT, ROGER-ARMAND. *Textiles en Europe sous Louis XV. Les plus beaux specimens de la collection Richelieu.* Preface in English by Valerie C. Sutton. Fribourg: Office du Livre, 1964.

WESCHER, H. "Rouen, French Textile Center." *CIBA Review* 135 (1959): 2–33.

WHARTON, ANNE H. *Colonial Days and Dames.* Philadelphia: J. B. Lippincott Co., 1895.

WHARTON, EDITH, and OGDEN CODMAN, JR. *The Decoration of Houses.* New York: Charles Scribner's Sons, 1897. Reprint ed., introduction by John Barrington Bayley and William A. Coles, New York: W. W. Norton, 1978.

WHEELER, CANDACE. *The Development of Embroidery in America.* New York: Harper & Bros., 1921.

————. *Principles of Home Decoration.* New York: Doubleday, Page, 1903.

WHITAKER, HENRY. *House Furnishing and Decorating Assistant.* London and Paris: H. Fisher & Son, 1847.

WHITAKER, HENRY, and MICHAEL ANGELO NICHOLSON. *The Practical Cabinetmaker, Upholsterer and Decorator's Treasury of Designs in the Grecian, Italian, Renaissance, Louis-Quatorze, Gothic, Tudor, and Elizabethan Styles.* London: Peter Jackson, 185[?].

WHITE, GILBERT. *The Natural History and Antiquities of Selborne, in the County of Southampton.* London: Printed by T. Bensley for B. White & Son, 1789.

White House Historical Association. *The White House: An Historic Guide.* Text by Mrs. John N. Pearce. Washington, D.C., 1962.

WHITE, MARGARET E. "The Pattern Books of Weavers." *Antiques* 53 (1948): 134–35.

WHITTOCK, NATHANIEL. *The Complete Book of Trades; or, The Parents' Guide and Youths' Instructor.* London: John Bennett, 1837.

[Wickersham catalogue of 1857]. Hutchinson and Wickersham. *A New Phase in the Iron Manufacture . . . Descriptive Catalogue of the Manufacturers of the New York Wire Railing Company.* New York, 1857. Reprint ed., *Victorian Ironwork: The Wickersham Catalogue of 1857,* introduction by Margot Gayle, Philadelphia: Athenaeum Library of Nineteenth-Century America, 1977.

WIEDERKEHR, ANNE-MARIE. "Le Cirsaka d'après les textes du XVIII siècle." *CIETA,* no. 49 (1979): 90–98.

Willing and Shippen Ledger. Philadelphia, 1730. Historical Manuscript Collection, Yale University, New Haven, Conn.

WILSON, CHARLES HENRY. *Anglo-Dutch Commerce and Finance in the Eighteenth Century.* Studies in Economic History, edited by M. M. Postan. Cambridge: At the University Press, 1941. Reprint ed., edited by Mira Wilkins, New York: Arno Press, 1977.

WINGATE, ISABEL B., ed. *Fairchild's Dictionary of Textiles.* New York: Fairchild Publications, 1967.

    A revision of the 1959 edition edited by Stephen S. Marks (q.v.). *See also* Louis Harmuth, *Dictionary of Textiles.*

[Winterthur Museum Library Catalogue]. *The Winterthur Museum Libraries' Collection of Printed Books and Periodicals.* 9 vols. Wilmington, Del.: Scholarly Resources in cooperation with the Henry Francis du Pont Winterthur Museum, 1973.

WISTAR, RICHARD. Letter book, 1759–72. Original owned by Elizabeth Wistar. Joseph Downs Manuscript and Microfilm Collection, M-220, Winterthur Museum Library.

    Wistar (1727–81) was a Quaker merchant of Philadelphia and Alloways, New Jersey. At the latter site, he continued operating the Wistarburgh glassworks begun by his father, Caspar Wistar, in 1739. This was the only successful glasshouse in colonial America.

Wistar Papers. Philadelphia, ca. 1750–ca. 1825. Joseph Downs Manuscript and Microfilm Collection, 56 x 17.1–87, Winterthur Museum Library.

This collection of over 400 manuscript items (totaling several thousand pages) and some 70 manuscript record books documents the business activities of Adam Konigmacher and Company; Miles and Wister; William Rotch; J. H. Stevenson and Company; Charles J. Wister; John Wister; William Wister; Wister and Aston; and Wister, Price and Wister.

[WISTER, SALLY]. "The Journal of Sally Wister." *Pennsylvania Magazine of History and Biography* 9 (1885): 318–33, 463–78; 10 (1886): 51–60.

The Workwoman's Guide. 2d ed. London: Simpkin, Marshall; Birmingham: Thomas Evans; 1840. Reprint ed., Owston Ferry, Doncaster, South Yorkshire: Bloomfield Books & Publications, 1975.

YAPP, G. W., ed. *Art Industry: Furniture, Upholstery, and House-Decoration*. 3 vols. 1879. Reprint. Westmead, Farnborough, Hants.: Gregg International Publishers, 1972.

Yorkshire pattern book. Owned by Mrs. George R. Stansfeld, Field House, Triangle, Sowerby Bridge, Halifax, Yorkshire.

Inscribed "Book of Patterns from Richard Hill to His much esteemed friend Mr. Francis Bequerrel of Boulogne Sur-mer, Merchant. 1770." The book is fully described by Frank Atkinson in *Woollen and Worsted Trade in Halifax* (q.v.).

YOUNG, ARTHUR. *A Six Months Tour through the North of England*. 4 vols. London: W. Strahan, 1770.

————. *A Six Weeks Tour through the Southern Counties of England and Wales*. London: W. Nicoll, 1768.

————. *A Tour in Ireland: . . . Made in the Years 1776, 1777, 1778, and . . . 1779*. Dublin: G. Bonham, 1780.

————. *Travels in France . . . during the Years 1787, 1788, 1789*. London: W. Richardson, 1794.